Frommer's®

Ecuador & the Galápagos Islands

1st Edition

by Eliot Greenspan

Here's what the critics say about Frommer's:

"Amazingly easy to use. Very portable, very complete."
—*Booklist*

"Detailed, accurate, and easy-to-read information for all price ranges."
—*Glamour Magazine*

"Hotel information is close to encyclopedic."
—*Des Moines Sunday Register*

"Frommer's Guides have a way of giving you a real feel for a place."
—*Knight Ridder Newspapers*

WILEY
2007
BICENTENNIAL

Wiley Publishing, Inc.

About the Author

Eliot Greenspan is a poet, journalist, musician, and travel writer who took his backpack and typewriter the length of Mesoamerica before settling in Costa Rica in 1992. Since then, he has worked steadily as a travel writer, freelance journalist, and translator, and has continued his travels in the region. He is the author of *Frommer's Belize, Costa Rica For Dummies, Frommer's Cuba, Frommer's Guatemala,* and *The Tico Times Restaurant Guide to Costa Rica,* as well as the chapter on Venezuela in *Frommer's South America.*

Published by:

Wiley Publishing, Inc.

111 River St.
Hoboken, NJ 07030-5774

ISBN: 978-0-470-12002-6
Editor: Matthew Brown
Production Editor: Suzanna R. Thompson
Cartographer: Andrew Murphy
Photo Editor: Richard Fox
Anniversary Logo Design: Richard Pacifico
Production by Wiley Indianapolis Composition Services
Appendix C illustrations by Kelly Emkow, Joni Burns, and Ronda David-Burroughs

Front cover photo: Galápagos giant tortoise
Back cover photo: San Rafael or Coca Falls on the Quijos River in the Amazon

For information on our other products and services or to obtain technical support, please contact our Customer Care Department within the U.S. at 800/762-2974, outside the U.S. at 317/572-3993 or fax 317/572-4002.

Wiley also publishes its books in a variety of electronic formats. Some content that appears in print may not be available in electronic formats.

Manufactured in the United States of America

5   4   3   2   1

Contents

List of Maps   vi

1 The Best of Ecuador   1

1 The Best Purely Ecuadorian
Travel Experiences 1

2 The Best of Natural Ecuador 4

3 The Best Historical Sites &
Museums 5

4 The Best Outdoor Adventures 7

5 The Best Bird-Watching 8

6 The Best Destinations for Families ...9

7 The Best Luxury Hotels 9

8 The Best Moderately Priced &
Budget Hotels 10

9 The Best Ecolodges & Haciendas 11

10 The Best Bed-and-Breakfasts &
Small Inns 12

11 The Best Restaurants 13

12 The Best Shopping & Markets 14

13 The Best After-Dark Fun 15

14 The Best Websites about Ecuador ...16

2 Planning Your Trip to Ecuador   17

1 The Regions in Brief 17

2 Visitor Information & Maps 19

3 Entry Requirements 19

4 When to Go 20

Ecuador Calendar of Events 21

5 Getting There 22

Getting Through the Airport 24

6 Money & Costs 26

*The U.S. Dollar, the British
Pound & the Euro* 27

What Things Cost in Ecuador 28

7 Travel Insurance 29

8 Health 30

9 Safety 32

10 Specialized Travel Resources 33

11 Sustainable Tourism/Ecotourism 36

*Frommers.com: The Complete
Travel Resource* 37

12 Staying Connected 38

Online Traveler's Toolbox 39

13 Packages for the Independent
Traveler 40

Ask before You Go 41

14 Escorted General-Interest Tours 41

15 Spanish-Language Programs 42

16 Getting Around 43

Car-Rental Tips 45

17 Tips on Accommodations 46

18 Tips on Dining 47

Fast Facts: Ecuador 48

3 Suggested Ecuador Itineraries   55

1 Ecuador in 1 Week 55

2 Ecuador in 2 Weeks 58

3 Ecuador for Families 60

4 Ecuador for Adventure Travelers 61

5 Quito in 3 Days 63

4 The Active Vacation Planner   66

1 Organized Adventure Trips 66
2 Activities A to Z 68
   Hummingbird Heaven 71
   The Big Peaks 80
3 Ecuador's Top National Parks &
   Bioreserves 84

Searching for Wildlife 89
4 Tips on Health, Safety & Etiquette
   in the Wilderness 89
5 Ecologically Oriented Volunteer &
   Study Programs 90

5 Quito   92

1 Orientation 92
   The Neighborhoods in Brief 96
   Breaking the Code 97
2 Getting Around 97
   Fast Facts: Quito 99
3 Where to Stay 102
4 Where to Dine 109
5 What to See & Do 114

The Quito School of Art 116
Getting High in Quito 118
6 Outdoor Activities &
   Spectator Sports 123
7 Shopping 124
8 Quito After Dark 126
   *Plaza Foch: Ground Zero
   in Mariscal* 130
9 Side Trips from Quito 133

6 The Northern Sierra   139

1 Otavalo .139
   Otavalo Globalized 144
   Tree Tomato 153

2 Ibarra 155
   The Minga 156
3 Tulcán 161

7 The Central Sierra   164

1 Cotopaxi National Park 164
   Andean Condor 168
2 Latacunga 173
3 Ambato .180

It's Chicha Time 184
4 Baños 185
   Tungurahua: Back with a Bang 191
5 Riobamba 195

8 Cuenca & the Southern Sierra   203

1 Cuenca 203
   The Panama Hat 211
2 Loja 221

The Virgin of El Cisne 224
3 Vilcabamba 228

9 Guayaquil & the Southern Coast   233

1 Guayaquil 233
La Rivalidad: Quito & Guayaquil . . .235
A Meeting of Giants 239
If You're Short on Time 240
2 Salinas & The Santa Elena
Peninsula 249
3 Montañita 254

4 Puerto López & Machalilla
National Park 256
Having a Whale of a Time 257
5 Machala & South to the
Peruvian Border 261
Going Bananas 262

10 Northern Pacific Coast & Lowlands   268

1 Manta .268
The Manta Airbase 272
2 Bahía de Caráquez 277
3 Canoa 283
4 Esmeraldas 286

*Esmeraldas: Ecuador's
African Coast?* 287
5 Atacames & the Beaches
West of Esmeraldas 291
6 Santo Domingo de los Colorados . . .295
Red-Haired Boys 297

11 El Oriente   300

1 Lago Agrio & Cuyabeno
Nature Reserve 302
Down & Dirty in the Jungle 303
Cofán Chief Randy Borman 305
2 Coca & the Lower Río Napo 308

Orellana's Journey of Discovery 310
3 Tena & the Upper Napo River 315
4 Puyo & the Southern
Amazon Basin 320

12 The Galápagos Islands   324

1 Essentials 325
The Islands in Brief 328
*Not Your Typical Passenger: Charles
Darwin & the Galápagos Islands* . . .330
2 Cruises .331
*Organizing a Last-Minute Trip
to the Galápagos* 338

3 Puerto Ayora & Santa
Cruz Island 339
Unwanted Guests 340
4 Puerto Baquerizo Moreno &
San Cristóbal Island 350
An Island Whodunit? 355
The Galápagos Tortoise 357

Appendix A: Ecuador in Depth   358

1 Ecuador Today 358
2 History 101 360
Dateline .361
3 The Natural Environment 367

4 Ecuadorian Culture 368
5 *Llapingachos, Cuy* & Pilsener:
Ecuadorian Food & Drink 370
6 Recommended Books & Films 372

Appendix B: Glossary of Spanish Terms & Phrases   374

1 Basic Words & Phrases 374
2 Menu Terms 376
3 Hotel Terms 378

4 Travel Terms 378
5 Typical Ecuadorian Words & Phrases 379

Appendix C: Ecuadorian Wildlife   380

1 Mammals 380
2 Birds 387
3 Amphibians 391

4 Reptiles 393
5 Invertebrates 396
6 Sea Life 397

Index   400

List of Maps

The Best of Ecuador   2

Ecuador in 1 Week   57

Ecuador in 2 Weeks   59

Ecuador for Families   61

Ecuador for Adventure Travelers   63

Quito in 3 Days   64

Ecuador's National Parks & Protected Areas   67

Quito   94

Side Trips from Quito   103

The Northern Sierra   140

Otavalo   141

Around Otavalo   145

The Central Sierra   165

Cotopaxi National Park   167

Quilotoa Loop   179

Baños   187

Riobamba   197

The Southern Sierra   204

Cuenca   205

Vilcabamba   229

The Southern Coast   234

Guayaquil   237

Machalilla National Park   259

Northern Pacific Coast & Lowlands   269

Manta   271

Bahía de Caráquez   279

El Oriente   301

Río Napo   309

The Galápagos Islands   325

Puerto Ayora   341

Acknowledgments

I got some very valuable support and input on this book from friends and experts in Ecuador and abroad. Jim Shapiro, Danielle Leyla Walters, David Dudenhoefer, Timothy Pertz, Vicky Longland, and Amanda Vlastas all made valuable contributions and corrections. I also must thank Nathalie Pilovetzky and Kristin Giroux of Latitude PR and Patricio Tamariz and Natalia Santa Maria of the Fondo Mixto de Promoción Turística del Ecuador for major logistical support. Finally, big thanks are due to Matthew Brown, my editor, for his patience, deft editorial touch, and personal expertise in Ecuador.

—Eliot Greenspan

An Invitation to the Reader

In researching this book, we discovered many wonderful places—hotels, restaurants, shops, and more. We're sure you'll find others. Please tell us about them, so we can share the information with your fellow travelers in upcoming editions. If you were disappointed with a recommendation, we'd love to know that, too. Please write to:

Frommer's Ecuador, 1st Edition
Wiley Publishing, Inc. • 111 River St. • Hoboken, NJ 07030-5774

An Additional Note

Please be advised that travel information is subject to change at any time—and this is especially true of prices. We therefore suggest that you write or call ahead for confirmation when making your travel plans. The authors, editors, and publisher cannot be held responsible for the experiences of readers while traveling. Your safety is important to us, however, so we encourage you to stay alert and be aware of your surroundings. Keep a close eye on cameras, purses, and wallets, all favorite targets of thieves and pickpockets.

Other Great Guides for Your Trip:

Frommer's South America

Frommer's Peru

Frommer's Argentina

Frommer's Chile & Easter Island

Frommer's Brazil

Frommer's Panama

Frommer's Star Ratings, Icons & Abbreviations

Every hotel, restaurant, and attraction listing in this guide has been ranked for quality, value, service, amenities, and special features using a **star-rating system.** In country, state, and regional guides, we also rate towns and regions to help you narrow down your choices and budget your time accordingly. Hotels and restaurants are rated on a scale of zero (recommended) to three stars (exceptional). Attractions, shopping, nightlife, towns, and regions are rated according to the following scale: zero stars (recommended), one star (highly recommended), two stars (very highly recommended), and three stars (must-see).

In addition to the star-rating system, we also use **eight feature icons** that point you to the great deals, in-the-know advice, and unique experiences that separate travelers from tourists. Throughout the book, look for:

Finds	Special finds—those places only insiders know about
Fun Fact	Fun facts—details that make travelers more informed and their trips more fun
Kids	Best bets for kids and advice for the whole family
Moments	Special moments—those experiences that memories are made of
Overrated	Places or experiences not worth your time or money
Tips	Insider tips—great ways to save time and money
Value	Great values—where to get the best deals
Warning	Warning—traveler's advisories are usually in effect

The following **abbreviations** are used for credit cards:

AE	American Express	DISC	Discover	V	Visa
DC	Diners Club	MC	MasterCard		

Frommers.com

Now that you have this guidebook to help you plan a great trip, visit our website at **www.frommers.com** for additional travel information on more than 3,500 destinations. We update features regularly to give you instant access to the most current trip-planning information available. At Frommers.com, you'll find scoops on the best airfares, lodging rates, and car rental bargains. You can even book your travel online through our reliable travel booking partners. Other popular features include:

- Online updates of our most popular guidebooks
- Vacation sweepstakes and contest giveaways
- Newsletters highlighting the hottest travel trends
- Online travel message boards with featured travel discussions

The Best of Ecuador

Ecuador likes to boast that it is really four distinct destinations: the Galápagos Islands, the Amazon basin, the high Andean Sierra, and the Pacific coast. In fact, it's much more. Quito offers up both colonial gems and modern pleasures. Cuenca is yet another colonial treasure, with the Inca ruins of Ingapirca nearby. You can visit not only the rainforests of the Amazon basin, but also the cloud forests of Mindo and Bellavista, the dry forests of the southern Pacific lowlands, and the high-altitude paramo of the Central highlands. Active travelers can ride horses on the Andean plains, or mountain bike down the slopes of active volcanoes. Bird-watchers can add to their list from the more than 1,600 species found here. With so much physical and cultural variety, there are plenty of excellent experiences and adventures for any type of traveler. Below is a selective list of some of the best that Ecuador has to offer.

1 The Best Purely Ecuadorian Travel Experiences

- **Stepping Back in Time in Colonial Quito:** Founded in 1534, Quito was the first city to be declared a World Heritage Site by UNESCO. Its Old Town seems in many ways to have changed little over the centuries. Walk the rough cobblestone streets and visit the numerous, beautifully restored colonial-era churches, monasteries, convents, private mansions, and public plazas—you'll feel as if you've traveled back in time. See chapter 5.

- **Straddling the Equator:** The country isn't called Ecuador for nothing—the equator passes right through it. Don't miss the chance to have your photo taken with one foot in either hemisphere. There are several popular tourist attractions and marked spots where you can do this. My favorite, though, is the new **Quitsato Mitad del Mundo Monument** (© 09/9701-133; www.quitsato.org), located just off the highway from Quito to Otavalo. See p. 135.

- **Eating *Cuy*:** You'll see them roasting on spits at little stands along the highways, or on sidewalks in cities and towns. You'll also find them on the menus of some of Ecuador's fanciest restaurants. It's guinea pig to me and you. The skin is served crisp and crackling, and you'll have to work to get much meat from *cuy*. But when it's good, it's moist and flavorful. See restaurant reviews throughout the book.

- **Searching for the Fountain of Youth in Vilcabamba:** The small and isolated village of Vilcabamba is said to have a disproportionately high number of centenarians. Most folks credit the clean water, air, and living. While it may not actually add years to your life, this is a great place to come for a quiet getaway with superb scenery. And whether or not there's any science behind it, a spa treatment or two at **Madre Tierra** (© 07/2640-269; www.madretierra1.com) or **Hostería**

The Best of Ecuador

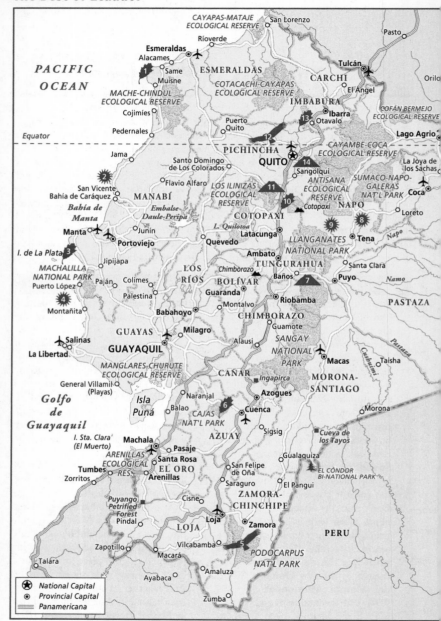

PACIFIC
OCEAN

CAYAPAS-MATAJE
ECOLOGICAL RESERVE   San Lorenzo
Ríoverde   Pasto

Esmeraldas
Alacames
Same   ESMERALDAS   Tulcán   Orilo
Muisne   CARCHI
COTACACHI-CAYAPAS   El Ángel
MACHE-CHINDUL   ECOLOGICAL RESERVE
ECOLOGICAL RESERVE   IMBABURA   COFÁN BERMEJO
Cojimíes   ECOLOGICAL RESERVE
Puerto   13 Ibarra
Pedernales   Quito   Otavalo   Lago Agrio

Equator   CAYAMBE-COCA
Jama   ECOLOGICAL RESERVE
12
PICHINCHA   La Joya de
Santo Domingo   los Sachas
de Los Colorados   QUITO   14
San Vicente   Flavio Alfaro   Sangolquí   ANTISANA   SUMACO-NAPO-
Bahía de Caráquez   MANABÍ   LOS ILINIZAS   11   ECOLOGICAL   GALERAS   Coca
Bahía de   ECOLOGICAL   RESERVE   NAT'L PARK
Manta   Embalse   RESERVE   10   Cotopaxi   NAPO   Loreto
Daule-Peripa   COTOPAXI
Manta   Junín   9   8   Tena   Napo
Portoviejo   Quevedo   Latacunga   LLANGANATES
I. de La Plata 3   NATIONAL PARK
Jipijapa   Ambato   TUNGURAHUA   Santa Clara
MACHALILLA   Chimborazo   Baños   7   Puyo
NATIONAL PARK   Colimes   LOS   BOLÍVAR
Pajan   RÍOS   Namo
Puerto López   Palestina   Guaranda   Riobamba   PASTAZA
4   Babahoyo   Montalvo
Montañita   CHIMBORAZO
GUAYAS   Milagro   Guamote
Salinas   Alausí   SANGAY
La Libertad   NATIONAL
GUAYAQUIL   PARK   Macas   Taisha
MANGLARES-CHURUTE
ECOLOGICAL RESERVE   CAÑAR   MORONA-
General Villamil   Ingapirca   SANTIAGO
(Playas)   Naranjal   Azogues
Golfo   Isla   Balao   6   Morona
de   Puná   CAJAS   Cuenca
Guayaquil   NAT'L PARK
I. Sta. Clara   AZUAY   Sigsig   Cueva de
(El Muerto)   Machala   los Tayos
ARENILLAS   Pasaje
Tumbes   ECOLOGICAL   Santa Rosa   San Felipe   Gualaquiza
Zorritos   RES.   Arenillas   EL ORO   de Oña   EL CÓNDOR
Saraguro   El Pangui   BI-NATIONAL PARK
Puyango   Cisne   ZAMORA-
Petrified   Pindal   CHINCHIPE
Forest   Loja
LOJA   Zamora   PERU
Zapotillo   Vilcabamba
Talára   Macará   5   PODOCARPUS
Amaluza   NAT'L PARK
Ayabaca
Zumba

★ National Capital
◉ Provincial Capital
═══ Panamericana

THE BEST OF NATURAL ECUADOR

The Beaches West of Atacames 1
Cajas National Park 6
Cotopaxi National Park 10
Cuicocha Lake 13
The Galápagos Islands 19
Isla de la Plata 3
The Rainforests of
    Ecuador's El Oriente 15

THE BEST OUTDOOR ADVENTURES

Climbing Cotopaxi Volcano 9
Playing Cowboy or Cowgirl
    on the High Mountain Paramo 9
Scuba Diving in the
    Galápagos Islands 20
Surfing Lonely Waves
    Along Ecuador's Pacific Coast 2
Watching Whales Breach &
    Breed off the Pacific Coast 4
White-Water Rafting & Kayaking 8

THE BEST BIRD-WATCHING

The Cloud Forests of
    Mindo and Bellavista 12
El Oriente 16
The Galápagos Islands 17
Podocarpus National Park 5

THE BEST FAMILY DESTINATIONS

Baños de Agua Santos 7
El Telefériqo & Vulqano Park 14
The Galápagos Islands 18
Hacienda La Alegría 11

Izhcayluma (© **07/2640-095** or 09/ 9153-419; www.izhcayluma.com) will definitely cure whatever's ailing you at the moment. See chapter 8.

- **Starting Off Your Day with a Glass of Tree-Tomato Juice:** Don't be put off by the name, nor think that it tastes anything like a traditional tomato. A tree tomato (*tomate de árbol* or *tamarillo*) is a unique fruit served just about every which way in Ecuador. My favorite is the juice, although you'll also find tree tomatoes in salads; cooked into jam; or boiled, peeled, sweetened, and served as dessert.

- **Riding on the Roof of a Train Past the Devil's Nose:** Earthquakes, landslides, and volcanic eruptions have wiped out most of the rail-line that used to connect Quito to Guayaquil. The one remaining operational section is also one of the most spectacular, a white-knuckle ride of sharp switchbacks and hairpin turns down the side of a steep rock mountain affectionately known as The Devil's Nose. See p. 199.

- **Buying a Panama Hat:** You shouldn't leave the country without buying one of these stylish straw wonders, which are made in Ecuador, not Panama (for

an explanation, see p. 211). Cuenca is currently the primary center for production of Panama hats; **Homero Ortega P. & Hijos** (© **07/2809-000;** www.homeroortega.com) is that city's top manufacturer, and also has shops in Quito. True aficionados might even head to the small towns of Montecristi or Jipijapa to find their special *superfino* headpiece. See chapter 8.

- **Drinking** *Chicha:* Homebrewed liquor made from fermenting corn, potatoes, yuca, and just about anything else on hand, *chicha* is consumed by indigenous peoples throughout the Andean highlands as well as in the lowland forests of El Oriente. Most *chicha* is relatively mild, but if you drink enough of it you'll definitely feel its effects—especially at high altitudes. See chapters 7 and 11.

- **Taking a Tour through the Amazon with an Indian Chief:** Born to missionary parents and reared among the Cofán people of Ecuador's Amazon basin, Randy Borman is the tribe's official chief. He'll guide you on a multiday tour through the Cofán lands and villages, and you'll learn about and experience Cofán traditions, skills, cuisine, and culture. See p. 305.

2 The Best of Natural Ecuador

With natural delights ranging from the Galápagos Islands to snowcapped volcanic peaks, and from Amazon lowland rainforests to high Andean paramo, Ecuador is a naturalist's wonderland. Whether or not you want to hike or climb, bird-watch or simply admire the innate beauty, you'll find plenty of natural wonder here.

- **Cuicocha Lake:** Formed thousands of years ago in the extinct crater of a massive volcano, this beautiful, clear blue lake is a popular destination. You can choose between hiking around the rim of the crater, or

scrambling down for a boat ride on the waters of the lake. The lake is named after the popular dish *cuy* (guinea pig), because locals thought the islands in its center resembled guinea pigs. See p. 146.

- **Cotopaxi National Park:** Comprising 33,393 hectares (82,480 sq. miles) surrounding the park's namesake and emblematic volcano, this is Ecuador's most popular national park, after the Galápagos. At 5,897m (19,348 ft.), the snow-covered Cotopaxi is the country's second highest peak, and allegedly the highest active volcano in the world. Tour options here range from leisure hikes at lower elevations, to full-on summit climbs, with a range of other options, from mountain biking to horseback riding to camping. The best general tour operators running trips to Cotopaxi are **Metropolitan Touring** (© 02/2988-200; www.metropolitan-touring.com); and **Surtrek** (© 02/2231-534; www.surtrek.com). For hard-core climbing and adventures, try **Cotopaxi.com** (© 02/2909-640; www.cotopaxi.com) or **Safari Ecuador** (© 02/2222-505; www.safari.com.ec). See chapters 4 and 7.

- **Cajas National Park:** Located just outside Cuenca, this beautiful national park is famous for its 232 high montane lakes and misty cloud forests. It is also an excellent place for hiking and bird-watching. Easily accessible, it's a great change of pace from the cobblestone streets, colonial-era churches, and Panama hat shops of Cuenca. See p. 219.

- **Isla de la Plata:** The crowning jewel of **Machalilla National Park** is Isla de la Plata, an offshore island often touted as "the poor man's Galápagos." Whether or not that's an appropriate or even worthy moniker, Isla de la Plata offers excellent bird and wildlife viewing and snorkeling. What's more, late June through early October, you have the good chance of seeing humpback whales on the boat ride out to the island. On land, Machalilla has some fabulous trails and beaches. See chapter 9.

- **The Beaches West of Atacames:** In general, Ecuador is not a great beach destination. It certainly can't hold a candle to beaches found in the Caribbean, South Pacific, or even Mexico or Costa Rica. However, the relatively short section of Pacific coast west of Atacames has several small and beautiful beaches. Sua and Same are my favorites, but Atacames itself, as well as Tonsupa, Tonchigue, and Galera, are also pretty. And for someplace really unique and isolated, you can head to the small island of Muisne. See chapter 10.

- **The Rainforests of Ecuador's El Oriente:** When Amazon rainforests are mentioned, most people think of Brazil. But Ecuador's El Oriente is a vast area of lowland tropical rainforest that is part of the Amazon basin which feeds and forms the Amazon River. In fact, Francisco Orellana, who first named and navigated the Amazon River, began his long journey here in Ecuador. Over 500 species of birds and some 15,000 species of flora can be found here, as well as fresh-water dolphins, 11 different species of monkeys, anacondas, caimans, and jaguars. See chapter 11.

- **The Galápagos Islands:** Ecuador's prime attraction is a naturalist's paradise. In fact, if we were talking religion, this would be Holy Ground. It was here that Charles Darwin developed many of his ideas that would later emerge as the *Theory of Natural Selection* and the *Theory of Evolution*. Not only are the Galápagos famous for their wildlife—on land, in the sea, and in the air—but this unique and isolated volcanic archipelago is a unique living geology laboratory. See chapter 12.

3 The Best Historical Sites & Museums

From the ruins and relics left behind by pre-Columbian peoples to the ornate colonial-era churches, monasteries, and convents built by the Spanish conquistadors—not to mention the work of iconic Ecuadorian artist Oswaldo

Guayasamín—Ecuador contains a wealth of fascinating historical sites and museums.

- **Iglesia de San Francisco** (Old Town; Quito): Quito's first church, San Francisco remains one of its most impressive, especially when you factor in the attached monastery, museum, massive altar, and wide stairway ascending from the plaza. The church and its ornate interior are in the midst of a major restoration, which should only make this classic, colonial-era church that much more impressive. See p. 118.

- **La Compañía de Jesús** (Old Town; Quito): There's so much gold and gold leaf adorning this unbelievably ornate 17th-century baroque church that I often feel the need for sunglasses. In fact, the Jesuits who built this church incorporated several sun symbols, which some say was a nod to the Incas who preceded them on this spot. The level of detail and artistry on display here is unparalleled. See p. 120.

- **Museo Nacional del Banco Central del Ecuador** (New Town; Quito): Ecuador's largest museum is also arguably its best. The anthropological and historical displays of the pre-Columbian inhabitants are extensive, interesting, and beautifully displayed. There are also very good collections of colonial-era and religious art, as well as a fine representation of Ecuador's best modern art and artists. See p. 122.

- **Fundación Guayasamín** (Bellavista, Quito): Oswaldo Guayasamín was Ecuador's greatest and most famous modern artist. His striking large paintings, murals, and sculptures had an impact on artists across Latin America and around the world. This extensive museum displays both his own work and pieces from his collection. Combined with the neighboring **Capilla del Hombre,** this is a must-see for any art lover or Latin American history buff. See p. 123.

- **Catedral Nueva** (Cuenca): This massive cathedral took over 80 years to complete. Its two towering blue domes dominate the skyline of Cuenca, especially when viewed from one of the hillside lookouts outside town. Don't miss a chance to tour its beautiful inside, which has white marble floors, stained-glass windows, and a Renaissance-style main altar. See p. 207.

- **Museo del Banco Central** (Cuenca; ℂ **07/2831-255**): This modern museum features an excellent collection of archaeological finds and relics, ethnographic displays, and colonial-era figurative and religious art; it's also built right on top of a major Inca ceremonial site that has been semi-excavated. As if that weren't enough, there are extensive botanical gardens here, a small aviary, and llamas roaming the grounds. See p. 208.

- **Ingapirca** (outside of Cuenca): Ingapirca is the greatest surviving Inca ruin in Ecuador. A visit here will allow you to appreciate the famous Inca masonry, with its seemingly impossibly tight joints. Even before the Incas arrived, this spot was inhabited by the Cañari, and some of their original constructions are also on display. The site is believed to have been sacred to both the Cañari and Incas. See p. 220.

- **La Tolita** (North Pacific coast): This unique archaeological site is found on a small island outside San Lorenzo. It is believed to have been inhabited by one of the oldest pre-Columbian cultures, a people skilled at working with gold, silver, and even platinum. One whole beach here contains millions of shards of ancient pottery. See p. 290.

- **Museo Antropológico y de Arte Contemporáneo** (Guayaquil; ☎ 04/2327-402): Large, modern, and well laid out, this is Guayaquil's best museum. There are extensive archaeological collections here from all over Ecuador, as well as a wonderful wing dedicated to contemporary Ecuadorian art. One of the best features of this museum is its prized location at the northern end of Guayaquil's Malecón 2000, allowing easy access (before and/or after) to both the popular riverside boardwalk and neighboring Cerro Santa Ana. See p. 240.

4 The Best Outdoor Adventures

Ecuador's varied landscape, ecosystems, and natural wonders make it a prime destination for adventure travelers, with opportunities to participate in a wide range of adventure sports and activities.

- **Climbing Volcán Cotopaxi:** Although it's actually only the second highest peak in the country, Cotopaxi is Ecuador's most coveted summit. At 5,897m (19,348 ft.), this is no leisurely climb, yet most people in reasonably good condition, with the proper guides and acclimation, can reach the top. The views on the way up, at the summit, and coming back down are spectacular. **Cotopaxi.com** (☎ 02/2909-640; www.cotopaxi. com) and **Safari Ecuador** (☎ 02/2222-505; www.safari.com.ec) are two excellent operators who can get you to the snowcapped summit. See chapters 4 and 7.
- **Playing Cowboy or Cowgirl on the High Mountain Paramo:** In Ecuador, cowboys are called *chagras,* and the *chagra* tradition is alive and well. Whether you sign on for a short ride or actually get to join in a round-up of wild bulls or horses, you'll feel like a *chagra* as you ride your steed over the rugged scrub of the high Andean paramo. **Hacienda La Alegría** (☎ 02/2462-319; www.haciendaalegria.com) offers multiday rides. See chapters 4 and 7.
- **Watching Whales Breach & Breed off the Pacific Coast:** From late June to early October, humpback whales congregate in large numbers off Ecuador's Pacific coast. They come to the warmer waters from Antarctica to mate, give birth, feed, and nurse their young. The whales here are very social, and often give spectacular displays of breaching. Whale-watching tours are offered up and down this coastline, but **Salinas** and **Puerto López** are your best bases for setting out on a whale-watching excursion. See chapter 9.
- **Surfing Lonely Waves along Ecuador's Pacific Coast:** Surfers love isolated or undiscovered breaks, and Ecuador is loaded with them. In fact, even the most crowded breaks here could be considered deserted by California standards. Beach and point breaks can be found up and down the Pacific coast. Montañita and Canoa are the country's top surfing destinations, and good bases to use for your search for the perfect wave. See chapters 4, 9, and 10.
- **White-Water Rafting & Kayaking:** With high Andean peaks plunging down to coastal lowlands in two directions, Ecuador is blessed with a host of white-water rivers perfect for rafting and kayaking. The small town of Tena, in El Oriente, is the country's hot spot for these sports, with easy access to everything from Class III to Class V rapids. The most popular rivers are the Upper Napo, or Río Jatunyacu, and the Río Misahuallí. There are also opportunities accessible

from Quito and other cities around the country. **Ríos Ecuador** ★★ (© 06/2886-727; www.riosecuador. com) is an excellent operator with offices in both Tena and Quito. See chapters 4 and 11.

- **Scuba Diving in the Galápagos Islands:** While most visitors spend their time marveling at the turtles, iguanas, boobies, and finches, diving the Galápagos may just provide the archipelago's most rewarding wildlife-viewing opportunities. The rich and

protected waters here are home to large quantities of sealife, from schools of hammerhead sharks, to manta rays, to large masses of jacks, barracuda, and other schooling fish. Lucky divers enjoy playful encounters with sea lions and penguins. Your best bet for enjoying the diving is to sign up for a cruise on a dedicated dive boat. You can also book dive trips out of Puerto Ayora or Puerto Baquerizo Moreno. See chapters 4 and 12.

5 The Best Bird-Watching

Ecuador is home to some 1,600 species of resident and migratory birds. With such a wide range in ecosystems, altitude, terrain, and habitat, you'll have to travel around the country some to get a full sense of the diversity. Many of the popular birding destinations in Ecuador have species counts well over 300 to 400. Below, I list some of the top bird-watching spots. See chapter 4, and the individual destinations, for more information.

- **Enjoying the Mists and Multitude of Species Found in the Cloud Forests of Mindo & Bellavista:** Cloud forests are unique ecosystems, renowned for their biological abundance. Located under 2 hours north of Quito, the cloud forests of Mindo and Bellavista are rich and rewarding stops for birders and nature lovers of all stripes. Over 400 species of birds have been recorded here, and experts believe the actual count is much higher. **El Monte** (© 09/3084-675; www.ecuadorcloudforest.com) and **Bellavista Cloud Forest Reserve** (© 02/2116-232; www.bellavista cloudforest.com) are two excellent lodges from which to base your bird-watching expeditions of this area. See p. 136, as well as chapter 4.
- **Spotting Some of the More Than 600 Species in Podocarpus National**

Park: This remote national park runs from a high of 3,700m (11,811 ft.) down to some 1,000m (3,281 ft.) above sea level, and contains ecosystems that range from high paramo to cloud forest and rainforest. The most common jumping-off points for visiting here are Loja and Vilcabamba. If you're looking for an excellent personal guide, contact Jorge Luis at **Caminatas Andes Sureños** (© 07/2673-147) See p. 227.

- **Catching Sight of Hundreds of Species in El Oriente:** The mid-elevation and lowland rainforests of Ecuador's El Oriente are prime bird-watching areas. Many lodges in this region have on-site bird-species lists that number 400 or more. Several species of macaws frolic overhead, while the prehistoric hoatzin inhabits the low branches of riverside trees. Just about any of the lodges in El Oriente can be considered top bird-watching destinations, but I recommend the **Napo Wildlife Center** (www.napowildlifecenter.com), which has a couple of parrot licks right on their grounds, where as many as several thousand mixed flock parrots may gather on any day to extract minerals and nutrients from an exposed clay river bank. See chapter 11.

- **Seeing Endemic Species on the Galápagos Islands:** What can you say? From the 13 species of Darwin's finches, to the only subtropical penguin, to the unique flightless cormorant, the Galápagos provide the greatest one-stop spot to check off a whole host of once-in-a-lifetime birds from your life's list. In fact, around half of all the bird fauna on the Galápagos is endemic, meaning you can only see them here. See chapter 12.

6 The Best Destinations for Families

- **El Telefériqo & Vulqano Park** (Quito; ☎ 02/3250-076; www.teleferiqo.com): If you spend any time in Quito, and if you have kids in town, this is a must-stop. The fast and thrilling ride up the mountain in this cable-car gondola is usually enough to put a smile on most kids' faces, and there's also an amusement park (Vulqano Park) at the base of the cable car. See p. 118.
- **Hacienda La Alegría** (Aloag; ☎ 02/2462-319; www.haciendalaalegria.com): This beautiful old hacienda is also a working farm. Kids can watch and even lend a hand when the cows are milked. Horseback riding is the specialty, and they have particularly good horses, trails, and trainers for introducing young riders to the sport. Their safety concern and record are exemplary. See p. 171.

- **Baños de Agua Santa:** While best known as a backpacker and adventure-travel hot spot, Baños is also great for kids. Vacationing Ecuadorian families come here, and many of the hotels and resorts cater to families. **Sangay Spa-Hotel** (☎ 03/2740-490; www.sangayspahotel.com) has a ton of excellent facilities and activities geared towards all ages. See chapter 7.
- **The Galápagos Islands:** Many of the Galápagos cruise ships and tour companies offer specific family-oriented tours. There is tons to see and do, and plenty of science, nature, and adventure to keep the whole family interested and entertained. **Tauck** ★★ (☎ 800/788-7885 in the U.S. and Canada; www.tauck.com) is an excellent soft-adventure company with distinctive family package tours to the Galápagos. See chapter 12.

7 The Best Luxury Hotels

- **JW Marriott Hotel** (Quito; ☎ 800/228-9290 in the U.S. and Canada, or 02/2972-000 in Ecuador; www.marriotthotels.com): With an imposing glass-atrium-covered lobby, gorgeous rooms, attentive service, and good restaurants, this is the best large luxury hotel not only in Quito but in all of Ecuador. The pool, spa, and recreational facilities are excellent, as are the business services. See p. 103.
- **Plaza Grande** (Quito; ☎ 02/2566-497; www.plazagrandequito.com): One of Quito's newest hotels is housed in an old classic-colonial home that was once the residence of one of the city's founding fathers. The meticulous restoration here is complemented by over-the-top luxury and personalized service. In addition to that you will be sleeping in the heart of Old Town, right off the Plaza de la Independencia (Plaza Grande). See p. 107.
- **Hotel Dann Carlton** (Quito; ☎ 02/2249-008; www.hotelesdann.com): The Dann Carlton is in many ways two hotels in one, combining the ambience and attention of a small boutique hotel with all the amenities,

facilities, and services of a luxury business-class hotel. Higher-floor rooms have excellent views. See p. 109.

- **La Mirage Garden Hotel & Spa** (Cotacachi; © 800/327-3573 in the U.S. and Canada, or 06/2915-237; www.mirage.com.ec): Arguably the most exclusive and opulent boutique hotel in the country, La Mirage offers refined accommodations, fine dining, and a spectacular spa. If that's not enough, a range of excellent hikes and adventure activities is available, and Otavalo is just a few minutes away. See p. 151.

- **Luna Runtun** (outside of Baños de Agua Santa; © 03/2740-882 or 03/2740-665; www.lunaruntun.com): With a breathtaking setting in the shadow of Volcán Tungurahua, this luxury spa offers up relaxations and rejuvenation, as well as a full plate of adventure activities and tours. The views from the rooms and suites are spectacular, and the spa here is one of the best in the country. See p. 191.

- **Hilton Colón Guayaquil** (Guayaquil; © 800/445-8667 in the U.S. and Canada, or 04/2689-000 in Ecuador; www.guayaquil.hilton.com): Guayaquil gets a lot of business travelers and hordes of folks overnighting on their way to and from the Galápagos Islands; this is the top hotel in town. The large rooms are well-appointed and some have good views. There are plenty of restaurant and nightlife options here, including a modern casino, and the hotel provides easy access to both the airport and downtown Guayaquil. See p. 243.

- **Royal Palm Hotel** (Santa Cruz Island, Galápagos; © 05/2527-409; www.royalpalmgalapagos.com): This is the most luxurious hotel on the Galápagos, and one of the plushest in the whole country. Every room here is gorgeous, but you'll want to splurge and get either a villa or a suite. See p. 346.

8 The Best Moderately Priced & Budget Hotels

- **Hotel Vieja Cuba** (Quito; © 02/2906-729; viejacuba@andinanet.net): Beautifully restored and wonderfully located, this Mariscal-district hotel provides great value. Hardwood floors, mosaic-tile bathrooms, a central courtyard fountain, and an excellent restaurant are just some of the perks. See p. 105.

- **Hotel San Francisco de Quito** (Quito; © 02/2287-758; www.sanfranciscodequito.com.ec): Offering tidy and comfortable rooms in a wonderfully preserved 17th-century converted home, this is my favorite budget option in Quito. This hotel is situated in the heart of Old Town. You get colonial charm and a great deal all in one. See p. 108.

- **Hacienda Guachala** (Cangahua, Cayambe; © 02/2363-042; www.guachala.com): Dating back to 1580, this rustic old hacienda provides all the colonial-era vibe and experience offered up by its more fancy brethren, at very reasonable prices. Granted, the rooms are quite rustic, but you'll have the undeniable feeling of staying at what was once a thriving colonial-era hacienda. A host of tours and activities are available, including a number of horseback-riding adventures. See p. 152.

- **Finca Chamanapamba** (Baños de Agua Santa; © 03/2742-671; www.chamanapamba.com): With a perfect setting, awe-inspiring views, neighboring Chamana waterfall, and comfortable accommodations, this is an excellent choice in the Baños area. I particularly like the waterfall-view balconies found around the grounds. The owners can arrange a number of tour and adventure options. See p. 192.

- **Posada del Angel** (Cuenca; ✆ 07/2840-695; ✆/fax 07/2821-360; www.hostalposadadelangel.com): It's hard to believe you can find such a charming room in such a charming converted old colonial home for such a bargain. The building is over 120-years old, yet the place is lively and cheery. There are a couple of classic interior courtyards, and second floor lounge areas. If you want more privacy, and a bit of a view, ask for a room on the third or fourth floor. See p. 215.

- **Hostería Alándaluz** (south of Puerto López; ✆ 04/2780-686; www.alandaluzhosteria.com): An environmentally conscious and eclectic collection of rooms and bungalows on a beautiful spot along the Pacific coast, this is one of my favorite beach hotels in all of Ecuador. Rooms come in a wide range of styles and prices, from semi-rustic doubles to almost opulent suites. Even the least expensive options are quite nice. Heck, you can even camp here. See p. 261.

- **Hotel Sol y Mar** (Puerto Ayora, Isla Santa Cruz; ✆ 05/2526-139): When you can score an ocean-front room with a balcony on the Galápagos Islands for under $50 (£25), you know you've found a good deal. Accommodations here have tasteful decor, and the common areas are wonderfully inviting. See p. 348.

8 The Best Ecolodges & Haciendas

Two distinct, yet in some ways similar, lodging options in Ecuador are small, converted old haciendas and isolated ecolodges. While the haciendas tend to be located on the high Andean plains, the ecolodges are mostly found in the Oriente or the Amazon basin. Both tend to be small and isolated, and nature-viewing and active adventure activities are the order of the day.

- **Hacienda Cusín** (San Pablo del Lago, Otavalo; ✆ 06/2918-013; www.haciendacusin.com): This 17th-century hacienda was sold originally at auction in Spain by King Phillip II. It's located just outside of Otavalo, beside the pretty San Pablo Lake. Accommodations, food, and service are all top-draw, and the surrounding gardens and volcano views are delightful. See p. 150.

- **Hacienda Zuleta** (Angochahua, Imbabura; ✆ 02/2228-554; www.zuleta.com): With sprawling grounds;

a working cheese, cattle, and horse farm; and the largest original entrance plaza of any hacienda in Ecuador, this place exudes authenticity. Once the home of President Galo Plaza, and still in his family, the hacienda offers wonderful and comfortable rooms, tasty family-style meals, and a host of tour options. Horseback riding is excellent here. They also have a condor rescue project on their grounds. See p. 154.

- **Black Sheep Inn** (Chugchilán, Cotopaxi; ✆ 03/2814-587; www.blacksheepinn.com): This isolated high-altitude eco-lodge is built on a hillside overlooking a beautiful river canyon. Situated about midway along the famed Quilotoa Loop, this is hands-down the best place to stay while taking part in the hiking, biking, trekking, and other adventures available in this pretty and pristine area. See p. 178.

- **Hacienda Leito** (outside Patate, Baños; ℰ **03/2859-328;** www. haciendaleito.com): This isolated hacienda provides a fabulous mix of old and new. The original ranch building, with its original cobblestone driveway, central fountain, and antique artworks and furnishings, is a classic example of a colonial-Spanish hacienda. But the brand-new and extensive spa, up-to-date rooms, and free Wi-Fi let you know you're in the 21st century. See p. 183.
- **Hacienda San Augustín de Callo** (Lasso, Cotopaxi; ℰ/fax **02/2906-157;** www.incahacienda.com): My pick for the most unique hacienda in Ecuador, this place is built inside the ruins of both an Inca palace and a colonial-era monastery. Some of the rooms here have walls laid by Inca masons, with their distinctive stone work. All are stunning and unique, with artistic touches that range from hand-painted murals to working stone fireplaces. See p. 170.
- **Hostería La Andaluza** (Chuquipogyo, Chimborazo; ℰ **03/2949-370;** www.la-andaluzaec.com): Located on the outskirts of Riobamba, in the shadow of Chimborazo peak, this converted old hacienda is the best hotel for many miles around. A relaxed and cozy vibe and colonial-era authenticity are prevalent. The restaurant here is excellent, and a number of activities are available. See p. 200.
- **Kashama** (outside of Santo Domingo de los Colorados; ℰ **02/2773-193;**

www.kashama.com): This is a beautiful and relaxing jungle lodge and spa set on the shores of the Río Blanco. Creative design elements and arty touches abound. The inviting pool features a tall, sculpted waterfall, and the excellent spa here offers a wide range of treatments and cures. All sorts of tours and adventures are also offered. See p. 298.
- **Napo Wildlife Center** (lower Río Napo; ℰ/fax **02/2897-316;** www. napowildlifecenter.com): Run as a joint venture with the local Añangu Quichua community, this, like Kapawi (see below), is one of the top ecolodges in the Amazon basin. The 10 lakefront bungalows are rustically luxurious, and the guides, food, and service are superb. Tours and adventures are offered, including visits to local indigenous communities and tours of the rivers, lagoons, and creeks of this lowland rainforest region. See p. 312.
- **Kapawi Ecolodge & Reserve** (on the Río Pastaza; ℰ **800/613-6026** in the U.S. and Canada, or 04/228-5711 in Ecuador; www.kapawi.com): This pioneering ecolodge is located deep in the Amazon rainforest among the villages of the Achuar tribe. You can only reach Kapawi on a private charter flight, and the isolation is part of the charm. Beautiful cabins (built on stilts over a black-water lagoon), great food, and fantastic guides don't hurt, either. This place provides a top-notch Amazon rainforest experience. See p. 322.

10 The Best Bed-and-Breakfasts & Small Inns

- **Mansión del Angel** (Quito; ℰ **800/ 327-3573** in the U.S., or 02/2557-721 in Quito; www.mansiondel angel.com.ec): With crystal chandeliers, Oriental rugs, and four-poster

beds, this boutique hotel offers all the elegance and style of a bygone era, in the heart of Quito's New Town. Located steps away from the bustle and blur of all the restaurants and clubs of the Mariscal district, this place is a quiet and calm oasis inside. See p. 104.

- **Hotel Café Cultura** (Quito; ✆/fax **02/2224-271;** www.cafecultura.com): Hip and European in feel, this cozy Mariscal hotel features unique, artistically designed and decorated rooms, an excellent restaurant, and super service. Hand-painted murals abound, and many of the bathrooms are works of art in themselves. See p. 104.

- **Hotel Santa Lucía** (Cuenca; ✆ **07/ 2828-000;** www.santaluciahotel. com): Set right in the heart of colonial Cuenca, in a house that dates to 1859, this is one of the best boutique hotels in Ecuador. The colonial vibe is maintained throughout, but the rooms also feature plasma-screen televisions and free Wi-Fi. The central courtyard here is home to a towering magnolia tree, as well as an excellent restaurant. See p. 214.

- **Mansión Alcázar** (Cuenca; ✆ **800/ 327-3573** toll-free in the U.S. and Canada, or 07/2823-918 in Ecuador;

www.mansionalcazar.com): Like the Santa Lucía (above), this charming little hotel is housed in a remarkably well-restored old colonial mansion. The Alcázar has a pretty garden and several sumptuous sitting areas and lounges. See p. 213.

- **Madre Tierra** (Vilcabamba; ✆ **07/ 2640-269** or 09/3096-665; www. madretierra1.com): This fun, funky, and arty little hotel is a great retreat. The accommodations, featuring creative design touches, are all unique. There are stunning views from many of the rooms as well as from the common areas, and the hearty, healthy cuisine here is legendary. See p. 231.

- **Vistalmar** (Manta; ✆ **05/2621-671;** www.vistalmarecuador.com): From the two large jade horses near the entrance to the large Buddha sculpture in the main lounge area, you'll be struck at every turn by the art, sculpture, and decor here. When that stops piquing your interest, you can marvel at the ocean views from the hillside perch. See p. 275.

11 The Best Restaurants

- **Café Mosaico** (Quito; ✆ **02/2542- 871**): With an eclectic menu, convivial ambience, and outstanding view over Old Town Quito, the Café Mosaico is a must-visit spot. Come a bit before sunset and hopefully you'll be able to snag a table with a view. It gets very crowded here, and for good reason. See p. 113.

- **El Nispero** (Quito; ✆ **02/2226- 398**): While Ecuadorian cuisine is tasty enough, this upscale place takes the traditional fare and, in the words of a famous TV chef, "kicks them up a notch." Traditional dishes and ingredients are treated to creative preparations and pairings, although the chef never strays too far from his source. See p. 114.

- **Zazu** (Quito; ✆ **02/2543-559**): Brash and bold, Quito's hippest new restaurant is also one of its most satisfying. The Peruvian-born chef uses his native sensibility, fresh local ingredients, and ample imagination to create a consistently successful string of new and exciting dishes. Just about everything on the menu shines, but my favorite way to dine here is to trust the chef and sign on for his nightly tasting menu. See p. 114.

- **Hotel Ali Shungu** (Otavalo; ✆ **06/ 2920-750**): Housed inside a popular hotel, this is my favorite restaurant in Otavalo. The healthy and creative international cuisine is served in a cozy and inviting ambience. Locally grown organic produce is used wherever possible. This is a welcome treat for breakfast, lunch, or dinner. See p. 149.

- **Café Hood** (Baños de Agua Santa; ℂ 03/2740-573): A popular backpacker hangout, this cozy restaurant serves everything from Mexican burritos to Pad Thai, with a wide range of international and vegetarian dishes filling out the long menu. After eating you can browse the book-swap library, play a board game, or mingle with fellow travelers. See p. 193.

- **Villa Rosa** (Cuenca; ℂ 07/2837-944): Excellent Ecuadorian cuisine is matched with an elegant setting and superb service in this Cuenca restaurant. Although traditional Ecuadorian dishes are the mainstay here, they often are given little twists and turns that set them above what you'll find at most other local joints. This place is almost always busy—and it's closed on most weekend evenings—so reservations are essential. See p. 217.

- **Lo Nuestro** (Guayaquil; ℂ 04/2386-398): Elegant and relaxed, this is the best place in Guayaquil to enjoy classic Ecuadorian cooking in a refined setting. The restaurant is located a little outside downtown, but it's definitely worth the ride. See p. 246.

- **Sea Flower Restaurant** (Same; ℂ 06/2733-369): It's almost worth a trip to Ecuador's Pacific coast just to dine at this delightful spot. Presentations are eye-catching, and the food served lives up to the fanfare. Be sure to have a reservation—this place fills up fast. See p. 294.

- **The Marquis Restaurant** (Tena; ℂ 06/2886-513): You'll be as surprised as I was to find a relatively fine dining experience in such a remote and rural town. Grilled meats are the specialty here, and the restaurant does an excellent job with them. The nightly three-course prix-fix menu is an excellent deal. See p. 318.

- **La Garrapata Restaurante** (Puerto Ayora; ℂ 05/2526-264): Good food and a relaxed ambience are what you'll find at what's probably the most popular restaurant on the Galápagos. You're just steps from the ocean, and the seafood here is excellent. On weekends there's often live music. See p. 349.

12 The Best Shopping & Markets

Ecuador is renowned for its artisans and their craftsmanship. Woven products, made from sheep, alpaca, or even vicuña wool, are perhaps the most well known, but a wide range of arts and crafts is produced. The indigenous tribes of El Oriente weave bags and baskets and make ornamental jewelry from local products, while craftspeople and artists produce high-end art, silver jewelry, and *superfino* Panama hats in Cuenca.

- **Olga Fisch Folklore** (Quito; ℂ 02/2541-315; www.olgafisch.com): Olga Fisch was a pioneer in recognizing and promoting the artistry of Ecuador's artisans and craftspeople. She helped them refine and improve some of their designs. Today her shop-gallery remains the top place to go for the best selection of high-end products. You'll find everything here, from clothing to ceramics to paintings. You can get chess sets, with pieces carved from tagua nuts, or fine, one-off silver and gemstone jewelry. See p. 126.

- **Tianguez** (Quito; ℂ 02/2230-609; www.sinchisacha.org): Housed in a mazelike series of rooms that feel like catacombs under the San Francisco church, this is my favorite place to shop for handicrafts. Just about every corner and region of the country is represented here, with pieces from the various Amazon basin indigenous tribes, as well as primitive paintings from artisans of the central Sierra. You can buy trinkets for next to nothing, or fine works that will make a dent in your wallet. See p. 126.

- **Otavalo Market** (Otavalo): This is the most famous market in Ecuador, and perhaps in all of South America. Indeed, it's the place to come for all sorts of locally made crafts, including alpaca sweaters, rugs, and wall hangings, as well as a wide range of wood work, primitive paintings, and jewelry. Musicians can pick up some pan pipes or a *charango*. See p. 144.

- **San Antonio de Ibarra:** It seems as if everyone in this little town in Imbabura province is a woodcarver. Many of the works produced here are religious in theme, and often of monumental proportion. Still, you can get

plenty of decorative and functional pieces, and some that are easy enough to carry home with you (the others can be shipped). See chapter 6.

- **Cuenca:** From Panama hats to locally produced handicrafts, fine art works, and one-off jewelry, Cuenca holds its own against Quito and Otavalo as one of the top shopping cities in the country. Of particular interest are the visits to the actual Panama hat factories and the studio of renowned ceramic artist Eduardo Vega. See chapter 8.

- **Galápagos Jewelry** (Puerto Ayora; ⓒ 05/2526-044; www.galapagos jewelry.com): These folks have excellent one-off pieces, many in the shape and image of local flora and fauna. Cast silver is their strong suit, but they also work with stones and other metals. They also have a couple of outlets in Quito. See p. 345.

13 The Best After-Dark Fun

- **Mariscal District** (Quito): The 4- to 5-square-block area known as Mariscal, in the heart of Quito's New Town, is chock-full of bars, clubs, discos, and restaurants. It's busy here every night of the week, but especially Thursday through Saturday. Consider starting off on the Plaza Foch with a pub crawl, but be careful and use common sense, because crime against tourists is not unheard of here. See p. 130.

- **Baños de Agua Santa:** As befits a bustling backpacker and adventure-tourist town, Baños has a rocking nightlife. If the rumblings of Volcán Tungurahua keep you up at nights here, stroll down Calle Eloy Alfaro, where you'll find a string of bars, clubs, discos, and *peñas*. See p. 185.

- **Café Eucalyptus** (Cuenca; ⓒ 07/ 2849-157): Great tapas, an excellent wine list, locally produced tap beer, and top-notch call liquors combine

with a warm and welcoming ambience to make this hands-down the top after-dark gathering spot in Cuenca. I like the couch seating near the fireplace, but the bar is also a good place to settle in. Or, if you're looking for a little more privacy, head to the second floor. See p. 217.

- **Montañita** (South Pacific coast): In addition to their prowess on the sea, surfers are legendary for their après-surf sessions. Montañita is the top surfer town in Ecuador, and the raucous nightlife it has is fed by the flood of local and international surfers. See p. 254.

- **Puerto Ayora** (Galápagos): Puerto Ayora has a surprisingly lively, albeit limited, nightlife and bar scene. **Bongo Bar** (ⓒ 05/2526-264) is the most happening place in town at night. It's located on a rooftop and opens at 4pm but usually doesn't get busy until after 8pm. See p. 349.

14 The Best Websites about Ecuador

- **Latin America Network Information Center** (http://lanic.utexas.edu/la/Ecuador): This site contains a collection of diverse information about Ecuador. It's hands-down the best place for Web browsing, with helpful links to a wide range of tourism and general-information sites.

- **Vive Ecuador** (www.vivecuador.com): This is the official website of the Ecuadorian Ministry of Tourism. There's a lot of information here, although much of it is quite basic and the format can be hard to navigate at times.

- **Ecuador.US** (www.ecuador.us): This is a large and comprehensive tourism English-language site, with loads of useful information, history, and links.

- **Quito Cultura** (www.quitocultura.com): Although this site is in Spanish, it's the place to go to find out what concerts, art exhibits, and cultural activities and events are happening in Quito.

2

Planning Your Trip to Ecuador

A large majority of tourists coming to Ecuador do so as part of an organized package tour to the Galápagos, often with an "add-on" excursion to some other popular destination in the country. Whether or not you are traveling on your own or with a package, there are many factors to take into consideration, from the basics of where and when to go, to more subtle decisions about how to get around and how to stay in touch with loved ones while on the road—or the high seas. This chapter will answer these questions, and many more.

1 The Regions in Brief

The Republic of Ecuador sits near the northwestern corner of South America. It's bordered by Colombia to the north, Peru to the south and east, and the Pacific Ocean to the west. The Galápagos Islands, which straddle the equator, are located about 966km (618 miles) to the west in the Pacific Ocean. The country covers an area of 272,046 sq. km (105,037 sq. miles), making it roughly the same size as Colorado.

QUITO Situated at some 2,850m (9,300 ft.), Quito is the second-highest capital city in the world (after La Paz, Bolivia). It may be the capital of Ecuador, but it's only the second-most populous city in the country (after Guayaquil). It's a major transportation hub, so most visitors begin and end their trips to Ecuador here. Quito is one of the more charming cities in South America, and there's plenty to see and do. **Old Town,** with its wonderfully preserved colonial-style buildings, was declared a World Heritage Site by UNESCO in 1978—the first city to earn the designation. **New Town** is a lively cosmopolitan area, with all the

modern amenities you would expect to find in a world-class destination.

THE NORTHERN SIERRA Just north of Quito, the equator cuts across Ecuador and forms the border that roughly defines the country's northern Sierra, or highlands. **Imbabura** is the first province you hit, and one of the country's prime tourism destinations. In Imbabura, you can explore the colorful artisans market of **Otavalo** as well as nearby towns, where you'll find the workshops and homes of many of the artisans who supply this fabulous market. In addition, this region is one of high volcanic mountains and crater lakes. There are great hiking opportunities, especially at such beautiful spots as **Cuicocha Lake** and **Mojanda Lakes.** Farther north lies the province of Carchi and the small border town of **Tulcán,** a gateway, albeit a rather dangerous one, to Colombia.

THE CENTRAL SIERRA The central Sierra covers the area south of Quito. **Cotopaxi National Park** is a little more than an hour south of Quito, and it's one of the most popular attractions on mainland Ecuador. Active travelers can climb to the summit of the highest active volcano in the world, while anybody can marvel at its imposing beauty from the high-altitude paramo all around the park. The central Sierra contains many isolated, colonial-era haciendas that have been converted into fabulous hotels and lodges. Most offer a variety of active tour options, with horseback riding often being the mainstay. **Baños** and **Riobamba** are the primary tourist towns of the central Sierra. Travelers head to Baños mainly for both relaxation and active adventures. The city, which is nestled at the bottom of active Volcán Tungurahua, offers great hiking and biking opportunities, as well as easy access to great white-water rafting. You can also take a soothing soak in one of the hot springs, or pamper yourself with spa treatments. Riobamba is more of an industrial city, and there's not much to do here besides catching the popular **Nariz del Diablo (Devil's Nose)** tourist train, which involves a spectacular journey along the winding switchbacks of a steep rock face.

CUENCA & THE SOUTHERN SIERRA

Cuenca is the largest and most interesting city in the southern highlands. Like Quito, it was declared a World Heritage Site by UNESCO. Cuenca was the second-most important city in the Inca empire (after Cusco). Nearby, you can explore **Ingapirca**, an archaeological site with both Inca and pre-Inca ruins. Cajas National Park is located only an hour outside Cuenca, and farther south lies the small city of **Loja**, one of the oldest cities in Ecuador. South of Loja is the even-more-remote village of **Vilcabamba**, famed for the health and longevity of its residents. Many come here seeking to sip from the town's fountain of youth; others use it as a jumping-off point to visit the wild **Podocarpus National Park.**

GUAYAQUIL & THE SOUTHERN COAST

Guayaquil is Ecuador's largest city. Chiefly a port and industrial city, Guayaquil is reinventing itself at a dizzying pace. The city's attractive riverside walk, **Malecón 2000,** has served as the anchor for a mini-renaissance. Guayaquil boasts several excellent museums as well as top-notch hotels, restaurants, and bars. To the west of Guayaquil lies the Ruta del Sol (Route of the Sun), a string of beach resorts, small fishing villages, and isolated stretches of sand. Surfers come here to find that endless wave, and sun worshippers can get the perfect tan. At the north end of the Ruta del Sol is **Machalilla National Park.** The sleepy town of Puerto López, just outside the park, is a gateway to its mainland sections, as well as to **Isla de la Plata,** which is home to a rich variety of wildlife, and which is often called the "Poor Person's Galápagos."

NORTHERN PACIFIC COAST & LOWLANDS

Ecuador's northern coast and its surrounding lowlands are often neglected or avoided by most tourists, although Ecuadorians are well aware of this area's charms. The beaches around **Esmeraldas** and **Atacames** are by far the prettiest in the country. The seaside city of **Bahía de Caráquez** is a picturesque and peaceful place with a safe and scenic bayside Malecón. At the southern end of this section of coast is **Manta,** the country's second-largest port and home to a controversial U.S. airbase. **Santo Domingo de los Colorados,** a bit inland, serves as a major crossroads and little-known gateway to a couple of beautiful and isolated nature lodges.

EL ORIENTE

The eastern region of Ecuador, known as El Oriente, is a vast area of lowland tropical rainforests and jungle rivers. It is considered part of the Amazon basin because the rivers here all feed and form the great Amazon River just a little further downstream. The wildlife and bird-watching here are phenomenal;

visitors have a chance to see hundreds of bird species and over a dozen monkey species, as well as anaconda, caiman, and fresh-water dolphins. For the most part, the indigenous people in this region escaped domination by both the Incas and the Spanish, so they have been able to hold on to their ancient rituals and traditions. Most visitors explore this area by staying at one of many remote jungle lodges, some of which are surprisingly comfortable. English-speaking guides will take you to local villages, as well as show you the incredible diversity of wildlife here.

THE GALAPAGOS ISLANDS The Galápagos Islands, located about 966km (618 miles) off the coast of Ecuador, are one of nature's most unique outdoor laboratories. The unusual wildlife here helped Charles Darwin formulate his *Theory of Natural Selection.* Fortunately for modern-day visitors, not much has changed since Darwin's time, and the islands still offer visitors the chance to get up close and personal with a wide variety of unique and endemic species, including giant tortoises, marine iguanas, penguins, sea lions, albatrosses, boobies, and flightless cormorants. The best way to explore the area is on a cruise ship or yacht. You should note, however, that this isn't your typical cruise destination—the trips involve packed days of tours and activities, some of them strenuous. A more relaxing option would be to base yourself at a resort in Santa Cruz (the most populated island in the Galápagos) and take select day trips to the islands of your choice.

2 Visitor Information & Maps

The Ecuadorian Ministry of Tourism has limited resources, and there are virtually no government-sponsored tourist offices outside Ecuador. But the Ecuador Tourist Board has two similar websites, **www. vivecuador.com** and **www.purecuador. com**. Both have some basic information, as well as forms to fill out to have a brochure sent to you. I've been told a redesign and improvements are scheduled for the latter site, so keep checking back. For a list of some of the better websites and links, see chapter 1, "The Best Websites About Ecuador."

The **Corporación Metropolitana de Turismo (Metropolitan Tourism Corporation;** www.quito.com.ec) hands out excellent city maps of Quito and the entire country at all their desks, which includes those at both the major international airports in Quito and Guayaquil. The most detailed map available is produced by **International Travel Maps** (www.itmb.com), available online from the website listed or from www.amazon. com.

3 Entry Requirements

PASSPORTS

A valid passport is required to enter and depart Ecuador. For information on how to get a passport, go to "Passports" in the "Fast Facts" section of this chapter—the websites listed provide downloadable passport applications as well as the current fees for processing passport applications. For an up-to-date, country-by-country listing of passport requirements around the world, go to the "Foreign Entry Requirement" Web page of the U.S. State Department at **http://travel.state.gov**.

VISAS

Ecuadorian visas are not required for citizens of the United States, the United Kingdom, Canada, Australia, New

Ecuadorian Embassy Locations

In the U.S.: 2535 15th St. NW, Washington, DC 20009 (*(C)* **202/234-7200**; fax 202/667-3482)

In Canada: 50 O'Connor St., Suite 316, Ottawa, ON K1P 6L2 (*(C)* **613/563-8206**; fax 613/235-5776)

In the U.K.: 3 Hans Crescent, Knightsbridge, London, SW1X 0LS (*(C)* **020/7584-8084**; fax 020/7823-9701)

In Australia: 6 Pindari Crescent, O'Malley, ACT 2606 (*(C)* **628/64021**; fax 628/61231)

Zealand, South Africa, France, Germany, and Switzerland. Upon entry, you will automatically be granted permission to stay for up to 90 days. Technically, to enter the country you need a passport that is valid for more than 6 months, a return ticket, and proof of how you plan to support yourself while you're in Ecuador, but I've never seen a Customs official ask for the last two requirements. If you plan on spending more than 90 days here, you *will* need to apply for a visa at your local embassy (see "Ecuadorian Embassy Locations," above). Requirements include a passport valid for more than 6 months, a police certificate with criminal record from the state or province in which you currently live, a medical certificate, a return ticket, and two photographs.

MEDICAL REQUIREMENTS

For information on medical requirements and recommendations, see "Health" on p. 30.

4 When to Go

PEAK SEASON

The peak seasons for travelers to Ecuador last from mid-June to early September and from late December through early January, because most American and European visitors have vacation time during these months. Cruises in the Galápagos are booked solid during these times of year. But since Ecuador is hardly Disney World, you'll always be able to find a room (or a berth on a ship), and the country never feels overcrowded. I find that Ecuador is great throughout the year, so whenever you visit, you won't be disappointed.

CLIMATE

There are four distinct geographical zones in Ecuador, all subject to their own weather patterns.

In the **Galápagos,** June through September, the air and water are chilly and the winds can be a bit rough. October through May, the air and water temperatures are warmer, but you can expect periodic light rain almost daily.

On the **coast,** the rainy season lasts December through May; this season is marked by hot weather and high humidity. The cooler air temperature June through September attracts whales and dolphins to the waters off the coast. In an odd anomaly, it's actually much sunnier during the rainy season, with a pattern of sunny mornings and early afternoons, followed by distinct and heavy showers or storms in the afternoons. The dry season is often characterized by dense and heavy overcast skies that feel as if they want to let loose, but never do.

In **Quito and the highlands,** the weather is coolest June through September (the dry season), but it's only a few degrees colder than during the rest of the year. Keep in mind that although Quito is practically on the equator, the temperature can get quite cool because it's at such a high altitude. The city has an average high of 19°C (67°F) and an average low of 10°C (50°F). Throughout the rest of the highlands, the temperature is similarly consistent, with average highs and lows mostly determined by the altitude.

In the rainforests and lowlands of **El Oriente** it rains year-round, but the rain is especially hard late December through April. The driest period is October through December. The temperature in the jungle can reach 27° to 32°C (80°–90°F) during the day; it's a bit cooler at night.

HOLIDAYS

Official holidays in Ecuador include New Year's Day (Jan 1), Easter, Labor Day (May 1), Simón Bolívar Day (July 24), National Independence Day (Aug 10), Guayaquil Independence Day (Oct 9), All Souls' Day (Nov 2), Cuenca Independence Day (Nov 3), and Christmas Day (Dec 25). The country also closes down on some unofficial holidays, including Carnaval (Mon and Tues prior to Ash Wednesday), Battle of Pichincha (May 24), Christmas Eve (Dec 24), and New Year's Eve (Dec 31). Foundation of Quito (Dec 6) is observed as a holiday only in Quito.

ECUADOR CALENDAR OF EVENTS

Most of the events listed below are more traditions than organized events—there's not, for instance, a Día de los Muertos PR Committee that readily dispenses information. In many cases, I've given a more detailed description of the events listed below in the appropriate destination chapters throughout the book. Beyond that, you can contact the **Ecuadorian Tourism Ministry** (© 02/2507-559; www.vivecuador. com). Your best bet is probably to contact hotels or tour agencies in the destination where the event or festivities take place.

February

Carnaval (Carnival), nationwide. Public concerts, parades, city fairs, and heavy drinking are all part of the festivities. In many cities, water, egg, and/or flour fights are part of the tradition. The city of Guaranda (p.201) is particularly famous for its Carnaval celebrations, as is Esmeraldas (p. 285) and Ambato (p. 180). During the week or so just before the start of Lent.

April

Holy Week, countrywide. Religious processions are held in cities and towns throughout the country. Quito's Good Friday procession through Old Town is especially large and ornate, with large floats, thick clouds of incense, and numerous devotees, some of whom quite vigorously flagellate themselves. Week before Easter.

June

Inti Raymi, countrywide. The indigenous peoples of South America have always revered the sun. The Inca have left intact their celebration of the summer solstice, or Inti Raymi. It is celebrated nationwide, but especially throughout the northern Sierra, with Otavalo having the most famous celebrations. In Otavalo, Inti Raymi festivities blend into and overlap with the Catholic celebration of San Juan de Batista (St. John the Baptist) on June 24.

July

Fiestas de Guayaquil, Guayaquil. The country's largest city throws a large party for itself each July. Wild street parties, concerts, fireworks, and overall festivities last for at least a week on and around the official holiday, although in many ways, this party is merely a prelude to the October celebrations of the city's Independence Day. July 26.

September

Fiestas de Mama Negra, Latacunga. This generally sleepy central Sierra city comes alive with a vengeance during its celebrations of the Virgen de la Merced (Virgin of Mercy), better known locally as Mama Negra (Black Mama). Each year, Ecuadorians flock to Latacunga and fill its streets with dancing and parades, fireworks and carnival rides. The festivities are unique in their mixing of indigenous, Spanish, and even African influences. September 23 and 24.

October

Independencia de Guayaquil (Guayaquil Independence Day), Guayaquil. Some say these are the largest civic parties in the country. Quiteños would probably disagree, but suffice it to say that Ecuador's largest city throws an appropriately large party to celebrate its independence day. Festivities include parades, rodeos, fireworks, and street parties, for several days on either side of the actual date of October 9.

November

Día de los Muertos (Day of the Dead), countrywide. Ecuadorians honor their dead with flowers and joyful remembrances. Many head to cemeteries, but the vibe is far from somber. November 2.

December

Fiestas de Quito, Quito. The capital city pulls out all the stops in early December to commemorate the city's founding. Celebrations last throughout the first, and most of the second, week of December. Concerts and street fairs can be found all over the city. Bullfights are held in the Plaza de Toros, with famous bullfighters coming from Spain and Mexico. A general air of celebration pervades the entire city. December 6 is the official date.

Christmas Eve, Cuenca. Obviously, the entire country celebrates Christmas, but the colonial city of Cuenca is famous for its Christmas Eve tradition of holding elaborate parades, with nativity scenes and other religious iconography on massive floats. December 24.

Años Viejos (Old Years), countrywide. In addition to the general debauchery and celebration, New Year's Eve is marked by an interesting tradition throughout Ecuador: Puppets and effigies symbolizing all that is bad or negative from the previous year are constructed, using old rags, sawdust, gunpowder, and fireworks as stuffing. Throughout the night, they sit on doorways and sidewalks. They are set on fire at the stroke of midnight, as part of celebrations. December 31.

5 Getting There

BY PLANE

There are two international airports in Ecuador. All flights into Quito land at the **Aeropuerto Internacional Mariscal Sucre** (© 02/2430-555; www.quito airport.com; airport code: UIO). Most international flights also touch down in Guayaquil's **José Joaquín de Olmedo International Airport** (© 04/2169-209; airport code GYE). If you plan to go to the Galápagos immediately after you arrive in Ecuador, it's best to fly into

Guayaquil. All international passengers leaving by air from Ecuador must pay a $38 (£19) departure tax.

FROM NORTH AMERICA American Airlines (© 800/433-7300 in the U.S. and Canada, or 02/2995-000 in Ecuador; www.aa.com) has one daily direct flight from Miami. **Continental Airlines** (© 800/231-0856 in the U.S. and Canada, or 02/2250-905 in Ecuador; www.continental.com) has one daily direct flight from Houston and another

New Quito Airport

Construction is under way at the sprawling new Quito airport, located 24km (15 miles) east of the current facility. The new airport will be 15 times larger, and is expected to open in 2009. Taxi fares to many hotels will likely double, and the trip to town will take about 40 to 50 minutes.

from Newark. **Delta** (✆ 800/241-4141 in the U.S. and Canada, or 1800/101-060 inside Ecuador; www.delta.com) has daily direct flights from Atlanta. And **LAN Chile/LAN Ecuador** (✆ 866/435-9526 in the U.S. and Canada, or 1800/526-328 in Ecuador; www.lanchile.com) offers direct service from JFK in New York to Guayaquil as well as direct service from Miami to Quito. **Taca** (✆ 800/400-8222 in the U.S. and Canada, or 1800/008-222 in Ecuador; www.grupotaca.com) has regular service to Ecuador from North America, via El Salvador or Costa Rica, while **Copa Airlines** (✆ 800/359-2672 in the U.S. and Canada; 02/2273-082 in Ecuador; www.copaair.com) offers daily flights from both Los Angeles and Miami to Ecuador with a quick stop in Panama City. Presently, there are no direct flights from Canada to Ecuador, so Canadians have to take a connecting flight via the United States.

FROM THE U.K. There are no direct flights from the United Kingdom to Ecuador. British travelers can fly to the United States (Atlanta, Miami, Houston, or New York) and then hook up with a direct flight (see "From North America," above). **Iberia** (✆ 0845/2601-2854; www.iberia.com) and **LAN Chile/LAN Ecuador** (see above) both offer daily, nonstop service between Madrid and Ecuador; convenient daily connections are available from London and a plethora of other European cities including Dublin, Paris, and Berlin. **KLM** (✆ 08705/2074-074; www.klmuk.co.uk) offers service from many cities in England to both Guayaquil and Quito via Amsterdam and Bonaire.

FROM AUSTRALIA & NEW ZEALAND To get to Ecuador from Australia or New Zealand, you'll first have to fly to Los Angeles, and then on to Miami or Houston, where you can connect with an American Airlines, Continental, or LAN Chile/LAN Ecuador flight to Ecuador. See "From North America," above, for more information.

FLYING FOR LESS: TIPS FOR GETTING THE BEST AIRFARE

- Passengers who can book their ticket either **long in advance** or **at the last minute,** or who **fly midweek** or **at less-trafficked hours** may pay a fraction of the full fare. If your schedule is flexible, say so, and ask if you can secure a cheaper fare by changing your flight plans.
- Search **the Internet** for cheap fares. The most popular online travel agencies are **Travelocity.com** (www.travelocity.co.uk); **Expedia.com** (www.expedia.co.uk and www.expedia.ca); and **Orbitz.com.** In the U.K., go to **Travelsupermarket** (✆ 0845/345-5708; www.travelsupermarket.com), a flight search engine that offers flight comparisons for the budget airlines whose seats often end up in bucket-shop sales. Other websites for booking airline tickets online include **Cheapflights.com, SmarterTravel. com, Priceline.com,** and **Opodo** (www.opodo.co.uk). Meta search sites (which find and then direct you to airline and hotel websites for booking) include **Sidestep.com** and **Kayak. com**—the latter includes fares for budget carriers like Jet Blue and

Spirit as well as the major airlines. **Site59.com** is a great source for last-minute flights and getaways. In addition, most **airlines** offer online-only fares that even their phone agents know nothing about. British travelers should check **Flights International** (© **0800/0187050;** www.flights-international.com) for deals on flights all over the world.

- Keep an eye on local newspapers for **promotional specials** or **fare wars,** when airlines lower prices on their most popular routes.
- Try to book a ticket **in its country of origin.** If you're planning a one-way flight from Johannesburg to New York, a South Africa–based travel agent will probably have the lowest fares. For foreign travelers on multi-leg trips, book in the country of the first leg; for example, book New York–Chicago–Montréal–New York in the U.S.

- **Consolidators,** also known as bucket shops, are wholesale brokers in the airline-ticket game. Consolidators buy deeply discounted tickets ("distressed" inventories of unsold seats) from airlines and sell them to online ticket agencies, travel agents, tour operators, corporations, and, to a lesser degree, the general public. Consolidators advertise in Sunday newspaper travel sections (often in small ads with tiny type), both in the U.S. and the U.K. They can be great sources of cheap international tickets. On the downside, bucket shop tickets are often rigged with restrictions, such as stiff cancellation penalties (as high as 50%–75% of the ticket price). And keep in mind that most of what you see advertised is of limited availability. Several reliable consolidators are worldwide and available online. **STA Travel** (www.statravel.com) has been the world's leading consolidator

---

Tips Getting Through the Airport

- Arrive at the airport 1 hour before a domestic flight and 2 hours before an international flight; if you show up late, tell an airline employee and he or she will probably whisk you to the front of the line.
- Beat the ticket-counter lines by using airport electronic kiosks or even online check-in from your home computers, from where you can print out boarding passes in advance. Curbside check-in is also a good way to avoid lines.
- Bring a current, government-issued photo ID such as a driver's license or passport. Children under 18 do not need government-issued photo IDs for flights within the U.S., but they do for international flights to most countries.
- Speed up security by removing your jacket and shoes before you're screened. In addition, remove metal objects such as big belt buckles. If you've got metallic body parts, a note from your doctor can prevent a long chat with the security screeners.
- Use a TSA-approved lock for your checked luggage. Look for Travel Sentry certified locks at luggage or travel shops and Brookstone stores (or online at www.brookstone.com).

Tips Don't Stow It—Ship It

Though pricey, it's sometimes worthwhile to travel luggage-free. Specialists in door-to-door luggage delivery include **Virtual Bellhop** (www.virtualbellhop. com), **SkyCap International** (wwww.skycapinternational.com), **Luggage Express** (www.usxpluggageexpress.com), and **Sports Express** (www.sportsexpress.com).

---

for students since purchasing Council Travel, but their fares are competitive for travelers of all ages. **Flights.com** (© 800/TRAV-800; www.flights. com) has excellent fares worldwide, particularly to Europe. They also have "local" websites in 12 countries. **FlyCheap** (© 800/FLY-CHEAP; www.1800flycheap.com) has especially good fares to sunny destinations. **Air Tickets Direct** (© 800/ 778-3447; www.airticketsdirect.com) is based in Montreal and leverages the currently weak Canadian dollar for low fares; they also book trips to places that U.S. travel agents won't touch, such as Cuba.

- Join **frequent-flier clubs.** Frequent-flier membership doesn't cost a cent, but it does entitle you to free tickets or upgrades when you amass the airline's required number of frequent-flier points. You don't even have to fly to earn points; **frequent-flier credit cards** can earn you thousands of miles for doing your everyday shopping. But keep in mind that award seats are limited, seats on popular routes are hard to snag, and more and more major airlines are cutting their expiration periods for mileage points—so check your airline's frequent-flier program so you don't lose your miles before you use them. *Inside tip:* Award seats are offered almost a year in advance, but seats also open up at the last minute, so if your travel plans are flexible, you may strike gold. To play the frequent-flier game to your best advantage, consult the community bulletin boards on **FlyerTalk** (www. flyertalk.com) or go to Randy Petersen's **Inside Flyer** (www.inside flyer.com). Petersen and friends review all the programs in detail and post regular updates on changes in policies and trends.

GETTING INTO TOWN FROM THE AIRPORT

It's easy and inexpensive to get from both of the international airports to their respective downtown areas. Depending upon whether you are arriving in Quito or Guayaquil, see the corresponding "Getting There: By Plane" sections for more details.

All the major rental-car agencies operating in the country have desks at these airports. See "Getting Around: By Car," later in this chapter, for more information.

LONG-HAUL FLIGHTS: HOW TO STAY COMFORTABLE

Long flights can be trying; stuffy air and cramped seats can make you feel as if you're being sent parcel post in a small box. But with a little advance planning, you can make an otherwise unpleasant experience almost bearable.

- Your choice of airline and airplane will definitely affect your leg room. Find more details about U.S. airlines at **www.seatguru.com**. For international airlines, the research firm Skytrax has posted a list of average seat pitches at **www.airlinequality.com**.
- Emergency exit seats and bulkhead seats typically have the most legroom. Emergency exit seats are usually left unassigned until the day of a flight

(to ensure that someone able-bodied fills the seats); it's worth getting to the ticket counter early to snag one of these spots for a long flight. Many passengers find that bulkhead seating (the row facing the wall at the front of the cabin) offers more legroom, but keep in mind that bulkheads are where airlines often put baby bassinets, so you may be sitting next to an infant.

- To have two seats for yourself in a three-seat row, try for an aisle seat in a center section toward the back of coach. If you're traveling with a companion, book an aisle and a window seat. Middle seats are usually booked last, so chances are good you'll end up with three seats to yourselves.
- Ask about entertainment options. Many airlines offer seatback video systems where you get to choose your movies or play video games—but only on some of their planes. (Boeing 777s are your best bet.)
- To sleep, avoid the last row of any section or the row in front of an emergency exit, as these seats are the least likely to recline. Avoid seats near highly trafficked toilet areas. Avoid seats in the back of many jets—these can be narrower than those in the rest of coach. You also may want to

reserve a window seat so you can rest your head and avoid being bumped in the aisle.

- Get up, walk around, and stretch every 60 to 90 minutes to keep your blood flowing.
- Drink water before, during, and after your flight to combat the lack of humidity in airplane cabins. Avoid alcohol, which will dehydrate you.
- If you're flying with kids, don't forget to carry on toys, books, pacifiers, and chewing gum to help them relieve ear pressure buildup during ascent and descent.

BY CAR

It's possible, but very difficult and impractical, to travel to Ecuador by car. For all intents and purposes, this is not an option for travelers. For more information about driving in Ecuador, see "Getting Around: By Car," later in this chapter.

BY BUS

It is possible to travel by bus to Ecuador from Peru. (I don't recommend traveling from Colombia due to kidnapping incidents near the border.) From Peru, the most popular border crossing is from Tumbes to Huaquillas in Ecuador. See chapter 9 for more information.

6 Money & Costs

It's always advisable to bring money in a variety of forms on a vacation: a mix of cash, credit cards, and traveler's checks. You should also exchange enough petty cash to cover airport incidentals, tipping, and transportation to your hotel before you leave home, or withdraw money upon arrival at an airport ATM.

Tips Small Change

Before coming to Ecuador, and whenever you make a purchase, get some smaller bills and coins. Petty cash will come in handy for tipping and public transportation. Many taxi drivers and small shop owners have trouble making change for a $20 bill. Consider keeping the change separate from your larger bills, so that it's readily accessible and you'll be less of a target for theft.

The U.S. Dollar, the British Pound & the Euro

US $	UK £	Euro €
0.50	0.28	0.39
1.00	0.55	0.77
5.00	2.75	3.85
10.00	5.50	7.70
25.00	14.00	19.00
50.00	28.00	39.00
100.00	55.00	77.00
250.00	138.00	193.00
500.00	275.00	385.00
1,000.00	550.00	770.00
2,500.00	1,375.00	1,925.00

In many international destinations, ATMs offer the best exchange rates. Avoid exchanging money at commercial exchange bureaus and hotels, which often have the highest transaction fees.

CURRENCY

Since 2000, the official unit of currency in Ecuador has been the **U.S. dollar.** You can use American or Ecuadorian coins, both of which come in denominations of 1¢, 5¢, 10¢, 25¢, and 50¢. Otherwise, all the currency is in the paper form of American dollars, in denominations of 1, 5, 10, 20, 50, and 100. It's very hard to make change, especially for any bill over $5, especially in taxis. If you are retrieving money from an ATM, be sure to request a denomination ending in 1 or 5 (most ATMs will dispense money in multiples of $1) so that you won't have to worry about breaking a large bill. If you are stuck with big bills, try to use them in restaurants to make change.

ATMs

The easiest and best way to get cash away from home is from an ATM (automatedteller machine), sometimes referred to as a "cash machine," or a "cashpoint." **Cirrus**

(*©* **800/424-7787;** www.mastercard.com) and **PLUS** (*©* **800/843-7587;** www.visa.com) networks span the globe. Go to your bank card's website to find ATM locations at your destination. Be sure you know your daily withdrawal limit before you depart. *Note:* Many banks impose a fee every time you use a card at another bank's ATM, and that fee can be higher for international transactions (up to $5 or more) than for domestic ones (where they're rarely more than $2). In addition, the bank from which you withdraw cash may charge its own fee. For international withdrawal fees, ask your bank.

Note: Banks that are members of the **Global ATM Alliance** charge no transaction fees for cash withdrawals at other Alliance member ATMs; these include Bank of America, Scotiabank (Canada, Caribbean, and Mexico), Barclays (U.K. and parts of Africa), Deutsche Bank (Germany, Poland, Spain, and Italy), and BNP Paribus (France).

ATMs are ubiquitous in Ecuador. You'll even find them in remote areas such as the Galápagos. Some of the major banks include **Banco de Guayaquil, Banco del Pichincha,** and **Banco del**

What Things Cost in Ecuador	US$	UK£
Taxi from the airport to New Town	5.00	2.75
Taxi from New Town to Old Town	2.00–3.00	1.10–1.65
Double room, expensive	80.00–120.00	44.00–66.00
Double room, moderate	40.00–80.00	22.00–44.00
Double room, inexpensive	20.00–40.00	11.00–22.00
Dinner for one without wine, expensive	10.00–20.00	5.50–11.00
Dinner for one without wine, moderate	6.00–10.00	3.30–5.50
Dinner for one, inexpensive	4.00–6.00	2.20–3.30
Bottle of Pilsner beer	1.00–1.50	0.50–0.83
Bottle of Coca-Cola	1.00	0.55
Cup of coffee	1.00–1.50	0.55–0.83
Gallon of premium gas	1.60	0.88
Admission to most museums	1.00–2.00	0.55–1.10
Admission to Galápagos National Park	100.00	55.00
Airport exit tax	38.00	21.00

Pacífico. Most ATMs accept cards from both the **Cirrus** and **PLUS** networks, but some can't deal with PINs that are more than four digits. Before you go to Ecuador, make sure that your PIN fills the bill.

If your ATM card doesn't work and you need cash in a hurry, contact **Western Union** (©1800/989-898 in Ecuador; www.westernunion.com), which has numerous offices around Quito and other major towns and cities. It offers a secure and rapid (although pricey) money-wire and telegram service. A $100 wire costs around $15, and a $1,000 wire costs around $50.

CREDIT CARDS

Credit cards are another safe way to carry money. They also provide a convenient record of all your expenses, and they generally offer relatively good exchange rates. You can withdraw cash advances from your credit cards at banks or ATMs, but high fees make credit-card cash advances a pricey way to get cash. Keep in mind that you'll pay interest from the moment of your withdrawal, even if you pay your monthly bills on time. Also, note that many banks now assess a 1% to 3% "transaction fee" on **all** charges you incur abroad (whether you're using the local currency or your native currency).

TRAVELER'S CHECKS

You can buy traveler's checks at most banks. They are offered in denominations of $20, $50, $100, $500, and sometimes $1,000. Generally, you'll pay a service charge ranging from 1% to 4%.

The most popular traveler's checks are offered by **American Express** (© 800/807-6233, or 800/221-7282 for card holders—this number accepts collect calls, offers service in several foreign languages, and exempts Amex gold and platinum cardholders from the 1% fee.); **Visa** (© 800/732-1322)—AAA members can obtain Visa checks for a $9.95 fee (for checks up to $1,500) at most AAA offices or by calling © 866/339-3378; and **MasterCard** (© 800/223-9920).

Be sure to keep a record of the traveler's checks serial numbers separate from your checks in the event that they are stolen or lost. You'll get a refund faster if you know the numbers.

American Express, Thomas Cook, Visa, and **MasterCard** offer **foreign currency traveler's checks,** useful if you're traveling to one country or to the Euro zone; they're accepted at locations where dollar checks may not be.

Another option is the new prepaid traveler's check cards, reloadable cards that work much like debit cards but aren't linked to your checking account. The **American Express Travelers Cheque Card,** for example, requires a minimum deposit, sets a maximum balance, and has a one-time issuance fee of $14.95. You can withdraw money from an ATM (for a fee of $2.50 per transaction, not including bank fees), and the funds can be purchased in dollars, euros, or pounds. If you lose the card, your available funds will be refunded within 24 hours.

7 Travel Insurance

The cost of travel insurance varies widely, depending on the destination, the cost and length of your trip, your age and health, and the type of trip you're taking, but expect to pay between 5% and 8% of the vacation itself. You can get estimates from various providers through Insure-MyTrip.com. Enter your trip cost and dates, your age, and other information, for prices from more than a dozen companies.

U.K. citizens and their families who make more than one trip abroad per year may find an annual travel insurance policy works out cheaper. Check **www. moneysupermarket.com**, which compares prices across a wide range of providers for single- and multitrip policies.

Most big travel agents offer their own insurance and will probably try to sell you their package when you book a holiday. Think before you sign. **Britain's Consumers' Association** recommends that you insist on seeing the policy and reading the fine print before buying travel insurance. **The Association of British Insurers** (© 020/7600-3333; www.abi.org. uk) gives advice by phone and publishes *Holiday Insurance,* a free guide to policy provisions and prices. You might also shop around for better deals: Try **Columbus Direct** (© 0870/033-9988; www. columbusdirect.net).

TRIP-CANCELLATION INSURANCE

Trip-cancellation insurance will help you retrieve your money if you have to back out of a trip or depart early, or if your travel supplier goes bankrupt. Trip cancellation traditionally covers such events as sickness, natural disasters, and State Department advisories. The latest news in trip-cancellation insurance is the availability of **expanded hurricane coverage** and the **"any-reason"** cancellation coverage—which costs more but covers cancellations made for any reason. You won't get back 100% of your prepaid trip cost, but you'll be refunded a substantial portion. **TravelSafe** (© **888/885-7233;** www.travelsafe.com) offers both types of coverage. Expedia also offers any-reason cancellation coverage for its air-hotel packages.

For details, contact one of the following recommended insurers: **Access America** (© 866/807-3982; www.accessamerica. com); **Travel Guard International** (© 800/826-4919; www.travelguard. com); **Travel Insured International** (© 800/243-3174; www.travelinsured. com); and **Travelex Insurance Services** (© 888/457-4602; www.travelex-insurance.com).

MEDICAL INSURANCE

For travel overseas, most U.S. health plans (including Medicare and Medicaid) do not provide coverage, and the ones that do often require you to pay for services upfront and reimburse you only after you return home.

As a safety net, you may want to buy travel medical insurance, particularly if you're traveling to a remote or high-risk area where emergency evacuation might be necessary. If you require additional medical insurance, try **MEDEX Assistance** (© 410/453-6300; www.medex assist.com) or **Travel Assistance International** (© 800/821-2828; www.travel assistance.com; for general information on services, call the company's **Worldwide Assistance Services, Inc.,** at © 800/777-8710).

Canadians should check with their provincial health plan offices or call **Health Canada** (© 866/225-0709; www. hc-sc.gc.ca) to find out the extent of their coverage and what documentation and receipts they must take home in case they are treated overseas.

LOST-LUGGAGE INSURANCE

On international flights (including U.S. portions of international trips), baggage coverage is limited to approximately $9.07 per pound, up to approximately $635 per checked bag. If you plan to check items more valuable than what's covered by the standard liability, see if your homeowner's policy covers your valuables, get baggage insurance as part of your comprehensive travel-insurance package, or buy Travel Guard's "BagTrak" product.

If your luggage is lost, immediately file a lost-luggage claim at the airport, detailing the luggage contents. Most airlines require that you report delayed, damaged, or lost baggage within 4 hours of arrival. The airlines are required to deliver luggage, once found, directly to your house or destination free of charge.

8 Health

STAYING HEALTHY

Staying healthy on a trip to Ecuador is predominantly a matter of being cautious about what you eat and drink, and using common sense. Know your physical limits, and don't overexert yourself in the ocean, on hikes, or in athletic activities. Many people need a day or two to acclimate to higher altitudes.

No specific shots or vaccines are necessary before traveling to Ecuador, although vaccinations against Hepatitis A are always a good idea.

GENERAL AVAILABILITY OF HEALTH CARE

In general, the health care system in Ecuador is pretty good and can handle most emergencies and common illnesses. For a list of hospitals around the country, check the "Fast Facts" section of the destination chapters, or see "Hospitals," in "Fast Facts: Ecuador," later in this chapter.

Although pharmacies are well-stocked and widespread, you should still carry with you sufficient supplies of any prescription medicines you may need. Most over-the-counter remedies commonly available at home should be relatively available in all but the most remote destinations around Ecuador, although you may have some trouble figuring out what the local equivalent is.

Contact the **International Association for Medical Assistance to Travelers** (**IAMAT;** © 716/754-4883, or 416/ 652-0137 in Canada; www.iamat.org) for tips on travel and health concerns in the countries you're visiting, and for lists of local, English-speaking doctors. The United States **Centers for Disease Control and Prevention** (© 800/311-3435; www.cdc.gov) provides up-to-date information on health hazards by region or country and offers tips on food safety.

Travel Health Online (www.tripprep. com), sponsored by a consortium of travel medicine practitioners, may also offer helpful advice on traveling abroad. You can find listings of reliable medical clinics overseas at the **International Society of Travel Medicine** (www.istm.org).

COMMON AILMENTS

DIETARY RED FLAGS Travelers to Ecuador should be very careful about contracting **food-borne illnesses.** Always drink bottled water. Avoid beverages with ice unless you are sure that the water for the ice has been previously boiled. Be very careful about eating food purchased from street vendors. Some travelers swear by taking supplements such as super bromelain, which helps aid in the digestion of parasites; consult your doctor to find out whether this is a good option for you. In the event you experience any intestinal woe, staying well-hydrated is the most important step. Be sure to drink plenty of bottled water, as well as some electrolyte-enhanced sports drinks, if possible.

HIGH-ALTITUDE HAZARDS Of concern in areas of high altitude is **altitude sickness.** Common symptoms include headaches, nausea, sleeplessness, and a tendency to tire easily. The most common remedies include taking it easy, abstaining from alcohol, and drinking lots of bottled water. To help alleviate these symptoms, you can also take the drug acetazolamide (Diamox); consult your doctor for more information.

TROPICAL SUN Limit your exposure to the sun, especially during the first few days of your trip and, thereafter, from 11am to 2pm. Use a **sunscreen** with a high protection factor, and apply it liberally. Remember that children need more protection than adults do. Don't be deceived by cool weather or cloud cover. I've been foolish enough to think I didn't need sunscreen on a severely overcast day, and paid the price with a painful sunburn.

MALARIA Fortunately, since mosquitoes can't live at high altitudes, **malaria** is not a risk in Quito, Cuenca, Baños, or Otavalo. Although located at sea level, there's no malaria risk in the Galápagos, either. But because there is a small risk of malaria for travelers who plan on spending time in the jungle areas of El Oriente or the Pacific lowlands, the CDC recommends that you protect yourself by taking the drugs mefloquine, doxycycline, or Malarone. Insect repellent is probably your best protection against malaria.

WHAT TO DO IF YOU GET SICK AWAY FROM HOME

The best and most modern hospitals can be found in Quito and Guayaquil. Most other major cities and towns will have a hospital or two. Your home country's embassy or consulate can provide a list of area doctors who speak English. If you get sick, consider asking your hotel staff or concierge to recommend a local doctor—even his or her own. I list **hospitals** and **emergency numbers** in "Fast Facts" (later in this chapter), as well as in the "Fast Facts" sections of each destination section throughout the book.

Healthy Travels to You

The following government websites offer up-to-date health-related travel advice.

- **Australia:** www.dfat.gov.au/travel
- **Canada:** www.hc-sc.gc.ca/index_e.html
- **U.K.:** www.dh.gov.uk/PolicyAndGuidance/HealthAdviceForTravellers/fs/en
- **U.S.:** www.cdc.gov/travel

You may have to pay all medical costs upfront and be reimbursed later. Medicare and Medicaid do not provide coverage for medical costs outside the U.S. Before leaving home, find out what medical services your health insurance covers. To protect yourself, consider buying medical travel insurance (see "Medical Insurance," under "Travel Insurance," above).

Very few health insurance plans pay for medical evacuation back to the U.S. (which can cost $10,000 and up). A number of companies offer medical evacuation services anywhere in the world. If you're ever hospitalized more than 150 miles from home, **MedjetAssist** (© **800/ 527-7478;** www.medjetassistance.com) will pick you up and fly you to the hospital of your choice virtually anywhere in the world in a medically equipped and staffed aircraft 24 hours day, 7 days a week. Annual memberships are $225 individual, $350 family; you can also purchase short-term memberships.

U.K. nationals will need a **European Health Insurance Card (EHIC)** to receive free or reduced-costs health benefits during a visit to a European Economic Area (EEA) country (European Union countries plus Iceland, Liechtenstein, and Norway) or Switzerland. The European Health Insurance Card replaces the E111 form, which is no longer valid. For advice, ask at your local post office or see www.dh.gov.uk/travellers.

We list **hospitals** and **emergency numbers** in "Fast Facts," later in this chapter.

If you suffer from a chronic illness, consult your doctor before your departure. Pack **prescription medications** in your carry-on luggage, and carry them in their original containers, with pharmacy labels—otherwise they won't make it through airport security. Carry the generic name of prescription medicines, in case a local pharmacist is unfamiliar with the brand name.

9 Safety

STAYING SAFE

Robberies and pickpocketing are the greatest problem facing most tourists to Ecuador. Crowded markets, public buses, and busy urban areas are the prime haunts of criminals and pickpockets. Never carry a lot of cash or wear very valuable jewelry. Men should avoid having a wallet in their back pants pocket. A woman should keep a tight grip on her purse. (Keep it tucked under your arm.) Thieves also target gold chains, cameras and video cameras, prominent jewelry, and nice sunglasses. Be sure not to leave valuables exposed or unattended in your hotel room.

Rental cars generally stick out, and they are easily spotted by thieves. Don't ever leave anything of value in a car parked on the street. Also be wary of solicitous strangers who stop to help you change a tire or bring you to a service station. Although most are truly good Samaritans, there have been reports of thieves preying on roadside breakdowns. Public intercity buses are also frequent targets of stealthy thieves. Never check your bags into the hold of a bus if you can avoid it. If this can't be avoided, when the bus makes a stop, keep your eye on what leaves the hold. If you put your bags in an overhead rack, be sure you can see the bags at all times. Try not to fall asleep during the trip. For more information on car and road safety, see "Getting Around: By Car," later in this chapter.

The Ecuadorian indigenous people are very uneasy about having their picture taken. Many, in the more touristy areas, have parlayed this into a means of earning a few dollars, by charging to have their picture taken. In the more remote and rural areas, a rude or disrespectful foreign shutterbug can earn the strong and sometimes vocal disdain of the local population. Always ask permission before taking photographs of people.

Political gatherings to protest current economic and social conditions are not uncommon. The most common form of this is the blockading of roads and highways. There's really little you can do to avoid this, though a fair amount of patience and some compassion will ease the bother and lower your stress levels. Many of these protests and blockades are announced in advance in the newspapers. If you have an important flight or connection, and you have a long ride to the airport, ask your hotel to check on any alerts, and be sure to leave plenty of time for your drive to the airport.

10 Specialized Travel Resources

TRAVELERS WITH DISABILITIES

Most disabilities shouldn't stop anyone from traveling. There are more options and resources out there than ever before. But Ecuador is severely behind the times in making structural changes to address the needs of its own citizens with disabilities—not to mention visitors with disabilities. In most cities, sidewalks are narrow, crowded, and uneven. Few hotels offer wheelchair-accessible accommodations, and there are no public buses equipped to handle those in wheelchairs. The Quito trolley system can handle wheelchair passengers, although its near constant overcrowding makes this better in theory than in practice. A few of the higher-end large hotels in Quito and Guayaquil have specific wheelchair-accessible rooms and bathrooms.

Organizations that offer a vast range of resources and assistance to disabled travelers include **MossRehab** (© 800/CALL-MOSS;** www.mossresourcenet.org); the **American Foundation for the Blind (AFB;** © 800/232-5463;** www.afb.org); and **SATH (Society for Accessible Travel & Hospitality;** © 212/447-7284;** www.sath.org). **AirAmbulance Card.com** is now partnered with SATH and allows you to preselect top-notch hospitals in case of an emergency.

Access-Able Travel Source (© 303/232-2979;** www.access-able.com) offers a comprehensive database on travel agents from around the world with experience in accessible travel; destination-specific access information; and links to such resources as service animals, equipment rentals, and access guides.

Many travel agencies offer customized tours and itineraries for travelers with disabilities. Among them are **Flying Wheels Travel** (© 507/451-5005;** www.flying wheelstravel.com); and **Accessible Journeys** (© 800/846-4537** or 610/521-0339; www.disabilitytravel.com).

Flying with Disability (www.flying-with-disability.org) is a comprehensive information source on airplane travel. **Avis Rent a Car** (© 888/879-4273) has an "Avis Access" program that offers services for customers with special travel needs. These include specially outfitted vehicles with swivel seats, spinner knobs, and hand controls; mobility scooter rentals; and accessible bus service. Be sure to reserve well in advance.

Also check out the quarterly magazine *Emerging Horizons* (www.emerging horizons.com), available by subscription ($16.95 per year in the U.S., $21.95 outside U.S.).

The "Accessible Travel" link at **Mobility-Advisor.com** (www.mobility-advisor.com) offers a variety of travel resources to disabled persons.

British travelers should contact **Holiday Care** (© 0845-124-9971** in U.K. only; www.holidaycare.org.uk) to access a

wide range of travel information and
resources for disabled and elderly people.

GAY & LESBIAN TRAVELERS

Ecuador is a predominantly Catholic,
socially conservative country, and in general terms the nation is considerably
homophobic. Public displays of same-
sex affection are rare. For these reasons,
the local gay and lesbian communities
are pretty discreet. While Quito and
Guayaquil have something of a gay and
lesbian scene, with several bars and clubs
catering to this clientele, the situation
gets radically worse outside these large,
modern metropolitan centers. For good,
comprehensive information on the current situation, check out **http://quito.
queercity.info**, the best English-language
online resource for gay travelers to
Ecuador, although the site is almost
exclusively geared toward men. The website **http://grupocanela.tripod.com** is
another good resource, with some pages
in English and some specific information
for the local and visiting lesbian and
bisexual populations. **Galápagos Traveller** (www.galapagostraveller.com) is a
recommended GLB-friendly Ecuadorian
travel agency.

The **International Gay and Lesbian
Travel Association** (IGLTA; © 800/448-
8550 or 954/776-2626; www.iglta.org) is
the trade association for the gay and lesbian travel industry, and offers an online
directory of gay- and lesbian-friendly
travel businesses and tour operators.

Many agencies offer tours and travel
itineraries specifically for gay and lesbian
travelers. **Above and Beyond Tours**
(© 800/397-2681; www.abovebeyond
tours.com) are gay Australia tour specialists. San Francisco–based **Now, Voyager**
(© 800/255-6951; www.nowvoyager.
com) offers worldwide trips and cruises.
Olivia (© 800/631-6277; www.olivia.
com) offers lesbian cruises and resort
vacations.

Gay.com Travel (© 800/929-2268 or
415/644-8044; www.gay.com/travel or
www.outandabout.com) is an excellent
online successor to the popular *Out &
About* print magazine. It provides regularly updated information about gay-
owned, gay-oriented, and gay-friendly
lodging, dining, sightseeing, nightlife,
and shopping establishments in every
important destination worldwide. British
travelers should click on the "Travel" link
at **www.uk.gay.com** for advice and gay-
friendly trip ideas.

The Canadian website **GayTraveler**
(**gaytraveler.ca**) offers ideas and advice
for gay travel all over the world.

The following travel guides are available at many bookstores, or you can
order them from any online bookseller:
*Spartacus International Gay Guide,
35th Edition* (Bruno Gmünder Verlag;
www.spartacusworld.com/gayguide) and
*Odysseus: The International Gay Travel
Planner, 17th Edition* (www.odyusa.
com); and the *Damron* guides (www.
damron.com), with separate, annual
books for gay men and lesbians.

SENIOR TRAVEL

Members of **AARP,** 601 E St. NW, Washington, DC 20049 (© 888/687-2277;
www.aarp.org), get discounts on hotels,
airfares, and car rentals. AARP offers
members a wide range of benefits, including *AARP: The Magazine* and a monthly
newsletter. Anyone over 50 can join.

Many reliable agencies and organizations target the 50-plus market. **Elder-
hostel** (© 877/426-8056; www.elder
hostel.org) arranges tour and study programs for those aged 55 and over (and
a spouse or companion of any age) in
the U.S. and in more than 80
countries around the world, including
Ecuador. Most courses last 7 to 14 days,
and many include airfare, accommodations, meals, and tuition. **ElderTreks**
(© 800/741-7956; www.eldertreks.com)

offers small-group tours to off-the-beaten-path or adventure-travel locations, restricted to travelers 50 and older. ElderTreks usually has at least one trip per year touching down in mainland Ecuador or cruising the Galápagos.

Those over 65 are eligible for various discounts in Ecuador, including reduced admissions to museums, some national parks, movies, and public transport. Be sure to ask before paying if this applies to you.

Recommended publications offering travel resources and discounts for seniors include: the quarterly magazine *Travel 50 & Beyond* (www.travel50andbeyond.com); and the bestselling paperback *Unbelievably Good Deals and Great Adventures That You Absolutely Can't Get Unless You're Over 50 2005–2006, 16th Edition* (McGraw-Hill), by Joann Rattner Heilman.

FAMILY TRAVEL

Hotels in Ecuador often give discounts for children under 12, and children under 3 or 4 are usually allowed to stay for free. This varies according to the hotel, but in general, don't assume that your kids can stay in your room for free.

Hotels offering regular, dependable babysitting service are few and far between. If you will need babysitting, make sure that your hotel offers it, and be sure to ask whether the babysitters are bilingual. In most cases, they are not. This is usually not a problem with infants and toddlers, but it can cause problems with older children.

All children, no matter how young, will need a valid passport to enter Ecuador. By law, minors under 18 need no special permission to enter or leave Ecuador. However, I recommend that adults traveling with children who are not their own carry documented permission from the parent or guardian of record, and contact a local Ecuadorian embassy or consulate before traveling.

To locate accommodations, restaurants, and attractions that are particularly kid-friendly, refer to the "Kids" icon throughout this guide.

Recommended family travel websites include **Family Travel Forum** (www.familytravelforum.com), a comprehensive site that offers customized trip planning; **Family Travel Network** (www.familytravelnetwork.com), an online magazine providing travel tips; and **TravelWithYourKids.com** (www.travelwithyourkids.com), a comprehensive site written by parents for parents offering sound advice for long-distance and international travel with children.

WOMEN TRAVELERS

As is common throughout Latin America, Ecuador can be considered a typically "macho" nation. Misogyny and violence against women, while not rampant, are part of the social fabric. In general, the most prominent expression of this machismo is a steady stream of come-ons and catcalls. Ignoring them is often the best tactic. Still, women should be careful walking alone at night in big cities, and throughout the country.

Check out the award-winning website **Journeywoman** (www.journeywoman.com), a "real life" women's travel-information network where you can sign up for a free e-mail newsletter and get advice on everything from etiquette and dress to safety. The travel guide *Safety and Security for Women Who Travel* by Sheila Swan and Peter Laufer (Travelers' Tales Guides), offering common-sense tips on safe travel, was updated in 2004.

AFRICAN-AMERICAN TRAVELERS

Black Travel Online (www.blacktravelonline.com) posts news on upcoming events and includes links to articles and travel-booking sites. **Soul of America**

(www.soulofamerica.com) is a comprehensive website, with travel tips, event and family-reunion postings, and sections on historically black beach resorts and active vacations.

Agencies and organizations that provide resources for black travelers include: **Rodgers Travel** (© 800/825-1775; www.rodgerstravel.com); the **African American Association of Innkeepers International** (© 877/422-5777; www.africanamericaninns.com); and **Henderson Travel & Tours** (© 800/327-2309 or 301/650-5700; www.hendersontravel.com).

Go Girl: The Black Woman's Guide to Travel & Adventure (Eighth Mountain Press) is a compilation of travel essays by writers including Jill Nelson and Audre Lorde. *The African-American Travel Guide* by Wayne C. Robinson (Hunter Publishing; www.hunterpublishing.com) was published in 1997, so it may be somewhat dated. *Travel and Enjoy Magazine* (© 866/266-6211; www.travelandenjoy.com) is a travel magazine and guide. The well-done *Pathfinders Magazine* (© 877/977-PATH; www.pathfinderstravel.com) includes articles on everything from Rio de Janeiro to Ghana to upcoming ski, diving, golf, and tennis trips.

STUDENT TRAVEL

The **International Student Travel Confederation** (ISTC; www.istc.org) was formed in 1949 to make travel around the world more affordable for students. Check out its website for comprehensive travel services information and details on how to get an **International Student Identity Card (ISIC),** which qualifies students for substantial savings on rail passes, plane tickets, entrance fees, and more. It also provides students with basic health and life insurance and a 24-hour help line. The card is valid for a maximum of 18 months. You can apply for the card online or in person at **STA Travel** (© 800/781-4040 in North America; www.statravel.com), the biggest student travel agency in the world; check out the website to locate STA Travel offices worldwide. If you're no longer a student but are still under 26, you can get an **International Youth Travel Card (IYTC)** from the same people, which entitles you to some discounts. **Travel CUTS** (© 800/592-2887; www.travelcuts.com) offers similar services for both Canadians and U.S. residents. Irish students may prefer to turn to **USIT** (© 01/602-1904; www.usit.ie), an Ireland-based specialist in student, youth, and independent travel.

11 Sustainable Tourism/Ecotourism

For more on ecotourism, see "Ecologically Oriented Volunteer & Study Programs," on p. 90, in chapter 4.

Each time you take a flight or drive a car, CO_2 is released into the atmosphere. You can help neutralize this danger to our planet through "carbon offsetting"—paying someone to reduce your CO_2 emissions by the same amount you've added. Carbon offsets can be purchased in the U.S. from companies such as **Carbonfund.org** (www.carbonfund.org) and **TerraPass** (www.terrapass.org), and from **Climate Care** (www.climatecare.org) in the U.K.

Although you could argue that any vacation that includes an airplane flight can't be truly "green," you can go on holiday and still contribute positively to the environment. You can offset carbon emissions from your flight in other ways. Choose forward-looking companies that embrace responsible development practices, helping preserve destinations for the future by working alongside local people. An increasing number of sustainable

Frommers.com: The Complete Travel Resource

It should go without saying, but we highly recommend **Frommers.com,** voted Best Travel Site by *PC Magazine.* We think you'll find our expert advice and tips; independent reviews of hotels, restaurants, attractions, and preferred shopping and nightlife venues; vacation giveaways; and an online booking tool indispensable before, during, and after your travels. We publish the complete contents of over 128 travel guides in our **Destinations** section covering nearly 3,800 places worldwide to help you plan your trip. Each weekday, we publish original articles reporting on **Deals and News** via our free **Frommers.com Newsletter** to help you save time and money and travel smarter. We're betting you'll find our new **Events** listings (http://events. frommers.com) an invaluable resource; it's an up-to-the-minute roster of what's happening in cities everywhere—including concerts, festivals, lectures and more. We've also added weekly **podcasts, interactive maps,** and hundreds of new images across the site. Check out our **Travel Talk** area featuring **Message Boards** where you can join in conversations with thousands of fellow Frommer's travelers and post your trip report once you return.

tourism initiatives can help you plan a family trip and leave as small a "footprint" as possible on the places you visit.

Responsible Travel (www.responsible travel.com) contains a great source of sustainable travel ideas run by a spokesperson for responsible tourism in the travel industry. **Sustainable Travel International** (www.sustainabletravelinternational.org) promotes responsible tourism practices and issues an annual Green Gear & Gift Guide.

You can find eco-friendly travel tips, statistics, and touring companies and associations—listed by destination under "Travel Choice"—at the TIES website, www.ecotourism.org. Also check out **Conservation International** (www. conservation.org)—which, with *National Geographic Traveler,* annually presents **World Legacy Awards** (www.wlaward. org) to those travel tour operators, businesses, organizations, and places that have made a significant contribution to sustainable tourism. **Ecotravel.com** is part online magazine and part ecodirectory

that lets you search for touring companies in several categories (water-based, land-based, spiritually oriented, and so on).

In the U.K., **Tourism Concern** (www. tourismconcern.org.uk) works to reduce social and environmental problems connected to tourism and find ways of improving tourism so that local benefits are increased.

The **Association of British Travel Agents** (ABTA; www.abtamembers.org/ responsibletourism) acts as a focal point for the U.K. travel industry and is one of the leading groups spearheading responsible tourism.

The **Association of Independent Tour Operators** (AITO; www.aito.co.uk) is a group of interesting specialist operators leading the field in making holidays sustainable.

For information about the ethics of swimming with dolphins and other outdoor activities, visit the **Whale and Dolphin Conservation Society** (www.wdcs. org) and **Tread Lightly** (www.tread lightly.org).

12 Staying Connected

TELEPHONES

To call Ecuador: If you're calling Ecuador from the United States:

1. Dial the international access code: 011 from the U.S.; 00 from the U.K., Ireland, or New Zealand; or 0011 from Australia.
2. Dial the country code 593.
3. Dial the one-digit area code; for Quito, the area code is 2.
4. Dial the seven-digit number. The whole number you'd dial for a number in Quito, Ecuador, would be 011-593-2-0000-000.

To make calls within Ecuador: If you are calling within the same area code inside Ecuador, you simply dial the seven-digit number. However, if you are calling from one area code to another, you must dial "0" and then the area code.

To make international calls: To make international calls from Ecuador, first dial 00 and then the country code (U.S. or Canada 1, U.K. 44, Ireland 353, Australia 61, and New Zealand 64). Next you dial the area code and number. For example, if you wanted to call the British Embassy in Washington, D.C., you would dial 00-1-202-588-7800.

To reach an international operator, dial ℰ 116 or 117. Major long-distance-company access codes are as follows:

- **AT&T:** ℰ 1800/225-528
- **Bell Canada:** ℰ 999-175
- **British Telecom:** ℰ 999-178
- **MCI:** ℰ 999-170
- **Sprint:** ℰ 999-171

For directory assistance: Dial ℰ 104.

For operator assistance: If you need operator assistance in making a call, dial ℰ 105.

Toll-free numbers: While all toll-free numbers in Ecuador begin with **1800,** there's no hard and fast rule about how many digits you'll find following them. Many toll-free numbers are just six digits long (after the 1800), while others are seven digits long. Calling a toll-free number in the United States from Ecuador is not toll-free. In fact, it costs the same as an overseas call.

Most mid- to high-end hotels in Ecuador have international direct-dial and long-distance service and in-house fax transmission. But these calls tend to be quite expensive, especially since hotels often levy a surcharge.

The least expensive way to make local phone calls is to go to one of the many *cabinas telefónicas* offices found in every Ecuadorian town. There, you'll have a private booth where you can make all your calls and pay the attendant after you are done.

You must pay in cash at the *cabinas.* Cost is roughly 5¢ to 30¢ (3p–15p) per minute for calls within Ecuador.; 40¢ (20p) per minute to the U.S. and 60¢ (30p) to the U.K.

Your best bet for making international calls, though, is to head to any Internet cafe with an international calling option. These cafes have connections to Skype, Net2Phone, or some other VoIP service. International calls made this way can range anywhere from 5¢ to $1 (3p–55p) per minute. If you have your own Skype or similar account, you just need to find an Internet cafe that provides a computer with a headset.

CELLPHONES

The three letters that define much of the world's wireless capabilities are **GSM** (Global System for Mobile Communications), a big, seamless network that makes for easy cross-border cellphone use throughout Europe and dozens of other countries worldwide. In the U.S., T-Mobile, AT&T Wireless, and Cingular use this quasi-universal system; in Canada,

Microcell and some Rogers customers are GSM, and all Europeans and most Australians use GSM. GSM phones function with a removable plastic SIM card, encoded with your phone number and account information. If your cellphone is on a GSM system, and you have a world-capable multiband phone such as many Sony Ericsson, Motorola, or Samsung models, you can make and receive calls across civilized areas around much of the globe. Just call your wireless operator and ask for "international roaming" to be activated on your account. Unfortunately, per-minute charges can be high—usually $1 to $1.50 in Western Europe and up to $5 in places like Russia and Indonesia.

For many, **renting** a phone is a good idea. While you can rent a phone from any number of overseas sites, including kiosks at airports and at car-rental agencies, we suggest renting the phone before you leave home. North Americans can rent one before leaving home from **InTouch USA** (© 800/872-7626; www. intouchglobal.com) or **RoadPost** (© 888/ 290-1606 or 905/272-5665; www.road post.com). InTouch will also, for free,

advise you on whether your existing phone will work overseas; simply call © **703/222-7161** between 9am and 4pm EST, or go to **http://intouchglobal. com/travel.htm**.

Unfortunately, per-minute charges can be high—usually $1 to $4 (55p–£2.20) in Ecuador. There are several competing cellphone companies in Ecuador. All have numerous outlets and dealers around the country. They sell pre-paid GSM chips that can be used in any unlocked triband GSM cellphone, as well as new phones with or without calling plans. Many also rent phones. **Telefonia Celular** (© **02/3301-757**) at the Mariscal Sucre International airport offers cellphone rental for $2.50 to $3 (£1.40–£1.65) per day, with a $50 (£28) deposit. However, if you're not carrying your own GSM phone, you are probably best off just buying one either before you travel or even in Ecuador. Most of the cellphone outlets around the country, including Telefonia Celular at the airport, sell already activated phones, with a few dollars of calling time loaded onto the chip. After that you simply buy pre-paid

Online Traveler's Toolbox

Veteran travelers usually carry some essential items to make their trips easier. Following is a selection of handy online tools to bookmark and use.

- **Airplane Food** (www.airlinemeals.net)
- **Airplane Seating** (www.seatguru.com or www.airlinequality.com)
- **Foreign Languages for Travelers** (www.travlang.com)
- **Maps** (www.mapquest.com)
- **Subway Navigator** (www.subwaynavigator.com)
- **Time and Date** (www.timeanddate.com)
- **Travel Warnings** (http://travel.state.gov, www.fco.gov.uk/travel, www. voyage.gc.ca, or www.dfat.gov.au/consular/advice)
- **Universal Currency Converter** (www.xe.com/ucc)
- **Visa ATM Locator** (www.visa.com), **MasterCard ATM Locator** (www. mastercard.com)
- **Weather** (www.intellicast.com or www.weather.com)

minutes in denominations of $3, $6, or $10 (£1.65–£5.50). The cheapest of these phones—a fully functional Siemens A71—costs just $36 (£20) activated and ready to go.

The main cellphone companies in Ecuador are **Porta, Movistar,** and **Alegro.** According to my Ecuadorian friends, Porta has the best coverage.

VOICE-OVER INTERNET PROTOCOL (VOIP)

If you have web access while traveling, you might consider a broadband-based telephone service (in technical terms, **Voice over Internet protocol,** or **VoIP**) such as Skype (www.skype.com) or Vonage (www.vonage.com), which allows you to make free international calls if you use their services from your laptop or in a cybercafe. Check the sites for details.

INTERNET/E-MAIL WITHOUT YOUR OWN COMPUTER

To find cybercafes in your destination, check **www.cybercaptive.com** and **www. cybercafe.com.** Quito's Mariscal district has an abundance of Internet cafes.

Most major airports have **Internet kiosks** that provide basic Web access for a per-minute fee that's usually higher than cybercafe prices. Check out copy shops like **Kinko's** (FedEx Kinko's), which offers computer stations with fully loaded software (as well as Wi-Fi).

WITH YOUR OWN COMPUTER

More and more hotels, resorts, airports, cafes, and retailers are going **Wi-Fi** (wireless fidelity), becoming "hotspots" that offer free high-speed Wi-Fi access or charge a small fee for usage. Most laptops sold today have built-in wireless capability. To find public Wi-Fi hotspots at your destination, go to **www.jiwire.com**; its Hotspot Finder holds the world's largest directory of public wireless hotspots.

For dial-up access, most business-class hotels throughout the world offer dataports for laptop modems, and a few thousand hotels in Europe now offer free high-speed Internet access.

Wherever you go, bring a **connection kit** of the right power and phone adapters, a spare phone cord, and a spare Ethernet network cable—or find out whether your hotel supplies them to guests.

13 Packages for the Independent Traveler

Package tours are simply a way to buy the airfare, accommodations, and other elements of your trip (such as car rentals, airport transfers, and sometimes even activities) at the same time and often at discounted prices.

One good source of package deals is the airlines themselves. Most major airlines offer air/land packages, including **American Airlines Vacations** (© 800/ 321-2121; www.aavacations.com), **Delta Vacations** (© 800/654-6559; www.delta vacations.com), **Continental Airlines Vacations** (© 800/301-3800; www. covacations.com), and **United Vacations**

(© 888/854-3899; www.unitedvacations. com). Several big **online travel agencies**— Expedia, Travelocity, Orbitz, Site59, and Lastminute.com—also do a brisk business in packages.

Before you book your package through a tour company, remember that with a few phone calls and e-mails, you can often organize the same thing on your own without having to pay the sometimes hefty service fee. This book contains all the information and resources you need to design and book a wonderful trip, tailored to your particular interests and budget. Moreover, package vacations

> **Tips Ask before You Go**
>
> Before you invest in a package deal or an escorted tour:
> - Always ask about the **cancellation policy.** Can you get your money back? Is a deposit required?
> - Ask about the **accommodations choices and prices** for each. Then look up the hotels' reviews in a Frommer's guide and check their rates online for your specific dates of travel. Also find out what types of rooms are offered.
> - Request a complete **schedule.** (Escorted tours only.)
> - Ask about the **size** and demographics of the group. (Escorted tours only.)
> - Discuss what is included in the **price** (transportation, meals, tips, airport transfers, and the like.). (Escorted tours only.)
> - Finally, look for **hidden expenses.** Ask whether airport departure fees and taxes, for example, are included in the total cost—they rarely are.

are still a budding industry in Ecuador and do not offer the same kinds of amazing bargains as those to Cancún or the Caribbean. In fact, many come with hidden charges and costs, so shop carefully.

Your best bet is often to do it yourself or to go with an Ecuadorian–based specialist; many of these companies emphasize adventure travel or ecotourism and can put together a complete custom itinerary for you. For a complete listing of tour companies servicing Ecuador, see "Organized Adventure Trips," in chapter 4.

Travel packages are also listed in the travel section of your local Sunday newspaper. Or check ads in national travel magazines such as *Arthur Frommer's Budget Travel Magazine, Travel + Leisure, National Geographic Traveler,* and *Condé Nast Traveler.*

14 Escorted General-Interest Tours

Escorted tours are structured group tours, with a group leader. The price usually includes everything from airfare to hotels, meals, tours, admission costs, and local transportation.

Despite the fact that escorted tours require big deposits and predetermine hotels, restaurants, and itineraries, many people derive security and peace of mind from the structure they offer. Escorted tours—whether they're navigated by bus, motor coach, train, or boat—let travelers sit back and enjoy the trip without having to drive or worry about details. They take

you to the maximum number of sights in the minimum amount of time with the least amount of hassle. They're particularly convenient for people with limited mobility and they can be a great way to make new friends.

On the downside, you'll have little opportunity for serendipitous interactions with locals. The tours can be jam-packed with activities, leaving little room for individual sightseeing, whim, or adventure—plus they often focus on the heavily touristed sites, so you miss out on many a lesser-known gem.

15 Spanish-Language Programs

Ecuador is one of the most popular places to study Spanish in South America. It is also one of the least expensive. A vast majority of the schools are found in Quito, although many have sister institutions in other cities and tourist towns around the country, such as Baños, Manta, Cuenca, and Otavalo.

If you are just looking to brush up on your existing knowledge of the language or to learn the basics to get by during your stay, most schools are happy to tailor their programs according to your requirements, offering courses ranging in length from 1 week to a year, from 2 to 8 hours a day. The majority of Spanish institutes also offer programs combining home-stays with local Ecuadorian families, as well as volunteer placements, workplace internships, cultural activities, and/or excursions to Ecuador's coastal, Amazon, and Andean regions included with the language tuition. The home-stays include a private room and either two or three meals daily taken with the family. One-on-one tuition or group classes, always with native speakers, cost approximately $5 to $10 (£2.75–£5.50) an hour depending on the institution and the specific program.

Qualifications obtained on completion of courses range from diplomas accredited by the Ecuadorian Ministry of Education and Culture, to those recognized on an international level and accredited by Spain's Instituto Cervantes. Some of the schools have reciprocal relationships with U.S. and European universities, so, you can even arrange for college credit.

Listed below are some of the better established Spanish-language institutes in Quito, many of which have sister-schools in other popular tourist destinations. Study programs in such destinations are usually organized through their Quito offices. Guayaquil has very few Spanish institutes, primarily because most tourists head for Quito, and the *castellano* spoken in Guayaquil is generally more difficult to understand, particularly for the beginner.

The popular **Amazonas Spanish School** ★★, Jorge Washington 718 and Avenida Amazonas, Edificio Rocaforte, Quito (© 02/2504-654; www.edu amazonas.com), was established in 1989. This academy boasts that all of its teachers have a minimum of 6 to 7 years of teaching experience. They emphasize language study combined with travel, offering home-stays, tours, and voluntary programs.

Beraca Spanish School, Av. Amazonas 11–14 and Pinto, 2nd floor; in Quito's New Town; and García Moreno 858 no. 3, between Sucre and Espejo, in Quito's Old Town (© 02/2906-672; www. beraca.net), has been operating since 1993. They provide the option of studying at either of their well-located campuses. Courses usually run from 9am to 1pm or 2 to 6pm, but personalized schedules can be organized. Home-stays with Ecuadorian families, or in private apartments, can also be arranged.

Bipo & Toni's ★★, Carrión E8–183 and Leonidas Plaza, Quito (© 02/2556-614 or 02/2500732; www.bipo.net), is a Spanish academy with small-group and private classes for $100 (£55) for 20 hours per week of classes. They also offer organized excursions, Latin dance classes, volunteer work opportunities, and home-stays. The institute has a good library, a garden with BBQ, and its own restaurant-bar, providing a friendly and interactive environment for its students.

Cristóbal Colón Spanish School, Colón 2088 and Versalles, Quito (© 02/2506-508; www.colonspanishschool. com), offers classes from $5 (£2.75) per hour; it's one of Quito's most popular modern Spanish schools. They only offer one-to-one classes, but they also have organized excursions, volunteer work opportunities, and the option of studying in several sister schools located around the country. Classes usually last 4 hours, but more flexible schedules can be arranged.

Escuela de Español Atahualpa, Pinto E5-08 375 and Juan León Mera, Quito (© 02/2545-914; www.atahualpa.com), with a pleasant, family-like atmosphere, school offers volunteer opportunities, home-stays, and cultural and tourist activities. Teachers possess a minimum of 5 years of experience, and courses cost $230 to $280 (£115–£140) per week including 20 hours' tuition and accommodations with local families.

Galápagos Spanish School, Av. Amazonas 1004 and Wilson, Quito (© 02/2565-213; www.galapagos.edu.ec), offers one-on-one instruction through 10 levels, or personalized courses, with the option of completing the Ministry's diploma. Classes cost around $5 (£2.75) an hour. Private accommodations with 20 hours' tuition costs from $120 (£66) per week; a variety of optional tours and activities are also available.

Instituto Superior de Español $\mathcal{R}\mathcal{R}$, Darquea Terán 1650 and Avenida 10 de Agosto, Quito (© 02/2223-342; www.instituto-superior.net), has been in business since 1988 and offers flexible Spanish courses in six locations around the country. They emphasize the importance of extracurricular activity through an extensive program of excursions and events. Specialized courses in business Spanish and Latin American literature and history are also on the agenda.

Quito Spanish Institute $\mathcal{R}$, Av. Orellana 1515 and 9 de Octubre, Quito (© 02/2550-377; www.quitospanish.com), is the only institute in Ecuador offering the internationally recognized DELE qualification from Spain's Instituto Cervantes. One-on-one or group classes can be combined with home-stays and volunteer placements. The institute also runs internship programs and organizes excursions. The school is extremely flexible and willing to adapt courses to students' needs. Prices start from $170 (£94) for a 20-hour-per-week program; home-stays cost an additional $16 (£9) per day, including three meals daily and laundry service.

Simón Bolívar $\mathcal{R}\mathcal{R}$, Mariscal Foch E9–920 and Avenida 6 de Diciembre, Quito (© 02/2234-708; www.simonbolivar.com), advertises that it is rated as "one of Ecuador's top schools" by members of the reputable South American Explorers club. They offer home-stays and volunteer placements, a "Discover Ecuador" program, and various excursions. Courses start at around $120 (£66) per week. The institute also has schools in Cuenca, in El Oriente, and along the Pacific coast.

16 Getting Around

Because Ecuador is one of the smallest countries in South America, traveling from one end to the other is not too difficult. The bus routes are comprehensive. The roads, however, can be a bit rough, and the buses are often hot and crowded. If you're short on time, I really recommend flying, which is cheap and efficient. If you're traveling only a short distance, though, say from Quito to Otavalo (around 2 hr.) or Riobamba (under 4 hr.), then a bus, shuttle, rental car, or car and driver may be your best bet.

BY PLANE
Most of Ecuador's major cities and tourist destinations are serviced by regular and reliable commuter air traffic. In some places, remote destinations can best be reached by charter flights, organized by the lodges themselves.

Aerogal (© **1800/2376-425** toll-free nationwide; www.aerogal.com.ec), **Icaro**

(© **1800/883-567** toll-free nationwide; www.icaro.com.ec), and **Tame** (© **02/ 2909-900** in Quito, or 04/2310-305 or 04/2310-305 in Guayaquil; www.tame. com.ec), are the main commuter airlines.

With the exception of the Galápagos, which is quite expensive, most flights cost between $50 and $80 (£28–£44) for a one-way fare. See the destination chapters for detailed information on flight schedules, times, and fares.

BY BUS

In Ecuador, all roads lead to Quito. From Quito, you can find a bus to every corner of the country, but don't expect to get anywhere quickly. Locals seldom board buses at the actual bus terminals. Instead, buses leave the station empty, and then drive very slowly through the outskirts of town, picking up passengers along the way. This adds considerable time onto most bus rides. Still, for relatively short distances, buses are your best, and cheapest, option. The journeys between Quito and Riobamba, Baños, Otavalo, and Cotopaxi are best served by buses, which leave frequently for these destinations. The road between Cuenca and Guayaquil is also a popular bus route. For specific information on bus schedules, fares, and companies, see the destination chapters throughout this book.

BY CAR

In general, I don't recommend renting a car in Ecuador. For the most part, the roads are in bad condition, and since signs are nonexistent it's very easy to get lost. For short-distance journeys, it's much more economical to take a bus, or even a taxi.

Nevertheless, if you're an adventurous type and you want to see the country from the privacy of your own car, you can certainly get a rental.

Avis (© **02/2440-270**; www.avis. com.ec), **Budget** (© **02/3300-979**; www.budget-ec.com), **Hertz** (© **1800/ 227-767** toll-free within Ecuador, or

02/2254-257; www.hertz.com.ec), and **Localiza** (© **02/3303-265**; www1. localiza.com.ec) are the main rental-car agencies, with offices at both major international airports. As a national company, Localiza also has numerous offices in other cities and tourist destinations around Ecuador.

Because the roads are so poorly maintained, I recommend that you rent a 4WD. All the agencies listed above rent four-wheel drive vehicles. Rates run between $40 and $150 (£11–£83) per day, with unlimited mileage and insurance, depending upon the type of vehicle you rent.

One very interesting option is to use **Rent 4WD.com** ⚡ (© **02/2544-719**; www.rent-4wd.com), which gets you a large, modern four-wheel drive vehicle, unlimited gas and mileage, and driver, for just $150 (£83) per day. They even cover the driver's lodging expenses.

GASOLINE Gasoline, or *gasolina* in Spanish, is sold as *extra* and *super,* both of which are unleaded. *Super* is just higher octane. Diesel is available at almost every gas station as well. Most rental cars run on premium, but always ask your rental agent what type of gas your car takes. Gas stations are widely available along the highways, and in all major cities, towns, and tourist destinations. But make sure to have a full tank when you're heading to a remote destination. At press time a gallon of *super* costs around $1.60 (90p) per gallon.

ROAD CONDITIONS Most of the major highways in Ecuador are in pretty decent shape. But once you venture off the major thoroughfares, the situation deteriorates dramatically.

Even the major highways and tourist destinations are only sporadically marked with up-to-date signs and markers. And once you get off the beaten path, you may not encounter any signs or indications as you pass intersection after intersection.

Always keep an eye out for the sudden appearance of a pedestrian, bicycle rider, dog, or cow, even on major highways. It's best to avoid driving at night, since very few roads or highways are illuminated.

MAPS Car-rental agencies and the Ministry of Tourism information centers at the airport and in downtown Quito have adequate road maps. For more information on maps, see "Visitor Information & Maps," earlier in this chapter.

DRIVING RULES A current foreign driver's license is valid for the length of your 90-day tourist visa. Seat belts are required for the driver and front-seat passengers.

Official driving rules are often ignored. Drivers seldom use turn signals or obey posted speed limits. Transit police are a rarity, but they will bust you for speeding. So keep to the speed limit (usually 60–90kmph/37–56 mph) if you don't want to get pulled over. Never pay money directly to a police officer who stops you for any traffic violation. Speeding and traffic tickets are usually charged to your credit card by your rental-car company.

BREAKDOWNS Emergency services, both vehicular and medical, are extremely limited once you get far from Quito, Guayaquil, or any of the major tourist destinations. If you are an AAA member,

contact the local affiliate **Aneta** (© **1800/556-677;** www.aneta.org.ec), which can provide free towing, as well as other emergency services.

If you're involved in a breakdown or accident, you should contact the police. Throughout Ecuador, you can reach the police by dialing © **101** in an emergency. The tourist police may be of help, and are more likely to have someone on hand who speaks English. In Quito, the number for the tourist police is © **02/2543-983.**

If you don't speak Spanish, expect added difficulty in any emergency or stressful situation. Don't expect rural (or urban) police officers, hospital personnel, service-station personnel, or mechanics to speak English.

If your car breaks down and you're unable to get well off the road, check to see whether there are reflecting triangles in the trunk. If there are, place them as a warning for approaching traffic, arranged in a wedge that starts at the shoulder about 30m (98 ft.) back and angle gradually toward your car. If your car has no triangles, try to create a similar warning marker using a pile of leaves or branches. Finally, although not rampant, there have been reports of folks being robbed by seemingly friendly good Samaritans who stop to give assistance.

Car-Rental Tips

Although it's preferable to use the coverage provided by your home auto-insurance policy or credit card, check carefully to see if the coverage really holds in Ecuador. Many policies exclude 4WD vehicles and off-road driving—much of Ecuador can, in fact, be considered off-road. It's possible at some car-rental agencies to waive the insurance charges, but you will have to pay all damages before leaving the country if you're in an accident. If you do take the insurance, you can expect a deductible of $750 to $2,000 (£415–£1,100). At some agencies, you can buy additional insurance to lower the deductible. To rent a car in Ecuador, you must be at least 21 years old and have a valid driver's license and a major credit card in your name.

17 Tips on Accommodations

You'll find a whole range of accommodations in Ecuador. There are very few truly high-end luxury hotels and resorts. Most are in Quito or Guayaquil, and are geared toward business travelers. Two exceptions are the Royal Palm Hotel (p. 346), on the Galápagos; and La Mirage Garden Hotel & Spa, just outside Otavalo (p.151).

The country's strong suit is in elegant, mid-range boutique hotels, many housed in old colonial-era homes or haciendas. The antique furnishings and cozy rooms will make you feel as though you are an Ecuadorian aristocrat living in the 18th century. In fact, throughout the Andean highlands, you will find a string of these lovely converted haciendas, which are among the best and most unique accommodations to be found. Some are in buildings over 200 years old.

On the other end of the spectrum are jungle lodges, usually built in the style typical to the Amazon basin (thatched roofs, bamboo walls, and so on). Accommodations are usually basic; the more expensive ones, such as Kapawi Ecolodge & Reserve (p. 322) and Napo Wildlife Center (p. 312), have private bathrooms, but hot showers are a rarity.

In general, inexpensive accommodations are easy to find. In Quito, you can rent a clean room with private bathroom and television for little more than $20 (£11); in smaller towns, you can find a bed for as little as $10 (£5.50) a night.

In the Galápagos, most visitors spend their nights sleeping on ships. The general rule is that if you don't pay a lot, you won't get a lot. The least-expensive boats have dorm-style common sleeping rooms and one shower for everyone onboard.

One good website and Ecuadorian travel operator, **Exclusive Hotels & Haciendas of Ecuador** (www.exclusive hotelshaciendasecuador.com), functions as a one-stop booking agent for various high-end boutique hotels and haciendas around the country.

Tip: If you're traveling on a budget and staying in some of the less-expensive hotels, one item you're likely to want to bring with you is a towel. Your hotel might not provide one, and even if it does, it might be awfully thin.

Throughout this book, I've separated hotel listings into several broad categories: **Very Expensive,** $120 (£66) and up; **Expensive,** $80 to $120 (£44–£66); **Moderate,** $40 to $80 (£22–£44); and **Inexpensive,** under $40 (£22) double. Unless otherwise noted, rates given in this book do not include the 12% IVA and 10% service tax. These taxes will add considerably to the cost of your room, so do factor them in.

Frommer's uses a zero- to three-star rating system. A truly special bed-and-breakfast, run with style and aplomb, may get two or three stars, even though the rooms do not have televisions or air-conditioning. Likewise, a large resort with a host of modern amenities may receive one or no stars. Every hotel listed is in some way recommended. This book is selective, and I've done my best to list the best options in each price range and each region.

SURFING FOR HOTELS

In addition to the online travel booking sites **Travelocity, Expedia, Orbitz, Priceline,** and **Hotwire,** you can book hotels through **Hotels.com; Quikbook** (www.quikbook.com); and **Travelaxe** (www.travelaxe.net).

HotelChatter.com is a daily webzine offering smart coverage and critiques of hotels worldwide. Go to **TripAdvisor.com** or **HotelShark.com** for helpful independent consumer reviews of hotels and resort properties.

It's a good idea to **get a confirmation number** and **make a printout** of any online booking transaction.

Heads-Up

When hotels quote prices, they rarely include the hefty tax. Unless otherwise noted, expect to pay an additional 22% in taxes on the prices quoted by hotels and listed throughout the book.

SAVING ON YOUR HOTEL ROOM

The **rack rate** is the maximum rate that a hotel charges for a room. Hardly anybody pays this price, however, except in high season or on holidays. To lower the cost of your room:

- **Ask about special rates or other discounts.** You may qualify for corporate, student, military, senior, frequent flier, trade union, or other discounts.
- **Dial direct.** When booking a room in a chain hotel, you'll often get a better deal by calling the individual hotel's reservation desk rather than the chain's main number.
- **Book online.** Many hotels offer Internet-only discounts, or supply rooms to Priceline, Hotwire, or Expedia at rates much lower than the ones you can get through the hotel itself.
- **Remember the law of supply and demand.** You can save big on hotel rooms by traveling in a destination's off season or shoulder seasons, when rates typically drop, even at luxury properties.
- **Look into group or long-stay discounts.** If you come as part of a large group, you should be able to negotiate a bargain rate. Likewise, if you're planning a long stay (at least 5 days), you might qualify for a discount. As a general rule, expect 1 night free after a 7-night stay.
- **Sidestep excess surcharges and hidden costs.** Many hotels have adopted the unpleasant practice of nickel-and-diming its guests with opaque surcharges. When you book a room, ask what is included in the room rate, and what is extra. Avoid dialing direct from hotel phones, which can have exorbitant rates. And don't be tempted by the room's minibar offerings: Most hotels charge through the nose for water, soda, and snacks. Finally, ask about local taxes and service charges, which can increase the cost of a room by 15% or more.

18 Tips on Dining

In major cities such as Quito, Cuenca, and Guayaquil, you'll find tons of Ecuadorian restaurants, as well as an excellent selection of international cuisines. In Quito, there is everything from cutting-edge fusion cuisine to Thai food and sushi. Throughout the country, you'll also be able to find authentic pizza joints, as well as Chinese restaurants, known as *chifas*.

While you're in Ecuador, you should definitely try *comida típica* (typical food). *Ceviche de camarones* (shrimp cooked in a tangy lemon juice and served with onions and cilantro) is one of the most popular dishes in Ecuador—you'll find it on almost every menu. *Ceviche* is often served with a side of salty popcorn, fried corn, and fried plantains. The salt complements the tart lemon flavor. Other local specialties include *seco de chivo* (goat stew in a wine sauce), *empanadas de verde* (turnovers made with fried green bananas and filled with cheese), *tortillas de maíz* (small round corn pastries, served with avocado), and *humitas* (a sweet corn mush mixed with eggs, served in a corn husk). In the Sierra, where it can get very cold, locals often have a soup called *locro de papas* (a creamy potato soup with cheese). In Cuenca, *mote pillo con carne* (huge potato-like pieces of corn, mixed with onions and eggs, served with a fried piece of meat and *tortillas de papa*—the Ecuadorian version of potato pancakes) is one of the more popular local dishes.

Fixed-price lunches *(almuerzo del día)* are also common in smaller restaurants. For about $2.50 to $3 (£1.40–£1.65), you will get soup, a main course, dessert, and fresh juice.

Ecuadorians tend to eat three meals a day, in similar fashion and hours to North Americans. Breakfasts are usually served from 6:30 to 9am; lunch from noon to 2pm; and dinner from 6 to 10pm. Soup is served at nearly every lunch and dinner. Most meals and dining experiences are quite informal. In fact, there are only a few restaurants in the entire country that can be considered semi-formal, and none require a jacket and tie, although you could certainly wear them.

I have separated restaurant listings throughout this book into three price categories based on the average cost per person of a meal, including tax and service charge. The categories are **Expensive,** more than $20 (£11); **Moderate,** $10 to $20 (£5.50–£11); and **Inexpensive,** less than $10 (£5.50). Prices on menus don't include tax or tip. Expect to pay an extra 22% in tax and service charges, above the prices listed on menus and in this chapter. Although a 10% tip is typically included in the bill, if the service is particularly good and attentive, you should probably leave a little extra.

For a more detailed discussion of Ecuadorian cuisine and dining, see *"Llapingachos, Cuy* & Pilsener: Ecuadorian Food & Drink"* in appendix A.

FAST FACTS: Ecuador

American Express There are two American Express travel offices in Ecuador— one in Quito, the other in Guayaquil—both run by **Global Tours** (www.global tour.com.ec). In **Quito,** the office is located on Av. República El Salvador 309 and Calle Suiza (© 02/2265-222). In **Guayaquil,** the office is located in the Edificio Las Cámaras, on Avenida Francisco de Orellana and Alcivar (© 04/2680-450).

Area Codes Cities and provinces across Ecuador have single-digit area codes (Pichincha province and Quito, 2; Guaya province and Guayaquil, 4; Azuay province and Cuenca 7; and so on). In some cases, a single area code will cover several provinces. If you are calling from one area code to another you must dial "0" before the area code, while neither the "0" nor the area code is used if calling within the area. To call a cellphone, you must first dial "09" and then the seven-digit number.

ATM Networks Ecuador has a well-developed network of ATMs. Just about every bank branch in the country, particularly in the major cities, towns, and tourist destinations, has an ATM or two. While many of Ecuador's ATMs will work fine with five- and six-digit PINs, some will only accept four-digit PINs. Before traveling, it is wise to change your PIN to avoid any unexpected hassles in getting access to quick cash.

Business Hours In general, business hours are weekdays from 9am to 1pm and 2:30 or 3 to 6:30pm. In Quito and Guayaquil, most banks stay open all day from about 9am to 5pm, but some still close in the middle of the day, so it's best to take care of your banking needs early in the morning. Most banks, museums, and stores are open on Saturday from 10am to noon. Everything closes down on Sunday.

Cameras & Film Film is generally more expensive in Ecuador, so bring as much as you will need from home. I also recommend that you wait to have your film processed at home, but if you must develop your prints down here or need to pick up film, batteries, or storage cards, try **Ecuacolor** (© 02/2526-982; www.ecuacolor.com), **Fuji Foto** (© 02/2551-275), or **Foto Quick** (© 02/2229-982), all of which have numerous outlets around Quito and in most major tourist destinations. For more serious photographic needs (equipment, repairs, and so on), **Difoto** (© 02/2224-676), on Foch 864 in Quito, is your best bet. Some of the chain stores mentioned above have technicians on hand, and carry a limited range of replacement and repair parts.

Car Rentals See "Getting Around," p. 43.

Cashpoints See "ATM Networks," above.

Currency See "Money & Costs," p. 26.

Customs **What You Can Bring into Ecuador:** Visitors to Ecuador are legally permitted to bring in up to $1,250 worth of items for personal use, including cameras, portable typewriters, video cameras and accessories, tape recorders, personal computers, and CD players. You can also bring in up to 2 liters of alcoholic beverages and 200 cigarettes (1 carton).

What You Can Take Home from Ecuador: It is illegal to bring out any pre-Columbian artifact from Ecuador, whether you bought it, you discovered it, or it was given to you. Do not traffic in ancient artifacts.

U.S. Citizens: For specifics on what you can bring back and the corresponding fees, download the invaluable free pamphlet *Know Before You Go* online at **www.cbp.gov**. (Click on "Travel," and then click on "Know Before You Go! Online Brochure.") Or contact the **U.S. Customs & Border Protection (CBP),** 1300 Pennsylvania Ave. NW, Washington, DC 20229 (© 877/287-8667) and request the pamphlet.

Canadian Citizens: For a clear summary of Canadian rules, write for the booklet *I Declare,* issued by the **Canada Border Services Agency** (© 800/461-9999 in Canada, or 204/983-3500; www.cbsa-asfc.gc.ca).

U.K. Citizens: For information, contact **HM Customs & Excise** at © 0845/010-9000 (from outside the U.K., 020/8929-0152), or consult their website at **www.hmce.gov.uk**.

Australian Citizens: A helpful brochure available from Australian consulates or Customs offices is *Know Before You Go.* For more information, call the **Australian Customs Service** at © 1300/363-263, or log on to **www.customs.gov.au**.

New Zealand Citizens: Most questions are answered in a free pamphlet available at New Zealand consulates and Customs offices: *New Zealand Customs Guide for Travellers, Notice no. 4.* For more information, contact **New Zealand Customs,** The Customhouse, 17–21 Whitmore St., Box 2218, Wellington (© 04/473-6099 or 0800/428-786; www.customs.govt.nz).

Driving Rules See "Getting Around," p. 43.

Drug Laws If you're caught possessing, using, or trafficking drugs in Ecuador, expect severe penalties, including long jail sentences and large fines. If you're arrested in Ecuador, you should also prepare yourself for a lengthy delay in prison before your case is tried before a judge. It's not uncommon to detain prisoners without bail.

Drugstores A drugstore or pharmacy is called a *farmacia* in Spanish. **Fybeca** has the largest chain of pharmacies in Ecuador. You can call Fybeca's toll-free line (© **800/2392-322**) 24 hours a day for home delivery in most major cities in the country.

Electricity The majority of outlets in Ecuador are standard U.S.-style two- and three-prong electric outlets with 110/120V AC (60 Hz) current.

Embassies & Consulates In Quito: **United States,** at the corner of Avenida 12 de Octubre and Avenida Patria, across from the Casa de la Cultura (© **02/2562-890,** ext. 480); **Canada,** Av. 6 de Diciembre 2816 and Paul Rivet (© **02/2232-114**); and **United Kingdom,** Avenida Naciones Unidas and República de El Salvador, Edificio Citiplaza, 14th floor (© **02/2970-800**). There is no Australian Embassy in Ecuador, but there is an **Australian Honorary Consul** in Guayaquil, in the Kennedy Norte neighborhood on Calle San Roque and Avenida Francisco de Orellana (© **04/2680-823**).

Emergencies In an emergency, call © **911,** or **101** for the police only.

Etiquette & Customs There are no overarching etiquette or customs concerns for visitors to Ecuador. However, it is very important to respect the prominent and pervasive indigenous culture

Appropriate Attire: In business situations, a suit or dressy women's clothing is appropriate. In all other situations, casual clothing is the norm, although short pants are almost never worn by men in urban centers, including in steamy Guayaquil.

Avoiding Offense: In rural areas, Ecuador's indigenous population can be relatively reserved and private. Most indigenous Ecuadorians are very wary of having their photographs taken, and it is considered impolite and even aggressive to do so without asking permission first. In many tourist destinations, locals will readily allow themselves to be photographed, for a small fee

Gestures: Almost all Ecuadorians use a handshake for greeting, men and women alike. However, don't expect or give anything like handshake common in North America; the Ecuadorian handshake can be very light, with almost no grasping, especially in the more remote indigenous towns and villages.

The Global Etiquette Guide to Mexico and Latin America (Wiley Publishing, Inc.) has a short chapter on Ecuador.

Holidays See "Calendar of Events," earlier in this chapter.

Hospitals **Hospital Vozandes** (© **02/2262-142;** www.hospitalvozandes.org; Villalengua 267 and 10 de Agosto) and **Hospital Metropolitano** (© **02/2261-520;** www.hospitalmetropolitano.org; Mariana de Jesús and Occidental) are the two most modern and best equipped hospitals in Quito. Both have 24-hour emergency service and English-speaking doctors. For hospitals in other cities, see the "Fast Facts" for each individual city.

Internet Access Internet service is available almost everywhere in Ecuador, including in the Galápagos. But don't expect to see anything resembling a computer in the jungle. Connections in major cities cost 80¢ to $1 (44p–55p) per hour. In smaller, more remote towns and the Galápagos, the connection can cost up to $3 to $4 (£1.65–£2.20) per hour.

Language Spanish is the language most commonly used in business transactions. Indigenous languages such as Quichua are also widely spoken throughout the country. Shuar is common in the Amazon basin. It's best to come to Ecuador with a basic knowledge of Spanish. Outside the major tourist sights, it can be difficult to find people who speak English.

Laundry Most folks rely on their hotel's laundry and dry-cleaning services, although these can be expensive. The more popular tourist destinations have self-service and full-service Laundromats as alternatives.

Legal Aid In the event you need legal help, immediately contact your embassy or consulate. See "Embassies & Consulates," above, for contact information.

Liquor Laws The legal drinking age is 18, although it's almost never enforced. At discos, however, you often need to show a picture ID for admittance. Everything from beer to hard spirits are sold in specific liquor stores as well as at most supermarkets and even convenience stores.

Lost & Found Be sure to tell all of your credit card companies the minute you discover your wallet has been lost or stolen, and file a report at the nearest police precinct. Your credit card company or insurer may require a police report number or record of the loss. Most credit card companies have an emergency toll-free number to call if your card is lost or stolen; they may be able to wire you a cash advance immediately or deliver an emergency credit card in a day or two. To report a lost or stolen **American Express** card, call ✆ **02/2560-488** in Ecuador, or ✆ 910/333-3211 collect in the U.S.; for **Diners Club,** call ✆ **02/2981-300** in Ecuador, or 303/799-1504 collect in the U.S.; for **MasterCard,** call ✆ **02/2262-770** in Ecuador, or 314/542-7111 collect in the U.S.; and for **Visa,** call ✆ **02/2459-303** in Ecuador, or 410/581-9994 collect in the U.S.

If you need emergency cash over the weekend when all banks and American Express offices are closed, you can have money wired to you via **Western Union** (✆ **1800/989-898** in Ecuador; www.westernunion.com).

Identity theft and fraud are potential complications of losing your wallet, especially if you've lost your driver's license along with your cash and credit cards. Notify the major credit-reporting bureaus immediately; placing a fraud alert on your records may protect you against liability for criminal activity. The three major U.S. credit-reporting agencies are **Equifax** (✆ **800/766-0008;** www.equifax.com), **Experian** (✆ **888/397-3742;** www.experian.com), and **Trans Union** (✆ **800/680-7289;** www.transunion.com). Finally, if you've lost all forms of photo ID, call your airline and explain the situation; they might allow you to board the plane if you have a copy of your passport or birth certificate and a copy of the police report you've filed.

Measurements Ecuador uses the metric system, although gasoline is sold by the gallon. See the chart on the inside front cover of this book for details on converting metric measurements to nonmetric equivalents.

Newspapers & Magazines There are several Spanish-language daily papers in Ecuador. The most popular and prominent are *El Mercurio, El Universo,* and *El Comercio.*

At the airports in Quito and Guayaquil, and at the high-end business hotels, you can find the latest edition of the *Miami Herald* for around 50¢ to $1 (25p–55p). English-language copies of *Time* or *Newsweek* are also available at some newsstands in the most touristy areas of Quito.

Passports Allow plenty of time before your trip to apply for a passport; processing normally takes 3 weeks but can take longer during busy periods (especially spring). And keep in mind that if you need a passport in a hurry, you'll pay a higher processing fee.

For Residents of Australia: You can pick up an application from your local post office or any branch of Passports Australia, but you must schedule an interview at the passport office to present your application materials. Call the **Australian Passport Information Service** at © **131-232,** or visit the government website at www.passports.gov.au.

For Residents of Canada: Passport applications are available at travel agencies throughout Canada or from the central **Passport Office,** Department of Foreign Affairs and International Trade, Ottawa, ON K1A 0G3 (© **800/567-6868;** www.ppt.gc.ca).

For Residents of Ireland: You can apply for a 10-year passport at the **Passport Office,** Setanta Centre, Molesworth Street, Dublin 2 (© **01/671-1633;** www.irl gov.ie/iveagh). Those under age 18 and over 65 must apply for an €12 3-year passport. You can also apply at 1A South Mall, Cork (© **021/272-525),** or at most main post offices.

For Residents of New Zealand: You can pick up a passport application at any New Zealand Passports Office or download it from their website. Contact the **Passports Office** at © **0800/225-050** in New Zealand or 04/474-8100, or log on to www.passports.govt.nz.

For Residents of the United Kingdom: To pick up an application for a standard 10-year passport (5-year passport for children under 16), visit your nearest passport office, major post office, or travel agency; or contact the **United Kingdom Passport Service** at © **0870/521-0410** or search its website at www. ukpa.gov.uk.

For Residents of the United States: Whether you're applying in person or by mail, you can download passport applications from the U.S. State Department website at **http://travel.state.gov.** To find your regional passport office, either check the U.S. State Department website or call the **National Passport Information Center** toll-free number (© **877/487-2778)** for automated information.

Police Throughout Ecuador, you can reach the police by dialing © **101** in an emergency. The tourist police can also help sort out problems. In Quito, the number for the tourist police is © **02/2543-983.**

Post Offices & Mail A post office is called *correos* in Spanish. Most towns have a central post office, usually located right on the central park or plaza. In addition, most hotels will post letters and post cards for you. Most post offices in Ecuador are open Monday through Friday from 8am to 12:30pm and 2:30 to 6pm, and Saturday from 8am to 2pm. It costs 90¢ (50p) to mail a letter to the United States or Canada, and $1.10 (60p) to Australia and Europe. From time to time, you can buy stamps at kiosks and newsstands. But your best bet is to mail your letter and buy your stamps from the post office itself, especially since there are no public mailboxes.

However, it is best to send anything of value via an established international courier service. Most hotels, especially in major cities and tourist destinations, can arrange for express mail pickup. Alternately, you can contact **DHL** (© **02/ 2485-100**; www.dhl.com), **Fed Ex** (© **02/2909-201**; www.fedex.com), **EMS** (© **02/2561-962**), or **UPS** (© **02/3960-000**; www.ups.com). *Note:* Despite what you may be told, packages sent overnight to U.S. addresses tend to take 3 to 4 days to reach their destination.

Restrooms The condition of public facilities is surprisingly good in Ecuador. In museums, the toilets are relatively clean, but they never have toilet paper. If you have an emergency, you can also use the restrooms in hotel lobbies without much problem. Note that most buses don't have toilet facilities, and when they stop at rest stops, the facilities are often horrendous—usually smelly squat toilets. It's always useful to have a roll of toilet paper handy.

Safety Pickpocketing is a problem in all large cities. But if you keep an eye on your belongings at all times, you should be fine. Never put anything valuable in your backpack. Also be careful on the Trole (trolley). At night, Quito can be dangerous, especially in the touristy areas—take a taxi, even if you're only going a short distance. Because the streets in Quito are often deserted at night, I recommend walking in the middle of them to prevent someone from jumping at you from a hidden doorway. Guayaquil used to hold the award for being the most dangerous city in Ecuador, but in the past few years, the city has cleaned up its act. Cuenca is the safest large city in Ecuador and residents routinely walk around at night, especially on weekends. Report all problems to the tourist police (© **02/2543-983**).

Smoking By law, smoking is prohibited in all indoor public spaces, including restaurants, shops, cinemas, and offices. (Bars and discos are exempt.) That said, enforcement is virtually nonexistent. While not as bad as most of Europe, a large number of Ecuadorians smoke, and smoke-filled public spaces are common. Bars, discos, and clubs are often especially smoke-filled in Ecuador.

Taxes All goods and services are charged a 12% value-added tax. Hotels and restaurants also add on a 10% service charge, for a total of 22% more on your bill. There is an airport departure tax of $38 (£19).

Time Zone Mainland Ecuador is on Eastern Standard Time, 5 hours behind Greenwich Mean Time (GMT). The Galápagos Islands are on Central Standard Time, 6 hours behind GMT. Daylight saving time is not observed.

Tipping Restaurants in Ecuador add a 10% service charge to all checks. It's common to add 5% to 10% on top of this, especially if you feel the service merits it. Taxi drivers don't expect tips. Hotel porters are typically tipped 50¢ to $1 (28p–55p) per bag.

Useful Phone Numbers **U.S. Department of State Travel Advisory** (© 202/647-5225, manned 24 hr.); **U.S. Passport Agency** (© 202/647-0518); **U.S. Centers for Disease Control International Traveler's Hot Line** (© 404/332-4559).

Water Always drink bottled water in Ecuador. Most hotels provide bottled water in the bathroom. You can buy bottles of water on practically any street corner. Small bottles cost about 25¢ (15p). The better restaurants use ice made from boiled water, but, to be on the safe side, always ask.

3

Suggested Ecuador Itineraries

Ecuador is a varied, rich, and rewarding destination, with numerous natural attractions and a broad selection of stunning historical sights and exhilarating adventure activities to keep you busy. On a trip to Ecuador, you can visit rainforests, cloud forests, lowland mangrove forests, snowcapped peaks, high Andean paramo, active volcanoes, perfectly preserved colonial-era churches, and Inca and Cañari ruins. You can go horseback riding, mountain biking, trekking, surfing, and white-water rafting. The birdwatching is world-class. And, of course, there are the Galápagos Islands. Ecuador is also a relatively compact country, which makes visiting several destinations during a single vacation both easy and enjoyable.

By far the fastest and easiest way to get around the country is by small commuter aircraft. Most major tourist destinations in Ecuador are either serviced by reasonably priced domestic airlines, or are commonly reached on a package tour that includes charter air transportation.

Driving around is another option, though one that demands serious consideration. Most major destinations are at least 3 to 5 hours from Quito by car, and some are even farther. Moreover, the roads here are often in terrible shape and unmarked (as are many intersections), and Ecuadorian drivers can be reckless and rude. One interesting option is **Rent 4WD.com** ✦ (© **02/2544-719;** www.rent-4wd.com), where $150 per day gets you a large, modern, 4WD vehicle; unlimited gas and mileage; and a driver. See p. 44 for more information on driving around Ecuador.

The following itineraries are blueprints for fabulous vacations. You can follow them to the letter; or you might decide to use one or more of them as outlines and fill in the blanks with other destinations, activities, and attractions that strike your fancy.

1 Ecuador in 1 Week

Let me level with you: Unless you are coming here only to visit the Galápagos, a week is just not enough time to see what Ecuador has to offer. If you are coming just to visit the Galápagos, however, 1 week is perfect—and you might even get to squeeze in a day or so in Quito and/or Guayaquil.

Having said this, I'm not including the Galápagos in the following itinerary. Instead, it takes you to several of Ecuador's top destinations and attractions, with everything from high-altitude hiking in the paramo to a rainforest extravaganza in the Amazon basin.

Note: The following 1-week itinerary includes 8 days, the first of which is considered a "travel day," when you'll likely arrive in Quito in the evening.

Days ❶ & ❷: Quito

Many international flights arrive in Quito in the late afternoon or early evening, so you'll need to book yourself into a hotel for 2 nights to enjoy 1 full day of sightseeing in the capital. Get to bed as early as possible so you can be rested and out the door early on Day 2. After breakfast at your hotel, spend the morning touring **Old Town.** Visit the magnificent **Iglesia de San Francisco** ❦❦ (p. 118), which dates back to 1535, and allow yourself a good 45 minutes to get a feel for the city's oldest church and its attached museum.

A few minutes' walk away, **La Compañía de Jesús** ❦❦❦ (p. 120) Jesuit church features an incredibly ornate interior that shows baroque and Moorish influences. Nearby, **Casa Museo María Augusta Urrutia** ❦ (p. 115) is a perfectly preserved 19th-century mansion worthy of at least a 45-minute visit. As the sun warms the cool morning air, take some time to stroll around Old Town, ending up at **La Plaza de la Independencia** (p. 120), which was the city's main square in the 16th century. Break for a cup of coffee at a sunny cafe on or around the plaza—there are plenty to choose from here.

Next, grab a taxi and head to **El Panecillo,** where you'll see the Virgin of Quito (p. 117). It's a 10-minute ride up a steep hill. From here, standing below the immense winged Virgin, you have a sweeping view of Old Town and the rest of the city. Right next to the monument is **PIM's Panecillo** (p. 112), a great place to enjoy local cuisine for lunch while you continue to enjoy the view. Remember to drink lots of bottled water, especially in the early afternoon, when the sun is at its highest and the atmosphere its driest.

After lunch, take a taxi to the **Fundación Guayasamín** ❦❦ (p. 123), named after the country's most famous and influential artist, Oswaldo Guayasamín. Expect to spend at least 1½ hours here and at the nearby **Capilla del Hombre** ❦. At both, you'll find original works by Guayasamín, as well as pieces from his personal collection.

You should be pretty beat by now, so head to **Plaza Foch** (p. 130) in the **Mariscal district** of **New Town** for a late-afternoon or early evening cup of coffee or a cocktail. If the weather is good, grab an outdoor table on the plaza at **Coffee Tree** (② 02/2565-521; see p. 130). If you're lucky, a jazz band will be playing right in front of you.

For dinner, be sure to have reservations at **Zazu** ❦❦❦ (p. 114), the best and hippest spot in Quito. You can end the meal with dessert or with a drink at their popular little laid-back bar. If you have the energy, pull out all the stops and head back to the Mariscal district's many bars and clubs to see where the night and your whims lead you.

Days ❸ & ❹: Otavalo & Imbabura Province

After your grueling sightseeing day in Quito, it's time to leave the city behind and unwind in the highlands of the northern Sierra for a couple of days. The roughly 2-hour drive is leisurely and scenic, and should include a stop at the new **Quitsato Mitad del Mundo** (② 09/9701-133; www.quitsato.org), where you can have your photo taken with one foot in each of the earth's hemispheres.

I recommend **Hacienda Cusín** ❦❦ (p. 150), a rambling, serene inn set amid 4 hectares (10 acres) of lush gardens, on the outskirts of **Otavalo** ❦❦. In the distance, Volcán Imbabura makes for a breathtaking backdrop. Have lunch on the sun-splashed terrace and perhaps take

Galápagos Islands
Darwin   Pinta
Wolf   Genovesa
      Marchena   Equator
   Santiago
GALÁPAGOS   Santa
NAT'L PARK   Cruz
Fernandina   Puerto   San
          Ayora   Cristóbal
Isabela
   Santa María   Española
0   50 mi
0   50 km

San Lorenzo
Esmeraldas   **COLOMBIA**
        Tulcán
   Ibarra
   Otavalo   **3-4**
1-2   Lago Agrio
QUITO   SUMACO-NAPO-   CUYABENO
Equator   GALERAS   WILDLIFE RES.
Bahía de   **8**   NAT'L PARK   Coca   **5-7**
Manta   Cotopaxi
Manta   LLANGANATES   Tena   YASUNÍ
   NAT'L PARK   NATIONAL
I. de   Chimborazo   PARK
la Plata   Puyo
MACHALILLA   Riobamba   Pastaza
NATIONAL PARK

PACIFIC   SANGAY
OCEAN   NATIONAL
   GUAYAQUIL   PARK
Golfo   CAJAS
de   NAT'L PARK
Guayaquil   I. Puná   Cuenca
      Machala
         PERÚ
1-2 Quito   Loja
3-4 Otavalo &   PODOCARPUS
      Imbabura Province   Vilcabamba   NATIONAL PARK
5-7 El Oriente   0   60 mi
8 Quito   0   60 km

a siesta afterward. In the afternoon, choose from a variety of activities, including horseback riding in the nearby hills, a Spanish lesson, or a meander in the lovely gardens. A candle-lit dinner is served in the cozy dining room, which makes for a perfect ending to a relaxing day. If you feel like going out for a gourmet dinner, make reservations at and take a taxi to **La Mirage Garden Hotel** ✸✸✸ (p. 151), one of the finer restaurants in Ecuador. The drive takes about 20 minutes.

On Day 4, spend your morning perusing the artisans market at **Otavalo** ✸✸✸ (p. 144), a 15-minute taxi ride away, and shop to your heart's content. Then stop by **Peguche** (p. 147) to visit some of the best weavers in Ecuador, before heading up to **Hacienda Pinsaquí** ✸ (p. 151) for lunch at one of the region's most picturesque and historic old haciendas. If you have the energy after lunch, you can take a taxi up to **Lago Cuicocha** ✸ and hike around the rim of this beautiful volcanic-crater lake, or take a more relaxing boat ride on its waters.

In the evening you can either spend a quiet night at Hacienda Cusín, or head back into Otavalo for dinner at **Hotel Ali Shungu** ✸✸ (p. 153), and maybe catch some live music at **Amauta Peña Bar** ✸ (p. 154). Whatever you choose, be sure to get a good night's rest, because you'll have to wake early in order to drive back to the Quito airport for your flight to the Amazon.

Days **5** to **7**: Head for the Amazon Basin

Just about all the rainforest lodges in Ecuador's El Oriente offer 4-day/3-night package excursions perfect for giving you a good sense of the culture, environment, and wildlife of this amazing region. I recommend either **Kapawi Ecolodge & Reserve** ✸✸✸ (✆ **800/613-6026** in the U.S. and Canada, or 04/228-5711 in Ecuador; www.kapawi.com; see p. 322) or **Napo Wildlife Center** ✸✸ (✆/fax **02/2897-316;** www.napowildlifecenter.com; p. 312). Both have excellent facilities, guides, and tour options.

Day ❽: Saying *Adios*

Your flight back to Quito from the Amazon won't get in until around mid-day, which is probably too late for your connecting flight back home. If you have extra time, head to the **Mercado Artesanal La** Mariscal (Mariscal Artisans Market; p. 125) to buy some last-minute souvenirs and gifts; or squeeze in a visit to **Museo Nacional del Banco Central de Ecuador** ⟨⟨ (p. 122).

2 Ecuador in 2 Weeks

While it may seem like a lot of time, you'll still just be scratching the surface if you spend 2 weeks in Ecuador. You'll visit Quito and the Sierra, the lovely colonial city of Cuenca, and then, after spending a week in the enchanting Galápagos Islands, you'll have just enough time for an overnight in Guayaquil, one of South America's most up-and-coming cities. If you can tack on a few more days, or opt for just a 3-day cruise of the Galápagos, then you'll have enough time to take a 4-day/3-night tour to El Oriente, Ecuador's lush Amazon region (chapter 11), spend some time at one of the beautiful old haciendas found throughout the central Sierra (chapters 6 and 7), or head out to the Pacific coast from Guayaquil (chapter 9).

Days ❶ to ❹: Quito, Otavalo & Imbabura Province

This itinerary starts off exactly as "Ecuador in 1 Week" does. Follow the first 4 days of that itinerary, as described above.

But, on Day 5, instead of leaving early from Hacienda Cusín for a flight to the Amazon, you'll leave early for a flight to Cuenca.

Day ❺: Cuenca ⟨⟨⟨

Your 1-hour flight will bring you to Cuenca, one of Ecuador's most charming colonial cities. If you're seated on the left side of the plane, and if there's a break in the clouds, you'll probably got a great view of Volcán Cotopaxi on the way.

By the time you arrive and settle into your hotel, you should be ready for lunch. I recommend that you head to **El Maíz** ⟨ (p. 217), a lovely indoor-outdoor restaurant serving top-notch Ecuadorian cuisine. After lunch, visit the **Museo del Banco Central** ⟨⟨ (p. 208), just steps away from El Maíz. The museum contains an extensive art and archaeology collection, and is located on the site of a major Cañari and Inca ceremonial center.

After touring the museum, be sure to walk around the ruins and their botanical gardens.

From the museum, take a taxi to **Mirador de Turi,** a strategic lookout with a beautiful view of Cuenca and its broad valley. Be sure to combine a visit here with a stop at **Taller E. Vega** ⟨⟨ (p. 210), the gallery and workshop of one of the country's most prominent ceramic artists.

At some point during the day, be sure to sign up for a half-day tour to Ingapirca for the following day. Your hotel desk is probably your best bet. Otherwise, contact **Hualambari Tours** ⟨ (℗ **07/ 2848-768;** www.hualambari.com) or **TerraDiversa** ⟨ (℗ **07/2823-782;** www. terradiversa.com).

For dinner, you should splurge and head for the best restaurant in town, **Villa Rosa** ⟨⟨⟨ (p. 217), which serves creative takes on classic Ecuadorian dishes in a refined and elegant setting.

If you have any energy left, head for a nightcap at the **Wunderbar Café** ⟨⟨ (p. 219), located just off Calle Larga midway down a flight of steep stairs to the Río Tomebamba.

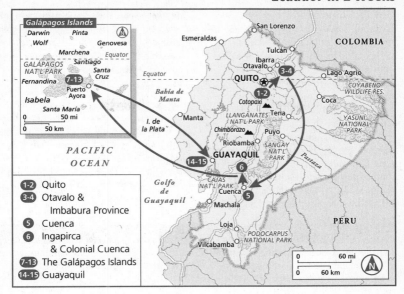

1-2 Quito
3-4 Otavalo &
        Imbabura Province
5 Cuenca
6 Ingapirca
        & Colonial Cuenca
7-13 The Galápagos Islands
14-15 Guayaquil

Day **6**: Ingapirca 🏛 & Colonial Cuenca ★★★

You'll probably leave just after breakfast for your trip to Ingapirca 🏛 (p. 220), the Machu Picchu of Ecuador. Located about a 2-hour drive north of Cuenca, Ingapirca is the largest and most significant archaeological site left by the Incas in Ecuador. It was built on the ruins of a Cañari settlement, and you will see evidence of their culture and architecture here as well. Your tour will likely include lunch, but you should be back in Cuenca with plenty of time to further explore its colonial core.

Start at the colorful **Flower Market** (p. 207) and continue from there to the main square, **Parque Calderón** (the heart of Cuenca). Be sure to visit the Gothic-Romanesque **Catedral Nueva** ★★ (p. 207), with its exquisite white-marble floors. Then catch a taxi from the square to the most interesting and best-known factory in the country. **Homero Ortega P. & Hijos** ★★★ (p. 211) makes some of the highest-quality Panama hats in the world. You'll get to see how they do it, as well as shop at slightly discounted prices in their showroom store.

For your last night, I recommend combining dinner and nightlife by heading to **Café Eucalyptus** ★★ (p. 217), where you can dine on a range of exotic tapas while mingling with the crème de la crème of Cuenca.

Days **7** to **13**: The Galápagos Islands ★★★

Getting to the Galápagos from Cuenca will require an early-morning departure with a change of planes in Guayaquil. The flight to Guayaquil is only 30 minutes, and from there to the Galápagos it's exactly 1½ hours. A 7-day cruise on one of the 100 vessels plying the waters of these magical islands is the best way to visit the Galápagos; the typical itinerary includes a visit to two islands a day— one in the morning and one in the afternoon.

Day ⑭: Guayaquil ⭑
Since all flights from the Galápagos first land in Guayaquil, spend your last night in Ecuador in this economically vibrant and up-and-coming city, the country's largest. Flights from the Galápagos arrive in the early afternoon, leaving you enough time to check into your hotel and stroll over to the **Malecón 2000** ⭑⭑ (p. 238). You may want to visit the MAAC, the **Museo Antropológico y de Arte Contemporáneo** ⭑⭑ (Museum of Anthropology and Contemporary Art; see p. 240), or take a long walk in the interesting neighborhood of **Cerro Santa**

Ana ⭑⭑⭑ (p. 239). Climb to the top for a sweeping view of the city. For your last evening in Ecuador, head over to **Lo Nuestro** ⭑⭑ (p. 246), the city's best restaurant, which focuses on traditional cuisine.

Day ⑮: Fly Home
It's unlikely you'll have much time during your last morning in Guayaquil, but if you do, head to **Parque Histórico Guayaquil** ⭑⭑ (p. 241), a small theme-park with a re-creation of old colonial-era homes and haciendas, as well as lovely gardens.

3 Ecuador for Families

Ecuador is not a particularly kid-friendly destination. There are few attractions and activities that appeal to youngsters, and very few hotels here have well-developed kids' programs. But youngsters and teens, especially the adventurous and inquisitive, will do great in Ecuador. The biggest challenge to families traveling with children is travel distances, as well as the logistical difficulties of moving around within the country, which is why I recommend going with two organized-tour options, combined with a stay at a hacienda near Quito.

Day ❶: Arrive & Head for Happiness
Alegría means "happiness" in Spanish, and I'd make my family's first stop **Hacienda La Alegría** ⭑ (p. 171). This colonial-era hacienda, still a working farm, specializes in horseback-riding tours, including a comprehensive and conscientious program for teaching beginners and young riders. The hacienda is only an hour or so from Quito's airport, making it possible to come here from all but the latest-arriving flights.

Days ❷ & ❸: Saddle Up, Partners
Depending on the skills, experience, and abilities of your family, a wide range of horseback rides can be arranged. Beginners will probably stay pretty close to the hacienda, at least on the first day or so. More experienced riders can venture farther afield, through neighboring towns, villages, and countryside, and even up into the high Andean paramo.

In addition to riding, kids can take part in various farm chores, including milking cows.

You'll probably want to spend your third night in Quito, since early the following morning you'll be catching a flight to the Galápagos.

Days ❹ to ⑪: Cruise the Galápagos Islands ⭑⭑⭑
The Galápagos Islands are an excellent destination for families. Kids of all ages—as well as adults—can't help being awed by the close and constant contact with wildlife. Several cruise operators specialize in family packages to the Galápagos; this is a good way to give your kids some extra-curricular class time in the natural sciences. They'll have so much fun, they won't realize how much they're learning. **Tauck** ⭑⭑ (© **800/788-7885** in the U.S. and Canada; www.tauck.com) is a first-rate tour company with several

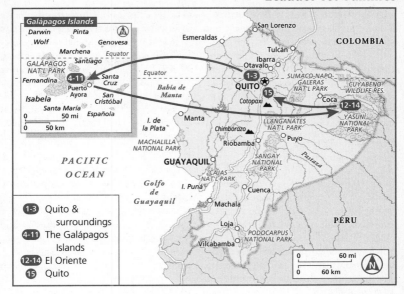

Galápagos Islands

Darwin   Pinta
Wolf   Genovesa
     Marchena   Equator
GALÁPAGOS   Santiago
NAT'L PARK
Fernandina   **4-11**   Santa
            Puerto   Cruz   San
Isabela   Ayora   Cristóbal
   Santa María
0   50 mi   Española
0   50 km

PACIFIC
OCEAN

Golfo
de
Guayaquil

San Lorenzo
Esmeraldas
                    Tulcán
                  Ibarra
               Otavalo
Equator   **1-3**   SUMACO-NAPO-
          QUITO ✪   GALERAS
Bahía de   **15**   NAT'L PARK
Manta   Cotopaxi ▲   Coca   **12-14**
                    LLANGANATES   YASUNÍ
     Manta   NAT'L PARK   NATIONAL
I. de   PARK
la Plata   Chimborazo ▲
MACHALILLA   Riobamba   Puyo
NATIONAL PARK
GUAYAQUIL   SANGAY
        CAJAS NATIONAL
        NAT'L PARK PARK
I. Puná   Cuenca
     Machala

Loja
     PODOCARPUS
Vilcabamba NATIONAL PARK

COLOMBIA

CUYABENO
WILDLIFE RES.

PÉRU

0   60 mi
0   60 km   N

1-3 Quito &
       surroundings
4-11 The Galápagos
        Islands
12-14 El Oriente
15 Quito

family-oriented itineraries to the Galápagos (p. 333).

Days ⑫ to ⑭: The Amazon Basin

You can continue your clandestine classes in the natural sciences by following the Galápagos with a 3-day tour to one of the isolated nature lodges in Ecuador's Amazon basin. I recommend **Kapawi Ecolodge & Reserve** ✸✸✸ (**©** **800/ 613-6026** in the U.S. and Canada, or 04/228-5711 in Ecuador; www.kapawi. com; see p. 322), which has excellent guides, comfortable accommodations, and a wide range of tour and activity options. In addition to the chance to see wild caiman, anacondas, bats, and an amazing abundance of bird and insect life, you can take night hikes, and try your hand at fishing for piranhas.

Day ⑮: Quito

Your return flight to Quito from the Amazon won't get you in until around mid-day, which is probably too late for your connecting flight back home. If you have time, take everyone to **El Teleférico** (**©** **02/3250-076;** www.teleferiqo.com), a high-speed cable car that will whisk you to the top of Volcán Pichincha. At the base of the cable car is **Vulqano Park,** where your family can enjoy amusement-park rides and mingle with Quiteño families (p. 118).

4 Ecuador for Adventure Travelers

Ecuador is an up-and-coming and under-exploited adventure-tourism destination. The following itinerary packs a lot of adventure punch into a single week. This is a basic outline; if you want to do more high-altitude climbing, trekking, mountain biking, horseback riding, or kayaking, schedule that in place of one of the activities that doesn't get your adrenaline pumping.

Day ❶: Arrive & Settle into Quito

If your flight gets in early enough and you have time, head to Old Town and visit some of the colonial-era treasures this UNESCO World Heritage Site has to offer. See the suggested itinerary "Quito in 3 Days," below, for suggestions on sights to see and restaurant recommendations.

Days ❷ to ❹: Head for the Hills

Parque Nacional Cotopaxi is Ecuador's premier high-mountain park, and home to the country's second highest peak. The rustic yet very comfy **Hacienda El Porvenir** ❀ (p. 172), right at the northern entrance to the national park, makes an excellent base for exploring this area. You'll need at least a day or two to acclimate if you plan on climbing Cotopaxi. The hacienda can arrange a number of adventures, including high-altitude trekking and camping, mountain biking, horseback riding, and, of course, summit climbs of Cotopaxi and several other nearby peaks. They also have a zip-line canopy tour at one of their sister lodges.

You'll want to head back to Quito for your final night of this leg, because you'll be getting up early to head to the Galápagos.

Days ❹ to ❻: Dive with Hammerhead Sharks

Sure, the wildlife viewing and natural history are fabulous draws and reason enough to visit the Galápagos Islands, but scuba divers know that this is one of the prime diving destinations on the planet. The isolated location, fishing regulations, and ocean currents have blessed this archipelago with abundant sea life. Large schools of all sorts of fish are the mainstay, and it's common to encounter hammerhead sharks—I've seen them on every one of my dives here. If you're lucky you might also bump into a manta ray, whale shark, sea turtle, or dolphin. You'll almost certainly have a sea lion swim right up to

your face. If you're going specifically to dive, I recommend staying in Puerto Ayora and doing daily dives with one of the local operators like **SCUBA Iguana** ❀ (© 05/2526-497; www.scubaiguana.com; see p. 345). Since you're not supposed to fly soon after diving, talk with your dive master, and if necessary, spend your final day surfing **Ola Escondida (Hidden Wave)** and **Punta Barba Negra (Black Beard Point)**.

Days ❼ to ❿: Go Native in the Amazon Basin with the Cofán Nation

No adventure tour to Ecuador would be complete without a visit to the lowland rainforests of El Oriente. Ecuadorian-born to American parents, Randy Borman is the current chief of the remote, indigenous **Cofán Nation** ❀❀ (© 02/2470-946; www.cofan.org; see p. 305). Randy and fellow Cofán guides lead multiday tours through the area around **Cuyabeno Wildlife Reserve** ❀❀, emphasizing hands-on experiences that get you into the lifestyle, tradition, and culture of the Cofán people.

Days ⓫ & ⓬: Get Wet & Wild

From the northern part of El Oriente, head south to Tena and spend some time on the rivers. Tena is Ecuador's capital for white-water rafting and kayaking. There are a number of local operators in town; **Ríos Ecuador** ❀❀ (© 06/2886-727; www.riosecuador.com) is one of the most reputable, with options ranging from relatively gentle Class III floats to kayak outings on raging Class IV and Class V sections (p. 317).

Day ⓭: Return to Quito & Prepare to Say Goodbye

If you're traveling by land, make a stop at Papallacta on your way back to Quito. After all your adventure travel, you'll appreciate—and perhaps desperately need—a few hours soaking in the hot

Ecuador for Adventure Travelers

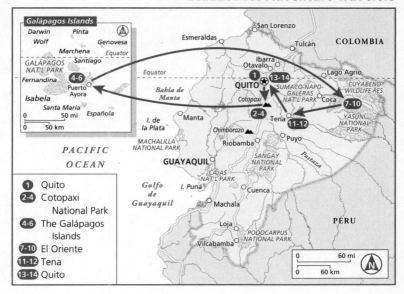

springs at **Termas de Papallacta** ✶✶ (© **06/2320-620;** www.termaspapallacta. com; p. 137). Papallacta is just off the road, along the main route between Tena and Quito.

Day ⑭: Fly Home
Your flight will probably leave early in the morning, but if you have time, head to the **Mercado Artesanal La Mariscal (Mariscal Artisans Market)** to buy last-minute souvenirs and gifts.

5 Quito in 3 Days

Surrounded by towering Andean peaks and volcanoes, Quito is a compact and accessible city with a host of interesting sights, as well as great dining and shopping opportunities. Three days is a perfect amount of time to visit many of the capital's best museums and attractions, while sampling some of the city's many great restaurants. You even have time to visit the artisans market in nearby Otavalo, and to have your picture taken straddling the equator.

Day ①: Taking In Old Town
Many international flights arrive in Quito in the late afternoon or early evening, so this actually begins the day after your arrival. Following breakfast at your hotel, spend the morning touring Old Town. Visit the magnificent **Iglesia de San Francisco** ✶✶ (p. 118), which dates back to 1535, allowing a good 45

minutes to get a feel for the city's oldest church and its attached museum.

A few minutes' walk from here is **La Compañía de Jesús** ✶✶✶ (p. 120) Jesuit church, which features an incredibly ornate interior mixing baroque and Moorish influences. Nearby, **Casa Museo María Augusta Urrutia** ✶ (p. 115) is a perfectly preserved 19th-century mansion

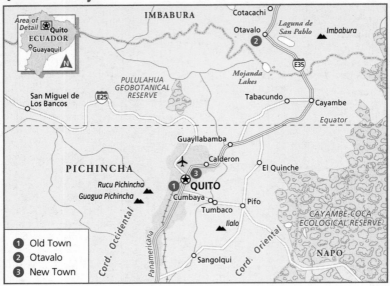

IMBABURA

Cotacachi

Laguna de San Pablo

Otavalo ②

Imbabura

Area of Detail · ⊛ Quito

ECUADOR

Guayaquil

E35

PULULAHUA GEOBOTANICAL RESERVE

Mojanda Lakes

San Miguel de Los Bancos

E25

Tabacundo

Cayambe

Equator

Guayllabamba

PICHINCHA

Calderon

El Quinche

Rucu Pichincha

③

Guagua Pichincha

① ⊛ QUITO

Cumbaya

Pifo

Tumbaco

CAYAMBE-COCA ECOLOGICAL RESERVE

Ilalo

① Old Town

② Otavalo

③ New Town

Sangolqui

Cord. Occidental

Panamericana

Cord. Oriental

NAPO

worthy of at least a 45-minute visit. Pope John Paul II visited here, so you shouldn't miss it. When the day begins to warm up, take an hour to stroll around **Old Town,** ending at **La Plaza de la Independencia** (p. 120), which was the city's main square in the 16th century. (Old Town is safe to get lost in during the day, but at night I don't advise venturing far from the Plaza de la Independencia on foot.) Break for a cup of coffee at a sunny cafe on or around the plaza—there are plenty of spots to choose from.

While walking around the Plaza de la Independencia, see if there's a show on that night at the **Teatro Nacional Sucre;** if there is, buy a ticket and make a pre-show dinner reservation at **Mea Culpa** ⋆ (p. 111) or **Theatrum** ⋆ (p. 112).

El Panecillo (p. 117) is where you'll want to head next; it's a 10-minute ride up a steep hill. From here, standing below the immense winged virgin, you have a sweeping view of Old Town and the rest of Quito. Right next to the monument is

PIM's Panecillo (p. 112), a great place to enjoy local cuisine and the view. I suggest returning to your hotel for a rest, because your body is probably not acclimated to the altitude and you may get tired easily. Remember to drink lots of bottled water, too, especially in the early afternoon, when the sun is at its highest and the atmosphere its driest.

After your dinner (and hopefully a show), sit at the bar in stylish **La Cueva del Oso** for a nightcap.

Day ②: A Side Trip & Some Shopping

For your second day I recommend signing up for a day trip to **Otavalo,** home to Ecuador's most famous **artisan market** ⋆⋆⋆ (p. 144). The market is most extensive and active on Saturday, but it's pretty impressive any day of the week.

Your tour should include lunch at one of the area's historic haciendas as well as stops at any number of nearby attractions, such as Lago Cuicocha, Cascada Peguche,

Lagunas de Mojanda, and Parque Condor. Be sure your tour includes a stop at the new **Quitsato Mitad del Mundo Monument** (© **09/9701-133**; www.quitsato. org; see p. 135).

For dinner, head to **El Nispero** ★★ (p. 114), the best restaurant in Quito, for a taste of cutting-edge New Ecuadorian cuisine.

Day ❸: Time for New Town

After breakfast, head for **Parque El Ejido** and work off a few calories walking around this pretty city park. If it's a weekend, you'll have a chance to shop for Ecuadorian crafts and clothing at the outdoor market here. Otherwise, you can head to the nearby **Mercado Artesanal La Mariscal (Mariscal Artisans Market),** or to **Olga Fisch Folklore** ★★, a high-end shop nearby. This is a good chance to pick up any last-minute gifts, in case you hesitated on pulling the trigger in Otavalo.

Next, head to **Museo Nacional del Banco Central del Ecuador** ★★ (p. 122), the country's biggest and most extensive museum.

It's now time to get one more fabulous view of Quito. So for lunch head to the perfectly perched **Café Mosaico** ★★★, which offers up a great vista of the city.

After you eat, take a taxi to the **Fundación Guayasamín** ★★ (p. 123), named after the country's most famous and influential artist. Expect to spend at least 1½ hours here, which may include a brief stop at the charming museum-cafe for a coffee and a sweet empanada.

Make sure you have a dinner reservation at **Zazu** ★★★ (p. 114), the city's best and hippest place for cutting-edge fusion cooking. You can choose to start or end things at their popular little laid-back bar; or if you have the energy, pull out all the stops and do a bar-and-club crawl in the **Mariscal** district of New Town. Begin at **Plaza Foch** (p. 130), and see where the night takes you.

4

The Active Vacation Planner

Ecuador's varied landscapes, biodiversity, culture, and natural beauty combine to make it a world-class destination for everything from bird-watching to sport fishing, from scuba diving to white-water rafting. Outdoor outfitters take full advantage of the country's diversity: For example, horseback-riding tours include stays in colonial haciendas; mountain-biking excursions stop at indigenous markets; and a golf course doubles as a bird-watching garden.

The fact that Ecuador's ocean, islands, mountains, forests, rivers, lakes, and beaches are packed into a relatively small territory allows travelers to sample an array of outdoor activities on a single trip. This chapter lays out the options, lists the best tour operators for each activity, and provides an overview of the country's national parks and protected areas. I've also listed some volunteer programs and other options for those who want to contribute to the preservation of the country's natural treasures.

1 Organized Adventure Trips

Organized ecotourism or adventure-travel packages, arranged by operators in either the United States or Ecuador, are a popular way of combining varied activities. Bird-watching, horseback riding, biking, and hiking can done in conjunction with visits to national parks or indigenous communities.

Traveling with a group has several advantages over traveling independently: Your accommodations and transportation are arranged, and most (if not all) of your meals are included in the cost of a package. If your tour operator has a reasonable amount of experience and a decent track record, you should proceed to each of your destinations quickly, without the snags and long delays that those traveling on their own can occasionally face. You'll also have the opportunity to meet like-minded souls who are interested in nature and active sports. Of course, you'll pay more for the convenience of having all your arrangements handled in advance.

In the best cases, groups are small (8–15 people), and tours are escorted by knowledgeable, bilingual guides. Be sure to ask about difficulty levels when you're choosing a tour. Although most companies offer "soft adventure" packages for those in moderately good but not phenomenal shape, others focus on more hard-core activities geared toward seasoned athletes or adventure travelers.

U.S.-BASED ADVENTURE TOUR OPERATORS

These agencies and operators specialize in well-organized and coordinated tours that cover your entire stay. Many travelers prefer to have everything arranged and confirmed before arriving in Ecuador, and this is a good idea for first-timers and during the high season.

Ecuador's National Parks & Protected Areas

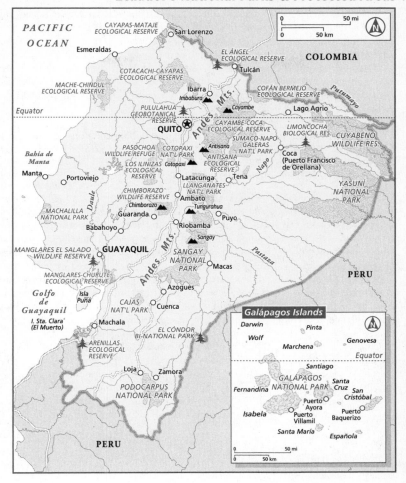

Abercrombie & Kent ✈ (© **800/554-7016** in the U.S. and Canada; www. abercrombiekent.com) is a luxury-tour company that offers upscale trips around the globe, and it has several Ecuador tours on its menu. It offers a selection of Galápagos cruises in combination with attractions on the Ecuadorian mainland or in Peru. Service is personalized and the guides are top-notch. The cost runs from around $5,400 (£2,970) to $9,400 (£5,170) per adult, not including international airfare.

Holbrook Travel ✈ (© **800/451-7111** in the U.S. and Canada; www.holbrook travel.com) is a small, Florida-based company that specializes in ecotourism and educational tours in Latin America They offer several Ecuador options ranging from traditional Galápagos cruises, starting at around $2,300 (£1,265), to an 18-day package that combines the Galápagos with the highlands and Amazon basin, which costs around $5,600 (£3,080) per person.

Latin Trails (☎ 800/747-0567 in the U.S. and Canada; www.latintrails.com), of New Jersey, specializes in adventure and off-the-beaten-path tourism of Ecuador and other Andean nations. They offer a selection of Galápagos cruises as well as overland adventures and Amazon expeditions at competitive prices.

Overseas Adventure Travel ☆☆ (☎ 800/493-6824 in the U.S. and Canada; www.oattravel.com) has good-value natural-history and "soft adventure" itineraries with small groups and naturalist guides. They offer 11-day packages in the Amazon rainforest and a package that combines the Amazon with the Galápagos Islands; prices range from $2,100 (£1,155) to 2,800 (£1,540).

In addition to these companies, many environmental organizations, including the **Sierra Club** (☎ 415/977-5522 in the U.S. and Canada; www.sierraclub.org) and **Smithsonian Institute** (☎ 877/338-8687 in the U.S. and Canada; www.smithsonian journeys.org) periodically offer organized trips to Ecuador.

ECUADORIAN TOUR OPERATORS

Because most U.S.-based operators subcontract their tours to established Ecuadorian companies, travelers can sometimes save money by booking directly with those outfitters in Ecuador. Packages may be 20% to 30% less expensive this way, but still not cheap—you still pay for the convenience of having all your arrangements handled for you.

Scores of agencies in Quito offer a selection of adventure options that ranges from white-water rafting to mountain climbing to bird-watching at a nature lodge in the Amazon basin. Although it's generally quite easy to arrange a day trip at the last minute, longer tours often leave on set dates or when there are enough interested people. So it pays to check websites or to call companies before you leave home.

Cotopaxi.com ☆☆ (☎ 02/2909-640; www.cotopaxi.com), one of Ecuador's leading adventure outfitters, has a selection of multisport packages with different combinations of mountain biking, hiking, camping, bird-watching, mountain climbing, horseback riding, white-water rafting, and visits to indigenous communities.

Safari Ecuador ☆☆ (☎ 02/2552-505; www.safari.com.ec) offers various Galápagos cruises, an array of Amazon adventures, Andean camping safaris, and mountain climbing.

Surtrek ☆ (☎ 02/2231-534; www.surtrek.com), one of the country's biggest tour operators/wholesalers, offers everything from mountain-bike tours to white-water rafting, and can customize combination tours.

2 Activities A to Z

This section describes the best places to participate in a given sport or activity, and lists tour operators and outfitters. If you want to focus on only one active sport during your stay in Ecuador, these companies are your best bets for quality equipment and knowledgeable service.

Adventure activities and ecotourism, by their very nature, carry risks and dangers, which vary according to the sport. Over the years, there have been deaths and dozens of minor injuries from white-water rafting and mountain climbing, which is why I include only the most reputable companies here. If you have any doubt about the safety of the guide, equipment, or activity, opt out. Moreover, know your limits and abilities, and don't exceed them.

BIKING

Ecuador offers varied biking options. Rentals in Baños and certain beach towns provide the option of heading off on your own. The highlands have a better climate for biking and are traversed by countless dirt tracks, with seemingly unlimited options for mountain biking, but there is a real potential for getting lost, which makes guided tours a good option. Some travelers fly their bike down and explore on their own, avoiding the country's main roads. Various tour companies—most of them based in Quito—provide the highway transport, bilingual guides, and logistical support.

TOUR OPERATORS & OUTFITTERS

Adventure Planet Ecuador (© 02/2871-105; www.adventureplanet-ecuador.com) runs a selection of mountain-bike tours lasting from 3 to 16 days. The shorter trips explore the scenery around Cotopaxi and Otavalo, whereas the 1-week trip combines exploration of protected areas with stops at indigenous markets, and the 2-week trips go from the highlands down to the Amazon basin or Pacific coast.

Andes World Bike (© 02/2352-769; www.ecuadorbikingclimbing.com) offers tours ranging from a pedal down the slopes of Cotopaxi to a 2-week trip that combines biking with other activities in and around Quito, Otavalo, Ambato, and Cuenca. They also run a 1-week ride from the highlands to the Pacific coast.

Aries Bike Company (© 02/2906-052; www.ariesbikecompany.com) has an array of guided tours that last anywhere from 1 day to 2 weeks. Those itineraries range from challenging rides over the rugged countryside surrounding Ecuador's highest peaks, or around the crater lake of Quilotoa, to more leisurely downhill routes.

Cotopaxi.com ✸✸ (© 02/2909-640; www.cotopaxi.com) offers custom-tailored mountain-biking trips through the highlands and rainforest as well as multisport tours that combine biking with other outdoor activities.

Ecole Travel Ecuador (© 02/2231-595; www.ecoletravel-ecuador.com) has a 2-day mountain-bike tour on the slopes of Volcán Chimborazo, which includes an overnight in a nearby hostel.

Luna Runtun ✸✸ (© 03/2740-882; www.lunaruntun.com), the hotel and spa perched in a hillside above Baños, has a selection of day tours through the surrounding countryside that vary in difficulty, but all include amazing views.

Quinde Expeditions (© 02/2257-924; www.quinde.com) runs tours ranging from 1 to 5 days in various regions. Shorter trips explore the slopes of Cotopaxi and Chimborazo volcanoes, or the cloud forests of Mindo, whereas longer ones traverse the highlands north of Quito, or the tropical dry forest of Machalilla National Park on the Pacific coast.

Safari Ecuador ✸✸ (© 02/2552-505; www.safari.com.ec) offers mountain-bike safaris around Volcán Cotopaxi and to indigenous villages, including a back-road trip from Quito to the market town of Otavalo.

Surtrek ✸ (© 02/2231-534; www.surtrek.com), one of the country's biggest tour operators/wholesalers, has mountain-bike tours ranging from 1 day to 2 weeks.

BIRD-WATCHING

Ecuador is one of the best places in the world for bird-watching. With approximately 1,600 species, counting resident species and migrants, the country has a greater diversity of birds than China or India, and nearly twice as many bird species as the United States. Though the neighboring nations of Colombia and Peru may boast more species, no nation in the world has as great a diversity of birdlife in as small an area as Ecuador. The country holds approximately one-sixth of the world's bird species in an area about the size of Colorado, and gives birders the possibility of spotting more different species in a week or two than they would have just about anywhere else.

Ecuador's varied feathered creatures are scattered across its main geographical regions: the Sierra, Oriente, Pacific coast and lowlands, and Galápagos Islands. For birding purposes, the Andes could be further broken down into the highlands, Pacific cloud forest, and Amazon cloud forest. The Andean condor may be the **Sierra**'s avian king, but the highland's smaller species are also quite impressive, and much easier to see, especially the varied tanagers and hummingbirds. Birdlife in the Andes varies depending on the altitude, with some species found only around the peaks and high-altitude paramo, and others found only in the Sierra's valleys. There is also a good bit of difference between the birdlife of the northern highlands and that of the country's southern mountains.

The **cloud forests** of the Ecuador's Andes are considered one of the planet's biodiversity hot spots, with a greater diversity of birds than just about anywhere else in the world.

The **Oriente,** or Amazon basin, is home to some amazing birds, including colorful toucans, macaws, and jacamars, as well as the unusual hoatzin. Whereas the Oriente is relatively homogenous, the country's **Pacific lowlands** have a greater variety of habitats, which translates into more bird species, with the Chocó rainforest to the north giving way to tropical dry forest in the southwest, which is home to such species as the Pacific parrolet and the Ecuadorian trogon. The **Galápagos Islands** are often a birder's top spot in Ecuador, with a mix of endemic species, such as Darwin's famous finches, and such common species as the blue-footed booby and the red-billed tropicbird.

If you're serious about birding, you'll definitely want pick up a copy of the *Birds of Ecuador Field Guide,* by Robert Ridgely, Paul Greenfield, and Frank Gill, as well as a pair of gas-sealed binoculars. While the field guide is helpful, you'll get much more out of your time in the woods if you are accompanied by a naturalist guide, and fortunately Ecuador's best tour operators and nature lodges have some very experienced, dedicated birding guides. The following specialty tour operators tend to use designated lodges, several of which organize their own tours.

U.S.-BASED TOUR OPERATORS

Exotic Birding (© 877/247-3371 in the U.S. and Canada; www.exoticbirding.com) specializes in bird-watching tours with very small groups (usually six people) to several Latin American countries. The company offers occasional 2-week tours in Ecuador that combine the highlands, cloud forest, and Amazon basin.

Field Guides (© 800/728-4953 or 512/263-7295 in the U.S. and Canada; www. fieldguides.com), a specialty, bird-watching travel operator, offers long tours of Ecuador and stays at nature lodges for small groups accompanied by expert guides. The company's 18-day "Jewels of Ecuador" tour travels across the highlands and Pacific slope for a cost of about $4,400 (£2,420), not including airfare. They also offer a 2-week "Rainforest & Andes" trip, as well as tours that concentrate on the highlands, Galápagos, and southwest Ecuador.

Victor Emanuel Nature Tours ⚘ (© 800/328-8368 or 512/328-5221 in the U.S. and Canada; www.ventbird.com), a well-respected, small-group operator specializing in bird-watching, runs several Ecuador trips. The company's 10-day hummingbird extravaganza concentrates on the northern Andes and costs about $3,100 (£1,705).

Hummingbird Heaven

The first winged creatures to capture a traveler's imagination may be the legendary condor or the multicolored macaws, but Ecuador's varied and abundant hummingbirds could well be its most impressive avian attraction. With more than 130 different species of hummingbirds, the country vies with Colombia for the distinction of having the most hummingbird species in the world. And because that diversity is spread from one end of the nation to the other, you are likely to encounter hummingbirds wherever you travel—from the rugged mountain slopes, to the lush jungles, to the patio of your Quito hotel.

The world's 330 hummingbird species are all found only in the Americas, and they can be spotted anywhere from Alaska to Tierra del Fuego, but Ecuador lies at the center of the region. With more than a third of the planet's hummers packed into tiny fraction of its landmass, Ecuador is nothing less than hummingbird heaven.

It is feasible for a birder to spot more than a dozen different kinds of hummingbirds in one morning. The best places to observe them are gardens, plenty of which can be found on the grounds of the country's best hotels. Ecuador's hummingbird rainbow includes the green-crowned wood nymph, the sparkling violet-ear, the amethyst-throated sun angel, the purple-crowned fairy, and the violet-tailed sylph, which has long, blue-green tail feathers that trail behind it when it flies.

The country is home to the Andean swordbill, which has the proportionally longest beak of any bird in the world—a 10-centimeter (4-in.) bill on a 13-centimeter (5-in.) body—which allows it to suck nectar from the long tubular flowers that it pollinates. Ecuador also has several species with inordinately long tails, such as the black-tailed trainbearer and the booted racket-tail, which has two bare-shafted tail feathers tipped with green discs. The country is also home to the largest species in the hummer family, called the giant hummingbird, though with a length of 20 centimeters (8 in.) and a weight of two-thirds of an ounce, the name does seem an exaggeration.

It may be hard to focus your binoculars on them before they zip away, but when you get a good look at one of the country's hummingbirds in direct sunlight, its colors are simply amazing. As they hum about from blossom to blossom and chase each other around, these high-powered, iridescent beauties are bound to impress you, and if you find a spot where several species congregate to feed, you are set for an entertaining morning.

Their southern Andes transect costs about $3,500 (£1,925) and can be combined with a 10-day stay at the Napo Wildlife Center, in the Amazon basin, which costs $2,800 (£1,540).

Wings (© **888/293-6443** or 520/320-9868 in the U.S. and Canada; www.wingsbirds.com) is a specialty bird-watching travel operator with more than 28 years of experience in the field. Its offers various 1-week packages with small groups at nature lodges in the cloud forest and Amazon basin.

ECUADORIAN TOUR OPERATORS & LODGES

Andean Birding (© 02/2244-426; www.andeanbirding.com) is run by an Ecuadorian operator started by an American and a Swede who have dedicated most of their lives to studying birds. They invest 10% of their profits in conservation and research. Trips they offer include a 1-week cloud-forest and paramo tour, a 10-day Amazon-to-the-Andes package, and 2 intensive weeks in northern Peru. Their trip costs average $1,400 (£770) to $3,000 (£1,650).

Andean Paths (© 09/9808-469; www.andeanpaths.com) is a small tour operator specializing in outdoor activities. They offer four single-destination tours to some of northern Ecuador's best birding spots.

Bird Ecuador (© 02/2228-902; www.birdecuador.com) is a small tour company owned by the same people who run Cabañas San Isidro, one of Ecuador's best birding spots. They offer various tours that combine stays at San Isidro, which is in the cloud forests of eastern Andes, with time at lodges in other parts of the country.

San Jorge Eco-Lodge & Biological Reserve ⅋ (© 02/2247-549; www.eco-lodge sanjorge.com) is a lodge near Quito that offers a "magic bird circuit" tour to its private forest reserves that protect various forest types.

Mindo Bird Tours (© 09/9183-015; www.mindobirds.com.ec) is an Ecuadorian tour operator, started by a British biologist, that also uses tourism profits to finance research and conservation. They have a good selection of tours to different regions of Ecuador for groups of no more than 10 people for competitive prices. Custom tours are also available.

Surtrek ⅋ (© 02/2231-534; www.surtrek.com), one of the country's biggest adventure and eco-tour companies, offers an array of birding tours at very competitive prices. Their 2-week Andes-to-the-Amazon tour costs just $2,600 (£1,430), and their 2- to 5-day tours cost from $200 (£110) to $800 (£440).

Tinalandia ⅋ (© 02/2449-028; www.tinalandia.com) is a luxury lodge set in private cloud-forest reserve in northwest Ecuador; bird-watching is the specialty here. More than 350 bird species have been spotted on that hotel's grounds, among them an array of hummingbirds, tanagers, manikins, cotingas, parrots, and other colorful creatures. They also offer day trips to other birding spots in the area.

Tropic Journeys (© 703/879-1575 in the U.S. and Canada, or 02/2234-594 in Ecuador; www.tropicoeco.com) can book stays at the rustic Maquipucuna Lodge, in a private reserve that stretches from the cloud forest into the Chocó rainforest; at the Alándaluz Ecolodge, near Machalilla National Park; and at various Amazon-basin lodges—three regions that together hold most of the country's bird species.

BUNGEE JUMPING

Andes Adrenaline Adventures (© 09/9900-300; bungeezone.cjb.net) offers 100m (330-ft.) jumps from a bridge over the Río Chiche every Sunday from 10am to 3pm, and with groups of 10 or more any other day of the week. The jump site is located just 25 minutes from Quito, between the towns of Tumbaco and Puembo, and can be reached on public bus (to Puembo, or to El Quinche); see above website for directions. Reservations are required.

CAMPING

During the dry months, the Andes and Pacific coast provide excellent camping conditions. Camping is allowed in many of the country's protected areas, but infrastructure is largely lacking and access is often difficult. Outdoor outfitters offer tours that include overnights in tents, usually at the end of a day of hiking, biking, horseback riding, or white-water rafting.

Safari Ecuador ☆☆ ((℃ **02/2552-505;** www.safari.com.ec) runs a series of African-style safaris in the Andean paramo using 4WD vehicles. In addition to high-altitude camping, activities include day hikes and horseback riding easy enough to be appropriate for families. Expeditions last anywhere from 2 days to 2 weeks, and costs range from $200 (£110) to $2,600 (£1,430).

Surtrek ☆ ((℃ **02/2231-534;** www.surtrek.com), one of the country's biggest adventure and eco-tour companies, offers various Andes and Amazon hiking tours that include the option of camping, and cost anywhere from $800 (£440) to $2,600 (£1,430).

CANOPY TOUR

The canopy tour—an activity that involves gliding along steel cables between platforms perched high in trees—was invented in Costa Rica, but has spread to other countries, Ecuador among them. It is estimated that some two-thirds of the tropical rainforest's species live in the canopy (the uppermost, branching layer of the forest), and biologists who pioneered study of that biodiversity developed some of the techniques now used in canopy tours. Nevertheless, the tours are more about adrenaline rushes than about observing or learning about wildlife.

Ecole Travel Ecuador ((℃ **02/2231-595;** www.ecoletravel-ecuador.com) offers a canopy tour through the treetops of a private reserve 2 hours from Quito. The tour includes an exhilarating flight down a 400m (1,310-ft.) cable strung over a canyon, and a visit to an 85m (280-ft.) waterfall. The price of the tour is $55 (£30) per person, including transportation, breakfast, and lunch, with a two-person minimum.

CRUISING

Most of Ecuador's cruising options are centered in the Galápagos (see chapter 12), where dozens of yachts and catamarans offer 1- to 2-week tours to the archipelago's attractions. These cruises are focused on the fascinating fauna, and most offer the option of snorkeling or scuba diving, whereas some boats cater explosively to scuba divers (see "Diving & Snorkeling," below).

Galacruises Expeditions ((℃ **02/250-9007;** www.galacruises.com) has four boats in the Galápagos, ranging from older, less-expensive yachts to luxury catamarans. They can also book Galápagos cruises on various other vessels.

Linblad Expeditions ☆☆ ((℃ **800/397-3348** in the U.S. and Canada; www.expeditions.com), a luxury-oriented agency committed to environmental protection, offers first-class Galápagos cruises with highly trained naturalist guides on the smaller M/V *Islander* and M/V *Polaris.* The 10-day cruise costs $3,650 to $6,280 (£2,008–£3,454).

Metropolitan Touring ☆☆ ((℃ **02/2988-200;** www.galapagosvoyage.com) offers affordable Galápagos cruises on the 72m (237-ft.) M/V *Santa Cruz,* a 46-cabin ship, and more comfortable trips on the 50m (166-ft.) *Isabela II,* which has 20 air-conditioned cabins. They offer the option of pairing a cruise with time at their Finch Bay Hotel, on Santa Cruz Island, or with an array of packages on the mainland.

The rustic *Manatee Amazon Explorer* ☆ ((℃ **02/2448-985;** www.manateeamazon explorer.com) runs 3-, 4-, and 7-night eco-cruises on the **Napo River,** the Amazon tributary where Francisco de Orellana began his journey that led to the big river's discovery. Accommodations are snug, but the guides and itinerary are first-class. The cruise includes daily boat trips up smaller rivers and hikes into the rainforest where you are likely to see everything from wooly monkeys to blue and gold macaws.

Tauck *★★* (*✆* **800/788-7885** in the U.S. and Canada; www.tauck.com) is a soft-adventure company catering to higher-end travelers. They offer various Galápagos cruises, including a family package, and an add-on to package to Peru.

DIVING & SNORKELING

In addition to being a phenomenal place to spot fauna on hikes and boat rides, the **Galápagos Islands** are a world-class scuba-diving destination. Unlike popular areas such as the South Pacific and Caribbean, the Galápagos don't have coral reefs, because the water is too cold. They do have a lot of marine life, including manta rays, sea lions, penguins, sea turtles, iguanas, at least five species of sharks, and hundreds of other fish species, many of them endemic to the archipelago. Galápagos cruises generally offer snorkeling or scuba diving; keep in mind that the water is chilly and most people need a wet suit. A handful of boats catering to experienced divers offer cruises that include any of 30 dive sites over the course of a 1 to 2 weeks. Two to four daily dives are complemented with island excursions. All divers must pay the one-time, $100 (£55) national park admission fee and port fees.

The best months for diving are November to April, when seas are calmer and the water is less cold: 18° to 23°C (65°–73° F). However, even then, many dive sites experience strong currents, surges of cold water that can get as low as 10° C (50°F), and visibility that can get as low as 3m (10 ft.), though it averages 6 to 24m (20–80 ft.). Many of the dives are relatively deep. Night dives are prohibited in the Galápagos. Divers consequently need to prove that they are experienced and have been diving recently in order to join trips. They will also need to use a full wet suit, often with hood. Because of the nature of the diving here, I personally recommend taking a dive boat with Nitrox facilities. If you aren't already Nitrox certified, you can take the course onboard and dive with Nitrox tanks during the trip. Nitrox will allow you increased time below the surface, an important consideration with these predominantly deep dives.

Various ships offer dive cruises to the northern islands that include comfortable accommodations, good food, and creature comforts. The best and most challenging dive spots are located around the archipelago's northern islands, especially **Wolf Island** and **Darwin Island,** but since the main attractions are on the southern islands, excursions that combine divers with non-divers tend to stay in the south.

A less-expensive option is to stay on Santa Cruz or on San Cristóbal and take day trips with a local dive operator. Though the best dive spots are too far north to reach on anything other than a live-aboard ship, there are dozens of excellent dive spots within a 20- to 90-minute boat trip from **Santa Cruz,** including Gordon's Rocks, where schools of hammerhead sharks sometimes congregate. The conditions in the south are also less demanding, and local dive schools offer basic certification and resort dives for novices. See chapter 12 for more about diving in the Galápagos.

Though the Galápagos has Ecuador's best diving, the **Pacific coast** also has its dive spots, the best of which is around **Isla de la Plata,** an offshore island about 2 hours by boat from Puerto López. Dubbed the "poor man's Galápagos," Isla de la Plata has many of the same fish, including white-tipped sharks and manta rays, as well as plentiful birdlife. From June to October, dive trips to the island can be complemented with whale watching. See chapter 9.

DIVING BOATS & OPERATORS

***Aggressor* Fleet Limited** ☆☆ (© 800/348-2628 in the U.S. and Canada, or 04/ 2681-950; www.aggressor.com) runs 1-week cruises for 14 divers to the islands' best spots on its two 30m (100-ft.) boats: the *Galápagos Aggressor I* and *II*. Boats include Nitrox facilities, film developing, and underwater-camera rental. A 1-week trip costs $3,300 to $3,600 (£1,815–£1,980) plus airfare, and the $100 (£55) national park and $70 (£39) port fees.

Exploramar Diving ☆☆ (© 02/2563-905 or 05/2300-123; www.exploradiving. com), an Ecuadorian company with dive centers on Santa Cruz Island and in Puerto López, Manabí, offers a selection of diving packages for the Galápagos and Isla de la Plata, as well as PADI certification courses.

Galápagos Divers (© 800/426-0802 in the U.S. and Canada; www.galapagos divers.com) is a Miami-based company that offers 7- and 10-day live-aboard cruise and land-based diving packages. Prices for live-aboard cruises range from $2,500 to $3,500 (£1,375–£1,925), whereas land-based packages cost less than $2,200 (£1,210), plus the $100 (£55) national park fee and international airfare.

Galápagos Sub-Aqua (© 05/2526-633; www.galapagos-sub-aqua.com), an Ecuadorian company in Puerto Ayora, is the archipelago's oldest dive center. They offer PADI certification courses, land-based packages, and cruises custom-designed to divers' experience levels.

Machalilla Tours (© 05/2300-234 or 09/6109-185; machalillatours@yahoo.com) is an excellent local operator based out of Puerto López. They offer diving trips to sites around Isla de la Plata, as well as off the coast of Manabí.

M/S *Lammer Law* (© 800/247-2925 in the U.S. and Canada, or 02/2446-996 in Ecuador; www.quasernautica.com), a large, luxury trimaran with eight staterooms, is one of the best options for dive cruises in the Galápagos. A 1-week cruise with unlimited diving, meals, and beverages costs $2,750 to $3,050 (£1,513–£1,678) per person, double occupancy, plus airfare, $100 (£55) national park fee, and transfers.

M/S *Sky Dancer* ☆ (© 800/932-6237 in the U.S. and Canada, or 04/2207-177; www.peterhughes.com), part of the international Peter Hughes Diving fleet, is a 30m (100-ft.) vessel with eight staterooms. Top-notch dive masters, food, and Nitrox facilities make this the Galápagos' second-best diving option, after the *Aggressor* boats (see above). A 1-week cruise with several daily dives and meals and beverages costs $3,195 to $3,395 (£1,757–£1,867) per person, double occupancy, plus airfare, $100 (£55) national park admission, and transfers.

Scuba Iguana ☆ (© 05/2526-497; www.scubaiguana.com) is an excellent operator, offering an array of day trips out of Puerto Ayora, as well as diving certification courses.

FISHING

Ecuador is one of the world's great overlooked deep-sea-fishing destinations. The ocean is remarkably rich in marine life thanks to the Humboldt current, which pulls nutrients off the ocean bottom through a process called upwelling, keeping the water full of plankton. A vibrant food chain ends in massive marlins, sailfish, sharks, and whales. The country has few sport-fishing operators, but their catch logs are as impressive as those of charter boats in the Caribbean, Mexico, or Costa Rica. The Galápagos archipelago and Pacific coastal waters hold abundant Pacific sailfish, tuna, wahoo, mahimahi, and blue, black, and striped marlin.

The calmest conditions are from December to May, but the fishing stays good from June to November, when it can be chilly in the Galápagos. Temperatures are more consistently tropical along the coast, where marlin and sailfish abound, especially around Isla de la Plata. Ecuador's excellent angling is complemented by a usually pleasant climate, nice beaches, and natural wonders, making the country one of sport fishing's best-kept secrets.

SPORT-FISHING CHARTERS

Art Marina ☆ (✆ **305/663-3553** in the U.S.; www.artmarina.com), a Miami-based company, offers Galápagos sport-fishing packages that include 3 days of fishing, 5 nights in hotels, and the flight to Galápagos from Guayaquil for around $3,000 to $4,500 (£1,650–£2,475), depending on the group size.

The Blue Marlin Lodge ☆ (✆ **09/9460-907;** www.bluemarlinmanta.com), in the port of Manta, specializes in daily fishing charters in the rich coastal waters around Isla de la Plata, dubbed the "marlin boulevard" for its abundant billfish. Charters on their 11m (36-ft.) Hatteras cost $1,000 (£550) for up to five people. The "lodge" in their name is misleading, but they will arrange first-class hotel accommodations in Manta for you.

Machalilla Tours ☆ (✆ **05/2300-234** or 09/6109-185; machalillatours@yahoo. com) are the folks to contact for sport fishing out of Puerto López, and along the Manabí coast.

Magellan Offshore Fishing Tours ☆☆ (✆ **877/426-3347** in the U.S. and Canada; www.magellanoffshore.com), of Miami, offers sport-fishing packages in the rich coastal waters of Manta and around Isla de la Plata from a base at the beach town of Salinas. Fishing is from 11m (36-ft.) and 14m (46-ft.) yachts.

Pesca Tours ☆ (✆ **04/2443-365;** www.pescatours.com.ec) offers sport-fishing charters out of the beach town of Salinas.

GOLF

Ecuador is not much of a golfing destination. The country has seven private clubs near Quito, Guayaquil, or Cuenca, some of which allow visitors to play (ask the concierge at your hotel to call). The easiest option for travelers, however, is to stay at one of the two resorts that have 9-hole courses. The upside is that those resorts are surrounded by impressive tropical scenery, and one is just a chip shot away from the beach.

Although the course is rather run-down, the best option for golfers remains the **Casablanca Beach Hotel & Golf Club** ☆ (✆ **06/2733-159;** www.casablanca.com), located near the beach resort of Atacames, which has a 9-hole course designed by Jack Nicklaus.

Another option is **Hacienda La Carriona** (✆ **02/2331-974** or ✆/fax 02/2332-005; www.lacarriona.com), just outside Quito, which has an agreement allowing guests to play at a nearby private country club with a regulation 18-hole course.

One final alternative is to stay at **Hacienda Tinalandia** (✆ **02/2449-028;** www. tinalandia.com), set in the cloud forests west of Quito. The 9-hole course here, designed in the 1970s, is a bit of a botanical garden and could easily double as a bird-watching refuge.

HANG GLIDING & PARAGLIDING

Hang gliding and paragliding are popular from the mountains above Quito—namely, Pichincha—and the cliffs above Canoa and the tiny town of Crucita, both on the

Manabí coast. While experienced pilots should be happy with the conditions, novices can also try the paragliding on a tandem flight, which can provide an unforgettable, bird's-eye view of the coast or highlands.

The Belgian-owned operator **Terranova Trek** (© **02/2253-327**; www.terranova trek.com) offers tandem flights in the Quito area, advice, transportation and support for pilots with their own gear, various paragliding courses, and a package tour for experienced pilots that includes flights in both the mountains and coast, as well as visits to national parks and other attractions. Tandem flights cost just $40 (£22), whereas the 16-day tour costs $1,300 (£715).

Parapente Crucita (© **05/2340-334**; www.parapentecrucita.com), in the paragliding mecca of Crucita, has a hostel and flight school, rents equipment, provides transportation to the bluffs, and offers 10-minute tandem flights for $16 (£8.80). A 5-day paragliding course costs $250 (£138).

HIKING

From its jungle trails to its highland tracks, Ecuador's hiking options are virtually limitless. In many places, the terrain is challenging, the altitude a serious consideration, or the forest thick, which is why organized hikes are quite popular. Stays at the nature lodges of the Oriente and the cruise down the Napo River include guided hikes through the rainforest, while Andean hiking options range from short hikes through the countryside around mountain lodges to acclimation and summit hikes on the slopes and peaks of snowcapped volcanoes and full-on trekking safaris to some of the country's most remote protected areas.

Popular trips include walks on the well-marked trails of the Pasochoa Reserve, near Quito; treks up the slopes of Cotopaxi or Chimborazo; or hikes around the crater lake of Cuicocha or down a section of the old Inca trail to the ruins of Ingapirca. Hikers who want to do it on their own should pick up the book *Trekking in Ecuador,* by Robert and Daisy Kunstaetter. When planning a hiking expedition, it is good to pay attention to the country's regional rainy seasons. Though the Sierra is largely sunny from June to September, and partially sunny in December and January, the eastern peaks and valleys are influenced by the inclement climate of the Oriente, where the wettest months are June, July, and August. The wettest months on the country's Pacific side are February through May.

HIKING OUTFITTERS

Andean Paths ✦ (© **09/9808-469**; www.andeanpaths.com) offers several multiday hiking tours in the southern part of the country: Sangay National Park; Cajas National Park, near Cuenca; and one of the surviving stretches of the Inca Trail to the archaeological site of Ingapirca.

Cotopaxi.com ✦✦ (© **02/2909-640**; www.cotopaxi.com), a Quito-based outdoor and mountaineering outfitter, offers a few 3- and 4-day high-altitude treks for outdoor enthusiasts in good shape that alternate camping with nights in lodges.

Ecole Travel (© **02/2231-595**; www.ecoletravel-ecuador.com) offers a selection of treks around the crater lake of Quilotoa, or along the Inca Trail; and a 5-day hike from the Andes down to the jungle along a pre-Incan trail.

Eco Trails ✦ (© **02/2465-916**; www.adventureinecuador.com) runs a series of day hikes out of Quito in areas such as Pasochoa, Cotopaxi National Park, Quilotoa Lake, and the slopes of Volcán Cayambe.

Luna Runtun ✿✿ (℃ **03/2740-882;** www.lunaruntun.com), a luxury resort in the mountains above Baños, has organized a dozen day hikes in and around Sangay National Park to waterfalls, indigenous villages, spots with panoramic views, and stretches of the old Inca Trail.

Moggely Climbing ✿ (℃ **02/2554-984;** www.moggely.com), a Danish-owned mountaineering outfitter, offers economical hiking tours of Cotopaxi National Park and the area around Papallacta, as well as ascents of such secondary peaks as extinct Volcán Pasochoa (approximately 5,000m/15,000 ft.).

Safari Ecuador ✿✿ (℃ **02/2552-505;** www.safari.com.ec) runs multiday hiking trips for serious hikers to the remote indigenous village of Tigua, around Cotopaxi and Antisana national parks, and up several of the country's secondary peaks that can serve as acclimatization hikes for further mountaineering expeditions.

Surtrek ✿ (℃ **02/2231-534;** www.surtrek.com) offers a dozen 3- to 6-day treks through some of the country's most spectacular regions, complete with pack horses and a cook. Among the tours are a 5-day trek around Volcán Cotopaxi and the Ilinizas peaks, a trek on the Inca Trail, and 4 days in Podocarpus National Park.

The Black Sheep Inn ✿✿ (℃ **03/2814-587;** www.blacksheepinn.com), in Chugchilán, Cotopaxi, offers guests guided day hikes around Quilotoa Lake and through the surrounding countryside.

HORSEBACK RIDING

Ecuador's horseback-riding tradition stretches back to 1534, when Spanish conquistadors rode the first horses into the country. During the colonial era, a thriving ranching culture developed in the Sierra, where cattle and horses took over pastureland that once supported herds of llamas and alpacas. That heritage is still visible at the country's traditional haciendas, where *chagras,* or Ecuadorian cowboys, round up cattle in traditional garb.

For visitors, horseback-riding opportunities range from an array of day trips to equestrian packages that let you ride from hacienda to hacienda, or to participate in a roundup. Trail rides can take you past amazing scenery, including the highland paramo, snowcapped volcanoes, Andean dwarf forest, or lush cloud forest. Horseback-riding enthusiasts have the option of staying at one of the country's traditional cattle ranches, such as Hacienda La Alegría or Hacienda Zuleta, or joining one of various horseback tours that visit two or more haciendas.

HORSEBACK OUTFITTERS

Andean Paths ✿ (℃ **09/9808-469;** www.andeanpaths.com) offers various horseback-riding tours ranging from 1-day riding on a ranch near Quito to 5- or 8-day tours of colonial haciendas. They also offer a 7-day ride between Cotopaxi and Chimborazo volcanoes that combines nights at haciendas with camping. Shorter tours cost from $60 to $700 (£33–£385), according to the number of days and riders, whereas longer tours cost around $1,300 (£715) with a minimum of four riders.

Equitours (℃ **800/545-20019** in the U.S. and Canada; www.ridingtours.com), of Wyoming, sells a 9-day horseback tour of Ecuador, which includes 7 days of riding and overnights at various historic haciendas, for $2,250 (£1,238), with a minimum of four riders.

Hidden Trails (℃ **888/987-2457** in the U.S. and Canada; www.hiddentrails. com), a U.S. tour agency that specializes in equestrian vacations, offers various riding packages in Ecuador that combine nights in traditional haciendas with camping or overnights in rustic farmhouses. Their tours include rides through cloud forest and highland paramo, trips around Volcán Cotopaxi, overnights at various historic haciendas, and participation in traditional horse or cattle roundups. The cost of a 5-day tour is $600 (£330), whereas the cost of 8- to 11-day tours ranges from $1,500 to $2,300 (£825–£1,265)

Ilalo Expeditions (✆ **09/7778-399;** www.ilaloexpeditions.com), an Ecuadorian outfitter, offers 1-day rides near Volcán Cotopaxi or to the summit of extinct Volcán Ilalo, and an 8-day ride along the Avenue of the Volcanoes, with overnights in historic haciendas and country inns. They also have a 2-week Inca Imperial tour that combines horseback riding in Ecuador and Peru with trips to the Galápagos and Machu Picchu.

HACIENDAS

Hacienda La Alegría ⚲ (✆ **02/2462-319** or 09/9802-526; www.haciendaalegria. com), a 20th-century horse ranch south of Quito, offers guests various horseback-riding tours though the surrounding countryside, as well as other outdoor activities.

Hacienda Pinsaqui ⚲ (✆ **06/2946-116;** www.haciendapinsaqui.com), near the market town of Otavalo, is a historic hacienda, founded in 1790, that specializes in horseback riding, with trips to nearby indigenous communities or to the summit of Volcán Imbabura.

Hacienda Zuleta ⚲ (✆ **02/2228-554** or 06/2662-182; www.zuleta.com), a colonial, 1,780-hectare (4,400-acre) hacienda, about 2½ hours north of Quito, has more than 90 horses. Guests can choose from an ample selection of guided trail rides through pasture, cloud forest, and paramo.

San Jorge Eco-Lodge & Biological Reserve ⚲ (✆ **02/2247-549;** www.eco-lodge sanjorge.com), in the mountains near Quito, has more than 20 horses and various trail rides from which guests can choose.

MOUNTAIN CLIMBING

Ecuador may not have the world's highest mountains, but thanks to the accessibility of the country's big peaks and its supply of experienced, bilingual climbing guides, it is one of the great mountaineering destinations. The country's popularity among climbers has grown steadily since the British mountaineer Edward Whymper—the first to ascend many of Ecuador's mountains—chronicled his experiences in an 1892 book called *Travels Amongst the Great Andes of the Equator.* But you don't need to read Whymper to be inspired enough to want to climb one of Ecuador's massive snow-capped volcanoes, which dominate the landscape in much of the northern Sierra.

The country's highest peaks are divided between eastern and western cordilleras that flank a fertile central valley, known as the "Avenue of the Volcanoes." The view from the summit of one of those mountains on a clear morning is truly breathtaking—if you've got any breath left to take after making the climb. But even a hike to the edge of one of their glaciers, or an ascent that fails to reach the summit, can provide an unforgettable experience.

Ecuador has peaks that are technically difficult enough to challenge experienced climbers, but it is also an excellent place for an introduction to the sport, thanks to the existence of various mountaineering schools. Because the country's second highest peak, Cotopaxi, is a relatively young, conical volcano, it presents a technically simple climb that is accessible to climbers with various levels of experience. If you're in good shape and acclimate quickly, it is feasible for you to take an introductory course and end up climbing Cotopaxi within a week's time.

Whether you are an experienced climber or a mountaineering novice, safety is always the priority, which means climbing only with trained, experienced guides. The popularity of the sport has resulted in an over-abundance of companies offering climbing tours, many of which are of dubious quality. The minimum training your guide should have is that required for membership in ASEGUIM, the Ecuadorian Mountain Guides Association; it's preferable, though, that a guide has had some training abroad as well. That said, there is no substitute for experience, so if you are going to attempt an ascent of a big peak, make sure your guide has climbed it at least a dozen times.

The Big Peaks

Climbers have dozens of mountains to choose from in Ecuador, but most head up the same peaks, especially the two highest—Chimborazo and Cotopaxi—which may be ascended by several groups at once during the driest months. Here are the biggest and most popular peaks:

Chimborazo (6,310m/20,703 ft.) This massive glacier-encrusted peak, 150km (93 miles) south of Quito, has five summits, the highest of which is named for Whymper, who believed it was the tallest mountain in the world when he ascended it in 1880. It has claimed the lives of many climbers and requires experience and acclimation. Best weather: June to January.

Cotopaxi (5,897m/19,348 ft.) A perfectly conical, snowcapped volcano less than an hour south of Quito, Ecuador's second-highest mountain is also its most popular climb. Though technically straightforward, the ascent demands good physical conditioning, ice axes, crampons, and ropes. It can be climbed year-round, but the best weather is in December, January, and July to September.

Cayambe (5,790m/18,997 ft.) Ecuador's third-highest peak, this extinct volcano north of Quito is climbed less frequently than Cotopaxi because it has crevasses and suffers from more inclement weather and avalanches. Nevertheless, qualified mountain guides regularly lead successful ascents there. Best weather: July and August.

Antisana (5,704m/18,715 ft.) Ecuador's fourth-highest peak, Antisana towers over the eastern edge of the Andes, which means it is more influenced by Amazon-basin weather. The surrounding scenery of lakes and forest and the abundance of Andean condors make this a good area for hikers—but the frequent clouds and crevasses near the summit make it a difficult peak to climb. Best weather: December and January.

El Altar (5,319m/17,452 ft.) This massive, extinct volcano with nine summits is a challenging technical climb complicated by frequent inclement weather, but even if you don't make the summit, the scenery on the lower slopes is impressive. Best weather: December to May.

Tungurahua (5,023m/16,475 ft.) Located within Sangay National Park, remote Tungurahua is an active volcano that was part of the climbing circuit for years when it was dormant, but massive eruptions in 2006 knocked it off the circuit, at least for the time being.

The most popular peaks have large refuges at their bases with kitchen facilities and rooms full of bunks, where climbers hit the sack early in order to start their ascent around midnight. Climbing outfitters reserve bunks, provide transportation, and take care of dinner. Serious climbers will want to pick up a copy of the book *Climbing and Hiking in Ecuador,* by Rob Rachowiecki, Mark Thurber, and Betsy Wagenhouser.

MOUNTAINEERING OUTFITTERS

Adventure Planet Ecuador (© 02/2871-105; www.adventureplanet-ecuador.com) offers guided ascents of the country's highest peaks and mountaineering tours that range from to a 6-day "soft climbing" package to a 3-week tour that combines ascents of five volcanoes with a rainforest trip.

Climb Ecuador ⭐⭐ (© 212/362-4721 in the U.S.; www.climbecuador.com) is a New York–based mountaineering outfitter run by mountain guide Roger Kovary; they use experienced local guides who have passed various mountain rescue and first-aid courses. You have a choice of 2-week packages for experienced climbers that combine ascents of four summits with acclimation hikes and other activities.

Compañía de Guías de Montaña ⭐ (© 02/2901-551; www.companiadeguias. com.ec), started by a group of Ecuadorian climbing guides 15 years ago, offers guided ascents of most of the country's big mountains and 9- to 15-day packages that combine acclimation and ascents of several summits with general sightseeing.

Cotopaxi.com ⭐⭐ (© 02/2909-640; www.cotopaxi.com), a Quito-based adventure outfitter, has custom-tailored 2-day ascents of the country's main peaks as well as a 10-day basic mountaineering course and a 2-week, five-summit program for novices or climbers with limited experience.

Eco Trails (© 866/978-6287 in the U.S. and Canada, or 02/2909-640; www. adventureinecuador.com), a climbing outfitter, offers two multipeak climbing packages.

Ecuadorian Alpine Institute (© 02/2565-465; www.volcanoclimbing.com), a local climbing and trekking outfitter, organizes ascents for experienced climbers and offers mountaineering training for beginners and intermediate climbers.

International Mountain Climbing School (© 603/356-7064 in the U.S.; www. ime-usa.com), based in New Hampshire, organizes annual climbing tours to Ecuador.

Moggely Climbing (© 02/2554-984; www.moggely.com), a European-owned Ecuadorian outfitter, offers guided ascents of the country's principal peaks for very competitive prices, without cutting corners on safety. They also have 1-day glacier-climbing courses.

Safari Ecuador ⭐⭐ (© 02/2222-505; www.safari.com.ec) organizes ascents of the country's main climbing peaks and runs an Andes Climbing School that offers an introduction to the sport and acclimatization programs.

SPAS

Ecuador has a limited spa selection, but those that are listed here feature such unusual extras as hummingbird gardens, lush cloud forests, or the opportunity to complement massages and other treatments with outdoor activities.

Arasha Resort ⭐ (© 02/2449-881; www.arasharesort.com) is sequestered in the cloud forest near Mindo, about 2 hours from Quito. It offers an array of stress-relieving therapies as well as lot of exposure to soothing Mother Nature.

La Mirage Garden Hotel & Spa ⭐⭐⭐ (© 800/327-3573 in the U.S. and Canada, or 06/2915-237 in Ecuador; www.mirage.com.ec), on the outskirts of the tranquil colonial town of Cotacachi, is a luxury hotel and spa where the massages and aromatherapy can be complemented by contemplating the hummingbirds that abound in the hotel's extensive gardens. See p. 151.

Hotel Termas de Papallacta 🏆🏆 (© 02/2568-989; www.papallacta.com.ec), on the eastern slope of the Andes, is an hour from Quito. This hotel and hot springs offers an affordable spa experience in an attractive valley known for its bird-watching. See p. 137.

Luna Runtun 🏆🏆 (© 03/2730-882; www.lunaruntun.com), an attractive hotel and spa in the mountains above Baños, Luna Runtun offers a range of massages, skin care, and hair care, as well as a selection of outdoor activities that include hiking, horseback riding, and mountain biking. See p. 191.

SURFING

Ecuador is one of the world's best-kept surfing secrets. Between the Galápagos Islands and the Pacific coast, the country has at least 50 surf spots where the waves consistently break overhead. The coastal water is warm, especially from December to June, but the Galápagos are wet-suit territory pretty much year-round. The best surfing months are December to June, when the ocean is often glassy in the morning, and the sky is usually clear. From June till November, the water gets choppier and cold, especially in the Galápagos, and onshore winds can further complicate conditions, though the mainland experiences days with good conditions year-round.

Galápagos surfing is considerably more expensive, due to logistics and lodging costs, but the islands have few surfers and the waves are consistently overhead and uncrowded. San Cristóbal island has about five breaks, most of which are over volcanic-rock platforms; though pleasant from January through May, the water gets cold here during the June-to-December rainy season. The U.S. company **Wave Hunters Surf Travel** 🏆 (© 888/899-8823 in the U.S. and Canada; www.wavehunters.com) offers 1-week surfing packages that include the flight from Guayaquil, lodging at the Canoa Surf Resort, and transportation to surf breaks that cost $1,600 to $1,900 (£890–£1,045). See p. 344.

Pacific coast surfing is considerably less expensive and offers more options than that in the Galápagos. The coast has about 50 breaks, most of which lie between Manta and Salinas and along the coast south of Salinas. **Montañita,** a tubular right point break, is one of the best. **Casa Sol Surf Camp** (www.casasol.com), in Montañita, offers accommodations, surf tours of coastal breaks, and instruction for novice surfers. **Río Chico,** north of Montañita, has an excellent left when there is a southwest swell. Las Tunas, near Ayampé, is a fun beach break that can easily be surfed from **Finca Punta Ayampé** 🏆 (© 09/6273-458; www.fincapuntaayampe.com), an ecolodge that offers surf tours, whale-watching, and other activities. **Salinas** has several breaks nearby, the best of which is a reef break in front of a military base that is only accessible by boat. **San Mateo,** near Manta, is a long, consistent left that can get very big. **Canoa,** on the northern coast, has a good beach break that can be fun for beginners and experienced surfers alike. **Mompiche,** south of Esmeraldas, is an intense left that breaks over lava rock—for experienced surfers only.

Waterways Travel 🏆 (© 888/669-7873 in the U.S. and Canada; www.waterways travel.com) sells packages ranging from a week at Casa Sol, either surfing Montañita or touring nearby breaks, which cost $400 to $650 (£220–£358), to a more expensive package that combines a tour of various coastal breaks with a week in the Galápagos, to a 2-week stay in the Galápagos for $2,000 (£1,100).

WHALE-WATCHING

From late June through early October, the ocean off Ecuador's Pacific coast is the breeding area for hundreds of humpback whales, which migrate there from the icy waters around Antarctica. Boat tours out of Salinas, Puerto López, and other ports offer an opportunity to observe those amazing creatures, the largest of which are 15m (50-ft.) long and can weigh as much as 50 tons. Whale-watching tours may include a stop at Isla de la Plata, an offshore island where thousands of seabirds nest.

Exploramar Diving (© 02/2563-905; www.exploradiving.com), in Puerto López, offers whale-watching tours on one of two boats.

Guacamayo Bahía Tours ℜ (© 05/2961-412; www.riomuchacho.com) runs inexpensive whale-watching tours out of Bahía de Caráquez.

Guayatur (© 04/2322-442; www.guayatur.com), a Guayaquil-based tour operator, organizes whale-watching tours that head to sea from Salinas.

Machalilla Tours ℜℜ (© 05/2300-234 or 09/6109-185; machalillatours@yahoo.com) is my favorite operator in Puerto López; they offer whale-watching excursions throughout the whale-watching season.

Pesca Tours ℜ (© 04/2443-365; www.pescatours.com.ec) is the best operator to contact if you are staying in Salinas and want to head out to spot a whale.

WHITE-WATER RAFTING & KAYAKING

As might be expected from a country with massive mountains and copious rainfall, Ecuador has world-class conditions for white-water rafting and kayaking. What makes those sports even more exciting in Ecuador is the fact that its rivers flow though tropical forests that are home to hundreds of bird species and other animals. And some river trips can be combined with visits to traditional indigenous communities.

Thanks to almost year-round rainfall, the eastern slope of the Andes boasts one of the highest concentrations of rivers in the world. Those boulder-strewn waterways flow from the cloud forest down to the rainforest, winding through lush valleys and gorges, past waterfalls, massive trees, and an array of flora and fauna. The western slope of the Andes also has some popular rivers, which are more accessible, but their water levels are only high enough for rafting from January to May.

Río Toachi, in the western Andes, is conveniently close to Quito and easy enough for beginners, which makes it the country's most rafted river. A strong class III/IV river, it can be run from January to May but flows through inhabited areas and farmland, which means its waters suffer some pollution. **Río Mulaute,** a class III river to the north of the Toachi, can be run as a 1- or 2-day trip. The upper **Río Blanco,** another class III river farther north of the Toachi, flows through a less-developed, forested valley, making it a more pleasant trip. A good trip for beginners and experienced rafters alike, it is far enough from Quito to be a 2-day trip, and is only navigable from January to May. The lower Río Blanco, after its confluence with the Toachi River, can be run year-round, but is not as pristine as the Upper Blanco.

On the eastern slope of the Andes is the upper **Río Napo,** a class III Amazon tributary that flows past amazing tropical forest. Its 25km (15-mile) white-water route is an exhilarating day trip that can be done year-round from Tena. **Río Misahuallí,** another eastern Andes river, is a gorgeous class IV route that offers the country's most impressive and challenging white-water experience. Some rafting experience is required for this river, which can be navigated only at low water from October to March and which includes a portage around Casanova Falls. **Río Upano,** another

Amazon tributary that flows through dense rainforest and spectacular Namangosa Gorge, then past indigenous villages, is a multiday trip with rapids ranging from class II to class IV. **Río Jatunyacu** is a long and lively class III white-water route perfect for beginners and nature enthusiasts. **Río Anzu** has an easier class II/III white-water route that is perfect for families or beginners. **Río Quijos,** a difficult class IV river east of Quito, is a popular route for experienced rafters and kayakers; it was the site of the 2005 World Rafting Championship.

RAFTING OUTFITTERS

Agencia Limoncocha ⨏ (© 06/2887-583; limoncocha@andinanet.net) is a smaller Tena outfitter that runs trips on most of the local white-water routes.

Cotopaxi.com ⨏⨏ (© 02/2909-640; www.cotopaxi.com), a Quito-based adventure outfitter, offers day trips on the western Andes rivers and a 5-day paddle down the Río Upano that includes visits to Shuar Indian communities.

Ríos Ecuador ⨏⨏ (© 02/2904-054 in Quito, or 06/2886-727 in Tena; www.riosecuador.com) runs rafting trips down the Upper Napo and Misahuallí rivers, and an easy trip down the class II to III Río Anzu that is perfect for nature lovers and families. They also teach kayaking.

River People ⨏ (© 06/288-2349; www.riverpeopleraftingecuador.com), a small outfitter based in Tena, runs rafting and kayaking trips on the Napo and Misahuallí rivers and on the class IV Río Intag, east of Otavalo. They also have a kayaking school.

Small World Adventures (© 800/585-2925 in the U.S. and Canada; www.smallworldadventures.com), a Colorado company with a river lodge near Tena, runs multiday, advanced rafting and kayaking trips on the Quijos, Misahualli, and Jatunyacu rivers. An especially good company for kayakers, they have a good fleet.

Yacu Amu Rafting ⨏ (© 02/2904-054; www.raftingecuador.com), a well-established rafting and kayaking outfitter, with offices in Quito and Tena, offers rafting trips on the most popular rivers as well as a 2-day trip on the challenging Quijos and a 4-day trip down the wild Upano. They also offer kayaking tours and instruction.

3 Ecuador's Top National Parks & Bioreserves

Ecuador has nearly 30 national parks and preserves that together protect all of its varied ecosystems and approximately 17% of the national territory. Those protected areas cover everything from the country's highest mountains to the blue depths of the Galápagos archipelago, and include vast expanses of Amazon rainforest, misty cloud forest, and paramo, as well as the mangrove and threatened tropical dry forest of the Pacific lowlands. Several of the largest protected areas stretch from the Sierra down to the Pacific lowlands or Amazon basin, in which case they protect a series of different, but interconnected life zones—important for the many animals that migrate seasonally between the mountains and lowlands.

Most of the country's protected areas are remote, undeveloped tropical forests, with few services or facilities available for visitors. Others, however, offer easier access to the country's varied natural wonders. Because most parks have limited or no infrastructure, and access can be difficult, it's usually best—and in some cases obligatory—to visit them on an organized tour. Many parks have farms or villages within them, most of which existed before those protected areas were created. And as is all too common in developing countries, hunting, illegal logging, mining, and even oil exploration take place in some of Ecuador's parks and reserves.

Most of the national parks charge $10 to $20 (£5.50–£11) for admission, but it costs a hefty $100 (£55) to enter Galápagos National Park. At parks where camping is allowed, there is usually an additional charge of around $5 (£2.75) per person per day. The following section is not a complete listing of all of Ecuador's national parks and protected areas, but rather a selective list of those parks that are of greatest interest and accessibility. Those protected areas are grouped according to the regions they lie in: the Sierra, Oriente, Pacific Lowlands, and Galápagos. You'll find detailed information about food and lodging options near some of the individual parks in the regional chapters.

THE SIERRA

CAJAS NATIONAL PARK 🏞️🏞️   Located in the western Andes near the city of Cuenca, Cajas National Park comprises a vast expanse of paramo—a high-altitude ecosystem dominated by grasses and bushes—dotted with 232 lakes, rocky peaks, and patches of cloud forest. The area is generally cool and misty, but when the sun burns through, it can be quite warm, and the rugged landscape is impressive. It is home to several duck species, the gray-breasted toucan, and the Andean condor, as well as wild llamas. The park also holds the ruins of pre-Columbian buildings and the remains of the Inca trail. Guided tours to Cajas are recommended, since an expert's knowledge can help you spot and identify wildlife, and there is a real risk of getting lost there when it's foggy.

Location: 32km (20 miles) west of Cuenca. See chapter 8.

CAYAMBE-COCA ECOLOGICAL RESERVE   This important protected area stretches from the icy heights of Volcán Cayambe, the country's third-highest peak, down to the rainforest of the Amazon basin. It covers almost 403,103 hectares (1 million acres) and protects an array of ecosystems that when combined are home to a wealth of wildlife. More than 900 bird species have been identified in the park, ranging from the Andean condor to the cock of the rock. The park's western sector is centered on Cayambe, a glacier-topped giant that is one of the country's more difficult climbing peaks. Reventador Volcano, farther to the east, is a 2-day hike, but lies in a lush area rich in wildlife. The park's upper sector holds several popular lakes, such as Laguna de San Marcos and Laguna Puruhanta. Access to the park's lower forest is available near Papallacta and at Cascada San Rafael, a spectacular waterfall above Coca.

Location: 75km (45 miles) northeast of Quito.

COTACACHI-CAYAPAS ECOLOGICAL RESERVE   One of the country's biggest protected areas, covering more than 204,420 hectares (500,000 acres), the Cotacachi-Cayapas Reserve is also one of its most important, owing to the diversity of wildlife zones that it protects. The reserve stretches down from the paramo west of Ibarra to the lowland rainforest of the Chocó region, comprising a series of ecosystems that are home to such rare species as the spectacled bear, ocelots, and more than 500 bird species, including the Chocó toucan, great green macaw, and Andean condor. But most of the reserve's natural wonders are inaccessible to all but the most dedicated hikers. Other areas, however, are very accessible, such as the **Laguna Cuicocha** 🏞️🏞️, a beautiful crater lake that can be reached by a paved road, a short trip from Otavalo or Cotacachi. The lagoon has two islands that can be visited on a boat ride, and a trail that skirts the crater's edge provides impressive vistas. Admission costs $5 (£2.75). Nearby Volcán Cotacachi can be reached via a 4WD track that leaves the main road near the lake. The Lagunas de Pinan, another of the park's Sierra attractions, is surrounded by relatively well-preserved paramo.

Location: 18km (11 miles) west of Cotacachi. See chapter 6.

COTOPAXI NATIONAL PARK ⭑⭑⭑ This is one of Ecuador's most popular parks, thanks to its proximity to Quito and the majesty of its volcano. The park is dominated by awe-inspiring Volcán Cotopaxi, a 5,897m (19,348-ft.) snow-draped cone that is Ecuador's second-highest peak and its most popular mountaineering spot. The park's 33,393 hectares (82,480 sq. miles) are traversed by a series of dirt tracks that provide the opportunity for hiking, mountain biking, or horseback-riding trips, but most people visit spots close to the park's small museum and main ranger head-quarters. Other destinations inside the park include the Laguna de Limpiopungo, where you might see Andean gulls, American coots, Andean lapwings, paramo rabbits, or perhaps a herd of wild llamas or horses grazing in the nearby plains. El Salitre, a pre-Inca site near the northern entrance, has an excellent volcano view. A trail near the lake leads to the smaller Volcán Rumiñahui, a 2-hour hike away, which is sometimes visited by Andean condors. The pine forest near the park entrance is the product of a reforestation project, but hikers or riders who make it to the volcano's eastern slope can explore native cloud and Andean dwarf forests that hold an array of birdlife and other animals.

The park admission costs $10 (£5.50) and camping costs $2 (£1.10), but be fore-warned: It can get very cold at night. The climbers' refuge at the volcano's base is accessible by 4WD vehicle, plus a short hike; a bunk there costs $10 (£5.50). But few guests actually sleep here, since most summit attempts begin around 11pm to mid-night; you hike through the night to reach the peak in the early morning light and to descend before bad weather moves in.

Location: 60km (37 miles) south of Quito. See chapter 7.

ILINIZAS NATIONAL PARK Spread over 149,000 hectares (370,000 acres) in the country's northwest Sierra, the bulk of Ilinizas is remote, unexplored wilderness. Two of its sites, however, receive a fair amount of visitors: the crater lake Quilotoa and the twin Ilinizas peaks. The bright blue Laguna Quilotoa lies in a deep crater, a hiking trail around the edge of which makes for an excellent day hike—a popular tour offered by nearby lodges and outfitters. The ascent of the Ilinizas peaks, the highest of which stands at 5,263m (17,268 ft.), is popular with mountaineers. The smaller Iliniza Norte is a relatively easy limb good for acclimatization before attempting the country's highest peaks, but Iliniza Sur is an experts-only technical climb. A refuge at their base has two dozen bunk beds and a basic kitchen.

Location: Quilotoa is 15 minutes from the town of Zumbagua. See chapter 7.

PODOCARPUS NATIONAL PARK ⭑⭑ Off the beaten path, Podocarpus covers a vast swath of the southern Sierra stretching from the paramo down to the rainfor-est. Its 146,280 hectares (361,311 acres) consequently cover an array of life zones, giv-ing the park some of the greatest biodiversity of any of the country's protected areas. It is named for the endemic coniferous podocarpus trees that abound in its Andean forests, known locally as "romerillo." But those conifer forests are just one of an array of ecosystems protected within the park, which include highland lakes, paramo, cloud forest, and rainforest. Its resident flora and fauna include the rare mountain tapir, a tiny deer called the pudú, and more than 600 species of birds, such as threatened species like the umbrella bird, bearded guan, and coppery-chested jacamar. The park also protects a large petrified forest in Puyango, more than 100 Andean lakes, and the headwaters of southern Ecuador's principal rivers.

Podocarpus is best visited from Loja, which lies close to its upper sector, or Zamora, which is closer to its cloud forests. The park's Cajanuma Administrative Center is

14km (8 miles) south of Loja. A refuge 8km (5 miles) uphill from there has about 10 bunk beds, whereas the Lagunas del Compadre, a dozen lakes with a camping area, is about a 2-day hike in. Access to the park's lower sector is available via the Bombuscara ranger station near Zamora; the sector also has a shelter with dorm accommodations. The loop trail, called Sendero Higuerones, is an excellent bird-watching route. The admission fee is $10 (£5.50) per person per day; camping costs an additional $3 (£1.65) per person in a tent; and a bunk at one of the shelters costs $5 (£2.75) per person per night.

Location: 14km (8½ miles) south of Loja, or 6km (3¾ miles) south of Zamora. See chapter 8.

SANGAY NATIONAL PARK ✸✸   Sangay is one of the country's two parks to be declared a UNESCO World Heritage Site, along with the Galápagos. The park, which spreads out over almost 518,000 hectares (1.3 million acres) to the southeast of Baños, is a hiker's paradise, but is also accessible on horseback or mountain bike. Its natural attractions include 324 lakes; the volcanoes of Altar, Sangay, and Tungurahua; and a wealth of rare flora and fauna. Sangay and Tungurahua volcanoes are both sporadically active, and thus too dangerous to climb, though Tungurahua's occasional incendiary performances can by enjoyed from miles away. Altar, an extinct volcano that is Ecuador's fifth-highest peak, is a popular climbing and trekking destination where there are lush forests, waterfalls, and a crater lake. Together with adjacent Llanganates National Park, Sangay National Park protects an array of ecosystems ranging from Andean paramo to lush rainforest; these areas are home for hundreds of bird species and such rare and endangered fauna as the spectacled bear, mountain tapir, and condor. The Luna Runtun Hotel, near the park's northern border, offers a variety of hiking and riding excursions into it, as do various outdoor outfitters in Quito and Baños.

Location: This massive park can be entered from various points, but the most popular entrance is the northern entrance, located about 70km (43 miles) from Baños. See chapter 7.

EL ORIENTE

CUYABENO WILDLIFE RESERVE ✸✸   This wildlife reserve is one of the largest and richest in Ecuador, with over 655,781 hectares (1½ million acres) of lowland rainforest in the northeast corner of the country. It is very wet, with numerous ox-bow lagoons, streams, and rivers, the largest of which is Río Aguarico. Access to the park is by boat, and as you explore its smaller waterways you may see gray river dolphins, caimans, monkeys, marmosets, macaws, toucans, or hoatzins, an unusual bird found only in the Amazon basin.

This area also holds the Siona, Cofán, and Quichua indigenous communities, several of which are accustomed to receiving visitors. The best way to visit the reserve is on day trips from one of the lodges along the Aguarico River, which are several hours by bus and boat to the east of Lago Agrio, an oil town that is a 30-minute flight from Quito. Tour and lodging prices usually include the reserve's $20 (£11) admission fee.

Location: 30km (19 miles) east of Lago Agrio. See chapter 11.

YASUNI NATIONAL PARK ✸✸   Ecuador's biggest national park, Yasuni covers almost 962,000 hectares (2.5 million acres) of lowland rainforest to the south of Río Napo, in the country's eastern extreme. Its jungle is drained by hundreds of lakes, streams, and rivers, such as the Ríos Yasuni, Tiputini, and Shiripuno, all of which flow into Río Napo. Those smaller waterways offer the best access to Yasuni, and exploration of them offers opportunities to spot some of area's rare wildlife, which includes pink river dolphins, tapirs, capybaras, giant river otters, anacondas, harpy eagles, various types of macaws, and approximately 500 other bird species.

Yasuni is also home to the Huaorani, an indigenous group that has only had contact with western civilization since the mid–20th-century. The only way to visit the park is from one of the nearby nature lodges or on the *Manatee Amazon Explorer* (p. 73). Those companies will arrange payment of the $20 (£11) park entrance fee and provide naturalist guides who help spot wildlife and explain the local ecology. Unfortunately, Yasuni wilderness and its Huaorani inhabitants are threatened by oil companies, loggers, and poor farmers, all of which are slowly looting the park of its natural treasures.

Location: 250km (155 miles) east of Quito. See chapter 11.

THE PACIFIC

MACHALILLA NATIONAL PARK 🦝🦝   The only major protected area in the Ecuador's Pacific lowlands, Machalilla encompasses some of the last surviving expanses of tropical dry forest in the country. The park's approximately 55,000 hectares (136,000 acres) of dry forest includes a mix of endemic plants, such as the ivory palm, as well as more common cactuses and kapok trees. During the dry season, many of the park's trees and bushes drop their foliage, which gives the area a desertlike appearance but makes it easier to spot wildlife. The park is home to animals such as the black howler monkey, the collared peccary, and the endangered brocket deer, as well as some 270 bird species that include rarities like the gray-cheeked parakeet and the Esmeraldas wood star. The park also contains various archaeological sites of the pre-Columbian Valdivia culture.

In addition to the dry forest, Machalilla protects a stretch of coastline that contains sea-turtle nesting beaches and the offshore islands of Isla Santiago and Isla de la Plata, which are important seabird nesting sites. The park's more than 128,000 hectares (300,000 acres) of protected ocean is rich in marine life, offering the country's best scuba diving outside the Galápagos Islands, and is a feeding and breeding area for humpback whales from June to October. Tour companies in Puerto López and Salinas offer boat trips to Isla de Plata for whale-watching, snorkeling, or scuba diving. The park's forests, beaches, and archaeological sites can be easily visited on day trips from Puerto López, where the park administration is based. You can pay the $15 (£8.25) admission there.

Location: 224km (139 miles) northwest of Guayaquil. See chapter 9.

GALAPAGOS NATIONAL PARK 🦝🦝🦝   The crown jewel of Ecuador's national parks system, Galápagos is not just the country's most visited park—it is the reason most people travel to Ecuador. That 14,245,000-hectare (55,000-sq.-mile) marine park was the country's first protected area, and remains its most important. Its endemic birds, giant tortoises, and marine iguanas are biological icons, and their archipelago is of such global importance that UNESCO designated it a World Heritage Site. The ability to follow in Darwin's footsteps and marvel at such biological oddities as swimming iguanas, flightless cormorants, and finches that drink blood is a dream come true for many nature lovers. And the amazing thing about the park is that its penguins, sea lions, iguanas, and boobies remain as tame as when the father of evolutionary theory sailed into the archipelago on the *Beagle*. A week spent exploring this park, whether on a cruise or from one of the hotels, is one of the world's great outdoor experiences. Park admission costs $100 (£55).

Location: 966km (618 miles) west of continental Ecuador. See chapter 12.

Searching for Wildlife

Animals in the forests and paramos are predominantly nocturnal. When they are active in the daytime, they are usually elusive and on the watch for predators. Birds are easier to spot in clearings or secondary forests than they are in primary forests. Unless you have lots of experience in the tropics, your best chance of an enjoyable walk through the forest is with a trained and knowledgeable guide.

Here are a few helpful hints:

- **Listen.** Pay attention to rustling in the leaves; whether it's monkeys or birds up above or coatis on the ground, you're most likely to hear an animal before you see one.
- **Keep quiet.** Noise will scare off animals and prevent you from hearing their movements and calls.
- **Don't try too hard.** Soften your focus and allow your peripheral vision to take over. This way you can catch glimpses of motion and then focus in.
- **Bring your own binoculars.** It's a good idea to practice a little first, to get the hang of them. It would be a shame to be fiddling around and staring into space while everyone else in your group *oohs* and *aahs* over a trogon or honeycreeper.
- **Dress appropriately.** You'll have a hard time focusing your binoculars if you're busy swatting mosquitoes. Light, long pants and long-sleeved shirts are often your best bet. Comfortable hiking boots are a real asset, except where heavy rubber boots are necessary. Avoid loud colors; the better you blend in with your surroundings, the better your chances of spotting wildlife.
- **Be patient.** The jungle isn't on a schedule, though your best shot at seeing forest fauna is in the very early morning and late afternoon.
- **Read up.** Familiarize yourself with what you're most likely to see. Most nature lodges and ecotourism-based hotels have wildlife field guides and bird books, although if you're serious about this, it's always a good idea to have your own copy. The best of the bunch for most would be David Pearson and Les Beletsky's *Ecuador and the Galápagos Islands: Traveler's Wildlife Guide* (Arris Books, 2004). Also, bird-watchers will want to purchase a copy of *Birds of Ecuador Field Guide* (Comstock Publishing, 2001), by Robert Ridgely, Paul Greenfield, and Frank Gill. Be forewarned, though, that the latter book is extremely hefty.

4 Tips on Health, Safety & Etiquette in the Wilderness

Much of what is discussed below is common sense. For more detailed information, see "Health & Insurance," in chapter 2.

Although most tours and activities are safe, there are risks involved in any adventure activity. Know and respect your physical limits before undertaking any strenuous activity. Be prepared for extremes in temperature and rainfall and for wide fluctuations in weather. A sunny morning hike can quickly become a cold and wet ordeal, so it's usually a good idea to carry along some form of rain gear when hiking in the rainforest or high paramo, and to have a dry change of clothing waiting at the end of the trail.

Avoid sunburn and sunstroke—be sure to bring along plenty of sunscreen and a hat when you're not going to be covered by the forest canopy. And don't be fooled by an overcast sky; I've been burned to a crisp on what seemed to be extremely cloudy days in Ecuador.

Altitude sickness is perhaps the biggest concern for visitors to Ecuador, especially those taking part in active adventures in the highlands and paramos. Altitude sickness is caused by reduced concentrations of oxygen in the air at higher altitudes. Symptoms include headache, fatigue, stomach upsets, dizziness, and sleep disturbance. Shortness of breath, quickened pulse, and general malaise can also occur. Exertion and alcohol consumption can worsen the symptoms. Altitude sickness affects everyone differently. Some will feel its effects in Quito at 2,850m (9,300 ft.) above sea level, while others will find no noticeable effects in the capital. Almost everyone will feel some effects over 4,000m (12,000 ft.). It is essential to stay fully hydrated and, with time, often a day or two, most people will acclimate to all but the most extreme altitudes. In serious cases, you should try to head to a lower altitude as soon as possible.

If you visit any of the country's rainforests or cloud forests, particularly in the lowlands, remember that it really *is* a jungle out there. Don't go poking under rocks or fallen branches. Snakebites are very rare, but don't do anything to increase the odds. If you do encounter a snake, stay calm, don't make any sudden movements, and *do not* try to handle it. Also avoid swimming in major rivers or lagoons unless a guide or local operator can vouch for their safety. Those in El Oriente may have caimans, electric eels, or piranhas.

Bugs and bug bites will probably be your greatest health concern in the Ecuadorian lowlands and beaches, and even they aren't as much of a problem as you might expect. Bugs are primarily an inconvenience, although mosquitoes can carry malaria or dengue. A strong repellent and proper clothing will minimize both the danger and the inconvenience; you might also want to bring along some cortisone or Benadryl cream to soothe itching. At the beaches, you may be bitten by *pirujas* (sand fleas). These nearly invisible insects leave an irritating welt. Try not to scratch because this can lead to open sores and infections. *Pirujas* are most active at sunrise and sunset, so you might want to cover up or avoid the beaches at these times.

And remember: Whenever you enter and enjoy nature, you should tread lightly and try not to disturb the natural environment. There's a popular slogan well known to most campers that certainly applies here: "Leave nothing but footprints; take nothing but memories." If you must take home a souvenir, take photos. Do not cut or uproot plants or flowers. Pack out everything you pack in, and *please* do not litter.

5 Ecologically Oriented Volunteer & Study Programs

Below are some institutions and organizations working on ecology and sustainable-development projects.

Earthwatch Institute (© **800/776-0188**; www.earthwatch.org) organizes volunteers to go on research trips to help scientists collect data and conduct field experiments in a number of scientific fields. Expeditions to Ecuador range from studies of cloud-forest birds to aiding efforts to eliminate the exotic species that threaten the ecological equilibrium of the Galápagos Islands. Fees for food and lodging average around $2,200 (£1,210) for a 2-week expedition, excluding airfare.

Ecuador Volunteer (*C* **02/2564-488;** www.ecuadorvolunteer.org), a Quito-based organization that connects volunteers with nonprofit organizations, usually has positions available at local environmental organizations.

The **Idealist** *R* (www.idealist.org), a Web portal of volunteer and employment opportunities with nonprofit organizations around the world, often lists more than a dozen environmental volunteer positions in Ecuador.

Jatun Sacha (*C* **02/2432-240;** www.jatunsacha.org) is an Ecuadorian environmental foundation that manages private biological reserves in various parts of the country, and works with local communities to involve them in conservation. They accept a steady flow of volunteers who help with field research, teach English, and perform other tasks for fees that are a fraction of what big U.S. volunteer programs charge.

Maquipucuna (*C* **706/542-2923** in the U.S.; www.maqui.org) is a private biological reserve and ecotourism lodge in the northern Pacific lowlands that is administered by the University of Georgia. They accept volunteers to help with conservation and research projects; volunteers must pay $450 (£248) per month for food and lodging. The reserve protects an important expanse of the endangered Chocó rainforest.

5

Quito

Ecuador's capital, Quito, sits on a long, level plateau in a valley between towering Andean peaks. It is a city of striking beauty and stark contrasts. Sebastián de Benalcázar founded Quito in 1534. If he were to walk the streets of Old Town today, he might still feel right at home. Many of the original colonial structures here have been magnificently preserved and restored. Quito was—and still is—a city of grand churches with detailed, hand-carved facades and altars. It is a place where 500-year-old buildings, which have survived earthquakes and volcanic eruptions, open onto medieval-style courtyards, complete with columned archways and stone fountains. In 1978, Quito was declared a UNESCO World Heritage Site, the first city to earn that designation.

But that's only one side of Quito. If Benalcázar were to venture a few kilometers north, the glass skyscrapers, electric trolleys, and early-20th-century mansions would make his head spin. Quito is a city of wonderful juxtapositions and stark contrasts. It's a place where you can travel to the past but still enjoy modern-day comforts. The living museum of Old Town nicely complements New Town's modern-art and archaeology museums. Spend a few leisurely days here and you can enjoy the best of both worlds. You can also travel to colorful indigenous markets, a unique cloud forest, or the world's highest active volcano—all within 2 hours of the city.

Although Quito is Ecuador's capital, it is only the second-most-populous city in the country, with under two million residents; Guayaquil has more people and is more important to the country's economy. In fact, there's quite a rivalry between the two cities (p. 234). Still, Quito is far more charming and cosmopolitan, and it has more museums, sights, restaurants, and clubs. The city gets its name from the pre-Inca Quitu tribe that inhabited this valley. Before Benalcázar arrived, the Incas had converted Quito into a major city. Instead of allowing the buildings and treasures to fall into Spanish hands, though, Inca warrior Rumiñahui ordered the city razed and burned in 1526.

Remember that at 2,850m (9,300 ft.) above sea level, Quito is one of the highest capital cities in the world, and the air is much thinner here. Many visitors quickly feel the effects of the high altitude. Drink plenty of water and do not overdo it as your body acclimates. Fortunately, this is a great place for taking it easy.

1 Orientation

ARRIVING

BY PLANE All flights into Quito land at the **Aeropuerto Internacional Mariscal Sucre** (*©* **02/2430-555;** www.quitoairport.com; airport code: UIO). The airport is about 8km (5 miles) from the heart of New Town. Right before you exit the international terminal, you'll find several information desks. I recommend ordering and paying for your taxi here, then taking your receipt to one of the many taxis waiting outside the terminal. Taxis shouldn't cost more than $8 (£4.40). In fact, most rides to downtown hotels are around $5 (£2.75). Unfortunately, there are no information desks in the national terminal, but it's easy to find a yellow taxi as you exit anywhere in the airport.

For more information on arriving in Quito, see "Getting There," in "Planning Your Trip to Ecuador."

The new international airport being built in the outskirts of downtown is slated to open in 2009.

BY BUS   The **Terminal Terrestre de Cumandá** (© 02/2570-529), located on the edge of Old Town, is the main bus station in Quito. A long line of taxis is usually waiting at the arrivals area. A taxi to New Town should cost $5 to $6 (£2.75–£3.30); to Old Town, the fare should be only $2 (£1.10). If you don't have a lot of luggage, you can take the Trole (trolley) into the heart of Quito. From the terminal, you have to walk up a serious set of stairs to the Cumandá station. To get to both the Old and New Town, be sure to get on the Trole going toward LA Y.

VISITOR INFORMATION

The **Corporación Metropolitana de Turismo** (**Metropolitan Tourism Corporation;** www.quito.com.ec) runs a few helpful information desks at strategic spots around Quito. You'll find one of their desks at the **Mariscal Sucre airport** (© 02/2300-163), after you clear immigration and just before you exit Customs. This is a good place to pick up an excellent free map of Quito, as well as a host of promotional materials. These folks also have two separate desks in Old Town, as well as at the Museo Nacional del Banco Central and Telefériqo. At their **Old Town office** (© 02/2586-591) at Calle Chile and García Moreno (Pasaje Arzobispal), you can sign up for guided walking tours led by city policemen.

The nonprofit **South American Explorers** ✸✸ (© 02/2225-228; www.saexplorers.org/quito.htm), at Jorge Washington 311 and the corner of Leonidas Plaza, is perhaps the best source for visitor information and a great place to meet fellow travelers. The offices are staffed by native English-speakers who seem to know everything about Ecuador. Membership costs $50 (£28) a year per person ($80/£44 per couple). As a member, you will have access to trip reports (reviews of hotels, restaurants, and outfitters throughout Ecuador written by fellow travelers) and a trip counselor. If you aren't a member, the staff can give you basic information that will get you on your way.

The government-sponsored **Ministerio de Turismo** information center on Eloy Alfaro N32-300, 3rd Floor (at the corner of Carlos Tobar), is woefully inadequate. Do not go out of your way to visit here—you can buy a few maps, but don't expect to find much else. The staff is always too busy to help visitors.

Local travel agencies are excellent sources of information. **Cotopaxi.com** ✸✸ (© 02/2909-640; www.cotopaxi.com), **Metropolitan Touring** ✸✸ (© 02/2988-220), **Safari Ecuador** ✸✸ (© 02/2552-505; www.safari.com.ec), and **Surtrek** ✸ (© 02/2231-534; www.surtrek.com) are some of the best and most helpful.

CITY LAYOUT

Quito is a long and thin city, set in a long and thin valley. It runs 35km (22 miles) from north to south and just 5km (3 miles) from east to west. But if you were to combine the most visited areas, they would measure only about 1.5km (1 mile). Most of the city's attractions are located in two areas: **Old Town** and **New Town.** Old Town,

Quito

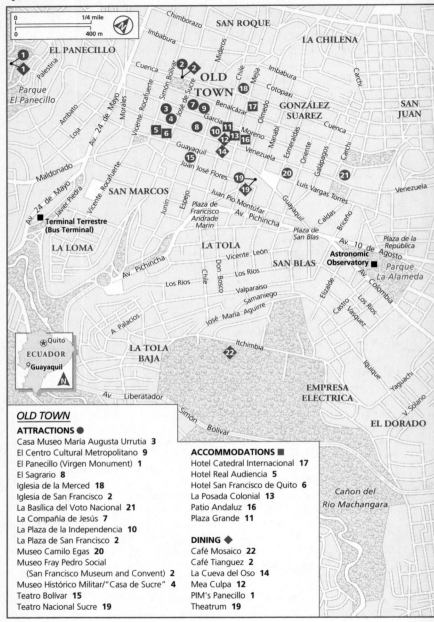

OLD TOWN

ATTRACTIONS ●
Casa Museo María Augusta Urrutia **3**
El Centro Cultural Metropolitano **9**
El Panecillo (Virgen Monument) **1**
El Sagrario **8**
Iglesia de la Merced **18**
Iglesia de San Francisco **2**
La Basílica del Voto Nacional **21**
La Compañía de Jesús **7**
La Plaza de la Independencia **10**
La Plaza de San Francisco **2**
Museo Camilo Egas **20**
Museo Fray Pedro Social
  (San Francisco Museum and Convent) **2**
Museo Histórico Militar/"Casa de Sucre" **4**
Teatro Bolívar **15**
Teatro Nacional Sucre **19**

ACCOMMODATIONS ■
Hotel Catedral Internacional **17**
Hotel Real Audiencia **5**
Hotel San Francisco de Quito **6**
La Posada Colonial **13**
Patio Andaluz **16**
Plaza Grande **11**

DINING ◆
Café Mosaico **22**
Café Tianguez **2**
La Cueva del Oso **14**
Mea Culpa **12**
PIM's Panecillo **1**
Theatrum **19**

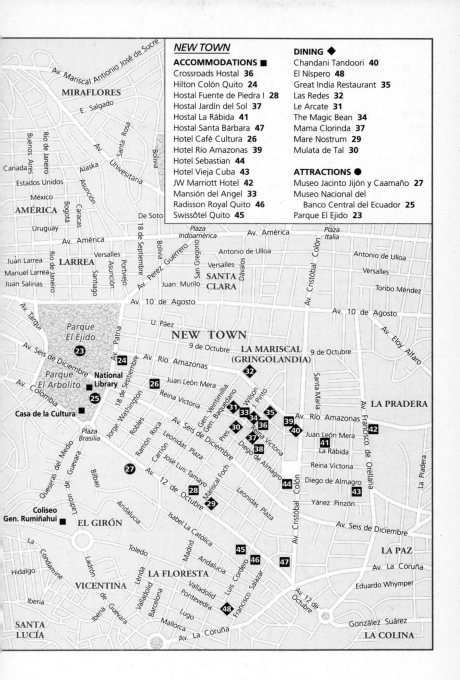

NEW TOWN

ACCOMMODATIONS ■
Crossroads Hostal **36**
Hilton Colón Quito **24**
Hostal Fuente de Piedra I **28**
Hostal Jardín del Sol **37**
Hostal La Rábida **41**
Hostal Santa Bárbara **47**
Hotel Café Cultura **26**
Hotel Río Amazonas **39**
Hotel Sebastian **44**
Hotel Vieja Cuba **43**
JW Marriott Hotel **42**
Mansión del Angel **33**
Radisson Royal Quito **46**
Swissôtel Quito **45**

DINING ◆
Chandani Tandoori **40**
El Níspero **48**
Great India Restaurant **35**
Las Redes **32**
Le Arcate **31**
The Magic Bean **34**
Mama Clorinda **37**
Mare Nostrum **29**
Mulata de Tal **30**

ATTRACTIONS ●
Museo Jacinto Jijón y Caamaño **27**
Museo Nacional del
  Banco Central del Ecuador **25**
Parque El Ejido **23**

at the southern end of the city, is where you'll find most of the historic churches, museums, and colonial architecture.

Warning: All parts of Quito can be dangerous at night. Avoid dark and deserted areas, and take taxis, even when traveling relatively short distances.

THE NEIGHBORHOODS IN BRIEF

Most visitors will not venture far from Old Town and New Town, except to head out of the city, or to and from the airport, which lies in the heart of northern Quito.

Old Town

Close to the southern extreme of downtown Quito lies Old Town. Also called **El Centro Histórico (Historic Center),** this is the colonial-era core of Quito. Much of it has survived, almost unchanged, over the centuries. Here you will find Quito's classic old churches, theaters, monasteries, and convents. Popular public plazas include the **Plaza de la Independencia, Plaza de San Francisco, Plaza de Santo Domingo,** and **Plaza del Teatro.** Although Old Town is hilly in places, it's easy to walk around the area and visit its major attractions on foot.

On the southern extreme of Old Town is the **Terminal Terrestre de Cumandá,** Quito's main bus terminal. And just to the southwest of Old Town is **El Panecillo,** a high hill crowned with a large sculpture of a winged Virgin.

New Town

New Town is located south of Parque La Carolina and north of Parque El Ejido. As the name suggests, this is a modern and mostly upscale section of Quito. Many of the city's better hotels are located here. New Town's main commercial street is **Avenida Amazonas,** where most of the banks and travel agencies are located.

La Mariscal, a subsection of New Town, is where you will find a dense concentration of bars, restaurants, Internet cafes, and backpacker hotels—the area is informally referred to as Gringolandia because of its popularity with tourists. **Plaza Foch** (also called Plaza del Quinde) is ground zero for La Mariscal district. La Mariscal is bounded by Avenida Amazonas, Calle Luis Cordero, Avenida 6 de Diciembre, and Calle Ventimilla.

La Floresta lies just to the east of La Mariscal, across Avenida 12 de Octubre, and up a small rise. It's an upscale section of downtown with a mix of high-rise apartments and condos, neo-colonial-style mansions, hotels, restaurants, and shops. The area gets its name from the former Urrutia family's Hacienda La Floresta that once occupied this area. **La Universidad Católica (Catholic University)** is located toward the southern end of La Floresta, while the **Swissôtel Quito** is at its northern edge.

North of New Town

While both Old Town and New Town lie toward the southern end of Quito's long, narrow valley, much of the city's almost two million inhabitants live north of New Town. This is also the area where much of the city's industry is located. Many of the neighborhoods here are crowded, poor, and working-class, and of little interest and considerable danger to most tourists. Exceptions include the trendy neighborhoods of **Guapulo** and **Bellavista.** The latter is where you find the **Fundación Guayasamín** and **Capilla del Hombre.**

The **Mariscal Sucre International Airport** is located north of New Town. But since the hotels of New Town are really just minutes away, there has been

Breaking the Code

Feeling a little bewildered by Quito's street-address system? Well you should be. While it's actually pretty logical, there are plenty of anomalies and certain addresses that correspond to a previous system. To add to the confusion, Ecuadorians only occasionally use the *calle* (street) and *avenida* (avenue) designation. More often than not, addresses are given with the street or avenue's name, but no indication if it's a street or avenue. Introduced in 1998, the capital's new street-numbering system is prefixed by one of the following letters: **N**, indicating that the street is situated north *(norte)* of Calle Rocafuerte in Old Town; **S**, meaning south *(sur)* of Old Town; or **E**, indicating east *(este)* and **OE**, meaning west *(oeste)*, depending on which side of 10 de Agosto the street is located. A hyphenated number follows, and then the name of the nearest cross-street or avenue. The first of these hyphenated numbers is actually the building number, while the second number indicates the number of meters the house or building is from the cross-street. For example, González Suárez N27–142 and 12 de Octubre. The building would be found on González Suárez street, north of Calle Rocafuerte. The building number is "27," and it is roughly 142m (460 ft.) from Avenida 12 de Octubre. This new street-numbering system has principally been adopted in the north of the city, and has proven difficult to implement in the south owing to the non-perpendicular streets. Addresses in Old Town may not have a letter indicator, nor a hyphenated number, although the nearest cross street will always be given. Both address systems are currently in use. Luckily, just about every taxi driver in Quito can find any direction using either the new or old system.

no real tourism or hotel development right near the airport. In fact, the area around the airport is mostly industrial and run-down.

The other main attraction and the geographic heart and civic soul of the area north of New Town is **Parque La Carolina,** a large, well-kept city park, with a host of facilities for sports and recreation.

2 Getting Around
BY TAXI

The streets of Quito swarm with yellow taxis, and they're my preferred means of transport here. Taxis are cheap, costing only $1 to $3 (55p–£1.65) for a ride within the Old or New Town and $4 to $6 (£2.20–£3.30) for longer distances. Drivers are required by law to use a meter, but it's obviously not a strict law because few taxis use them. If the taxi has a meter, insist that the driver use it. Alternatively, ask your hotel desk or a trusty local what your ride should cost and negotiate an appropriate price beforehand. Quito can be dangerous at night, so it's best to take a taxi wherever you go, no matter how short the distance. The staff at most restaurants, hotels, and bars will be

---

Tips If You Want a Guide

If you'd like ultra-personalized service, an English-speaking guide, a private car, or even a bodyguard or two to accompany you while you visit the city or the highlands, contact **Turisvision,** Ultimas Noticias N37–97 and El Espectador, Quito (© **02/2246-756;** fax 02/224-5741; www.turisvision.com). They will take care of you from the moment you arrive to the moment you depart.

---

happy to call a cab for you. In case you need to call one yourself, try **Taxi Amigo** (© **02/2222-222**) or **Taxi Jotajota** (© **02/2639-639**).

BY TROLLEY

Three electric trolley lines wind their way through Quito, running north-south, and connecting Old Town with New Town. In New Town, the **Trole** runs along Avenida 10 de Agosto, which is a few blocks west of Avenida Amazonas. When it reaches Old Town, it travels along Avenida Guayaquil. To reach Plaza de la Independencia, be sure to get off at the Plaza Grande stop. The **Ecovía** is much more convenient if you want to start your journey in New Town; it runs along Avenida 6 de Diciembre, which is one of the major streets. Unfortunately, when it reaches Old Town, it stops several blocks east of the colonial core, and it's a bit of an uphill hike to the heart of the action. If you want to avoid this hike, transfer to the Trole at the Simón Bolívar stop. **Metrobus** is the newest line and it runs along the western edge of town, along Avenida América. All three of these trolley lines cost 25¢ (15p) for a one-way trip. The turnstiles accept only exact change, but fortunately all stations have change machines. Trolleys run from around 5am until midnight.

Warning: Pickpockets frequently operate on crowded trolleys and buses, so be careful.

BY BUS

Quito has an extensive and very complicated system of city buses. In New Town, buses run along Avenida Amazonas and Avenida 12 de Octubre. If you're only going a short distance along these streets, it's easy to hop on a bus (just flag it down). But beware: Once you pass Avenida Colón, the buses go off in many convoluted directions. Short rides cost 25¢ (15p). Overall, it's much easier to travel through Quito by taxi, which is relatively inexpensive and safe, and will take you exactly where you need to go.

ON FOOT

Aside from walking around specific and compact neighborhoods or circuits, like Old Town or the Mariscal section of New Town, Quito is not a friendly city for walkers. Most of the streets are in a state of near-constant gridlock; sidewalks are narrow and irregular; and car and bus fumes, along with street crime, are real problems. Luckily, taxis are plentiful and very inexpensive (see above).

BY CAR

I highly discourage you from renting a car to get around Quito. Navigating a strange city is difficult as it is, and many of Quito's streets are narrow and in a nearly constant state of gridlock. Moreover, taxis (see above) are plentiful and inexpensive.

   If you're set on renting a car in Quito, **Avis** (© **02/2440-270;** www.avis.com.ec), **Budget** (© **02/3300-979;** www.budget-ec.com), **Hertz** (© **1800/227-767** toll-free within Ecuador, or 02/2254-257; www.hertz.com.ec), and **Localiza** (© **02/3303-265;** www1.localiza.com.ec) all have offices at the Mariscal Sucre International Airport, as well as downtown, and can deliver a car to most hotels in Quito. Car rentals will run you $20 to $90 (£11–£50) per day, depending upon the type of vehicle. For more information about renting a car in Ecuador, see p. 44.

FAST FACTS: Quito

Airport See "Arriving," earlier in this chapter.

American Express In Ecuador, American Express travel services is represented by **Global Tours** (© 02/2265-222; www.globaltour.com.ec), located on Av. República El Salvador 309 and Calle Suiza.

Babysitters Your hotel front desk is your best bet for finding a babysitter.

Banks You'll have no trouble finding a bank in Quito. Branches are common all over the city, especially in the more affluent and touristy areas. Numerous bank branches and ATMs can be found in the popular Mariscal and Old Town areas.

Bookstores **Café Libro,** Leonidas Plaza N23–56 (© 02/2234-265; www.cafelibro. com), and **Libri Mundi,** Hermano Miguel 8–14 and Mariscal Sucre (© 022843-783), are the two best bookstores in Quito. Both have excellent selections of tropical biology, bird, and flora books, as well as books on Ecuadorian history and culture, in both English and Spanish. For a wide selection of used books in English, **Confederate Books,** Calama 410 and Juan León Mera (© 02/2527-890), is your best bet.

Car Rentals See "Getting Around," above.

Cellphones There are several competing cellphone companies in Ecuador. All have numerous outlets and dealers across the city, including at the airport, and all these outlets and dealers sell pre-paid GSM chips that can be used in any unlocked triband GSM cellphone, as well as new phones with or without calling plans. Many also rent phones. **Telefonía Celular** (© 02/3301-757), at the airport, offers cellphone rental for $2.50 to $3 (£1.40–£1.65) per day, with a $50 (£28) deposit. And many hotels around the city will also rent out cellphones. But if you're not carrying your own GSM phone, you are probably best off just buying one. Most of the outlets around town, including Telefonía Celular at the airport, sell already activated phones, with a few dollars of calling time loaded onto the chip. After that you simply buy pre-paid minutes in denominations of $3, $6, or $10 (£1.65–£5.50). The cheapest of these phones—a fully functional Siemens A71—costs just $36 (£20), activated and ready to go.

The main cellphone companies in Ecuador are **Porta, Movistar,** and **Alegro.** According to my Ecuadorian friends, Porta has the best coverage.

Currency Exchange The U.S. dollar is the official currency of Ecuador. If you have euros, pounds, Canadian dollars, or any other currency, your best bet is to exchange them for dollars prior to leaving for Ecuador. However, all the major banks in Ecuador will exchange the major currencies for dollars, for a small service fee. And most ATMs in Ecuador will give you dollars at the official exchange rate, even if your home account is in another currency. See "Money & Costs," in chapter 2, for more information.

Dentists Call your embassy, which will have a list of recommended dentists, or check out the Consular Section of the website of the U.S. Embassy in Quito (www.usembassy.org.ec), which has a list of recommended dentists.

Doctors Contact your embassy for information on doctors in Quito, or check out the Consular Section of the website of the U.S. Embassy in Quito (www.usembassy.org.ec), which has a list of recommended doctors and specialists. You can also head to one of the major hospitals in town. See "Hospitals," below.

Drugstores A drugstore or pharmacy is called a *farmacia* in Spanish. **Fybeca** is the largest chain of pharmacies in Ecuador. You can call Fybeca's toll-free line (© **800/2392-322**) 24 hours a day for home delivery. The most centrally located Fybeca is at Avenida 6 de Diciembre and Cordero. **Rey de Reyes** (© **02/2557-357**) is a 24-hour pharmacy located at Jorge Washington 416, near the corner of 6 de Diciembre.

Embassies & Consulates See "Fast Facts: Ecuador," in chapter 2.

Emergencies In case of an **emergency,** call © 911. You can reach an **ambulance** at © 09/2739-801 or 02/2442-974; for **police assistance** call © 101. For the **tourist police** call © 02/2543-983; the headquarters are located at Roca and Reina Victoria. You can reach the **Cruz Roja (Red Cross)** by dialing © 131.

Express Mail Services Most hotels can arrange for express mail pickup. Alternatively, you can contact **DHL** (© **02/2485-100**; Av. Eloy Alfaro and Av. de los Juncos; www.dhl.com), **Fed Ex** (© **02/2909-201**; Av. Amazonas 517 and Santa María; www.fedex.com); **EMS** (© **02/2561-962**; Av. Eloy Alfaro 354 and 9 de Octubre); or **UPS** (© **02/3960-000**; Calle de los Cipreses Lote 26 and Av. de las Avellanas, between Eloy Alfaro and 10 de Agosto; www.ups.com).

Eyeglasses Look for the word *óptica*. There are *ópticas* all over Quito. Your best bet is to ask your hotel concierge or manager. Or head to **Cyber Optic** (© **02/2285-747**), on Venezuela N2-74, or **Multióptica** (© **02/2225-777**), on Reina Victoria N26-146. Just about any *óptica* can do everything from eye exams to repairs.

Hospitals **Hospital Vozandes** (© **02/2262-142**; www.hospitalvozandes.org), at Villalengua 267 and 10 de Agosto, and **Hospital Metropolitano** (© **02/2261-520**; www.hospitalmetropolitano.org), at Mariana de Jesús and Occidental, are the two most modern and best-equipped hospitals in Quito. Both have 24-hour emergency service and English-speaking doctors.

Internet Access Internet cafes can be found all over Quito, particularly in the Mariscal and Old Town neighborhoods. Rates run 70¢ to $2 (40p–£1.10) per hour. Many hotels either have their own Internet cafe or allow guests to send and receive e-mail. A few are starting to add wireless access, either for free or a small charge. If your hotel doesn't provide the service and there's no Internet cafe close by, head to the Mariscal district or Old Town, where you'll have a hard time walking more than a block without finding an Internet cafe.

Laundry & Dry Cleaning Most folks rely on their hotel's laundry and dry-cleaning services, although these can be expensive. Alternatively, head to the Mariscal district, where there are several self-serve and full-service laundromats.

Try **Rainbow Laundry** (© 02/2237-128), on Juan León Mera 1337 and García, or **Wash & Go** (© 02/2230-993), on Pinto 340 and Juan León Mera.

Maps The **Corporación Metropolitano de Turismo (Metropolitan Tourism Corporation;** www.quito.com.ec) hands out excellent city maps of Quito at all of their desks, including one at **Mariscal Sucre airport** (© 02/2300-163), located just before you leave the immigration and Customs area. Other map sources in Quito include hotel gift shops and bookstores.

Newspapers & Magazines See "Fast Facts: Ecuador," in chapter 2.

Photographic Needs Film is generally more expensive in Ecuador, so bring as much as you will need from home. I also recommend that you wait to have your film processed at home, but if you must develop your prints down here, or if you need to pick up film, batteries, or storage cards, try **Ecuacolor** (© 02/2526-982;** www.ecuacolor.com), **Fuji Foto** (© 02/2551-275), or **Foto Quick** (© 02/2229-982), all of which have numerous outlets around town. For more serious photographic needs (equipment, repairs, and so on), **Difoto** (© 02/2224-676), on Foch 864, is a good bet.

Police Throughout Ecuador, you can reach the police by dialing © 101 in an emergency. The tourist police can also help sort out your problems. In Quito, the number for the tourist police is © 02/2543-983.

Post Office The **main post office** is located in New Town (© 02/2561-218) at Av. Eloy Alfaro 354 and 9 de Octubre. There's also a convenient post office in Old Town (© 02/2282-175) on Calle Espejo 935, between Guayaquil and Venezuela. Perhaps the most conveniently located **post office** (© 02/2508-890) is on the ground floor of the Ecuatoriana Building, on the corner of Avenida Cristóbal Colón and Reina Victoria. Most are open Monday through Friday from 8am to 6pm and Saturday 8am to noon. It costs 90¢ (50p) to mail a letter to the United States or Canada, and $1.10 (60p) to Australia and Europe. From time to time, you can buy stamps at kiosks and newsstands. But your best bet is to see if your hotel will provide stamps and post your mail, or to do so yourself at the post office, especially since there are no public mailboxes. See "Mail," in "Fast Facts: Ecuador," in chapter 2 for more information.

Restrooms These are known as *sanitarios* or *servicios sanitarios.* You might also hear them called *baños.* They are marked *damas* (women) and *hombres* or *caballeros* (men). Public restrooms are rare to nonexistent, but most big hotels and public restaurants will let you use their restrooms.

Safety Pickpocketing and petty crime are problems in Quito. But if you keep an eye on your belongings and exercise caution, you should be fine. Never put anything valuable in your backpack. Also be careful on the Trole (trolley). At night, Quito can be dangerous, especially in the touristy areas—take a taxi, even if you're only going a short distance. Because the streets in Quito are often deserted at night, I recommend walking in the middle of them to prevent someone from jumping at you from a hidden doorway. Report all problems to the **tourist police** office, on Roca and Reina Victoria (© 02/2543-983). Also, see "Safety," in "Fast Facts: Ecuador," in chapter 2.

Taxes All goods and services are charged a 12% value-added tax. Hotels and restaurants also add on a 10% service charge, for a total of 22% more on your bill. There is an airport departure tax of $38 (£21).

Taxis See "Getting Around," above.

Time Zone Quito is on Eastern Standard Time, 5 hours behind Greenwich Mean Time (GMT). Daylight saving time is not observed.

Useful Telephone Numbers For directory assistance, call ℂ **100** or **104**; for a local operator dial ℂ **105**; and for an international operator, call ℂ **116** or **117**.

Water Always drink bottled water in Ecuador. Most hotels provide bottled water in the bathroom. You can buy bottles of water on practically any street corner. Small bottles cost about 25¢ (15p). The better restaurants use ice made from boiled water, but always ask, to be on the safe side.

Weather At 2,850m (9,300 ft.), Quito enjoys consistently mild to cool temperatures year-round. Daytime high temperatures average 18° to 21°C (65°–70°F), while evening lows average 7° to 13°C (45°–55°F). As with much of the rest of the Andean highlands, Quito experiences two distinct seasons: dry (June–Sept) and wet (Oct–May). The dry season is called summer *(verano),* the wet season winter *(invierno).* There's also a so-called "little summer" throughout much of December and early January. April is the rainiest month.

3 Where to Stay

Since the Mariscal Sucre airport is located in downtown Quito, and since there are really no good options right at the airport, I haven't included a section of hotels near the airport. The hotels in New Town and La Floresta are approximately 10 to 15 minutes from the airport, depending on traffic, while those in Old Town are some 20 to 25 minutes away.

IN NEW TOWN
EXPENSIVE

Hilton Colón Quito ⭐   In 1967, when the Hilton Colón opened it was the only high-end hotel in town. It quickly became a major cultural and business-meeting spot for both locals and visitors alike. While today it faces some stiff competition from both large chains and small boutique hotels, the Hilton is still a good and well-located choice—it's right near Parque El Ejido, Casa de la Cultura, and the business center of the city. It is particularly popular as a quick overnight base for folks heading to or from the Galápagos or other far-flung destinations in the country. The deluxe rooms are on the small side, with compact marble bathrooms to match. The superior rooms are a bit larger and more modern, but the real benefit of these rooms is free use of the business center (which includes a free continental breakfast and Internet access). The junior suites are similar to the superior rooms, except they have breakfast tables and two sinks in the bathroom. Suites have a separate sitting area and both a tub and shower in the bathrooms. The service here is quite good.

Av. Amazonas and Patria, Quito. ℂ **800/221-2424** in the U.S. and Canada, or 02/2560-666 in Ecuador. Fax 02/2563-903. www.hilton.com. 395 units. $115–$135 (£63–£74) double; $145–$165 (£80–£91) executive level; $300–$350 (£165–£193) suite. AE, DC, MC, V. Free parking. **Amenities:** 4 restaurants; bar; lounge; midsize outdoor pool; small health club; Jacuzzi; sauna; concierge; tour desk; free airport shuttle; business center; shopping arcade; salon; 24-hr. room service; in-room massage; babysitting; same-day dry cleaning; laundry service; smoke-free floors; executive/club floor; casino. *In room:* A/C, TV, minibar, hair dryer, safe, Wi-Fi for a fee.

JW Marriott Hotel ★★★ Quito's most luxurious large business-class hotel, the JW Marriott features perhaps the best rooms and facilities in town. Service is top-notch, the restaurants are fantastic, and the large pool with its central Jacuzzi island and waterfalls makes you feel as if you've escaped to a tropical resort. You enter each room through a carved wooden door that looks as though it should open onto an old-fashioned den. But instead of a den you'll find a large room with colorful bedspreads, heavy wood furniture, and comfy chairs. Most rooms offer views of either the city or of the volcanoes. (If you can, opt for the volcano view; my least favorite rooms have views of the glass-enclosed lobby.) The large marble bathrooms are wonderful—all have separate tubs and showers. **La Hacienda restaurant** offers delicious local specialties in an elegant setting, while **Bistro Latino** is the hotel's buffet restaurant. The lobby features a small sushi bar to round out the culinary offerings. The gym here is large and well-equipped with a regular slate of classes and activities. Executive-level rooms and suites include a buffet breakfast and other perks.

Av. Orellana 1172 and Av. Amazonas, Quito. ℰ 800/228-9290 in the U.S. and Canada, or 02/2972-000 in Quito. Fax 02/2972-050. www.marriotthotels.com. 257 units. $129–$159 (£71–£88) deluxe; $149–$189 (£82–£104) executive; $219–$259 (£120–£142) suite. AE, DC, MC, V. Free valet parking. **Amenities:** 3 restaurants; bar; large pool; health club; Jacuzzi; sauna; concierge; tour desk; business center; shopping arcade; salon; 24-hr. room service; massage; babysitting; same-day dry cleaning; laundry service; smoke-free floors; executive/club floors. *In room:* A/C, TV, dataport, minibar, hair dryer, iron, safe.

Mansión del Angel ★★ *(finds)* Mansión del Angel feels more like a friend's home than like a hotel. In fact, after you stay here for a few days, you will probably meet the owner, who will indeed become a friend. The staff distributes fresh flowers throughout the hotel daily, so everything smells lovely. The sitting areas on the first floor are full of gorgeous antiques, handmade wood furniture, unique art, crystal chandeliers, and gilded mirrors. All the rooms have brass canopy beds, hand-carved moldings, Oriental carpets, and plush bedspreads. The bathrooms are not especially spacious; none have tubs, but they all have very large showers. The larger rooms, on the top floor, have a separate sitting area. Since the rooms in the back of the hotel don't face the street, they are a bit quieter, although I've never found noise to be a problem, even in the street-side rooms. The breakfast, served on the enclosed rooftop terrace, includes fresh-baked breads, and at night the smell of baking bread permeates the entire hotel. Delicious! A formal English tea is served every afternoon, which is a good way to meet other guests.

Wilson E5–29 and Juan León Mera, Quito. ℰ 800/327-3573 in the U.S., or 02/2557-721. Fax 02/2237-819. www.mansiondelangel.com.ec. 11 units. $105–$127 (£58–£70) double. Rates include full breakfast and tax. MC, V. Parking nearby. **Amenities:** Enclosed rooftop breakfast terrace; afternoon tea; laundry service. *In room:* TV, hair dryer, safe.

MODERATE

Hostal La Rábida Hostal La Rábida is in an old home on a quiet street, away from the fray of the Mariscal neighborhood. The rooms are lovely, if a bit small, with brass or iron beds (one even has a canopy) and luxurious white down comforters. The spacious bathrooms come complete with old-fashioned wood sinks and antique fixtures. Room no. 11 has a patio and beautiful blue-and-white wallpaper, while room no. 2 is my favorite room because it has a large second-floor terrace. The beautiful breakfast room/restaurant opens onto a small garden. Overall, the hotel has a refined, British

feel—the walls are covered with botanical prints and old maps, Oriental carpets complement the hardwood floors, and every evening a fire burns in the very cozy living room.

La Rábida 227 and Santa María, Quito. ©/fax **02/2222-720.** www.hostalrabida.com. 11 units. $58 (£32) double. AE,
DC, MC, V. Free parking. **Amenities:** Restaurant; bar; room service 7am–10pm; laundry service. *In room:* TV, safe.

Hotel Café Cultura ★★ (Finds)

In the heart of New Town, the Café Cultura is def-
initely one of the most unique and interesting hotels in Quito. Formerly the French
Cultural Center, this old but beautifully renovated house is now the hippest hotel in
the city. It's truly an inner-city retreat, complete with a lush garden with resident hummingbirds and doves. All the rooms have hand-painted designs on the walls and their
own personal touches. For example, no. 25 has a tree growing through it; no. 1 has a
fireplace, French doors, painted furniture, and a claw-foot tub. My favorite room,
though, is no. 2, which has a beautiful sitting nook, with wraparound floor-to-ceiling
windows. Several of the rooms have sloped wooden ceilings; most have been renovated
in the past few years, and all the windows have been soundproofed. In general, the
bathrooms are also excellent; there are some rooms, however, where only a curtain separates the bathroom from the rest of the room. Note that all the rooms are smoke-free.

The charming owner, Laszlo Karolyi, has done a great job of making this hotel feel
like a real home. It's also one of the few hotels in the city not to charge the full 22%
service fee; it adds only the minimum tax of 12% to your bill—although you should
tip the service staff accordingly. There's a lovely restaurant adjacent to the lobby, complete with hardwood floors and flickering candles, and a roaring fireplace.

Robles and Reina Victoria, Quito. ©/fax **02/2224-271** or 02/2564-956. www.cafecultura.com. 26 units. $89 (£49)
double; $99 (£54) triple and junior suite; $109 (£60) suite. AE, DC, MC, V. Free parking. **Amenities:** Restaurant;
lounge; tour desk; free airport pickup if you book online; room service 7am–10pm; laundry service; free Wi-Fi; all
rooms smoke free. *In room:* Safe, no phone.

Hotel Río Amazonas

At 10 stories, this modern business hotel towers over the
Mariscal district. As you walk through the glass doors, marble floors and a broad marble reception desk greet you, and you'll immediately feel a sense of calm overtake
you—a stark contrast to the bustle of busy Avenida Amazonas just outside. Rooms are
tidy, spacious, and modern, with plenty of amenities. Try for a room on a higher floor,
to take advantage of the views. This hotel does a brisk business with tour and events
groups, and is often quite busy.

Cordero 1342, on the corner of Av. Amazonas, Quito. © **02/2556-666.** Fax 02/2556-670. www.hotelrioamazonas.
com. 74 units. $70 (£39) double; $90 (£50) suite. AE, DC, MC, V. Free parking. **Amenities:** Restaurant; bar; tour desk;
24-hr. room service; laundry service; free Wi-Fi. *In room:* TV, minibar, hair dryer, safe.

Hotel Sebastián ★ (Value)

This well-located business-class hotel offers tidy, well-
maintained rooms, excellent service, and good value. All of the rooms feature new carpeting and 29-inch flatscreen televisions. The decor is almost stately, with gold
bedspreads and subdued colors on the walls. Free Wi-Fi reaches just about every nook
and cranny in the hotel. Rooms on the higher floors have great views, especially those
on the south side, from which you can see Volcán Cotopaxi on a clear day. With their
own filtering system, this is one of the few hotels in Quito, or in the country for that
matter, to offer safe drinking water straight from the tap. The small gym here is surprisingly well equipped.

Diego de Almagro 822 and Cordero, Quito. ©/fax **02/2222-300** or 02/2222-400. Fax 02/2222-500. www.hotel
sebastian.com. 55 units. $79 (£43) double; $89 (£49) junior suite. AE, DC, MC, V. Free parking. **Amenities:** Restaurant; bar; small gym; tour desk; 24-hr. room service; laundry service; free Wi-Fi. *In room:* TV, hair dryer.

Hotel Vieja Cuba ★ *(Finds)*   This lovely old colonial house has been renovated with style and flair. The owner, a Cuban immigrant, has spared no expense in the redesign: A soothing fountain in the courtyard and gleaming hardwood floors lead to cozy rooms with exposed brick and modern wood beds. The rooms are simple but rustic and comfortable. Bathrooms have nice mosaic tiles, brand-new everything, and showers with great pressure. Everything is very clean and very new. The larger doubles come with either a sitting area or a fireplace; suite no. 11 has a nice sitting area downstairs and a loft bedroom upstairs with a small balcony. The attractive restaurant downstairs offers homemade Cuban dishes and great *mojitos.*

Diego de Almagro 1212 and La Niña, Quito. ℂ 02/2906-729. Fax 02/2520-738. viejacuba@andinanet.net. 24 units. $55–$85 (£30–£47) double; $95 (£52) suite. Rates include breakfast. MC, V. **Amenities:** Restaurant; bar; massage; room service 7am–10pm; laundry service. *In room:* TV, dataport, hair dryer.

INEXPENSIVE

Crossroads Hostal   This centrally located Mariscal hostel is everything a hostel should be: friendly, busy, safe, and funky. There are a shared kitchen and a large living area with a television surrounded by bean-bag chairs and a couch. One of the dorm rooms comes with a fireplace. Some of the rooms have wood floors, while others are carpeted. Nos. 16, 17, and 18 are my top choices; they're located in a quiet, newer section out back. Every guest gets a lock box in the office, but it's a bring-your-own-lock affair. This is a great place to meet and hook up with fellow travelers, and to arrange trips and adventure tours around the country. They offer free luggage storage, and you can leave some stuff here while you travel outside Quito.

Foch E5-23 and Juan León Mera, Quito. ℂ 02/2234-735 or 022545-514. www.crossroadshostal.com. 4 dorm rooms and 14 private rooms (9 with private bathroom). $6 (£3.30) per person in dorm room; $18 (£9.90) double with shared bathroom; $24 (£13) double with private bathroom. MC, V. Parking nearby. **Amenities:** Restaurant; bar; lounge; free Wi-Fi. *In room:* No phone.

Hostal Fuente de Piedra I *(Finds)*   Not to be confused with the less charming Hostal Fuente de Piedra II, this is a great find on a quiet street close to everything. A serene courtyard with a trickling fountain leads to small, simply furnished rooms with exposed stone in some and large picture windows in others. The bathrooms are clean and good-sized, though none have tubs. There's a small balcony with reading chairs for guests on the second floor and a very cozy restaurant with fireplace on the ground floor. This hotel has been open for over a decade, and the management still tries hard to please their guests.

Wilson 211 and Tamayo, Quito. ℂ 02/2525-314. Fax 02/2559-775. www.ecuahotel.com. 19 units. $40 (£22) double. Rates include full breakfast and taxes. AE, MC, V. **Amenities:** Restaurant; bar; lounge. *In room:* TV.

Hostal Jardín del Sol *(Value)*   The "garden of the sun" hotel offers inexpensive and basic accommodations and is conveniently located close to many of New Town's bars and restaurants. The friendly staff will welcome you with a smile and seems to genuinely care about making your stay as pleasant as possible. Units are small but clean and simply furnished with wood beds and tiny bathrooms with tiled floors. Some rooms have balconies with limited views of Quito; a few have yellow walls as bright as the sunshine (thus the hotel's name). Next to the lobby is a computer room with free Internet access for guests. Another nice touch is the complimentary transfer from the airport if you book directly with the hotel—but be sure to call the day before to confirm that you are being met.

Jose Calama 166 and Diego de Almagro, Quito. © **02/2230-941**. Fax 02/2230-950. www.hostaljardindelsol.com. 23 units. $37 (£20) double. Rates include full breakfast and taxes. AE, MC, V. Free parking. **Amenities:** Restaurant; bar; room service 7am–10pm; laundry service. *In room:* TV, dataport.

IN OLD TOWN

Quito's Old Town is in the midst of a major renaissance. Whereas just a couple of years ago I cautioned visitors from staying in this area, there are now several excellent hotel options in various price ranges, and the security situation has improved greatly. That said, you still need to be careful walking some of the streets around here at night, and taxis definitely should be used after nightfall.

VERY EXPENSIVE

Patio Andaluz *Finds* This stately boutique hotel is a fabulous option in the center of Quito's colonial core. Rooms are spread around the perimeters of two large central courtyard areas. The first courtyard houses the hotel's restaurant, while the second has a pretty garden bar. In addition, several common areas offer comfortable couches, or tables and chairs. The rooms are all large and elegant, with wood floors, Persian rugs, antique-style furniture and beds, large desks, and flatscreen televisions. Only a handful of units have windows facing the street; most have windows opening onto one of the central courtyards. The suites are all two levels, with a bedroom on one level and a comfortable sitting room on the other. But suites have only one bathroom, and sometimes it's located on the level with the sitting room, so if you like your bathroom just steps away from your bedroom, be sure to request one of these units. Service here is attentive and professional, although I wouldn't mind if the staff got rid of their colonial-period costumes.

Av. Garcia Moreno N6–52, between Olmedo and Mejía, Quito. © **02/2280-830**. Fax 02/2288-690. www.hotelpatio andaluz.com. 31 units. $150 (£83) double; $175 (£96) suite. Rates include breakfast buffet. AE, DC, MC, V. **Amenities:** Restaurant; bar; lounge; tour desk; laundry service; smoke-free rooms. *In room:* TV, safe.

Plaza Grande *Finds* Old Town's newest hotel is also its most plush and ambitious. Housed in the meticulously restored former home of one of Quito's founding fathers, Juan Díaz de Hidalgo, this stylish boutique hotel is opulent and grand. The all-suite hotel fronts the Plaza de la Independencia (Plaza Grande), and the best rooms have large windows and French doors overlooking the plaza. All rooms are beautifully done and feature such perks as soundproofed windows and doors, 107cm (42-in.) flatscreen televisions, Jacuzzi tubs in large bathrooms with heated floors, and fine cotton linens and down comforters. The decor is refined, with heavy drapes, plush furnishings, fine fabrics, and tasteful art and tapestries on the walls. The hotel's main restaurant and wine cellar match the high standards set by the rooms, and the small but delightful spa is a great place to pamper yourself. Service is prompt, attentive, and friendly. Because this place is new, their prices are well above those at most other high-end hotels in Quito—in most cases more than two to three times as high as other upscale options. But no other downtown hotel can match the Plaza Grande in terms of intimacy, location, and luxury.

On the Plaza de la Independencia, Av. García Moreno N5–16, and Chile, Quito. © **02/2566-497**. Fax 02/2559-203. www.plazagrandequito.com. 15 units. $500–$600 (£275–£330) suite; $2,000 (£1,100) presidential suite. AE, DC, MC, V. Free valet parking. **Amenities:** 2 restaurants; cafe; bar; lounge; small, well-equipped spa; sauna; concierge; tour desk; 24-hr. room service; in-room massage; laundry service. *In room:* A/C, TV, minibar, hair dryer, safe, free Wi-Fi.

MODERATE

Hotel Real Audiencia   This Old Town standby offers clean, comfortable rooms at good prices. The decor is quite dated and dour, however. The best rooms are spacious and come with views. No. 2A is a corner suite with a fabulous view of the Santo Domingo Plaza, while no. 301 is a floor higher up, with more panoramic views. In fact, the best feature of this hotel is its top-floor restaurant with wraparound picture windows and a view of Santo Domingo Plaza and El Panecillo. The owners aim to be socially and culturally conscious, with solar panels to heat their water, solid-waste recycling, and educational programs for local youths. You'll get a slight discount and free airport transfers if you book directly online with them.

Bolívar 220 at the corner of Guayaquil, Quito. 🕐 **02/2952-711.** Fax 02/2580-213. www.realaudiencia.com 32 units. $45 (£25) double; $55 (£30) suite. Rates include full breakfast and taxes. AE, DC, MC, V. **Amenities:** Restaurant; bar; tour desk; laundry service; free Wi-Fi. *In room:* TV.

INEXPENSIVE

In addition to the places listed below, **La Posada Colonial** (🕐 **02/2280-282;** posada colonial@yahoo.com) is a good option in this price range, just steps away from the Compañía de Jesus and Plaza de la Independencia.

Hotel Catedral Internacional   Backpackers and budget hounds will love the price, location, and cleanliness here. Others may want to spend a few more bucks for something with more style and a little less funk. Rooms are all compact and carpeted, and have tiny televisions. Nos. 1 through 4 front the street, and are some of the few options with exterior windows. While this brightens things up and adds a bit of charm, it also makes these rooms noisier. There's an atrium-covered central courtyard area, with a simple restaurant.

Mejía 638, between Cuenca and Benalcázar, Quito. 🕐 **02/2955-438.** Fax 02/2557-890. 15 units. $12 (£6.60). Rates include taxes. AE, MC, V. **Amenities:** Restaurant; laundry service. *In room:* TV.

Hotel San Francisco de Quito *Value*   This is my favorite budget option in Old Town. Housed in a 17th-century converted residence, the hotel's rooms are on the second, third, and fourth floors, which rise above a classic central stone courtyard with stone fountain. Rooms vary considerably in size, so try to see a few first if you can. Most have varnished wood floors, although a few are carpeted. No. 32 is the best room in the house. A large suite with fireplace and kitchenette, it's located on the fourth floor, and has excellent views in several directions.

Sucre 217, at the corner of Guayaquil, Quito. 🕐 **02/2287-758.** Fax 02/2951-241. www.sanfranciscodequito.com.ec. 32 units. $32–$36 (£18–£20) double; $45 (£25) suite. Rates include breakfast and taxes. AE, MC, V. **Amenities:** Restaurant; Jacuzzi; steam room; sauna; shopping arcade; laundry service. *In room:* TV.

IN LA FLORESTA
VERY EXPENSIVE

In addition to the Swissôtel (listed below), the **Radisson Royal Quito** (🕐 **888/201-1718** in the U.S. and Canada, or 02/2233-333; www.radisson.com), at Cordero 444 and 12 de Octubre, is another dependable high-end choice in La Floresta.

Swissôtel Quito ☆☆   This is the second-best large hotel in town, after the JW Marriott. It may be a Swissôtel, but the rooms here have much more of a Danish feel. The rooms are very modern with a touch of classic Danish design: sleek blond-wood paneling, cream-colored striated wallpaper, and stylish wood desks, dressers, and closets. The bathrooms are very spacious and have double sinks and brand-new fixtures.

The pool area is attractive but it's so tiny that only a few lounge chairs are available on the grass outside; on weekends there's hardly a vacant spot in which to stretch out. You'll get all the typical services and amenities of a high-end business hotel. About 15 years old, the Swissôtel doesn't feel as new or hip as the Marriott, but it does have a good location, as well as a handful of excellent, if overpriced, restaurants and perhaps the best hotel health club in Quito.

Av. 12 de Octubre 1820 and Luis Cordero, Quito. ⓒ 02/2567-600. Fax 02/2568-080. www.swissotel.com. 277 units. $155–$185 (£85–£102) standard; $195–$300 (£107–£165) deluxe; $300–$400 (£165–£220) suite. Free valet parking. AE, DC, MC, V. **Amenities:** 5 restaurants; bar; small indoor-outdoor pool; outdoor tennis court; racquetball and squash courts; state-of-the-art health club; spa; Jacuzzi; sauna; concierge; tour desk; business center; shopping arcade; salon; 24-hr. room service; massage; babysitting; same-day dry cleaning; laundry service; smoke-free floors; executive/club floor. *In room:* A/C, TV, dataport, minibar, coffeemaker, hair dryer, iron, safe.

MODERATE
Hostal Santa Bárbara   Here's an Ecuadorian hotel with Gothic trappings. The hotel is housed in a mansion from the 1940s, and guests can enjoy some of the old-fashioned details that the owners left behind. The rooms have hardwood or elegant parquet floors, dark-wood paneling, detailed moldings, archways, iron chandeliers, bay windows, and dark-hued furniture. Some of the rooms even have decorative stone fireplaces or sloped ceilings. All units are large and very comfortable; the bathrooms have good proportions and great showers. No. 23, with its enormous balcony and views of both the garden and the city, is one of my favorites. No. 20 is gigantic and has a kitchen, sink, and refrigerator. The rooms in the front of the hotel can sometimes be a bit noisy. The intimate restaurant here serves Italian and international cuisine.

Av. 12 de Octubre N26–15 and Coruña, Quito. ⓒ/fax **02/2225-121** or 02/2564-382. www.hotel-santabarbara.com. 16 units. $63 (£35) double; $76 (£42) triple. Rates include taxes. Free parking. AE, DC, MC, V. **Amenities:** Restaurant; bar; tour desk; laundry service. *In room:* TV.

NORTH OF NEW TOWN
VERY EXPENSIVE
Hotel Dann Carlton 🎯🎯 *Finds*   The Dann Carlton is probably the only high-rise in all of Quito to have more brick than glass. It's not brash or flashy, but rather understated and elegant. It bills itself as a boutique hotel because it offers all the charm and personal service that you'd find at a small hotel, although the Dann Carlton does have over 200 rooms. The accommodations are quite spacious and come with dark-wood furnishings, built-in closets, CD players, and subtle green, earthy tones. The marble bathrooms are sparkling. Rooms at the back of the hotel, especially those on the higher floors, have sumptuous views of the city, El Panecillo, Parque La Carolina, and the volcanoes. The location is a tiny bit out of the way, but the neighborhood is nice and the huge Parque La Carolina is just outside the door. Don't despair if you don't have your laptop to take advantage of the free Wi-Fi; every guest gets 30 free minutes of Internet time in the well-equipped business center. These folks offer free airport pickup and drop-off, too. The newest addition here is a casino.

Av. República de El Salvador N34–377 and Irlanda, Quito. ⓒ 02/2249-008. Fax 02/2448-807. www.hotelesdann. com. 212 units. $160 (£88) double; $190–$210 (£105–£116) suite; $220–$230 (£121–£127) executive rooms and suites. AE, DC, MC, V. Free valet parking. **Amenities:** Restaurant; bar; casino; Jacuzzi; sauna; well-equipped gym; concierge; business center; salon; 24-hr. room service; massage; same-day dry cleaning; laundry service; smoke-free floors. *In room:* TV, dataport, free Wi-Fi, minibar, hair dryer, safe.

4 Where to Dine
IN NEW TOWN
MODERATE

Mare Nostrum *(R)(R)* SEAFOOD   This dimly lit restaurant with a distinctly medieval feel is the best—and most expensive—place in Quito to enjoy fresh seafood. Specialties of the house include bouillabaisse, paella, and other seafood stews. *Arroz del capitán* (rice, prawns, mussels, clams, squid, octopus, and any other fresh seafood available that day mixed with coriander, soy sauce, and onions) is the only Ecuadorian dish on the menu. But the coconut shellfish is prepared with local tropical flavors. Also available are Chilean mussels, lobster, and calamari. The sea bass in a butter-and-garlic sauce is succulent. Whatever you order, you probably won't be disappointed— the chef has a knack for throwing together different flavors from the sea. And you certainly won't leave hungry, as portions are substantial. There are three separate dining rooms; I always try to get a seat within view, but not too close, to the fireplace in the principal dining room.

Mariscal Foch E10–5 and Tamayo. (C) 02/2528-686. Reservations recommended. Main courses $6–$20 (£3.30–£11). AE, DC, MC, V. Daily noon–5pm and 7–11pm.

Rincón La Ronda Restaurante *(R) (Overrated* ECUADORIAN   This restaurant takes its name from one of the most historic streets in the Old City, with colorful colonial buildings and old-time charm. The restaurant feels very Spanish colonial, with thick white-stucco walls, red carpeting, sloped wood ceilings, brick archways, dark-wood high-back chairs, and iron chandeliers. Tour buses bring hordes of diners nightly; indeed, very few locals come here. If you're looking to mingle with Quiteños, I suggest you skip this place and head to El Nispero or La Querencia (see below for both). That said, the food here is excellent, and the service professional. Highlights of the high-quality Ecuadorian cuisine include *langostinos del Pacífico* (Pacific jumbo shrimp in garlic or tarragon sauce); *brocheta mixta con lomo, pollo, y chancho* (grilled kabob with beef, chicken, and pork); and *pernil con llapingachos, mole, salsa de maní, y aguacate* (roasted leg of pork with mashed potatoes and cheese in a peanut sauce with avocados). For appetizers, I recommend the *ceviche,* chicken *tamales,* and famous Ecuadorian soup, *locro de papas con queso y aguacate* (creamy potato soup with cheese and avocado). On weekends they usually have live folkloric dance and music performances.

Belo Horizonte 400 and Diego de Almagro. (C) 02/2540-459. Reservations recommended. Main courses $6–$19 (£3.30–£10). AE, DC, MC, V. Daily noon–11pm.

INEXPENSIVE

In addition to the places listed below, a host of simple restaurants are geared toward the backpacker crowd. For tasty Indian food, try either **Chandani Tandoori** ((C) 02/2221-053), on Juan León Mera 1312, between Avenida Colón and Luis Cordero, or **Great India Restaurant** ((C) 02/2238-269), on José Calama E4–54, between Juan León Mera and Avenida Amazonas. For pastas and pizzas, head to **Le Arcate** ((C) 02/2237-659), on Baquedano 358 and Juan León Mera.

Las Redes *(R)* SEAFOOD   This is a great alternative to the more stuffy, and more expensive, Mare Nostrum. Plus, this place serves the best *ceviche* in Quito. You can order any type of *ceviche,* from clams to octopus to fish or shrimp. The chefs here also do an excellent job with all sorts of seafood. One of the specialties is the *gran mariscada,* an enormous, beautiful platter of assorted sizzling seafood. The *arroz con* *mariscos* (yellow rice with peppers, onions, mussels, clams, shrimp, calamari, octopus, and crayfish) is also delicious. Even though Las Redes is on one of the busiest streets of Quito, the simple wood tables and fishnets hanging from the ceilings make you feel as though you are at a local seafood joint on the coast.

Av. Amazonas 845 and Veintimilla. ℂ 02/2525-691. Main courses $5–$11 (£2.75–£6.05). AE, DC, MC, V. Mon–Sat 11am–11pm.

The Magic Bean *(Kids* BREAKFAST/INTERNATIONAL   The Magic Bean is a cozy cafe that would be right at home in any college district in the United States, say, in Santa Cruz, California, or Boulder, Colorado. It's not fancy, but it has a pleasant setting with a couple of small dining rooms and covered outdoor tables. Expect to see plenty of the city's expatriates here, especially at breakfast and lunch. The fare is typical cozy cafe food—pancakes, French toast, sandwiches, bagels, omelets, fresh fruit drinks, salads made with organic lettuce, and freshly brewed coffee. Overall, the food is quite good. Just beware: The pancakes are enormous! More substantial options range from grilled local mountain trout to filet mignon. They do a lot of kabobs here, with everything from steak, chicken, and pork, to mahimahi and shrimp grilled on a spear. They even have a children's menu. The Magic Bean unabashedly caters to foreigners, but it's comforting to find a place in Ecuador that reminds you of your favorite little spot at home. If you've got a laptop or PDA, this is a good place to come for a free Wi-Fi hookup. Though it's more popular as a restaurant, the Magic Bean also functions as a hostel.

Mariscal Foch 681 and Juan León Mera. ℂ 02/2566-181. www.magicbeanquito.com. Sandwiches $4–$6.50 (£2.20–£3.60); main courses $4.75–$11 (£2.60–£5.90). AE, DC, MC, V. Daily 7am–10pm.

Mama Clorinda ECUADORIAN   This enormously popular restaurant opened in 2004 and immediately garnered a loyal following—mostly of locals. Simplicity is the theme here; the food, not the atmosphere, is the attraction. The focus is on hearty and traditional recipes from the highlands, including *seco de chivo* (goat stew), *llapingachos* (homemade corn tortillas smothered with cheese), and *guatita* (beef, potato, and peanut stew). All varieties of grilled pork are also available, as well as roasted chicken served with *elote* (corn on the cob) and mashed potatoes. If you are a vegetarian, this is not a good place because even the mashed potatoes are cooked with pork fat (which is the traditional Ecuadorian way to cook them). But if you want a taste of what locals consider a fantastic meal, then this is one of your best bets. Round out your meal with a luscious coconut flan or a fresh-fruit salad.

Reina Victoria 1144 and Calama. ℂ 02/2544-362. Main courses $3.50–$6 (£1.90–£3.30). MC, V. Daily noon–9pm.

Mulata de Tal *☀* LATIN AMERICAN   Small and cozy, this new restaurant serves up a varied menu of Latin American dishes, with their origins ranging from Oaxaca, Mexico, to Buenos Aires. The main dining room is dimly lit, with dark, wash-painted walls, an L-shaped bar, and a fireplace in one corner. The *mole* is sweet and spicy, with hints of banana, almonds, and chocolate, and it comes served over pork. The Brazilian *moqueca* is a thick and creamy seafood stew in a coconut-milk base. The walls often feature rotating art exhibits, and a separate, less-cozy upstairs dining room is often used to host poetry readings, tango shows, or small concerts.

Diego de Almagro 2419, between Pinto and Wilson. ℂ 02/2229-980. Reservations recommended. Main courses $4.80–$10 (£2.65–£5.50). MC, V. Daily noon–9pm.

IN OLD TOWN

Only a few years ago there wasn't a single good restaurant in Old Town. But things are changing fast as the area becomes a bit safer. If you do come at night, though, I suggest taking a taxi directly here and then asking the restaurant to call you a taxi for your ride back to your hotel. Strolling on the Plaza de la Independencia (Plaza Grande) after dark is relatively safe, and it's the only place in Old Town where people linger late into the evening—but I don't recommend venturing into any of the side streets at night.

Two of the restaurants listed below, Café Mosaico and PIM's Panecillo, are actually located a little bit outside and above the center of Old Town, but for practical purposes—and for the views they provide of Old Town—they are included here. A taxi to either of these restaurants from Old Town should not cost more than $3 (£1.65).

EXPENSIVE

Mea Culpa ⊛ (Moments) INTERNATIONAL   This refined restaurant commands one of the most beautiful settings in Old Town. On the second floor of a building that overlooks the Plaza de la Independencia, also known as the Plaza Grande, Mea Culpa is one of the grandest restaurants in the entire city—so grand, in fact, that they require "business casual" attire. Sneakers and T-shirts are not allowed, although exceptions are sometimes made at lunch. Still, it's best to dress up if you come here. There are two large, formal dining rooms. You'll definitely want to be in the front room, with large windows overlooking the plaza. Be sure to reserve a window table, if at all possible. You can start things off with a soup, or opt for salmon carpaccio, but I recommend their house specialty, the frittata Mea Culpa (a crepe stuffed with octopus, shrimp, mussels, and calamari). Main courses include everything from simple pastas and steaks, to pork tenderloin in a raspberry sauce or an ostrich filet flambéed in brandy and served with a maple-soy-apple reduction. The modest wine list leans heavily on Chilean and Argentine vineyards, but with some interesting and less common selections. Those looking to really splurge can drop a little over $400 (£220) on a Château Latour 1997.

2nd floor of the Palacio Arzobispal, on the Plaza de la Independencia, Venezuela and Chile. (Ⓒ) **02/2951-190.** Reservations recommended. Main courses $10–$19 (£5.50–£10). AE, DC, MC, V. Mon–Fri 12:30–3:30pm and 7–11pm; Sat 7–11pm.

Theatrum INTERNATIONAL   Housed on the second floor of the Teatro Sucre, this elegant restaurant is more style than substance. The dining room is long and narrow and has high ceilings and stark decor, with bold black chairs, white-clothed tables, and heavy red drapes. Although fancy and formal enough, and certainly acceptable, both the service and cuisine fail to live up to expectations and the prices charged. The cumin-crusted tuna is a good bet, as is the rack of imported New Zealand lamb chops. Two separate five-course tasting menus are available for $33 (£18). This is certainly convenient if you're going to the theater here. Whether I'm going to the theater or not, though, I prefer simply coming to their new wine bar, where you can sample from their extensive wine list and cellar, and order a few appetizers to fill you up.

Teatro Nacional Sucre, Calle Manabí, between Guayaquil and Flores. (Ⓒ) **02/2571-011.** Reservations recommended. Main courses $9–$20 (£4.95–£11). AE, DC, MC, V. Mon–Fri 12:30–4pm and 7:30–11:30pm; Sat 7:30–11:30pm; Sun 12:30–4pm.

MODERATE

La Cueva del Oso (Finds) ECUADORIAN/INTERNATIONAL   While most of Quito's Old Town harkens back to the colonial era, this cozy spot is a tribute to the

Art Deco heyday of the early 1900s. Etched glass, plush high-backed leather booths, high ceilings with ornate stucco designs, and marble floors give this place a sophisticated feel. The menu and food are not nearly as upscale as the decor, but they are dependable. You can get a range of standard Ecuadorian fare and well-grilled steaks and a few Continental classics, like cordon bleu. The bar here is also a good choice if you're looking for a quiet watering hole.

Chile 10–46 and Venezuela. © 02/2583-826. Main courses $5–$14 (£2.75–£7.70). MC, V. Mon–Sat 12:30pm–12:30am, Sun 12:30–4pm.

PIM's Panecillo *(Moments* ECUADORIAN/INTERNATIONAL   You might recognize this spot from a segment of *The Amazing Race: All-Stars.* While rivaling the Café Mosaico (see below) in terms of view, it falls far short of its competition in the realms of ambience and cuisine. Still, you're coming here for the view. Located just off the *Virgen de Quito* monument, atop the Panecillo hill, it has plenty of seating with a view, both in the multileveled main dining room and the heated outdoor areas. The menu is massive and ranges from hamburgers and sandwiches to a wide selection of meat, poultry, and seafood options. You can get a pepper steak or trout in almond sauce. There's a small children's menu, which includes chicken nuggets and mini-hamburgers. This is a popular tourist destination, and the place is often filled with tour bus groups.

Calle Melchor Aymerich, on top of the Panecillo. © 02/3172-595. Reservations recommended. Main courses $6.60–$16 (£3.30–£7.75). AE, DC, MC, V. Mon–Sat noon–midnight, Sun noon–6pm.

INEXPENSIVE

Café Mosaico *(★★★ (Finds* INTERNATIONAL   Much more than a cafe and more like an elite gathering place, Mosaico is perhaps the most spectacular eatery in Ecuador. Set in an old house high up on a hill overlooking Old Town, Mosaico is run by an Ecuadorian-Greek-American family. The view is beyond belief—the entire city stretched at your feet and the place filled with the crème de la crème of Ecuadorian society. Settle at your beautiful table, inlaid with hand-painted mosaic tiles, and take in the view. Many people come here only for cocktails or dessert and coffee, but the food is surprisingly good. The Greek moussaka is delicious, as is the tender souvlaki. The vegetarian lasagna is divine and there's a good selection of delicious sandwiches including a turkey club. And this is the only place in Ecuador that serves real New York cheesecake. Reservations are not accepted and this place fills up fast; be prepared to wait for a table. The best time to come here is late afternoons during the week, before the after-work crowd arrives. That way you'll score a table fast, get to see the place during the day, and also take in the incredible view as the city lights up after dark. New additions here include free Wi-Fi service and a large telescope for stargazing at night and downtown spying during the day. A taxi here should cost under $5 (£2.75)—just tell the driver to take you to Itchimbia.

Manuel Samaniego N8–95 and Antepara, Itchimbia. © 02/2542-871. Reservations not accepted. Main courses $3.50–$8 (£1.90–£4.40). MC, V. Daily 11am–10:30pm.

Café Tianguez *(★ (Value* ECUADORIAN   This is the perfect place in which to have a quick meal when you're spending the day in Old Town visiting the sights. Just below the Iglesia de San Francisco, the large outdoor cobblestone patio has a sweeping view of the Plaza de San Francisco. The indoor dining room is very small and it can get quite cozy when it's full because you sit elbow to elbow with your neighbors; but the atmosphere is friendly and convivial and the staff works hard to keep everybody happy. The food here is simple and delicious. Order a *plato típico* and you'll get a sampling of local specialties: empanadas, *humitas,* fried yuca, and fried pork. For something lighter, there's a good selection of large salads and sandwiches and fresh-squeezed fruit juices.

Below the Iglesia San Francisco, Plaza de San Francisco. © 02/2570-233. Main courses $3.80–$6.50 (£2.10–£3.60). AE, DC, MC, V. Mon–Tues 9:30am–6:30pm; Wed–Sat 9:30am–11:30pm; Sun 9:30am–10pm.

IN LA FLORESTA
EXPENSIVE
Il Risotto ✿ ITALIAN   Semi-formal and almost always packed, this longstanding option is one of the top Italian restaurants in town. The menu is dauntingly long and covers the cuisines from all regions of Italy—I like coming with a group so I can taste a wide range of the choices. The heart and soul of the menu is a range of pastas and risi. Everything is very well done. I like the *risotto salmone e rucola* (salmon and arugula) and the house penne, which comes in a thick tomato sauce with eggplant, capers, anchovies, and both green and black olives. For something more exotic, you can try a risotto with frog's legs. More substantial entrees include *captretto alla messinese,* a goat dish cooked with tomatoes, rosemary, and potatoes, as well as veal Bolognese. There's an antipasti buffet ($8/£4.40 small; $14/£7.70 large), which is quite inviting, and a less-outstanding dessert buffet ($4.50/£2.50). The wine list is long, but much heavier on Chilean and Argentine offerings than on those from Italy. Try to grab a window table in the main dining room, which features wood floors and a few Tiffany-style lamps. There's a cozy but viewless dining room below the main room, which is used for overflow. *Note:* This place is closed on Saturday.

Eloy Alfaro N34–447 and Portugal. © 02/2246-850. Reservations recommended. Main courses $9–$21 (£4.95–£12). AE, DC, MC, V. Mon–Fri noon–3pm and 6:30–11:30pm; Sun noon–3:30pm and 6:30–10:30pm.

MODERATE
El Nispero ✿✿ *Finds* NEW ECUADORIAN   If you're looking for a high-end restaurant serving updated takes on traditional Ecuadorian cuisine, this is the place to come. The restaurant is housed in a charming old home that has been totally gutted and renovated with hardwood floors and blue and yellow walls; a serene, quiet atmosphere prevails throughout. Service is gracious and the food is very good. The focus here is on traditional ingredients and recipes updated with an eclectic twist. The roast pork is served with figs and a mint sauce; the fresh prawns with coconut sauce come with an Ecuadorian nut called *tocte;* pancakes are made from yuca flour; and the *humitas* (a kind of corn mush) are served like a pudding, in a bowl. For dessert, try the *oritas*—small Ecuadorian bananas drizzled with local honey—or the éclairs filled with *naranjilla* cream. If you like ice cream, be sure to ask about the *helado* special of the day—it's delicious.

Valladolid N24–438 and Cordero. © 02/2226-398. Reservations recommended. Main courses $8–$18 (£4.40–£9.90). AE, DC, MC, V. Tues–Sat noon–4pm and 7–11pm; Sun–Mon noon–4pm.

NORTH OF NEW TOWN
EXPENSIVE
La Querencia ✿ *Finds* ECUADORIAN   La Querencia offers delicious Ecuadorian cooking in a beautiful setting. If you're looking to try Ecuadorian specialties such as *seco de chivo* (lamb stew) or *ceviche* (marinated fish), but you're a bit apprehensive about venturing into a hole-in-the wall restaurant, La Querencia is for you. Both the

seco de chivo and *ceviche* here are excellent. Other unique dishes include *papas con cuero* (pork skins with potatoes in a peanut sauce) and *arroz con menestra* (a juicy filet served with rice, lentils, and fried bananas). I recommend starting your meal with *empanadas de verde* and *tortillas de maíz*. The locals eat the empanadas with their hands, so don't be bashful about using yours. From the outside, you can immediately tell that this is a place for wheelers and dealers. On the inside, you'll find large picture windows, which open onto a garden; brightly colored walls decorated with typical Ecuadorian crafts; a fireplace; and charming, large-planked hardwood floors. This is definitely the best restaurant in Quito for high-quality local dishes.

Eloy Alfaro 2530 and Catalina Aldaz. (℃ 02/2446-654. Reservations recommended. Main courses $6.50–$22 (£3.60–£12). AE, DC, MC, V. Mon–Sat 11am–10pm; Sun 11am–6pm.

Zazu ✦✦✦ *(Finds* FUSION   Hip and eclectic, this new restaurant avoids the common pitfalls of modern fusion restaurants, and gets just about everything right. The Peruvian-born chef, Alexander Laud, uses fresh, local ingredients whenever possible, and flavor always takes precedence over presentation and shock-value—although presentations are always creative and often unexpected. Start things off with the *ceviche martini,* a relatively traditional *ceviche* of sole served in a martini glass, with a freshly shaken passion-fruit martini poured over it as marinade. Don't miss the white-tuna appetizer, which comes baked in a delicate ginger and Peruvian hot chile broth, with bok choy and scallions. For a main dish, I recommend *langostinos Zazu,* which are first cooked tempura style and then served with a sauce made with six types of chiles—did I mention the chef is from Peru?—and a side salad made from green mangos. Perhaps the best way to dine here, though, is to go with the chef's nightly tasting menu ($30–$35/£17–£19) and to trust his skills and whims. Quito's hippest crowd gathers at the bar here, which serves up a wide range of martinis and mixed drinks, including a couple of very tasty original concoctions.

Mariano Aguilera 331 and La Pradera. (℃ 02/2543-559. Reservations recommended. Main courses $8–$18 (£4.40–£9.90). AE, DC, MC, V. Mon–Fri 12:30–11:30pm; Sat 7–11:30pm.

MODERATE

Los Troncos Steak House ARGENTINE STEAKHOUSE   Fronting the Parque La Carolina, this is where Ecuadorian businesspeople meet for power lunches, and where families come to sample some of the best grilled meat in town. When you walk into the restaurant, you'll pass the huge grilling area, where juicy steaks, pork loin, chicken breasts, sausages, and other savory meat specialties are roasting over hot coals. I recommend that you order the *parrillada* (grilled) special, so that you can sample everything on the menu, including the above-mentioned meats, plus *riñón* (kidney) and *morcilla* (blood pudding). You can also order everything individually. The charcoal fire gives all the meat a delicious flavor. Vegetarians can eat here, too—there's a large selection of pastas, soups, and salads, including an impressive salad bar.

Av. de los Shyris 1280 and Portugal. (℃ 02/2437-377. Main courses $6–$15 (£3.30–£8.25). AE, DC, MC, V. Mon–Sat noon–8pm; Sun noon–4pm.

5 What to See & Do

It's hard to hit all of Quito's major attractions in 1 day, although if you are real pressed for time, you can pack in a lot of them, especially if you focus first on Old Town. I recommend getting an early start and visiting Old Town highlights of the Iglesia de

San Francisco, La Compañía de Jesús, and Casa Museo María Augusta Urrutia. During the midday break, when many attractions close for lunch and siesta, you could head up to El Panecillo for panoramic views of the city and lunch at PIM's (see above). In the afternoon, head over to Fundación Guayasamín and the Capilla del Hombre. End your day with a sunset ride on the new cable car, El Teleférico, with its sweeping view of the city. This is a pretty good and packed 1-day tour, although it leaves out the Museo Nacional del Banco Central, which will take you several hours to tour properly.

IN OLD TOWN

Casa Museo María Augusta Urrutia 🖈   It's hard to have a favorite sight in Old Town—there are just so many amazing things to see. But this museum, which provides a nice break if you've been visiting churches all morning, ranks high on my list. It allows modern-day visitors to envision what it must have been like to live in a 19th-century Spanish-style mansion in Old Town. When you enter the house, you immediately find yourself in a gorgeous courtyard. Not much has been changed since Doña María Augusta Urrutia lived here, so the dramatic entry that you see is probably what the Pope and many other world leaders also experienced when visiting this home. (Doña María devoted much of her life to philanthropy with a Catholic bent.) The house is surprisingly modern, with a full bathroom and modern kitchen appliances; but there are also a cold storage room, a wood-burning stove, and the oldest grain masher in Ecuador. The interior is gorgeous, featuring antique European furniture, a bed that belonged to General Sucre, hand-painted wallpaper, stained-glass windows, handcrafted moldings, murals on the walls, and Belgian tiles. There is also an incredible collection of Ecuadorian art, much of it by painter Victor Hideros.

Note: Guided tours are available in English. Just ask for a guide when you enter. Most of the written display information is in both Spanish and English. Allow about 40 minutes to visit the whole house.

García Moreno N2–60, between Sucre and Bolívar. © 02/2580-103. Admission $2 (£1.10) adults; $1 (55p) students and seniors; 50¢ (30p) children under 12. Tues–Sat 10am–6pm; Sun 9:30am–5:30pm.

El Centro Cultural Metropolitano   This mildly interesting museum is worth a visit if you love colonial art; otherwise, I recommend a visit only if you have an extra hour on your hands. The bustling museum is housed in a 400-year-old complex that contains several extensive public libraries, a museum, and performance spaces. The galleries on the main floor are used for temporary exhibitions and are free to the public. One of my favorite gallery spaces is the large open courtyard, covered with a high glass ceiling. Upstairs, you'll find the **Museo Alberto Mena Caamaño.** Few museums in the world can boast that they were both a prison and a university—this museum is one of them. Instead of prisoners or students, however, this space now houses a modest collection of colonial art. Your entrance fee gets you a bilingual guided tour; the guide will also take you to the old Jesuit residences and the basement area that used to house the prisoners. There's a simple cafeteria on the ground floor that makes a good coffee-break spot.

Corner of Espejo and García Moreno. © 02/2584-362. www.centrocultural-quito.com. Free admission to the center; museum $1.50 (85p) adults; 75¢ (40p) students; 50¢ (30p) children and seniors. Tues–Sun 9am–5pm.

El Panecillo (Virgin Monument) *Moments*   From a distance, the hill that hosts a huge statue of the winged virgin does indeed look like a *panecillo* (small bread roll).

The Quito School of Art

The mid-16th-century Council of Trent mandate was clear: Art was to be used to convey Catholic doctrine and Christian themes to an illiterate, pagan populace. Early religious art that appeared throughout the Spanish colonies in South America carefully reflected traditional European themes and styles, as taught by Franciscan and Dominican monks to indigenous or *mestizo* artists.

After a century of standard, if uninspiring, copies of Christ on the cross and somber Virgins, a creative transition took place that the early Catholic fathers never envisioned. As the indigenous artists gained confidence and Catholicism became firmly rooted in the New World, religious paintings and sculptures became increasingly detailed and dramatic. In Quito, artists began incorporating more passionate elements into their works. Vivid crucifixes revealed Christ in excruciating detail—flayed, bones exposed, with a face distorted in its agony; it was an almost rebellious reflection of the suffering of a conquered people.

The Quito School of art matured into a distinctive original style known for its exquisite detail of expression—statues had glass eyes, real hair, and rich fabrics overlaid with layers of gold leaf, for example.

By the time the colonial stranglehold weakened over an increasingly free-thinking Latin America, this graphic suffering and drama gave way to more native influences; Christ became more swarthy and llamas and *cuyes* (guinea pigs), parrots and condors began to populate the landscapes in Catholic art.

Many of Quito's churches and museums display or are examples themselves of this idiosyncratic School: Visit the stunning, gold-draped **Iglesia de la Compañía de Jesus, Iglesia de San Francisco,** and **Museo de Arte Colonial** to see surviving examples.

Since it's directly south of the city, this hill was an ideal spot to construct the 45m-high (148-ft.) *La Virgen de Quito,* an enlarged copy of Bernardo de Lagarda's *La Virgen de Quito* sculpture that is on display on the main altar in the San Francisco church. The Panecillo stands at about 3,000m (9,840 ft.), so you can also see the sculpture from the center of Quito.

The significance of the Panecillo Hill dates back to Inca times, when it was known as Shungoloma (Hill of the Heart). Before the Spanish arrived, the Incas used this hill as a place to worship the sun. Later, from 1812 to 1815, the Spanish constructed a fortress, to control what was going on down below. These days, most people come up here for the 360° views of Quito. *Tip:* For the best vistas, try to get here early in the morning (around 10am), before the clouds settle in around the nearby mountains. On a clear day, you can see Cotopaxi in the distance. This is a relatively quick ride from Old Town, and a taxi should only cost about $3 (£1.65) each way. A half-hour is all you'll need to take in the sights.

El Panecillo, south of Old Town. Admission to enter the grounds $1 (55p); admission to climb to the top of the monument $1(55p). Mon–Fri 9am–6pm; Sat–Sun 9am–5pm.

El Sagrario   This 17th-century church was once part of the nearby cathedral. It's a mishmash of different architectural styles, from baroque to neoclassical. The Solomonic columns on the outside are both Ionic and Gothic. Inside, you can see the Moorish influence in the painted domes, with their striking frescos. As you enter El Sagrario, look down—you will see crypts. (Those with crossbones mean that the body buried there died of smallpox.) The second door is regarded as a colonial-era masterpiece; it was painted with liquid gold leaf and designed with vegetables and fruits, including pineapples, which are considered an indigenous welcome symbol. The intricate rococo altarpiece is also impressive—it took 12 years to build, and the details are quite lovely.

Around the corner from the cathedral on García Moreno near Espejo. Free admission. Mon–Sat 8am–noon and 2–5:30pm.

Iglesia de la Merced   It's believed that after the expulsion of the Moors from Spain, in 1492, many Moorish artists sought refuge in South America. The current Iglesia de la Merced, a delightful example of Moorish design, only dates from 1737, but it was originally built in 1538. The resplendent gold-leaf altar, designed by the great Bernardo de Legarda, is pure baroque, while the ornate stucco work is mainly Moorish. Many of the oil paintings are by Víctor Mideros, one of the greatest Ecuadorian artists of the 20th century. If you have the time (and it's still early in the morning), you can head around the corner to the convent, which dates back to the early 16th century and still houses the church's priests. Some of the highlights include the Neptune sculpture in the stone fountain and the 17th-century sun clock above the dome. The convent is open Monday through Saturday from 8 to 10:30am; the entrance is on Mejía near the corner of Cuenca.

Chile, near the corner of Cuenca. Free admission. Mon–Fri 6:30am–noon and 3–6pm; Sat 6:30am–noon.

Iglesia de San Francisco 🖈🖈   San Francisco was the first church built in Quito. Construction began in 1535, just 1 month after the Spanish arrived. (It took more than 100 years to finish.) You'll notice that Plaza San Francisco is distinctly sloped; for several hundred years, it was assumed that it followed the shape of the earth. However, a group of archaeologists recently discovered that San Francisco was built over an Inca temple, which is the reason the actual church is much higher than other structures in Quito. As you walk up the stairs from the plaza to the church, you can't help but realize how wide the stairs are. Supposedly, the architects designed the stairs this way so that as you approach the church, you have to keep your eyes on your feet to watch where you're going—in other words, you are forced to bow your head in respect.

Like La Compañía (see below), San Francisco is an important baroque church, but the latter is much larger and, for some reason, feels much more somber. The ceilings have a beautiful Moorish design. In the entryway, as in La Compañía, you will notice images of the sun, which were used to lure indigenous people to the Christian religion. Throughout the church are combinations of indigenous and Catholic symbols. For example, the interior is decorated with angels in the shape of the sun—and the faces of these angels have distinct Indian characteristics.

The baroque altar in the front of the church has three important sculptures: The top is *El Bautismo de Jesús (The Baptism of Jesus);* the bottom is a representation of *Jesús de Gran Poder (Almighty Jesus);* and the middle is probably one of the most important sculptures in Ecuador, the original *La Virgen de Quito (The Virgin of Quito),* designed

Getting High in Quito

One of the city's most popular attractions is **El Teleférigo** ⚓, six-person cable cars that transport you up the side of Volcán Pichincha to 4,050m (13,280 ft.). The quick climb over 1,000m (3,280 ft.) takes all of 8 minutes. At the top, you will have a magnificent view of the city and surrounding snow-covered mountain peaks. The air is thin up here, but don't worry: The ambitious and very modern complex includes an oxygen bar to replenish the weary traveler, along with several viewing platforms. You'll also find souvenir stands and shops, and a couple of restaurants and fast-food outlets.

If crowds bother you, avoid visiting here on the weekends (and public holidays), when it's packed to the gills. That said, this attraction is enormously popular with Ecuadorian families and it's a wonderful cultural experience just to be out among the locals. People wait patiently in line just to get a glimpse of their city from an elevated perspective. You can escape the crowds by taking one of the marked paths on a stroll through the shrubby highlands. If you have kids in tow, you might want to return to the base of the mountain where you'll find an amusement park, **Vulqano Park,** complete with roller coasters, all kinds of rides, arcades, and video games.

The cable car operates Monday to Thursday from 10am to 8pm and Friday through Sunday from 9am to 11pm. I strongly suggest you splurge for the Fast Pass ticket that will cut your wait time considerably. The cost for a regular ticket is $4 (£2.20) for adults and $3 (£1.65) for children; the Fast Pass ticket costs $7 (£3.85) for adults and $5 (£2.75) for children. Admission to Vulqano Park is free and prices for the rides average around 50¢ to $1 (30p–55p).

To get here, take a 15-minute taxi ride from the center of Quito. Tell the driver to take you to El Teleférigo at the Vulqano Park. The taxi ride should cost no more than $8 (£4.40). For more information, visit www.teleferiqo. com or call ☎ 02/3250-076.

by Bernardo de Legarda. (*La Virgen de Quito* was the model for the huge winged angel on the Panecillo; see p. 115.)

When I last visited, in 2007, the interior of the church was receiving a major restoration and face-lift. Scaffolding had been erected throughout much of the interior, and much of the overhead artwork was covered up, or under repair. The full restoration may take several years. But there's still plenty to see, making this church worth a visit.

Plaza San Francisco. Free admission. Mon–Sat 7am–noon and 3–5:30pm; Sun 7am–noon.

La Basílica del Voto Nacional   Work on the basilica began in 1883 and is still unfinished. Visitors are permitted inside this concrete marvel, which is modeled on Paris's Notre-Dame. The large central nave of this church feels cold, with so much unfinished concrete, but if you look up you'll see fabulous stained-glass works all around. Be sure to stop into the small side chapel, La Capilla de Sacramento, which features a mosaic tile floor, painted walls, columns, and a beautiful high altar of Mary. Most people, however, come here for the spectacular aerial views of the Old City and to see the *La Virgin de Quito* in the distance. For the best views, you have to pay to take the elevator, or climb the 90m (300 ft.) to the top of the towers. *Note:* The elevators don't always work and the final "ladders" to the top are very narrow and quite steep. As you cross the bridge to enter the towers, look for the carved condors—the stonework is impressive and the condors look as though they are about to fly away. The basilica is also famous for its mystical gargoyles in the form of local Ecuadorian icons such as pumas, monkeys, penguins, tortoises, and condors that guard the outsides of the church. There is a cafe on the third floor—a good place to catch your breath after taking in the breathtaking views.

Carchi 122, at the corner of Calle Venezuela. © 02/2289-428. Admission $2 (£1.10) to visit the top of the towers. Daily 9am–5pm.

La Compañía de Jesús ✸✸✸   This Jesuit church is one of the great baroque masterpieces in South America. All the work took 160 years to complete (1605–1765). The facade won't fail to impress you—the carvings are unbelievably detailed. Notice the Solomonic columns, which are symbolic of the Catholic doctrine that life's journey starts at the bottom (on earth), but by following the holy path, it ends at heaven.

Almost every inch of the interior has intricate decorations. When you enter La Compañía, look for the symbols of the sun in both the main door to the church and the ceiling. The sun was a very important Inca symbol, and the Spanish thought that if they decorated the entryway with indigenous symbols, it might encourage local people to join the church. The walls and ceilings of La Compañía are typical of Moorish design—you will only see geometric shapes but no human forms. The building has been under renovation for the past several years, and some of the gold leaf on the ceiling and walls has been restored to its original luster. Natural sunlight and candlelight really bring out an angelic brilliance.

Concerts are sometimes held inside this church, and the acoustics and setting are haunting. If you happen to be in Quito on November 1 (Day of the Dead), you can also visit the catacombs here.

On García Moreno near Sucre. Admission $2 (£1.10). Mon–Fri 10am–1pm and 2–5pm; Sat 10am–1pm.

La Plaza de la Independencia ✸   Also called La Plaza Grande, this became the main square of Quito in the 16th century. The Spanish were afraid that the Incas might poison their water supply, so the Spanish set up their own protected well here, and this plaza subsequently became the social center of town. It also served as a central market and bullfighting area. Today, Old Town's main square is bordered by the Government Palace on the west, City Hall to the east, the Archbishop's Palace on the north, and the cathedral to the south.

The **Government Palace** ✸ is the most interesting building on the plaza. Don't be intimidated by the chain-link fence in front of the palace; everyone is welcome to walk

---

⟨Tips⟩ Touring Iglesia de San Francisco

The Iglesia de San Francisco closes at noon, earlier than most of the other churches in Old Town, and it doesn't open again until 3pm. So if you're trying to see everything in Old Town in one morning, be sure to visit San Francisco first. If you can't make it before 11:30am, you can visit Museo Fray Pedro Gocial, the museum connected to the church (see above).

Fun Fact **Colorful Quito**

When a smallpox epidemic hit Quito in 1756, the government declared that all buildings must be painted with white limestone, which was then believed to be a disinfectant. From then until the late 1980s, all buildings in Quito were white. Everything changed when the mayor of Quito discovered that most Quiteños felt that Old Town was *too* white. Out came the art historians, who did extensive research, uncovering the true colors of all the colonial structures in the city. Now most of the buildings have been restored to their pre-1756 luster.

---

inside the main area—just tell the guard that you're a curious tourist. Once you walk into the main entry area, you can get a sense of the Spanish/Moorish architecture. If you look straight ahead, you'll see the impressive 1966 mural by Guayasamín, of Orellana discovering the Amazon.

The **City Hall** is probably the least impressive structure on the plaza. It was built in 1952, in the Bauhaus style. The **Archbishop's Palace** was built in 1852; it was formerly the mayor's house. You can now walk inside and see the Andalusian- and Moorish-inspired courtyard; note that the floor of the courtyard is made from the spines of pigs. This area is now an informal crafts market. The **cathedral** dates from the 16th century. Inside is a good collection of art from the Quito School, including works by Caspicara and Manuel Samaniego. You can visit the cathedral Monday through Saturday from 6 to 10am. The square is most beautiful at night, when all the buildings are lighted up.

Plaza de la Independencia is bordered by Calle Venezuela to the east, García Moreno to the west, Chile to the north, and Espejo to the south. To get to the plaza from the Trole, get off at the Plaza Grande stop and walk 1 block on either Calle Espejo or Chile.

Museo Camilo Egas (Camilo Egas Museum) ✿ Famed Ecuadorian *indigenista* (indigenist) painter Camilo Egas is featured in this small but striking museum. Housed in an old, colonial-era home, with massive adobe walls and a beautiful central courtyard, the collection features a broad selection of Egas's work. Part of the international vanguard of painters of the early 20th century, Egas spent time in New York, Rome, Madrid, and Paris, where his works were influenced by contemporary trends and styles—expressionism, surrealism, cubism, and abstract expressionism. He knew and hung out with Picasso, Braque, Matisse, and de Chirico. Throughout it all, his primary subject matter was the Andean indigenous peoples of Ecuador and neighboring countries.

Venezuela 1302, at the corner of Esmeraldas. ✆ 02/2572-012. Admission $1 (55p). Tues–Fri 9:30am–5pm; Sat–Sun 10am–4pm.

Museo Fray Pedro Gocial (San Francisco Museum and Convent) This museum, which is attached to the San Francisco church (see above), allows visitors to see the convent as well as the church's choir. Tour guides also will show you some of the pieces of the church's fantastic colonial art collection. I highly recommend a visit to the choir. Here you can see the church's original wood ceiling, as well as a beautiful wood inlaid "lyric box" that was used to hold up the music for the singers in the choir. You will also experience Manuel Chile Caspicara's famous crucifix, which dates

THE TRAVELOCITY GUARANTEE

...THAT SAYS EVERYTHING YOU BOOK WILL BE RIGHT, OR WE'LL WORK WITH OUR TRAVEL PARTNERS TO MAKE IT RIGHT, RIGHT AWAY.

*To drive home the point,
we're going to use the word "right" in every single sentence.*

Let's get right to it. Right to the meat! Only Travelocity guarantees everything about your booking will be right, or we'll work with our travel partners to make it right, right away. Right on!

Here's a picture taken smack dab right in the middle of Antigua, where the Guarantee also covers you.

The Guarantee covers all but one of the items pictured to the right.

Now, you may be thinking, "Yeah, right, I'm so sure." That's OK; you have the right to remain skeptical. That is until we mention help is always right around the corner. Call us right off the bat, knowing our customer service reps are there for you 24/7. Righting wrongs. Left and right.

For example, what if the ocean view you booked actually looks out at a downright ugly parking lot? You'd be right to call – we're there for you. And no one in their right mind would be pleased to learn the rental car place has closed and left them stranded. Call Travelocity and we'll help get you back on the right track.

Now if you're guessing there are some things we can't control, like the weather, well you're right. But we can help you with most things – to get all the details in righting,* visit travelocity.com/guarantee.

*Sorry, spelling things right is one of the few things not covered under the Guarantee.

I'd give my right arm for a guarantee like this, although I'm glad I don't have to.

travelocity
You'll never roam alone.

back to 1650–70. It is said that Caspicara tied a model to a cross to learn how to real-istically represent Christ's facial and body expressions; the glass eyes are piercing.

Plaza San Francisco, Cuenca 477 and Sucre. © 02/2952-911. Admission $2 (£1). Mon–Sat 9am–1pm and 2–6pm; Sun 9am–noon. Visits only by guided tour, which leave on an as-needed basis. English-language tours are available.

Museo Histórico Militar/"Casa de Sucre"   This museum will appeal to both history and military buffs. The house dates from the 17th century, but the house's namesake, the Independence hero Mariscal Antonio José de Sucre, lived here from 1828 until his death in 1830. On the ground floor, in the Sala de Armas, you can see swords, pistols, and bayonets that all belonged to him. There is also a stable with old-fashioned saddles on display. On the second floor, you can visit the original brick kitchen with two cold storage rooms. The *archivo* is where Sucre received visitors; the desk is original. Sucre's bedroom doesn't contain his original bed, but look at the walls—you'll notice that they have slats, which allowed Sucre to move the walls of his room closer together in order to preserve heat. Most of the tours are in Spanish, but even if you can't understand your guide, you can get a good picture of what it must have been like to live in Old Town in the 19th century. Plan on spending about 45 minutes here.

Venezuela 573, at the corner of Sucre. © 02/2952-860. Admission $1 (55p). Tues–Thurs 8:30am–4:30pm; Fri 8:30am–1pm; Sat 9am–1pm.

IN NEW TOWN

Museo Jacinto Jijón y Caamaño   This tiny museum holds the personal collection of Jacinto Jijón y Caamaño, an Ecuadorian who did extensive archaeological excava-tions in South America in the 20th century. In my opinion, the most interesting arti-facts are the *fardos funerarios,* or funeral bundles, that he discovered in Lima in 1925. You will see mummies and all sorts of jewelry and learn about pre-Columbian funeral rituals. Also impressive is the display of exquisite colonial furnishings. You can see the entire collection in about 30 minutes. Admission includes a guided tour; most of the guides are bilingual.

Av. 12 de Octubre and Roca (on the 3rd floor of the Edificio de la Biblioteca at the Universidad Católica). Admission $1 (55p). Mon–Fri 8:30am–4pm.

Museo Nacional del Banco Central del Ecuador 🎯🎯 *Kids*   This huge and enor-mously rich museum offers visitors an opportunity to learn about the evolution of Ecuador—its human and natural history, as well as its art. When you see all the arti-facts, archaeological finds, and works of art displayed chronologically, you get a pro-found sense of the country not commonly found in museums that focus on one era or type of exhibit. *Tip:* To see everything in this massive museum, you really need at least 4 hours; I recommend taking a guided tour.

If you visit the museum from beginning to end, you will start at the **Archaeological Gallery.** On display are artifacts dating from 11,000 B.C. Artifacts and dioramas explain the beliefs and lifestyle of a wide range of pre-Columbian and pre-Inca peoples. One of the most striking exhibits here is a Cañari mummy, though the **Golden Court** 🎯🎯 is my favorite exhibit. Because many indigenous groups worshipped the sun, they used gold to create masks, chest decorations, and figurines to represent the sun. The fine details are really amazing—many of the pieces in this gallery are a sight to behold.

You can see the influence of the sun and the veneration of women in the work dis-played in the **Colonial Art Gallery,** which contains pieces from 1534 to 1820. Much of the colonial art here combines the rich ornamentation popular in pre-Columbian art with the severe polychrome style of European art. You'll also probably notice that a lot of pieces in this gallery are quite bloody and gory—an attempt to scare the indigenous people into believing in the Christian God. I find the colonial-era art is displayed better here—with better lighting and explanations—than at the Museo Fray Pedro Gocial (see above).

After independence from Spain, Ecuadorian artists began to eschew religious symbolism. In the **Republican Art Gallery,** you can see this transition. Instead of gory religious art and paintings of the Virgin, for example, you'll find lifelike portraits of Ecuador's independence heroes. One of my favorites is *Retrato de Simón Bolívar (Portrait of Simón Bolívar).*

On a whole different plane is the **Contemporary Art Gallery.** Here you'll see everything from peaceful landscapes from the early 20th century to Oswaldo Guayasamín's tortured and angry portraits, as well as a wide range of modernist works by prominent Ecuadorian artists such as Pilar Bustos, Camilo Egas, Theo Constante, and Enrique Tabara. In addition to the above galleries, the museum also hosts temporary art exhibits. And in the same building, there is a **Museum of Musical Instruments,** which is a lot of fun if you're traveling with kids.

Av. Patria, between 6 de Diciembre and 12 de Octubre. ℂ 02/2223-258. Adults $2 (£1.10), students 50¢ (30p). Tues–Fri 9am–5pm; Sat–Sun and holidays 10am–4pm. Free multilingual guided tours are available throughout the day, and most of the displays are in both Spanish and English.

NORTH OF NEW TOWN

The two nearby attractions are expected to one day be joined in a relatively massive museum, workshop, and cultural center.

Capilla del Hombre (Chapel of Mankind) ℱ   A few blocks from the Fundación Guayasamín (see below), this impressive structure is in many ways the culmination of the work and dreams of Ecuador's great modern artist, Oswaldo Guayasamín. Guayasamín, who died in 1999 at the age of 90, had wanted to open the museum on the first day of the new century, but financial problems and construction delays postponed its opening until November 2002. Dedicated to "man's progress through art," the architecturally intriguing chapel houses many of the artist's paintings, murals, and sculptures, as well parts of the his personal collection of colonial art, archaeological finds, and contemporary art. Incan and indigenous mythological beliefs are incorporated into the design of the building, which is three levels and which uses the number 3 for various motifs and architectural elements. The eternal flame in the chapel's altar is dedicated to those who died defending human rights (or the rights of man, which explains the name of the museum). Guayasamín himself is buried here, beneath a tree he planted, which has been renamed El Arbol de la Vida (The Tree of Life). Allot yourself about an hour to view the museum.

Corner of Mariano Calvache and Lorenzo Chávez, Bellavista. ℂ 02/2448-492. Admission $3 (£1.65), or $5 (£2.75) combined with the Fundación Guayasamín. Tues–Sun 10am–5pm.

Fundación Guayasamín ℱℱ   This powerful museum displays the works and art collections of Oswaldo Guayasamín, one of Ecuador's most famous artists. The museum has three sections. **El Museo Arqueológico (Archaeology Museum)** houses Guayasamín's collection of pre-Columbian art. The artist once said, "I paint from 3,000 or 5,000 years ago." It's interesting to see both his collection and his inspiration.

Keep an eye out for the sitting shamans and tribal chiefs, and the jugs with the intricately carved faces.

Across the courtyard is the **Museo de Arte Moderno (Museum of Modern Art)** ⚔, which displays Guayasamín's own work. Most impressive is his art from 1964 to 1984 entitled "La Edad de la Ira" (The Age of Anger), which represents his dismay over violence in the world, and in South America in particular. One of the most dramatic pieces is the three-paneled *Homenaje a Víctor Jara (Homage to Víctor Jara).* Jara was a Chilean guitarist and Communist Party supporter who was tortured and killed by General Pinochet's army during the 1973 military junta. Military officers cut off his hands to try to stop his protest songs, but it took a machine gun to silence him. The images of a skeleton playing a guitar have a tremendous impact.

In the **Museo de Arte Colonial,** you can view Guayasamín's incredible collection of colonial art. The majority of the pieces are from the Quito School; they give viewers a good idea of the art created by the first inhabitants of Quito. The collection contains more than 80 crucifixes.

There is also a nice patio (with a great view) and a cafe on the premises. It doesn't take more than an hour to explore the whole museum. Take a taxi here (about $2/£1.10) from the heart of New Town.

Calle José Bosmediano E 15–68 Bellavista (Batán). ✆ 02/2465-265. Admission $3 (£1.65) or $5 (£2.75) combined with the Capilla del Hombre. Tues–Sun 10am–5pm.

6 Outdoor Activities & Spectator Sports

Quito is a large sprawling city, so it's hard to do anything truly outdoorsy within the city limits. The large, central Parque La Carolina is the best spot for outdoor sports and activities. Your best bet, though, is to travel an hour or two outside the city, where you'll find an abundance of outdoor pursuits. These include hiking, climbing, trekking, white-water rafting, and mountain biking. For a more complete listing of adventure tours and activities available close to Quito, see "Side Trips from Quito" (p. 133) and chapter 4.

BULLFIGHTING   The once-popular and -proud tradition of bullfighting is now very rarely performed publicly in Quito, except during the Fiestas de Quito the first week of December. Bullfights are held at the **Plaza de Toros** (✆ 02/2229-369), north of the intersection of Avenida Amazonas and 10 de Agosto. Tickets can be picked up right at the bullring and run $1 to $10 (55p–£5.50).

JOGGING   The downtown Parque La Carolina is your best bet for jogging. This large, central city park has several jogging paths, and you'll usually find plenty of fellow joggers around. The much smaller Parque El Ejido is another option.

SOCCER   Soccer, or *fútbol,* is the principal spectator sport in Ecuador. Soccer season in Quito lasts March through December. Most important games take place at the **Estadio Olímpico Atahualpa** (✆ 02/2247-510), on 6 de Diciembre and Avenida Naciones Unidas. Game day is usually Saturday or Sunday. General-admission seats cost $2 (£1.10); the good seats go for $10 to $12 (£5.50–£6.60). You can buy tickets at the stadium on the day of the game. To get there, take the Ecovía trolley line to the Estadio stop.

TENNIS   If you're not staying at a hotel with its own courts, the Parque La Carolina open-air public courts are your best bet. They are free of charge, and awarded on a first-come, first-served basis. They fill up very fast on weekends, and tend to be busy on weekdays as well.

7 Shopping

While the majority of Ecuador's most-famous and sought-after shopping occurs outside Quito—in Otavalo and Cuenca, and at small Andean markets—you can still find ample opportunities for successful and rewarding shopping in the capital.

THE SHOPPING SCENE   As in the rest of the country, the shopping scene in Quito mainly consists of local handicrafts (alpaca sweaters, tapestries, figurines, pottery, hats, and jewelry) made by indigenous Ecuadorian artists. Some of the stuff you'll find is mass-produced or of poor quality. But if you know where to go (see below), there are some great shops, which support local indigenous groups. You'll also find more high-end shops here than in other parts of the country.

A note on store hours: Unless indicated below, all stores are open from 9am to 1:30pm, and from 3 to 7pm. Most stores close for a siesta from 1:30 to 3pm, and most are closed on Sunday.

MARKETS   While nothing compares to the various weekly local markets held in towns and cities across the Andes, or the world-famous market in Otavalo (p. 133), a couple of longstanding markets are worth hitting in Quito, especially if you can't visit any of those I just mentioned.

In New Town, the **Mercado Artesanal La Mariscal (Mariscal Artisans Market)** is a tight warren of permanent booths selling all sorts of arts, crafts, and clothing. You should definitely be picky here—there are a lot of mass-produced and mediocre wares for sale. But if you shop carefully, you can find plenty of high-quality goods. You can bargain a little, but not too much. Located on Jorge Washington, between Reina Victoria and Juan León Mera, it's open daily from around 10am until 7pm.

A similar option is available on weekends all along the north end of **Parque El Ejido.**

MODERN MALLS   With globalization and modernization taking hold all across Latin America, much of the local shopping scene has shifted to large mega-malls. Modern multilevel affairs with cineplexes, food courts, and international brand-name stores are becoming ubiquitous. The biggest and most modern of these malls, called *centros comerciales* in Spanish, include the **Centro Comercial El Jardín** (© **02/2980-298**), at Avenida Amazonas and Avenida de la República; **Centro Comercial Iñaquito** (© **02/2253-508**), at Avenida Amazonas and Naciones Unidas; and **Centro Comercial Quicentro** (© **02/2464-526**), at Avenida 6 de Diciembre and Avenida Naciones Unidas. Although they lack the charm of small shops and galleries found around Quito, they are a reasonable option for one-stop shopping; most contain at least one or two art galleries and crafts shops, along with a large supermarket, which is always the best place to stock up on coffee, local liquors, and other nonperishable foodstuffs.

SHOPPING A TO Z
ART GALLERIES
Artes   This small stylish gallery has rotating exhibits of modern Ecuadorian and other Latin American artists. Veintimilla 560 and 6 de Diciembre. © **02/2548-494.**

LaPosta Art Forum   Quito is known as a center for artists in South America. At this gallery, you can see firsthand what local artists are producing in the form of jewelry, paintings, sculpture, pottery, and photos. Juan León Mera N23-106 and Wilson. ✆ 02/2544-185.

BOOKS

Café Libro ⍟⍟   This is my favorite bookstore in Ecuador. They have an extensive collection of books in Spanish and English, with loads of books on natural history and tropical biology, as well as a fabulous collection of Ecuadorian and Latin American literature. Poetry readings, lectures, and concerts are often held here. Leonidas Plaza N23-56. ✆ 02/2234-265. www.cafelibro.com.

Confederate Books   Specializing in English-language books, this place buys and sells just about anything you may want in English. As such, it offers the largest selection of English-language reading, especially novels and easy-reading books for travelers. Calama 410 and Juan León Mera. ✆ 02/2527-890. www.cafelibro.com.

Libri Mundi   Similar to Café Libro in terms of quality, quantity, and selection, this is another excellent bookstore in the Mariscal district. Housed in a rambling old home, it stays open through siesta. Hermano Miguel 8–14 and Mariscal Sucre. ✆ 02/2843-783.

HANDICRAFTS

Exedra   This not-for-profit community of stores helps support scholarships for poor children. You'll find a variety of artwork here, including ceramics, acrylics, books, lithographs, painted furniture, and tapestries. There are also several antiques stores and a cafe. Carrión 243 and Plaza. ✆ 02/2224-001.

Galería Latina   Like Olga Fisch (see below), Galería Latina specializes in high-quality handicrafts. You'll find great pottery and a nice selection of alpaca sweaters, in addition to silver and gold jewelry, textiles, and even some antiques. Open Sunday. Juan León Mera N23–69 (833), between Baquedano and Wilson. ✆ 02/2540-380.

Olga Fisch Folklore ⍟⍟ *(Finds)*   We have Olga Fisch to thank for recognizing and inspiring the creation of high-quality, locally made handicrafts. As an artist, Fisch had a very keen eye, and she worked with indigenous groups to create carpets, figurines, jewelry, and decorative arts based on their traditional understanding of the arts. Everything here is displayed in a gorgeous showroom. This store carries high-end art, crafts, and clothing, and the prices reflect the difference in quality that you'll find between the offerings here and those at the street markets. A nonprofit museum here supports the development of these arts in indigenous communities. I suggest that you visit the museum first to get an idea of the local artisan traditions—it will help you understand what you are looking at in the showroom. In addition to the main shop, Olga Fisch has several other storefronts around Quito, including inside the Quicentro and San Marino malls, as well as at the Hotel Patio Andaluz (p. 106), and inside both the Guayaquil and Quito airports. It's open during siesta. Av. Colón E10–53 and Caamaño. ✆ 02/2541-315. www.olgafisch.com.

Tianguez ⍟⍟   Tianguez showcases products similar to those you'll find at Olga Fisch and Galería Latina, including masks, ceramics, and all sorts of pieces inspired by pre-Columbian artisan traditions. Tianguez means "market" in Quichua, and it's an especially appropriate name because the store is housed in a sprawling, mazelike old market in Old Town under the San Francisco church. It feels like the catacombs in Rome. A not-for-profit organization, Sinchi Sacha, runs Tianguez and supports indigenous and *mestizo* artisan groups. It's open Sunday and during siesta. Plaza San Francisco. © 02/2230-609. www.sinchisacha.org.

JEWELRY

In addition to the places listed below, you'll find excellent artsy jewelry for sale at the Fundación Guayasamín (see above).

Ag Joyería   Featuring a broad selection of silver and stone jewelry from across Ecuador and other Latin American countries, this place also features antiques and other craft items. Reina Victoria and Juan León Mera 614. © 02/2550-276.

Galería Aymara   This beautiful jewelry store features a wide selection of fantastic rings, bracelets, earrings, and necklaces. Most of the jewelry is silver with semiprecious stones, and most of the designs are unique to this store. Reina Victoria 1110 and Cordero. © 02/2549-088.

LEATHER GOODS

Aramis   A small local chain, these folks carry a range of high-quality locally produced leather works and leather wear. In addition to the main shop listed here, there are outlets in the Centro Comercial Espiral, on Avenida Amazonas and Jorge Washington. Av. Amazonas N24–142 and Mariscal Foch. © 02/2542-559.

MUSIC

You'll see CDs of Ecuadorian pop and traditional Andean folk music for sale at many gift shops around Quito. You'll also see hawkers selling CDs on the streets around the city, though most of them are poor-quality bootlegs. For the best selection, head to the local outlet of **Tower Records** (© 02/2920-415; www.towerrecords.com.ec), in the Centro Comercial Quicentro.

PANAMA HATS

Ortega P. & Hijos ***   This is the local outlet for renowned Cuenca hat manufacturer Ortega and Sons. If you aren't able to get to Cuenca, or to the other traditional Panama hat–making cities of Montecristi and Jipijapa, this is where you should pick up your *super fino*. If you really wait until the last minute, you can visit their outlet at the airport, but the selection there is reduced, and the prices slightly inflated. Isable La Católica N24–100 and Madrid. © 02/2526-715; www.homeroortega.com.

TEXTILES

Magic Hand Crafts *   With an excellent selection of alpaca sweaters, this is the place to come if you're looking for something of better quality than that sold at the street markets. These folks work directly with weavers and producers, and have some unique designs you won't find elsewhere. Juan León Mera N24–237 and Cordero. © 02/2542-345.

Punto en Blanco *Finds*   This is one gorgeous linen store. You'll find beautiful lace place mats, towels, pillowcases, and wonderful baby clothing, all handmade. It's closed Saturday and Sunday. Veintimilla 560 and 6 de Diciembre. © 02/2541-843.

8 Quito After Dark

From elegant opera performances to dirt-cheap all-you-can-drink bars, Quito offers a range of nocturnal activities for visitors and locals alike. The Mariscal sector, the hub for partying and dining out, has restaurants and "here today, gone tomorrow" pubs and clubs pumping out popular salsa and infectious *reggaetón* beats until daybreak. To find out what's going on in Quito while you're in town, pick up a copy of *Quito Cultura* (www.quitocultura.com), a monthly Spanish-language events guide that includes theater listings, concerts, and general cultural events.

In 2001, the city government issued a new law stating that all bars and clubs must close at midnight on weekdays and 2am on weekends. But this is only sporadically enforced, and many clubs have found ways around it, including declaring themselves private parties.

Warning: Remember that, at night, Quito can be quite dangerous, especially near the bars and clubs. Take a cab, even if it's only for a few blocks; bartenders can call a taxi for you. If you have a cellphone, dial © **02/2222-222** for a taxi 24 hours a day.

THE PERFORMING ARTS

Quito has a relatively important performing-arts scene, and the majority of theaters are located in Old Town. Performances include traditional theater pieces, political satire, ballets, dance shows, classic opera, and comedies.

The **National Symphony** performs weekly in different venues around town, including some colonial churches; call © **02/2256-5733** for up-to-date information. Every Wednesday at 7:30pm, the **Ballet Andino Humanizarte** (© 02/2967-152) performs traditional Andean dances at the Fundación Cultural Humanizarte, on Leonidas Plaza N24–226 and Lizardo García. The **Ballet Folkórico Nacional Jacchigua** ★ (© **02/2952-025;** www.jacchiguaesecuador.com) performs traditional dances and songs on Wednesday and Friday nights at 7:30pm at the Teatro Aeropuerto. Tickets cost $12 to $14 (£6.60–£7.70), and are often easiest to buy through **Metropolitan Touring** (© **02/2988-200;** www.metropolitan-touring.com) or through your hotel tour desk or concierge.

The newly restored **Teatro Nacional Sucre** ★★ (© **02/2572-823;** www.teatrosucre.com), in Old Town's Plaza del Teatro Manabí N8–131, between Guayaquil and Flores, first opened its doors in 1867; it's Quito's most popular theater and offers a varied and exciting events program including contemporary theater, ballet, electronic-music performances, and opera. Free concerts and street shows put on by the theater frequently take place just outside, on the Plaza del Teatro. Despite being almost completely destroyed by a fire in 1999, the restored neoclassic **Teatro Bolívar** (© **02/2582-486;** www.teatrobolivar.org), at Flores 421 and Junín, continues to host and produce a range of cultural events including theater, dance, music, and Latin American cinema.

Another important outlet for the performing arts is the **Casa de la Cultura Ecuatoriana** (© **02/2902-272;** www.cce.org.ec). Founded in the 1940s by writer, politician, and diplomat Benjamin Carrión ("If we can't be a military or economic power, we can, instead, be a cultural power fed by our rich traditions"), the Casa offers an extensive repertoire of events including rock concerts, art exhibitions, and performances by the National Symphonic Orchestra. It also houses one of the city's most important museums, the **Museo Nacional del Banco Central del Ecuador** (p. 121), which contains important archaeological artifacts, as well as an extensive collection of Ecuadorian traditional and contemporary artwork.

The newly constructed **Teatro del CCI,** at CCI Iñaquito, Avenida Amazonas and Nacionas Unidas (© **02/2921-308**), which opened its doors in January 2006, is a fine example of a modern theater with the latest technology in sound and lighting, offering up a mix of contemporary dance, theater, and music.

Quito is becoming an ever-popular destination among international artists. Recent concerts have featured Shakira, electronic DJ Paul Van Dyke, and North American industrial-metal musicians Fear Factory. The majority of large blockbuster concerts are held at **Coliseo Rumiñahui** (Ladrón de Guevara and Toledo), **Casa de la Cultura Ecuatoriana** (see above), the **Plaza de Toros** (© 02/2229-369; north of the intersection of Av. Amazonas and 10 de Agosto), or the much larger **Estadio Olímpico Atahualpa** (© 02/2247-510; 6 de Diciembre and Naciones Unidas). Check local papers for listings and ticket outlets.

For a more mellow vibe, check out the recently inaugurated **Casa de la Música** (© 02/2261-965), at Valderrama and Avenida Mariana de Jesús. It hosts traditional, folkloric, classical, and jazz concerts and recitals including performances by visiting international artists and orchestras.

Quito's cultural panorama changes quite dramatically during the first week of December when the **Fiestas de Quito,** celebrating the founding of the capital, transform the city into one huge party. Festivities include profoundly Spanish traditions such as bullfighting in the Plaza de Toros and flamenco dancing. Copious amounts of alcohol consumption accompany live music in *chivas* (open-air trucks with traditional bands carrying beer-swigging partygoers through the city streets); revelers rock out at important alternative music festival **Quitofest,** and the city comes to a standstill with never-ending street parades.

For the duration of August, Quito is also host to a popular arts festival offering a substantial list of art exhibitions, theater, and dance in cultural institutions all over the capital. Almost all performing-arts events are done in Spanish. Consult www.quitocultura.com for an extensive guide, or www.quito.com.ec, which has listings in English.

LIVE MUSIC

Over the last few years, the live music scene has really started to evolve in Quito, and an increasing number of bars and clubs now have bands and musicians performing. The city's scene, popular with local musicians trying to gain a larger following, is varied and includes jazz, salsa, pop, rock, metal, and alternative among other musical styles.

Some live performances to watch out for are those by the jazz quartet **Plaza Foch** on Monday, Wednesday, and Saturday at Coffee Tree (Plaza Foch and Reina Victoria), and the Latin jazz band **Cabo Frío.** A good place to look for jazz is the restaurant and bar **El Pobre Diablo** (© 02/2235-194), in La Floresta on Isabel La Católica E12–06 and Galavis. Other groups to watch out for at various venues are some of Ecuador's most influential bands on the South American rock-and-metal scene: **Pulpo3, Muscaria,** and **Sal y Mileto.** Also worth a mention are the psychedelic pop-electronic group **Can Can** and, for a truly Caribbean flavor, **Hector Napolitano.**

THE CLUB, MUSIC & DANCE SCENE

There is certainly no shortage of places to let loose on the dance floor in Quito. Most popular among Quiteños are salsa, electronic, and *reggaetón* rhythms. You'll be harder pressed to find a decent selection of rock, alternative, or jazz clubs.

Quiteños and visitors alike mainly flock to the Mariscal sector to check out the capital's nightlife. With a range of restaurants, bars, and clubs, Mariscal is certainly Quito's hottest party spot. The majority of clubs are located around the streets Calama, Mariscal Foch, and Reina Victoria, or a few blocks north around Pinta and

Santa María. In addition to the places listed below, favorites among party-goers are **Tijuana** (© 02/2238-324), Reina Victoria and Santa María, a happening spot pumping out international dance and techno with a small cover charge; and **Blooms** (© 02/2600-324), Juan León Mera 1117 and Calama, a sweat-inducing and usually packed discothèque blasting typical South American party tunes; cover charge is usually around $7 (£3.85), which includes an open bar. Thursday night there's live Cuban music and dancing at **La Bodeguita de Cuba** ✦ (© 02/2542-476), Reina Victoria 1721 and La Pinta.

Beer House Café Concert   Mainly renowned for rock and metal concerts (see flyers posted around the city for the latest hard-core events), this is also a pop-dance haven. Open from Tuesday to Saturday, Beer House is relatively small with an intimate atmosphere and is almost always crowded. Cover charges average around $3 (£1.65), although rock and metal events usually cost around $6 (£3.30). Av. de los Granados E14–605 and Eloy Alfaro. © 02/2445-979.

Blues   One of Quito's most popular venues, this is a relatively large retro-style club playing classic rock until around 2am, when the music changes to a more electronic-cum-house vibe. Depending on the night, cover charges range from $5 to $10 (£2.75–£5.50); on Thursday there is an open bar and women get in free. República 476. © 02/2223-206.

Club Gia ✦✦✦ *(Finds)*   At the time of this writing, Gia is by far Quito's hottest and most happening club, with go-go dancers and a varied musical repertoire including anything from Offspring to Tiesto. Entrance costs $8 to $10 (£4.40–£5.50) on most nights, or as much as $15 to $20 (£8.25–£11) for special events. DJ Paul Van Dyke was recently here, and Shakira held her concert after-party at Gia. Jose María Ayora and Villalengua, behind the Quito Municipal administration building. © 02/2924-094. www.clubgia.com.

La Bunga   This is a hip party spot with a medium-size dance floor and a varied music selection including anything from Latino rhythms to rock. Guys are normally charged a $5 (£2.75) admission fee, while women get in free. Francisco de Orellana 899 and Yánez Pinzón. © 09/4837-666.

Macondo ✦✦   As one of the Mariscal's newest and trendiest bar-discothèques with minimalist decor, expect a variety of dance/house tunes, an exciting drinks menu, cocktail-shaking displays, and a positively uplifting atmosphere. Calama and Juan León Mera. © 02/2227-563.

No Bar ✦   Sweat-inducing and always packed to the gills on weekends, No Bar offers an energetic dance vibe, strong cocktails, and a meat-market scene. Entrance costs around $3 (£1.65), depending on the night. Calama 380 and Juan León Mera © 02/2545-145.

Seseribó ✦   Solely devoted to salsa, this is *the* club for salsa lovers. Probably the best and most popular *salsateca* in Quito, Seseribó pumps out infectious Latino beats in an intimate atmosphere. A cover charge of $6 (£3.30) is common. Veintimilla 352 and 12 de Octubre, basement of Edificio Girón. © 02/2563-598. www.seseribo.com.

THE BAR SCENE

Catering to all tastes, Quito's bar scene is extensive, offering options ranging from British-style beer pubs to sophisticated wine bars, and just about everything in between. The majority of places are situated in the Mariscal district. The newly renovated Plaza Foch is generally targeted toward those in search of classier venues (see "Plaza Foch: Ground Zero in Mariscal," below), while the majority of other bars, from

Plaza Foch: Ground Zero in Mariscal

The heart and soul of Quito's nightlife, the Mariscal district, has been dubbed "Gringolandia" by those who flock to the area to drink and dance the night away with the city's tourists and resident foreigners. The newly renovated Plaza Foch (also known as the Plaza del Quinde)—which during the last couple of years has been transformed from a seedy, run-down intersection to a pristine plaza—is the area's star attraction. Its excellent selection of bars and international restaurants target visitors in search of more upscale nightspots. In addition to hitting the bars, clubs, and restaurants right on the plaza, you can use the plaza as a great starting place for a bar or club crawl through the rest of the Mariscal district. Plaza Foch frequently hosts free, open-air live shows including performances by rock bands, dance groups, percussion and jazz ensembles; one group to watch out for is up-and-coming Jazz quartet XXL, who generally play on Wednesday and Saturday at 7pm outside the Coffee Tree (see below). With alfresco dining and tall heater lamps to keep the Quito nighttime chill at bay, the funky European-style Plaza Foch is especially packed on weekends, so arrive early to get a good outdoor seat. The following are a few of my favorite spots on the Plaza Foch, although the list is by no means exhaustive.

Coffee Tree ★   With front-row seats of the plaza's frequently staged live performances and a big screen showing all the important *fútbol* games, this cafe-bar is extremely popular among locals and tourists alike. Two-for-one offers change every day, the drinks list is extensive, and the menu is pretty good for bar food. Try their ice-cold Pilsener on tap. Plaza Foch and Reina Victoria. ✆ 02/2565-521.

Gaudí ★★   This is a new funky and stylish watering hole with an upbeat electronic vibe, friendly staff, trendy decor, and superb selection of wines, martinis, and extravagant cocktails. Grab a table on the outdoor terrace to enjoy a bird's-eye view of the plaza. Plaza Foch, 2nd floor. ✆ 02/2451-297.

Latitud ★★   It's always full to capacity and easy to see why: This increasingly popular Spanish-style wine-and-tapas bar guarantees an excellent night out. Choose from a variety of all-you-can-eat/all-you-can-drink menus, starting at $15 (£8.25). Lively Spanish music and dim lighting make for an intimate but upbeat atmosphere. Plaza Foch. ✆ 02/2528-919.

funky cafes to laid-back bars, are located in and around the streets Calama, Reina Victoria, and Juan León Mera. With such a variety of bars and pubs in one area, the Mariscal is perfect for a pub crawl, although it can sometimes get a little dodgy after dark, so it's advisable not to go alone. Bars usually only charge a cover if there is live music or another type of special event. The line between a bar and a club in Quito is sometimes a little blurry. Many bars pump up the volume as the night goes on, converting themselves into happening party spots.

Bungalow 6   The best thing about this bar-cum-club is that it frequently hosts live music, featuring some of Quito's best reggae artists such as Alma Rasta. Apart from that, this is a colorful party spot playing a selection of contemporary and classic tunes with a small dance floor, busy bar, and vibrant atmosphere. Corner of Calama and Diego de Almagro. ✆ 09/9810-209.

Huaina ✧   Dangerously strong $1 (55p) *cuba libres* and dance-floor craziness pretty much sum up this party spot. There is an ample seating area, and music depends on whatever takes the owner's fancy on a given night—requests are not uncommon. Cover is sometimes charged on weekends and the bar is closed on Monday. Calama and Reina Victoria, just past Sutra. ✆ 02/2526-468.

Naranjilla Mecánica ✧✧   The name of this club translates as "Clockwork Orange." Lavishly decorated and housing permanent art exhibitions, this is a great place for indulging in delicious cocktails while lounging on the comfy sofas and bean-bag chairs. They play ambient grooves here. Tamayo and Veintimilla. ✆ 02/2526-468.

Patatus ✧   Another place catering to the foreign customer, this pub-cum-disco has a friendly, English-speaking staff, two-for-one cocktail offers, and tasty $1 (55p) home-baked pizzas. Music varies from classic rock to hip-hop, but expect *reggaetón* and dance beats as the night progresses and the dance floor fills up. Theme nights are common and a cover is usually charged on weekends. Wilson E4-229 and Amazonas. ✆ 02/2505-233.

Red Hot Chili Peppers ✧   Although this is principally a Mexican restaurant renowned for its massive and mouthwatering fajitas, by night it is also a small and relatively laid-back bar serving the best frozen margaritas in the city. Foch 713 and Juan León Mera, ✆ 02/2557-575.

Reina Victoria   As Quito's most authentic British-style pub, with a fire place, pool table, and dartboard, Reina Victoria serves good old traditional pub grub and beer on tap in a genuinely comfy atmosphere. Check out their British-style pub quiz held every Wednesday. Reina Victoria 530 and Roca. ✆ 02/2226-369.

Six-Nine-Six   As one of Quito's few truly alternative bars, this hyper-hip music lounge with post-punk minimalist decor bangs out a selection of rock, metal, new wave, industrial, ska, trip-hop, reggae, and grunge. Frequent audiovisual tributes and live performances make this bar an alternative-music heaven. Most events are free of charge. Calama 454 between Amazonas and Juan León Mera.

Sutra   This bar-cafe is slightly larger and somewhat mellower than its sister-bar Sutra Lounge (see below). Extravagant decor complements the upbeat atmosphere with music to suit all tastes. Live ensembles generally play on the weekends; there is a heated outside seating area, a Sutra "gift shop," a diverse cocktail list, and a scrumptious menu. Calama 380 and Juan León Mera. ✆ 02/2509-106.

Sutra Lounge   With a laid-back, intimate atmosphere complemented by cozy sofas and beanbags, this bar-cafe is perfect for chilling out and sampling the delicious cocktails and traditional *canelazos*—a warm cinnamon tea-and-liquor concoction. Live music is sometimes on the agenda; if not, catch live-concert videos frequently shown on the big screen. Juan León Mera and Calama. ✆ 02/2509-106.

Turtle's Head   Boasting the best beer in town, with various options on tap, this British-American–style pub has its own on-site brewery, pool table, darts, and table soccer, as well as tasty pub food—ideal for homesick British or American visitors. La Niña 626 and Juan León Mera, ✆ 02/2565-544.

THE GAY & LESBIAN SCENE

Although 1998 saw important changes to the Constitution regarding the status of homosexuals in Ecuador, attitudes toward the gay and lesbian community still lag behind those of North America and Europe, partly owing to Ecuador's being a staunchly Catholic county. This is reflected in the fact that gay and lesbian nightlife is not particularly well publicized, although by no means nonexistent. Quito has a few homosexual hot spots, including those listed below. For a detailed lowdown and the latest happenings on Quito's gay and lesbian scene, check out **www.quitogay.net** or **http://quito.queercity.info**.

Bohemio　Quite popular among the younger gay crowd, and reputedly a good pick-up joint, Bohemio is Quito's longest-standing gay club. It pumps out popular dance tunes with a good party atmosphere. Admission is around $4 (£2.20) including a drink. Baquedano 188 and 6 de Diciembre. ✆ 02/2214-127.

La Boca del Lobo　A gay-friendly bar and restaurant in the heart of the Mariscal district, La Bova del Lobo has an English-speaking staff and is a trendy joint with dim lighting, imaginative decor, and electronic music, not to mention probably the most extensive cocktail list in Ecuador. Calama 284 and Reina Victoria. ✆ 02/2234-083.

Matrioshka　As one of Quito's best-established openly gay clubs, Matrioshka has a great party vibe and is one of Quito's better discos. This is definitely a popular party spots for gays and lesbians. Cover charge is around $5 (£2.75) with a drink included. Pinto 376 and Juan León Mera. ✆ 02/2275-617.

CINEMAS

As with most cities, Quito has its fill of mainstream cinemas as well as one or two alternative picture houses. Hollywood blockbusters, usually in their original English with Spanish subtitles, are most popular among moviegoers, along with Latin American cinema mainly consisting of Argentinean, Chilean, and Mexican productions. Two multiplex cinemas, **Multicines,** Av. Amazonas and Naciones Unidas, inside the CCI shopping mall (✆ 02/2259-677; www.multicines.com.ec), and **Cinemark,** Avenida de la República and América (✆ 02/2260-301; www.cinemark.com), are your best bet for new releases. Both have around seven or eight screens. If alternative cinema is more your cup of tea, check out the excellent **Ocho y Medio,** Valladolid N24–353 and Viscaya, near La Floresta (✆ 02/2904-720), Quito's only independent picture-house showing *cine arte,* classics, Latin American cinema, foreign films, and musical and dance productions. It also hosts the Eurocine film festival every May. Ocho y Medio also publishes the country's most extensive self-titled cinema guide, free of charge every month.

CASINOS

Gambling is legal in Ecuador and the majority of casinos operate a free entrance, free-of-charge drink policy. The city's most popular casinos are **Hotel Casino Plaza Caicedo,** Av. Shyris 1757 and Amazonas (✆ 02/2445-305), with 176 slots and 25 table games, and **Hotel Casino Hilton Colón Quito,** Avenida Patria and Amazonas (✆ 02/2501-919), with 91 slots and 12 table games.

9 Side Trips from Quito

The legion of Quito-based tour agencies and just about every hotel desk can arrange any number of tour options, like trips to Cotopaxi National Park. The most popular day trips out of Quito are probably to **La Mitad del Mundo** (see below and chapter 6), **Cotopaxi National Park** (see below and chapter 7), and the **market in Otavalo** (see below and chapter 6).

If you don't go with you hotel's tour desk or in-house agency, I recommend **Cotopaxi.com** (© 02/2909-640; www.cotopaxi.com), **Metropolitan Touring** (© 02/2988-220; www.metropolitan-touring.com), **Safari Ecuador** (© 02/2552-505; www.safari.com.ec), or **Surtrek** (© 02/2231-534; www.surtrek.com).

GUIDED TOURS & ADVENTURES

In addition to the tours and adventures listed below, see chapter 4 for detailed information on **mountain biking, bird-watching, white-water rafting, climbing and trekking,** and **horseback riding.** In each section, you will find recommended operators. In just about every case, you will find a Quito-based tour operator with day trips you can participate in for all of these different adventure sports and activities.

COTOPAXI NATIONAL PARK   Almost every travel agency in Quito offers some sort of day trip to Cotopaxi National Park. Most are only moderately strenuous and feature a hike from the parking lot to the *refugio*. You definitely will *not* have time to hike up to the summit. If you want to hike, horseback ride, or mountain bike around Cotopaxi National Park, be sure to ask your organizer what exactly the tour includes. A whole host of options are available. Most tours include lunch at a typical hacienda, or inside the park at Tambopaxi. *Note:* On almost all tours, you will have to pay an additional $10 (£5.50) national-park fee.

Guided tours to Cotopaxi run $30 to $60 (£17–£33) per person, depending on group size, length of tour, and other factors.

Alternatively, you can organize a day trip to Cotopaxi on your own. You can hire a taxi in Quito for about $60 to $80 (£33–£44) round-trip. The ride from Quito to the parking lot takes about 1½ hours. Once you reach the parking lot, you can then hike up to the *refugio* or glacier at your own pace while the taxi waits for you. This is my preferred way of visiting Cotopaxi. For more information on visiting the national park, see chapter 7.

OTAVALO MARKET   Though Saturday is the main market day, most Quito-based operators offer daily excursions to nearby Otavalo, and there's plenty of good shopping in Otavalo any day of the week. There's also a lot to see and do around the town. Most tours last all day, with a stop at the artisans market as well as visits to any number of nearby attractions including Cuicocha Lake, Peguche Waterfall, Mojanda Lakes, and Condor Park. Most tours include lunch at one of the area's historic haciendas.

Guided tours to Otavalo run $25 to $80 (£14–£44) per person. As with the tours to Cotopaxi, the price varies depending on group size, what's included, where you have lunch, length of tour, and other factors. For more information on Otavalo, the Otavalo market, and other attractions in the area, see chapter 6.

DESTINATIONS & ATTRACTIONS CLOSE TO QUITO
SAN JORGE ECO-LODGE & BIOLOGICAL RESERVE ✦

This mountain lodge just outside Quito gives you the best of several worlds. The original building here is an old hacienda once owned by former President Eloy Alfaro.

Formerly called the Hostería San Jorge, the San Jorge Eco-Lodge and Biological Reserve (© **877/565-2596** toll-free in the U.S. and Canada, or 02/2247-549; www.eco-lodgesanjorge.com) offers a range of room styles and a wide array of tours and activities. Bird-watching and horseback riding are the main draws here, and both are excellent. In addition, they have a pretty outdoor swimming pool, Jacuzzi, sauna, and steam room. The 300-hectare (740-acre) private reserve contains a number of ecosystems, including high barren plains, high-altitude rainforest, montane cloud forest, and subtropical mid-elevation rainforest. More than 800 species of birds have been recorded on the reserve.

Accommodations cost $65 to $132 (£36–£73). The owners have recently built a separate nature lodge in the cloud forests outside of Mindo (see below) and offer a range of combination tours.

GETTING THERE   The ecolodge is only around 20 minutes from Quito's Mariscal Sucre International Airport, making it a very reasonable alternative to city hotels, especially for nature enthusiasts. The hotel offers transportation to the lodge for $10 to $15 (£5.50–£8.25) per person each way.

LA MITAD DEL MUNDO (THE MIDDLE OF THE WORLD)

One of the most common souvenir photos taken in Ecuador is that which has a visitor with one foot in either hemisphere, straddling the equator. **Ciudad La Mitad del Mundo** (© 02/2394-806) is a tourist complex set up on the site where, in 1736, French explorer and scientist Charles-Marie de la Condamine made his final calculations to determine the precise equatorial line. With modern GPS technology, we now know that De la Condamine was close, but erred by some 180m (600 ft.). I find this tourist trap a bit cheesy and highly recommend you get your photo precise by visiting the new **Quitsato Mitad del Mundo Monument** (© 09/9701-133; www.quitsato. org), which is on the road to Otavalo (p. ###).

The centerpiece of this attraction is a large, trapezoidal monument topped with a large globe. At the top of the monument is a viewing area, reached by an elevator, with great views of the surrounding mountains and countryside. My favorite attraction here is the large scale model of colonial-era Quito, called **Museo del Quito en Miniatura (Quito in Miniature).** This is a great way to get your bearings before touring around the colonial core. On the site, there's also a separate **Museo de Etnografía (Ethnographic Museum),** with displays about Ecuador's various indigenous tribes and peoples, as well as a small **Planetarium.** All around are tourist shops and souvenir stands, snack bars, and restaurants. The whole place was built with a mock-colonial styling, sort of a miniature Epcot version of colonial Quito. Frequent shows of folkloric music and dance are performed. Quiteños flock here on Sunday.

Ciudad La Mitad del Mundo is open Monday to Thursday from 9am to 6pm, and from Friday to Sunday from 9am to 7pm. Admission is $3 (£1.65). Admission to the Ethnographic Museum, Planetarium, and Quito in Miniature is an additional $1.50 (85p) each.

Separate from the main attraction, but just a few hundred yards away, is the **Museo Solar Inti-Ñan (Inti-Ñan Solar Museum;** © 02/2395-122). This interesting attraction has a series of exhibits and ongoing experiments relating to the geography, astrology, and natural sciences of the region. Try your hand at balancing an egg on its end, and watch how water flows down a drain at the equator. This place is supposedly right on the equator, although I haven't yet checked this with a GPS. The museum is open daily from 9:30am to 5pm. Admission is $2 (£1.10).

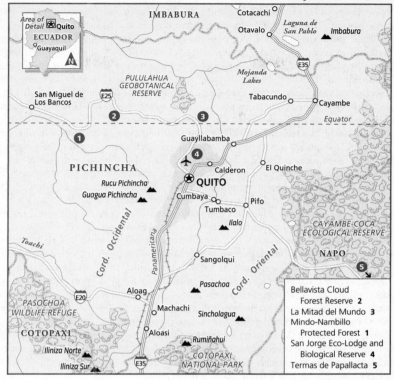

GETTING THERE Located some 23km (14 miles) north of Quito, near San Antonio de Pichincha, Ciudad La Mitad del Mundo is connected to Quito by a well-paved road. Just about every tour agency and hotel desk in Quito offers a half-day tour here. Prices range from $8 to $30 (£4.40–£17), depending on how exclusive the tour is, how many attractions it takes in, and whether or not lunch or admission fees are included in the price.

A taxi ride here from Quito should run about $12 to $15 (£6.60–£8.25) each way. Regular buses, marked MITAD DEL MUNDO, leave from the Cotocallao stop of the Metrobus trolley line. The trolley costs 25¢ (15p), and the bus costs an extra 40¢ (20p). Be sure to stay on the bus until you reach the actual monument, its final stop.

MINDO & BELLAVISTA CLOUD FOREST RESERVE ★★
Hiking through the forests of Mindo and Bellavista is one of the most exciting and rewarding side trips you can take from Quito. Within 2 hours, you will escape the city and find yourself in a cloud forest—a magical ecosystem where near-constant mist, as opposed to heavy rains, gives nourishment to a dense mix of trees, lichen, and epiphytes. Cloud forests are some of the most biologically diverse places on earth. Over 400 bird species have been recorded in the area, including the golden-headed quetzal, tanager finch and, my personal favorite, Chocó toucan. In addition, you will have the

opportunity to hike to remote waterfalls, ride inner tubes on pristine rivers, and marvel at the rich array of orchids, butterflies, bromeliads, and flowers.

While the under-2-hour drive makes this a potential (and popular) day-tour destination, I recommend spending at least a night or two. There are several lovely lodges in this region, with excellent naturalist guides, and a host of tour and activity options. In addition to bird- and wildlife-viewing, tour options include horseback riding, zipline canopy excursions, mountain biking, and visits to local butterfly farms.

Much of the cloud forest around Mindo is protected in the **Bosque Protector Mindo-Nambillo (Mindo-Nambillo Protected Forest),** which is administered by **Amigos de la Naturaleza** (© 02/2765-463). While most of the reserve is closed to the public, there are ample private reserves and publicly accessible trails through Mindo's cloud forests. The Mindo-Nambillo reserve was the source of controversy a few years ago, when the government ran an oil pipeline right through it, despite the objections of tourism and environmental groups. Today, the forest is recuperating and covering up much of the damage caused when the pipeline was pushed through.

Mindo is the more developed of these two cloud-forest destinations, with a host of hotels and lodges. The top hotel here is gorgeous **El Monte** ✛ (© 09/3084-675; www.ecuadorcloudforest.com). Accommodations are private, wood-and-thatch cabins set near the banks of the clear-flowing Río Mindo. This place is located a couple of miles south of Mindo, and the final leg of your journey to the lodge is via a handcranked cable car over the river. Accommodations are $86 (£47) per person, for a 2-day/1-night stay, including three meals, guided hikes and activities, and taxes. A new and similar choice is the lovely **Séptimo Paraíso** (© 02/2893-160 or 09/9934-133; www.septimoparaiso.com), which has its own private reserve.

The 720-hectare (1,778-acre) **Bellavista Cloud Forest Reserve** (© 02/2116-232 or 09/9490-891; www.bellavistacloudforest.com) is privately owned and has a variety of accommodations options, from private cabins to dorm rooms in the top of a large geodesic dome. It's not a fancy place, but the views over the forest canopy are dramatic, the food is excellent, and the nature guides will open up your eyes to a whole different world. Rates run $17 to $44 (£9.35–£24) per person, including three meals, but a whole host of package options are available, including meals, tours, and transportation.

GETTING THERE   If you're staying at a hotel here, you can usually arrange transportation with your hotel or lodge. Alternatively, a taxi from Quito should run around $40 to $50 (£22–£28). Mindo is serviced by a couple of daily buses from Quito. **Cooperativa Flor de Valle** (© 02/2527-495) has buses leaving Quito's main bus terminal, Terminal Terrestre, at 8am and 3:35pm, and returning at 6:30am and 2pm. On weekends there are additional buses and a slightly varied schedule. The ride takes around 2½ hours, and the fare is $2.50 (£1.40).

It's a little more complicated to travel to Bellavista on your own: You have to take the bus from Quito to the small town of Nanegalito, where you can arrange for a truck taxi to Bellavista. From Nanegalito, it's about a 45-minute ride to Bellavista. The ride should cost about $15 (£8.25) for the whole vehicle, which can hold up to six passengers. Any bus from Quito to Mindo, Puerto Quito, or San Miguel de los Bancos can drop you off in Nanegalito.

PAPALLACTA ✛✛

Situated at an altitude of 3,300m (18,825 ft.) and containing some wonderful lush green scenery, the small village of Papallacta boasts the country's cleanest, most picturesque **hot**

springs—a must while in Ecuador, especially if you've been doing any strenuous hiking or bumpy horseback riding. Papallacta is less than 2 hours from Quito by car or bus, but far from the hustle and bustle of the capital; it's along the road to Lago Agrio, and is an excellent, relaxing day trip from the city, or the perfect stop-off spot to or from El Oriente.

The mineral-rich baths are believed to possess healing powers; locals swear by them, claiming that they alleviate a number of medical conditions ranging from kidney ailments to arthritis. While there are a couple of inexpensive and basic hot-spring options in and around the village, I highly recommend the considerably larger and far better maintained **Termas de Papallacta** 🌟🌟 (✆ **06/2320-620** at the hot springs, or 02/2568-989 reservations in Quito; www.termaspapallacta.com), a couple of kilometers outside the center. They have exceptional pool and spa facilities, a hotel, and a restaurant. Take in the breathtaking views of the hilly landscape and, on a cloudless day, the majestic snowcapped Volcán Antisana (5,753m/18,874 ft.).

This complex houses various thermal pools ranging from frost-bitingly freezing to utterly scorching, all well-maintained and with water changed on a daily basis. You can opt to enter either the *balneario* (daily 6am–11pm; admission $6/£3.30; lockers 50¢/30p) or the **spa area** (daily 9am–5pm; admission $15/£8.25), which is generally less crowded and also has a sauna, steam room, and hydro-massage pools. In addition, the spa area offers a range of treatments, including massages, facials, clay body wraps, and aromatherapy at an extra charge. *Tip:* If at all possible, visit mid-week, because this place fills up most weekends.

Should you decide to stay overnight, lodging at **Termas de Papallacta** is an excellent option. The rustic rooms and cabins are spacious and comfy, with minimalist decor; large, cozy beds; and modern, well-equipped en-suite bathrooms. A double, including entrance to the *balneario* and breakfast, costs $90 (£50) per night. But the real advantage of spending the night here is that rooms are surrounded by scores of hot pools for the exclusive, around-the-clock use of hotel guests. And the tasty buffet breakfast is an ideal way to begin an oh-so-tiring day of lounging around the baths.

If you're looking for something less pricey, check out **Hostería La Pampa de Papallacta** (✆ **06/2320-624**), which has clean rooms with private bathrooms at $20 to $30 (£11–£17) for a double. An even cheaper alternative, just a stone's throw from the main hot-springs complex, is **Hostal Antisana** (✆ **06/2320-626**), which provides basic accommodations, perfect for backpackers on a budget, at around $8 (£4.40) per person.

Papallacta's surrounding areas are great for hikes and nature walks. Inquire at your hotel's reception desk, or at the Termas de Papallacta's own Exploratorio research center, located next the hot springs; they provide information on local flora and fauna, maps, and naturalist guides, and even organize excursions to the Cayambé-Coca Reserve or rafting tours on Río Quijos.

Since Papallacta is located at an altitude of over 3,000m (9,842 ft.), it can get pretty cold after dusk; be sure to pack warm clothing if you're staying overnight.

Your best bet for food is the excellent **restaurant** at the **Termas de Papallacta,** whose specialty is local, freshly caught trout. A snack bar sells sandwiches and light bites right at the hot springs. Outside the complex you can head down the dirt track to any of the relatively inexpensive *almuerzo* eateries, all of which offer typical Ecuadorian fare including fish; trout is on the menu everywhere. The **restaurant** at **Hostería La Pampa de Papallacta** serves rather tasty dishes.

GETTING THERE   The easiest ways to get here are to join an organized tour, or to arrange transportation and an overnight stay with the Termas de Papallacta itself. Alternatively, any bus heading to Baeza, Tena, or Lago Agrio (via Baeza) will drop you off in the village of Papallacta (or better yet, at the entrance road to the hot springs, a little before the village). From the well-marked turnoff here, it's a little over a mile to the hot springs. If you're coming by bus, you'll probably have to walk this last bit, unless you're lucky enough to flag down a ride. Buses leave from Quito's main terminal for Lago Agrio roughly every half-hour from 6am to 11:30pm. Two main bus lines, **Transportes Baños** (© 02/2570-884) and **Putamayo** (© 02/2583-316 in Quito, or 06/2833-819 in Lago Agrio), make the run and both will drop you off at the entrance to Termas de Papallacta. The ride takes around 2 hours, and the fare is $2.50 (£1.40).

If you're driving, take the highway (E20) east out of Quito toward Baeza. To get to E20 from downtown Quito, head north on Avenida Eloy Alfaro to Avenida de los Granados, and then turn right. This road becomes Highway E20. Follow any signs to Papallacta, Tumbaco Baeza, or El Oriente. Papallacta is about 65km (40 miles) southeast from Quito. The ride takes about 1½ hours.

The Northern Sierra

The equator cuts across Ecuador not far north of the Quito; besides delineating the planet's hemispheres—and determining which way water circles before heading down a drain—this line also forms the rough boundary for Ecuador's northern Sierra.

The crown jewel and most popular destination of these northern highlands is the small, busy city of **Otavalo,** which has a world-famous artisans market. Besides doing some shopping, be sure to visit a few of these artisans' workshops and studios, which are spread around a handful of neighboring towns and villages.

Several of the country's better haciendas and boutique resort hotels are here, too, and the area is great for hiking, mountain biking, or horseback riding. In particular, **Cuicocha Lake** and the **Mojanda Lakes** are fabulous spots for hikers of any ability, while the **Intag Cloud Forest Reserve** is a must-see destination for serious bird-watchers.

North of Otavalo lies the busy little city of **Ibarra** and its satellite suburb of **San Antonio de Ibarra,** where you'll find some of the best woodcarving craftsmen in all of Ecuador. From Ibarra, the Pan-American Highway continues north to Tulcán and the Colombian border.

1 Otavalo ✶✶

95km (59 miles) N of Quito, 515km (319 miles) NE of Guayaquil, 537km (333 miles) N of Cuenca

Otavalo is one of Ecuador's most popular destinations. The locals, known as Otavaleños, have been famous for their masterful craftsmanship for centuries, and the artisans market here is world-renowned. Otavaleños still wear traditional clothing and cling to their heritage. Men wear their long straight black hair in distinctive ponytails, and women wear multistranded, bead necklaces. Saturday is the main market day, when the impressive market spills out over much of this small city. Luckily for travelers with tight schedules, however, the market has become so popular that it now takes place on the other 6 days of the week, too, albeit on a smaller scale. In addition to shopping at Otavalo's market, you can explore the back roads of the province and visit local studios. Some of the smaller towns specialize in specific crafts: **Cotacachi,** for example, is known for leather work, **Peguche** for its weaving, and **San Antonio de Ibarra** for its age-old woodcarving techniques.

Even nonshoppers will love Otavalo and its surroundings. The town has an almost perfect setting. It's nestled in the Sunrise Valley in the shadow of two protective volcanoes, **Cotacachi** and **Imbabura.** According to local legend, Cotacachi is the area's symbolic mother, and Imbabura is the father standing watch. To feel the inspirational powers of Mother Nature, I recommend spending a few days exploring the area, breathing in the fresh air, gazing at the dark-blue waters of the local crater lakes, and

The Northern Sierra

standing in awe of the snow-covered volcanoes. Plus, after you find the perfect alpaca sweater, you can wear it as you stroll around **Cuicocha Lake** or hike in the mountains.

ESSENTIALS

GETTING THERE & DEPARTING

BY PLANE   The closest airport with regular traffic is Quito's **Aeropuerto Internacional Mariscal Sucre** (✆ 02/2430-555). See p. 22. From the airport you can hire a taxi or shuttle to Otavalo (see below).

BY BUS   Buses leave Quito's main bus terminal, Terminal Terrestre, roughly every 20 minutes between 5am and 10pm. Two former rivals, **Cooperativa Los Lagos** and **Cooperativa Otavalo** (✆ 02/2585-360 in Quito, or 06/2920-668 in Otavalo) have partnered and now have a monopoly on this route—although buses may be labeled with either name. The ride takes 2 to 2½ hours, and the fare is $2.60 (£1.45). Buses to Ibarra and Tulcán drop off folks along the highway just outside of town, and do not enter the main bus terminal of Otavalo.

Otavalo's main bus terminal, Terminal Terrestre, is located on Quito and Atahualpa, about 8 blocks—or a 15-minute walk—from Plaza de los Ponchos. Taxis are always available at the bus terminal.

Otavalo

ATTRACTIONS ●
Catholic church **4**
Instituto Otavaleño
  de Antropología **12**
Museo de Tejidos El Obraje **1**
Otavalo Market **10**

ACCOMMODATIONS ■
Hostal Rincón Viajera **9**
Hotel Ali Shungu **11**
Hotel El Indio Inn **5**
Hotel Otavalo **3**
Samay Inn **6**

DINING ◆
Hotel Ali Shungu **11**
Pizza Siciliana Otavalo **8**
Quino Restaurante **2**
Restaurante Mi Otavalito **7**

BY SHUTTLE   Every hotel desk and tour agency in Quito sells day tours to Otavalo and shuttle tickets aboard minivans and buses. The rate runs around $5 to $12 (£2.75–£6.60) per person each way for just transportation, and around $25 to $45 (£14–£25) for a day tour, including lunch. These shuttles and tours will pick you up at most hotels in Quito.

If your hotel desk can't set one up for you, contact **Grayline Ecuador** (© 02/2907-577; www.graylineecuador.com) or **Metropolitan Touring** ✦ (© 02/2988-200; www.metropolitan-touring.com).

BY TAXI   A taxi holding up to four passengers should cost $40 to $50 (£22–£28) from Quito to Otavalo.

BY CAR   To reach Otavalo by car, take the Pan-American Highway (E35) north out of Quito. It's a fairly straight shot, and Otavalo is located just off the highway. You will pass first through the towns of Calderón and Cayambe. There are two $1 (55p) tolls between Quito and Otavalo. The ride takes around 1½ hours.

GETTING AROUND

It's easy to get around Otavalo and the surrounding area by taxi and local bus. Taxis are plentiful. A ride anywhere in the city of Otavalo itself should cost only $1 (55p).

If you're traveling farther afield and looking to explore Imbabura province, taxis can be hired for $5 to $8 (£2.75–£4.40) per hour. A one-way taxi fare to Cotacachi or San Antonio de Ibarra should cost $5 to $6 (£2.75–£3.30).

If you need a taxi, call **Taxis El Jordán** (© 06/2920-298), **Taxi Otavalo** (© 06/2920-301), or **Taxilagos** (© 06/2923-203).

Most of the surrounding communities, towns, and cities are connected to Otavalo by **local bus service.** Buses leave Otavalo every 5 minutes or so for Ibarra. Other buses head to Intag, Cayambe, El Quinche, Peguche, and Cotacachi. Your best source of information is to simply head to the bus station on Quito and Atahualpa. Bus rides to nearby towns or villages run 15¢ to 50¢ (10p–25p)

ORIENTATION

Otavalo is a compact city. Streets here are set on a squared-off grid running at an approximately 45-degree angle to true north. The main arteries through town are the parallel streets of Sucre and Bolívar, which run from southwest to northeast. There are two main plazas of note. **Parque Bolívar** is located on the southwestern end of the city and is Otavalo's civic center, with the main Catholic church on its northwest side and the municipal hall on its southwest side. The streets that border Parque Bolívar are Sucre and Bolívar, on two opposite sides, and Juan Montalvo and García Moreno. Toward the northeastern edge of the city lies the **Plaza de los Ponchos,** which is ground zero for the weekly market, and which has become a de facto artisans market every day of the week. The Pan-American Highway skirts the city to the north.

VISITOR INFORMATION

The **Otavalo Chamber of Tourism (Cámara de Turismo de Otavalo; © 06/2921-994)** runs a helpful information office on Calle Sucre and Calle García Moreno. You'll find another, similar office run by the **Municipal Tourism Office (Oficina Municipal de Turismo; © 06/2921-313)** on Avenida Bolívar near Calle Juan Montalvo.

En Route: Straddling Two Hemispheres

The Pan-American Highway north of Quito passes right through the equator close to Km 55. On your left, as you drive toward Otavalo, you'll see a cluster of souvenir stands and a small concrete globe allegedly sitting right on the equatorial line. Avoid the temptation to pull over here, and head a few hundred feet farther to the new **Quitsato Mitad del Mundo Monument** (© 09/9701-133; www.quitsato.org), which is on the right-hand side of the road.

Opened in 2006, this attraction was built and is run by the folks at Hacienda Guachala (see later in this chapter). The centerpiece here is a tall spire that works as one of the world's most accurate sundials. Stone inlays mark the cardinal directions, as well as the solstice limits and the exact equatorial line. As far as I know, this is the most precise of the Mitad del Mundo (Middle of the World) attractions in Ecuador, and if you have a GPS, bring it to check. At noon, the spire casts absolutely no shadow in any direction, and on the equinox, the shadow falls exactly on the equatorial line, which is the same width as the spire. The monument is open daily during daylight hours, and admission is free, although a donation is encouraged. Future plans here include the addition of a small museum and a multimedia presentation space.

Your best bet, though, is your hotel tour desk or a local tour agency. My favorite local agency is **Runa Tupari Native Travel** ✦✦, located right on Plaza de los Ponchos, between Sucre and Quiroga (© **06/2925-985;** www.runatupari.com). They are not-for-profit and work to support rural indigenous communities.

FAST FACTS   If you need to contact the **police,** dial © **101,** or © 06/2920-101. The main hospital in Otavalo, **Hospital San Luis** (© **06/2920-444**), is located on Sucre and Estados Unidos. The **post office** is adjacent to Plaza de los Ponchos, on the corner of Salinas and Sucre; it's on the second floor of a dreadful building that is con-stantly under construction. Yes, it looks as though the building has been condemned, but it hasn't, so head up the stairway and walk past the miniconstruction site to the post office.

Banks are abundant in Otavalo. There's a **Banco Pichincha** (© **06/2920-214**) on Bolívar 614, near García Moreno, and a **Banco del Pacífico** (© **06/2923-300**) on the corner of Bolívar and García Moreno. You'll find another branch of Banco Pichincha just north of Plaza de los Ponchos, on Sucre between Quiroga and Quito.

There are plenty of pharmacies around downtown Otavalo. The **Farmacia Otavalo** (© **06/2920-716**), at Colón 510 between Sucre and Juan Jaramillo, is very helpful. Pharmacies work on a *turno* system, which means that each pharmacy periodically takes responsibility for being open 24 hours.

It's easy to find an Internet cafe in Otavalo; there are over a half-dozen within 2 blocks of the Plaza de los Ponchos. Fast connections can be found at **Native C@ffee Net** (© **06/2923-540**), on Calle Sucre between Colón and Morales. Rates run around 50¢ to $1.50 (25p–85p) per hour.

WHAT TO SEE & DO IN & AROUND OTAVALO

Aside from wandering around and shopping the outdoor markets (see below), there are few tourist attractions of note right in the town of Otavalo, although the sur-rounding towns, villages, and countryside are ripe with opportunities for sightseeing, shopping, and adventure activities.

IN TOWN

If you tire of the hustle, bustle, and commerce of the artisans market on the Plaza de los Ponchos, head for the more peaceful Parque Bolívar. You can grab a bench in the gardens here, or venture into the city's main **Catholic church.** Although very plain from the outside, the church features a small but ornate gold-leaf and gold-painted altar, as well as a pretty tiled ceiling.

If you want to learn about the process of weaving used by the artisans in and around Otavalo, head to the **Museo de Tejidos El Obraje** (© 06/2920-261), which was set up by Don Luis Maldonado and his wife, and has exhibits about the local weaving tools and techniques, as well as displays on the daily lives of the Otavaleños. This lit-tle museum is located on Calle Sucre 608, near Olmedo. It is open Monday to Satur-day from 9am to noon and 3 to 6pm. Admission is $2 (£1.10). They also offer classes on weaving.

On the campus of the University of Otavalo, just north of town across the Pan-American Highway, is the **Instituto Otavaleño de Antropología (Otavalo Institute of Anthropology;** © **06/2920-461**), which has a modest collection of archaeological relics and finds. But I recommend that you spend your precious time enjoying the other sites and activities around town, and get your archaeological fix at the Museo

Otavalo Globalized

There's a fair chance you'll have seen them on the streets or public plazas of cities around the world: a group of Otavaleños performing traditional Andean music and selling woven textile goods and other handicrafts. Known by both the Incas and Spanish conquistadores as talented weavers, Otavaleños are an indigenous group who live throughout much of Imbabura province, but who are named after the town with the world-famous Saturday textile market. They have woven their way into the history books, and their enduring culture stands out as a unique success story in a time of globalization and reduced ethnic identity.

With an official government seal of approval, Otavaleños and their craftsmanship were promoted—beginning in the 1950s—as part of a nascent tourism drive. Dutch artist Jan Schreuder, an Ecuadorian resident at the time, searched out pre-Columbian designs to incorporate into their rugs, hangings, and ponchos, and he is also, bizarrely, responsible for the Escher knock-offs and more modern motifs that are still seen today.

Things took off in the 1970s with increased international tourism. Peace Corps assistance helped hone styles and colors to suit "foreign" tastes, and the Otavalo market became a must-do for everyone visiting Ecuador. With typical enterprise, Otavaleño weavers have embraced market trends and set forth: to Colombia, the United States, Europe, and as far away as Asia and Australia. With a strong independent streak and plenty of business acumen, they use no middle men; the traditionally dressed couple sitting on an international flight to Amsterdam will have financed their flights, woven and bartered for their merchandise, and in turn, will keep all the profits from sales.

Otavaleños proudly display their culture; in fact, this is part of their successful "brand image." Quichua is their first language, although most also speak Spanish and many master other tongues as well. The men's long, braided hair is such a strong cultural symbol that Otavaleño men are not required to cut it off when they enter the Ecuadorian armed forces. Women wear embroidered white blouses, wool skirts, and many necklaces made of gold or red beads; the size, color, and quantity of the beads all carry cultural significance.

Many Otavaleño youngsters travel abroad—a rite of passage into the globalized world. The majority return home and add their experience and earnings to one of the world's most prominent indigenous groups.

Nacional del Banco Central in Quito (p. 121). The institute is open Tuesday through Friday from 9am to noon and 2:30 to 6pm, and on Saturday from 9am to noon. Admission is free.

OTAVALO MARKET &&&   Because there are often several, simultaneous markets taking place, it's probably most accurate to talk about Otavalo's "markets" (not "market"). The artisans market presents some of the best bargains in Ecuador and, just as importantly, some of the best people-watching. On Saturday, almost the entire city becomes one big shopping area, and itinerant vendors set up stalls on every available

COTACACHI-CAYAPAS
ECOLOGICAL RESERVE

0   4 mi
0   4 km

Teodoro Wolf   Yerovi

Cuicocha Lake

1

Cotacachi   To Ibarra   San Roque

2

Quiroga

E35

Carabuela

IMBABURA

Ambi

Ilumán   Imbabura ▲

Fuente de Salud **3**   Quinchuquí

Quito ★   Otavalo

ECUADOR

Guayaquil

Blanco

Peguche   Agato

Huarmi Imbabura ▲

San Juan **4**

Quichinche   San Vicente

Otavalo

6   **5**

Laguna de San Pablo

ACCOMMODATIONS & DINING ■

Eugenio Espejo   Araque **10** →

7

Cushnirumi

San Javier

Panamericana

San Pablo del Lago **9**

Itambi

Ali Shungu
     Mountain Lodge **6**
Casa Mojanda **7**
Hacienda Cusin **9**
Hacienda Guachala **11**
Hacienda Pinsaquí **3**
Hacienda Zuleta **10**
La Mirage Garden
     Hotel & Spa **2**

San Rafael
González Suárez

ATTRACTIONS ●

Mojanda
Lakes

E35

Fuya Fuya ▲ **8**

Laguna Negra

Cuicocha Lake **1**
Mojanda Lakes **8**
Parque Condor **5**
Peguche Waterfall **4**

PICHINCHA

Laguna Chiquit

To Quito ↘ **11** ↘

speck of sidewalk and alleyway. It's not just for tourists, either; Ecuadorians come here from miles away, to peddle and buy high-quality, handmade goods. The Otavaleños are extremely friendly and helpful, and they wear beautiful traditional clothing. Overall, this is one of the most colorful markets in Ecuador, and the handicrafts are of excellent quality.

Some of the most interesting buys available here include handmade alpaca sweaters, soft alpaca scarves, wool fedoras, colorful straw bags, hand-embroidered blouses, ceramics, tapestries, fresh pineapple, and llamas. *Yes,* llamas. Early in the morning on Saturday, there is an animal market, where you can exchange your cow for a llama or simply buy a dozen chickadees. To get to the animal market from the main plaza, walk down Sucre or Bolívar to Morales. Take a right on Morales and walk straight for about 5 blocks and cross the bridge. Turn right after the bridge and then take a left at the next main street. The animal market is about a half-block up. Get here early (around 7 or 8am) because the market closes down at 10am. There is also an excellent fresh-produce market in Plaza 24 de Mayo.

Though Saturday is market day, there is a relatively complete market every day in Plaza de los Ponchos. Whenever you visit, you'll find the same great crafts on sale here, and the same beautiful people selling them. *Tip:* I find that the Saturday market is a bit overwhelming; in fact, I prefer coming on a weekday, when I don't have to visit millions of stands to be sure that I have found the perfect bag or hat. You might also be able to bargain better on an off-day, since fewer tourists mean less demand, and sellers are often a bit more flexible if they really want to make a sale.

Shoppers should expect to do some bargaining, but I've found that prices will only drop a dollar or two (or 20% at most). Don't worry—the asking price is usually quite low, and everything here is already a bargain.

EXPLORING THE AREA

Many of the textiles and crafts sold in Otavalo's markets are produced in the towns and villages nearby. Outside Otavalo, you can visit weavers' studios in Peguche, leather shops in Cotacachi, and woodcarving workshops in San Antonio de Ibarra.

Nature lovers should also take note: With snow-covered Volcán Cayambe overhead and green mountains in the distance, Imbabura province is a place of stunning beauty. There are several excellent hiking possibilities in the area, including one from Otavalo to the Peguche waterfall, and a 4-hour hike around Cuicocha, a picturesque crater lake. All the travel agencies and tour desks in Otavalo can arrange hiking, trekking, and horseback-riding excursions to a range of beautiful and off-the-beaten-path spots in the area, as well as guided tours to the towns and artisans workshops all around outlying towns and villages.

Runa Tupari Native Travel 🏵🏵, located right on Plaza de los Ponchos between Sucre and Quiroga (✆ **06/2925-985;** www.runatupari.com), and **Dicency Viajes,** on the corner of Sucre and Colón (✆ **06/2921-217**), are the two best agencies in town. Both offer a wide range of tours, hikes, and adventure activities around the area, including guided tours to all the sites and destinations listed below as well as organized climbs of Mount Cotacachi (4,939m/16,200 ft.).

CUICOCHA LAKE 🏵🏵   Cuicocha is a sparkling blue crater-lake formed about 3,000 years ago, when the crater of the lake's namesake volcano collapsed during an eruption. The crater was covered with snow, which eventually melted and formed the lake. When the Incas came here, they thought that one of the islands in the middle looked like a *cuy* (guinea pig), hence the name Cuicocha (Guinea Pig Lake). You can take a motorized boat ride out and around the two islands in the middle of the lake, although you can't get off and hike on them. From the boat, along the shores and in the shallows, you will see *totora,* the reed used in this area for making baskets and floor coverings. A 20- to 40-minute boat ride should cost no more than $2 (£1.10) per person. Be sure to bring a warm sweater—the wind here can be vicious.

I prefer hiking here to riding around on a boat (although you can certainly do both). An 8km (5-mile) trail loops around the rim of the crater, which takes about 4 hours to circle. But even if you walk along it for only 5 or 10 minutes, you'll be able to see Otavalo, Cotacachi, Cayambe, and all the volcanoes of Imbabura province. The setting and views are consistently striking. There's a small visitor center, near the end of the road leading from Quiroga to Cuicocha, which has some basic exhibits on the geography, geology, and local history of the lake, and serves as the administration center for this entrance into the Cotacachi-Cayapas Ecological Reserve, of which Cuicocha is a part. Admission is $1 (55p) to visit the lake, $5 (£2.75) to visit other areas of the reserve. For more information on the Cotacachi-Cayapas reserve, see chapter 4.

Cuicocha Lake is located about 16km (10 miles) west of the town of Cotacachi. Although a paved road leads almost to the crater's edge, no public transportation is available from Otavalo directly to Cuicocha.

Tip: I recommend taking a guided tour here, since robberies of unaccompanied tourists have been reported. If you're doing it on your own, it's best to hire a taxi in Otavalo for the full trip, or to take a bus from Otavalo to Cotacachi or Quiroga, and then hire a cab. If you hire a cab, be sure to either pay for the wait time, or designate a time for your return ride.

COTACACHI   Cotacachi is a sleepy little pueblo with incredible vistas. From here, you can see snow-covered Volcán Cayambe and the lush green mountains in the distance. But no one comes here for the views, because Cuicocha, about 10 minutes up the road, offers much better views—perhaps the best in all of Imbabura province. People do, however, come here to shop. Cotacachi is famous for the leather stores that line Avenida 10 de Agosto. Offerings range from wallets and purses to shoes and clothing. Equestrian enthusiasts can shop for handmade saddles. The quality varies widely, but if you search hard enough you are bound to find some excellent work and great bargains. Cotacachi is about 15km (9½ miles), or 15 minutes, from Otavalo. You can easily take a public bus from the station in Otavalo, or hire a taxi for about $6 (£3.30) each way.

PEGUCHE   Peguche is home to some of the best weavers in Ecuador. If you stop in the main square, you can start off by visiting the gallery and workshop of José Cotacachi, a master weaver. Peguche is also famous for its musical instruments. You'll find various shops that specialize in making single-reed flutes and *rondadores* (panpipes), as well as guitars and *charangos* (a mandolin-like instrument with five pairs of strings). Traditionally, the back of a *charango* is made from an armadillo shell. If you visit the town on a guided tour (which I highly recommend), you will explore the back streets of Peguche and visit the homes of some of the town's best weavers while learning about the old-fashioned process of spinning wool.

Just outside the town is **Peguche Waterfall** ✸, a popular spot for tourists and locals alike. Peguche Waterfall is a tall and powerful torrent of water with lush vegetation on either side. Near the foot of the falls you'll find broad grassy areas with picnic tables and bench seating. Paths take you around the area, including one that goes to the top of the falls, with a sturdy wooden bridge taking you directly over the rushing water. The Peguche Waterfall plays an important role each year in the concurrent festivals of Inti Raymi and San Juan de Batista, which coincide with the summer solstice. Locals of both indigenous and Catholic faiths come to the falls for cleansing baths at this time of year.

A tiny town is located about 10 minutes by car from Otavalo. A taxi should cost $5 (£2.75) each way, and you can also walk to the falls from town in about 45 minutes. The route is well-worn and popular—just ask one of the locals to point you in the right direction.

Tips **Sunny Otavalo**

Otavalo is practically on the equator. It's also located at about 2,700m (9,000 ft.) above sea level. The sun here is extremely powerful. To top it all off, in the main market, there is not a trace of shade. Be sure to bring plenty of **sunscreen** and a **brimmed hat,** and carry water with you at all times. It gets very hot, so dress appropriately—light pants and a short-sleeved shirt will be fine. If you plan on heading out to Cuicocha Lake, you'll also need a sweatshirt (it gets cold up there).

MOJANDA LAKES 🎯   After Cuicocha Lake, the Mojanda Lakes offer some of the best and most scenic hiking around Otavalo. The extinct volcano Fuya Fuya stands majestically above the three high mountain lakes, creating a beautiful setting. This is a great spot for bird-watching—more than 100 species of birds are found here, including the giant hummingbird and the endangered Andean condor. Mojanda Lakes are located about 30 minutes south of Otavalo. A taxi here costs about $12 (£6.60) each way.

PARQUE CONDOR (CONDOR PARK) *Kids*   Although you'll find Andean condors on display here, you'll find a whole host of other bird species as well. The emphasis is on raptors, with a variety of local raptor species represented, including various different owls. Several large birds are brought out by trainers and allowed to fly each day at 11:30am and 4:30pm. The park is set on a high hillside with a lovely view over Laguna San Pablo, the Otavalo Valley, and Volcán Imbabura. There's a small restaurant with great views, as well as a children's playground.

Parque Condor (© 06/2924-429; www.parquecondor.com) is located outside Otavalo near El Lechero and Peguche. It is open Tuesday through Sunday from 9:30am to 5pm. Admission is $2 (£1.10). A taxi ride here should cost no more than $4 (£2.20) each way.

INTAG 🎯   This is a region of beauty and conflict. The hills, mountains, valleys, and ravines here are covered in rich cloud forests, and they're home to a wide array of wildlife and hundreds of bird species. Small communities get by on subsistence farming and coffee production. But large mining interests, led by Ascendant Copper, have their eyes and heavy machinery aimed at the mineral wealth that lies beneath the ground, and the Intag region has been ground zero for a tense and sometimes violent clash between local activists, environmental organizations, and Ascendant Copper. The **Intag Cloud Forest Reserve** (© 2648-509; www.intagcloudforest.com) is owned and run by Carlos Zorrilla, who has been a leader in trying to preserve the environment and ecosystems here. The bird-watching is phenomenal, and Carlos and his crew are great guides. Accommodations are available in rustic rooms inside the reserve. Water is heated by passive solar energy and all meals are vegetarian. Depending upon the size of your group, rates run $40 to $60 (£22–£33) per person per day, including three meals and a guided hike daily.

The Intag Cloud Forest Reserve is located several hours over rough dirt roads from Otavalo. You need a prior reservation to stay here. When making your reservation, Carlos and company will arrange transportation, or give you detailed information on how to arrive in your own vehicle or via public transportation.

Those looking to volunteer or help out with the conservation efforts should contact **DECOIN** (www.decoin.org), an organization that works closely with indigenous communities in the region on a range of environmental and social issues, including mining and sustainable tourism.

OUTDOOR ACTIVITIES

Hiking trails abound here. One of my favorite hikes is the 4-hour trek around Cuicocha Lake. Keep in mind, however, that robberies have been reported in the area, so it's best to do the trail with a guide. You can also hike from Cuicocha to the Mojanda Lakes, up Volcán Cotacachi, or around the Mojanda Lakes and up Mount Fuya Fuya. Both **Dicency Viajes** (© 06/2921-217) and **Runa Tupari Native Travel** 🎯🎯 (© 06/2925-985; www.runatupari.com) can provide experienced guides and help organize your hiking excursions. Both of these tour agencies also offer **horseback-riding** trips. One of the most popular is the trail around Cuicocha Lake. A half-day trip costs $40 to $60 (£22–£33) per person.

LEARN THE LANGUAGE

If you want to learn some Spanish, check in with the **Otavalo Spanish Institute** (✆ **02/2925-475;** www.otavalospanish.com), which offers a variety of intensive plans with one-on-one instruction, a home-stay with a local family and three meals daily, and various extra-curricular activities. They even offer classes in Quichua. Rates run $220 to $270 (£121–£149) per week, depending upon the number of hours of study per day.

WHERE TO STAY IN OTAVALO
MODERATE

Hotel Ali Shungu ★   This popular hotel is a definite step up from most of the downtown options. The large two-story building is built in a broad horseshoe around a large garden that attracts hummingbirds and other bird species. Ali Shungu translates as "good heart" in the native Quichua, and the owners are expatriated Americans who have put their hearts into this project and the area. The rooms are simple but comfortable, with firm beds and colorful art and handicrafts hanging from the walls. The two family suites are big, with two bedrooms and spacious living areas; they are located on the second floor and have large, inviting balconies. In addition to the rooms, all public indoor areas here are smoke-free. The most recent addition to the hotel has free Wi-Fi access, which extends to all the common areas and reaches most of the rooms as well. The **restaurant** here (see below) is one of the best in town.

Calle Quito and Calle Migue Egas, Otavalo. ✆ 06/2920-750. www.alishungu.com. 18 units. $40 (£22) double; $80 (£44) apt. No credit cards. Parking nearby. **Amenities:** Restaurant; bar; tour desk; laundry service; all rooms smoke free; free Wi-Fi. *In room:* No phone.

INEXPENSIVE

In addition to the places listed below, **Hotel Rivera Sucre** (✆ **06/2920-241;** www.rivierasucre.com) is another excellent option in this price range. This hotel is located in a lovely old building on Calle García Moreno 380, on the corner of Calle Roca.

Hostal Rincón Viajera *Finds*   There are scores of backpacker specials in Otavalo, but this place is my pick as the best of the bunch. The rooms are all kept clean and comfortable. About half have private bathrooms, worth the extra $1.50 (£85) per person. The public areas and friendly service set this place apart. There's a small central courtyard and a large third-floor rooftop terrace, with a separate covered area, featuring a game room and hammock area. Down below, guests gather nightly in a cozy lounge with a large brick fireplace.

Roca 11–07, between Quiroga and Quito, Otavalo. ✆ 06/2921-741. rincondelviajero@hotmail.com. 12 units; 6 with private bathroom. $16 (£8.80) double with shared bathroom, $19 (£10) double with private bathroom. Rates include breakfast and taxes. DC, MC, V. Free parking. **Amenities:** Restaurant; tour desk; laundry service. *In room:* No phone.

Hotel El Indio Inn   This glass-fronted high-rise hotel seems a little out of place in downtown Otavalo. The rooms are large, clean, and well kept, although lacking in any sense of style or personality. All come with a "minibar" selection of snacks and drinks, but without any fridge. Rooms are set around a pair of interior courtyards hung heavily with potted plants, and windows front only these interior courtyards. There's a game room with a pool table and an attached Internet cafe. The hotel's main restaurant,

La Cascada de Ensueños (The Waterfall of Dreams), serves good Ecuadorian and international cuisine in a pleasant room with a wall of glass facing the street, and an interior waterfall and garden, which gives the joint its name. This place should not be confused with the Hotel el Indio, which is a slightly older sister facility closer to the bus station.

Calle Bolívar 904 and Abdón Calderón, Otavalo. (✆ **06/2922-922** or (✆/fax 06/2920-325. hindioinn@andinanet.net. 33 units. $37 (£20) double. AE, MC, V. Free parking. **Amenities:** Restaurant; bar; tour desk; room service 7am–10pm; laundry service. *In room:* TV.

Hotel Otavalo *(Finds* This downtown option oozes colonial-era charm. Worn wooden floors, high ceilings, and rambling common areas are the highlights here. The large central courtyard area features a high atrium roof, and there are several lounge areas. I also really like the second-floor restaurant, which has seating in a series of rooms and around a central veranda. Accommodations here are simple, with minimal decorations and furnishings, although the beautiful woven bedspreads do brighten things up. No. 3 features a nice view over rooftops to the hills west of town.

Roca 504 and Juan Montalvo, Otavalo. (✆ **06/2920-416** or 06/2923-712. www.hotelotavalo.com.ec. 32 units. $30–$38 (£17–£21) double. DC, MC, V. Parking nearby. **Amenities:** Restaurant; bar; tour desk; 24-hr. room service; laundry service. *In room:* TV.

Samay Inn *(¥ (Finds* This simple, budget hotel, centrally located on Calle Sucre, just a block from the Plaza de Ponchos, is a great choice in Otavalo. The rooms all have wood floors and faux-stucco walls painted with bold primary colors and an aged-wash effect. All come with 53cm (21-in.) flatscreen televisions. A relaxing interior courtyard lounge on the second floor is enclosed by a tall brick wall. Interior brick arches and other design touches give this place more charm and class than you'd expect at this price. As with El Indio Inn, there are two Samay Inn sites in Otavalo—don't head to the one closer to the bus station.

Calle Sucre 1009 and Calle Colón, Otavalo. (✆ **06/2921-826.** samayinn@hotmail.com. 23 units. $20 (£11) double. DC, MC, V. Free parking. **Amenities:** Restaurant; bar; tour desk; laundry service. *In room:* TV.

WHERE TO STAY NEAR OTAVALO
VERY EXPENSIVE

Hacienda Cusín *(¥¥ (Kids* This 17th-century hacienda is a fabulous choice in the Otavalo area, especially if you're looking for a mix of luxury and history. Cusín sits on over 4 hectares (10 acres) of lush gardens and cobblestone courtyards overflowing with bougainvillea, orchids, and palm trees. Rooms are located in the renovated one-story hacienda and come with antique furnishings and high ceilings. The garden cottages are of somewhat recent construction, but have a wonderfully rustic feel; they're scattered throughout the lush grounds and come with working fireplaces and wood bed and armoires. The owner's suite is large enough for a family of four. All units have spacious bathrooms with lovely blue tiles. The friendly staff can help you arrange activities, including the popular overnight horseback-riding trip to Volcán Imbabura. Spanish-language classes are also available. There's a computer with Internet access for guests to use at the reception desk. The restaurant serves a wonderful dinner by candlelight so there's no need to leave the property after dark. A full meal plan here will run you $41 (£23) per day.

San Pablo del Lago, Otavalo. (✆ **06/2918-013.** Fax 06/2918-003. www.haciendacusin.com. 42 units. $105 (£58) double; $120 (£66) garden cottage; $250–$300 (£138–£165) suite. Suite rates include dinner. AE, DC, MC, V. **Amenities:** Restaurant; bar; tour desk; laundry. *In room:* No phone.

La Mirage Garden Hotel & Spa ★★★   If you're looking for luxury, you won't find a better hotel in the highlands than this member of the prestigious Relais & Chateaux. It's owned by Jorge Espinosa (the same guy who owns Mansión del Angel in Quito; p. 103); clearly, interior design and landscaping are his specialty. All the rooms are essentially suites, with separate sitting areas and fireplaces. Just about every one of them could be featured in the pages of *House & Garden*. Some rooms have brass canopy beds; others have antique wood frames. Crystal chandeliers brighten the rooms, while plush Oriental carpets decorate the floors. The spacious bathrooms come with extra-large showers. All the rooms have sloped wood ceilings, which gives them a rustic feel. Reina Sofía of Spain stayed in stately no. 114, and I'm sure she must have felt right at home. Room no. 109 overlooks a garden with a handful of colorful peacocks. You will surely be spoiled here: Turndown service consists of lighting the fire in your private fireplace and slipping two hot-water bottles in your bed. The spa here was the first one to open in Ecuador and it's a real classic. Indulge in clay baths and body massages, or treat yourself to a full-body purification performed by a local female shaman. The outdoor gardens are also magnificent. The outstanding restaurant offers the only fine-dining experience in the region.

At the end of Calle 10 de Agosto, Cotacachi. (C) **800/327-3573** in the U.S. and Canada, or 06/2915-237. Fax 02/2915-065. www.mirage.com.ec. 23 units. $250–$280 (£138–£154) double; $300–$700 (£165–£385) suite. DC, MC, V. Rates include breakfast and dinner. **Amenities:** Restaurant; bar; beautiful indoor pool; tennis court; tiny exercise room; full spa services; room service 7:30am–9pm; laundry service. *In room:* TV, hair dryer, safe.

EXPENSIVE

Hacienda Pinsaquí ★ (Moments)   Hacienda Pinsaquí is one of the great historic hotels of Ecuador. Simón Bolívar once stayed here. The over-200-year-old hacienda immediately transports you back in time with its antique floors that have the seasoned scent of old wood. The homey smell of well-worn fireplaces permeates the air. The narrow, old-fashioned hallways are filled with flowers fresh from the outdoor gardens. And the rooms are sumptuous; each one is unique, but all have a touch of old-fashioned country elegance. No. 8 has a magnificent canopy bed and beautiful antique furniture, as well as a separate sitting area where you can gaze out onto the property's wonderfully landscaped gardens. This room also has a sunken Jacuzzi tub set near a large window overlooking the gardens. Room nos. 9 through 30 are in a newer wing but are built to mimic the colonial-era style. In general, though, the bathrooms aren't perfect. Once you leave the comfort of your cozy room, you can walk around the property's gardens or explore the area by horseback—the hotel offers guided riding tours. Superb meals are served in an elegant dining room.

Pan-American Hwy., Km 5, Otavalo. (C) **06/2946-116** or 09/9727-652. Fax 06/2946-117. www.haciendapinsaqui. com. 30 units. $108 (£59) double. Rates include tax and breakfast. AE, DC, MC, V. **Amenities:** 2 restaurants; bar; tour desk; mountain bike rentals; room service 7am–10pm; laundry service. *In room:* No phone.

MODERATE

Ali Shungu Mountain Lodge ★   After decades in town, the owners of the popular and long-standing Ali Shungu Hotel have decided to seek some peace and quiet on a high hillside just outside Otavalo. Here you'll find four large, fully equipped houses; two have one bedroom, the others two bedrooms. Both have full kitchens and large comfortable living rooms. The one-bedroom units have a large dining room, which is used as the second bedroom in the other houses. There's a working woodstove and good views all around from the wraparound windows. Highest up the hill is the complex's main restaurant and lounge area. Excellent home-style meals are served here, and vegetarians can be heartily accommodated with advance notice. Locally produced organic fruits and vegetables are featured as much as possible. Sixteen hectares (40 acres) of private reserve surround the property. Several hours of guided horseback riding are included in the room rates, and there are trails through the neighboring cloud forest for self-guided hiking. A 2-night minimum stay is required.

1.9km (3 miles) outside Otavalo, near the village of Yambiro. ⓒ 06/2920-750. www.alishungumountaintoplodge. com. 4 units. $120 (£66) double. Rates include breakfast and a 4-course dinner. No credit cards. Free parking. **Amenities:** Restaurant; lounge; tour desk; laundry service; free Wi-Fi. *In room:* No phone.

Casa Mojanda *(Finds)*   Ever wonder what it would be like to stay in the middle of nowhere? Stay at the Casa Mojanda and you'll find out. The hotel is located only about 10 minutes outside of Otavalo, but the isolated 7.2-hectare (18-acre) property is nestled in a valley surrounded by mountains and rolling green hills. The vistas are phenomenal, unspoiled by any man-made structures. The cabins are rustic-chic; all have either tile or hardwood floors, antique dressers, small reed floor coverings, and tons of personal touches; several have their own fireplaces. You can enjoy the spectacular views from the comfort of your own bed. No. 6 is great for families—it has a kitchenette, a separate living room, and separate bedrooms. The gorgeous dining area, filled with antiques and local crafts, serves as the heart of the hotel. This is where you can enjoy scenic vistas as well as divine home-cooked meals, all made with food grown in the hotel's gardens. The English-speaking owners are charming and can help with kayak and mountain-bike rentals, as well as horseback-riding tours.

Mojanda Lakes (mailing address: Casilla 160), Otavalo. ⓒ 09/2731-737 or 06/2922-986. Fax 09/2731-737. www. casamojanda.com. 10 units. $140 (£77) double. Rates include breakfast and dinner. No credit cards. **Amenities:** Restaurant; lounge; wood-fire heated cedar hot tub; game room; massage; laundry service. *In room:* No phone.

INEXPENSIVE

Hacienda Guachala *(Value)*   Dating to 1580, this claims to be the oldest hacienda in Ecuador. One of the first structures built here was a little chapel, which is still standing, and features a faded fresco from the mid-1700s. At one point, the hacienda covered over 40,000 hectares (98,842 acres). It was here that García Moreno, who lived in the hacienda for 7 years, planted the first eucalyptus trees in Ecuador, many of which still flourish on the grounds. The hacienda then passed on to the family of Neptali Bonifaz, the country's first democratically elected president and founder of the Bank of Ecuador. The hacienda remains in the Bonifaz family.

Rooms here are more rustic than those at most of the other converted haciendas, but then again, the prices are substantially lower. All feature wood floors, working fireplaces, high ceilings, and rough wood beds and furnishings. Nos. 1 through 10 are slightly newer in feel and comfort. There's an inviting pool under a greenhouse roof, with tropical fruits and flowers planted around it. The hacienda's large church has been converted into a small museum that contains historic photos from the Bonifaz family and some pre-Inca pottery, including huge Cayambe pots. An old lounge area has a pool table on the grounds, and several computers offer Internet access. Horseback tours, specializing in nearby archaeological ruins, are offered. The owners were involved in the new Mitad del Mundo monument, Quitsato (p. 142). To reach this hotel, take the well-marked turnoff near Km 70 on the Pan-American Highway, and head another 2km (1½ miles) along the road to Cangahua.

Km 70 Pan-American Hwy., on the road to Cangahua, Cayambe. ⓒ 02/2363-042 or 09/8146-688. Fax 02/2362-426. www.guachala.com. 36 units. $40 (£22) double. AE, DC, MC, V. Free parking. **Amenities:** Restaurant; small, covered pool; tour desk; laundry service. *In room:* No phone.

Tree Tomato

When is a tomato not a tomato? When it's a tree tomato. Although the *Cyphomandra betacea* belongs to the same family as its more universally recognized bright red cousin, Solanaceae, the tree tomato grows as a small perennial shrub up in the hills, and looks like a colorful egg when ripe. Its succulent, tomato-like flesh is tart enough to pucker your lips—don't even think about eating the skin, which is more like a shell.

Tree tomatoes were cultivated by the Incas and probably originated in one of the Andean countries between Chile and Colombia. Today, they're grown commercially in New Zealand and Australia, as well as in Ecuador.

In Ecuador the tree tomato, or *tamarillo*, flourishes at 1,500 to 3,000m (5,000–10,000 ft.), and you will see them growing in the highlands. You can find both the tart golden-orange and smoother, deep-red varieties in any market around the country. Being rich in natural pectin, they make perfect setting agents for jellies and jams—orange and tree tomato are a sublime combination. You will most commonly find *tamarillo* served as a fruit drink or skinned and stewed as a dessert compote. It is also a popular local ice-cream flavor.

With supposed medicinal properties to treat everything from respiratory disease to obesity, stress, and colds—as well as improving your immune system and lowering cholesterol—the tree tomato seems to be a bit of a wonder fruit. And it's pretty good with rum, too.

WHERE TO DINE IN & AROUND OTAVALO

In addition to the places listed below, you can treat yourself to some fine dining, with advance reservations, at the restaurant at **La Mirage** (see above). You can also get great meals at **Casa Mojanda** (see above) and **Hacienda Cusín** (see above).

If you're looking for somewhere with a view, I suggest dining at a restaurant overlooking Lago San Pablo, a beautiful little lake considered sacred by the local indigenous populations. The restaurant of the **Hostería Puerto Lago** (© 06/2920-920; Lago San Pablo and Pan-American Highway, Km 5/12, Otavalo) sits right on the lake and serves delicious fresh grilled trout in addition to the usual Ecuadorian and Continental offerings. Almost every table has a lake view with magnificent Volcán Imbabura in the background. Main courses are $6 to $8 (£3.30–£4.40), and a set four-course meal runs $15 (£8.25). The restaurant is open daily from 7:30am to 9pm.

Hotel Ali Shungu 🌟🌟 ECUADORIAN/INTERNATIONAL   The cozy restaurant of this popular hotel is one of the best in the city. Heavy wooden tables are spread around the large central dining room, which features terra-cotta tile floors and a fireplace. Local and regional art and handicrafts serve as decor, and there's a small bar in one corner. I like to grab one of the tables near the long wall of picture windows, especially at lunchtime. The restaurant uses locally grown organic produce whenever possible. The tomato-basil soup is a house specialty and delicious. For a main dish, I recommend the Indian lamb curry or the spinach cheese pie. For lunch you can get excellent sandwiches on homemade bread, or one of their massive hamburgers.

Breakfasts are also excellent and worth it if you want a change from traditional Ecuadorian morning fare; this is the only place around where you can get fresh waffles with homemade raspberry syrup.

Calles Quito and Miguel Egas. ✆ 06/2920-750. Reservations recommended. Sandwiches $4.50–$5 (£2.50–£2.75), main courses $6.50–$7.50 (£3.60–£4.15). No credit cards. Daily 7:30am–8:30pm.

Pizza Siciliana Otavalo PIZZA/ITALIAN There are several pizza joints in Otavalo, but this is my favorite. The ambience is warm and cozy, with rugged wood tables and chairs, plenty of exposed wood all around, and a large brick fireplace in one corner. Pizzas have a medium-thin and crisp crust, and come with a wide range of possible toppings. There are also over a dozen pasta dishes on the menu, including a rich meat lasagna. In addition, you can get hamburgers, sandwiches, and even barbecued ribs. There's live Andean music here most Friday and Saturday nights.

Calle Morales 510, near Calle Sucre. ✆ 06/2925-999. Main courses $5–$6.50 (£2.75–£3.60). MC, V. Daily noon–10pm.

Quino Restaurante ECUADORIAN/SEAFOOD While seafood features prominently on the menu here, there's plenty more for you to try. You should definitely start things off with one of their excellent *ceviches*. But for a main course, I prefer the *steak a la criolla,* which comes bathed in onions and peppers. If you do opt for fish, I'd go for the fresh mountain trout, *trucha al ajo macho,* served in a rich garlic sauce. With simple, glass-topped tables and minimal decor, there's not much ambience here. Nevertheless, it's almost always full and lively.

Calle Roca 740, near Calle Juan Montalvo. ✆ 06/2924-994. Reservations recommended on weekends. Main courses $3.40–$5.90 (£1.90–£3.25). MC, V. Daily 8am–9:30pm.

Restaurante Mi Otavalito 👍 *Finds* ECUADORIAN This lively and popular place is my favorite option for local cuisine. The menu features a wide range of fish, meat, poultry, and specialty items. I especially like the simple grilled trout. For a real value, order the three-course daily special, which costs around $3.50 (£1.95). Tables are spread throughout several rooms connected by arched brick doorways. Some of the walls feature a mix of wood and woven mat paneling. There's a small brick fireplace in the back. During lunch and dinner most days, local bands play Andean folk music—they're working for tips, so don't be stingy.

Calle Sucre, near Calle Morales. ✆ 06/2920-176. Reservations recommended on weekends. Main courses $4.50–$5.90 (£2.50–£3.25). No credit cards. Daily 8am–10pm.

OTAVALO AFTER DARK

While not a raging party town, Otavalo has several cozy bars and clubs. It's easy to find a place with a local group playing traditional Andean music. One of my favorite spots is **Amauta Peña Bar** 👍 (✆ 06/2922-435), on Calle Morales 522, near Modesto Jaramillo. A band performs there every night and there's a minimal cover, which you can use toward the purchase of your first couple of drinks.

For dancing, check out the **Habana Club** (✆ 06/2920-493), on Calle Quito and 31 de Octubre. For a more mellow, boho scene, try **Casa de Arte Da Pinto** 👍 (✆ 06/2920-058), on Calle Colón 410, between Bolívar and Sucre. This place features creative artwork on the walls, tables, and floors, and serves up pizzas, burgers, beer, and wine.

AN ISOLATED & HISTORIC HACIENDA

Hacienda Zuleta 👍👍 *Finds* This elegant old hacienda belonged to the former president and diplomat Galo Plaza. The massive plaza at the still-working farm is quite impressive. The remodeled rooms are spread throughout the old building and are quite comfortable—most have a working fireplace or woodstove, which comes in handy in this high-mountain climate. Many units face an open-air courtyard or small garden. The majority of rooms carry the name of a prominent family member. "Galo," which is located in the oldest part of the hacienda, is a large room with a high-peaked ceiling featuring exposed beams that date back to 1691; there's a claw-foot bathtub in the bathroom. Be sure to ask to visit Galo Plaza's library, an impressive two-story room containing historic memorabilia, a massive book and art collection, and a portrait of the former president painted by Guayasamín. The farm here produces excellent cheeses, and the local community produces renowned embroidery works. First-rate meals are served family-style in the main old dining room. Horseback riding is taken seriously here—their horses are well trained and beautiful, and a wide range of tours are available. The hotel oversees a condor recovery project, where injured condors are cared for, and where wild condors often visit.

Hacienda Zuleta can arrange transportation for you. If you are coming on your own, there are several routes—your best bet is to check in with the hotel to find out which is in the best condition.

Angochahua, Imbabura. (℃ 02/2228-554 reservations office in Quito, or 06/2662-182 at the hacienda. www.zuleta.com. 12 units. $510 (£281) double. Rates include all meals, nonalcoholic drinks, guided tours and activities around the hacienda, and taxes. Children under 2 free; children 2–5 75% discount; children 5–12 50% discount. Slight discounts for multiday stays. AE, DC, MC, V. Free parking. **Amenities:** Restaurant; lounge; tour desk; free mountain bikes; massage; laundry service. *In room:* No phone.

2 Ibarra

115km (71 miles) N of Quito, 535km (332 miles) NE of Guayaquil, 20km (13 miles) N of Otavalo

Often overlooked by tourists, Ibarra is the capital of Imbabura province and the main business, transportation, and governmental hub for Ecuador's northern highlands. Founded in 1606, Ibarra was almost completely destroyed by a massive earthquake in 1868. Ibarra is nicknamed "La Ciudad Blanca" (The White City), owing to the surviving whitewashed colonial-era buildings that define its downtown. In fact, many of the newer constructions have also been built in a neo-colonial style and painted white.

Perhaps the biggest draw in Ibarra is its satellite burg, **San Antonio de Ibarra** ⚜ (5km/3 miles south of downtown), a small, artistic community renowned for its woodcarving and artisans. Another of Ibarra's biggest attractions, **Laguna Yahuarcocha,** also lies just outside the city.

ESSENTIALS
GETTING THERE & DEPARTING
BY BUS Buses leave Quito's primary bus terminal, Terminal Terrestre, for Ibarra roughly every 20 minutes between 5am and 10pm. Two main bus companies, **Cooperativa Andina** (℃ 02/2573-641 in Quito, or 06/2950-833 in Ibarra) and **Cooperativa Express Turismo** (℃ 02/2572-255 in Quito, or 06/2607-456 in Ibarra) alternate departures. The ride takes around 2½ hours, and the fare is $3 (£1.65).

The main bus terminal, Terminal Terrestre (℃ 06/2644-676) in Ibarra, is located southwest of downtown, on Calle Espejo. Taxis are always waiting at the bus station and charge just $1 (55p) for a ride to the city center.

In addition to the return buses to Quito, which follow the same schedule as their arriving counterparts, there are frequent buses from Ibarra north along the Pan-American Highway to Tulcán.

BY CAR   To reach Ibarra by car, take the Pan-American Highway (E35) north out of Quito. It's a fairly straight shot, and Ibarra is located just off the highway. You will pass first through the towns of Calderón and Cayambe, and then just skirt Otavalo. There are two $1 (55p) tolls between Quito and Ibarra. The ride takes around 2 hours.

BY TRAIN   The train between Ibarra and San Lorenzo, on the Pacific coast, no longer runs. Rumors are ongoing that it may be reopened one day, but as of press time, no discernible progress has been made.

ORIENTATION

Ibarra has a compact downtown, parts of which still feature rough cobblestone streets from the colonial period. The Pan-American Highway skirts the town to the west before turning north for Tulcán. The city's central park, Parque Pedro Moncayo, occupies a full city block and has well-tended gardens and plenty of benches. It is anchored on the north by the city's cathedral. One block west lies a similar little park, Parque La Merced, which fronts the Iglesia La Merced, while 1 block east is San Agustín church, which features its own little plaza out front.

GETTING AROUND

Ibarra's downtown is quite easily navigated on foot. Nonetheless, taxis are always available. If you can't flag one down, call **Aerotaxi** (© **06/2958-921**) or **Taxis Lagos de Ibarra** (© **06/2955-150**).

The *Minga*

If you want something done, you do it yourself, right? Not in the Ecuadorian highlands. The *minga* is a quintessentially South American phenomenon still strongly evident in many Andean communities. Derived from the Quichua word *minka,* meaning roughly "working together," it evokes the concept of a community's mutually collaborating to achieve a task for the benefit of everyone, and goes way back to before the Incas.

The *minga* can apply to many different projects from helping with the harvest, building or repairing a neighbor's house, or, in more modern times, picking up trash along a dirty city street or equipping a children's playground.

The Incas exploited the practice to great effect within the highland farming communes *(ayllus)* under their domain, which partly helps explain their success in expanding and supplying their once vast empire.

The work carried out is done free of charge and in shifts for the common good. *Mingas,* it's important to note, take place in addition to a worker's normal job. In the highland Andean villages, the communities decide what needs to be done: say, a new drainage ditch, road repair, or the potato harvest. Laborers bring their tools to the site of the task in question, and although the project may be backbreakingly hard, there is an almost festive atmosphere as the volunteers come and go.

The *minga* philosophy—that what you give, you get back—is still alive and well. Orphans, the elderly, and the infirm all make their contribution, too, however small, and receive shelter and food in return.

VISITOR INFORMATION

There's a helpful **tourism information office** (℃ **06/2608-409;** www.ibarraturismo. com) on Calle Sucre, between Oveido and Flores.

FAST FACTS   To contact the **police,** dial ℃ **101,** or ℃ 06/2641-029. The main **post office** (℃ **06/2643-135)** is located on Calle Salinas 4–56, between Oveido and Pedro Moncayo. The **Hospital San Vicente de Paul** (℃ **06/2957-272)** is located just west of downtown, on Luis Vargas Torres and Pasquel Moreno.

There are several banks and plenty of ATMs around the center of Ibarra. A branch of the **Banco Pichincha** (℃ **06/2643-097)** is just off Parque Pedro Moncayo on Calle Flores 5–18 near Calle Sucre, and a branch of **Banco del Pacífico** (℃ **06/2957-714)** is on the corner of calles Olmedo and Pedro Moncayo.

If you need an Internet cafe, try **Nando's Cyber Café** (℃ **06/2950-632),** on Av. Pérez Guerrero 6–50 and Bolívar, or **Internet Lago Azul** (℃ **06/2641-851),** on Calle Pedro Moncayo 5–78 and Bolívar.

WHAT TO SEE & DO IN IBARRA

Aside from visiting the local churches and people-watching from a bench at one of the several downtown parks, there's not very much of interest for tourists in Ibarra. The city's most popular attractions, San Antonio de Ibarra and Laguna Yahuarcocha (see below), are just outside the city limits.

While the **Iglesia de la Merced, Iglesia San Augustin, Iglesia Santo Domingo,** and the **Cathedral** are all worth a quick visit, my favorite church in Ibarra is the **Basílica de la Dolorosa** ⭐, which is located several blocks south of downtown, on Calle Sucre. This somber stone-and-brick church features two high clock towers, several large stained-glass murals, and a bright neon sign over the ornately carved wooden alter reading OH, MADRE, DOLOROSA.

The local branch of the **Museo del Banco Central de Ecuador (Ecuador Central Bank Museum;** ℃ **06/2644-087)** has a respectable collection of Inca and pre-Inca relics. The museum is located at the corner of calles Sucre and Oviedo. It is open Monday through Saturday from 9am until 5pm. Admission is $1 (55p).

There's also a small museum of colonial-era religious art attached to the **Iglesia Santo Domingo.** The church features large carved wooden doors and fronts a small park with a statue of Simón Bolívar. The museum is open daily from 9am till noon, and from 2 to 6pm. Admission is 50¢ (30p). This church is located north of downtown, on calles Bolívar and Troya.

Those not staying at the Hotel Montecarlo (see below), can use the pool, sauna, gym, and other facilities there for a daily fee of $3 (£1.65).

Tip: Try to catch a local match of *pelota de guante,* a popular game played with a soft ball and large circular leather paddles with large nails embedded in them. This is a team sport, played on a large field, whose rules can best be described as a rough blend of team tennis (without a net) and dodge ball. Ask around town and you should be able to find a game to watch, especially on Saturday afternoons, after the main market activity winds down.

WHAT TO SEE & DO NEARBY

SAN ANTONIO DE IBARRA ⭐   Cedar wood is abundant in Imbabura province. Take a trip to the small town of San Antonio de Ibarra and you can see how local woodcarvers transform this raw wood into high art. The town is full of galleries selling wood figurines in almost every shape and size; all are beautifully hand-painted.

Many are religious-themed, although there are plenty of artisans making secular decorative and functional pieces as well. The best stores are on the main street, 25 de Noviembre and along Calle Ramón Teanga, whose colonial-era charm has been restored. This cobblestone road now features brightly painted buildings, which are a mix of residential homes, tourist shops, galleries, and artisans' workshops. All along the street are broad brick sidewalks with iron, antique-style street lamps.

Tip: I recommend starting your tour of San Antonio de Ibarra near the church known locally as La Capilla del Barrio del Sur. This diminutive blue church is near the top of the restored section of Calle Ramón Teanga. Catty-corner to the church is **Escultura Cisneros** (✆ 06/2932-354), the workshop of Saul and Alfonso Cisneros, two of the more prominent local sculptors. From here, walk downhill for several blocks, stopping in at shops as they strike your fancy, before jogging over toward the town's central plaza and the main Avenue 25 de Noviembre. Heading out of town on this avenue, be sure to stop at the **Asociación de Artesanos** (✆ 06/2933-538). This large space exhibits works by a number of local artisans, and also has a large gallery area that often hosts traveling exhibitions. For a real treat, try calling on **Alcides Montesdeoca** (✆ 06/2932-106), a renowned maker of large Virgin Mary sculptures used in prominent Holy Week processions around the world. Alcides can usually be found at his home workshop, on Calle Bolívar 5–38.

GETTING THERE   San Antonio de Ibarra is located 5km (3 miles) south of Ibarra, just off the Pan-American Highway. Any bus from Ibarra to Quito or Otavalo will drop you off at the entrance to San Antonio de Ibarra, although it's 10 blocks or more uphill from here to the center of town, so be sure to hop on one of the similarly frequent direct buses to San Antonio proper. These leave roughly every 20 minutes from Ibarra's Terminal Terrestre throughout the day. The fare is 20¢ (10p). A taxi ride here should not cost over $3 (£1.65).

LAGUNA YAHUARCOCHA (YAHUARCOCHA LAKE)   Located a few miles outside the city, this small lake is a popular local spot for picnics and small-boat outings, but to my mind it holds more interest as a historical site. The lake's name means "Blood Lake," in reference to a fierce 1495 battle in which Inca King Huayna Capac massacred thousands upon thousands of the local Cara people. The massacre was so intense that the lake allegedly turned red.

GETTING THERE   Laguna Yahuarcocha is located 3.2km (2 miles) north of Ibarra, just off the Pan-American Highway. Frequent buses leave Ibarra's main bus terminal for Yahuarcocha. The fare is 30¢ (20p). Alternatively, a taxi ride here should cost around $3 (£1.65).

WHERE TO STAY IN IBARRA
MODERATE
Hacienda Chorlavi ★ *Kids*   Although it's located a few kilometers south of the city, this is your best hotel option around Ibarra. Dating from 1816, the hacienda was originally a Jesuit monastery. There are now over 50 rooms in a host of newer buildings, while only 12 of the rooms are housed in the original building, but the newer rooms maintain much of the same colonial-era style and feel. Accommodations here are comfortable and well done. The newer suites are very large, with king-size beds, modern bathrooms, and stylish floors featuring a mix of wood and stonework. My favorite is no. 55, a separate little cottage fronting a small garden plot; it has a claw-foot tub in the bathroom. For standard rooms, I recommend either those in the original building

or those in the block (nos. 26–35), which is located near the pool. Most of these come with wooden floors and ornate wallpaper.

This hacienda has extensive amenities, which include the above-mentioned pool, an indoor Jacuzzi, a sauna and steam-room area, tennis and squash courts, and a full soccer field. There's a pretty little chapel which gets good use for weddings and baptisms and which has weekly Sunday Mass. The hacienda has its own stable, and horseback riding is popular here. They have gentle, well-trained horses and specialize in rides for children.

Excellent **Ecuadorian cuisine** is served in an antique dining room as well as around the central stone courtyard of the main building. Even if you're not staying here, you might consider coming for a meal (see below).

5km (3 miles) south of Ibarra, on the Pan-American Hwy., Ibarra. © **06/2932-222** or 06/2932-223. Fax 06/2932-234. www.haciendachorlavi.com. 55 units. $50 (£28) double; $80 (£44) suite. DC, MC, V. Free parking. **Amenities:** Restaurant; small, outdoor pool; outdoor tennis court; outdoor squash court; Jacuzzi; sauna; steam room; tour desk; room service 7am–10pm; laundry service. *In room:* TV.

INEXPENSIVE
Hotel Giralda 🎖 *Value*   This modern, business-class hotel has the most comfortable rooms and best facilities in Ibarra proper. Indeed, it's the only hotel I know of at this price where you're greeted by a uniformed doorman. The rather tacky decor won't ever be featured in *Architectural Digest,* but it's not so garish as to be disturbing. Rooms are of good size, with two or three twin beds or one queen-size bed. Bathrooms feature sparkling black tile. This place is located slightly east of the city center, on Avenida Atahualpa, which is the start of the route to Hacienda Zuleta.

Av. Atahualpa and Francisco Bonilla, Ibarra. ©/fax **06/2956-002** or 06/2641-059. www.hotelgiralda.com. 32 units. $30 (£17) double. DC, MC, V. Free parking. **Amenities:** Restaurant; bar; swimming pool; tennis court; Jacuzzi, sauna, and steam room; room service 7am–11pm; laundry service. *In room:* TV, minibar.

Hotel Montecarlo   Located a few blocks from downtown, this hotel offers perfectly acceptable rooms at affordable prices, and has many of the same amenities you'll find at the Hotel Giralda (see above). The rooms and facilities, however, feel far more contemporary at the Giralda, though the Montecarlo has basically the same amenities. Most of the rooms have large picture windows, and those on the fourth floor have pretty good views. The owners and staff are extremely friendly and accommodating.

Calle Jaime Rivadeneira 5–55 and Oviedo, Ibarra. © **06/2958-182.** Fax 06/2958-266. montecarlohotel@gmail.com 35 units. $28 (£15) double; $36 (£20) suite. Rates include full breakfast. AE, DC, MC, V. Free parking. **Amenities:** Restaurant; bar; small indoor pool; small gym; Jacuzzi; sauna; steam room; room service 7am–10pm; laundry service. *In room:* TV.

WHERE TO DINE IN IBARRA
MODERATE
Hacienda Chorlavi 🎖 ECUADORIAN/INTERNATIONAL   Even if you're not staying here (see above), it's worth coming to for a meal. There's an elegant dining room in the old hacienda building, but I prefer the tables set on the veranda and patio of the central courtyard with its beautiful central fountain. The menu and offerings are far more refined than anything else you'll find in or around Ibarra. The Chorlavi trout comes in a rich cream sauce, while the *carne colorado* is a spicy beef stew served with *llapingachos* (potato and cheese patties) and *mote* (hominy). The *cuy de hacienda* (guinea pig) is a house specialty, and portions range from filling to huge. On weekends and holidays, local Andean bands accompany most lunches and dinners.

Helado de Paila

Ibarra is famous across Ecuador for its *helado de paila,* a handmade sherbet. Although *helado* translates as "ice cream," Ibarra's *helado de paila* is made simply from fruit juice, fruit pieces, ice, and sugar. The mixture is churned by hand, with a wooden paddle, in a large copper bowl, or *paila,* over ice and salt. My favorite flavors are *maracuyá* (passion fruit) and *tomate de árbol* or *tamarillo* (tree tomato). Other popular flavors include *mora* (blackberry), and *guanábana* (soursop).

The tradition was apparently begun in Ibarra in 1897, by Rosalía Suárez. Her descendants still run the original **Heladería Rosalía Suárez** (℃ **06/2950-107**), on Calle Oviedo 7–79 and Olmedo. Today there are shops and stands selling *helado de paila* throughout the country. But if you're in Ibarra, be sure to stop here, where they've been dishing up this treat for more than a century.

5km (3 miles) south of Ibarra, on the Pan-American Hwy. ℃ **06/2932-222.** Reservations necessary. Main courses: $5.50-$12 (£2.75–£6.15). DC, MC, V. Daily 7am–9pm.

INEXPENSIVE

Café Arte 🌟 *finds* ECUADORIAN/INTERNATIONAL   This eclectic and arty spot wears many hats. It's part gallery, part cafe, part bar, part performance space, and part restaurant. And it seems to excel on almost all fronts, so be sure to stop in here if you're in Ibarra. In addition to showing the owner's own work, this large space often has rotating exhibits of local and visiting artists. The menu ranges from sandwiches and burgers to grilled mountain trout and filet mignon. There are a host of Mexican-style plates, including tacos and burritos, and specialty drinks are named after famous painters. Expect to find some sort of live entertainment most nights, which might range from a poetry reading or cinema to a jazz combo or local punk-rock outfit.

Calle Salinas 5–43, between Flores and Oveido. ℃ **06/2950-806.** Reservations recommended on weekends. Main courses: $2.50-$5.80 (£1.40–£3.20). MC, V. Daily 9am–midnight.

IBARRA AFTER DARK

Ibarra is a quiet town after sundown. My favorite nightspot is **Café Arte** 🌟 (see above). Another popular bar is **El Encuentro** (℃ **06/2959-526**), on Calle Olmedo 9–59, near Calle Velasco. If you're looking to boogie, head to the nostalgically named **Studio 54** (℃ **06/2953-985**), located out on the highway to Laguna Yahuarcocha.

EN ROUTE NORTH: EL ANGEL ECOLOGICAL RESERVE 🌟

At altitudes ranging from 3,500 to 4,800m (11,500–15,750 ft.), this reserve comprises 15,700 hectares (38,795 acres). Visitors have been known to spot condors as well as Andean foxes and deer. The park is perhaps most famous for the fields of *frailejón* found here; the *frailejón* is a striking plant with soft, furry leaves and tall central stalks that can grow to heights of some 1.8m (6 ft.). A few small lakes dot the vast and varied topography as well.

The gateway to the park is the tiny town of El Angel, where there's a **park office** (℃ **06/2977-597**). Admission is $10 (£5.50) per person, per day, and camping is allowed. Note that the park is often cold and wet, so come prepared.

If you need a place to stay in El Angel, try **Hostería El Angel** (℃ **06/2977-584**); they can also help you arrange a guided tour of the reserve.

To get here, turn off the Pan-American Highway near Pusir and follow signs to Mira and El Angel. If you're coming from Tulcán, make your turn at San Gabriel and follow the signs to El Angel. The **Cooperativa Espejo** (© 06/2977-103) bus line has regular service to El Angel from both Ibarra and Tulcán. The ride is about 2 hours from Ibarra, and 1½ hours from Tulcán.

The principal entrance to the park, El Voladero, is 16km (10 miles) outside El Angel, along the old road to Tulcán. For a few dollars, you can hire a 4WD taxi in El Angel to take you there.

3 Tulcán

240km (149 miles) N of Quito, 660km (409 miles) NE of Guayaquil, 145km (90 miles) N of Otavalo

The capital of Carchi province, Tulcán is a small but bustling border city. At almost 3,000m (10,000 ft.), it's usually cool to quite cold here. This is the principal land crossing between Ecuador and Colombia, and Tulcán has become a predominantly commercial city, with a brisk business in cross-border trading. For tourists, it's likely just a transfer point on a journey either to or from Colombia.

ESSENTIALS
GETTING THERE & DEPARTING
BY PLANE   Tame (© 02/2909-900 central reservation number in Quito, or 06/2980-675 in Guayaquil; www.tame.com.ec) flies at 10:30am Monday, Wednesday, and Friday from Quito's international airport to the Aeropuerto Teniente Coronel Luis A Mantilla (© 06/2980-555; airport code: TUA). The flight takes 30 minutes and costs $38 (£21); it continues on to Cali, Colombia. The return flight to Quito leaves Tulcán at 2:45pm. Tulcán's airport is located 2km (1½ miles) north of the city center. Taxis are always waiting to meet incoming flights, and charge 50¢ to $1 (30p–55p) for the ride into town.

BY BUS   Cooperativa Express Turismo (© 02/2572-255 in Quito, or 06/2980-492 in Tulcán) buses leave Quito's main bus terminal, Terminal Terrestre, every hour between 5am and 10pm for the 5-hour ride to Tulcán. Several other bus lines also run this route, providing much more frequent service in the daytime, and at least one bus every half-hour around the clock. The fare runs $5 to $6 (£2.75–£3.30).

Tulcán's bus terminal is located at the southern end of the city, near the junction of Avenida General Arellano and Calle Bolívar. Taxis, which are plentiful, charge 50¢ to $1 (30p–55p) for the ride to the center.

BY CAR   To reach Tulcán by car, take the Pan-American Highway (E35) north out of Quito. Follow the directions above to Otavalo (p. 141)and Ibarra (p. 156), and then continue on to Tulcán. The ride takes 4 to 4½ hours.

ORIENTATION
Tulcán is a long, narrow city running roughly southwest to northeast. Avenida General Arellano is the main artery through town, although 1 block east of Arellano, Calle Bolívar, as well as its parallel Calle Sucre, are where the city's business and civic life happens. The central plaza, or Plaza de la Independencia, is bounded on either side by calles Sucre and Olmedo. About 5 blocks north, lying between Avenida General Arellano and Calle Bolívar, is the larger Parque Isidro Ayora.

The Colombian border is 6km (3¾ miles) north of downtown.

GETTING AROUND

You'll have no trouble flagging down a taxi. If you do, call **Cooperativa de Taxis Rápido Nacional** (© 06/2980-420). Rides around town should not exceed $1 (55p), and a trip to the border should cost around $4 (£2.20).

Minivans leave for the airport and the border throughout the day from the northeast corner of Parque Isidro Ayora. The fare is 50¢ (30p) to the airport and 75¢ (40p) to the border.

VISITOR INFORMATION

There's a basic **tourist information office** (© 06/2980-487) on the southeast side of the Parque de la Independencia, on Calle Olmedo. You'll also find a tourist information booth near the entrance to the Municipal Cemetery.

Tips: Tulcán has the reputation of being a rough and dangerous border city. Colombia's ongoing insurgency and narco-trafficking are no help, either. Use common sense—don't venture far from the city center or popular tourist spots, try not to travel alone, and use taxis to get around, especially at night.

FAST FACTS   To contact the **police,** dial © **101.** In the event of a medical emergency you can call the **Cruz Roja (Red Cross;** © **06/2980-100);** or head to the **Hospital de Lea** (© **06/2980-396)** on Calle Junín and Avenida General Arellano. The main **post office** (© **06/2980-552)** is on Calle Bolívar, between calles Junín and Boyaca.

For your banking needs, head to the **Banco del Pichincha** (© **06/2985-020),** on 10 de Agosto and Sucre. This bank will change money into Colombian pesos, as will the **Casa de Cambio** (© **06/2985-731),** on Calle Ayacucho and Calle Sucre. If the bank and Casa de Cambio are closed or inconvenient, you'll find plenty of individual money changers hanging out at Parque Isidro Ayora and on the Plaza de la Independencia. You'll probably get better rates for pesos in Tulcán—either at the official bank, Casa de Cambio, or with these money changers—than you will at the border.

As elsewhere in Ecuador, you'll have no problem finding an Internet cafe here. I like **Compu Café Net** (© **06/2984-949),** on calles Ecuador and Bolívar.

There is a **Colombian consulate** (© **06/2890-559)** in Tulcán, at Av. Manabí 58–087 (though you should be able to handle all immigration formalities at the border itself).

WHAT TO SEE & DO

Tulcán's greatest attraction is its **Cementerio Municipal (Municipal Cemetery)** ⭐, with its extravagant topiary gardens. These were begun in 1936 by José María Franco. In 1984 the Ecuadorian government designated the gardens a National Patrimony. Today, his sons carry on the tradition, and Franco is buried beneath some of his creations, with one of his quotes prominently displayed: A CEMETERY SO BEAUTIFUL, IT INVITES ONE TO DIE. While the cemetery is the town's crowning achievement, Franco's work and influence can be seen all over Tulcán, where locals have taken to shearing and shaping just about every bush and tree they can lay their clippers on. The Municipal Cemetery is located about 2 blocks north of Parque Isidro Ayora.

If you want to arrange a tour around this area or to El Angel, or if you just need help with logistical arrangements, contact **Eccotur** (© **06/2980-468),** on Calle Sucre 51–029.

WHERE TO STAY & DINE IN TULCAN

Hotel and restaurant options are rather bleak in Tulcán; tourists staying here are usually only in transit and not necessarily overnighting by choice. The best hotel options are **Hotel Azteca** (©/fax **06/2960-417**), on Calle Bolívar and Atahualpa, and **Hotel Sara Espindola** (© **06/2985-925**), on Calle Sucre and Ayacucho. Clean rooms with cable television run around $16 (£8.80) for a double at either of these places. The Sara Espindola gets the nod in terms of location, fronting the Parque de la Independencia. If you want to be real close to the border, try **Hostería Rumichaca** (© **06/2980-276**), which has a swimming pool and some hot springs, and is located just off the Pan-American Highway.

Tip: Hotel rooms fill up fast in Tulcán on weekends, when Colombian shoppers flock to town to take advantage of bargains their slightly stronger currency buys them in Ecuador. Therefore, if you're going to stay here on a weekend, be sure to make reservations.

In terms of dining, your best bets are probably the restaurants at the two downtown hotels mentioned above. Being this close to the border, be sure to look out for and sample some Colombian cuisine. *Pollo sudado,* which translates literally as "sweaty chicken," is a tasty braised chicken-and-potato dish, while *bandeja paisa* is a plate piled high with various fried foods, similar to the Ecuadorian dish *chugchucaras,* which is popular around Latacunga (p. 176)

TULCAN AFTER DARK

If you want to try your luck at blackjack, poker, or slots, head to **Rey Casino Internacional** (© **06/2980-952**), on Calle Sucre and Ayacucho. The Hotel Azteca (see above) has a popular disco that gets particularly packed on weekends. Another bar, disco, and restaurant that I like is **T-Kila** (© **06/2986-346**), on Calle Bolívar and Ayacucho.

CROSSING INTO COLOMBIA

The Pan-American Highway passes through Tulcán, over the Rumichaca bridge and on into Bolívar province of Colombia. The closest Colombian town to the border is Ipiales, about 2km (1½ miles) north of the bridge.

The border process is relatively painless and cost free. Both Ecuadorian and Colombian immigration officials have their stations on either side of the bridge. If you're heading into Colombia, you will have the option of either a 30- or 90-day visa. (Be sure to specify the latter if you think you'll need it.) The border offices are open daily from 6am until 9pm.

There are money changers on both sides of the border, but, as I advised above, you'd be best off changing for some Colombian pesos in Tulcán.

Given the precarious nature of security in Colombia, you should always check with your home consulate, fellow travelers, and knowledgeable locals before heading across.

7

The Central Sierra

Heading south out of Quito, the Pan-American Highway passes through high Andean terrain that Alexander von Humboldt called "La Avenida de los Volcanes," or the Avenue of the Volcanoes. This is some of Ecuador's most beautiful mountain territory, with snowcapped peaks, high-altitude paramos, and massive tracts of cattle and sheep pasture patrolled by Andean condors overhead. Volcán Cotopaxi is the most impressive and striking of the peaks here, owing to its near-perfect volcanic cone covered in glacial ice. This imposing behemoth is still active, and a must-summit for any serious mountain climber. This region features a host of other towering snowcapped peaks, including Volcán Rumiñahui and the twin Iliniza peaks. Throughout the area, you can find isolated haciendas that have been converted into fabulous little hotels. As you follow the Avenue of the Volcanoes south, you eventually hit the popular tourist towns of Riobamba and Baños. The latter is named after the hot springs, or *baños,* located at the foot of towering Volcán Tungurahua.

1 Cotopaxi National Park ★★★

60km (37 miles) S of Quito

At 5,897m (19,348 ft.), Cotopaxi is the world's highest continuously active volcano, and Ecuador's second-highest peak. Your first encounter with the almost perfectly cone-shaped and snow-covered Cotopaxi might be from overhead in a plane; I've been on planes that have flown terrifyingly close to the volcano, where I almost felt I could reach out and touch it. From above, it's hard to determine where the clouds end and where the glaciers begin. The snow glimmers in the sunlight and magically blends with the bright blue sky—and what a sight! On a clear day in Quito, even if you're not airborne, it's easy to see Cotopaxi rising high and mighty above the clouds.

The first documented summit of Cotopaxi was on November 28, 1872, by the German climber Wilhen Riess and his Colombian partner Angel Escobar.

ESSENTIALS
GETTING THERE & DEPARTING

BY PLANE   The closest airport with regular traffic is Quito's **Aeropuerto Internacional Mariscal Sucre** (© 02/2430-555). See "Quito: Orientation," on p. 92.

BY BUS & TAXI   Very frequent buses leave Quito's main bus terminal, Terminal Terrestre, heading south along the Pan-American Highway. **Latacunga** (© 03/2800-765), **Cooperativa CIRO** (© 03/2802-672), and **Cooperativa Cotopaxi** (© 03/2800-752) bus lines take turns running the route to Latacunga and Ambato, with a

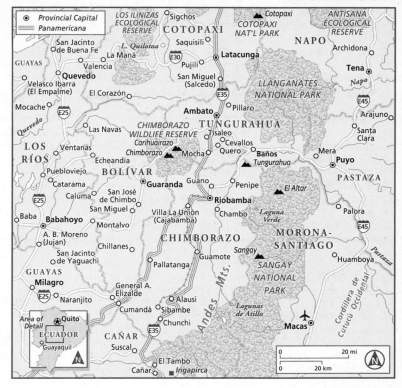

Map legend:
- ⊙ Provincial Capital
- ═══ Panamericana

bus leaving roughly every 10 minutes from 5am to 11pm, and somewhat less frequent service throughout the rest of the evening and early morning.

There are two main entrances to the park, and a third, lesser-used entrance. By far, most visitors use the main, southern entrance, also known as El Chasqui. If you are going to the park, be sure to ask the driver to drop you off at the El Chasqui entrance to Cotopaxi National Park. From here you can hire a taxi to take you to the park entrance and on to the museum or other spots inside the park for around $8 to $15 (£4.40–£8.25). Be sure to specify to the driver that you want to be dropped off at the museum or Lake Limpiopungo or other destination, as the entrance gate *(control sur)* is several miles before any of the more popular attractions inside the park.

If you're going to the northern entrance *(control norte),* you can get off any of the above buses at the entrance to Machachi, or, better yet, take the **Carlos Brito (© 02/ 2235-067)** bus from Quito's main terminal into Machachi; here you can transfer to one of the twice-daily local buses to El Pedregal, although that will still leave you several miles to go to the park entrance. Your best bet is to hire a truck-taxi in Machachi to take you all the way into the park for around $20 to $30 (£11–£17).

BY CAR   No matter which entrance you decide to use to access the park, begin by heading south out of Quito on the Pan-American Highway (E35).

To enter the park through the northern entrance, exit at Machachi and drive through the town, following the signs for El Pedregal and Cotopaxi National Park. This 21km (13-mile) stretch of dirt road is sometimes very rugged, especially during rainy periods, and a high-clearance 4WD is necessary. This is the route to take if you are staying at Hacienda El Porvenir or Tambopaxi (see below). Once inside the park, it's another 16km (10 miles) to the museum and parking area.

Although slightly longer in terms of mileage, the southern park entrance is more popular and has better roads. To reach this entrance, continue on the Pan-American Highway past Machachi for another half-hour or so, until just before the village of Lasso. You will see the signs on your left-hand side indicating the turnoff for the southern entrance to Cotopaxi National Park. This entrance and route are best if you plan to visit or base yourself out of the park's museum and nearby campsites.

There is a third entrance to the park located about 16km (10 miles) south of Machachi, before the principal southern entrance. This entrance is often referred to as El Boliche and is the least used and least convenient for most travelers visiting the park.

A 4WD vehicle is recommended whichever route you take, although if you drive slowly and carefully, a normal sedan can usually use the southern entrance route with no difficulty.

ORIENTATION

There are two main entrances to Cotopaxi National Park; see "Getting There & Departing," above, for more information on accessing these entrances. Most visitors use the principal southern entrance, or *control sur,* also known as El Chasqui. This is the closest entrance to the small museum and visitor center.

Inside the park is a series of trails, dirt roads, and campsites. The road from the southern entrance forms a very rough semicircle around the foot of Volcán Cotopaxi. About 10km (6 miles) from the entrance gate, you'll come to the museum, as well as a small restaurant, souvenir stand, and campsite. Beyond the museum to the north lies Laguna de Limpiopungo, a small, high-mountain lake with a pretty campsite beside it. Beyond Laguna de Limpiopungo, the road forks. The left-hand fork leads toward Tambopaxi (see below) and the northern entrance *(control norte).* This road actually forks again, with a secondary road leading into the much less frequently visited eastern area of the park. The main right-hand fork heads sharply south toward the cone of the volcano and the Refugio José Rivas, some 9km (5½ miles) away.

VISITOR INFORMATION

Whether you enter the park from the northern or southern entrance, you will be given a park map when you pay your entrance fee. Park rangers at each entrance gate can give basic information and recommendations, although their English may be limited or even nonexistent. Most travelers visit with a guide or as part of a guided tour, and unless you are a very experienced climber and hard-core camper, I recommend you do so as well.

There are no banks, shops, or other major services inside the park. The main ranger headquarters (© **09/9820-493** or 02/2812-768) is located by the small museum. The park admission is $10 (£5.50) per day, and camping costs another $2 (£1.10) per person per day. A bunk at the Refugio José Rivas costs $10 (£5.50) per night. This refuge is the most common jumping-off point for summit attempts.

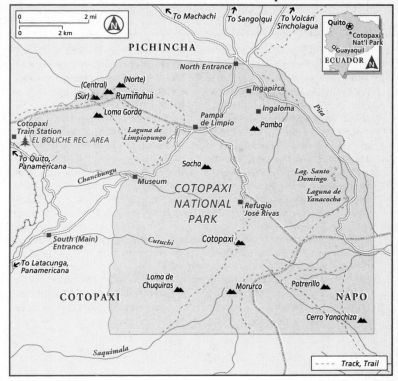

Cotopaxi National Park

WHAT TO SEE & DO IN COTOPAXI NATIONAL PARK ✿✿✿

Looking down from a plane at a volcano is one thing, but climbing it, camping on its flanks, riding a horse or mountain bike across the paramo, or hiking around it are much more rewarding. The high Andean paramo here features wild horses and llamas grazing. Below the volcano, the flat plains are peppered with volcanic boulders that give stark evidence of the power and fury of Cotopaxi's relatively recent eruptions. And everywhere you turn there are fantastic views of the snow-covered crater—that is, when it's not shrouded in low cloud cover.

Climbing to the summit is serious business, and not for those in merely average physical condition and with no experience at high altitudes. Nonetheless, every year, thousands of intrepid climbers take out their ice axes, strap on their crampons, and conquer the summit. An embarrassing admission: I've never done it. But according to those in the know, the climb is not terribly technical or difficult. On the other hand, I have met several experienced climbers who have been severely affected by the altitude and were forced to turn back early. Be sure to spend several days in Quito and at higher altitudes acclimating before you attempt to summit Cotopaxi. Even if you're feeling fine at 2,800m (9,184 ft.), remember that the air will feel a whole lot thinner at 5,000m (16,400 ft.), especially if you're exerting a lot of energy. You should also

Andean Condor

While hiking around Cotopaxi National Park, our guide pointed out a tiny pinprick silhouette almost beyond the scope of our sight. Was he right in assuring us it was an Andean condor? I don't know, but it was the nearest I've ever come to seeing one in the wild. *Vultur gryphus,* Ecuador's national bird, is not easy to find these days despite its 3m (10-ft.) wingspan, 25-pound body, and legs and claws the size of a man's forearm and fist. It is the biggest raptor on the planet, but according to estimates, a mere 70 birds remain in isolated populations around Antisana, Cotopaxi, El Altar, and El Angel, and near the Papallacta Pass.

Dating back to the Pleistocene age, the Andean condor once thrived in an era when mastodons were their primary source of carrion. They nearly went extinct along with their large food sources, but made a comeback when Spanish settlers began introducing massive sheep and cow herds on the high Andean paramo.

The condor boasts other impressive stats. Maturing at around 7 years of age, condors can live to 60. They mate for life, with both sexes incubating the egg, which is laid every 2 years (so junior gets nearly 2 years of parenting before leaving home). An overall glossy black plumage gives way to a neat, white neck ruff into which apparently high-soaring birds tuck their bald heads when flying at sub-zero temperatures. That lack of head and neck feathers ensures that the carrion-eating condor easily keeps itself free of germs after tucking into a carcass. The condor can spot a dead animal from miles away, and is known to follow smaller raptors on the hunt to

note that the climb typically starts at about 11pm to midnight and you will be going uphill on glaciers for about 8 continuous hours before you reach the top. This way, you reach the crater in the early morning light, before the clouds settle in.

Fortunately for the less adventurous and less fit, you really don't need to climb Cotopaxi to enjoy it. A host of outfitters in Quito, and all the hotels close to the volcano, organize day trips to the national park. Many day trips bring you to the small museum and visitor center, which has a somewhat sad collection of stuffed animals, including an Andean condor, as well as a relief map of the volcano and some explanatory materials. From here, these trips commonly take any number of short-to-mid-length hikes around the park, most commonly to the Laguna de Limpiopungo. The museum is located at 4,500m (14,760 ft.) above sea level, and most of the hikes around the park take place at this general altitude—note that even at this altitude, the air is quite thin and it's not uncommon to feel lightheaded.

ORGANIZING A CLIMB TO THE TOP   It's very important to make sure that you're climbing Cotopaxi with an experienced guide and good equipment. The best companies provide one guide for every two climbers. The finest and most experienced outfitters include: **Adventure Planet Ecuador** ✵ (© **02/2871-105;** www.adventure planet-ecuador.com), **Cotopaxi.com** ✵✵ (© **02/2909-640;** www.cotopaxi.com), get in on the meal—since no other bird will mess with a condor, it has a guaranteed a place at the table. Oh, and it turns out that the condor is not in the vulture family: Biochemical studies now place it genetically with storks!

As usual, the main threat to this magnificent creature is humans. Although it is a carrion feeder, the condor has historically had a reputation for preying on young animals, placing it in direct conflict with highland farmers. Most ranchers will kill condors on sight, and it has been a traditional rite of passage for a young man to bag a bird to prove his virility.

In the past, local communities would lure a condor into traps baited with rotting meat. The captive bird was then strapped to a bull depicting Spanish domination over the conquered native population. If the condor succeeded in flying free, it was a sign of good fortune for the community.

Condors need lots of air space and land to thrive, and evidence suggests that breeding programs and reintroductions into the wild can succeed. An ambitious Nature Conservancy/USAID–supported program embracing nearly 2.2 million hectares (5½ million acres) ranging from Antisana, Cotopaxi, Cayambe, and dropping to the Amazon rainforests to the east, might help tip the balance. With a multifaceted, functional-landscape approach, the **Condor Bioreserve** (www.biorresesrvadelcondor.org) aims to protect the main watershed providing Quito's drinking water, defend indigenous reserves, and encourage farmers to create wildlife corridors. Keep your eyes open, your head in the air, and hope.

and **Safari Ecuador** ☞☞ (© 02/2222-505; www.safari.com.ec). Rates run $125 to $200 (£69–£110) per person for a 2-day/1-night trip to the summit, depending upon the size of your group.

All the above companies also organize longer treks around the park, as well as climbs to the summits of other nearby peaks, including Rumiñahui, Iliniza Norte, and Iliniza Sur, all of which are good practice climbs to tackle before attempting Cotopaxi.

VISITING AS PART OF A DAY TRIP   Just about every tour desk and tour operator in Quito offers a day trip to Cotopaxi. The details may vary some, but most head first to the small museum and then spend anywhere from 1 to 3 hours hiking. In addition, most operators offer options for mountain biking or horseback riding.

The best general tour operators, in my opinion, are **Metropolitan Touring** ☞ (© 02/2988-200; www.metropolitan-touring.com); and **Surtrek** ☞ (© 02/2231-534; www.surtrek.com). Day trips to Cotopaxi run $30 to $50 (£15–£25), depending on size of your group and whether lunch is included. The park entrance fee is rarely included.

If you want to tour the park on a mountain bike, contact **Andes World Bike** (© 02/2352-769; www.ecuadorbikingclimbing.com), **Aries Bike Company** (© 02/2906-052; www.ariesbikecompany.com), **Cotopaxi.com** ☞☞ (© 02/2909-640; www.cotopaxi.com), or **Safari Ecuador** ☞☞ (© 02/2552-505; www.safari.com.ec).

For horseback-riding tours of Cotopaxi, I recommend **Andean Paths** (© 09/980-8469; www.andeanpaths.com), **Ilalo Expeditions** (© 09/777-8399; www.ilalo expeditions.com), or **Hacienda La Alegría** ✦✦ (see below).

Mountain-bike or horseback excursions to Cotopaxi run around $40 to $75 (£22–£41) depending upon the length of the tour and several other variables, like group size and equipment requirements.

VISITING BY CHIVA EXPRESS   For a unique ride and tour of Cotopaxi National Park, check out **Metropolitan Touring's Chiva Express** ✦ (© 02/2988-200; www.chivaexpress.com). A converted and brightly painted school bus that rides on old railroad tracks, this fun option runs day trips every Tuesday, Thursday, Saturday, and Sunday. They'll pick you up at your hotel and bring you to the train station. The Chiva Express leaves Quito at 9am, and takes a leisurely and picturesque ride to Cotopaxi. The bus-train stops along the way at Hacienda La Alegría (see below), for a brief tour of the milking operation, before continuing on to El Boliche station inside the national park. From here, traditional buses or minivans will take you to the park's little museum, after which there is a hike around the Laguna de Limpiopungo. Depending upon timing, weather, and the group's hunger, lunch at Tambopaxi (see below) is offered either before or after the hike.

The Chiva Express has 34 seats inside, and 20 more in seats on the roof. They only sell the 34 indoor seats, so folks can take turns riding on the roof. The tour costs $92 (£51) per person, including lunch. The $10 (£5.50) national park entrance fee is extra.

WHERE TO STAY & DINE IN & AROUND COTOPAXI

All the lodges and haciendas listed here are very isolated. If you're staying at one of them, you will most likely take all your meals there. The only real restaurant of note to visit separately while visiting the park is at **Tambopaxi** (see below). There's also a simple little restaurant next to the national park's museum.

VERY EXPENSIVE

Hacienda San Augustín de Callo ✦✦✦ (Finds)   Built inside the remains of an old Augustine monastery—which was itself built on top of an ancient Inca temple and residence—this is one of the most unique hotels in Ecuador. Accommodations here are large and beautifully appointed, and most units have hand-painted murals. My favorite rooms are those that still have exposed Inca stone walls, but every room has something going for it, including the brand-new units, which have Jacuzzi tubs and great views of Cotopaxi from large picture windows. Most rooms contain working fireplaces, some of which are impressive constructions. I like "Las Gordas," which has a huge bay window above a queen bed, a claw-foot tub, and a playful mural of the full-figured women for whom the room is named. The lounge area features an original portrait of the owner, Mignon Plaza, painted by Oswaldo Guayasamín. The main dining room is built inside a classic Inca structure, with trapezoidal window niches and a more modern large window overlooking the garden and perfectly framing the volcano. Meals are excellent, and many of the fruits and vegetables are grown right here. The hacienda offers most of the traditional tours, hikes, and horseback-riding adventures available in this area; these guided activities are included in the rates, as is the necessary equipment.

Lasso, Cotopaxi (mailing address: Veintimilla E8–125 y Av. 6 de Diciembre, Quito). ©/fax **02/2906-157** reservation office in Quito or ©/fax 03/2719-160 at the hacienda. www.incahacienda.com. 10 units. $214–$340 (£118–£187) double. Rates include 3 daily meals, and daily tours and activities. Rates higher during peak periods. AE, DC MC, V. **Amenities:** Restaurant; bar; mountain bikes; laundry service. *In room:* Dataport.

EXPENSIVE

Hacienda Hato Verde 🐎   Although this converted home is over 120 years old, it has a more modern feel than most of the other haciendas but retains its fair share of colonial-era charm. All the rooms have heavy iron beds, antique armoires, and wood-burning stoves; most units have dark, polished wood floors. In general, the bathrooms are on the small side, although they are very attractive, with interesting tile work and hip, modern fixtures. Paintings throughout the hacienda are by Sussy Palacio, the mother of one of the owners. The main lounge area is a beautiful room with heavy stone walls, high ceilings supported by exposed wood beams, and a massive stone fireplace. Televisions can be put into any room with advance notice. The owners are avid equestrians who specialize in horseback-riding tours and adventures. A full, hearty breakfast is included in the room rate, and three-course lunches and dinners are offered daily for an extra $20 (£10) per person per meal.

Km 78 of the Pan-American Hwy., on the entrance road to Mulalo, Lasso, Cotopaxi. ©/fax **03/2719-348** or 09/5978-016. www.haciendahatoverde.com. 6 units. $89 (£49) double. Rates include full breakfast. AE, DC MC, V. **Amenities:** Restaurant; bar; laundry service. *In room:* No phone.

Hacienda La Alegría 🐎 *Kids*   This lovely little hacienda is quite close to Quito. The entrance is striking, with a flowing fountain—made from a massive stone spewed out during one of Cotopaxi's many eruptions—and some pretty stained-glass work around the door. The owners are real equestrians, and horseback-riding is the specialty here. Multiday horse treks into the high paramo and exploration of Cotopaxi National Park are available. This is also a great place to learn how to ride; they take particularly good care of beginning and young riders. By far the best rooms are the two new units in back of the main building, with wood floors and a masonry fireplace. These rooms have a queen-size and twin bed downstairs and two more twins in a large loft with a small skylight. The rooms in the older main house have more character and an antique feel, but don't all have private bathrooms. Half of the still-working milking barn has been converted into a game room and lounge, which contains a Ping-Pong table and other diversions. Excellent Ecuadorian meals are served family-style in the main hacienda.

40km (25 miles) south of Quito, near the town of Aloag (mailing address: Alonso Torres N4302 y Beck Rollo, Edificio El Roble, Apartamento 201, Quito). © **02/2462-319** or 09/9802-526. www.haciendalaalegria.com. 6 units, 3 with private bathroom. $90 (£50) double. Rates include full breakfast and taxes. AE, DC MC, V. **Amenities:** Restaurant; bar; tour desk; laundry service. *In room:* No phone.

Hacienda La Carriona   This is one of the closest hacienda options to Quito. The rooms in this over-200-year-old farm vary widely; most have high ceilings, painted brick walls, and exposed beam ceilings. I like nos. 1 through 8, which are in the oldest part of the hacienda and have Persian rugs and antique beds and furniture. The best room in the house is no. 36, a large suite with a big stone fireplace. It opens onto to a small garden area in back. The hotel has a small outdoor pool, pretty gardens, and Wi-Fi in the public areas. There's even a small bullring, where nonfatal bullfights are sometimes held. The hacienda can arrange golf packages, too—one of Quito's better 18-hole golf courses is located just 5 minutes away, and there are two roughed-in practice holes on the hacienda's own expansive grounds. La Carriona is only about 40 minutes from Quito's airport; it will be even closer to the new airport, once it's open.

Km 2.5 on the road to Amaguana, Sangolquí. © **02/2331-974** or ©/fax 02/2332-005. www.lacarriona.com. 30 units. $80 (£44) double; $100 (£55) junior suite; $120 (£66) suite. Rates include full breakfast. AE, DC MC, V. **Amenities:** Restaurant; bar; small outdoor pool; Jacuzzi; sauna; steam bath; tour desk; small gym; laundry service; free Wi-Fi. *In room:* TV.

MODERATE

Hacienda El Porvenir ⟨ *Finds*   Located close to the northern entrance to Cotopaxi National Park, this is a working hacienda that specializes in dairy cattle and the traditional wild Andean fighting bull—there are more than 300 of the latter on the grounds. The main house here is only 18 years old but feels as if it's another of the colonial haciendas. Most of the simple, cozy rooms have space heaters, although a few have fireplaces or wood-burning stoves. A wonderful honeymoon suite on the second floor of the main building has a picture window, a woodstove, and a brass bed. A separate building contains a couple of rooms, which come with a communal kitchen downstairs. Of these, I like the Suite Cotopaxi, which features a great view of its namesake volcano from the large window and skylight. In the main building's second floor, there is a series of units with shared bathrooms and steeply pitched ceilings—in this case, though, there's no skylight, and the roof cuts into the space of the rooms. Units with private bathrooms all get nightly turn-downs and chocolates on the pillows. In general, the food here is excellent.

Besides treks and summits inside the national park, horseback riding and mountain biking are prime activities here, and the hacienda also runs a nearby zip-line canopy tour. El Porvenir is set at 3,600m (11,800 ft.), on the lower slopes of Volcán Rumiñahui. This hacienda is also known as Tierra de Volcanoes, although the owners actually run several small haciendas close to Cotopaxi under that brand name, and they organize a wide range of multiday adventure tours.

4km (2½ miles) from the park entrance, on the road between Machachi and the northern entrance to Cotopaxi National Park. ⟨C⟩ **02/2331-806** or 09/4980-115. www.tierradelvolcan.com. 17 units, 6 with private bathroom. $40 (£22) double with shared bathroom; $80–$120 (£44–£66) double with private bathroom. Rates include full breakfast. Lower rates in the off season. Camping $5 (£2.75) per person, not including any meals. AE, DC MC, V. **Amenities:** Restaurant; bar; mountain-bike rental; laundry service. *In room:* No phone.

Hostería La Ciénega ⟨   This is one of the older and more atmospheric of the hacienda hotels. The grand driveway leading up to the main building is flanked by tall pine trees. The hacienda has been in the family of the Marques de Maenza since the 17th century. It's said that the first true hotel guest here was Alexander von Humboldt, in 1802, who took up residence in unit no. 8, the massive top-floor suite, which still has soaring arched ceilings and crystal chandeliers. I actually prefer room no. 7, which is similar in size and feel, but which has a much larger balcony. The rest of the rooms vary considerably in size and details, and some are in severe need of major maintenance and overhaul. Nos. 30 through 35, located in a row close to the chapel, are all good bets. If you want a view of Cotopaxi, ask for no. 6, an end room on the second floor with a small balcony overlooking the volcano, and three oversized twin beds.

In addition to the main-entrance driveway, the central courtyard garden and beautiful private chapel are magnificent examples of the grand colonial-era opulence of this once massive estate. The restaurant serves excellent Continental cuisine, and is very popular with tour groups and day-trippers, so reservations are essential. Horseback riding is available for $8 (£4) per hour.

Lasso, Cotopaxi (mailing address: Calle Cordero 1442, Quito). ⟨C⟩ **02/2549-126** reservation office in Quito or 03/2719-053 at the hacienda. Fax 02/2228-820. www.hosterialacienega.com. 35 units. $70 (£39) double; $110–$150 (£61–£83) suite. Rates include full breakfast and taxes. AE, DC MC, V. **Amenities:** Restaurant; bar; tennis court; tour desk; laundry service.

INEXPENSIVE

Tambopari *(Finds)*   This simple lodging, located inside Cotopaxi National Park, makes a perfect base for folks looking for a modicum of comfort before and/or after climbing to the summit. It also makes a great base for less-strenuous hiking and trekking around the park. This place is busiest as a lunch stop for day-trippers to the park, but you will also find four clean and comfortable dorm rooms above the restaurant. These are large, but they have a mix of twin and bunk beds crammed in so tightly there is little walking room. For a bit more money, you can opt for one of the new private rooms in a separate building down near a running brook. The second-floor room on the south side of this building has a fabulous view of the volcano. Camping is also allowed here. The **dining room** features a red-tile floor, rustic wooden tables and chairs, and wraparound picture windows with views over the paramo and of the volcano. The menu features a range of Ecuadorian and international dishes. I recommend the fresh grilled trout in a butter and herb sauce.

Inside Cotopaxi National Park, 9km (5½ miles) from the village of El Pedregal (mailing address: Foch E7-46 y Reina Victoria, Quito). ℭ 02/2220-241 reservation number in Quito, or 09/9448-223 at the lodge. www.tambopaxi.com. 7 units, 3 with private bathroom. $5 (£2.75) per person camping; $15 (£8.25) per person in dorm room; $50 (£28) double private bathroom. MC, V. **Amenities:** Restaurant; bar; laundry service. *In room:* No phone.

2 Latacunga

89km (55 miles) S of Quito; 47km (29 miles) N of Ambato; 335km (208 miles) N of Guayaquil

Latacunga is a midsize city located just across a river from the Pan-American Highway, southwest of Cotopaxi. The snowcapped volcano towers imposingly and impressively over the city, forming a beautiful backdrop from many spots. It is the capital of Cotopaxi Province and a major market and industrial center for this region. Few tourists use it as a base for exploring Cotopaxi National Park, and I highly recommend the more picturesque and inviting nearby haciendas listed above—though real budget travelers and those depending on buses for transportation may find themselves by design or by chance needing to overnight in Latacunga. If that is the case, don't despair: This is a pleasant and friendly city. Latacunga is also the main jumping-off point for those touring the so-called Quilotoa Loop.

Although Cotopaxi is relatively quiet at the moment, it has pretty much completely destroyed Latacunga on three occasions, in 1742, 1768, and 1877. Stubborn or stupid, the undeterred residents have continued to rebuild in this precarious spot.

ESSENTIALS
GETTING THERE & DEPARTING

BY BUS   Very frequent buses leave Quito's main bus terminal, Terminal Terrestre, heading south along the Pan-American Highway to Latacunga. **Cooperativa CIRO** (ℭ 003/2802-672), **Cooperativa Cotopaxi** (ℭ 03/2800-752), and **Latacunga** (ℭ 03/2800-765) bus companies take turns running the route, with a bus leaving roughly every 10 minutes between 5am and 11pm and somewhat less frequent service throughout the rest of the evening and early morning. The ride costs $1.50 (85p) and takes around 2 hours.

Alternatively, you can also catch any bus heading to Ambato or Baños—just ask to be let off in Latacunga.

BY CAR   To reach Latacunga by car, simply head south out of Quito on the Pan-American Highway (E35). Latacunga is located just off the highway, across the Río Cutuchi. The ride takes a little over an hour and a half.

ORIENTATION

The heart and majority of the city lies on the eastern side of the Río Cutuchi, with the Pan-Americana passing along the western bank of this river. There are several bridges over the river: The most popular one, farthest to the north, takes you on to Calle Felix Valencia, which runs along the northern edge of the market and Plaza El Salto. A second bridge crosses the river on Avenida 5 de Junio, which runs along the southern edge of this large market area. The main north-south thoroughfare through town is Avenida Amazonas; this broad avenue is dotted with monuments, sculptures, and antique-style lamp posts strung along the central divider. Most of the hotels, restaurants, shops, and bars are clustered around or near Parque Vicente León, the town's main plaza.

GETTING AROUND

You can easily walk anywhere in Latacunga, but taxis are plentiful. A ride to anyplace in town should be $1 to $2 (55p–£1.10). If you can't flag down a taxi, call **Cooperativa de Taxis El Salto** (© 03/2801-288) or **Taxis Padre Salcedo** (© 03/2800-995).

The main bus terminal is right on the Pan-American Highway, near one of the bridges into downtown, a couple of blocks away. Taxis are always waiting around the bus terminal and along the southern edge of the main market.

VISITOR INFORMATION

There's a basic tourist information booth inside the main bus terminal, as well as an official **Captur** (© 03/2814-968) tourist information office on Avenida Sánchez de Orellana, between Guayaquil and Echeverría. At both places, you can get maps and brochures, but your best source of information will probably be any one of the local tour agencies.

FAST FACTS   The main **police station** (© 03/2812-666) is located on Calle San Martín. The main **post office** is located at the corner of calles General Maldonado and Quevedo. The **Hospital General Latacunga** (© 03/2812-398) is near the southern edge of the city, on Calle Hermanas Paez.

You'll find a branch of **Banco de Guayaquil** (© 03/2813-900) on calles General Maldonado and Orellana, and a branch of **Banco del Pichincha** (© 03/2810-304) on Calle Quito 71–95, across from the Parque Vicente León.

Internet cafes are abundant in Latacunga, especially around the downtown. If you don't simply stumble into one that looks good to you, head to **OJ Sistem** (© 03/2803-442), on Avenida Amazonas near Sucre; or to **Universo.com** (© 03/2802-869), on Avenida Félix Valencia and 2 de Mayo.

WHAT TO SEE & DO

Aside from strolling the city and visiting its few parks and churches, there's not terribly much of interest for tourists in Latacunga. The main plaza or park, **Parque Vicente León,** has pretty gardens, including some topiary sculptures. On the south side of Parque Vicente León is the city's main **Cathedral,** a rather unspectacular large church that is most notable for the tile mosaics atop its spires and domes.

Los Molinos de Monserrat (© 03/2813-247) is the city's main museum. It features a modest collection of Inca and pre-Inca artifacts, as well as colonial-era art. This place is housed in the ruins of an old river-powered mill, and has a beautiful setting just above the river. Reached by a footbridge is the museum's sister institution, the **Casa de la Cultura.** The art gallery and theater make this a good place to check for any music, theater, or dance performance. You'll find Los Molinos de Monserrat and Casa de la Cultura on Antonia Vela 3–49 and Padre Salcedo. They're open Tuesday through Saturday from 8am to noon and 2 to 6pm, and Sunday from 9am to noon. Admission is 50¢ (30p). They're also open in the evenings whenever there is a function at the Casa de la Cultura.

The **Casa de los Marqueses de Miraflores** is a colonial-era mansion—one of the few that has survived—which has been converted into a small museum, with the various rooms dedicated to exhibits ranging from archaeological finds to religious art. There's a good display and explanation of the city's Mama Negra festival and celebrations. The museum, located on Sánchez de Orellana and Abel Echeverría, is open Monday through Saturday from 8am to noon and 2 to 6pm. Admission is free.

Tuesday and Saturday are market days in Latacunga, when the already substantial Plaza El Salto market swells with vendors who take over Plaza Chile and every bit of sidewalk and alley nearby. This is a working local market heavy on fruits, vegetables, housewares, and clothing, but you can find some artisans' wool clothing as well as assorted handicrafts.

If you're feeling energetic, head out east of town on Calle Maldonado, to the **Mirador de la Virgen del Calvario,** a high lookout point with great views of the city countryside. Several blocks east of the small Parque Bolívar you'll see a steep flight of steps, and above and beyond that the sculpture of the Virgin of Calvary. Another good place to walk during the day is on the paved walkway that runs along the river.

Several tour agencies in town offer guided tours, treks, and expeditions to Cotopaxi National Park. The best local operators are **Expediciones Tovar** (© 03/2811-333), on Calle Guayaquil 5–38, near Quito; and **Metropolitan Touring** (© 03/2810-334), on Calle Guayaquil 5–26, near Quito. Both these agencies are excellent. Tovar is probably better for climbing and adventure tourism, while Metropolitan is best for traditional tourism, soft adventure, and onward travel arrangements. See "What To See & Do In Cotopaxi National Park," above, for more details on the types of tours and adventures available to park visitors. These operators also offer guided tours to Laguna Quilotoa and around the Quilotoa Loop. For more information on this excursion, see "The Quilotoa Loop," below.

Fiesta de la Mama Negra

Latacunga is known across Ecuador for its celebration of the Virgen de la Merced (Virgin of Mercy), better known locally as Mama Negra (Black Mama). Each year on September 23 and 24, Latacunga's streets host a wild party, with dancing and parades, street food, fireworks, and carnival rides. The festivities exhibit a mix of indigenous, Spanish, and even African influences. Mama Negra is also celebrated, to slightly lesser extent, every November 11, which is Latacunga's independence day.

WHERE TO STAY IN LATACUNGA

Keep in mind that nearly all the hotels in Latacunga fill up every Wednesday night, and often on Thursday night too, due to the Thursday market in **Saquisilí** (see below). On these nights, and during the Mama Negra festivities (see above), it's absolutely imperative that you have a reservation.

Hotel Makroz   This is arguably the plushest hotel in Latacunga, although that certainly isn't saying much. The three-story downtown building is painted a bright white, and the carpeted rooms are comfortable and well equipped. Most have large picture windows that let in plenty of light. Some units come with minifridges and small stereo systems. *Note:* This hotel is right on one of the busiest avenues in Latacunga, and the street-facing rooms can be noisy.

Av. Félix Valencia 8–56 and Calle Quito, Latacunga. (*ℂ* **03/2800-907.** Fax 03/2807-274. 26 units. $25–$35 (£14–£19) double. Rates include breakfast. MC, V. **Amenities:** Restaurant; bar; laundry service. *In room:* TV, hair dryer.

Hotel Rodelu   If you're spending the night right in Latacunga, this is your best option. The rooms are bright and almost cheery, although the decor is definitely dated. Still, they have clean tile floors, cable television, and wooden headboards and furnishings. Ask to see a few units because some are pretty compact. The hotel is located right near Parque Vicente León and has a popular pizzeria on the ground floor, as well as its own little garden area.

Calle Quito 16–31, Latacunga. (*ℂ* **03/2800-956.** Fax 03/2812-341. www.rodelu.com.ec. 18 units. $25–$40 (£14–£22) double. AE, DC, MC, V. **Amenities:** Restaurant; bar; 24-hr. room service; laundry service. *In room:* TV.

WHERE TO DINE IN LATACUNGA

Latacunga's local specialty, *chugchucaras,* won't win any fans at the American Heart Association. This insane concoction is served up with piles of fried pork skins, fried plantains, fried potatoes, fried white-corn kernels that are pretty close to popcorn, some fried cheese empanadas, and seemingly anything else they can dig out of the deep fryer. *Chugchucara* restaurants abound in Latacunga. A massive *chugchucara* plate should run $3.50 to $5 (£1.95–£2.75). If you want to try this local treat—and if you think your heart can take it—head to **Chugchucaras Mama Negra** (*ℂ* **03/2805-401**), on Ordóñez 1–67 and Quijano, although there are a dozen or more dedicated *chugchucara* restaurants around town.

For good Chinese fare, head to **Chifa China** (*ℂ* **09/4579-982**), on Antonia Vela 6–85 and 5 de Junio. For Italian fare and pizza try **Pizzería Buon Giorno** (*ℂ* **03/2801-488**), on Sánchez de Orellana and General Maldonado.

Parrillada Los Copihues *※* ECUADORIAN/INTERNATIONAL   This is my favorite restaurant in Latacunga. Steaks, chicken, and fish are grilled over wood charcoal. You can also get a range of pastas and some local Ecuadorian fare. I like the fresh Andean trout simply sautéed with garlic. The dining room is large and sometimes crowded, especially on weekends. This is a great place to come for the filling *menú ejecutivo* lunch special which will run you just $2.50 (£1.40).

Calle Quito 70–83, between Maldonado and Tarqui. (*ℂ* **03/2802-962.** Main courses $3–$6 (£1.65–£3.30). MC, V. Mon–Sat 11am–10pm.

LATACUNGA AFTER DARK

Latacunga is a relatively quiet city, which only really gets going on Thursday, Friday, and Saturday nights. After dark, I recommend heading to the popular bar **Galaxi** (*ℂ* **03/2811-185**), located up the hill east of town in Barrio el Calvario. Another hot nightspot is the nearby **Sky Bar** (© **03/2813-016**), on Avenida Oriente, which has either karaoke or dancing most weekend nights.

THE QUILOTOA LOOP ⚑

One of the most popular trips based out of Latacunga is a circuit known as the **Quilotoa Loop.** The entire loop is about 200km (125 miles). While it is possible to do the trip in 1 day, I recommend spending a night or two at the **Black Sheep Inn** (see below). The roads, rough and rugged for much of the loop, pass through a beautiful series of isolated mountain villages and hamlets, many of whose inhabitants cling close to their ancient indigenous heritage and ways. You can make the trip in either direction.

Whichever direction you choose, **Laguna Quilotoa** ⚑⚑, a beautiful, high mountain lake formed in the broad crater of an extinct volcano, is roughly the halfway point and prime destination of this route. The views of the emerald-green lake are striking from the parking area, but many folks are tempted to hike down the steep slopes of the crater to the water's edge. The distance to the water seems deceptively short, and the climb down is relatively quick. But the climb back up is quite steep and can take over an hour. Local vendors, touts, and guides are always on hand in the parking lot, and several will offer to sell you a mule ride back to the top. If you want to save yourself the hike, be sure to arrange this before you head off downhill. The mule ride should cost around $4 to $5 (£2.20–£2.75). Other hiking options include the narrow and rugged trail around the crater rim, where the views are spectacular. There's a $1 (55p) entrance fee to visit the Quilotoa lagoon and crater.

Of the towns strewn along the Quilotoa Loop, perhaps the most famous is **Saquisilí,** a small indigenous village on the northeastern end of the loop, not very far from the Pan-American Highway. The weekly **Thursday market** ⚑ is perhaps the most authentic in Ecuador, and quite distinct from what you find in Otavalo, which many feel has become far too touristy. This market is a traditional highland market with scores of vendors, and hundreds, if not thousands, of locals arriving from villages throughout the central Sierra to buy, barter, and trade for foodstuffs, household items, herbs, tools, animals, and just about anything and everything else imaginable. A similar market, albeit somewhat smaller, is held every Saturday in the town of Zumbahua, and is easily combined with a visit to Laguna Quilotoa.

GETTING THERE   The Quilotoa Loop can done by rental car, organized tour, or local buses. Most folks first head west out of Latacunga toward Tigua, and then on to Zumbahua, where the loop goes north before reaching Laguna Quilotoa. Heading north from Quilotoa, the first major village is Chugchilán, followed by Sigchos, after which the route begins heading east again toward Saquisilí, close to where you meet up again with the Pan-American Highway, a little bit north of Latacunga.

If you're doing the loop by bus, arm yourself with some patience, plenty of warm clothing, snack food and energy bars, a good map of the region, and a sense of adventure. Local buses plying this circuit run erratic schedules, are often overcrowded, and occasionally break down. Still, every day, scores, if not hundreds, of locals make the various legs of this journey between the many small villages, and if you wait long enough you will be able to catch an onward ride in a bus or pickup truck.

For really comprehensive and up-to-date information on bus schedules, check the websites of, or contact directly, the Black Sheep Inn or Hostal Llullu Llama (see below). Alternatively, you can head to the main bus terminal in Latacunga and inquire there. **Transportes Iliniza** (© 03/2716-055) has two buses with daily departures making the entire loop in 2 days. The 11:30am bus leaves Latacunga and heads coun-terclockwise, via Sauislilí, Sigchos, and Chugchilán, where it spends the night and departs the next morning to complete the loop. The noon bus heads in the opposite direction and follows the same route. The ride around half the circuit takes about 4 hours. The buses from Chugchilán leave between the ungodly hours of 3 and 4am. **Cooperativa Vivero** (© 03/2723-251) has a couple of buses daily that head to Isin-livi, Saquisilí, Quilotoa, Chugchilán, and Zumbahua. **Cooperativa Cotopaxi** (© 03/ 2800-752) buses leave roughly every hour for Quevedo and will take you as far as Zumbahua, from where you can make onward connections around the circuit. The fare for the entire circuit should cost about $6 (£3.30), with the current one-way fare between Latacunga and Chugchilán costing about $2.25 (£1.25).

WHERE TO STAY ALONG THE QUILOTOA LOOP

There are a host of small, humble hostels and budget hotels all along the Quilotoa Loop; most are very basic and cater to locals and rugged backpackers. The two places listed below are striking exceptions, however, and I highly recommend that you choose one of these as your overnight midpoint, or better yet, as a base for exploring the area.

Black Sheep Inn ★★ *(Finds)* Environmental awareness and all-around greater global consciousness are the primary ideas motivating the owners of this unique Andean lodge. All meals are vegetarian. The bathrooms feature composting toilets and they recycle every type of container and material possible. The lodge has its own extensive organic permaculture gardens, as well as llamas, guinea pigs, and, of course, black sheep. There's a large dorm room that can hold up to 10 guests, and nine private rooms with sleeping lofts, wood-burning stoves, and straw and red tile roofs. Immac-ulate shared bathrooms and showers are located outside the rooms, and private bath-rooms have been added to five of the units.

The hotel is built on a high hillside just outside the village of Chugchilán, with a fabulous view over the Río Toachi canyon. There's a small swimming pond with a waterslide, along with a hot tub and wood-fired sauna. Other recent additions include a yoga room with a climbing wall, some gym equipment, and weights, as well as a 9-hole Frisbee golf course. The Black Sheep makes a great base for exploring the area, and a wide range of hikes and llama-accompanied treks are available. One of their most popular day tours begins with a car ride to Quilotoa Lake, from where you hike back to the hotel.

P.O. Box 05-01-240, Chugchilán, Cotopaxi. © 03/2814-587. www.blacksheepinn.com. 10 units; 5 with private bath-room. $25 (£14) per person in dorm room; $80 (£44) double with shared bathroom; $100 (£55) double with private bathroom. Rates include breakfast and dinner, and taxes. No credit cards. **Amenities:** Restaurant; bar; hot tub; sauna; small exercise room; tour desk; laundry service. *In room:* No phone.

Hostal Llullu Llama ★ If you simply remember that the double "L" in Spanish is pronounced as a *y*, you'll have no problem saying the name of this delightful moun-tain retreat. Housed in a converted farm house, the rooms here are bright and cheer-ful, and come with a mix of bed options from bunks to twins to double beds for couples. Most units have thick adobe walls and varnished wooden floors with woven reed mats used as throw rugs—and in some instances as wallpaper. The decor is com-plemented with local handicrafts. The Llullu Llama features a wood-fired sauna and a range of tours and treks. Though the hotel is located slightly off the actual

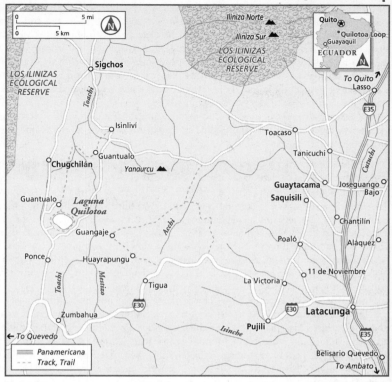

Quilotoa Loop

Quilotoa Loop, it still makes a great base for exploring the area. Your best bet for transportation, if you don't have your own rental car, is to arrange things with the lodge in advance. In fact, Llullu Llama is closely connected to **Safari Ecuador** ☆☆ (✆ **2/2222-505;** www.safari.com.ec), one of the better adventure tour operators in the country, which offers a host of organized tours and adventures to this lodge and around the area.

Isinliví, Cotopaxi. ✆ **03/2814-790** or 08/5737-829. www.llullullama.com. 9 units; 4 with private bathrooms. $6 (£3.30) per person in dorm room; $14 (£7.70) double with shared bathroom; $18 (£9.90) double with private bathroom. No credit cards. **Amenities:** Restaurant; bar; sauna; tour desk; laundry service. *In room:* No phone.

EN ROUTE SOUTH: A COUPLE OF QUICK STOPS

You'll know you've reached **San Miguel de Salcedo** when you see the large sculpture of one of the locally produced ice-cream sticks, or *helados de paila.* These somewhat conical treats are sold all over this small roadside city, which places a lot of civic pride in them (although most Ecuadorians will tell you that *helados de paila* are native to Ibarra). You can pretty much stop anywhere and find a shop selling *helados de paila.* Flavors vary, and include staples like vanilla, chocolate, and strawberry. I like some of the local fruit varieties, like *granadilla,* a tart member of the passion-fruit family. Salcedo is located about 15km (9 miles) south of Latacunga.

Located just off the Pan-American Highway, another 12km (7½ miles) south of Salcedo, the **Laguna de Yambo** is a popular spot to stop, stretch your legs, and take a gander down into the lime-green waters of this lake formed in an extinct volcanic crater. Unlike Quilotoa, however, this lake appears stagnant and polluted to me. The lake's greatest claim to fame is the legend that it "swallowed a train"; if you look down the steep sides of the extinct crater you can see still see the railroad tracks that run alongside it. Apparently at one point a train derailed and disappeared into the lake, and divers and salvage workers never found a trace.

On a clear day, you can look beyond the lake and catch a glimpse of Volcán Tungurahua in the distance. If you're heading to Baños, this is a good reference point and marker.

3 Ambato

138km (86 miles) S of Quito; 47km (29 miles) S of Latacunga; 288km (179 miles) N of Guayaquil

Despite its reputation as a cultural center that gave birth or was home to various prominent authors and intellectuals, and the fact that it is the largest city in the central Ecuadorian highlands, Ambato is rightly bypassed by most tourists. While it's an important commercial hub for the region, Ambato holds little of interest for visitors. Most folks breeze through Ambato on their way to someplace else. Moreover, with Baños (see below) and a couple of truly beautiful haciendas nearby, I see very little reason to overnight in Ambato.

Ambato is known as the "City of Flowers and Fruits," and you can find an overwhelming abundance of both in the city's markets. Ambato is also sometimes called the "City of the Three Juans," because three prominent Ecuadorian writers and intellectuals—Juan Leon Mera, Juan Montalvo, and Juan Benigno Vela—either hailed from the city, or spent much time living and writing there. Montalvo was a prominent novelist who some have called "the Cervantes of South America," while Mera was both a poet and novelist, but is most famous for writing the country's national anthem. Benigno Vela is best known as a critic and essayist.

ESSENTIALS
GETTING THERE & DEPARTING
BY BUS   Buses frequently leave Quito's main bus terminal, Terminal Terrestre, heading south along the Pan-American Highway to Ambato throughout the day. **Cooperativa Ambato** (© **02/2570-038** in Quito, or 03/2849-504 in Ambato) and **Cooperativa Transandina** (© **02/2572-265** in Quito, or 03/2849-566 in Ambato) are the main bus lines, although another half-dozen or so companies are in the mix, all taking turns to spread out the departures, with a bus leaving roughly every 15 minutes from 5am to 11pm and somewhat less frequent service throughout the rest of the evening and early morning. The ride takes about 2½ hours and costs about $2 (£1.10).

From Ambato there are frequent bus connections to most other major destinations around Ecuador.

The main bus terminal in Ambato, **Terminal Terrestre** (© **03/2821-481**), is located a little over 1.5km (1 mile) northeast of downtown, on Avenida Colombia. Frequent local buses connect the bus terminal and downtown Ambato—look for a bus that says CENTRO. The fare should be around 25¢ (15p). You can also take one of the many taxis you will find waiting at the bus terminal; a ride anywhere in Ambato should not exceed $2 (£1.10), and most rides are just $1 (55p).

BY CAR   To reach Ambato by car, simply head south out of Quito on the Pan-American Highway (E35). The ride takes just over 2 hours. There's a bypass around Ambato, but the Pan-American Highway itself, and most of the flow of traffic, actually goes right through the heart of downtown on its way south and toward Riobamba.

ORIENTATION

If you enter Ambato from the north, you'll pass by a traffic circle with the sculpture of a large, naked woman holding some flowers and welcoming you to the city. The main downtown area is bounded by the parallel avenidas Rocafuerte and 12 de Noviembre, and by the calles Sevilla and Olmedo. All the city's major parks, churches, and markets are found within this compact area.

GETTING AROUND

The city is large, spread out, and located on relatively hilly terrain, making walking long distances problematic. Luckily, taxis are abundant and inexpensive. If you can't simply flag one down, call **Cooperativa Mera** (*(C)* **03/2821-460**) or **Cooperativa 12 de Noviembre** (*(C)* **03/2820-280**).

Ambato has an extensive network of local urban buses. For most tourists the only bus route of importance is the one between downtown and the main bus terminal. Buses from the center to the bus station are marked TERMINAL, and leave from the south side of Parque Cevallos.

If you want to rent a car here, contact the local branch of **Localiza** (**03/2420-415;** www.localiza.com.ec).

VISITOR INFORMATION

The Ministry of Tourism runs a friendly **tourist information office** (*(C)* **03/2821-800**), right next to the Hotel Ambato (see below). They can provide information on local attractions and tours.

FAST FACTS   To reach the **police** dial *(C)* **101** or 03/2846-400. The main office is on Av. Atahualpa 568 and Avenida Quisquis. The **Hospital Municipal** (*(C)* **03/2821-058**) is on Avenida Pasteur and Unidad Nacional.

You'll find a branch of **Banco de Guayaquil** (*(C)* **03/2422-587**) on the corner of calles Sucre and Mera, and a branch of **Banco del Pichincha** (*(C)* **03/2422-031**) on Calle Lalama 3–20 and Cevallos. The **post office** (*(C)* **03/2823-332**) is located on Calle Castillo 04–10, near Avenida Bolívar.

Internet cafes abound in Ambato, especially around downtown and Parque Montalvo. I like the fast connections at **Net Place Ambato** (*(C)* **03/2826-178**), at Montalvo 558 and Cevallos; **La "L" Internet** (*(C)* **03/2822-731**), at Montalvo and Cevallos; and **Megaplanet** (*(C)* **03/2423-725**), at Cevallos 2154 and Olmedo. Hourly rates are 50¢ to $1.50 (30p–85p).

WHAT TO SEE & DO IN AMBATO

Ambato's main downtown park, **Parque Juan Montalvo,** is a solid-square block area with tall palm trees, pretty gardens, plenty of bench seating, and footpaths crisscrossing it. It's very busy on weekdays during lunch and in the early evening, as well as throughout the day and into the night on weekends. On the northeast side of the park is the city's massive modern **cathedral** with its soaring domes.

On the northwest corner of Parque Juan Montalvo is the **Casa de Montalvo** (*(C)* **03/2824-248**), the restored birthplace and residence of one of the town's famous Juans. This house is open daily from 9am until noon and 2 until 6pm. Admission is $1 (50p).

La Quinta de Juan León Mera (© 03/2820-419) is the home and retreat formerly belonging to one of the three Juans. Today, the small estate is a beautiful place to get away from the bustle of downtown Ambato and admire stunning views over the Ambato River. Located on Avenida Los Capuiles, the house is open Wednesday through Sunday from 9am until 6pm. Admission is $1 (55p). La Quinta is located a little over 1.5km (1 mile) north of the downtown area. You can walk here, or take a taxi for around $1 (55p).

For an even better view, head to the **Monumento A La Primera Imprenta (Monument to the First Printing Press),** which is located on a high point northwest of downtown. On a clear day you'll have no problem seeing the plume of smoke from Volcán Tungurahua. A taxi here should run you $2 (£1.10) each way.

Ambato is famous for its markets. These are working traditional markets where locals and highland dwellers sell and barter for food, clothing, tools, animals, seeds, spices, and just about everything else imaginable. The city is particularly well known for its fruits and flowers. The biggest market day is Monday, with Wednesday and Friday not far behind. Really, though, Ambato's bustling **Mercado Central** and **Mercado Modelo** have ample offerings pretty much every day of the week. The Mercado Central is located on Avenida 12 de Noviembre, a block northeast of Parque 12 de Noviembre. The Mercado Modelo is located on the southeastern side of Avenida Cevallos, about 2 blocks northeast of Parque Cevallos. On Monday and other market days, vendors fill the city streets all around these two markets. A small amount of art and craftworks is available, but you can certainly buy hand-woven wool clothing and traditional Andean headwear.

For any organized tours, contact your hotel tour desk, **Metropolitan Touring** (© 03/2820-211), inside the Centro Comercial Caracol on Avenida Los Capuiles, or **Delgado Travel** (© 03/2423-070), on Juan León Mera 6–13 and Calle Sucre. Options range from city tours to trips to Cotopaxi or Baños or other destinations around the central highlands.

WHERE TO STAY & DINE IN AMBATO

In addition to the places listed below, the **Hotel Miraflores** (© 03/2843-224l; www.hmiraflores.com.ec), located in an upscale neighborhood southwest of downtown, is another good mid-range option.

There are really no standout restaurants in Ambato, and most visitors are here by necessity on a 1-night stay as part of a longer itinerary. Most tourists simply have dinner at their hotel restaurant, though the restaurants at both hotels listed below are quite acceptable. If you want to venture out, you can get good pizzas and Italian fare

---

Flowers & Fruit

Befitting a town known as the "City of Flowers and Fruits," Ambato celebrates the yearly Carnaval season with a major blowout party known as La Fiesta de las Flores y de las Frutas. For 2 solid weeks, Ambato hosts a near-constant stream of parades, open-air concerts, beauty contests, bull fights, and street fairs with portable amusement park rides. The exact dates vary, but the celebrations coincide with traditional Latin American Carnaval periods, and tend to occur around mid-February and early March, preceding Ash Wednesday and the beginning of Lent. During this fiesta, hotel rooms are sold out long in advance.

at **Pizzería Fornace,** on Cevallos 17–28 (© **03/2823-244**); and decent Continental fare and local Ecuadorian cuisine at the popular **Restaurante El Gran Alamo,** on Sucre 15–21 and Juan León Mera (© **03/2821-710**).

EXPENSIVE

Hotel Casino Emperador ⚞ Easily the most luxurious option in Ambato, this high-rise of reflective glass is well located, wonderfully equipped, and very comfy. Rooms are large and well done, with more sense of style than you will find at many modern hotels in Ecuador. On the top of this six-story building, you'll find a small spa with a rooftop pool and Jacuzzi under an atrium-glass open-air roof. The hotel's restaurant also enjoys a high perch, with walls of windows providing a fabulous view. On-site is a somewhat refined little piano bar, as well as a small but spiffy casino.

Av. Cevallos 10–14 and Lalama. © 03/2424-460. www.hotelcasinoemperador.com. 63 units. $108 (£59) double; $140–$180 (£77–£99) suite. Rates include breakfast buffet. Lower rates in the off season. Free parking. AE, DC, MC, V. **Amenities:** Restaurant; bar; casino; pool; small well-equipped exercise room; Jacuzzi; steam bath; sauna; tour desk; room service 7am–midnight; massage; laundry service. *In room:* TV, minibar, hair dryer, safe.

MODERATE

Hotel Ambato This is a fairly run-of-the-mill, modern business-class hotel located downtown. Most of the rooms come with two twin beds, so if you're a couple, be sure to specify that you want a *matrimonial.* The rooms on the higher floors have great views of the surrounding mountains and river below. There's one presidential suite, which is large and has a separate sitting area featuring a plush sofa and a couple of chairs as well as a private little bar. The hotel's restaurant is good and dependable, one of the best in Ambato. There's even a small casino on-site, which is popular with locals and visiting businesspeople.

Guayaquil 1–08 and Rocafuerte. © 03/2421-791. Fax 03/2421-790. www.hotelambato.com. 59 units. $60 (£33) double; $80 (£44) suite. Rates include breakfast. Free parking. AE, DC, MC, V. **Amenities:** Restaurant; bar; casino; tour desk; room service 7am–11pm; laundry service. *In room:* TV.

AMBATO AFTER DARK

Ambato's nightlife is pretty tame. It picks up some on Thursday and through the weekend. The most popular nightclub in town is the **Coyote Disco Club,** located on Av. Bolívar 20–57, near Guayaquil (© **03/2822-424**). This is a large club with loud music and dancing. A young crowd dominates **Cervecería Búfalo,** on Olmedo 681 and Juan León Mera (© **03/2841-685**). For hard-core dancing, head to **Discoteca Ilusiones,** on Av. Quis Quis and Madrid (© **03/2851-826**).

If you're in a gaming mood, the casinos at the **Hotel Ambato** and **Hotel Casino Emperador** (see above) are good bets.

EN ROUTE TO BAÑOS: TWO HACIENDAS IN THE HILLS

About halfway between Ambato and Baños, a side road heads toward the small village of Patate. Beyond Patate are two delightful haciendas. The road on which these two haciendas are located connects to an alternative and rugged gravel road to Baños, a little over 16km (10 miles) away.

Hacienda Leito ⚞⚞ (Finds) This is a classic old hacienda with plenty of modern touches and comforts. There's a beautiful central fountain near the entrance to the main building, at the end of the centuries-old stone driveway. The main building, where you'll find the restaurant and lounge area, is filled with antiques and colonial-era artwork. Most of the rooms are either brand new or recently remodeled. All have

It's *Chicha* Time

If you drive through the Ecuadorian countryside at night, you may notice a red light in a window or the doorway of a home, which usually means the owners are selling homemade *chicha:* a fermented beverage popular in the Andes since the days of the Incas.

Sometimes considered a beer, though it lacks carbonation, *chicha*—the Spanish pronunciation is *chee*-cha—is made and consumed by indigenous groups across the Americas. It can be brewed from various fruits and vegetables, but in the Andes it is usually made from yellow corn and sometimes called *chicha de jora.*

To make *chicha,* corn kernels are soaked in water until they germinate, then are boiled and fermented for several days, usually in large clay vessels. The result is a milky yellow liquid, sweet at the beginning of fermentation and becoming sour as it progresses. The alcohol content increases the longer the liquid is fermented, but it never gets any stronger than beer.

Chicha is used in Andean indigenous rituals as a sort of holy water that is drunk, and it's copiously consumed during traditional village festivals (though it's steadily being replaced by beer). It is also given to visitors as an act of respect, and if you are offered an earthenware cup of the beverage upon arriving at an Ecuadorian village, Emily Post would probably recommend that you drink it whether you like it or not.

If you visit an indigenous village in the Oriente, you may be given *chicha* made from cassava, a tropical tuber known as *yuca* in Spanish. The cassava *chicha* is thicker and doesn't have much flavor, but that doesn't keep folks in the rainforest from consuming it on a regular basis. Another point of etiquette is that in the Oriente, you are expected to place your cup upside down on the ground when you've finished your *chicha.*

If you travel to other parts of Latin America, you'll find that the word *chicha* is also used to refer to nonalcoholic fruit drinks. In Peru, a traditional beverage is *chicha morada,* which is made by boiling purple corn, pineapple rinds, and an applelike fruit called *membrillo,* and is especially popular with children because it leaves the tongue and lips lavender.

The uncertainty created by the existence of alcoholic and nonalcoholic beverages with the same name is sometimes clarified by using the term *chicha fuerte,* or "strong chicha," to distinguish the alcoholic beverage. And to make things just a little more confusing for outsiders, there is the popular Latin American idiomatic expression *"ni chicha, ni limonada,"* which translates as "neither *chicha* nor lemonade," and means about the same thing as "neither fish nor fowl." Now, put that in your cup and drink it!

fireplaces, polished wood floors, exposed beams on the ceilings and walls, and separate tubs and showers. Each suite, in addition to being bigger than a standard room, comes with a balcony that has a view of Volcán Tungurahua, as well as with a large bathroom and private Jacuzzi. The meals here are excellent, with elegant candle-lit dinners every night. Early 2007 saw the inauguration of a sumptuous spa, which has a large indoor swimming pool under a broad, high roof with loads of skylights and expansive lounge areas. There are several massage and treatment rooms, as well as a natural hot-spring fed Jacuzzi, a sauna, and a steam room. A small museum contains pre-Columbian artifacts and archaeological finds. Horseback riding is excellent here, and a wide range of tours around the hacienda and Baños area is offered.

8km (5 miles) from Patate, Baños. ℂ 03/2859-328. ℂ/fax 03/2859-329. www.haciendaleito.com. 18 units. $70 (£39) double; $86 (£47) suite. Rates include full breakfast. AE, DC MC, V. **Amenities:** Restaurant; bar; indoor pool; Jacuzzi; sauna; steam room; mountain bikes; tour desk; massage; laundry service; free Wi-Fi. *In room:* No phone.

Hacienda Manteles ⋆   This beautiful hotel has the feel of a homey mountain lodge. There are seven rooms in the main building, while the rest of the units are spread between two buildings slightly below. The best room in the house is the end unit on the main floor of the main building. This room has a king-size bed facing a large picture window with a view of Volcán Tungurahua. It also features a modern Jacuzzi-style shower with two main shower heads and a row of jets. I find the attic rooms, in the main house, a bit cramped, while the four-bedroom Casa Chiquita (Little House) is an excellent option for a family or group of friends; its two front rooms have great views of the volcano. All around the hacienda you'll find beautiful gardens, with fruit trees, organic vegetable gardens, and ornamental flowers and orchids. Meals are served family-style in the main dining room, and usually feature plenty of produce from the gardens. There's a small library of Ecuadorian history and natural history books in the main hacienda lounge, where you will also find a television that has a host of cable stations. These folks own 200 hectares (494 acres) of primary cloud forest, and specialize in tours of their own private reserve and neighboring (and seldom-visited) Llanganates National Park. The bird-watching is excellent. One of the great features here is a nearby waterfall.

11km (7 miles) from Patate, Baños. ℂ/fax 02/2233-484 reservation office in Quito, or 09/8715-632 cellphone at the hacienda. www.haciendamanteles.com. 15 units. $72 (£40) double; $83 (£45) mini-suite. Rates include breakfast and a guided hike to the nearby waterfall. AE, DC MC, V. **Amenities:** Restaurant; bar; tour desk; laundry service. *In room:* No phone.

4 Baños ⋆⋆

176km (109 miles) S of Quito; 55km (34 miles) N of Riobamba; 288km (179 miles) N of Guayaquil

Strategically located on the jungle's doorstep and at the foot of Volcán Tungurahua, the charismatic town of Baños de Agua Santa offers both adventure and relaxation. Indeed, it's extremely popular among local and international tourists alike. Tourism is well established and a wide variety of activities are offered, ranging from adrenaline-pumping extreme sports to a soothing soak in the hot springs. Situated at an altitude of 1,800m (5,900 ft.), Baños has a warm and mostly sunny climate, and is an excellent base from which to explore the jungle and neighboring protected areas such as Parque Nacional Sangay, a UNESCO World Heritage Site since 1983.

Although Tungurahua's recent and somewhat unexpected return to activity has rather overshadowed the town's main attraction of late, Baños is chiefly famous for its thermal pools (hence the name Baños, or Baths), which are nourished by the mineral-rich naturally heated springs of Tungurahua itself. Locals rave about the health benefits of taking a soak, claiming that the springs, with their high mineral and sulfur content, can alleviate anything from muscular pain to kidney ailments.

ESSENTIALS

GETTING THERE & DEPARTING

BY BUS   **Transportes Amazonas** (© **02/2571-747** in Quito, or 03/2740-242 in Baños) and **Transportes Baños** (© **02/2570-884** in Quito, or 03/2740-382) leave from Quito's main bus terminal, Terminal Terrestre, approximately every 15 to 20 minutes from 4am to midnight. The return buses follow roughly the same schedule. The trip takes around 4 hours and costs $3.50 (£1.95) each way.

Baños is also connected, with less frequent service, to Tena, Coca, Puyo, and Guayaquil. The main bus terminal in Baños is located on calles Reyes and Espejo, just a short walk from the town's center.

BY CAR   To reach Baños by car, begin by heading south out of Quito on the Pan-American Highway (E35) to the city of Ambato. The highway weaves its way right through the center of Ambato. Near the southern end of Ambato you'll see the well-marked turn-off for Pelileo and Baños. Follow the signs and Highway E50 to Baños. The ride takes around 3½ hours. Along the final stretch between Pelileo and Baños, you'll pass fallen ash, volcanic rocks, and destroyed houses from an eruption in August 2006. Be aware that mudslides (lahars) from heavy rains can occasionally cause the temporary closure of this route.

From Guayaquil, take the Pan-American Highway northeast through Riobamba and Penipe, and cross Río Chambo into Baños. The road between Penipe and Baños is also subject to mudslides from Volcán Tungurahua; it's best get the all-clear before setting off. The Guayaquil-Baños route takes approximately 5 hours.

ORIENTATION

Baños is a compact little town nestled right against the flanks of the Tungurahua Volcano. The downtown area is only about 11 by 7 blocks, and the main roads through the city run in an east-west direction. The Río Pastaza runs just outside the downtown area. The center features two small, pretty parks, **Parque Palomino Flores (Parque Central)** and **Parque Sebastian Acosta (Parque de la Basílica)**; the majority of tourist infrastructure is along the main streets either side of these two parks. The bus terminal, located near the center of town on calles Reyes and Espejo, is a short walk from most hotels and hostels. The hills of Bellavista are located towards the south, accessible by following a trail south off Calle Maldonado.

GETTING AROUND

It's unlikely you'll need bus transportation to get around Baños, except perhaps to go to El Salado thermal baths, which are located a couple of kilometers outside the center. The bus to El Salado departs from Calle Rocafuerte, just beside the artisans market. The fare is 15¢ (10p).

Getting around in a taxi is extremely convenient—many cooperatives offer a set rate to tourist attractions. A trip to the town *mirador* (lookout point) costs $8 (£4.40); a taxi trip to and from the volcano *mirador* will set you back around $15 (£8.25); a waterfall tour costs approximately $20 (£11) and lasts 2½ to 3 hours. If you can't flag down a taxi, call **Cooperativa de Taxi 16 de Diciembre** (© **03/2740-416**).

VISITOR INFORMATION

Tourist information is easily accessible in Baños. The friendly **official tourist office** (© **03/2740-483**) is located on calles Halflants and Ambato, by the Parque Central; there you can get detailed information, maps, tourist guides, or general help with your

ACCOMMODATIONS ■
Finca Chamanapamba **5**
Hospedaje Santa Cruz **9**
Hostal Los Nevados **6**
Hostal Plantas y Blanco **8**
Hostería Monte Selva **11**
Luna Runtun **5**
Sangay Spa-Hotel **14**

DINING ◆
Café Hood **2**
Café Mariane **3**
Le Petit Restaurant **10**
Restaurant Moni **4**

ATTRACTIONS ●
Balneario Las Peñas **15**
Basílica de Nuestra Señora
de Agua Santa **7**
La Piscina de la Virgen **13**
Piscina El Salado **1**
Piscinas Santa Clara **12**
Zoológico San Martín **1**

- - - - *Track, Trail*

trip. The office is open Monday to Friday 8am until 4pm, and there is usually some-one on duty who speaks English. Most tour operators are also a good source of tourist information and are willing to help without any commitment on your part. In busi-ness over 20 years, **Expediciones Amazónicas** ⚘, calles Thomas Halflants and Ori-ente (© **03/2740506;** www.amazonicas.banios.com), is one of the town's most experienced tour operators, specializing in a wide range of extreme sports. **Geotours** (calles Ambato and Thomas Halflants; © **03/2741-344;** www.geotoursecuador.com) also comes highly recommended for adventure and extreme sports, especially rafting; they provide bilingual, professionally trained and certified guides. Another leading operator is **Rainforestur,** calles Ambato and Maldonado (© **03/2740-743;** www. rainforestur.com), known for its excellent jungle and mountain expeditions and trilin-gual guides. They also have an office in Quito, at Av. Amazonas 420 and Robles (© **02/2239-822**).

FAST FACTS If you need to contact the local **police,** dial © **03/2740-251** (or © 101 in an emergency); the police station is located on Calle Oriente 251 and Juan León Mera. In the case of a medical emergency, head to the local **hospital** (© **03/2740-443**) on Montalvo and Pastaza. There are a number of **pharmacies** located along the main street, Calle Ambato.

Banco del Pichincha (© **03/2740-961**) is on the corner of calles Ambato and Thomas Halflants. **Banco del Pacífico** (© **03/2740-336**) is on the corner of Thomas Halflants and Rocafuerte. Both have ATMs accepting international cards and can change traveler's checks.

The **post office** (© **03/2740-901**) is located on Calle Ambato by the Parque Central.

Internet cafes are plentiful in Baños, with rates starting at 25¢ (15p) for 15 minutes; just head along Ambato or surrounding streets and you'll find a spot. Most Internet cafes have cheap international-call capabilities and are generally open from around 8am until 11pm. Most hotels and hostels offer **laundry service;** alternatively, **Laundry Service Carina** (Martínez and Alfaro) is a good, quick option, charging 80¢ (45p) per kilo for a full-service same-day wash and dry.

WHAT TO SEE & DO

It's worth taking a peek inside the town's semi-gothic **Basílica de Nuestra Señora de Agua Santa** ⊛, which was finally completed in 1944 after Belgian priest Thomas Halflants had begun construction 40 years earlier. The interior displays interesting pictures telling stories of the supposed miracles performed by the Virgin of Holy Water in and around the town. There are always hawkers selling candles and religious trinkets outside, and it gets pretty crowded on Sundays and during religious festivals. Upstairs from the church is a small museum (50¢/30p) with religious artifacts, paintings, and, for some odd reason, stuffed animals. You won't be missing much if you skip the museum.

Housing a wide variety of local fauna and several endangered species, **Zoológico San Martín** ⊛ (© **03/2741-166**) is perhaps the best zoo in Ecuador. If you can't make it to the Galápagos, you can at least see one of the giant tortoises here. Located some 3km (2 miles) outside Baños in the San Martín sector along the road to the parish of Lligua, the zoo is perfect for a half-day trip and great for kids. It's open daily 8am to 5pm. Admission is $1.50 (85p).

All the local tour agencies and hotel desks offer sightseeing tours to the nearby waterfalls and other nearby attractions. Your best bet is to sign on for an organized *chiva* **tour,** either to the waterfalls during the day or to the volcano lookout at night. These take place in open-air, brightly painted buses. Waterfall tours cost around $8 (£4.40), take about half a day, and end up at the rushing giant waterfall **El Pailón del Diablo (The Devil's Cauldron).** Along the way you can take a short ride on a *tarabita,* a cable car crossing the river, which is a fun and slightly thrilling way to appreciate the splendid scenery. Volcano tours usually leave around 9pm and cost around $4 (£2.20). These last a few hours, and, if you're lucky, you'll get to see the red glow of Tungurahua's erupting molten lava.

SOAKING IN THE HOT SPRINGS

No trip to Baños is complete without a visit to the town's namesake hot springs. The most popular—and therefore busiest—thermal pools are **La Piscina de la Virgen,** Martínez and Montalvo (© **03/2740-462**), which has three large pools of differing temperatures, from pretty cool to very hot. Like Goldilocks, many people find the medium-temperature pool just right. This place is located near the waterfall by the Sangay Spa-Hotel, and brave bathers can take a cold shower in the waterfall before and/or after a hot soak. It is open daily 4:30am to 5pm and 6 to 10pm. Admission is $2 (£1.10).

Just a little bit beyond La Virgen, **Balneario Las Peñas** 🐟 (end of Martínez) is the town's largest and most modern thermal bath complex, which is popular with local families. This place features several pools, one that's very large, with crisscrossing water slides that children love. It is open Friday through Sunday from 8am until 5pm. Admission is 50¢ (30p).

Piscinas Santa Clara, Ibarra and Viera, next to Empresa Eléctrica (© **03/2740-349**) has cooler pools of clear mineral water, as opposed to the muddy, colored sulfuric waters found at the other hot springs. Although not as soothing to tired muscles, these mineral waters are also reputed to be healthy and healing. This place is also known locally as El Cangrejo. It's open daily 8am to 5pm, and admission is $2 (£1.10).

If you prefer a quieter atmosphere, head a mile or so out of town to **Piscina El Salado** 🐟, Avenida El Salado, off the road to Ambato (© **03/2740-493**). This is a mid-size and well-tended complex, with several different pools fed by both cloudy sulfuric waters and clear mineral waters. These pools are open daily from 4am to 5pm. Admission is $1 (55p). To get here, take a taxi (about $3/£1.65) or catch the bus from Rocafuerte outside the artisans market.

In addition to the above-mentioned pools and baths, which are my top choices, you'll see signs for other options.

If you're looking to pamper yourself entirely, and aren't staying at a hotel with an in-house spa, head to **Stay in Touch,** Martínez and Eloy Alfaro (© **03/2742-138**), which offers full-body and deep-tissue massages, facials, and shiatsu from $15 (£8.25). Alternatively, opt for Carmen Sánchez's treatments at **Chakra,** Eloy Alfaro and Martínez (© **03/2742-027**) for Swedish massage and reflexology.

ACTIVE ADVENTURES & OUTDOOR ACTIVITIES

Baños is a popular and, in many ways, perfect destination for those looking to participate in outdoor adventure pursuits, especially extreme sports such as white-water rafting, bridge jumping, canyoning, mountain climbing, horseback riding, and mountain biking. Tour operators and experienced guides are plentiful and prices are extremely reasonable. See above, under "Visitor Information," for recommended and reputable operators that can organize just about any of the tours and activities listed below.

Whatever you sign up for, be sure to know your own physical limits before setting out. Also, always bring plenty of water and sunscreen.

WHITE-WATER RAFTING 🐟   The majority of white-water rafting trips offered out of Baños are half-day tours on Río Pastaza or Río Patate. Rates run around $30 (£17) per person. Novices are welcome and all gear is provided by the operator. Most of these trips spend about 2 hours on the river, in class II to class III waters. Some operators also offer full-day excursions. If you have some experience, ask about the full-day tours on a class IV and V section of the Pastaza.

CANYONING & BRIDGE JUMPING   If you'd prefer to climb the waterfall rather than navigate the river at the foot of it, try **canyoning,** a new sport proving to be increasingly popular among visitors. Canyoning involves hiking in a mountain canyon, through rivers, with periodic rappel descents, usually on the face of a waterfall. Around Baños, canyoning is possible on the Chamana, San Jorge, Río Blanco, and Cashuano waterfalls. Half-day tours cost around $30 to $35 (£17–£19). Try the excursions organized by **Geotours.**

Bridge or **swing jumping** has recently sprung up as one of the most daring outdoor pursuits in the area. A rope is fastened to one end of a bridge and clipped to the jumper's harness; unlike in bungee jumping, the jumper pushes outward from the bridge, swinging pendulum-like when the rope becomes taut. Jumps, which cost $10 to $15 (£5–£7.50), take place off the San Francisco bridge by the bus terminal or off the bridge crossing the Río Blanco (along the road to Puyo), with different platform heights available, depending on how bold you are. During the week you should organize jumps through local operators. On weekends and holidays you can head straight to the bridge.

CLIMBING, HIKING & TREKKING   The forests, mountains, volcanoes, and national parks around Baños offer opportunities for all sorts of hiking, climbing, and trekking adventures. Hiking up to Bellavista, to the white cross overlooking town, is a popular option. Take the trail which begins at the southern end of Maldonado.

Volcano climbing is also an old favorite, although **ascending Volcán Tungurahua is not recommended at present** owing to recent activity and the imminent threat of eruption. Many operators have limited their climbing tours on Tungurahua because of the summer 2006 and February 2007 eruptions and the danger of mud flows. But volcanoes El Altar and El Sangay can be ascended; check with local tour guides for up-to-date information on climbing conditions. All-inclusive trips usually range in duration from 2 days to a week and cost around $90 (£50) per person per day. A minimum of two participants is usually required. Lower-altitude trekking on the flanks of these volcanoes, as well as inside Sangay and Llanganates national parks, is better suited to those seeking shorter, less-strenuous trips. Day trips with relaxed hiking start at around $50 (£28).

HORSEBACK RIDING & MOUNTAIN BIKING   All the local tour agencies and hotel desks can help you arrange horseback-riding and mountain-bike tours through the lush mountainous terrain here. Rates run around $5 to $10 (£2.75–£5.50) per hour for a guided tour.

If you're going mountain biking, one popular option is the so-called Ruta de las Cascadas (Route of the Waterfalls), ending up at El Pailón del Diablo, which is predominantly a descent. With some coordination, your tour company will pick up you and your bikes, so you can make the more arduous ascent back to Baños.

TRIPS TO THE AMAZON   Situated on the Oriente's doorstep, Baños makes for a superb base from which to explore Puyo and Cuyabeno. From 1-day to 10-day trips deep into the heart of the rainforest, expect to pay approximately $30 (£17) per day per person for budget-oriented tours. The summer months of June to September are usually the most popular for jungle tours, so book in advance if possible. Come prepared if embarking on longer trips; be sure to have appropriate clothing, waterproofing, insect repellent, sunscreen, and malaria tablets. **Rainforestur** (see above) probably offers the best jungle tours around.

BRUSH UP ON YOUR SPANISH

With its host of language schools, Baños is a great place to brush up on your rusty Spanish or to dive in for some intensive, first-time learning. Schools here offer courses

---

Party Time in the Old Town

An excellent time to visit Baños is during its celebration of Nuestra Señora de Agua Santa (Our Lady of Holy Water), held each year throughout October, which features fireworks, parades, dancing in the streets, and all-out revelry. The city's founding is also celebrated heartily on and around December 16. Book accommodations in advance if you're planning a trip during these dates.

Tungurahua: Back with a Bang

After an 80-year period of inactivity, which led many experts and inhabitants to believe that the volcano was dormant, Tungurahua unexpectedly returned to life with a bang in October 1999, spurting ash and lava for 2 weeks. Baños and surrounding villages were evacuated, and roads leading to and from the area were closed. While the eruptions were relatively minor, evacuees spent not weeks but months waiting for a major eruption, which never materialized.

Impatient to return to their beloved homes, locals began to pour back into the town after a showdown with the military, and by summer 2000 Baños was back to business as usual. The first half of 2006, nevertheless, marked a period of increased seismic activity, and August 2006 saw the biggest eruption since 1916, with lava flows and incandescent rocks destroying nearby villages and causing several fatalities. Following months of relative calm, February 2007 saw increased activity once again, with ash, gases, lava flows, and lahars (volcanic mudslides) prompting authorities to close roads.

The volcano remains on orange-red alert and at present **climbers are strongly advised against ascending Tungurahua** because a large eruption is imminent. The refuge, situated at 3,800m (12,470 ft.), remains partly destroyed. Tungurahua is constantly monitored and security measures are in place with a number of designated "safe spots" in the town's surrounding hills in the event of evacuation. Visitors to the area should be aware of the possibility of eruption; although in this case seismologists estimate that Baños would not be in the immediate path of danger due to its position. For further information on Volcán Tungurahua's current status, check out www.volcano.si.edu.

for all levels, and you can opt for group or one-on-one classes. Check out **Ciudad de Baños Language School** (© 03/2740317; www.escueladeidiomas.banios.com) or **Mayra's Spanish School** (© 03/2742-850; www.mayraschool.com). Classes run around $100 (£55) per week, for 4 hours of lessons per day, including a home-stay and three daily meals.

WHERE TO STAY IN BAÑOS
VERY EXPENSIVE

Luna Runtun ✿✿✿ Located some 6km (3¾ miles) above the town, Luna Runtun offers spectacularly breathtaking views of Baños, Llanganates National Park, and the smoking Volcán Tungurahua. The hotel is located within Sangay National Park. With a well-deserved reputation as one of the top hotels in the country, and billing itself an "Adventure Spa," Luna Runtun promises a luxurious stay, whether you decide to lie around and indulge in relaxing spa treatments or opt to partake in challenging outdoor activities, such as rafting, trekking, and horseback riding. The spaciously cozy and enchanting rustic rooms all offer views of the stunning landscape, with the choice of either deluxe, superior, or presidential suites. The food here is excellent. Homegrown, organic ingredients are used in a range of delicious dishes, with European cuisine as the restaurant's specialty. The spa, however, is the hotel's principal attraction. This is where you should head to unwind and luxuriate in a wide range of treatments that include clay wraps, honey exfoliation, various massages, depilation, and hydrating baths. Some of the treatments incorporate volcanic ash and rocks from neighboring Tungurahua. The entire complex is surrounded by lush gardens and also houses an art gallery, two conference centers, and a bird-watching platform.

Caserío Runtun, Km 6 (mailing address: P.O. Box 18-02-1944), Baños de Agua Santa. (C) **03/2740-882** or 03/2740-665. Fax 03/2740-376. www.lunaruntun.com. 30 units. $207 (£114) double; $270 (£147) superior double; $330 (£181) presidential suite. Rates include breakfast; dinner; use of pool, sauna and Jacuzzi; and taxes. AE, DC, MC, V. **Amenities:** Restaurant; bar; cafe; lounge with fireplace; 5 outdoor swimming pools; Jacuzzi; sauna; steam bath; tour desk; laundry service; babysitting; free Wi-Fi. *In room:* Minibar, hair dryer, safe.

MODERATE

Finca Chamanapamba ★★ Set in beautiful rustic cabins right beside the Chamana waterfall, this intimate, homey lodge, run by German couple Regine and Dietrich Heinke, offers excellent views of the River Ulba and Volcán Tungurahua. A quiet hide-out, with two of its own man-made waterfalls, the Finca is located 4km (2½ miles) outside the central hub of Baños, and is the perfect choice if you wish to escape the hustle and bustle of the town but still be within reach of main attractions and activities. The two-story cabanas are spacious and stylishly decorated with king-size beds, private bathrooms, and balconies exuding a real country-style feel about the place. The owners will gladly help you arrange climbing or horseback-riding trips, or will give advice on how best to explore the natural beauty of the area; you can even go trekking right from the ranch itself, or bathe in the cool waters at the foot of the falls. The ranch's restaurant is quite good and the menu features several German specialties. Given space restrictions, try to book in advance.

Km 4, Ulba, Chamana, Baños de Agua Santa. (C) **03/2742-671.** www.chamanapamba.com. 3 units. $80 (£44) double. Rates include full breakfast. Credit cards not accepted. **Amenities:** Restaurant; tour desk; room service. *In room:* No phone.

Hostería Monte Selva ★ *Kids* Established in 1993 and set on 5 hectares (12 acres) of green hillside, Monte Selva boasts lush gardens and comfortable accommodations in pretty, rustic wooden cabins at the foot of the mountain. Spa facilities are offered here, including mud baths, steam baths, and massages. They even have their own natural hot pools, fed by springs heated near Tungurahua. For those with a sweet tooth, the on-site *chocolatería* is an absolute must. If adventure is more your thing, try one of the many tour and activity options. And if you need to release some pent-up aggression, let loose on the lodge's very own paintball ground. The Monte Selva group also runs the small zoo, Zoohogar, and Monte Selva Ecopark in Puyo, with daily excursions there. Monte Selva is just 7 blocks away from the bus terminal and within easy walking distance of the town center.

Andes and Amazonia, Baños de Agua Santa. (C) **03/2740-244** or 03/2740-566. www.monteselvaecuador.com. 39 units. $63 (£35) double. Rates include: breakfast and taxes. AE, DC, MC, V. **Amenities:** 2 restaurants; bar; 2 outdoor swimming pools; Jacuzzi; steam bath; sauna; spa treatments; tour desk; laundry service. *In room:* TV.

Sangay Spa-Hotel ★ *Value Kids* Situated underneath the waterfall Cascada de la Virgen, and right on the doorstep of the hot springs of the same name, this is one of the town's most popular moderately priced hotels among Ecuadorian and foreign tourists alike. Rooms are pleasantly decorated and relatively spacious. You can choose from either colonial, cabana, or executive suites. Established in 1930, and currently run by English climber Brian Warmington, Sangay offers both recreation and relaxation, with tennis and squash courts, a large swimming pool with a water slide, and spa facilities that include Jacuzzis, steam baths, a sauna, and a wide range of massage and spa treatments. This hotel is popular with tour groups and families, which may put off those looking for a romantic getaway, although it's well located and a good deal for the money.

Plazoleta Isidro Ayora 10, Baños de Agua Santa. © **03/2740-490** or 03/2740-917. Fax 03/2740-056. www.sangays pahotel.com. 65 units. $40–$70 (£22–£39) double; $98 (£54) suite. Rates include buffet breakfast and taxes. AE, DC, MC, V. **Amenities:** Restaurant; bar; swimming pool; lighted outdoor tennis court; squash court; Jacuzzi; sauna; steam baths; spa treatments; tour desk; room service 7:30am–10pm; laundry service. *In room:* TV, hair dryer.

INEXPENSIVE

In addition to the places listed below, I've gotten good reports about the new budget hostel **Hospedaje Santa Cruz** (© **03/2740-648;** santacruzhostal@yahoo.com), on calles 16 de Diciembre and Martínez.

Hostal Los Nevados *Value*   This pleasant hostel, just a block down from the pretty basilica, is an excellent choice for those on a budget. Rooms are spacious, modern, and clean, and all have private bathrooms, hot water, and cable television. On the top floor you'll find the cafe-restaurant serving breakfast and showing the occasional movie. Breakfast here will cost about $2 (£1.10). Friendly service is guaranteed, as is real value for money—the same room rates are charged by other run-down, less-attractive alternatives.

Ambato and Hermano Mideros Ciudadela El Rosario, Baños. © **03/2740-673.** 18 units. $6 (£3.30) per person. No credit cards. **Amenities:** Restaurant; lounge; laundry service. *In room:* TV, no phone.

Hostal Plantas y Blanco   Certainly one of the town's nicest budget hostels, Plantas y Blanco has a convivial backpacker atmosphere and attractive rooftop terrace decorated with plants, plants, and more plants (hence the name). Double rooms are fairly spacious and comfortable and some offer pretty views of town; the singles, however, are on the small side. Try to book in advance because it tends to get quite full here. The management's "No Ecuadorians" policy is discriminatory and off-putting, but you'll be sure to meet a number of foreign tourists from all parts. The rooftop restaurant serves up tasty breakfasts and offers entertainment with a great collection of board games, music, and free Internet.

Martínez and 12 de Noviembre. © **03/2740-044.** 22 units. $7.50 (£4.15) per person. No credit cards. **Amenities:** Restaurant; rooftop terrace; steam bath; laundry service. *In room:* No phone.

WHERE TO DINE IN BAÑOS

There is no shortage of restaurants in Baños. Most cater to budget travelers and international backpackers, and serve a range of Italian, Ecuadorian, Mexican, French, Chinese, Mediterranean, and vegetarian fare at reasonable prices. If you are feeling really adventurous, you can try the local specialty, *cuy* (roasted guinea pig), which is sold from stalls near the market.

Café Hood *Finds* INTERNATIONAL   This eclectic joint exudes a backpacker's vibe and dishes up delicious international cuisine including pastas, curry, Mexican, Thai, Greek, Turkish, and vegetarian options. You can opt to chill out with a hot chocolate while playing board games or browsing the book exchange. Don't be confused or fooled: There's a Casa Hood (also good) and Café Good (not quite as good), both serving similar fare.

Maldonado and Rocafuerte. © **03/2740-573.** Main courses $2.80–$6.20 (£1.55–£3.40). MC, V. Daily 10am–10pm.

Café Mariane *(★)* *(Value)* MEDITERRANEAN   This inconspicuous downtown eatery offers an impressive selection of mouthwatering Mediterranean and French dishes in an attractive yet rustic setting. The steak au poivre is excellent. With main courses averaging around $5 (£2.75) and excellent service, this restaurant offers a real value. Be sure to save room for a dessert crepe.

Halflants and Rocafuerte. © **03/2740-911.** Main courses $3.50–$7 (£2–£3.85). MC, V. Daily 6–10pm.

Le Petit Restaurant FRENCH   This upscale Baños restaurant serves tasty French fare—everything from crepes and hors d'oeuvres to fondue and chateaubriand. On a cold evening, their French onion soup can't be beat. Portions aren't huge, though. The decor is warm and cozy, with dim lighting and a mix of wood paneling, woven mats, and exposed bricks on the walls. The relaxing and rustic ambience makes it the perfect place for a romantic meal, or you can relax and enjoy a drink and fondue with friends.

16 de Diciembre 240 and Montalvo, inside the hotel Le Petit Auberge. © **03/2740-936.** www.lepetitbanos.com. Main courses $4–$14 (£2.20–£7.70). MC, V. Tues–Sun 8am–3pm and 6–10pm.

Restaurant Moni INTERNATIONAL   While this place specializes in Mexican food, it offers international options. Really, the breakfasts are the crowning glory of this restaurant. Try their delicious ranch-style *desayuno mexicano* (Mexican breakfast) or go for their homemade pancakes, which are to die for.

Rocafuerte, between 16 de Diciembre and Eloy Alfaro. © **03/2741-044.** Reservations not accepted. Main courses $3–$10 (£1.65–£5.50). No credit cards. Daily 7am–10pm.

AFTER DARK

For a small town, Baños has a very vibrant nightlife. In fact, it feels a lot like Quito's Mariscal district in miniature. Stroll down Eloy Alfaro, off Ambato, and you'll find a string of bars and dance clubs pumping out pop, rock, salsa, and *reggaetón* until the early hours. *Peñas*—bars hosting traditional live music—are also popular among locals and visitors alike. Dance clubs and *peñas* charge an average of around $2 (£1) admission.

For dancing, **Buenavista,** Eloy Alfaro, between Espejo and Oriente (© **03/2741-096**), boasts the town's largest dance floor and a diverse drink menu. **Reventador** (at Hotel Sangay; see above) has the best setting, just beside a waterfall. **Leprechaun** *(★)*, Eloy Alfaro and Oriente (© **03/2741-537**) is another popular party joint, especially among foreigners, with an upbeat atmosphere and a diverse musical repertoire, while **Santo Pecado,** Eloy Alfaro and Ambato (© **03/2740-703**), blasts out Latin beats, including *reggaetón,* and gets pretty full. **Trébol** *(★★)*, Montalvo and 16 de Diciembre, opposite Parque Montalvo (© **03/2741-501**), is open till near dawn and is an excellent "after-hour" spot.

Recommended *peñas* are **Mocambo** *(★)*, Eloy Alfaro and Ambato (© **03/2742-733**), which extends over three floors, is dedicated to live Latino music, and has a great cocktail menu; and **Ananitay,** 16 de Diciembre and Espejo (© **03/2741-713**), which has excellent live Andean bands playing salsa, merengue and *cumbia.* **Café-Bar Barbass,** Eloy Alfaro and Ambato (© **03/2742-470**), and **Jack Rock** *(★)*, Eloy Alfaro 541 and Ambato (© **03/2741-329**), are the town's rock bars. **La Abuela,** Eloy Alfaro and Ambato (© **03/2740-923**), is a smaller, cozier, more subdued cafe-bar, perfect for a chilling out with a cold beer or cocktail, while **La Casa del Loco,** Eloy Alfaro and Espejo (no phone), is just one of the town's many pool bars, with more of a local clientele. For karaoke, head to **Why Not?,** Eloy Alfaro and Espejo (no phone); **Fun,** Eloy Alfaro and Martínez (✆ **03/2741-996**); or **Luna Azul,** Eloy Alfaro and Martínez (✆ **03/2742-238**).

5 Riobamba

188km (117 miles) S of Quito; 55km (34 miles) S of Baños; 233km (145 miles) N of Guayaquil

Shadowed by five spectacular snowcapped peaks in the heart of the Ecuadorian central highlands, Riobamba is an enchanting small city, with attractive 18th-century architecture, pretty, peaceful parks, interesting museums, and charming churches. Situated at an altitude of 2,750m (9,000 ft.), the town enjoys a principally springlike climate, similar to that of Quito, with plenty of cloudless days perfect for taking in the stunning views of the surrounding landscape. As capital of **Chimborazo province** and a commercial hub, Riobamba boasts a fair amount of hustle and bustle, particularly at weekends, when the town comes alive with street traders and indigenous market sellers arriving from surrounding villages to hawk their goods and produce.

Founded in 1534 and known, perhaps a tad pompously, as "The Sultan of the Andes," Riobamba was the original Ecuadorian capital under Spanish rule before suffering a devastating earthquake in 1797. The earthquake almost destroyed the town and led to its relocation to the current site. Popular among tourists who principally come here to experience the exhilarating **Nariz del Diablo (Devil's Nose)** train ride, which famously zigzags up a solid rock face, Riobamba also serves as the perfect base from which to embark on climbing and trekking tours and trips to the beautiful lakes nearby.

Situated close to several towering peaks, including the country's tallest, **Chimborazo** (6,310m/20,703 ft.), Riobamba is a bit of a mini-mecca for serious mountain and rock climbers.

ESSENTIALS
GETTING THERE & DEPARTING
BY BUS   Buses depart Quito's main bus terminal, Terminal Terrestre, for Riobamba roughly every 15 minutes between 3am and 10pm. **Transportes Riobamba** (✆ **02/ 2571-879** in Quito, or 03/2960-766 in Riobamba) is one of a half-dozen or so bus lines that take turns running this route. The return bus schedule is pretty much the same. The ride takes a little under 4 hours and the one-way fare is $4 (£2.20).

Riobamba's main bus terminal, **Terminal Terrestre** (✆ **03/2962-005**), is located on the northwestern outskirts of town, on Avenida de la Prensa and Avenida León Borja. There is regular service to and from this terminal to Guayaquil, Cuenca, Guaranda, and Santo Domingo de los Colorados. Taxis always await arriving passengers, and a ride into the town center should cost you only $1 (55p).

Buses heading for Baños, Puyo, Macas, Tena and jungle destinations need to be caught at the **Terminal Oriente** (no phone), on Espejo and Luz Elisa Borja, several blocks northeast of downtown.

BY CAR   From Quito, head southbound on the Pan-American Highway (E35) and continue along this route, passing through Latacunga and Ambato, until you reach Riobamba. The ride takes around 3½ hours.

If setting out from Guayaquil, take E70 east to El Triunfo, passing by Durán on the way. At El Triunfo, head northeast on E60 to Riobamba. This ride takes around 4 hours.

Keep abreast of the latest travel information if you plan on journeying between Riobamba and Baños, as the road running parallel to Río Chambo is subject to closure by authorities due to mud flows (lahars) from the currently active Volcán Tungurahua.

BY TRAIN   Currently, train service to and from Riobamba is limited to the popular Devil's Nose run, round-trip between Riobamba and Alausí. See below for more details.

ORIENTATION

Riobamba has an orderly gridlike layout; streets, particularly around the central area, have an attractive colonial appearance, with pretty 18th- and 19th-century buildings. The main avenues through town, running in a northeast-to-southwest direction, are León Borja (also called 10 de Agosto) and Primera Constituyente.

The town center has several parks. **Parque Sucre,** occupying a square city block, is pretty much the center of town, although the Catholic Cathedral, post office, and local museum are all clustered around **Parque Maldonado.** The largest park, **Parque Guayaquil,** is located toward the northern end of León Borja, next to the **Estadio Municipal** soccer stadium, a little bit up from the **Plaza de Toros** (bullring).

Trains for the famous Devil's Nose train ride leave from the main train station in the heart of downtown, on Carabobo and León Borja.

Riobamba itself is situated along the central plain high up in the Andes, shadowed by several snowcapped volcanoes, which makes for spectacular views on clear days.

GETTING AROUND

Even though Riobamba is a bit spread out, it's easy to get around town. Local buses run up and down Avenida León Borja. From a small terminal a couple of blocks away from the main bus station, buses depart to surrounding areas that you may wish to visit. Fares cost 20¢ to 30¢ (10p–15p).

But since taxis are so plentiful and economical, I still recommend them as the preferred means of travel. A ride anywhere around the city or to the bus terminals should usually be around $1 and never exceed $2 (55p–£1.10). Rides to outlying hotels and restaurants listed below should only cost a few dollars. If you can't flag down a cab, call **Cooperativa de Taxis San Francisco** (© 03/2966-011) or **Cooperativa de Taxis Terminal Terrestre** (© 03/2966-990).

VISITOR INFORMATION

For general tourism inquiries, maps, and helpful advice, visit the **municipal tourist office,** on León Borja and Pasaje Municipal (© 03/2947-389; uniturismorio@ yahoo.es).

Local tour agencies are also excellent sources of information. For all-purpose tours and to book the Devil's Nose (see below), head to **Metropolitan Touring,** on León Borja and Lavalle (© 03/2969-600; www.metropolitan-touring.com). For hiking, trekking, mountain biking, or other adventure tours, see the companies recommended below.

FAST FACTS   Should you need to contact local **police,** dial © 03/2961-913 or © 911 in an emergency. There are two police stations in the town, the main one located on Primera Constituyente; alternatively, there is a more centrally located station on León Borja.

For medical attention head to the **Hospital Policlínico,** toward the south end of town on Olmedo 11–01 (© 03/2961-705); or to the **Clínica San Juan,** on Veloz and

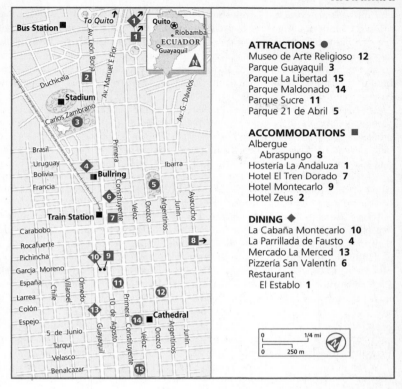

ATTRACTIONS ●
Museo de Arte Religioso **12**
Parque Guayaquil **3**
Parque La Libertad **15**
Parque Maldonado **14**
Parque Sucre **11**
Parque 21 de Abril **5**

ACCOMMODATIONS ■
Albergue
  Abraspungo **8**
Hostería La Andaluza **1**
Hotel El Tren Dorado **7**
Hotel Montecarlo **9**
Hotel Zeus **2**

DINING ◆
La Cabaña Montecarlo **10**
La Parrillada de Fausto **4**
Mercado La Merced **13**
Pizzería San Valentín **6**
Restaurant
  El Establo **1**

Duchicela (© **03/2944-636**). There are **pharmacies** all over town, with several on the main drag of León Borja.

You'll find the major branches of both **Banco de Guayaquil** (© **03/2945-001**) and **Banco del Pichincha** (© **03/2967-416**) near each other on Primera Constituyente, between García Moreno and Pichincha, as well as **Banco del Pacífico,** on the corner of León Borja and Carlos Zambrano (© **03/2942-242**). All have ATMs and foreign-currency-exchange facilities.

The main **post office** is at Espejo and 10 de Agosto (© **03/2969-942**). There are plenty of **Internet cafes** around the center; one of the best is **El Puente Informático,** on Guayaquil and Carabobo (© **03/2960-292**). I also like **@internet,** on the corner of León Borja and Zambrano (© **03/2969-135**). Internet rates run around 80¢ to $2 (45p–£1.10) per hour. Most hotels and hostels offer laundry services, but as an alternative check out **Lavendería Donini,** on León Borja and Uruguay (© **03/2961-063**).

WHAT TO SEE & DO
Riobamba has a couple of minor city attractions, but most folks use the city as a base for tours, activities, and excursions outside of town.

Riobamba's city parks are perfect for people-watching. Re-landscaped in 1911, **Parque Maldonado** has pretty gardens, tall trees, and flowing fountains, and it fronts the city's picturesque cathedral. **Parque Sucre** has a splendid fountain of Neptune, while **Parque La Libertad** fronts the pretty 19th-century basilica. Toward the north end of the city, **Parque Guayaquil** (also called **Parque Infantil,** or **Children's Park**) is the largest in Riobamba, with a small lagoon, row boats, and a large abstract sculpture strangely resembling a cow; there's also a children's playground. For a panoramic view, head to the **Parque 21 de Abril,** from where you can marvel at the scenery, particularly the plumes of smoke coming off Volcán Tungurahua.

The **Museo de Arte Religioso** ⍟, on Argentinos and Larrea (② **03/2965-212**), is the town's most prestigious museum, with a fine collection of 18th-century religious artifacts and a priceless gem-encrusted .9m-tall (3-ft.) monstrance. Housed in a former convent, the **Convento de la Concepción,** the collection here is large and spread out, some of it in the rooms, known as cells, which were occupied by the prospective nuns. It is open Tuesday through Saturday from 9am to noon and 3 to 6pm, and Sunday from 9am to noon. Admission is $2 (£1.10). Ask at the entrance and you should be able to hire a bilingual guide for a few more bucks.

Riobamba really comes alive on Saturday, with its famously colorful regional market, as villagers from all over the province pour into the city to sell their produce and handicrafts to locals and tourists alike. The most activity occurs around the streets 5 de Junio and Argentinos, where vendors principally sell produce. Tourists are better off heading to the charming market in **Parque La Concepción** (Orozco and Colón). **La Condamine** is a smaller daily market situated on Carabobo and Colombia. On non-market days, you can find **handicrafts** in a number of shops located along León Borja close to the train station. Check out **The Tagua Shop,** at León Borja 35–17 (② **03/2942-215**), which sells a wide range of handicrafts carved from the extremely hard nut of the *tagua* tree; or nearby on the same street, try **Almacén Taller Rescate Artesanías de Chimborazo,** which specializes in woven bags and woolen goods.

While in Riobamba, don't miss out on a trip to the region's beautiful lakes. The **Lagunas de Ozogoche,** composed of 60 lakes, is a stunning spot, as is the **Lagunas de Atillo,** both of which are situated about a 3-hour drive outside the city. Slightly closer is the **Laguna de Colta,** just 20 minutes away. All the local tour agencies and hotel tour desks can arrange these trips.

From Riobamba, you can also visit surrounding indigenous villages. The small village of **Guano,** famous for its weaving industry, is located some 9km (5½ miles) north of the city. You can also head a few kilometers farther to **Santa Teresita** to visit the **Balneario Los Helenes** hot springs.

An excellent time to come and experience the typical Ecuadorian highland culture of Riobamba is during its annual fiestas, on and around April 21, when the town comes alive with music, drinking, dancing, street parades, and fireworks to commemorate its 1822 independence from Spanish rule.

GETTING BUSY OUTDOORS

Several operators organize climbing, trekking, and mountain-biking tours to the surrounding snowcapped peaks and their outskirts.

CLIMBING & TREKKING   For climbers, Chimborazo is the prized peak: At 6,310m (20,703 ft.) it's the tallest mountain in Ecuador. This is a very high-altitude climb and somewhat technical, too. Only those in good shape and with sufficient skills and experience should attempt it. Trips can also be arranged to Sangay, the Ilinizas, Cotopaxi, and other peaks. If high-altitude climbing is beyond your reach, you can do a multiday trekking-and-camping tour at slightly lower elevations. Destinations include the flanks of Chimborazo, as well as sections of the ancient Inca trail. Organized tours usually last from 2 to 7 days and cost from around $60 to $120 (£33–£66) per person per day. Be sure to go with a reputable, licensed guide, particularly if you are a novice. Recommended operators are **Expediciones Julio Verne** ✦ (© **03/2963-423;** www.julioverne-travel.com), **Andes Climbing and Trekking** (© **03/2940-963;** www.andes-trek.com), and **Alta Montaña** (© **03/2942-215**).

MOUNTAIN BIKING & HORSEBACK RIDING   The terrain and scenery here make this a top-notch spot to go mountain biking or horseback riding. Local operators arrange everything from half-day to multiday tours—depending upon on your fitness level! The most popular destinations are the Ozogoche and Atillo lakes, Chimborazo, and El Altar. Expect to pay $40 to $60 (£21–£33) per day, depending on the number of participants. These rates usually do not include admission to national parks or protected areas. Check out **Biking Spirit** (© **03/2942-215;** www. bikingspirit.com), the biking arm of Alta Montaña; **Pro-Bici** (© **03/2961-923;** www.probici.com); or **Metropolitan Touring** (© **03/2969-600;** www.metropolitan-touring.com).

THE DEVIL'S NOSE TRAIN RIDE ✦✦

Most tourists come to Riobamba to embark on the exhilarating **Nariz del Diablo (Devil's Nose) train ride** ✦✦, which winds through some fantastic scenery and daring zigzags up a solid 100m (330-ft.) rock face. The tight switchbacks and sheer drop-offs are enough to make the hairs stand up on the back of anyone's neck. The journey is an absolute must for visitors to Riobamba. Most travelers choose to ride on the roof of the train—be sure to bring your camera and dress warmly, especially if you plan to ride up top.

The journey is a round-trip run from Riobamba to Sibambe and back, with the Devil's Nose itself on the stretch between Alausí and Sibambe. The train leaves at 7am on Wednesday, Friday, and Sunday, but check locally before going because sometimes there are changes or cancellations. Tickets go on sale the day before at the **administration office,** on Espejo next to the post office (© **03/2961-909**). You can also sometimes buy the tickets at the train station the day of your trip, but it pays to reserve in advance. I've heard you need a passport to purchase your tickets, although I've done so without showing one. The fare is approximately $20 (£11) for the round-trip—you should be back in Riobamba around 5pm. On the day of your trip, try to arrive early to get a good seat. Local touts will rent you a cushion for the trip for $2 (£1.10), a well-recommended investment. *Tip:* If you choose to sit on the roof, head toward the rear of the train; those sitting closest to the front get the worst of the soot and fumes from the train's exhaust.

WHERE TO STAY IN RIOBAMBA
MODERATE

Albergue Abraspungo ✦   This pleasant, country-style inn, housed in a pretty whitewashed building, offers splendid accommodations, attentive service, and great dining. Decorated in a *mestizo* (mixed) architectural style, as the owners like to call it, the warm, spacious rooms—most have fireplaces—show a mix of decor and design influences, relying most heavily on Spanish colonial and local Ecuadorian styles. The walls all around the hotel are adorned with antique photographs of the breathtaking regional landscape. Located on the outskirts of Riobamba along the road to Guano, this is the perfect spot to relax away from the hustle and bustle, but close enough to explore the town and take advantage of all the local tours and activities. The friendly tour desk here will happily help you plan excursions.

Km 3.5 Via Guano, outskirts of Riobamba. © 03/2940-820. Fax 03/2940-819. www.abraspungo.com.ec. 26 units. $63 (£35) double. Rates include taxes. Free parking. AE, DC, MC, V. **Amenities:** Restaurant; bar; lounge; tour desk; laundry service.

Hostería La Andaluza (★★ (Finds)   Located some 16km (10 miles) outside the town center in the small indigenous village of Chuquipogyo, this hotel is housed in a charming hacienda dating back centuries. Surrounded by lush gardens and featuring stunning views, the whole operation has a relaxed, homey atmosphere. The spacious rooms are decorated in a classic colonial style with wooden beams, cast-iron beds, and open fireplaces—a good thing because it can get pretty chilly at night. The standard rooms are found in the old part of the hacienda, while the suites and junior suites are in a new wing. All have the same colonial-era decor. With 55 rooms, the hacienda is relatively large, although it manages to preserve an intimate ambience, which is perfect for couples, families, and tourist groups alike. Relaxation and recreation are both offered here: Take a stroll around the gardens; unwind in the Turkish baths: sweat it out in the sauna; let loose in the game room; or meander through the *hostería*'s surroundings on horseback. The superb **El Establo restaurant** (see below) is located here.

Pan-American Hwy., Km 16, Vía Ambato, Chuquipogyo, Chimborazo. © 03/2949-370. www.la-andaluzaec.com. 55 units. $50–$60 (£25–£30) double; $70 (£35) suite. Free parking. AE, DC, MC, V. **Amenities:** Restaurant; bar; gym; sauna; steam room; room service 7am–10pm; laundry service. *In room:* TV, hair dryer.

INEXPENSIVE

In addition to the places below, backpackers, especially those leaving early on the Devil's Nose train ride, swear by **Hotel El Tren Dorado** (© 03/2964-890; htren dorado@hotmail.com), which is right near the train station and charges $16 (£8.80) for a double room with private bathroom.

Hotel Montecarlo (Value   This pretty 19th-century house offers comfortable accommodations in the center of town with elegant, cozy rooms, an attractive court-yard, and a good restaurant. Trips to Chimborazo mountain can be arranged at the tour desk here. This is definitely one of the better budget options in Riobamba, and it's only a couple of blocks from the train station.

10 de Agosto 25–41, between García Moreno and España, Riobamba. © 03/2960-557 or 03/2953-204. Fax 03/2960-557. www.hotelmontecarlo-riobamba.com. 20 units. $24 (£13) double. Rates include continental breakfast. Free valet parking. MC, DC, V. **Amenities:** Restaurant; bar; tour desk; laundry service. *In room:* TV.

Hotel Zeus (★   A somewhat large, contemporary place, this is probably the best downtown hotel. The rooms are colorful and attractively decorated and, from the upper floors, there are splendid views of the surrounding landscape. I recommend that you opt for one of the executive rooms or suites, rather than a standard. It's worth paying a little extra so you can enjoy the stunning views of snowcapped volcanoes while you take a soak in the bathtub, which is set beside a picture window. In the suites, these tubs are Jacuzzi tubs, and there's also a minibar. This hotel even has a small, on-site ethno-anthropologic museum.

León Borja 41–29, Riobamba. © 03/2968-036 or 03/2968-037. www.hotelzeus.com.ec. 65 units. $40 (£22) double; $60 (£33) executive; $73 (£40) suite. Rates include breakfast and taxes. Free parking. AE, DC, MC, V. **Amenities:** Restaurant; bar; small gym; room service 7am–10pm; laundry service. *In room:* TV.

WHERE TO DINE IN RIOBAMBA

Inexpensive restaurants serving typical Ecuadorian fare are found all over town, particularly close to the train station where there are several *almuerzo* (lunch) eateries, as well as in the relatively tidy **Mercado La Merced** (**La Merced Market;** on Guayaquil between Colón and Espejo).

If you want a slightly more varied menu or a touch more ambience, head to one of the following restaurants listed below. In addition to these, **La Cabaña Montecarlo** (✆ 03/2962-844), on García Moreno 24–10, comes highly recommended for a wide range of Ecuadorian and international fare.

La Parrillada de Fausto STEAKHOUSE/GRILL   This cozy place offers steaks and a variety of chicken and fish dishes grilled over a charcoal flame. The fresh grilled mountain trout is excellent. The ambience here is warm and inviting, and the restaurant is ideally located right in the center of Riobamba.

Uruguay 20–30 and León Borja. ✆ 03/2967-876. Main courses $3.50–$8 (£1.95–£4.40). MC, V. Mon–Sat noon–3:30pm and 6–10pm.

Pizzería San Valentín ✷ ITALIAN/PIZZA   This is an excellent local Italian restaurant with a lively atmosphere. The menu features a range of tasty pizzas, pastas, and lasagnas, as well as a varied selection of Mexican dishes. You can also get hamburgers and a few vegetarian items. While I often come here to eat, this place also serves as a local pub or club.

León Borja and Torres. ✆ 03/2963-137. Reservations not accepted. Main courses $2.50–$6 (£1.40–£3.30). MC, V. Mon–Sat 5pm–midnight.

Restaurant El Establo ✷✷ INTERNATIONAL   This rustic place in the Hostería La Andaluza (see above) has open log fires and serves some real culinary treats such as roasted lamb with apple sauce, scrumptious spaghetti, and tasty Chilean empanadas. Be sure to try their home-cured Spanish-style ham. Vegetarian options are available. The breakfasts are simply delicious. During the day, large picture windows offer stunning views.

Pan-America Hwy., Km 16, inside the Hostería La Andaluza (see above), Chuquipogyo. ✆ 03/2949370. Reservations recommended. Main courses $6–$12 (£3.30–£6.60). AE, MC, V. Daily 7am–10pm.

AFTER DARK

Unlike Baños, Riobamba is not exactly renowned for its nightlife—your best bet is to venture to and around the eastern end of León Borja, where there are a handful of bars and discothèques, mainly frequented by locals and principally open on the weekends. If clubbing is your style, check out the town's largest disco, **La Romeo** ✷, on León Borja (no phone). **Vieja Guardia,** on E. Flor 40–43 and Zambrano (✆ 03/2940-735), is also well established and a pretty popular bar-disco. Or head to **Ronny's,** at Nueva York 16–45 and Alvaredo (✆ 03/2966-683). All blast out a variety of Latin, *reggaetón,* pop, rock, and electronic tunes. The best laid-back bar for drinks is **Pizzería San Valentín** ✷ (see above). Karaoke-lovers should check out **Amigos,** at Primera Constituyente and Cuba (✆ 03/2941-595).

A DETOUR WEST: GUARANDA

As the capital of the province of Bolívar, **Guaranda** is a charming, relatively small town set among seven lush green hills—hence its nickname "Rome of the Andes." It has pretty views of the surrounding rolling pastures. While there isn't an extensive repertoire of things to do, Guaranda is a perfect place for taking leisurely walks and hikes, doing some horseback riding, and visiting the colorful Saturday market. It also makes for an excellent base from which to explore the giant Volcán Chimborazo or the nearby village of Salinas, where you can indulge in chocolate and cheese to your heart's content. Other popular local activities include picnics and barbeques at Las Cochas Lake and visiting El Indio de Guaranga, a large monument towering over the town, in honor of its namesake Indian chief.

Guaranda's claim to fame, however, is its annual **Carnaval** ★★, arguably the country's best. Local and international visitors alike pour into the town by the hundreds to celebrate in traditional Guarandeño style with music, dancing, street parades, beauty contests, and plenty of alcohol, as well as water, egg, and flour fights. *Fritada con mote* (fried pork with white Andean corn) is typical Carnaval fare in Guaranda, traditionally accompanied by a shot of the infamous Pájaro Azul (Blue Bird), a local drink that would work well as paint stripper. But it's extremely popular: The locals won't let you go home without trying it! Carnaval is 5 solid days of crazy festivities leading up to Ash Wednesday.

If you decide to stay the night, your best bet for accommodations is **Hotel Cochabamba,** on García Moreno and 7 de Mayo (© **03/2981-958**), which charges around $30 (£15) for a double and is the most luxurious hotel in downtown Guaranda. Alternatively, check out the slightly more expensive **Hotel La Colina,** at Guayaquil 177 (© **03/2980-666**), a 10- to 15-minute walk up the hill, but the splendid views are worth it. A double room here costs approximately $45 (£23) and includes use of pool and Jacuzzi. For those on a budget, **Hotel Bolívar,** at Sucre 704 and Olmedo (© **03/2980-547**), has clean, inexpensive rooms with a pretty patio area, as does **Hostal de las Flores,** at Pichincha and Rocafuerte (© **03/2980-644**), which is set in a charming building and has rooms with a balcony and cable TV. Both of these budget places charge around $8 (£4.40) per person. Try to book in advance if you plan to travel to Guaranda during Carnaval—the town gets packed.

When hunger strikes, check out the numerous, inexpensive restaurants around the town near the Plaza Roja; most serve typical Ecuadorian cuisine, including the region's specialty, *cuy* (roasted guinea pig). **Restaurante Cochabamba,** at García Moreno and 7 de Mayo (© **03/2981-958**), belongs to its namesake hotel, serves some great international dishes, and is one of the town's more upmarket restaurants. Café-bar **Los 7 Santos,** on Convención de 1884 and 10 de Agosto (© **03/2980-612**), is without a doubt the trendiest eatery, with tasty, inexpensive international and Ecuadorian fare; the open fire makes for a cozy ambience and the artsy decor is a welcome change of pace for Guaranda. For Italian cuisine, try the excellent **Pizzería Buon Giorno,** Circunvalación, 2 blocks from the Plaza Roja; locals rave about the scrumptious lasagna and delicious pizzas. As for nightlife, Guaranda has few discothèques; check out **No Bar,** at Azuay and Pichincha, which pumps out typical electronic tunes and infectious *reggaetón* vibes.

GETTING THERE   The drive to Guaranda, by bus or car, certainly makes for some breathtaking views, particularly at dawn or dusk. Along the way, you'll ascend 4,000m (13,000-ft.) mountain passes, with huge ravines dropping off from the roadside, and pass right by Volcán Chimborazo.

Flota Bolívar (© **03/2982-061** in Guaranda; 02/2570-699 in Quito; 03/2941-832 in Riobamba) is the main bus line serving Guaranda, with buses running roughly every 90 minutes between Guanada and Riobamba from 4am until 5pm. The ride takes about 2 hours and costs around $2 (£1.10). They also offer several daily buses from Quito (5 hr.; $4.50/£2.50). If you're coming from anywhere else in the country, your best bet is to head first to Riobamba and connect from there.

8

Cuenca & the Southern Sierra

Most visitors to Ecuador don't take the time to explore the **Southern Sierra,** which is a shame. This region, often called **El Austro,** offers rich and varied rewards for all sorts of travelers. The colonial city of **Cuenca** is the region's de facto hub, not to mention its main attraction. One of South America's best-preserved and most charming colonial-era cities, Cuenca is compact and vibrant, and readily offers up its many charms: a wide range of wonderful boutique hotels in restored mansions, a plethora of excellent restaurants and bars, and some of Ecuador's best shopping outside of Otavalo. A few hours from Cuenca sits **Ingapirca,** Ecuador's principal Incan ruins, as well as **Cajas National Park,** a nature-lover's and bird-watcher's paradise.

South of Cuenca is the city and province of Loja. The Andean mountain peaks aren't quite as high or imposing here as they are in the Central Sierra, but they still provide numerous opportunities for hiking, trekking, wildlife-viewing and camping. **Loja** is one of the oldest cities in Ecuador, and thanks to its remoteness it retains much of its old-world ambience. Just outside Loja are **Podocarpus National Park** and the isolated mountain hamlet of **Vilcabamba.** Podocarpus is one of the country's richest national parks in terms of biodiversity and a must-see for any serious bird-watcher. Vilcabamba, for its part, is world renowned for the remarkable longevity of its inhabitants, and it's become a pilgrimage destination for those seeking a bit of spiritual healing.

1 Cuenca ★ ★

442km (274 miles) S of Quito, 250km (155 miles) SE of Guayaquil, 254km (157 miles) S of Riobamba

Cuenca is Ecuador's third-largest city, but it feels much more like a charming old-world town, with cobblestone streets and a rich collection of colonial-era churches, plazas, and buildings. A good deal of the city's colonial architecture remains intact—Cuenca is a UNESCO World Heritage Site. Before the Spanish arrived here, Cuenca was the second-largest city in the Inca empire (after Cusco). The foundations of former Inca palaces became foundations for the city's churches and government buildings. Amazingly, when the Incas conquered the area, in the late 1400s, the Cañari had already been living here for centuries. The Incas—not unlike what the Spanish would eventually do—used stones from the Cañari structures to build their palaces. Several excellent museums here are dedicated to the city's rich and varied past. The **Museo del Banco Central** sits right next to the **Pumapungo** archaeological site, which was an Inca palace. Not only can you see the artifacts on display in the museum, but you can also tour the ruins of the palace, as well as its accompanying botanical gardens. A few blocks away, the **Todos Los Santos** archaeological site literally symbolizes the three layers of history—in one single area, you'll see structures built by Cañari, Incan, and Spanish settlers.

The Southern Sierra

The mysterious Cañari (also spelled Kañari) people were the first known inhabitants of Cuenca, building a city here, around A.D. 500, called Guapondeleg. Their language and customs are largely a mystery, although several nearby villages do have names that end in -*deleg,* a common Cañari suffix. Around 1480 the Cañari were conquered by the Incas, who called the city Tomebamba, which is the current name of one of the rivers that runs through its center. Tomebamba was one of the preferred cities of Inca King Huayna Capac, who spent much time here. But the Inca reign was short-lived—they were vanquished by Pizarro and the Spanish conquistadors in 1534. The Spanish city of Santa Ana de los Cuatro Ríos de Cuenca was founded here in 1557.

Outside Cuenca, there's also plenty to see and do. **Ingapirca,** for example, Ecuador's most impressive Incan ruins, are only 2 hours away; and **Cajas National Park,** which is full of scenic hiking trails and peaceful blue lagoons, is an hour north of the city.

ESSENTIALS
GETTING THERE & DEPARTING
BY PLANE   Tame (🕾 **02/2909-900** central reservation number in Quito, or 07/ 2889-581 in Cuenca; www.tame.com.ec), **Icaro** (🕾 **1800/883-567** toll-free nationwide; www.icaro.com.ec), and **Aerogal** (🕾 **1800/2376-425** toll-free nationwide; www. aerogal.com.ec) all offer daily flights to Cuenca from both Quito and Guayaquil.

Cuenca

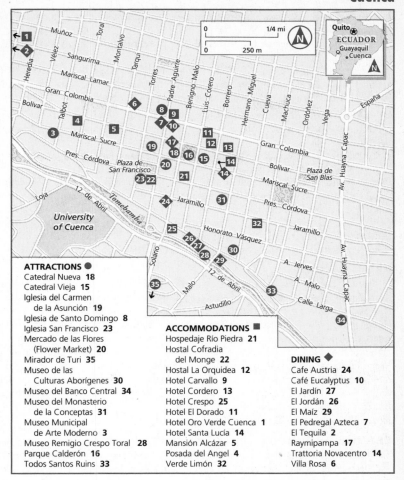

ATTRACTIONS ●
Catedral Nueva **18**
Catedral Vieja **15**
Iglesia del Carmen
de la Asunción **19**
Iglesia de Santo Domingo **8**
Iglesia San Francisco **23**
Mercado de las Flores
(Flower Market) **20**
Mirador de Turi **35**
Museo de las
Culturas Aborígenes **30**
Museo del Banco Central **34**
Museo del Monasterio
de la Conceptas **31**
Museo Municipal
de Arte Moderno **3**
Museo Remigio Crespo Toral **28**
Parque Calderón **16**
Todos Santos Ruins **33**

ACCOMMODATIONS ■
Hospedaje Río Piedra **21**
Hostal Cofradia
del Monge **22**
Hostal La Orquidea **12**
Hotel Carvallo **9**
Hotel Cordero **13**
Hotel Crespo **25**
Hotel El Dorado **11**
Hotel Oro Verde Cuenca **1**
Hotel Santa Lucía **14**
Mansión Alcázar **5**
Posada del Angel **4**
Verde Limón **32**

DINING ◆
Cafe Austria **24**
Café Eucalyptus **10**
El Jardín **27**
El Jordán **26**
El Maíz **29**
El Pedregal Azteca **7**
El Tequila **2**
Raymipampa **17**
Trattoria Novacentro **14**
Villa Rosa **6**

One-way tickets cost $45 to $52 (£25–£29) to or from Guayaquil; $55 to $65 (£30–£36) to or from Quito. All planes arrive at the **Aeropuerto Mariscal LaMar** (© 07/2862-203; airport code: CUE), which is located on Avenida España, about 1.6km (1 mile) northeast of downtown. Taxis are always waiting for incoming flights, and a ride from the airport to the center of town cost about $4 (£2.20).

BY BUS Cuenca is connected to the rest of Ecuador by frequent bus service. Several bus lines leave from Quito's main bus terminal at least every hour, around the clock, for the 9-hour ride. **Flota Imbabura** (© 02/2572-657 in Quito, or 07/2839-135 in Cuenca) is the main company making this run. The fare runs around $10 (£5.50). From Guayaquil, a cooperative of five different bus lines takes turns departing from the main bus terminal roughly every half-hour throughout the day. The buses use two different routes, alternating each departure either via Cajas or Cañar. The former route is faster, taking about 4 hours, while the latter route takes around 5 hours. The fare costs around $8 (£4.40).

Cuenca is also connected by frequent bus daily service to Loja, Macas, Machala, and Sigsig.

The Cuenca bus terminal (© **07/2843-888**) is on Avenida España, about 1.6km (1 mile) northeast of the center of town, just before the airport. Taxis are always waiting here. A ride from the terminal to the center of town costs about $4 (£2.20).

BY CAR   If you are driving from Quito, take the Pan-American Highway (E35) south through Latacunga, Ambato, and Riobamba, all the way to Cuenca. The drive takes about 8 hours.

Coming from Guayaquil, the best route is to take E70 east out of town to the junction with E25 south. Near the town of Jesús María, take the exit for Miguir and El Parque Nacional Cajas, and follow this scenic road through to Cuenca. The ride should take around 3½ hours. *Note:* In the rainy season (mid-Oct to early May), this route is sometimes hit with landslides.

Alternatively, you can take E70 east all the way to the town of Zhud, where it connects with E35 south, which will take you in to Cuenca. This route should take you about 4½ hours.

ORIENTATION

In Spanish, *cuenca* means river basin, and four separate rivers run through the broad flat valley here, eventually merging southeast of the city to form the Río Cuenca. The **Río Tomebamba** runs right through Cuenca, and the central core of the city lies along, and a few blocks north of, this river's bank. Three blocks north of the river, **Parque Calderón** is for all intents and purposes the heart of Cuenca. On the southwest corner of the park is the **Catedral Nueva,** and on the southeast corner is the **Catedral Vieja.** From here, you can easily walk to all the hotels, restaurants, banks, and attractions in town. Running parallel to the Río Tomebamba is **Calle Largo,** where you will find several hotels and restaurants, as well as the **Todos Santos ruins** and **Museo del Banco Central.** Several sets of stairs lead down from Calle Largo to **Calle 3 de Noviembre,** where you'll find a pretty riverside pathway.

GETTING AROUND

Taxis are abundant in Cuenca. A ride anywhere in town should cost no more than $2 (£1.10). A ride up to the **Mirador de Turi** should cost from $4 to $5 (£2.20–£2.75). If you can't flag one down, call **Radio Taxi Patrimonio** (© **07/2853-593**).

If you want to rent a car while in Cuenca, contact **Inter Rent A Car** (© **07/2863-915;** www.interentacar.com) or **Localiza** (© **07/2803-198;** www.localiza.com.ec), both of which have offices at the airport.

VISITOR INFORMATION

The main **tourist office** (© **07/2821-035**) is located on Mariscal Sucre on the south side of Parque Calderón. The friendly staff can give you maps and help you get your bearings. But for even better information, you should head to **TerraDiversa** ⚐, on Calle Hermano Miguel, 1½ blocks north of Calle Larga (© **07/2823-782;** www. terradiversa.com); or try **Hualambari Tours** ⚐, Av. Borrero 9–69, next to the post office (© **07/2848-768;** www.hualambari.com). The owners of TerraDiversa are former tour guides who know all of Ecuador like the backs of their hands, while Hualambari is the local representative of Grayline Tours. Both companies can provide a wealth of information and can arrange a wide variety of tours around Cuenca, the region, and the entire country.

FAST FACTS   The main **police station** is located on Calle Luis Cordero, near Córdova (© **101**). The main office of the National Police is on Avenida Vallejo and Calle Espejo. You'll find the **post office** on the corner of Borrero and Gran Colombia (© **07/ 2838-111**). It's open Monday through Friday from 8am to 12:30pm and 2:30 to 6pm, and Saturday from 9am to noon.

Banks and ATMs are ubiquitous in Cuenca and you'll find more than a half-dozen outlets within a block or two of Parque Calderón. You'll find **Banco de Guayaquil** at Calle Sucre and Hermano Miguel (© **07/2837-700**), **Banco del Pichincha** on the corner of Calle Sucre and Avenida Borrero (© **07/2836-932**), and **Banco del Pací-fico** on Benigno Malo 9–75 near Gran Colombia (© **07/2831-144**).

Clínica Hospital Monte Sinai, M. Cordero 6–111 and Avenida Solano (© **07/ 2885-595;** www.hospitalmontesinai.org), is the best hospital in Cuenca. **Fybeca** is a 24-hour pharmacy with several locations, including one at Avenida Huayna Capac 6–15, on the corner of Juan Jaramillo (© **07/2844-501**), and the other on the corner of Gran Colombia and Unidad Nacional (© **07/2839-871**). **Farmacia Los Andes,** at Borrero 7–57 (© **07/2839-029**), is a little closer to the center of town.

Internet cafes are abundant in Cuenca; two of my favorites are **Hol@net,** located at Borrero 5–90 and Juan Jaramillo (© **07/2843-126**), and **Cuenc@net Café,** on Calle Larga 602 and the corner of Hermano Miguel (© **07/2837-347**).

For laundry service, your best and cheapest bet is **La Química Automática,** located at Borrero 7–34, on the corner of Presidente Córdova (© **07/2823-945**).

WHAT TO SEE & DO
PARQUE CALDERON & NEARBY ATTRACTIONS

Parque Calderón is the historical heart of Cuenca and the center of the action. Here you'll find both the Catedral Nueva and the Catedral Vieja. The **Catedral Vieja,** also known as the Iglesia del Sagrario, is the oldest structure in the city. It dates from 1557 and was built over the Inca ruins of Pumapungo. Because cities can't have two cathedrals, once the New Cathedral opened in 1967, the old one went out of business. It was closed to the public when I last visited, although I was told a major interior renovation and plans to open a museum of religious art should be completed sometime in 2007. Construction began on the **Catedral Nueva** ✦✦, also known as the Catedral de la Inmaculada Concepción, in 1885, but it wasn't completed for almost another 80 years. It has a mix of styles—Romanesque on the outside with Gothic windows. It is modeled on the Battistero (Baptistery) in Florence. The two massive blue domes are distinctive and visible from various vantage points around the city. The floors are made of white marble imported from Italy, while the stained-glass windows contain a mix of Catholic and indigenous symbols (the sun and the moon, for example). In 1985, when the Pope visited this cathedral and saw the Renaissance-style main altar (which is modeled on the one in St. Peter's in Rome), he looked confused and asked, "Am I in Rome?" The cathedral is open Monday through Friday from 7am to 4:30pm and Saturday from 9am to noon.

Around the corner, on Padre Aguirre and Sucre, is the **Iglesia del Carmen de la Asunción.** The church is not open to the public, but from the outside you should take note of its unique stone entrance and neon-lit altar. The church sits on the delightful and colorful **Mercado de las Flores (Flower Market).** In the early part of the 20th century women weren't allowed to work. To create a diversion for them, the men of the city decided to set up this little market for the use of women only. Nowadays, anyone can wander around the fresh-smelling market. Ecuador is one of the world's largest exporters of flowers, and some beautiful varieties are found here. At the market, you'll find folk remedies for all sorts of illnesses, too. Nearby, on Presidente Córdova and Padre Aguirre, is the **Iglesia y Mercado de San Francisco.**

Purple Petals Aplenty

Beginning in late October and lasting through much of November, majestic jacarandas bloom across Cuenca. These tall trees, with broad canopies and a striking purple flower, have been planted in abundance throughout the city, especially along the Rio Tomebamba and the long, broad Avenida Huayna Capac.

In addition to the places mentioned below, if you're interested in archaeological finds, stop by the small **Todos Los Santos** (✆ **07/2821-177**) archaeological site. Discovered in 1972, the short loop path here takes you through overlapping constructions by the Cañari, Inca, and Spanish cultures. The site is located at the intersection of Calle Large and Avenida Todos Los Santos (a few blocks down from the Museo del Banco Central). When I last visited, the museum, recently taken over by a university archaeological program, was closed for inventory. But it should be open again by the time this book goes to press. If not, you should be able to talk somebody into letting you take a quick stroll through it—just walk in and ask. As you walk the path, you will see the remains of massive Spanish milling stones, alongside an Inca-period wall with four of the style's classic trapezoidal niches, as well as pieces of wall that date to the era of the Cañari. It will only take you about 20 minutes to tour this site.

For a bird's-eye view of Cuenca, take a taxi up to the **Mirador de Turi.** In Quichua, *turi* means twins, and from this sight you can see twin mountains in the distance. A taxi here should cost about $4 to $5 (£2.20–£2.75) each way. You can—and really should—combine a visit here with a visit to the ceramic gallery **Taller E. Vega** (see below).

Museo del Banco Central ★★ *(Kids)*   This massive museum, archaeological site, and botanical gardens is the pride and joy of Cuenca. The museum itself covers several floors in a modern building next to the Central Bank building. Exhibits range from rooms filled with colonial and religious artwork, to walk-through re-creations of typical dwellings from the various regions of Ecuador, to an entire numismatic section that chronicles the country's currency from spondylus shells through the now-defunct sucre. The **Tomebamba Hall** ★ is a highlight. The museum was constructed over the ruins of an Inca palace—Pumapungo—and in this room, you will learn the history of the Incas in Cuenca, as well as see archaeological artifacts found in the area. Afterwards, you can exit and walk behind the museum to see the actual archaeological site, which has a few llamas wandering around it. The complex is set on a high hillside, from which the views are wonderful. In addition to the Inca archaeological excavations, the Museo del Banco Central has recently added some beautiful botanical gardens and a small aviary. This museum complex is huge, and you really need 2 to 3 hours to see it. Groups of more than four people can ask for a free bilingual guide.

Calle Larga and Av. Huayna Capac. ✆ **07/2831-255.** Admission $3 (£1.65) adults, $1.50 (85p) children 6–18, children under 6 free. Mon–Fri 9am–6pm; Sat 9am–1pm.

Museo del Monasterio de la Conceptas ☆ This small museum was a former monastery. The nuns' rooms and common areas of the two-story adobe structure, which dates to the 17th century, are now all wonderfully curated art galleries; the theme is religious art. One of the highlights is an impressive collection of gruesome crucifixes by local artist Gaspar Sangurima. In one of these sculptures, you can see the carved heart through the gaping wounds in Christ's chest. The central courtyard is lushly planted and features a cherimoya tree that bears fruit each fall. Don't miss visiting the back patios, where you'll find the monastery's kitchen, as well as the old indoor cemetery with empty burial crypts.

Calle Hermano Miguel 6–33, between Presidente Córdova and Juan Jaramillo. ℂ 07/2830-625. Admission $2.50 (£1.40), children 8–18 $1.50 (85p). Mon–Fri 9am–5:30pm; Sat–Sun and holidays 10am–1pm.

Museo de las Culturas Aborígenes ☆ This amazing private collection includes more than 8,000 Ecuadorian archaeological pieces dating as far back as 500 B.C. Some of the most interesting are the pre-Inca urns that were used to bury the dead in an upright position, and the flutes made from the bones of different animals. The collection ranges far and wide, with works by the Valdivia, Machalilla, Tolita, Yasuni, and Quitis peoples. Near the entrance, there's an excellent gift shop and a pleasant little courtyard cafe and bakery.

Av. 10 de Agosto 4–70 and Rafael Torres Beltrán. ℂ 07/2880-010. Admission $2 (£1.10). Mon–Fri 8:30am–noon and 1–6pm, Sat 8:30am–12:30pm.

Museo Municipal de Arte Moderno Art and sculpture adorn the many rooms and hallways of this old adobe home. It's hard to predict what type of art you'll see when you visit this museum—there are no permanent exhibits. But the museum does display the best of Ecuadorian modern art—previous shows have included works by Guayasamín, Tábara, and Oswaldo Muñoz Mariño. The museum is also famous for hosting the **Bienal Internacional de Pintura,** a biannual exposition of Ecuadorian and American art. Even if you're not an art-lover, it's nice to come here and relax in the peaceful colonial courtyard.

Calle Sucre 1527 and Coronel Tálbot. ℂ 07/2831-027. Free admission. Mon–Fri 8:30am–1pm and 3–6:30pm; Sat 9am–1pm.

Museo Remigio Crespo Toral The exhibits here focus on the history of both Cuenca and Ecuador. The museum possesses a large collection of archaeological pieces, a massive coin and metalworks collection, and a good selection of colonial art. The first museum founded in Cuenca, this is a great place for history buffs. Perhaps the best reason to visit is simply for the chance to tour through the neo-baroque French-style palace overlooking Río Tomebamba that currently houses it.

Calle Larga 7–27 and Presidente Borrero. ℂ 07/2833-208. Free admission. Mon–Fri 8:30am–1pm and 3–6:30pm; Sat 10am–1pm.

LEARNING SPANISH

Whether you want to just brush up on your rusty Spanish skills or dive in for intensive instruction, contact **Nexus Language & Culture** (ℂ 07/2841-927; www. nexus.edu.ec), which offers group and private classes. The school is located on a hill overlooking Río Tomebamba. Prices run around $8 (£4.40) per hour for private lessons, $5 (£2.75) per hour for small-group classes. A home-stay with a local family can be arranged for just $13 (£7.15) per day, which is quite a bargain, considering it includes three full meals. Nexus can also help arrange volunteer opportunities in and around Cuenca.

SPORTS & OUTDOOR ACTIVITIES

Cuenca may be Ecuador's third-largest city, but if you venture just a few miles outside the city center, you'll find yourself at one with nature. For the best hiking in the area, head to **Cajas National Park** (see "Side Trips from Cuenca," later in this chapter). **Hualambari Tours** (© 07/2848-768; www.hualambari.com) and **TerraDiversa** (© 07/2823-782; www.terradiversa.com) both offer horseback-riding and mountain-biking expeditions through the outlying mountains and forests, stopping at small towns along the way. Day trips run $40 to $80 (£22–£44) per person, including lunch, equipment, and transportation. Multiday trips and expeditions can also be arranged.

SHOPPING

Cuenca is a shopper's paradise. Ceramics and Panama hats are the best buys here, but, in general, you can find an excellent selection of folksy handicrafts, as well as some higher-end art and ceramic works. If you happen to here on a Sunday, you should hop on a bus to or sign up for a tour of the nearby villages of **Sigsig, Chordeleg,** or **Gualaceo.** They all host active Sunday markets where you can buy some very high-quality locally produced handicrafts. All the local tour agencies offer day trips to these villages, and even on non-market days, you can find good arts and handicraft works here. If you make it to Chordeleg, be sure to check out the fine silverwork and jewelry at **Mar de Plata** (© 09/2932-706).

ARTS & HANDICRAFTS   Walk down any street in the center of Cuenca and you are sure to find scads of stores specializing in handmade crafts. **Tejemujeres**, on Hermano Miguel and Presidente Córdova (© 07/2839-676), sells beautiful hand-crafted sweaters. **Galería de Arte 670,** at Hermano Miguel 6–70 (© 07/2845-631), showcases works of local artists. I also especially like **Arte con Sabor a Café** (© 07/2849-828), a gallery and coffee shop with a good rotating selection of local art works and crafts; it's located down by the river, on Paseo 3 de Noviembre 1–48 and Coronel Talbot. In the evenings, this place sometimes has live music.

CERAMICS   For hundreds of years, Cuenca has been a center for ceramics. Walk into any museum in the area (see above), and you'll see examples of beautiful pre-Inca jugs and vases. **Artesa**, at the corner of Gran Colombia and Luis Cordero (© 07/2842-647), keeps the tradition alive. This is the best place in the city for hand-painted ceramics.

For a more personalized experience, I recommend visiting **Taller E. Vega**, located just below the Mirador de Turi (© 07/2881-407). Eduardo Vega is a ceram-icist and one of Ecuador's most famous artists. Monumental ceramic sculptures and murals by Vega can be found around Cuenca, as well as in Quito. A visit to his hill-side workshop and gallery is worthwhile just for the views, but you'll also have a chance to glimpse a bit of his production process, and to buy from his regularly chang-ing collection of decorative and functional works, handicrafts, and wonderful jewelry. Most organized city tours stop here. If you're coming to Taller E. Vega on your own, I recommend calling in advance to be sure it's open.

JEWELRY   The spondylus shell was used as currency by early civilizations of Ecuador. At the custom jewelry shop **Spondylus** (© 07/2820-689), you'll find the shiny shell integrated into a wide range of pendants, earrings, and bracelets. You'll also find plenty of beautiful pieces in silver, either plain or with assorted gemstones. This shop is located on Gran Colombia 20–85, on the western edge of town.

PANAMA HATS   You may be surprised to know that Panama hats have always been made in Ecuador: For generations, the people on the coast have been using local straw to create finely woven hats. The trade was moved inland, and Cuenca is now the major hub for the production of Panama hats. **Homero Ortega P. & Hijos** ✸✸✸ makes the highest quality Panama hats in the world; patrons include the queen of England.

The Panama Hat

If a rose by another name would still smell as sweet, then a hat, invented, designed, and manufactured in Ecuador, would look as stylish and protect you from the sun just as well if, for example, it were called a **Panama hat.**

The Panama hat is endemic to Ecuador, with Panama mistakenly receiving credit for the hat's origin over a century ago. These lightweight woven hats made a splash at the 1855 World's Fair in Paris. When they were shipped from Ecuador, they went via Panama, their last port of call before landing in Europe. By the end of the World's Fair, Panama had gotten the credit for producing the hat, and the Emperor Napoleon III became perhaps the first in a long line of celebrities associated with the headpiece.

As far back as the 16th century, Ecuadorians were wearing and weaving hats from *paja toquilla,* a fiber from the leaves of the *Carludovica palmata* palm. The fibers from these plants were boiled and dried and then painstakingly crafted into the final product. Cities in Manabí province—Azogues, Biblian, Sigsig, Montecristi, and Jipijapa—developed into major centers for the production of these hats. A single artisan can take anywhere from 3 to 6 months to craft just one *superfino* (super-fine) hat. Major production was moved to Cuenca in 1836, and then spread throughout the provinces of Azuay and Cañar, now the largest centers of hat production in Ecuador. The popular style of today is still called Montecristi, after the town where to this day the finest quality panamas are still woven (p. 273).

After taking Paris by storm, the hats began covering the heads of American troops during the Spanish-American war (1898). Gold miners who arrived in California by way of the Isthmus of Panama also donned these light and breathable hats, whose popularity escalated further when a photograph circulated of U.S. President Theodore Roosevelt wearing one. Other prominent politicians to wear Panama hats included Winston Churchill and Nikita Khrushchev. The Panama hat also has its fare share of Hollywood cred, having graced the heads of stars as diverse as Clark Gable, Humphrey Bogart, Orson Welles, Sean Connery, Paul Newman, Bruce Willis, and Danny Glover.

Today, despite the popularity of the Panama hat, few, except those who visit Ecuador, know its true origins. But like a rose, a *toquilla* straw hat, by any name, keeps the sun off your head and looks pretty sharp to boot.

You can visit the factory and learn how the hats are made, and afterwards you can browse in the elegant boutique. The store is located a few minutes outside the center of town, at Av. Gil Ramírez Dávalo 3–86 (© **07/2809-000;** www.homeroortega. com); **Sombreros Barranco,** at Calle Larga 10–41, between General Torres and Padre Aguirre (© **07/2831-569**); and **K. Dorfzaun** ✦, Av. Gil Ramírez Cávalos 4–34 (© **07/2807-563;** www.kdorfzaun.com), also sell finely crafted hats.

Panama hats in Cuenca vary greatly in price and quality, running from around $10 to $12 (£5.50–£6.60) for a basic version, to around $150 to $250 (£83–£138) for a *superfino.* That *superfino,* though, may cost over $1,000 (£500) in a boutique shop in New York, Los Angeles, or London.

WHERE TO STAY
EXPENSIVE

Hotel El Dorado ✦✦   If you're looking for some serious contrast to quaint, colonial Cuenca, check into this hip new hotel. Opened in 2005, and built inside the shell of the former Mercure hotel, El Dorado is bold and brash, with lots of glass and polished stainless steel in the entrance and lobby. A glass-and-steel staircase leads up to the rooms, and there are several waterfalls scattered around the building. The rooms—all spacious and well lit, have a clean and minimalist decor. Some units on the higher floors have good views. I particularly like no. 512, which has a good view of the cathedral dome. The presidential suite is a two-room affair with a Jacuzzi tub, glass sinks and elegant bathroom fixtures, a Zen-style water fountain on the writing desk, and a small Buddha sculpture on the bureau. Several floors have been designated smoke-free, and there's one very well set up room for travelers with disabilities. The entire building has free Wi-Fi access. There's a small spa here, too, which covers the necessary bases, but isn't quite as large or well equipped as I would have expected. On the ground floor is a large, chic restaurant with nothing but full-length walls of glass separating it from the busy sidewalk outside.

Gran Colombia 7–87 and Luis Cordero, Cuenca. © **07/2831-390.** Fax 07/2831-663. www.eldoradohotel.com.ec. 42 units. $90 (£50) double; $125 (£69) junior suite; $160 (£88) presidential suite. Rates include buffet breakfast. AE, DC MC, V. Free parking. **Amenities:** Restaurant; bar; small, well-equipped health club; sauna; steam room; 24-hr. business center; room service 6am–11pm; massage; babysitting; laundry service; smoker-free rooms. *In room:* TV, minibar, hair dryer, safe, free Wi-Fi.

Hotel Oro Verde Cuenca ✦   This hotel is great if you're looking for a large, luxurious resort that feels a little like a country retreat. The Oro Verde offers some of the largest rooms in Cuenca, all of which are decorated with local art and have a sitting area where you can enjoy views of the lagoon, home to lively swans and ducks. The executive suite is appropriately named—it has a conference table, large desk, and fax machine. The free Wi-Fi connection here reaches most of the rooms and common areas. This place has extensive grounds and facilities, including a pool and perhaps the best health club in the city. The Oro Verde, however, is located on the outskirts of the city, and you can't walk from there to the colonial center of Cuenca. Fortunately, a taxi costs only about $3 (£1.65) each way. Free airport pickup can be arranged if you contact the hotel a day before. Discounts abound here, so be sure to ask for "promotional" or "corporate" rates when making your reservations.

Av. Ordóñez Lazo, Cuenca. © **07/2831-200.** Fax 07/2832-849. www.oroverdehotels.com. 79 units. $100 (£55) double; $130 (£72) suite. Rates include buffet breakfast. AE, DC MC, V. Free parking. **Amenities:** 2 restaurants; 2 bars; small outdoor pool; well-equipped health club; sauna; room service 6:30am–11pm; massage; babysitting; laundry service; free Wi-Fi. *In room:* TV, minibar, hair dryer, safe.

Mansión Alcázar ★★ This is an elegant oasis in the heart of Cuenca, a meticulously renovated 1870s house that once belonged to the president of Ecuador. Behind a large gate you'll enter into a world of old colonial living. A beautifully tiled enclosed courtyard with a fountain leads to plush accommodations on two floors. Out back there's a lovely garden ringed with palm trees and filled with lavender and rose bushes; a few resident hummingbirds complete the picture. Each room is different from the next in size and decor, but they all have one thing in common: Every piece of furniture was made in Cuenca. Elegant antiques and fine objets d'art give the rooms that old colonial feel. The suites have wrought-iron four-poster beds; no. 207 has a mural of angels on its ceiling, but no. 202 is my favorite, with a view over the garden. Bathrooms have Cuencan marble and each one has distinctly hand-painted walls. I think it's worth the splurge for one of the suites, as several of the standard rooms, especially those on the first floor, are quite small. The beautiful dining area overlooks the garden and there are a few tables outside for alfresco dining on warm days. The elaborate breakfast here includes rolls and fruitcakes baked on the premises. The owners are welcoming and friendly.

Calle Bolívar 12–55 and Tarqui, Cuenca. ✆ **800/327-3573** toll-free in the U.S. and Canada, or 07/2823-918 in Ecuador. Fax 07/2823-554. www.mansionalcazar.com. 14 units. $110 (£61) double; $160 (£88) suite. Rates include full breakfast and afternoon tea. AE, DC, MC, V. Free parking. **Amenities:** Restaurant; bar; lounge; room service 7am–10:30pm; laundry service; free Wi-Fi. *In room:* TV, hair dryer, safe.

MODERATE

Hotel Carvallo ★ The intimate Carvallo is full of understated elegance. Yet another lovingly restored old house in the heart of the downtown, the Carvallo boasts cozy rooms with blue walls and armoires made from local black walnut wood. Some come with terrific views of the city; no. 303 has a lovely view of the red-tiled rooftops of Cuenca. The bathrooms are small but well equipped and very clean. If you request a bathrobe at check-in, they'll deliver one to your room. The honeymoon suite comes with a king-size bed, plush comforter, and giant candelabra. The hotel is linked to the hip **Café Eucalyptus restaurant** (see "Where to Dine," below) across the street and they'll deliver snacks or meals to your room if you're too tired to venture out.

Gran Colombia 9–52 and Padre Aguirre, Cuenca. ✆/fax **07/2832-063.** 30 units. $50–$60 (£28–£33) double; $85–$100 (£47–£55) suite. Rates include full breakfast. MC, V. Parking nearby. **Amenities:** Lounge; room service noon–midnight; laundry service. *In room:* TV, minibar, hair dryer.

Hotel Cordero This is a modern, high-rise business-class hotel in the heart of the old colonial center. The rooms are all of good size and well equipped, although they lack any sense of style or flair. All have at least one queen-size bed, and many come with a bidet in the spacious bathroom. Most units have large windows, or even walls of glass, and those on the third and fourth floors have good views. Room no. 403 is a huge suite with a Jacuzzi in a large glass-enclosed room with its own wet bar. The suite has a sitting room, bedroom, and principal bathroom. The hotel has a small gym and indoor parking. If you don't have a room with a view, be sure to visit the rooftop terrace, which provides a sweeping 360° panorama of the city. There's a small shopping arcade just off the lobby, and the hotel is just a block from Parque Calderón.

Bolívar 6–50 and Antonio Borrero, Cuenca. ✆ **07/2825-363.** ✆/fax 07/2825-834. hotelcordero@etapaonline. net.ec. 22 units. $61(£34) double; $130 (£72) presidential suite. Free parking. AE, DC MC, V. **Amenities:** Restaurant; bar; tour desk; business center; room service 7am-10pm; laundry service. *In room:* TV, minibar, safe.

Hotel Crespo   This hotel is a real classic, having been in business since 1942. The original building is more than 140 years old, and built on the steep hillside leading down to the Río Tomebamba. The rambling structure covers some five stories, and there's no elevator, so ask for a room close to the lobby if climbing several flights is a problem for you. The rooms have an old-fashioned charm, with wood paneling, classic green walls, dark furniture, and colorful hand-painted moldings, although some feel a bit dated in their furnishings and decor. The ceilings are charming, too—they are designed to look like antique tin ceilings. The nice bathrooms feature marble tiles, lots of counter space, and a second telephone. The best rooms have views of the river down below. Room no. 408 is my favorite—it has both river and mountain views. The free Wi-Fi reaches most of the units, as well as assorted nooks and crannies here. Overall, this is a good choice but not nearly as elegant or as intimate as Mansión Alcázar (see above) or the Santa Lucía (see below). These folks will cover your cab fare to and from the airport, if you ask.

Calle Larga 7–93, Cuenca. © **07/2842-571.** Fax 07/2839-473. www.hotel-crespo.com. 39 units. $70 (£39) double. Rates include full breakfast. AE, DC MC, V. **Amenities:** Restaurant; bar; tour desk; business center; room service 7am–3pm and 7–10pm; laundry service; free Wi-Fi. *In room:* TV, minibar, hair dryer.

Hotel Santa Lucía ★★★ *(Finds)*   In 2002, after a 2-year renovation of this enchanting 1859 house, the lovely Hotel Santa Lucía was awarded the prize of "best restoration of a historical building" by the city of Cuenca. What you can expect here is meticulous attention to detail—in both the decor and the service. The owner hails from an old Cuenca family and he will go out of his way to make sure your stay is as exquisite as possible. The large, enclosed courtyard, which contains a 100-year-old magnolia tree and beautiful baby palms, leads to spacious, comfortable accommodations. Rooms, which have the amenities of a large, luxury hotel, include plasma-screen televisions, and the suites have sleeping lofts, hardwood floors, and Persian carpets. Room no. 212 has a view of the cathedral, and a small, private balcony overlooking the street. All but four of the spacious bathrooms have tubs, and many feature luxurious multiheaded spa showers. On the second floor, there's a huge private salon with a fireplace for guests to gather around; antiques adorn the hallways and fresh flowers are arranged daily. The whole complex has free Wi-Fi.

The airy Trattoria Novacentro (see below), in the courtyard, serves authentic Italian cuisine, while the cozy street-side **Bacchus Café** is very popular for its inexpensive Ecuadorian meals.

Antonio Borrero 8–44 and Sucre, Cuenca. © **07/2828-000.** Fax 07/2842-443. www.santaluciahotel.com. 20 units. $83 (£46) double; $110 (£61) suite. Rates include full breakfast and tax. AE, DC, MC, V. Parking nearby. **Amenities:** 2 restaurants; lounge; room service 7am–10:30pm; tour desk; laundry service; dry cleaning. *In room:* TV, minibar, hair dryer, safe, free Wi-Fi.

INEXPENSIVE

In addition to the places listed below, there are plenty of really inexpensive hostels aimed at the backpacker and student crowds. Of these, I recommend **Verde Limón** (© **07/2831-509;** www.verdelimonhostal.com), on Juan Jaramillo 4–89 and Mariano Cueva, which offers a range of accommodations from dorm-style, with shared bathrooms, to private rooms with private bathrooms.

Hospedaje Río Piedra   Unlike many of its competitors, this hotel is not housed in a restored colonial-era home. The rooms in this sleek four-story building are large, clean, and well equipped; those facing the street have huge picture windows. Many units, however, only have frosted windows opening onto the interior hallways. Some rooms come with kitchenettes, and most have fairly small bathrooms. The hotel has attractive artwork and stained-glass pieces in the public spaces, and a small cheerful restaurant.

Presidente Córdova 8–40 and Luis Codero, Cuenca. © **07/2843-821.** ©/fax 07/2839-679. riopiedrahosp@yahoo. com. 36 units. $30 (£17) double. Rates include full breakfast and taxes. AE, DC, MC, V. Free parking. **Amenities:** Restaurant; bar; lounge; laundry service. *In room:* TV, minifridge.

Hostal Cofradia del Monge *Finds*   A local tour agency turned me on to this excellent budget option. Located across from the Plaza San Francisco, and right next to the San Francisco church, this new hostel inhabits yet another meticulously restored old home. The rooms are on the second floor, and the atrium-covered central courtyard houses the hostal's popular restaurant. All rooms have polished wood floors with Persian rugs, flatscreen TVs, and small bathrooms. They also feature hand-painted wall murals, high ceilings, and ornate steel light fixtures. Room nos. 1 through 5 have views of the cathedral and the lively market on Plaza San Francisco. Your best bet is to ask for room no. 2, a corner unit that has French doors opening onto two little balconies— one on each side of the corner.

Presidente Córdova 10–33 and Padre Aguirre, Cuenca. ©/fax 07/2831-251. cofradiadelmonje@hotmail.com. 7 units. $36 (£20) double. Rates include full breakfast. MC, V. Parking nearby. **Amenities:** Restaurant; bar; lounge; laundry service. *In room:* TV.

Hostal La Orquídea   Take a moment to marvel at the ornate and beautifully restored facade before entering this wonderful budget option. Once you're inside, a high atrium roof lets plenty of light in to the central lobby area. The rooms are simple and plain, with wood floors and minimal decorations. Most have anywhere from two to four twin beds, so be sure to specify that you want a *matrimonial,* or queen, if you're traveling as a couple. Room nos. 11 and 12 have small balconies overlooking the street. The suite here is really better described as an apartment with three bedrooms, two bathrooms, a full kitchen, and living and dining rooms. This suite also has a private rooftop terrace with a view of the San Alfonso Church steeple. There's a small restaurant tucked into the back of the ground floor serving inexpensive Ecuadorian cuisine, as well as a full breakfast for $1.50 (85p).

Antonio Borrero 9–31 and Bolívar, Cuenca. © **07/2824-511.** ©/fax 07/2835-844. www.hostalorquidea.com. 14 units. $20 (£11) double; $80 (£44) suite. MC, V. Parking nearby. **Amenities:** Restaurant; lounge; laundry service. *In room:* TV, minifridge.

Posada del Angel *Value*   If you're looking for a bit of colonial charm with artistic touches—all at budget prices—then this is the hotel for you. After an extensive renovation of the 120-year-old large colonial house, the Posada del Angel is a whimsical, airy place. Bright yellow and blue are the themes here. You enter through a large enclosed courtyard, and most of the rooms, which come in all shapes and sizes, are found around the first two floors. All are simply furnished and very clean, and all but three have beautiful hardwood floors. Some rooms have wrought-iron lamps made in Cuenca and attractive wooden armoires. The tiled bathrooms are tiny but sparkling. If you're looking for some privacy, ask for one of the remote rooms located on the third or fourth floors. Free Internet access at a few computers is available for guests in the lobby. Several lounge areas and covered courtyards are spread around the rambling structure.

Bolívar 14–11 and Estévez de Toral, Cuenca. © **07/2840-695.** ©/fax 07/2821-360. www.hostalposadadelangel.com. 17 units. $30–$34 (£17–£19) double. Rates include full breakfast. MC, V. Free parking. **Amenities:** Lounge, laundry service. *In room:* TV.

WHERE TO DINE

Cuenca has excellent restaurants, inviting cafes, and wonderful bakeries so you'll eat well here. In addition to the places listed below, there's plenty of street food available all over town. You'll see *cuy* (guinea pig) and whole pigs on spits, or recently roasted, as well as *empanadas* and *llapingachos,* all for sale by street vendors. While not an option for those with sensitive stomachs, if you've got a sturdy intestinal tract, this is a tasty and inexpensive way to go.

MODERATE

El Jardín ⭐ *Finds* INTERNATIONAL   This elegant restaurant is located inside the Hotel Victoria. The dimly lit dining room features a wraparound wall of glass with views of the Río Tomebamba and the lights of Cuenca below. Tables feature abundant place settings and overlapping gold-on-green tablecloths. There are stained-glass fixtures overhead as well as on the entrance door. The menu is hand-drawn on an oversize piece of thick parchment paper. Options range from spaghetti carbonara to veal cordon bleu. There are usually one or two daily specials, as well as a daily pie or cake for dessert. Everything is wonderfully prepared and presented. The wine list is relatively short and relies heavily on Chilean vineyards.

Calle Larga 6–93, inside the Hotel Victoria. ✆ 07/2831-120. Reservations recommended. Main courses $6–$19 (£3.30–£10). AE, DC, MC, V. Daily noon–10pm.

El Jordán ⭐⭐ INTERNATIONAL/MIDDLE EASTERN   Not your typical falafel joint, this is one of the more upscale and elegant restaurants in town. In fact, there's no falafel on the menu, but there is tabbouleh and baba ghanouj. While Middle Eastern cuisine is the core of the cooking here, the menu ventures off into less-traditional realms as well. There's plenty of seafood available, and you can even get a lobster thermidor. But I like staying closer to the restaurant's roots, and ordering the salmon in Arabian herbs or shrimp shish kabobs. The presentations are often artful, and the food is excellent. The dining room is as ornate and opulent as you'll find in Cuenca, with fancy table settings, heavy pewter goblets, Moorish architectural touches, and handpainted murals on the walls. The best seats are those along the wall of picture windows fronting the Río Tomebamba.

Calle Larga 6–111 and Borrero. ✆ 07/2850-517. Main courses $4–$15 (£2.20–£8). AE, DC, MC, V. Daily noon–11pm.

Trattoria Novacentro ⭐⭐ *Finds* ITALIAN   Occupying the sunken central courtyard area of the classy Hotel Santa Lucía (see above), this place serves the best Italian fare in the city and holds its own as an elegant and refined choice any night of the week. Service is formal and attentive. White linens cover the tables, and the seating is in uniquely designed steel chairs, with plush white cushions. The high atrium courtyard is beautiful by day but is particularly romantic, with its dim lighting, at night. There's a wide range of classic Italian antipasti and pasta dishes. For a main course, I like the perfectly grilled steak and arugula. Be forewarned: Ask for a pasta substitution, or the steak will come incongruously with French fries. You can also get freshgrilled fish expertly prepared, or spicy shrimp fra diavolo. The wine list is extensive and fairly priced. For dessert, order a piping-hot shot of espresso and classic tiramisu.

Antonio Borrero 8–44 and Sucre, Cuenca. ✆ 07/2828-000. Reservations recommended. Main courses $5–$17 (£2.75–£9.35). AE, DC, MC, V. Mon–Sat noon–10:30pm; Sun noon–4pm.

Villa Rosa ★★★ *Finds* ECUADORIAN/INTERNATIONAL   The loveliest restaurant in Cuenca is owned and managed by the friendly Berta Vintimilla. The setting is divine: the enclosed courtyard of an old Cuencan home elegantly refurbished into a restaurant. Marble floors, crisp white tablecloths, and comfortable wooden chairs may make this place feel more like a restaurant in Paris than one in Cuenca, but the creative cuisine here has its roots in Ecuador. Mrs. Vintimilla bakes the delicious empanadas herself and they are excellent as an appetizer; the recipes for many of the Ecuadorian specials come from her family. If you're in the mood for something really hearty, try the amazingly good *locro de papas* (potato soup served with a slice of avocado). Main courses include sea bass with crab sauce served with rice and vegetables, tenderloin of beef, jumbo langoustines with fennel, and a variety of daily specials. The service is excellent, the wine list is reasonable, and every ingredient used in the kitchen is of the highest quality. Note that the restaurant is closed on weekends, except for groups of a substantial size who have made reservations.

Gran Colombia 12–22 and Tarqui. ℂ **07/2837-944.** Reservations recommended. Main courses $5–$14 (£2.75–£7.70). AE, DC, MC, V. Mon–Fri noon–3pm and 7–10:30pm.

INEXPENSIVE

Cafe Austria INTERNATIONAL   This pleasant little corner of Old Europe is a great place for a breakfast, coffee break, drink, or full meal. The menu features some Austrian classics like Wiener schnitzel and Viennese goulash. You can also get pastas, sandwiches, or empanadas. For dessert, they've got the requisite apple strudel, as well as Linzer torte and other goodies. The restaurant is spread around a large room on two levels. Some arty black-and-white photos adorn the wall, as does a bust of Amadeus Mozart. I recommend grabbing a table by one of the wraparound windows, to take in the passing parade as you enjoy your food and drink. There's a small bar near the entrance; happy hour is every weekday from 8 to 9pm.

Benigno Malo 5–95 and Juan Jaramillo. ℂ **07/2840-899.** Main courses $3.75–$5.50 (£2.05–£3). V. Daily 7:30am–11pm.

Café Eucalyptus ★★ *Finds* TAPAS/INTERNATIONAL   This is Cuenca's hippest and most happening restaurant and bar. The crème de la crème of the city flock here (especially on weekend nights) to gather for drinks and appetizers. There's seating on two floors—head upstairs if you want to find a somewhat quieter table, or stick to the main floor and bar area to people-watch and mingle. The food here is tapas-style and tapas-sized; most people order several and share them. Selections are truly international (more than 50 dishes from 20 different countries) and include hot Cuban sandwiches, cheese quesadillas, Pad Thai, French bread with tapenade, and stuffed peppers with rice, raisins, and parsley. This is the only place in the city to offer sushi and sashimi, although the rest of their menu is much better. The call liquor and wine list is quite impressive, and there are a number of wine choices by the glass. Eucalyptus also has the only draft beer in the city, including Llama Negra, which is made in Quito and is a dark stout beer like a Guinness.

Gran Colombia 9–41 and Benigno Malo. ℂ **07/2849-157.** Tapas $4.50–$10 (£2.50–£5.50). AE, DC, MC, V. Sun, Tues–Thurs 11am–midnight; Fri–Sat 11am–1am.

El Maíz ★ ECUADORIAN   This is the place to come for local cooking; it's set in a beautifully renovated old house, with a lovely outdoor patio for alfresco dining. The indoor dining room feels like somebody's house with wood floors, red tablecloths, and a gracious waitstaff. There are actually two outdoor seating areas: a lower patio, with colorful tiles, overlooking a courtyard full of plants, and an upper terrace with a lovely view of the green hills. Appetizers include the usual offerings of *humitas,* empanadas, and *locro de papas.* The main courses are terrific and unique. My favorites include the chicken in pumpkinseed and white-wine sauce, beef medallions in a pear sauce, and *hornado cuencano* (roasted pork served with *llapingachos*—mashed potatoes with cheese). Rotating monthly specials are tied to national holidays and celebrations. For dessert, try the *almíbar de babaco* (a compote of a local fruit, tart and sweet).

Calle Larga 1–279 and Calle de los Molinos. ℭ 07/2840-224. Main courses $4.50–$6 (£2.50–£3.30). MC, V. Mon–Sat noon–9pm.

El Pedregal Azteca ℛ MEXICAN

This could very well be the best Mexican restaurant in Ecuador. Since 1989, María and Juan Manuel Ramos have welcomed diners into their cozy restaurant with smiles. Everything is homemade—even the tortillas—the owners bring some of the ingredients back from Mexico to ensure that the food is of the highest quality. The *enchilada de mole* is delicious, as are the tacos filled with your choice of stuffing. The huge burrito comes with spicy sausage and egg, based on an old Mexican recipe. For dessert, the *arroz con leche* (rice pudding) is divine and comes with fresh vanilla and plump raisins, although I sometimes prefer the sweet, fried beignet-like *buñuelos.* Live music on Friday and Saturday nights fills the place with a youngish crowd; weekday nights, on the other hand, are quiet.

Gran Colombia 10–29 and Padre Aguirre. ℭ 07/2823-652. Main courses $3.50–$8 (£1.90–£4.40). MC, V. Mon–Sat noon–3pm and 6–11pm.

El Tequila *Value* CUENCAN

Locals flock to this simple place that serves the best roasted pork in the city. If you're looking for a taste of true Cuencan cuisine, not diluted for foreign tastes, then this your place. You'll dine in a simple room with red tile, wooden tables and chairs, and bright yellow walls. Outside, the local women roast the pork on the grill along with baby potatoes and fava beans. Here's how it works: You order a serving of pork and choose several sides to share with your dining companions. Sides include fresh steamed corn on the cob, *tamales,* fresh local cheese, and mashed potatoes. Do like the locals do and order a *canelazo* (warm wine and cinnamon drink) to round out your meal.

Gran Colombia 20–59 and León. ℭ 07/2822-807. Main courses $3–$7.50 (£1.65–£4.15). MC, V. Mon–Sat noon–10pm.

Raymipampa ℛ *Value* ECUADORIAN/CUENCAN

This popular local institution is located right next to the new cathedral. The cozy dining room features a loft area with tables under a low ceiling made of exposed log beams over much of the main dining area. The walls feature imitation baroque bas-reliefs. I like grabbing a table near the front windows, which have a view of Parque Calderón. The menu features a range of meat, poultry, and seafood. You can also get traditional Ecuadorian fare, such as *humitas* and *tamales de maíz.* I like the complete breakfast, which is an excellent deal at $2 (£1.10), including coffee, fresh juice, two eggs, two fresh-baked croissants, and local cheese. Broken plates and bent silverware have been fashioned into an interesting little sculpture hanging near the entrance.

Benigno Malo 8–59, between Sucre and Bolívar. ℭ 07/2824-169. Reservations not accepted. Main courses $3.50–$6 (£1.95–£3.30). MC, V. Daily 8:30am–11pm.

Fanesca—Holy Week Soup

If you're lucky enough to be in Cuenca for Semana Santa, or Holy Week, be sure to try the seasonal specialty, *fanesca*, a thick soup of salted cod. The soup contains 12 different beans or grains, representing the 12 apostles. It has a cream or milk base and is thickened with ground pumpkin seeds. *Fanesca* is usually served with a hard-boiled egg in the bowl, and often with an empanada and some tubers like yuca or plantain. The traditional meal in Ecuadorian homes on Good Friday, *fanesca* is served in the majority of local restaurants for most of Holy Week.

CUENCA AFTER DARK

Cuenca used to be a sleepy, provincial city, but in recent years local young people and visiting tourists have turned this into a respectable little party city. For quiet drinking and conversation, **Wunderbar Café** ✺✺, right off the stairs below Calle Larga and Hermano Miguel (✆ 07/2831-274), and **El Cafecito,** at Honorato Vásquez 7–36 (✆ 07/2832-337), are both popular spots. Early birds will appreciate the Wunderbar Café's happy hour, which begins at 11am and runs until 7pm. For live music, head to the **San Angel** ✺, on Hermano Miguel at the corner of Presidente Córdova (✆ 07/2839-090), or **Blanco & Tinto,** on Av. Jose Peralta 2–132 and Cordero (✆ 09/8832-510). On any given night, both of these places might have anything from a folk singer or small combo to a DJ spinning electronic dance tunes. The 20- and 30-something who's-who of Cuenca gather at **Eucalyptus** ✺✺ (see "Where to Dine," above), which has a popular Ladies' Night every Wednesday and a rowdy salsa night every Saturday.

If you're looking to go dancing, **La Fábrica** ✺, on Presidente Córdova and Manuel Vega (✆ 07/2861-984), is one of the best discos in town, and **La Mesa Salsoteca** ✺, on Gran Colombia between Machuca and Ordóñez (✆ 07/2833-300), is the best place in town for salsa. Other good spots for mingling with the local crowd include **Tal Cual** (✆ 09/9722-906), next to the Hotel Crespo (p. 214), and **Tinku** ✺, on Calle Larga at the corner of Alfonso Jerves (✆ 07/2838-520).

Note: Many venues are only open Wednesday to Saturday. Sunday, Monday, and Tuesday are very quiet nights in Cuenca and hardly anybody ventures out late. Covers are sometimes charged and usually range from $2 to $5 (£1.10–£2.75), which may include a drink or two.

SIDE TRIPS FROM CUENCA

Hualambari Tours ✺ (✆ 07/2848-768; www.hualambari.com), **TerraDiversa** ✺ (✆ 07/2823-782; www.terradiversa.com), and **Metropolitan Touring** (✆ 07/2837-000; www.metropolitan-touring.com) all offer a wide range of day trips out of Cuenca, including trips to the two attractions listed below.

PARQUE NACIONAL CAJAS (CAJAS NATIONAL PARK) ✺✺

After you've seen the museums and historic sights in Cuenca, it's great to get away from the city and immerse yourself in the area's natural wonders. Cajas is only about 32km (20 miles) west of the city (about a 1-hr. drive), but it feels worlds away. Unlike many other areas in Ecuador, the park was formed by glaciers, not volcanic activity. Covering about 29,000 hectares (71,630 acres), the park has 232 lakes. The terrain and ecosystems are varied here, allowing for an impressive variety of flora and fauna.

In high-elevation cloud forests, bird species range from the masked trogon and gray-breasted mountain toucan, to the majestic Andean condor. The famed Inca Trail runs right through the park. One of my favorite hikes is up **Tres Cruces,** which offers spectacular views of the area and the opportunity to see the Continental Divide. I also recommend the hike around Laguna Quinoa Pato; the vistas of the lake are impressive, and as you walk on the trails you'll have a good chance of spotting ducks. From the main visitor center, you can explore the flora of the humid mountain-forest climate—mosses, orchids, fungi, and epiphytes are common. The forest is full of polylepis trees, one of the few trees in the world that grows to about 3,000m (9,840 ft.). *Note:* It can get extremely cold here, so wear warm clothing.

GETTING THERE & VISITING THE PARK   Cajas is huge and much of its wildlife is elusive. I highly recommend exploring the park with a guide. Both Hualambari and TerraDiversa (p. 219) have excellent naturalist guides. If you want to go on your own, head to the main terminal in Cuenca and catch any Guayaquil-bound bus that takes the route via Molleturo and Cajas. These buses leave roughly every hour throughout the day. Ask to be dropped off at La Toreadora. Return buses run on a similar schedule and are easy to catch from the main road outside the visitor center. Admission to the park is $10 (£5.50) for adults, $5 (£2.75) for children under 12. If you have any questions, call the park office (© **07/2829-853**).

INGAPIRCA ⌖

Ingapirca is the largest pre-Columbian architectural complex in Ecuador, and it's definitely the most interesting. However, anyone familiar with the massive ruins of Machu Picchu or of the Mesoamerican Maya will find this site rather small by comparison. The Incas arrived here around 1470. Before then, the Cañari people had inhabited the area. It's believed that both the Cañari and Incas used Ingapirca as a religious site. It was common for the Incas to build their religious palaces over the ruins of a conquered culture. When the Incas conquered the area, they ordered all Cañari men to move to Cusco. In the meantime, Inca men took up residence with Cañari women, to subtly impose Inca beliefs on the local culture. Ingapirca, then, is a mix of Cañari and Inca influences. For example, many of the structures here are round or oval-shaped, which is very atypical of the Incas. In fact, Ingapirca is home to the only oval-shaped sacred Inca palace in the world.

Ingapirca means "the wall of the Inca," and you can see some fine examples of the famed Inca masonry here. The highlight of the site is **El Adoratorio/Castillo,** an elliptical structure which is believed to be a temple to the sun. It is built from east to west, and if you're here on June 21, you can watch as the sun projects light on certain symbols. Nearby are the **Aposentos,** rooms made with tight stonework, thought to have been used by the high priests. Most of the remains from the Cañari culture have been found at **Pilaloma,** at the south end of the site (near where you first enter). Pilaloma means "small hill," and some archaeologists surmise that this was a sacred spot, especially because it is the highest point in the area. Eleven bodies (mostly of women) have been found here—perhaps the circle of stones was some sort of tomb. On a hill behind the entrance, near the parking area, is a small museum with a relief map of the site and a collection of artifacts and relics found here.

This site is administered and run by the local community. Llamas graze amongst the archaeological ruins. If you're lucky enough to visit before or after the large tour buses arrive, you'll find the place has a very peaceful vibe to it.

GETTING THERE   The site (© **07/2215-115**) is open daily from 8am to 6pm; admission is $6 (£3). It's best to visit Ingapirca with an experienced guide because most of the resident guides here do not speak English, and all the explanations inside the museum are in Spanish only. A full-day trip to Ingapirca out of Cuenca, including transportation, lunch, and guided tour of the ruins, but not the admission fee, should cost $30 to $45 (£17–£25). If you want to go to Ingapirca on your own, catch a bus from the main bus terminal in Cuenca. **Cooperativa Cañar** (© **07/2844-033**) operates buses that stop at the site; they depart at 9am and 1pm, and the 2-hour ride costs $3 (£1.65) each way. The return buses leave Ingapirca at 1 and 4pm.

Staying near the Site

Posada Ingapirca *(Finds*   Perched on a hill just above its namesake ruins, this converted farmhouse has cozy rooms in a remote, rural setting. Perfectly fitted Inca stones form the hearth of the beautiful fireplace here. The rooms are all carpeted, have exposed rustic log-beam ceilings, and come with little electric heaters. The decor features colorful woven blankets and local handicrafts. Some rooms have their own fireplaces. The views are great from the large picture windows of the second-floor rooms, but those on the ground floor have a wonderful tile-and-stone shared veranda. Posada Ingapirca is located just a couple of hundred yards from the entrance to the archaeological site.

Ingapirca, Cañar Province. © 07/2215-116 or 09/8060-223. santaana@etapaonline.net.ec. 22 units. $43 (£24) double. Rates include full breakfast. AE, DC, MC, V. **Amenities:** Restaurant; bar; lounge; laundry service. *In room:* TV.

EN ROUTE SOUTH: SARAGURO

Located 141km (88 miles) south of Cuenca and 64km (40 miles) north of Loja, **Saraguro,** as well as a handful of neighboring towns, is home to a unique and traditional indigenous group known by the same name. The Saraguro are most recognized for their use of black ponchos and shawls, which some claim they wear in memory and mourning of Atahualpa, who was killed by the Spanish in 1533. Both Saraguro men and women wear their hair in a single, long braid, and the women often wear beautiful beaded necklaces. The Saraguros also are known for using distinctive broad-brimmed hats. The everyday use of their traditional dress, however, is greatly decreasing with globalization, and the Atahualpa legend has been called into doubt recently. Today, Saraguros can be found throughout the region, particularly in Loja and Vilcabamba (see below). The forests and hills surrounding the town of Saraguro are a rich area for bird-watching and a beautiful spot for those wanting to see a bit of rural Ecuador.

Of interest in Saraguro is the fact that the principal church and other public buildings are built using Inca stones cut, carved, and transported from Cusco during the reign of Huayna Capac. The stones were part of a temple destined for Quito. But when a lightning storm struck the convoy transporting them near Paquishapa and Saraguro, it was thought to be a bad omen and the project was abandoned.

Hotel options are severely limited in Saraguro. Your best bet is probably **Samana Wasi** (© **07/2200-315**), which is on Avenida 10 de Marzo near the Pan-American Highway; it's a simple and inexpensive hostel, with clean rooms and a friendly staff.

2 Loja

647km (401 miles) S of Quito, 415km (257 miles) SE of Guayaquil, 205km (127 miles) S of Cuenca

Off the beaten track and not on most traditional tourist itineraries, Loja is the capital city of the southern province of the same name. This small burg is little-visited, and serves predominantly as a gateway to the more popular and even more remote village of Vilcabamba (see below). That said, Loja is a clean, quiet, and pleasant city nestled between two rivers. In addition to a colonial-era vibe, there's a whimsical side to Loja: At the entrance to the city, you'll see a castlelike bridge and clock tower, which show both medieval and Tudor architectural influences and feature various public murals.

Founded in the beautiful Cuxibamba Valley in 1548 by Alonso de Mercadillo, Loja is one of the oldest cities in Ecuador. It was also the country's first to be wired for electricity, in 1896, using electricity generated by a nearby hydroelectric dam. As you enter the city, a large sign over the main road in proclaims Loja THE MUSICAL CAPITAL OF ECUADOR, owing to the fact that the city has produced its fair share of popular artists.

ESSENTIALS
GETTING THERE & DEPARTING
BY PLANE   **Tame** (© **02/2909-900** central reservation number in Quito, or **07/2585-224** in Loja; www.tame.com.ec), **Icaro** (© **1800/883-567** toll-free nationwide; www.icaro.com.ec), and **Saereo** (© **02/3302-280** in Quito, or 07/2579-810 in Loja; www.saereo.com) all have daily service between Quito and Loja's **Aeropuerto Camilo Ponce Enríquez** (© **07/2677-140;** airport code: LOH)—also known as La Toma—in Catamayo, about 45 minutes outside of Loja. Fares run $70 to $85 (£39–£47) each way, and the flight takes around 1 hour and 10 minutes.

There are always taxis waiting for arriving flights. A cab ride from the airport to Loja should cost $5 to $7 (£2.75–£3.85). From the airport into Loja, buses also run about every hour between 6am and 9pm. The fare is around $1 (55p).

BY BUS   **Cooperativa Loja** (© **02/2581-240** in Quito, or 07/2571-861 in Loja), **Cooperativa Santa** (© **02/2572-899** in Quito, or 07/2579-017 in Loja), and **Pullman Viajero** (© **02/2953-872** in Quito, or 07/2571-626 in Loja) all have direct service to Loja, via Cuenca, from Quito's main bus terminal. About a dozen different buses leave between 1:30pm and midnight for the 12-hour journey. The fare is around $14 to $18 (£7.70–£9.90).

Cooperativa Loja and **Pullman Viajero** have roughly hourly service round the clock between Loja and Cuenca. This ride takes about 4½ hours and the fare is $7 (£3.85). Cooperativa Loja also has regular service to Guayaquil, which, like Quito, is a 12-hour ride.

In Loja, the main bus station, Terminal Terrestre (© **07/2570-407**), is on Avenida 8 de Diciembre and Juan José Flores. In addition to the major cities listed above, you can find regular bus connections between Loja and Huaquillas, Machala, and Vilcabamba.

BY CAR   If you're driving to Loja from Quito, follow the directions to Cuenca (p. 206). In Cuenca, stay on the Pan-American Highway (E35), which takes you right in to Loja.

If you are coming from Guayaquil, follow the directions to Machala (p. 263). From Machala, continue south on E25 until the town of La Avanzada, where you will take the well-marked exit for E92 to Loja.

ORIENTATION
The highways into Loja from Cuenca, Machala, and the airport enter the city from the north, near the divergence of the Malacatus and Zamora rivers—the heart of the city lies between these two rivers. The main north-south thoroughfares in town are avenidas Iberoamérica and Universitaria, which are parallel and straddle the Malacatus River.

The Parque Central (Central Park) is the physical and social center of Loja, with every major hotel, restaurant, shop, and attraction of note within easy walking distance. The Universidad Nacional de Loja (National University of Loja) is located south of downtown.

GETTING AROUND

Local buses and *taxi rutas* (shared taxis that cruise a specific route, picking up and dropping off passengers as necessary) circulate around the city. Fares run 10¢ to 40¢ (5p–20p). You can also find numerous traditional taxis. A ride anywhere in town, including to or from the bus terminal, should be just $1 (55p). If you can't flag one down, call **Radio Taxi** (© 07/2588-532).

If you want to rent a car while in Loja, contact **Bombuscaro Rent A Car** (© 07/2577-022; www.bombuscarorentacar.com), on 10 de Agosto, between Avenida Universitaria and 18 de Noviembre. Rates run $30 to $80 (£17–£44) per day, with 150km (93 miles) of mileage included and a charge of 30¢ (15p) per km above that.

FAST FACTS   The main **police station** is located outside of the center of town, on Avenida Argentina, near Avenida Bolívar (© **101** or 07/2579-030). The main **post office** is located on the corner of calles Colón and Sucre. The **Hospital Loja** is located on Avenida Samaniego and San Juan de Dios (© **07/2570-540**). At Av. Valdivieso 8–22 and Avenida 10 de Agosto, on the southwest corner of the main plaza, you'll find the **Ministry of Tourism** (© 07/2572-964).

Several banks are located near the central park, and other branches and various ATMs are spread around town. There's **Banco del Pichincha** branch on Valdivieso and 10 de Agosto (© **07/2571-699**), and one of **Banco de Guayaquil** on Jose Antonio Eguiguren and Olmedo (© **07/2585-025**).

Internet cafes and *cabinas telefónicas* can be found all over Loja, particularly around downtown, as well as at or near any hotel. Recommended Internet cafes include **Cybersat,** on Rocafuerte 13–41 near Bolívar, and **Jungle Net,** on Miguel Riofrío 13–64, between Valdivieso and Bolívar. Rates run 70¢ to $1.20 (40p–65p) per hour.

WHAT TO SEE & DO

For most visitors, the first sight to catch their eye is the **Puerta de la Ciudad (Door to the City),** a castlelike clock tower that actually forms a bridge over the main road into town. The tower, which features a couple of side turrets, displays a re-creation of the coat of arms granted the city by King Phillip II of Spain in 1571. It was from here that expeditions were to be launched to conquer the Amazon and to seek the mythical city of El Dorado. Inside this structure you'll find a few shops and galleries, as well as a simple little second-floor cafe. The top of the tower provides a nice lookout point from which to take in the lay of the land in Loja.

Public parks and plazas abound in Loja. The **Parque Central** ⊛ is a classic colonial-era construction with the city's Catholic church on the eastern side, and the Palacio Municipal (Municipal Palace) on its north side. The main cathedral, or **Catedral** ⊛, which has an ornately painted interior, is worth a visit. This is one of the largest churches in Ecuador, and received a major overhaul and restoration in 2004. In mid-August, the famous statue of the Virgin of El Cisne is brought to the cathedral for the celebrations in her honor. On the south side of the central plaza is the **Museo del Banco Central** (© 07/2963-004), which has a collection of archaeological relics and displays illustrating local historical events. This museum has seven rooms, with sections dedicated to the Incan and pre-Incan civilizations, colonial-era art, natural history, and significant Loja citizens. The museum is open Monday to Friday from 9am to 5pm and Saturday from 9am to 1pm. Admission is $2 (£1.10).

Located about 5 blocks south of the Parque Central is the **Plaza San Sebastián** ✪, also known as the Plaza de la Independencia (Independence Square). It was here, on November 18, 1820, that the local populace gathered to declare independence from Spain. At the center of the plaza stands a towering 32m-tall (105-ft.) clock tower. Around the plaza, colonial-era buildings have been lovingly restored, and on the south side of the plaza stands the pretty blue-and-white Iglesia de San Sebastián and its attached convent. Both are beautifully maintained.

Another notable little city park, the **Plaza San Francisco,** gets its name from the neighboring **San Francisco church and convent.** At the center of this plaza is a large sculpture of Alonso de Mercadillo, the city's founder, mounted on a marvelous steed.

Perhaps Loja's most striking church is the **Iglesia de Santo Domingo** ✪✪, located at **Plaza Santo Domingo.** Dating to 1557, this church features interior paintings and frescos by Fray Enrique Mideros, who also painted the churches in Ibarra, Latacunga, and Baños.

Much of Loja's colonial architecture has been destroyed by earthquakes, fire, and the passage of time, so you absolutely must take a stroll up **Calle Lourdes** ✪, which has a picturesque row of well-restored and -maintained colonial homes and buildings with ornate plaster facades, carved wood window frames and doors, cobblestone streets, and stone and tile sidewalks. Antique street lamps and fresh paint complete the picture. Scattered among the residential homes you'll find art galleries and other shops. Calle Lourdes is located south of the center of town; the best section is found between Avenida Bolívar and Avenida 18 de Noviembre.

There are excellent hiking and bird-watching opportunities all around the mountains and forests outside of Loja. The primary destination for these activities is Podocarpus National Park (see below). If you want to do any serious hiking, bird-watching,

The Virgin of El Cisne

Located some 70km (43 miles) northwest of Loja, El Cisne is one of Ecuador's major religious-pilgrimage sites. The impressive Basílica del Cisne (El Cisne Basilica) here is home to a famous sculpture of the Virgin Mary carved by Diego de Robles in the 16th century. Locals call the sculpture *La Churona,* which translates roughly as "the curly headed girl." The first church to house this holy figure was begun in 1594; the current basilica was finished in 1934, and is impressive in size and the amount of detailed craftsmanship. The beautiful church sits on a high hillside in a remote rural area. The main celebrations for the Virgin del Cisne take place on August 15. Two days later, carried by thousands of devotees, she begins a 3-day trek to Loja, where she will stay for the next couple of months. Based out of the main cathedral in Loja, during this period, the statue is taken to various churches in the region. In Loja, the main celebration for the Virgin del Cisne occurs on September 8, a celebration that was officially decreed by Simón Bolívar himself on a visit to Loja in 1822. On November 1, the Virgin and her followers begin their return pilgrimage to El Cisne.

or any other adventure activity in the area, I recommend that you contact **Biotours** (© 07/2579-387), **Metropolitan Touring** (© 07/2578-671), or **Vilcatur** (© 07/2571-443). All have trained bilingual guides, and a wide range of possible tour options.

Loja isn't a particularly great shopping town, but if you want to browse some excellent local arts, handicrafts, and handmade clothing, head to **Arte Sano** ☆, on Calle Lourdes, between Sucre and Bolívar (© 07/2574-242).

WHERE TO STAY IN LOJA

In addition to the hotels listed below, the **Grand Hotel Loja** (© 07/2572-200; www.grandhotelloja.com) is another downtown option offering good value, if somewhat dated rooms, with plenty of modern amenities.

MODERATE

Bombuscaro Hotel   The exterior of this hotel is striking, with three spires of tinted glass rising six stories over Loja. Inside the entrance, the elegant lobby features an abundance of shiny marble. Rooms are large and well appointed, and have firm beds and attractive furnishings. The two presidential suites come with a private Jacuzzi in a large bathroom. Some of the units on the higher floors have really wonderful views. The hotel provides free daily newspaper delivery, and has a modest little business center.

Av. 10 de Agosto, between Av. Universitaria and 18 de Noviembre, Loja. © 07/2577-021. Fax 07/2570-136. www. bombuscaro.com.ec. 35 units. $48 (£26) double; $57 (£31) junior suite; $75 (£41) presidential suite. Rates include continental breakfast. AE, DC, MC, V. Free parking. **Amenities:** Restaurant; bar; tour desk; 24-hr. room service; laundry service. *In room:* TV.

Hotel La Castellana ☆   One of the newer hotels in Loja, this high-rise business-class hotel provides comfortable, well-equipped rooms at a good price. Most have carpeted floors, two queen-size beds, and good views from large windows. The decor is understated, but tasteful and contemporary. The junior suites are obviously larger and come with a king-size bed, a sitting area with a plush couch, and a stocked minibar. The hotel has a Jacuzzi, steam room, and sauna, as well as a dependable little restaurant serving local and international fare. The Castellana is located just west of downtown, across the Río Malacatus.

Av. Lauro Guerrero 10–57, between Azuay and Miguel Riofrío, Loja. © 07/2585-592. Fax 07/2573-844. www. lacastellana.com.ec. 32 units. $40 (£22) double; $60 (£33) junior suite. Rates include continental breakfast. AE, DC, MC, V. Free parking. **Amenities:** Restaurant; bar; Jacuzzi; sauna; tour desk; room service 7am–10pm; laundry service. *In room:* TV.

Hotel Libertador ☆☆   This is the fanciest hotel in Loja, with the best facilities and amenities. The carpeted rooms are large and tastefully decorated; most have large picture windows that let in lots of light. The junior suites actually have small solarium sitting areas that are quite inviting. On the fourth floor you'll find the hotel's pool and spa area, which has a small but pretty pool under an arched atrium ceiling. In addition to the pool, a small gym, Jacuzzi, sauna, and steam bath, this pleasant oasis also has pretty views of the city.

Colón 14–30 and Av. Bolívar, Loja. © 07/2560-779. Fax 07/2572-119. www.hotellibertador.com.ec. 58 units. $51 (£28) double; $67 (£37) suite. Rates include buffet breakfast. AE, DC, MC, V. Free parking. **Amenities:** Restaurant; bar; small indoor pool; exercise room; Jacuzzi; sauna; steam bath; tour desk; room service 7am–11pm; laundry service. *In room:* TV, hair dryer.

INEXPENSIVE

Hotel Acapulco   The Hotel Acapulco has definitely seen better days, but it remains a safe bet and good value. While the furniture and paint may be a tad tired, the service is friendly and attentive. In fact, in its day this was once considered an almost upscale hotel in Loja, and today it is certainly one of the better budget options in town. Very few of the rooms have exterior windows—most unit windows face interior hallways. Many rooms are quite compact; ask to see a few and you may be able to snag a larger room, or at least one with more warmth and light.

Calle Sucre 07–61 and Av. 10 de Agosto, Loja. ℂ 07/2570-651. Fax 07/2571-103. 43 units. $26 (£14) double. Rates include continental breakfast. MC, V. Free parking. **Amenities:** Restaurant; bar; tour desk; laundry service. *In room:* TV.

WHERE TO DINE IN LOJA

Loja is a midsize city with plenty of restaurants, although most cater to the local crowd, and very few stand out. The local specialty is the *tamal lojano,* a large *tamal* of fresh ground corn filled with a mix of shredded pork or chicken and other goodies, which include hard-boiled eggs, beans, carrots, and onions—all of which is wrapped in the local *achira* plant leaf.

In addition to the local joints listed below, Loja has its share of international restaurants. The best of these include **A Lo Mero Mero,** on Sucre 06–22, near Colón (no phone), for traditional Mexican fare; **Pizzería Forno di Fango,** on Bolívar 10–98 near Azuay (ℂ 07/2582-905), for pizza, pastas, and Italian cuisine; and **Mar y Cuba,** on Rocafuerte 09–00 and 24 de Mayo (ℂ 07/2585-154), for Cuban cooking and fresh seafood. Vegetarians should head to **Paraíso Vegetariano,** on Calle Quito, between Sucre and Bolívar (ℂ 07/2576-977), which has a good menu of meat-free entrees and snacks.

Casa Sol 🏵 *Finds* ECUADORIAN/LOJANO   This is the place to come for Lojano cooking. Grab a seat on the second-floor balcony and start things off with the local specialty, *tamal lojano,* or some *empanadas de yuca.* If you want to really go native, order fresh roasted *cuy,* or guinea pig—it's prepared as well here as it is anyplace in Ecuador. A daily *menú ejecutivo* for around $2 (£1.10) makes for a filling lunch.

24 de Mayo 07–04, on the corner of José Antonio Eguiguren. ℂ 07/2588-597. Main courses $3–$9 (£1.65–£4.95). DC, MC, V. Daily 11am–11pm.

Diego's *Value* ECUADORIAN/INTERNATIONAL   This local institution is a great choice any time of day, for any occasion. You can come for breakfast in the morning and then return for an afternoon beer. The menu features a daily selection of soups, including the ever popular *locro de papa,* as well as sandwiches and pastas, and more substantial fare including steaks, grilled chicken, and shrimp dishes. The service is semi-formal, with waiters decked out in starched white shirts and black bow-ties. Housed in a restored colonial-era home, the restaurant's best seats are in the open-air patio.

Calle Colón, between Sucre and Bolívar. ℂ 07/2560-245. Main courses $3.50–$6 (£1.95–£3.30). MC, V. Mon–Sat 7:30am–10pm; Sun 9am–4pm.

LOJA AFTER DARK

Loja has two universities and the self-proclaimed reputation of being the country's music capital. Indeed, there is a vibrant music scene here. On weekends, bands often play in the Parque Central.

In addition to offering French-language classes, the local branch of the French cultural center, **Alianza Francesa** (ℂ 07/2571-166), on Avenida Iberoamérica and Miguel Riofrío, frequently hosts film cycles and live concerts.

The most popular bars in town are **Casa Tinku** ☆☆, on Calle Lourdes, between Avenida Bolívar and Sucre, and **La Fiesta** ☆, on Av. 10 de Agosto 10–59, between 24 de Mayo and Juan José Pena. Casa Tinku attracts a young, college crowd and sometimes has live rock and folk bands, and even the occasional dance, theater piece, or poetry reading, while La Fiesta is Loja's all-out salsa and merengue dance club. Expats will feel comfortable at the new **Free Days,** on Río Zamora and 24 de Mayo, which has the feel of an American-style sports bar and gets people going with nightly karaoke. For a more quiet time, try **La Siembra** (across the street from Free Days), an intimate bar that serves local fare, grilled meats, and pizzas; or **El Viejo Minero** ☆, on Sucre 10–76 near Azuay, a down-home, no-frills watering-hole popular with local college students.

BETWEEN LOJA & VILCABAMBA: PODOCARPUS NATIONAL PARK ☆☆

Naturalists and bird-watchers covet this little-visited national park. **Podocarpus National Park** begins just south of Loja and covers a vast area that descends down toward the Amazon basin. The park runs from a high of 3,700m (11,811 ft.) down to some 1,000m (3,281 ft.), and contains ecosystems that range from high paramo (moor) to cloud forest and rainforest—with a total area of 146,280 hectares (361,311 acres). The sheer size and variety of ecosystems contained in Podocarpus make this an incredibly rich park in terms of biodiversity. Over 600 species of birds have been identified here. The park is named after several endemic species of the *Podocarpus* genus. Other park residents include the spectacled bear, jaguar, sloth, and tapir. For overnight stays, camping is allowed at several campsites in the park, and there are a few rustic cabins located near each of the entrance ranger stations. For more information on these, contact the **park office** (☎ 07/2571-534 or 07/2577-125) in Loja.

Several well-marked and -maintained trails leave from the Cajanuma park-ranger station. The terrain is mostly moist cloud forest and high-altitude paramo, and rain is common throughout much of the year. A short loop trail leads through the cloud forest to a beautiful lookout point. Longer hikes, which require overnight camping, bring you to a series of stunning small mountain lakes. I recommend that you visit with a guide. In Loja, contact **Biotours** (☎ 07/2579-387), **Metropolitan Touring** (☎ 07/2578-671), or **Vilcatur** (☎ 07/2571-443). In Vilcabamba, contact Jorge Luis at **Caminatas Andes Sureños** (☎ 07/2673-147). A full-day tour of the park, with transportation, lunch, and naturalist guide, should run around $25 to $40 (£14–£22) per person.

Mining firms and loggers covet this park as much as naturalists and bird-watchers do. Much of the park has been ceded to mining interests, and mining activities and illegal logging pose a major threat to the delicate ecosystems here. Both the **Nature Conservancy** (www.nature.org) and the Ecuadorian **Fundación Ecológica Arcoiris** (www.arcoiris.org.ec) are working to protect the park. Contact either of these organizations for more information, or if you are interested in volunteering in the park.

GETTING THERE & VISITING THE PARK The principal entrance to the park is the Cajanuma entrance, some 14km (8 miles) south of Loja, on the road to Vilcabamba. From the highway turnoff, a rugged road leads another 8km (5 miles) to the park-ranger station. A taxi from Loja all the way to the ranger station should cost around $6 to $8 (£3.30–£4.40) each way. If you want to arrange a round-trip ride, set a pick-up time with a driver you trust. Alternatively, any of the many buses running the Loja-to-Vilcabamba route will drop you off and pick you up near the exit to the park entrance. See "Vilcabamba: Getting There," below, for more details. There's a bit of a hike into the park from where you'll be dropped off. Admission is $10 (£5.50) per person per day. Camping costs an additional $3 (£1.65) per person in a tent, and $5 (£2.75) for a bunk in one of the cabins.

ON TO PERU

Loja is often used as a land-based jumping-off point for onward travel into Peru. The border crossing here is less commonly used than that at Huaquillas (p. 266). From Loja, the Pan-American Highway heads first west, then south, to the Ecuadorian border town of Macará. The Peruvian town on the other side of the border is La Tina. Both of these towns are tiny and of little interest to travelers. In fact, the first Peruvian city that most travelers head to is Piura, several hours south of the border. **Cooperativa Unión Cariamanga** (*© 07/257-1340*) has a half-dozen buses daily from Loja's main bus terminal to Macará. The ride takes around 5 hours, and the fare is $4.50 (£2.50). This same bus company also has two daily direct buses to Piura, Peru. I highly recommend you book one of these, since the bus will wait for you to complete immigration formalities (otherwise you'll have to take two different buses). These buses leave at 3am and 6am, and the ride takes 8 to 9 hours. The fare is around $11 (£6.05).

If you decide to head first to Macará, the border formalities are relatively straightforward and painless, and the entire scene is mellower than that at Huaquillas. The Ecuadorian immigration office is just before the bridge over the river that separates the two countries. There's a Peruvian checkpoint on the other side of the bridge, but you will have to take care of formal Peruvian immigration procedures in Sullana, 130km (80 miles) to the south. There is plenty of taxi and onward bus service between Macará and La Tina, and from La Tina on to Sullana and Piura.

3 Vilcabamba ⭐⭐

40km (25 miles) S of Loja

The remote and picturesque valley of Vilcabamba has earned the nickname "Valley of Longevity" because residents here allegedly live to ripe old ages far beyond the norm. The reasons given for this range from clean air, clean water, and clean living, to extraterrestrial influences, to the work of the gods—in Quichua, Vilcabamba, sometimes spelled Huilcobamba or Huilco Pamba, means "Sacred Valley." Recent scientific studies have cast doubt on any quantifiable longevity effects here. I doubt a visit to Vilcabamba will add any years to your life, but if stress and the daily grind have been getting you down, it just might cure what ails you.

Located at 1,470m (4,900 ft.), Vilcabamba enjoys a pleasant, temperate climate, with warm days and slightly cool nights. There's great hiking, bird-watching, and horseback riding all around the area.

ESSENTIALS
GETTING THERE & DEPARTING

BY PLANE   The nearest airport to Vilcabamba is **Aeropuerto Camilo Ponce,** outside of Loja. See "Loja: Getting There," above, for details. Taxis are always waiting for incoming flights. A ride from the airport to Loja costs about $4 (£2.20). From Loja you can take one of the very frequent buses or minivans to Vilcabamba (see below). A direct taxi ride from the airport to Vilcabamba should cost around $25 to $30 (£14–£17).

BY BUS   **Vilcabamba Turis** (*© 07/2640-065*) and **Sur Oriente** (*© 07/2571-755*) make the run between Loja and Vilcabamba roughly every 15 to 20 minutes between

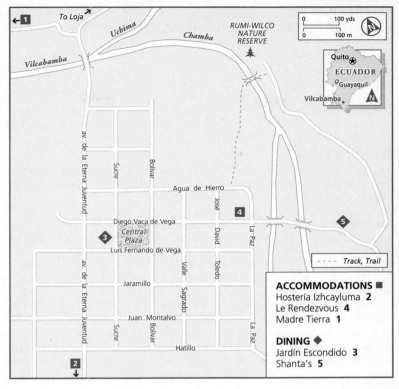

6am and 7pm. The fare is $1 (55p) and the ride takes a little over 1 hour. Sur Oriente uses large, traditional buses, while Vilcabamba Turis uses slightly faster minivans. Both leave from the main terminal in Loja, and in Vilcabamba they arrive at and leave from the corner of Avenida Eterna Juventud and Jaramillo, 1 block south and 1 block west of the central plaza.

BY CAR   If you are driving to Vilcabamba, follow the directions to Loja (see above), and then take E39 south to Vilcabamba. Historically, this road has been in horrendous shape, but it received major refurbishing in 2006 and 2007. It remains to be seen how long it will stay in good shape. Currently, the drive takes around 45 minutes.

ORIENTATION
Vilcabamba is a tiny town. The main downtown area measures only 4 square blocks or so, with a main plaza at its core. The town's principal Catholic church is on the south side of this plaza.

GETTING AROUND
You can easily walk anywhere in town. Walking and horseback riding (see below) are the main means of transportation here. Numerous vans and shared taxis make the run to Loja, and a few locals with pickup trucks serve as taxis for runs around the valley. Most rides cost $1 to $3 (55p–£1.65).

FAST FACTS   There's an **information office** (📞 07/2580-890) on the northeast corner of the main plaza, and a small **hospital** (📞 07/2673-188) 1 block north of the main plaza.

There are no banks in Vilcabamba, but a **Banco de Guayaquil** ATM lies just off the main plaza, next to the tourist information office. This machine sometimes runs out of money or goes on the blink, so I recommend you stock up in Loja, or you could be making an emergency run back there for cash. There are a couple of Internet cafes in town, although when tourism is running high, the terminals fill up fast. The best option is **Vilcanet** (📞 07/2673-124), on the southwest side of town on Huilcopamba near Juan Montalvo.

WHAT TO SEE & DO

The most popular activity here is horseback riding. Horses, with riders and without, are common in the streets. Various individuals and small tour companies offer guided horseback tours around the area, and most hotels here either have their own horses and guides, or can set you up. If you want to do it on your own, check in with **Centro Equestre** (📞 07/2673-151) or **Gavilan Tours** (📞 07/2640-281). Rides run around $15 to $20 (£8.25–£11) for a half-day tour, to $35 to $50 (£19–£28) for a full-day tour, including lunch.

The same terrain that makes horseback riding so rewarding is also perfect for mountain biking. If you prefer pedal power to horse power, ask at your hotel, or contact the information office (see above).

There's plenty of good hiking all around the Vilcabamba valley. Perhaps the most popular hike is to the top of the Mandango rock formation. From the town and several vantage points around the valley, this rock formation looks quite a bit like a face staring up towards the sky, and locals call it "The Sleeping Giant" or "The Sleeping God." It's a sometimes steep and strenuous 2-hour hike to the top, but the views are worth it. Another popular hiking destination is Podocarpus National Park (see above). If you want to do any guided hiking, a longer trek, or some serious bird-watching, contact Jorge Luis at **Caminatas Andes Sureños** (📞 07/2673-147). Jorge Luis is an extremely knowledgeable and enthusiastic guide.

Long Strange Tripping

It's a long way to Vilcabamba, but for many visitors here, this is where their tripping begins. The San Pedro cactus grows heartily here. Known as the Holy Cactus, San Pedro is a bucket term given to some 30 different species of Andean *Trichocereus* cacti. All are tall columnar cacti that contain the psychotropic alkaloids used to make mescaline. Its ritual and shamanic use in Ecuador and Peru dates to at least 1400 B.C. Locals and expatriates around Vilcabamba often offer to guide travelers on a San Pedro cactus trip. These trips run the gamut from very conscientious and well-guided ritual experiences to bonfire party scenes. In most cases, it is illegal, and considered a jailable offence, to take San Pedro cactus. However, apparently some shamans are licensed to provide the experience. I cannot advocate or recommend any specific guides or shamans, but only caution you that if you do decide to venture into this realm, be forewarned that this is a very strong psychedelic substance, and you should be very sure you trust and feel comfortable with whomever you choose to guide you.

If you're sore from hiking, biking, or horse-back riding, you should consider heading to **Madre Tierra** ★★ (see below) for a massage or spa treatment. Individual treatments begin at around $8 (£4.40) for an aromatherapy session, to $40 (£22) for a 90-minute massage. Other options range from hot mud treatments, to facials, to Reiki sessions. **Hostería Izhcayluma** ★ (see below) has very similar offerings.

If you're spending any serious time in Vilcabamba and run out of good reading material, head about 1 kilometer out of town towards Yambarara for **Craig's Book Exchange.**

For some reason, people from across Ecuador flock to Vilcabamba in late February for the annual **Carnaval** celebrations. During this period, the sleepy and peaceful little town becomes a major party destination, with bands and parades and street vendors and pretty much nonstop partying.

WHERE TO STAY IN VILCABAMBA
INEXPENSIVE
Hostería Izhcayluma ★   Very much like Madre Tierra (see below), and clearly an attempt at matching the magic made there, this place has a range of room styles in a range of prices, from shared bath dorm rooms to private cabins. The latter are the top choice here. Each of the five cabins is set on the edge of a hillside, with plenty of room and privacy. Each also has a large balcony, with some chairs and a hammock, overlooking spectacular views. Still, even the dorm rooms here are pleasant; they have high ceilings, plenty of light, and no bunk beds. The beautiful outdoor pool was designed to resemble a natural pond, with lush plantings all around and a small waterfall. The open-air restaurant and dining room features panoramic views of the Vilcabamba valley. These folks have a small spa offering massage, mud treatments, and Reiki sessions. For less holistic pursuits, there's a bar with a pool table and dart board. The outdoor fire pit is a popular reunion spot.

2km (1½ miles) south of Vilcabamba, on the road to Zumba. © **07/2640-095** or 09/9153-419. www.izhcayluma. com. 15 units. $8 (£4.40) per person in dorm room; $24 (£13) double room; $30 (£17) double cabin. Rates include breakfast and taxes. No credit cards. **Amenities:** Restaurant; bar; outdoor pool; small spa; free mountain bikes; tour desk; laundry service. *In room:* No phone.

Le Rendezvous ★ *(Value*   Located 2½ blocks from the central plaza—and close to the river—this is my favorite hotel right in the town of Vilcabamba. The rooms are spotless, with whitewashed adobe walls and terra-cotta tile floors. All are of good size and feature firm beds. Each opens onto the hotel's lush and perpetually flowering gardens, and comes with a hammock hung on its front veranda. The French owners are extremely personable and knowledgeable, and they care a good deal about the area. The complex is wired for Wi-Fi, so if you're carrying a laptop or PDA, for $3 (£1.65) per day you can have unlimited use.

Diego Vaca de Vega 06–43 and La Paz, Vilcabamba. © **09/2191-180.** www.rendezvousecuador.com. 8 units. $18 (£9.90) double. Rates include breakfast and taxes. Rates lower in the off season and for longer stays; and higher during peak periods. No credit cards. **Amenities:** Restaurant; bar; tour desk; laundry service. *In room:* TV, Wi-Fi, no phone.

Madre Tierra ★★ *(Finds*   Whether or not there's any fountain of youth in Vilcabamba, it's worth the journey to stay at this unique retreat. To say artistic touches abound would be an understatement. Carved wood, eclectic tile work and stone masonry, stained glass, and hand-painted art are everywhere. Every room is distinct here: Many have exposed brick walls; some have glass skylights, and most have interesting stone, tile, and brick floors. The range in room prices reflects both the size and location of the room. The best rooms come with their own private balcony, with a hammock and fabulous view. But even if you don't get a room with a view, there are excellent views from all around the hotel's common grounds. There's an inviting outdoor pool with fabulous landscaping and stone work, and a beautiful tiled Jacuzzi. The small spa here offers a range of treatment and beauty options, and the hotel has satellite Internet access available via house computers or plugging in a laptop.

Organic and wholesome foods are served, much of it grown on-site. Thick whole-grain breads are baked daily. Don't be surprised if after dinner there's a jam session, or some fire juggling, or an impromptu dance performance. The owners also rent out two beautiful, fully equipped cottages, off the hotel grounds.

2km (1½ miles) before the town of Vilcabamba, on the road to Loja. ✆ 07/2640-269 or 09/4465-073. www. madretierra1.com. 24 units, 5 with shared bathroom. $12 (£6) double with shared bathroom; $29–$89 (£16–£49) double. Rates include breakfast and dinner. AE, DC, MC, V. Amenities: Restaurant; bar; midsize outdoor pool; Jacuzzi; steam bath; tour desk; laundry service. In room: Hair dryer.

WHERE TO DINE IN VILCABAMBA

Two of the best restaurants in Vilcabamba are those at the **Madre Tierra** and **Hostería Izhcayluma** (see above). Both serve excellent international fare, with an emphasis on fresh, healthy ingredients. The views from the restaurant at Izhcayluma are particularly beautiful. Just make sure you call ahead and make reservations.

INEXPENSIVE

Jardín Escondido *(Finds* MEXICAN/INTERNATIONAL   The Jardín Escondido, or Hidden Garden, has wonderful covered and open-air seating in a large, central garden and courtyard at the interior of its namesake hotel. When it's not raining, I love the heavy wrought-iron tables out in the center of this spread, with canvas shade umbrellas. The heart of the menu is Mexican cuisine, with everything from burritos and enchiladas to spicy, dark, chicken *mole.* On a cool night, the tortilla soup is a perfect tonic, and a welcome change from the more traditional Ecuadorian soups served everywhere else. On Saturday nights there's usually live music.

Calle Sucre, between Agua de Hierro and Diego Vaca de la Vega. ✆ 07/2640-281. Reservations recommended during high season. Main courses $3–$7 (£1.65–£3.85). MC, V. Daily 8am–11pm.

Shanta's *(Finds* ECUADORIAN/INTERNATIONAL   This small thatch-roof place looks as if it might fall down with the first stiff wind. This is probably more bar than restaurant, but they serve good food. Grab one of the several tables, or sit at the bamboo bar. The main offerings include a range of pizzas and pastas, which are well prepared, although they probably wouldn't wow them in Naples or Rome. You can also get a thick steak or grilled chicken. The signature appetizer here is the sautéed frog's legs, which are almost as much of a novelty as the owner's long handlebar mustache.

Diego de la Vaca, east of downtown, over the 2nd bridge. ✆ 07/2640-296. Main courses $3–$6 (£1.65–£3.30). No credit cards. Daily noon–2am.

VILCABAMBA AFTER DARK

Vilcabamba is a remote town known for its peace and tranquillity. The nightlife here is very subdued. But the recent and rapid increase in tourism has given rise to a few bars in town. **Shanta's** (see above) is my favorite spot, with a laid-back drinking scene; the drink specialty is shot of a local cane liquor kept in a bottle with a coral snake pickling inside it.

9

Guayaquil & the Southern Coast

Quito may be the historical and political capital of Ecuador, but **Guayaquil** is the country's largest city and its economic center. It's also the primary gateway to the Galápagos Islands, with virtually every flight to and from the archipelago touching down here. While Guayaquil hasn't totally shed its image of being a dangerous, dirty, and inhospitable city, the truth is that this riverside port has undergone an impressive transformation in recent years. Today, Guayaquil boasts a beautiful riverfront promenade, the **Malecón 2000,** and a host of excellent hotels, restaurants, shops, clubs, and casinos.

In addition to the Galápagos, Guayaquil is also the gateway to vast stretches of Ecuador's Pacific Coast and several prime beaches. This area has been dubbed the **Ruta del Sol,** or Route of the Sun, with everything from large, resort destinations to tiny beach getaways to secret surf spots. At the northern end of the Ruta del Sol lies **Machalilla National Park** and **Isla de la Plata,** a lovely offshore island which is often described as an alternative to the Galápagos Islands. While this is a stretch, the wildlife viewing and snorkeling at Isla de la Plata are superb. Tourists and Ecuadorians looking for some fun in the sun aren't the only ones to take advantage of this section of coast. Late June through September, the waters here are a prime mating and breeding ground for humpback whales, and an excellent place to get up close and personal with these amazing mammals.

Finally, since I'm talking about gateways, just 253km (157 miles) south of Guayaquil lies Peru—many travelers heading by land down to Machu Picchu, Cusco, and Lima will pass through here en route.

1 Guayaquil ⁄★

250km (155 miles) NW of Cuenca, 420km (260 miles) SW of Quito, 966km (618 miles) E of the Galápagos

Guayaquil is Ecuador's most populous and economically vibrant city. Still, most visitors to Ecuador only look upon Guayaquil as a necessary overnight stop on the way to the Galápagos Islands. But that is changing, and the city continues to reinvent itself at a dizzying pace. At the helm since 2000, Mayor Jaime Nebot has instituted a far-reaching urban renewal project that has already had impressive results. The **Malecón 2000,** the city's main riverfront promenade, and **Cerro Santa Ana (Santa Ana Hill)** are emblematic of Nebot's plan. Whereas crime was once rampant and problematic, Guayaquil is now a relatively safe and tourist-friendly city. Perhaps the city's greatest problem is the sometimes oppressive heat and humidity. Nevertheless, if you avoid the mid-day heat, you'll find the early mornings, late afternoons, and evenings all very agreeable for taking in the city's pleasures.

The Southern Coast

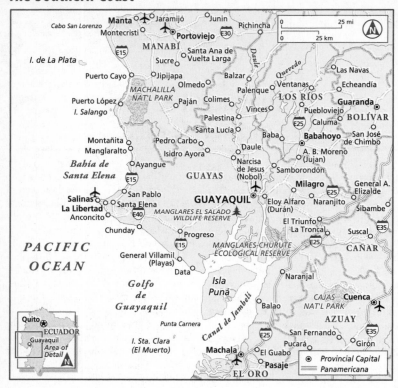

Although Guayaquil was founded in 1537, it lacks the colonial architecture that you find in Quito and Cuenca. A devastating fire ravaged the city in 1896, almost completely leveling it. Virtually no buildings escaped the blaze, and today the city has a more modern and contemporary feel than any other major city in Ecuador.

ESSENTIALS
GETTING THERE

BY PLANE   All international and national flights arrive at the new **José Joaquín de Olmedo International Airport** (© **04/2169-209;** airport code: GYE), which is located about 10 minutes north of downtown Guayaquil, just next door to the now-defunct Simón Bolívar International Airport. Many international flights to Quito first touch down in Guayaquil, and outgoing international flights often similarly stop in Guayaquil to pick up and discharge passengers.

   Tame (© **02/2909-900** central reservation number in Quito, or 04/2310-305 in Guayaquil; www.tame.com.ec), **Icaro** (© **1800/883-567** toll-free; www.icaro.com.ec), and **Aerogal** (© **1800/2376-425** toll-free; www.aerogal.com.ec) all offer daily flights between Guayaquil and both Quito and Cuenca. One-way tickets range from $55 to $66 (£30–£36) to or from Quito, and from $45 to $52 (£25–£29) to or from Cuenca.

La Rivalidad: Quito & Guayaquil

The fierce and ongoing political rivalry between the country's two principal cities, Quito and Guayaquil, was first publicly expressed in 1830 by independence heroes Juan José Flores and Vicente Rocafuerte, during the Republic's declaration of independence. During the latter half of the 19th century, García Moreno's decision to grant the Catholic Church almost absolute authority over Conservative Quito increased the polarization between the sierra and coastal regions. This regional division was even more firmly entrenched with the rise to power of Liberal leader Eloy Alfaro, who reversed García Moreno's act and called for the separation of church and state. The back-and-forth battle for presidential power between the Liberals from Guayaquil and Conservatives from Quito dominated the political landscape during the late 19th and early 20th centuries.

The rivalry inevitably spread from politics and religion to include nearly every aspect of the social, economic, and cultural life of the country. And it is still raging strong today—both Quito and Guayaquil claim to be the country's most important city. Guayaquil bases its case on the fact that it is the country's largest and most economically important city, functioning as Ecuador's major shipping port and commercial center. Quito, on the other hand, claims its supremacy on the basis of its hold on political power, its better educational opportunities, and its role as the country's physical and administrative center. Stereotypes also exist: Those from Guayaquil consider themselves much more open-minded, liberal, cheerful, and boisterous than their counterparts in the capital, while Quiteños regard themselves as more hardworking, better educated, and generally calmer than Guayaquileños. Today, one of the fiercest battlegrounds for this historic rivalry takes place on the fields and in the stands whenever the cities' *fútbol* teams compete.

If your hotel doesn't provide a shuttle service from the airport, it's incredibly easy to catch a taxi. As you exit the Customs area in the international arrivals area, there is a desk with friendly staff who will arrange a taxi for you. You pay at the desk and receive a voucher, which you then present to a driver, who will be waiting for you once you exit the terminal. A taxi to the downtown area should cost no more than $8 (£4.40).

Tip: Feel free to break out your laptop or PDA—the new airport provides free wireless connections throughout the terminal.

BY BUS   Guayaquil is connected to the rest of the country by extensive and frequent bus service. From Quito, buses leave the main terminal (Terminal Terrestre) at least every half-hour for Guayaquil; the 8-hour ride costs $10 (£5.50). Buses from Cuenca leave on a very frequent schedule as well; the 5-hour bus ride costs $8 (£4.40). **Flota Imbabura** (© 02/2572-657 in Quito, or 04/2140-649 in Guayaquil) and **Panamericana** (© 02/2570-425 in Quito, or 04/2296-171 in Guayaquil) are the two main companies making the Quito-Guayaquil run.

The new Guayaquil bus station, **Terminal Terrestre** (© 04/2140-166), is a few minutes north of the airport. All buses to and from Guayaquil leave from this terminal.

Note: If possible, it's best to travel through the Guayas province during daylight hours. While night buses are now generally considered safe, in recent years some bus hijackings have occurred after dark.

BY CAR   To reach Guayaquil by car from Quito, you will need to start off heading south on the Pan-American Highway (E35) until the intersection at Aloag. From here, you will head west on E30 towards Santo Domingo de los Colorados. In Santo Domingo, take the well-marked exit for E25 south to Quevedo. This road continues on to Guayaquil via Babahoyo.

If you're going to make this drive, I strongly recommend you do so during the daytime—road and weather conditions can make this route treacherous and hair-raising after dark.

GETTING AROUND

Guayaquil is a compact city, and it's easy to walk most places around the downtown and Malecón 2000. However, a fair amount of the hotels, shopping centers, and restaurants are located outside of the downtown area. In Guayaquil, taxis are the cheapest and most efficient way to get around. It's easy to find them on any street corner. If you can't flag one down, call **Cooperativa de Taxis Bucaram** (© 04/ 2403-592), **Cooperativa de Taxis Centro Cívico** (© 04/2450-145), or **Cooperativa de Taxis Paraíso** (© 04/2201-877). Rides within the center of the city cost only $2 to $4 (£1.10–£2.20).

Most of the major rental-car agencies have offices in Guayaquil: **Avis** (© 04/ 2285-498; www.avis.com) on Avenida Kennedy and Avenida de las Américas; **Budget** (© 04/2284-559; www.budget-ec.com) at the airport and on Av. de las Américas 900; **Hertz** (© 04/2293-011; www.hertz.com) at the airport; and **Localiza** (© 04/2395-236; www.localiza.com.ec) on Av. Franciso Boloña 713.

VISITOR INFORMATION

The Ministry of Tourism runs a **tourist information office** (© 04/2568-764) on Pedro Icaza 203, between Pedro Carbo and Panamá, on the sixth floor. The office is open Monday through Friday from 8:30am to 5pm, and provides a city map as well as other useful information on tours and attractions. The city itself maintains an excellent website crammed with information at **www.visitaguayaquil.com**.

ORIENTATION

Guayaquil is located on the western bank of the Guayas River. Avenida 9 de Octubre is the main street, running west to east through the center of the city and dead-ending at the Malecón 2000, the large pedestrian mall on the river. Avenida Malecón runs along the river as well as the Malecón 2000 development. The central downtown area and most of the museums are located within a block or two of the Malecón. The airport and bus terminal, as well as several major malls and popular hotels, restaurants, and bars, are located north of downtown in the neighborhoods of Urdesa and Nueva Kennedy.

FAST FACTS   In an **emergency**, dial © **911.** To dial the **police** call © **101,** and for the **Cruz Roja (Red Cross)** © **131.**

Most banks in Guayaquil are clustered around the intersection of Pedro Icaza and General Córdova; you'll find branches of **Banco del Pichincha** and **Banco de Guayaquil** here. You'll also find ATMs all over the city and in all the modern malls and shopping centers. The local **American Express** office is run by **Global Tours**

Guayaquil

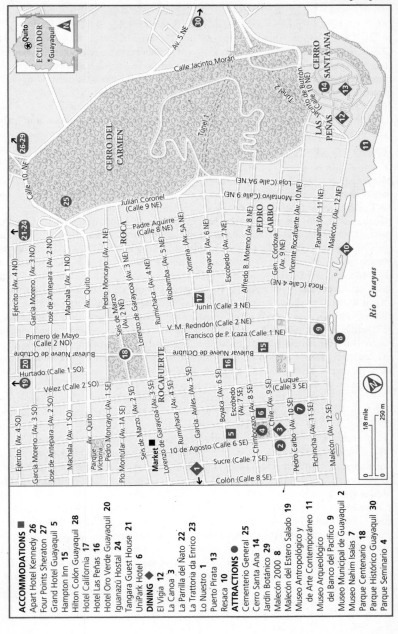

ACCOMMODATIONS ■
Apart Hotel Kennedy **26**
Four Points Sheraton **27**
Grand Hotel Guayaquil **5**
Hampton Inn **15**
Hilton Colón Guayaquil **28**
Hotel California **17**
Hotel Las Peñas **16**
Hotel Oro Verde Guayaquil **20**
Iguanazú Hostal **24**
Tangara Guest House **21**
UniPark Hotel **6**

DINING ◆
El Vigía **12**
La Canoa **3**
La Parrilla del Ñato **22**
La Trattoria da Enrico **23**
Lo Nuestro **1**
Puerto Pirata **13**
Resaca **10**

ATTRACTIONS ●
Cementerio General **25**
Cerro Santa Ana **14**
Jardín Botánico **29**
Malecón 2000 **8**
Malecón del Estero Salado **19**
Museo Antropológico y
de Arte Contemporáneo **11**
Museo Arqueológico
del Banco del Pacífico **9**
Museo Municipal de Guayaquil **2**
Museo Nahim Isaías **7**
Parque Centenario **18**
Parque Histórico Guayaquil **30**
Parque Seminario **4**

(© 04/2680-450) in the Edificio Las Cámaras, on Avenida Francisco de Orellana and Alcivar. The main **post office** is located on Clemente Ballén and Pedro Carbo.

The best hospital in Guayaquil is the **Hospital Clínica Kennedy** (© 04/ 2286-963), located north of the city in the Mall Policentro on Avenida del Periodista; the hospital runs a 24-hour pharmacy. There are scores of other pharmacies around town. The chain **Pharmacy's** (© 1800/9090-909) has various outlets, is open 24 hours, and offers delivery.

There are scores of Internet cafes in Guayaquil. Rates run around 50¢ to $1.50 (30p–85p) per hour. Many city hotels also provide reasonably priced or complimentary Internet connections.

WHAT TO SEE & DO

If you're short on time, it's still possible to get a feel for Guayaquil rather quickly, since the important attractions are quite close together (see "If You're Short on Time," below, for more information).

The **Malecón 2000 (Dos Mil)** ✈✈ is the shining star of the new and improved Guayaquil. It's impressive to enter the Malecón 2000 from Avenida 9 de Octubre, where you are greeted by a 1937 statue of the independence heroes Simón Bolívar and San Martín shaking hands. On either side of the statue, you can climb up lookout towers, which afford great views of the city and the river. Walk south and you'll hit the Moorish Clock Tower, Glorious Aurora's Obelisk, a McDonald's, a mini-mall, and tons of inexpensive food stalls. As you head in this direction, look across the street: You'll see the impressive neoclassical Palacio Municipal. If you walk north from the Bolívar-Martín statue, you'll come across a lively playground and an exercise course.

On the western end of Avenida 9 de Octubre is a separate, newer riverside promenade, along the narrow Estero Salado (Salt Water Estuary), known appropriately as the **Malecón del Estero Salado** ✈. Like its more extravagant brethren, the Malecón here is a pleasant riverside pedestrian walkway sprinkled with little parks and plazas, benches for resting, and a few restaurants, shops, and food stands.

In addition to the Malecón 2000, Malecón Salado, and attractions listed below, you can visit a few parks and an interesting cemetery. **Parque Seminario** ✈ dates from 1880, and is adjacent to the city's principal church, a neo-Gothic cathedral whose most recent and primary construction dates from 1948. Parque Seminario is also called "Iguana Park" because a healthy population of these prehistoric-looking reptiles inhabit its trees and grounds. Much larger, **Parque Centenario** is in the middle of the city, bisected by Avenida 9 de Octubre. This park is a very popular lunchtime spot for downtown workers and is a pleasant place to relax and people-watch.

The massive **Cementerio General (General Cemetery)** ✈ is north of the downtown area (© 04/2293-849). It's also called La Ciudad Blanca, or the White City, because of its abundance of shiny white marble. The cemetery has some impressive aboveground marble tombs and mausoleums, in a variety of styles ranging from neoclassical Greco-Roman to baroque to Moorish. The tombs are spread across a vast hillside area and connected by paths and even streets. The cemetery was opened in 1843 and has become a major emblem of the city. The entrance is at Avenida Pedro Menéndez Gilber and Julian Coronel. The Cementerio General is open daily from 8am to 6pm.

One good way to get a feel for the city is to hop on one of the red double-decker tourist buses run by **Guayaquil Vision** (© 04/2885-800; www.guayaquilvision.com). These folks offer several options, including a 1½-hour loop around and through the city, passing its most important landmarks, as well as a 3-hour Gran Guayaquil tour,

A Meeting of Giants

Not long after being appointed "Protector of Peru," and with the supposed hope of annexing Guayaquil into the newly forming Peruvian nation, Argentine independence leader **José de San Martín** met with **Simón Bolívar**— El Libertador—in the city of Guayaquil on July 26, 1822. They were also to discuss the broader future of South America, now free from Spanish rule. Precise details of the "closed-door" meeting remain the subject of much debate among historians. But soon after the famous Guayaquil encounter, San Martín decided to abandon the independence struggle in Peru and retire to Argentina. He later went into self-imposed exile in France, leaving Bolívar to finish the Peruvian campaign.

According to some, San Martín wanted Bolívar's assistance in supplying troops for the swift conclusion of the faltering Peruvian independence struggle. Despite their common objectives, Bolívar's refusal to cooperate, even when San Martín offered to serve under him, resulted in San Martín's withdrawal from the independence struggle. Other historians suggest that Bolívar and San Martín clashed on the fundamental subject of how the new South American nations should be organized: Bolívar favored the idea of independent republics, while San Martín wanted to retain, in some measure, the European monarchy system. San Martín was thus supposedly pressured by Bolívar to resign, as he was a hindrance to Bolívar's vision of a free and independent South America. Although a failure for San Martín, the Guayaquil meeting, which lasted no more than a few hours, was followed by a banquet and a ball at which the two independence heroes made toasts to the hasty conclusion of the war and Bolívar's health and success in future undertakings. Today, a prominent **sculpture and monument** on the Malecón 2000 commemorates the historic meeting.

which makes three stops for visits at Las Peñas neighborhood, Parque Seminario, and the handicraft market. Fares run around $5 (£8.25) adult, and $3 (£1.65) for children, students, and seniors, for the basic loop trip; and $15 (£8.25) adult, $12 (£6.60) children, students, and seniors for the Gran Guayaquil tour.

GUAYAQUIL'S MAIN ATTRACTIONS
Cerro Santa Ana (Santa Ana Hill) ✷✷✷   The 465 stairs leading up Cerro Santa Ana are clearly marked, so you can keep track of your progress. And while the climb is vigorous in spots, it shouldn't take more than 20 to 25 minutes from bottom to top. If you avoid the mid-day heat and sun, you'll find the views worth the effort. The entire length of the steps are strung with a series of restaurants, cafes, bars, art galleries, and shops, mixed in with residential housing. Many of the buildings are painted in bright and contrasting primary colors, creating a beautiful effect. At the top, you'll find the chapel of Santa Ana, along with a beautiful lighthouse. Both were built in 2002, atop the foundations of a 17th-century fort. Cerro Santa Ana is where the city of Guayaquil was first established in the mid-1500s.

At the north end of Malecón Simón Bolívar. No phone. Free admission. Daily 24 hr.

If You're Short on Time

Many visitors find themselves with only a few hours in Guayaquil as they connect to or from the Galápagos. If you fall into that category, don't despair: You can still get a good feel for the city in just a few hours.

Grab a cab (or walk, if you're close) from your hotel to the Malecón 2000. The Malecón area is ideally enjoyed on foot, so prepare yourself for a good 3.2km (2-mile) hike and bring protection from the sun. It's best to begin at the southern end, the corner of the Malecón and Avenida Olmedo. Here you can browse the shops selling local artifacts, and the boardwalk is breezy and airy on this end. As you walk north, you'll find many food shops (and more people). Take a break halfway; most of the food stalls here sell freshly squeezed juice that makes an excellent pick-me-up; small bottles of water are also readily available and there are impressively clean public restrooms here, too. At the end of the Malecón, just past the MAAC (see below), you'll find **Las Peñas** neighborhood—a narrow street filled with art galleries and funky shops. After you walk around Las Peñas, climb to the top of **Cerro Santa Ana** ✸✸ (see below) to get a fantastic view of the entire city, the river, and the surrounding countryside. You'll find many places to eat and drink on the stairs leading up to the top. This is one of the city's safest areas, with specially trained tourist police patrolling the stairs day and night.

Jardín Botánico (Botanical Gardens) ✸   Opened in 1979, Guayaquil's botanical gardens are home to over 500 species of native and imported tropical flora. Well-tended paths wind through sections of ornamental plants, orchids, and bromeliads, as well as medicinal plants and herbs, fruit and lumber trees, and various crops. The orchid collection is particularly beautiful. This is a great place for urban bird-watching, with over 70 avian species on record, as well as over 60 species of butterflies. The gardens are north of the city center, out along the main Avenida Francisco de Orellana, and a taxi here should cost around $5 (£2.75).

Cerro Colorado, Urbanización Las Orquídeas, Av. Francisco de Orellana. ✆ **04/2560-519** or 09/8076-029. Admission: $3 (£1.65) adults; $1.50 (85p) children under 12, students, and seniors. Daily 9am–4pm.

Museo Antropológico y de Arte Contemporáneo (Museum of Anthropology and Contemporary Art) ✸✸   Commanding a spectacular location on the tip of the Malecón, and known simply as the MAAC, this large and impressive museum opened in late 2004. It focuses on the archaeological finds from around Ecuador (including some relatively recent discoveries from the coastal regions). However, one wing is dedicated to a large collection of Ecuadorian contemporary art, as well as to a smattering of international artists. Constantly changing temporary exhibits focus on local contemporary artists—usually accompanied by short films about those artists, which are quite interesting and worth your while. There's also a library, a bookstore, and a pleasant cafe. It will take you about 2 hours to visit the museum, though plan to spend a little longer if you are interested in the archaeological finds and the films about the artists.

Malecón Simón Bolívar and Calle Loja. ✆ **04/2327-402**. Admission $3 (£1.65) adults, $1(55p) children. Tues–Sat 10am–5:30pm; Sun 10am–4pm.

Museo Arqueológico del Banco del Pacífico ✦ This museum runs a close second to the MAAC as my favorite museum in Guayaquil. Like at the MAAC (and unlike at the two museums listed below), *all* the exhibits here have explanations both in English and Spanish. The museum is small, but it does a good job of showing what life must have been like in the coastal areas of Ecuador thousands of years before Europeans arrived there. You will learn about food, clothing, tools, music, and the use of hallucinogenic drugs in pre-Columbian cultures. The most interesting artifacts come from the Chorrera Period (1000–300 B.C.). Keep an eye out for the double-chambered whistling bottle and the descriptive figurines from this period.

Calles Pedro Icaza 113 and Pichincha. ✆ 04/2566-010. Free admission. Mon–Fri 9am–6pm; Sat–Sun 11am–1pm.

Museo Municipal de Guayaquil If you're wondering about the history of Guayaquil, head to this museum. It starts off with pre-Columbian history, displaying artifacts similar to those found in the Museo Nahim Isaías (see below). Then, as you move through the museum, you'll learn about colonial history, the independence movement, the republic, and the 20th century. On display are pistols, army uniforms, coins, and an old-fashioned car. *Note:* The exhibits are in Spanish, although some pamphlets are available in English.

Calle Sucre between calles Chile and Pedro Carbo. ✆ 04/2524-100. Free admission. Tues–Sat 9am–5pm; Sun 10am–2pm.

Museo Nahim Isaías This small museum displays some amazing pieces of pre-Columbian arts and functional relics found along the coastal areas near Guayaquil. Some date as far back as 4200 B.C. You'll see ceramic jugs, wonderfully expressive figurines, gold jewelry, and—my personal favorite—carved seashells in the shape of fish. On the second floor is a collection of colonial art, including many prominent works from the Quito School, as well as gold and silver altar pieces, and wooden sculptures.

Calles Clemente Ballén and Pichincha. ✆ 04/2324-182. Admission $1.50 (85p). Free for children under 12. Free admission Sun. Wed–Sat 10am–5pm; Sun 11am–3pm.

Parque Histórico Guayaquil ✦✦ *Moments* This historical theme park is a great place to spend an afternoon and learn more about southern Ecuador. Here, you can walk in a large "forest" filled with regional flora (including endangered plants and trees) and through rows of different banana plants, some endemic to Ecuador (remember that Ecuador is the world's largest banana exporter). A traditional country house replicates how rural farmers lived and what farming utensils they used. In the courtyard of a beautiful old hacienda, plays, staged twice daily, depict life on a farm in the 19th century. The boardwalk here is dubbed Malecón 1900, and gives you a glimpse into how the city looked some 100 years ago. An old-fashioned bakery and cafe serves traditional dishes in a lovely outdoor setting. An old trolley completes the picture. I recommend coming here on a weekday if possible; weekends are very crowded—this theme park has become extremely popular with Ecuadorian families.

Vía Samborondón, between avs. Esmeraldas and Central. ✆ 04/2833-807. www.parquehistorico.com. Tues–Sat $3 (£1.65) adults; $1.50 (85p) children under 12; Sun and public holidays $4.50 (£2.50) adults, $3 (£1.65) children. Tues–Sun and holidays 9am–4:30pm.

NEARBY ATTRACTIONS & TOURS

A number of agencies in town offer a wide range of area tours. Guayaquil is surrounded by banana, coffee, and cocoa plantations; if you have an extra half-day or day, consider taking a tour to see how these farms operate. You might also want to take a bird- and wildlife-watching tour through some nearby mangroves. The best and most established agencies include **Canodros** (© 04/2285-711; www.canodors.com), **Global Tours** (© 04/2680-450; www.globaltour.com.ec), and **Metropolitan Touring** ★ (© 04/2286-565; www.metropolitan-touring.com). All of these agencies, as well as most of the city's hotels, offer visits to the places listed below, among many other possibilities.

Bosque Protector Cerro Blanco   This place has a network of trails through mangrove and primary forests, which vary vastly with the seasons—flowing rivers and streams and an abundance of lush vegetation in the rainy season (Jan–May), and a more typical dry-forest feel during the rest of the year. I recommend you hire one of their bilingual guides—you'll see a lot more wildlife and learn a lot more in the process. Guides cost $7 to $12 (£3.85–£6.60), depending upon the length of your hike, and can handle a group of up to eight people. Resident mammals include the howler monkey, wild peccary, and ocelot. Over 200 species of birds have been spotted here, including the scarlet macaw, which is being actively protected at the Bosque. There's a restaurant, and you can use their campground or rent a rustic two-bedroom bamboo bungalow. These folks also run the nearby **Puerto Hondo,** which is set on the banks of a broad mangrove, where you can rent canoes and kayaks (either solo or accompanied by a guide).

Km 16, on the road to the coast (Vía a La Costa). © 04/2874-946. www.bosquecerroblanco.com. Admission $4 (£2.20); $3 (£1.65) children under 12. Daily 9am–4pm. Reservations recommended.

Hacienda El Castillo   If you're interested in visiting a working farm, check out this hacienda. Although not as historic or traditional as the haciendas found in the central and northern highlands, this large estate covers over 300 hectares (741 acres). Some of the land is devoted to growing cacao, mangos, and hardwoods, but there are also large tracts of primary and secondary forests. The tour takes you through the process of harvesting and processing cacao, as well as the making of chocolate. Lunch is served on the grounds of the hacienda, which is a mostly modern building with a couple of towers at the entrance made to resemble those of an ancient castle, or *castillo.* Horseback riding is offered, and they actually have some luxury rooms for rent.

Urdenor 2 Manzana, Villa 9, Guayas. © 04/2887-492 or 09/7195-162. Admission $25 (£14); $15 (£7.65) students, seniors, and children under 12. Rates include tour, transportation, and lunch. Horseback riding $10 (£5.50). Daily 9:30am–5pm. Reservations necessary.

SHOPPING

The **Mercado Artesanal** (© 04/2306-266), on Baquerizo Moreno, between calles Loja and Juan Montalvo, is the best place to buy local handicrafts. You'll find over 280 stalls and shops run by area businesspeople as well as by the artisans themselves. Everything from tagua nut—also called vegetable ivory—carvings to Otavaleño textiles to Panama hats and ceramics is available.

As a throbbing metropolis, Guayaquil is full of modern shopping malls that include the **San Marino Mall** (© 04/2083-178), **Mall del Sur** (© 04/2085-000), and **Mall del Sol** (© 04/2690-100). Each has scores of shops, a couple of department stores, a food court and independent restaurants, and a multiplex cinema. The **Malecón 2000** shopping center is one of the town's newest and most frequented by visitors. It's located on the Malecón near Calle Junín.

WHERE TO STAY

If there's no space at the hotels below, the **Hampton Inn** ⟨ (© **1800/4267-866;** www.hampton.com.ec) and **Four Points Sheraton** ⟨⟨ (© **04/2691-888;** www. sheraton.com) are two good options.

VERY EXPENSIVE

Hilton Colón Guayaquil ⟨⟨⟨   This hotel is housed in a modern high-rise and it's definitely the best hotel in the city. It has a charming ambience and is extremely comfortable. The hotel has become an institution in Guayaquil—its restaurants, banquet halls, and bars are frequented by the crème de la crème of Ecuadorian society. The rooms are large with big windows—some rooms offer views of planes taking off and landing at the nearby airport. The suites and executive doubles have new plasma-screen televisions. The corner suites are the most desirable—each has a lovely balcony with a great view. The marble bathrooms are huge and sparkling. The beautiful outdoor pool has a swim-up bar and a snack bar for alfresco dining. The coffee shop serves excellent Ecuadorian specials at reasonable prices; and the Portofino restaurant is the best and most elegant Italian eatery in Guayaquil. Several airline offices, including LAN Chile, TACA, and KLM, are located in the shopping arcade adjacent to the hotel lobby, as is a little sushi bar. *Tip:* The Hilton Colón is located close to the airport, which makes it an ideal place for people trying to catch an early flight to the Galápagos. Be sure to book online or through an agency, where you can get rates far, far better than the rack rates listed here.

Av. Francisco de Orellana, Guayaquil. © 800/445-8667 in the U.S., or 04/2689-000 in Ecuador. Fax 04/2689-149. www.guayaquil.hilton.com. 294 units. $290–$350 (£160–£193) double; $390–$450 (£215–£248) suite; $1,200 (£660) presidential suite. AE, DC, MC, V. Free parking. Free airport shuttle (reserve in advance). **Amenities:** 4 restaurants; 2 bars; beautiful large pool; exercise room; Jacuzzi; sauna; concierge; business center; shopping arcade; salon; 24-hr. room service; massage; babysitting; laundry service; same-day dry cleaning; smoke-free floors; executive/club floors. *In room:* A/C, TV, dataport, Wi-Fi, minibar, coffeemaker, hair dryer, safe.

Hotel Oro Verde Guayaquil ⟨   The Oro Verde commands a central location on Avenida 9 de Octubre, and is located right next to the U.S. Consulate. It looks and feels like a typical high-end business hotel. The public areas, cafes, and restaurants are attractive and the service is excellent. The whole place has been updated in the past couple of years. Most rooms are spacious and have recessed lighting, moldings on the walls, and smallish marble bathrooms. Suites come with two bathrooms and an extra sitting room; some even have kitchenettes. For business travelers working downtown, the location is good, but if you want to visit the Malecón and the museums, you'll have to walk about 15 blocks or take a taxi. I prefer the rooms and service at the Hilton Colón. All guests get free use of the Internet at the business center, Wi-Fi in the public areas, and access to an excellent health club. For distraction, there's a casino on-site. There's also an hourly complimentary shuttle to the airport.

Av. 9 de Octubre and García Moreno, Guayaquil. © 04/2327-999. Fax 04/2329-350. www.oroverdehotels.com. 230 units. $240–$260 (£132–£143) double; $320 (£$176) executive suite; $600 (£165–£330) presidential suite. AE, DC, MC, V. Free parking. **Amenities:** 4 restaurants; 2 bars; casino; tiny outdoor pool; modern exercise room w/new machines; Jacuzzi; sauna; concierge; business center; 24-hr. room service; massage; babysitting; laundry service; same-day dry cleaning; smoke-free floors; executive/club floors. *In room:* A/C, TV, dataport, minibar, hair dryer, safe.

EXPENSIVE

Grand Hotel Guayaquil ⟨   There are two reasons to stay at this hotel. First, the location: It's only a few blocks from the Malecón and close to all the major attractions in the downtown area. Second, the gorgeous swimming pool: Take one look at the magnificent waterfall cascading into the clear blue water and you'll feel as though you are in a tropical resort. It provides a great escape from the heat, noise, and pollution of Guayaquil. Unfortunately the rooms, though comfortable and generously sized, aren't as fancy as the pool. The walls are a bit thin, so to avoid hearing your neighbors as they traipse through the hallway, request a room as far from the elevator as possible. This hotel is not as luxurious or well-kept as the Hilton Colón or Oro Verde, but it does offer similar amenities, and for the price it's a great deal.

Boyacá and 10 de Agosto, Guayaquil. ⓒ **04/2329-690.** Fax 04/2327-251. www.grandhotelguayaquil.com. 180 units. $100–$110 (£55–£61) double; $145–$175 (£80–£96) suite. AE, DC, MC, V. Free parking. **Amenities:** 3 restaurants; 2 bars; outdoor pool; 2 air-conditioned squash courts; exercise room; Jacuzzi; sauna; small business center; salon; 24-hr. room service; massage; laundry service; smoke-free floors; executive/club floors; free Wi-Fi. *In room:* A/C, TV, minifridge, hair dryer, safe.

UniPark Hotel 🐱 *Value*   This large, luxury hotel is located right downtown and connected to the UniPark mall, across from Parque Seminario and the cathedral and just 3 blocks from the Malecón. The rooms are everything you would want and expect in this category. The hotel lacks the pool and extensive facilities of the Hilton Colón and Grand Hotel Guayaquil, but thanks to the local glut of rooms and competition, they've made up for this by dropping their rates substantially. The UniPark has several restaurants, including a sushi bar, and there are scores more in the adjacent mall.

Calle Clemente Ballén 406 and Calle Chimborazo, Guayaquil. ⓒ **04/2327-100.** Fax 04/2328-352. www.unipark hotel.com. 139 units. $80–$90 (£44–£50) double. Rates include breakfast buffet and free airport shuttle. AE, DC, MC, V. Free parking. **Amenities:** 3 restaurants; 2 bars; small gym; sauna; concierge; business center; 24-hr. room service; massage; laundry service; smoke-free rooms; free Wi-Fi. *In room:* A/C, TV, dataport, minibar, hair dryer, safe.

MODERATE

Apart Hotel Kennedy 🐱 *Value*   Catering to business travelers, the Kennedy is located catty-corner to the much fancier Hilton Colón. Rooms are cool, sleek, and spacious. The large suites have separate sitting rooms and kitchenettes, which come in handy if you're here for several days. The decor aims to be elegant, but comes across as a bit kitschy. Still, this is a great value. The entire hotel features free wireless Internet for guests. *Tip:* The rates I list below are their "corporate" rates, which are half of their rack rates. That said, all you have to do is say you work for any company—heck, make one up—and they are usually more than happy to apply the corporate rate.

Calles Nahum Isaías and Vicente Norero, Kennedy Norte, Guayaquil. ⓒ **04/2681-111.** Fax 04/2681-060. www.hotelkennedy.com.ec. 49 units. $65 (£36) double; $80 (£44) suite. Rates include buffet breakfast. AE, DC, MC, V. Free parking. **Amenities:** Restaurant; bar; business center; salon; room service 7am–10pm; laundry service; free Wi-Fi. *In room:* A/C, TV, minifridge, hair dryer, safe.

Hotel Las Peñas *Value*   Don't be fooled: This hotel isn't located in its namesake neighborhood. However, Las Peñas is an intimate business-class hotel and a great value. And it's wonderfully located, just a block off Avenida 9 de Octubre, and 5 blocks in either direction from the Malecón 2000 and the Plaza del Centenario. The rooms are rather spartan and the furnishings feel as though they were selected by someone's aging spinster aunt, but you get plenty of space, a privileged location, and enough modern amenities to make your stay perfectly enjoyable. I like the higher floors, where rooms have a bit of a view and are also a bit above the fracas and fray of the street below. The hotel runs a free airport shuttle, with advance notice, and allows guests 30 minutes of free Internet usage at their small business center.

Calle Escobedo 1215 at the corner of Calle Vélez, Guayaquil. ©/fax **04/2323-355**. www.hlpgye.com. 30 units. $47 (£26) double. Rates include full breakfast. AE, DC, MC, V. Parking nearby. **Amenities:** Restaurant; bar; business center; room service 7am–11pm; laundry service. *In room:* A/C, TV, minifridge, safe.

INEXPENSIVE

There are plenty of run-down and seedy budget hotels in Guayaquil, but I really can't recommend any of them. Given the heat and humidity, I think it's worth the splurge for someplace with air-conditioning and a sense of style, like the places listed below.

Hotel California This place lacks the charm and hominess of the two other options listed below, but it's a good choice if you're looking for a comfortable, well-equipped room in a semi-modern building right downtown. The rooms and their decor are rather dated, though at these prices you really can't complain. A few come with somewhat classy marble sitting tables. This place is located just 3 blocks from the Malecón, on the north end of downtown.

Calles Luis Urdaneta 529 and Ximena, Guayaquil. © **04/2302-538**. Fax 04/2562-548. 54 units. $16–$20 (£8.60–£11) double. Rates include full breakfast. AE, DC, MC, V. Free parking. **Amenities:** Restaurant; bar; tour desk; room service 7am–10pm; laundry service. *In room:* A/C, TV, minibar.

Iguanazú Hostal *(Value)* This cozy hideaway is located in a northern suburb at the base of a forested hill that has been declared a city reserve. Accommodations here range from a large dormitory-style room with four bunk beds and a fan, to air-conditioned rooms with private bathrooms. Everything is kept spic-and-span, and is decorated with a sense of style. The hostel has extensive grounds, which include well-tended gardens, a pretty and refreshing pool, and a large terrace and barbecue area. The suite is a lovely room with its own Jacuzzi, television, and private entrance to the shared terrace with a good view of the city below. Guests have full run of the converted home's full kitchen. The owners run a good little tour agency.

Calzada La Cogra, Manzana 1, Villa 2, Km 3.5 Av. Carlos Julio Arosemena, Guayaquil. © **04/2201-143** or 09/9867-968. www.iguanazuhostel.com. 5 units. $9.75 (£5.35) per person in dorm room; $33 (£18) double room; $50 (£27) suite. Rates include full breakfast. AE, DC, MC, V. Free parking. **Amenities:** Lounge; small outdoor pool; tour desk; laundry service. *In room:* No phone.

Tangara Guest House *(★)* If you're looking for homey accommodations with gracious, knowledgeable hosts (who happen to run an excellent small tour operation), this is the place for you. Housed in a converted home in a residential neighborhood, the rooms are nothing fancy, but they are bright, cheery, and immaculate. There's a common lounge area with cable television, and guests can use the house's kitchen facilities. This little bed-and-breakfast is located very close to both the airport and bus terminal.

Manuela Saenz and O'Leary Block F, House 1, Ciudadela Bolivariana, Guayaquil. ©/fax **04/2282-828** or 04/2282-829. www.tangara-ecuador.com. 6 units. $40 (£22) double. Rates include full breakfast. AE, DC, MC, V. Free parking. **Amenities:** Lounge; tour desk; laundry service. *In room:* A/C.

WHERE TO DINE
EXPENSIVE
La Trattoria da Enrico *(★★ Finds)* ITALIAN It's worth a meal here just to marvel at the fish tanks embedded in the ceiling. However, the Mediterranean-tinged trattoria-style cuisine is also very good. Start with some grilled octopus or a mixed antipasti. There's a wide range of pasta dishes, and the gnocchi here are light and tender. Sure, you can get a steak pizzaiola or veal marsala, but I recommend sticking with the

seafood options, which are extensive. In fact, if you want the pizzaiola sauce, you can have it over scallops, snook, or shrimp. A group can share the mixed seafood platter, which has a little bit of almost everything, from prawns and langoustines to fish and calamari. This place has an excellent wine list. The floral tablecloths are a bit schmaltzy, as is the roving trio of violins and guitar, but they do add to the charm of this local favorite.

Calle Bálsamos 504, between Ebanos and Las Monjas. © 04/2387-079. Reservations recommended. Main courses $6–$24 (£3.30–£13). MC, V. Daily 12:30–11:30pm.

MODERATE

La Parrilla del Ñato ✮ ECUADORIAN/STEAKHOUSE   This local mini-chain serves up excellent grilled meats in a lively setting. Portions are legendarily large, and easily shared. The dining room is also large and often as "loud" as the large neon signs out front. Still, the food is excellent. I'd stick to the simply grilled meats and seafood, though if you're feeling adventurous you can order a dove breast. I don't know where they get their doves, but they're big. The *brocheta mixta* is a massive shish kabob with a couple of whole sausages and large cuts of meat interspersed with grilled onions and peppers. Avoid the pastas and pizzas, which are not the strong suit here. Other outlets around town can be found in Barrio Kennedy on Avenida Francisco de Orellana and Nahim Isaías (© 04/2682-338), and at Km 2.5 on the road to Samborondón (© 04/2834-326).

Av. Estrada 1219 and Laureles. © 04/2387-098. Main courses $5.80–$14 (£3.20–£7.70). AE, DC, MC, V. Daily noon–midnight.

Lo Nuestro ✮✮ ECUADORIAN   The best Ecuadorian restaurant in the city, located 10 minutes from downtown (a taxi will cost about $4/£2.20), is a small, elegant eatery whose walls are filled with historical photos of Guayaquil. Ask what the fresh fish is: Seafood reigns supreme here. *Ceviches* make for the best appetizers. The grilled sea bass with crab sauce is my favorite main course. There are myriad daily specials, but traditional favorites include homemade empanadas, *seco de chivo* (goat stew), and shrimp served several different ways. Everything is of the highest quality—and meticulously prepared. This is the kind of place where you enjoy a 3-hour meal and where the waiters wheel over a liquor tray to offer you an after-dinner drink. Don't come here if you're pressed for time! These folks also offer home delivery.

Av. Estrada 903 and Higueras. © 04/2386-398. Reservations recommended. Main courses $6–$14 (£3.30–£7.70). MC, V. Mon–Thurs noon–3:30pm and 7pm–midnight; Fri–Sun noon–midnight.

INEXPENSIVE

El Vigia *Finds* ECUADORIAN/INTERNATIONAL   This funky hole-in-the-wall sits on a small rise about midway up Cerro Santa Ana. You'll definitely want to grab a table on the narrow front balcony fronting the steps, a fantastic spot for people-watching. This place serves equally well as a coffee shop and snack joint during the day, and as a bar and restaurant at night. The food is surprisingly good, with everything from traditional Ecuadorian fare, like *humitas* and *hayacas*, to spaghetti Bolognese and *tortilla española*. You can order a plate of mixed appetizers *(piqueo)* to share, or head right for the main courses. I recommend the grilled tilapia, which is done in a simple garlic and olive oil sauce. All main courses come with crisp *patacones* and salad.

Callejóns Diego Noboa and del Tesoro, Cerro Santa Ana. © 04/2300-218. Main courses $4–$8 (£2.20–£4.40). MC, V. Sun–Thurs 10am–midnight; Fri–Sat 10am–2am.

La Canoa ⟨✦⟩ ECUADORIAN   You'll have a hard time believing that La Canoa is attached to a hotel. During lunchtime, it's one of the most happening places in town. Locals come here for the inexpensive but very satisfying Ecuadorian food. Recommended dishes include *seco de chivo, humitas, ceviche,* grilled chicken, and delicious milkshakes. There's also a large selection of soups, salads, and sandwiches. A great place to take a break if you're seeing the sights of Guayaquil, La Canoa is close to most of the museums and only a few blocks from the Malecón 2000. Before noon, you can choose from a large selection of breakfast specialties.

In Hotel Continental, Chile 510 and 10 de Agosto. ⟨✆⟩ **04/2329-270.** Main courses: $3.50–$9 (£1.90–£4.95). AE, DC, MC, V. Daily 24 hr.

Puerto Pirata ⟨*Kids*⟩ ECUADORIAN   Located just below the chapel and lighthouse on the top of Cerro Santa Ana, this restaurant is housed inside a faux-pirate ship, hence *"pirata"* in the name. A shallow tile pool serves as a moat around the outside, where you'll also find a small playground, some pirate mannequins, and bronze cannons. The best seats are those on the second floor, with a view out the windows of the false stern of this fantasy ship. The food is pretty standard fare, but at least it's very inexpensive, and what you're coming for are the view and atmosphere, anyway. You can get simply grilled meats and fish, as well as a wide range of appetizers and *ceviches.* Some nights there's live music, which might be anything from a mellow jazz trio to a full-on salsa band.

Stair 384, El Fortín Naval Museum, Cerro Santa Ana. ⟨✆⟩ **09/3105-299.** Main courses $3.75–$7.50 (£2.05–£4.10). AE, DC, MC, V. Daily noon–midnight.

Resaca ⟨*Finds*⟩ ECUADORIAN/INTERNATIONAL   There are scores of restaurants along the Malecón 2000, but this is my top choice. If the weather's nice, head straight upstairs for the second-floor, open-air patio and grab a seat close to the river. When it's too hot or windy or rainy, you can opt for a table near one of the large picture windows that ring the main dining room. The menu here leans heavily on bar-food staples, with nachos, fried calamari, *patacones,* and onion rings to choose from. You can also get main-course plates of fresh fish or grilled steaks and chicken. For lunch, try the three-course *menú ejecutivo* for $2.50 (£1.40). On Monday, Wednesday, and Friday, they have an all-you-can-eat crab special for $10 (£5.50), and weekend nights usually feature live bands. *Resaca* translates as "hangover," and the late-night scene here has certainly caused its fair share of them.

North end of Malecón 2000, near Junín. ⟨✆⟩ **04/2631-068.** Reservations recommended. Main courses $4.50–$8 (£2.50–£4.40). AE, DC, MC, V. Daily noon–midnight.

GUAYAQUIL AFTER DARK

Guayaquil has made great strides in reducing crime and insecurity in recent years, and its nightlife has benefited greatly. Bars, cafes, and restaurants are sprouting like mushrooms around the **Zona Rosa** and **Cerro Santa Ana** (both located toward the end of the Malecón). This is the best area to experience the city's nightlife. Have a taxi drop you off by the MAAC, on the tip of the Malecón, at **La Proa Bar** (⟨✆⟩ **09/4267-061**). This modern club, with its long bar and large outdoor patio, is a good spot for a drink; patrons tend to be young and trendy—things don't get going here till after 10 or 11pm—and occasionally there are live bands. For more mellow options, you can stroll up the Cerro Santa Ana, where you'll find a plethora of bars and pubs flanking the steps leading to the top of the hill. Around the corner from the steps, in Las Peñas, is the boho standout **La Paleta** (⟨✆⟩ **04/2312-329**).

For dancing and a more lively time, try the Zona Rosa, a several-square-block area bordered by the Malecón to the east and Avenida Rocafuerte to the west, and by Calle Juan Montalvo to the north and Calle Manuel Luzarraga to the south. You'll find a score of bars here, and it's a relatively safe area to bar-hop. Down here, I like **Heineken Bar Music** ✪, Rocafuerte and Padre Aguirre (© 08/5234-129), which has atmospheric brick walls and often features live music; most Thursdays, this is a good place to find a local rock band playing.

Locals like to head to the handful of clubs and discos found in the neighborhood Kennedy Norte, at the **Mall Kennedy.** These clubs attract a broad mix of Guayaquil's young and restless. There's plenty to choose from, but if you want an all-out party, try **Ibiza Evolution** (© 09/7422-925).

Live theater, poetry, art cinema, and other performances can be found at **La Alianza Francesa de Guayaquil** ✪, on José Mascote and Hurtado (© 04/2532-009; www.afgye.com). Alternatively, you can check out the **Casa de la Cultura Ecuatoriana (Ecuadorian House of Culture)** on the corner of Avenida 9 de Octubre and Quito (© 04/2304-998). These folks show art movies most nights at 7pm, and often schedule other cultural events.

Located at the northern end of the Malecón 2000 is a four-plex **IMAX theater** ✪ (© 04/2563-079; www.imaxmalecon2000.com), showing late-run IMAX-specific films. For more traditional movie fare, there are **Cinemark** multiplex theaters in both **Mall del Sur** (© 04/2085-000) and **Mall del Sol** (© 04/2690-100).

If you're in the mood for some gambling, there are large modern casinos at both the **Sheraton Four Points** and **Hilton Colón.**

PLAYAS: THE CLOSEST BEACH TO GUAYAQUIL

On weekends and holidays, Guayaquileños (Guayaquil natives) flock to the beach at **Playas General Villamil,** better known as simply Playas. Located 97km (60 miles) south of Guayaquil, this laidback fishing village has taken the popularity with a sense of indifference, and the town lacks the feel of full-on beach destinations like Salinas or Atacames. It also lacks the stylish and varied lodging options you can find in those resort towns. The beach itself is long and wide, with a gentle curve and hard-packed light-colored sand. Still, on weekends and holidays, this place is packed, and the restaurants and bars that line the seafront Malecón bustle and buzz. The beach is popular with surfers, who come for the well-formed point break.

Artisans in Playas still produce ancient-style balsa fishing rafts, as well as finely crafted balsa surfboards. The unique fishing rafts are usually made by joining together three long balsa logs, and then fitting them with a triangular sail.

Good lodging options are very limited in Playas. The best hotels in town are the beachfront **Hostería Bellavista** (© 04/2760-600; hoteriabellavista@hotmail.com), located toward the quieter eastern end of town; and the **Hotel Arena Caliente** (© 04/2761-580; www.hotelarenacaliente.com), which is 1 block inland, but near the center of the action. Both of these hotels have air-conditioned rooms and swimming pools—two very important perks down here.

Playas is easily reached by heading out of town on the coastal highway and taking the well-marked turnoff for General Villamil. Buses leave Guayaquil's main terminal for Playas roughly every 15 to 20 minutes from 6am to 8pm, with less frequent departures during the few hours on either end of that time frame. **Transportes Villamil** (© 04/2760-190) and **Transportes Posoria** (© 04/2140-284) both run this route. The ride takes about 1½ hours and the fare is around $2 (£1.10).

2 Salinas & The Santa Elena Peninsula ⭐

163km (101 miles) W of Guayaquil, 570km (354 miles) SW of Quito

Salinas and the **Santa Elena Peninsula** anchor the southern end of **La Ruta del Sol (The Sun Route),** a string of fishing and beach towns stretching up the southern Pacific coast. Salinas is the most developed resort destination on this stretch, with high-rise luxury hotels, casinos, vacation condos, and a prominent yacht club. Sailboats, yachts, and fishing vessels fill the protected bay here. Many of these boats can be chartered out for fishing excursions, whale-watching tours, or simple cruises.

During high season, which runs from December to April, this area gets very crowded. Hotel reservations are necessary on weekends throughout this period. In contrast, the beaches and hotels here are often deserted during the off season, especially September through November.

ESSENTIALS
GETTING THERE

BY PLANE   There's a small airport in **Salinas** (airport code: SNC) located at the very tip of the Santa Elena peninsula. **VIP** (© **1800/847-847;** www.vipec.com) flies there from Quito on Wednesday at 6:35pm, and on Sunday at 5:45pm. Return flights leave Salinas Wednesday and Friday at 7:55pm, and Sunday at 7:30pm. There's one flight on Sunday from Guayaquil to Salinas at 6:45pm, and the Sunday return flight to Quito stops first in Guayaquil. The fare is $45 to $60 (£25–£33).

Many people fly into Guayaquil and continue on to Salinas by car, bus, or taxi. See "Getting There: By Plane," under "Guayaquil," for details.

BY BUS   Buses leave Guayaquil's main bus terminal regularly for Salinas between 3am and 11pm every day. During busy daytime hours, a bus leaves nearly every 5 minutes. The schedule is somewhat reduced during off-hours, but there are still frequent buses. Two companies run this route, **CICA** (© **04/2140-664**) and **Libertad Peninsular** (© **04/2140-975**). The ride takes about 2½ hours. The fare is around $3.40 (1.90).

Transesmeraldas (© **04/2786-670** in Salinas, or 02/2505-099 in Quito) has three direct buses daily between Quito and Salinas. The ride takes 11½ hours, and the fare is $10 (£5.50).

The bus station in Salinas is beside the main market, 1 block in from the Malecón.

BY CAR   Salinas and the Santa Elena Peninsula are connected to Guayaquil by a well-traveled and well-marked highway. Calling it a highway, however, may seem a misnomer to some. The road is only two lanes wide in many points, and passes directly through a string of small towns and villages, where you may have to slow down for a stop sign, speed bump, or passing cow. As mentioned, though, the route is well-marked, heading out of Guayaquil to the west. Salinas is 163km (101 miles) from Guayaquil. The ride takes about 2 hours.

GETTING AROUND

Local buses run continuously along the main route that connects Salinas, Santa Elena, La Libertad, and Ballenita. Fares cost from 30¢ to 50¢ (15p–30p) depending on how long your ride is.

This route is also covered by so-called *taxi rutas,* which are taxis that operate almost like the buses, following the same set route and picking up and discharging passengers. But with a maximum of five passengers, these tend to be much faster, since they make fewer stops.

Traditional taxis are also abundant—flag one down on the street or call Taxis Ruta del Sol (© 04/2770-358). A taxi between Salinas and La Libertad should cost no more than $3 (£1.65), and a ride around either town should be under $2 (£1.10).

ORIENTATION

As you drive toward the coast from Guayaquil, you will arrive at the town of **Santa Elena,** which is considered Km 0 on the highway (E15) that runs in both directions along the coastline—and which should not be confused with the highway *to* the coast (called *carretera a la costa*) that runs from Guayaquil to Santa Elena (E70). Santa Elena sits on a small rise above the ocean. The beach and tiny town just below it are called **Ballenita.** Located at the western tip of the Santa Elena peninsula, 13km (8 miles) west of Santa Elena and Ballenita, is **Salinas.** La Libertad lies about halfway between Ballenita and Salinas. As this area develops, the distinctions may start to fade and the resorts will start to flow one into the next, but for now there is still some separation between these beach towns, although the distances are quite short.

Heading farther east and then north up the coast, the beach stretches for miles and miles almost uninterrupted—except for the odd rocky point and headlands—with only a few small fishing villages, tiny towns, and the periodic isolated beach hotel. Beach towns along this coast include **Punta Blanca, Montañita,** and **Olón.**

The beach in Salinas itself is divided almost perfectly in half by the jetty and docks of the **Salinas Yacht Club.** One block inland from the jetty is the town's main plaza and its pretty Catholic church.

FAST FACTS   To reach the **police,** dial © **101** or © 04/2775-813. In the case of any **emergency,** call © **911.** The **Hospital Alcivar** (© **04/2778-807;** www.hospital alcivar.com) in La Libertad is the most modern and best-equipped facility on this coast. It has 24-hour emergency services, as well as a 24-hour pharmacy.

The **post office** is located on the Malecón and Calle 2, next to the Barceló Mira-mar Colón hotel (© **04/2770-097**).

There are several banks and even more ATMs along the Malecón in Salinas and in La Libertad. **Banco de Guayaquil** has branches at Malecón 417 and Avenida Bolívar (© **04/2772-552**) in Salinas, and at the Paseo Shopping complex in La Libertad (© **04/2785-892**). **Banco del Pichincha** has branches in Salinas on the Malecón, between calles 29 and 30 (© **04/2772-468**), and in La Libertad at Avenida 4 and Calle 23 (© **04/2782-294**).

There are a number of Internet cafes all along the Malecón and on the *calles* and *avenidas* just inland. **Café Planet,** on Avenida 10, between calles 25 and 26 (© **04/ 2772-211**), is my favorite, with a fast connection and cool, cozy ambience. Rates run around 50¢ to $1.50 (30p–85p) per hour.

WHAT TO SEE & DO

Most of the activity here focuses on the sand and sea. Aside from swimming and sun-bathing, there are plenty of waterborne activities. Most of the beach resorts have their own watersports equipment; if yours doesn't, you'll have no trouble finding someone renting out sailboards, Hobie cats, windsurfers, jet skis, and the like. The beach of this large, curving bay is made of a rather coarse golden sand. All along the shore you'll find beach umbrellas, portable shade cabañas, and chaise lounges for rent. A beach umbrella and two chaise lounges should cost you $10 (£5.50) per day. Waves are rather mellow toward the center of town, but they pick up as you head farther out in either direction.

Surfers will want to head out to the far western end of the peninsula, which is also called **La Chocolatera.** This is a naval-base territory, and you may have to ask permission to enter (it's almost always granted). Several shops along the Malecón rent out **surf and body boards,** and offer lessons. Board rentals run from $3 to $10 (£1.65–£5.50) per hour, depending upon the quality of the equipment. Lessons cost around $8 to $10 (£4.40–£5.50) per hour.

If you want to go **sport fishing,** you can head to the **Puerto Lucía Yacht Club** (© 04/2783-190; www.puertolucia.com.ec) on the waterfront between Salinas and La Libertad) and ask around; or contact **Pesca Tours** ✪, which has an office on the Malecón and Calle 20 (© 04/2443-365; www.pescatours.com.ec). Offshore fishing provides good opportunities to catch black and blue marlin, sailfish, albacore tuna, and a whole host of other big game fish. Rates run from $250 to $800 (£138–£400) per day for up to four people, depending upon the size and quality of the boat, and how far offshore you go.

The small **Museo de Ballenas (Whale Museum;** © 04/2778-329; www.femm.org) features an interesting collection of exhibits about the biology and natural history of whales and dolphins. The centerpiece of the museum is a 12m (39-ft.) complete skeleton of a humpback whale. They also have partial and complete skeletons and skulls of other species, as well as explanatory materials in both English and Spanish. The museum is located on Avenida General Enriques Gallo, between calles 47 and 50. The museum is open daily from 10am until 5pm, but it's wise to call in advance because they often close if there aren't many visitors. Admission is free, but a donation is requested.

The **Museo Salinas Siglo 21 (Salinas 21st Century Museum;** © 04/2771-279) is another option, with a collection of local maritime relics and displays, including coins recovered from the wreck of a Spanish galleon that sank in 1664. This museum also has a good collection of regional archaeological finds of the Valdivia, Machalilla, and Chorrera peoples dating back as far as 4200 B.C. Located on the Malecón, between calles Guayas and Quil, the museum is open Wednesday through Sunday from 10am to 1pm and from 3 to 6pm. Admission is $2 (£1.10).

June through September, the waters off Salinas are a fantastic place to **spot humpback whales** ✪✪✪ (see "Having A Whale of A Time," below). Most hotels offer whale-watching excursions, or you can contact **Costa Tour** (© 04/2770-095 or 09/7544-444) or **Pesca Tours** ✪ (© 04/2443-365; www.pescatours.com.ec). When the whales aren't around, all of the above operations can arrange simple half-day, full-day, and sunset cruises or sailboat outings.

WHERE TO STAY IN & AROUND SALINAS
EXPENSIVE
Barceló Colón Miramar ✪✪   This is the largest and most luxurious resort in Salinas. Rooms are big and inviting, with clean lines, stylish furnishings, and lots of amenities. Most have a small sitting area with a couple of rattan chairs and a couch. Views from the oceanfront balconies are fabulous, and you should definitely specify that you want one of these units, preferably on a higher floor. The only downside here is the food, which is mediocre at best. Since they only offer an all-inclusive system, most guests are hesitant to spend extra money outside the hotel on food, but believe me, the few dollars you spend for some fresh seafood at one of the many simple oceanfront restaurants around Salinas will be well worth it. The beach right in front of the hotel is pretty narrow and hard packed, but the pools are easily the nicest in the area.

Malecón, between avs. 38 and 40, Salinas. © **04/2771-610.** Fax 04/2773-806. www.barcelo.com. 95 units. $150–$300 (£83–£165) double. Rates are all-inclusive, and include 3 buffet meals daily, unlimited soft drinks and national liquors, and nonmotorized watersports equipment. AE, DC, MC, V. Free parking. **Amenities:** 2 restaurants; 3 bars; casino; 2 outdoor pools; watersports equipment; well-equipped gym; Jacuzzi; sauna; tour desk; salon; in-room massage; laundry service; smoke-free rooms. *In room:* A/C, TV, minibar, hair dryer, iron, safe.

MODERATE

Hotel Calypsso   This place is located on the ocean, close to all the action near the center of Salinas's Malecón. Rooms are large and generally tidy. But the decor seems a bit sterile and uninspired, and things felt neglected and in need of fresh paint the last time I visited. Most of the accommodations here are two-bedroom units they call master suites, but which are clearly meant for families traveling with children. Many have excellent ocean views and private balconies. The hotel's open-air and ocean-facing restaurant serves good seafood and local cuisine, although it's a bit pricey by Ecuadorian standards. During the high season and on weekends, this hotel's popular disco, **Club 21,** can be a problem for light and early sleepers.

Malecón, next to the Capitanía del Puerto, Salinas. © **04/2772-425.** Fax 04/2773-431. www.hotelcalypsso.com. 48 units. $65–$80 (£36–£44) junior suite; $135–$155 (£74–£85) master suite. Rates lower in the off season; higher during peak periods. AE, DC, MC, V. Free parking. **Amenities:** Restaurant; bar; outdoor pool; Jacuzzi; salon; room service 7am–midnight; laundry service; smoke-free rooms. *In room:* A/C, TV, minifridge, safe.

Puerto Lucía Yacht Club Hotel ⭐   The high-rise hotel attached to this marina and yacht club offers up modern, luxury rooms, with plenty of perks, at great prices. The rooms are big, bright, and airy, each with a large-screen television, pretty bathroom, and private balcony overlooking the ocean. In addition to the adjacent marina, the hotel has a host of facilities and services, including a couple of pools, two lit tennis courts, a small gym and spa, and a private little patch of beach between two stone jetties. There's also a children's playground, as well as a beach-volleyball court. There are two restaurants in-house, and even a karaoke disco bar.

Av. Puerto Lucía, La Libertad. © **04/2783-180** or 04/2783-190. www.puertolucia.com.ec. 24 units. $60–$80 (£33–£44) double. Rates higher during peak periods. AE, DC, MC, V. Free parking. **Amenities:** 2 restaurants; 2 bars; 2 outdoor pools; 2 lit outdoor tennis courts; well-equipped gym; Jacuzzi; tour desk; watersports equipment rental; room service 7am–11pm; laundry service. *In room:* A/C, TV, minibar, coffee maker, hair dryer, safe.

INEXPENSIVE

Farallón Dillon ⭐ *(Finds*   This is my favorite hotel along this stretch of coast. The rambling whitewashed structure is built above a quiet section of beach in Ballenita on a small hillside that almost qualifies as a cliff. The rooms aren't as fancy as those at some of the higher-end resorts in Salinas, but they have plenty of style and character. Moreover, all face the ocean. I prefer those on the second floor, though these cost a little more. The shaded, open-air balcony restaurant is delightful, with a beautiful perch and perfect views. You can sometimes even see whales blowing their spouts from this spot. The hotel has a wonderful covered area strung with a half-dozen or so hammocks where guests can sneak a midday siesta, and there's a wonderful collection of nautical memorabilia and antiques throughout. Farallón Dillon is close enough to Salinas that guests here have easy access to all the restaurants, shops, clubs, and activities available to folks staying in the more popular and crowded resort town.

Lomas de Ballenita, Ballenita. © **04/2953-611.** Fax 04/2953-643. www.farallondillon.com. 7 units. $30–$42 (£17–£23) double. Rates lower in the off-season; higher during peak periods. DC, MC, V. Free parking. **Amenities:** Restaurant; bar; unlit outdoor tennis court; laundry service. *In room:* A/C, no phone.

Hotel Chipipe   This midsize hotel is located 2 blocks from the beach, in the center of town. The rooms are standard, with plenty of light, cool and shiny white tile floors, simple furnishings, solid green bedspreads and curtains, and mostly unadorned walls. Most have balconies, and a few have ocean views. I find the rooms here much more comfortable and inviting than those at the Sunbeach (see below). The pool area is a welcome oasis, with a wide tile deck area and the hotel's open-air restaurant nearby.

Calle 12, between avs. 4 and 5, Salinas. © 04/2770-553. Fax 04/2770-556. www.hotelchipipe.com. 49 units. $32–$40 (£18–£22) double. Rates include continental breakfast. Rates lower in the off season; higher during peak periods. MC, V. Free parking. **Amenities:** Restaurant; bar; small outdoor pool; laundry service. *In room:* A/C, TV.

Hotel Sunbeach   In many ways, the public areas—the pool, lounge, and restaurant— of this downtown hotel are more cheery and comfortable than its rooms. Some of the rooms, in fact, are quite tiny and cramped. Look at a few and grab one of the larger ones, if possible. Still, all are pretty well-maintained and up-to-date, with clean tile floors, colorful bedspreads, and minimal furnishings. They all come with televisions and air-conditioning—although these are older, wall-mounted air-conditioning units that can be a bit loud.

Main road into Salinas, Salinas. © 04/2930-193-425 or 04/2930-261. www.hotelsunbeachsalinas.com. 44 units. $30–$50 (£17–£28) double. Rates include continental breakfast. Rates lower in the off season; higher during peak periods. MC, V. Free parking. **Amenities:** Restaurant; bar; small outdoor pool; laundry service. *In room:* A/C, TV.

WHERE TO DINE IN & AROUND SALINAS

There are scores of restaurants along the Malecón serving mostly *ceviche,* fresh seafood, and typical Ecuadorian fare. The best of these include **Mar y Tierra** (© 04/ 2774-193) and **Vrouw María** (© 04/2770-214).

INEXPENSIVE

Caída del Sol *(Finds* SEAFOOD   While you can do fine at any number of seaside seafood joints and *cevicherías* in Salinas, I like to take a taxi the few miles to the more remote beach of Ballenita and grab one of the outdoor tables set in the sand at this open-air restaurant. The restaurant itself and each of the outdoor tables have thatched roofs. In the daytime heat, mixed *ceviche* is certainly in order to start things off. Beyond this, you can get whole grilled fish—fresh from the sea—or shrimp, crab, and even lobster. This restaurant's name translates as "sunset," which is spectacular here.

Malecón, next to Club Ballenita, Ballenita. © 04/2953-061. Main courses $3–$8 (£1.65–£4.40). MC, V. Daily noon–11pm.

La Bella Italia *(* ITALIAN/SEAFOOD   Besides great pizzas and pasta dishes, these folks serve up excellent seafood. The thin-crust pizza is cooked in a wood-burning oven and comes with a wide range of toppings. I especially like the grilled shrimp. There's an indoor dining room, with air-conditioning, but I prefer the seats on the outdoor front patio overlooking the Malecón and beach.

Malecón and Calle 19. © 04/2771-361. Main courses $3.50–$8 (£1.95–£4.40). MC, V. Daily noon–midnight.

SALINAS & THE SOUTHERN COAST AFTER DARK

Most of the after-dark activity in Salinas, and all along the coast, is located close to the beach on the Malecón. **Choclo's** *(* (on the Malecón and Calle 23, next to Empanadas Milanis) is one of the most popular spots, with neon lights over the bar and a mixed crowd. It's open Wednesday through Sunday from 8pm on. The **Oystercatcher Bar,** on Avenida 2, between calles 47 and 50 (© **04/2778-329**), is another good bet, popular with expatriates. For live music, especially on weekends, check out **Peña El Colonial,** on the Malecón between calles Guayas and Quil (© **04/2771-949**).

For dancing, head to **Abatawa,** on Avenida 11 and Calle 53 (© **04/2777-220**); **Cancún,** on Malecón and Calle 3 (© **04/2560-628**); or **Club 21,** in the Hotel Calypsso (© **04/2772-425;** see above).

3 Montañita

180km (111 miles) NW of Guayaquil; 59km (37 miles) N of Santa Elena; 27 miles (44km) S of Puerto López

Montañita is a tiny beach town that has garnered a fair amount of fame among surfers and backpackers. The few dirt streets here are densely packed with rock-bottom budget hostels, cheap eats, lively bars, and a handful of surf shops. You'll also find a fair amount of bohemian artisans, from Ecuador and other Latin American locales, selling their wares or offering to braid hair, pierce some body part, or lay on a henna tattoo. If you're an avid surfer, looking to learn how to hang ten, or just want to party with folks who can, you'll probably love it here. If not, you may find Montañita a bit seedy and certainly limited.

ESSENTIALS
GETTING THERE
BY BUS   Libertad Peninsular (© **04/2140-975**) buses leave Guayaquil three times daily for Montañita at 5:30am and at 1 and 4:30pm. The ride takes around 3½ hours. The fare is $3.80 (£2.10).

Local buses run between Santa Elena and Puerto López roughly every 15 to 20 minutes throughout the day. All of these buses stop in Montañita to pick up and drop off passengers. If you're coming from Puerto López, hop on at the main bus stop in town, or anywhere along the highway heading south. If you're in Salinas, grab a taxi to Santa Elena and ask them to drop you off at the bus stop for Puerto López. The fare is around $1 (55p).

BY CAR   To drive to Montañita, follow the directions for driving to Salinas (see above). Montañita is located at Km 59 on the E15 coastal highway.

GETTING AROUND
You can easily walk anywhere in Montañita. That said, taxis usually hang around town to take surfers up and down the coast in search of secret spots. If you can't flag one down, have your hotel or any local business call one for you.

ORIENTATION
Montañita is a tiny town roughly 10 blocks long (running along the ocean), and 4 blocks deep (from the coastal highway to the sea). Erosion has claimed much of the beach right in front of the town, and a large stone-barrier wall has been put in to try to slow the ocean's advance. I think some of the closest beachfront properties here may lose their looming battle with the sea.

FAST FACTS   There are no banks in Montañita, but there is an ATM in the center of town. Still, I recommend you stock up on cash before heading to Montañita. Very few hotels or restaurants here accept credit cards. There are also no medical services, and very limited supplies. Local general stores carry aspirin and other basic remedies, but the closest real pharmacies and medical care are in Santa Elena, Salinas, and Puerto López.

There are several Internet cafes in town. I recommend the computers and relatively fast connection found at the **Hotel Balsa y Tortora** (© **09/7153-871**).

WHAT TO SEE & DO IN MONTAÑITA

Surfing reigns supreme here, and there are rideable beach breaks up and down the coast. The most popular is the point break formed by a rocky headland at the north end of town. Surf competitions are often held here. The best surfing is December through May, though throughout the year you can find waves which can be big and powerful and accompanied by strong rip tides. Be careful and sure of yourself before heading out. If you want to take a lesson or rent a board, stop in at one of the little surf shops in town, or ask at your hotel. I like **Hotel Tiki Limbo** (© **09/9540-607**). For a surf-camp learning package, try **Casa del Sol** (see below).

Aside from surfing and hanging out on the beach, several hotel tour desks and in-town tour operators offer trips up to Puerto López, from where you can head out to **Isla de la Plata** to see the whales in season, or visit **Machalilla National Park** and **Los Frailes** beach. See below for descriptions of these types of tours and activities.

WHERE TO STAY & DINE IN MONTAÑITA

Plenty of budget hostels and funky hotels cater to surfers right in town. Most charge around $7 to $10 (£3.85–£5.50) per person for a bed in a simple room, usually with a shared bathroom. If you really want to save some dollars, walk around the tiny town and check out a few to see if any suit your fancy. The hotels listed below are a step up from most of these hostels, though.

Not surprisingly, Montañita is packed with small, simple restaurants serving the backpacker and surfer crowd. Most are pretty good, and all are inexpensive. In general, the hotel restaurants are your best bet; in addition, **El Tiburón,** which means "the shark," is a good spot for fresh seafood, as well as for pizzas and pastas. **Viejamar** (© **09/3721-433**), with its nautical decor and open-air sidewalk seating, is another good spot for a meal.

INEXPENSIVE

Cabañas Arena Guadua *(Finds)*   These individual bungalows on the beach just north of town are my favorite lodging option in Montañita. Built on raised stilts out of wood and thatch, the cabins are large and relatively cool, with plenty of windows for cross-ventilation. Each cabin can sleep up to five people with a mix of beds that range from a queen on a built-in concrete platform to bamboo bunk beds. Every bed has a mosquito net over it. The restaurant and bar here are popular hangouts for surfers.

500m (1,640 ft.) north of town, on the beach, Montañita. © 09/7029-417. www.montanita.com. 3 units. $30 (£17) double. Rates lower in the off season; higher during peak periods. No credit cards. **Amenities:** Restaurant; bar; laundry service. *In room:* No phone.

Casa del Sol   This is a large, rambling complex on the north end of the beach, built by and for surfers. It consists of several connected buildings, with weathered thatch roofs and interconnecting verandas-cum-walkways. The owners here specialize in surf camps at this, their home base in Montañita, as well as up and down the coastline and even in the Galápagos. Rooms are designed for groups to pile in, and many can accommodate up to six people. In some cases, the beds are packed in pretty tight, leaving very little floor space. Most of the rooms have air-conditioning, but only a few have ocean views, which are the best bets. The dimly lit restaurant features a high ceiling, stone walls and pillars, and large, heavy wooden tables. The food is good, and definitely filling.

On the beach, north of town. © 05/2624-784 or ©/fax 05/2624-782. www.casasol.com. 17 units. $24 (£13) double; $40 (£22) double with A/C. Rates include full breakfast. Rates lower in the off season; higher during peak periods. No credit cards. **Amenities:** Restaurant; bar; laundry service. *In room:* No phone.

Charo's Hostal ⓖ   At three stories, this place qualifies as a high-rise in Montañita. One of the newer and plusher hotels in the area, Charo's rooms all have large balconies with ocean views—although some are from the side of the building, while others face the ocean. I like the top-floor penthouse, which has a private balcony and the best view in the house. The hotel has relatively large grounds, which include gardens, strategically placed hammocks, and a blue tile fountain. You'll also find a popular restaurant and bar here. The latter can get rowdy at times.

On the beach, Montañita. ⓒ 09/9386-474. www.charoshostal.com. 15 units. $14–$20 (£7.70–£11) double. Rates lower in the off season; higher during peak periods. MC, V. **Amenities:** Restaurant; bar; laundry service. *In room:* No phone.

MONTAÑITA AFTER DARK

With a high concentration of young surfers, international backpackers, and Ecuadorian hippies, you'll find a lively nightlife in Montañita. The scene is pretty informal. Dancing is done in shorts and flip-flops, and there are no fancy clubs here. Just walk around the town until you find a bar that best suits you.

4 Puerto López & Machalilla National Park ⓖⓖ

224km (139 miles) NW of Guayaquil; 103km (64 miles) N of Santa Elena; 44km (27 miles) N of Montañita

Although it's little more than a small coastal fishing village, **Puerto López** is the largest town on this section of the Pacific coast as well as the gateway to **Machalilla National Park** ⓖⓖ. Scores of fishing and tour boats bob at anchor just off the shore, and many more are hauled up on the sands each day. The town itself is rather rundown and unappealing, but this is the best place to come to book whale-watching cruises and trips out to **Isla de la Plata** ⓖⓖⓖ, as well as tours to the land-based attractions of the popular park.

ESSENTIALS
GETTING THERE

BY PLANE   The nearest airport with regular service is in **Manta** (see p. 268 for information on flying into Manta), some 122km (76 miles) away, although many folks also fly into **Guayaquil** (see "Getting There: By Plane," under "Guayaquil," for information on flying into Guayaquil).

BY BUS   Turismo Manta (ⓒ 05/2627-770 in Manta, or 05/2300-150 in Puerto López) operates bus service between Puerto López and Manta roughly every hour between 7:30am and 5:30pm. The fare is $3.80 (£2.10) and the ride takes 3 hours. If you're traveling to or from Quito, you should head first to Manta and then take an onward bus. For information on bus connections to and from Manta, see p. 269.

Libertad Peninsular (ⓒ 04/2140-975) buses leave Guayaquil three times daily for Puerto López at 5:30am, 1, and 4:30pm. The ride, which takes around 4 hours, costs $4.20 (£2.30).

Local buses run between Santa Elena and Puerto López roughly every 15 to 20 minutes throughout the day. If you're coming from Puerto López, pick one up at the main bus stop in town, or anywhere along the highway heading south. If you're in Salinas, grab a taxi to Santa Elena and ask them to drop you off at the bus stop for Puerto López. The fare is around $2 (£1.10).

BY CAR   To reach Puerto López by car from Quito, you will need to start off heading south on the Pan-American Highway (E35) until the intersection at Aloag. From

Having a Whale of a Time

If you are lucky enough to find yourself traveling late June through early October, you have an excellent chance of catching the marvel of this coast's annual humpback whale–mating celebration. Each year, Ecuador welcomes a large population of humpback whales, who migrate from the chilly polar waters of Antarctica. Arriving off the Ecuadorian coast in June, pregnant mothers promptly give birth, while single adults find a mating partner for the next 4 months.

Humpback whales grow to about 16m (50 ft.) in length and can weigh between 30 and 50 tons. The babies are born about 3 to 4.5m long (10–15 ft.) and can weigh over 2 tons. The Pacific humpback whales—called *ballenas jorobadas* in Ecuador—are an especially acrobatic species and it's not uncommon to see them breach, wave their tail fins, or even pop their heads up for a look around. It is believed that their acrobatics may be a part of their mating dance.

Humpbacks have been known to travel up to 8,050km (4,000 miles) each way on their annual breeding and feeding excursions. Because calves (young whales) aren't born with blubber, a protective layer of fat, they need to be birthed and reared in the warmer tropical waters, feeding on as much as 100 pounds of their mother's milk each day in order to develop the protective fatty layer of insulation necessary for survival. A female humpback will calve approximately every 2 to 3 years.

Humpbacks can travel at a speed of 8 to 14km per hour (5–9 mph). But during long journeys, they average only 1.6km per hour (1 mph), stopping to rest and socialize along the way. They navigate back to the freezing waters to feast on crustaceans and small fish. While in the warmer, tropical waters, they don't eat at all—but live off their blubber.

During the whale-watching months, all the hotels and tour agencies in town offer outings to see these magnificent mammals up close. Most charge $20 to $30 (£11–£17). Some of the trips combine whale-watching time with a visit to Isla de la Plata. But be careful—the boats are small and the water can be rough. If you're prone to seasickness, be sure to take some sort of anti-motion-sickness medication before you board the boat.

here, head west on E30 toward Santo Domingo de los Colorados. In Santo Domingo, take the well-marked exit for E25 south to Quevedo. From Quevedo you will head west again on E40 to Puerto Viejo, where you will take E9 south to Jipijapa. In Jipijapa there is an exit for the coastal highway, E15, which runs south from Puerto Cayo, through Machalilla, and on to Puerto López. The drive should take between 10 and 11 hours.

If you're driving from Guayaquil, you can either take Highway E9 to Jipijapa and then jog down the coast on E15, or take E70 west out of Guayaquil to Santa Elena, where you will join E15, which follows the coast north all the way to Puerto López. Either one of these routes should take between 3½ and 4 hours.

GETTING AROUND

Puerto López is compact and you can easily walk anywhere in town. That said, there's an abundance of motorcycle-powered "ecotaxis" that will take you anywhere in town for $1 (55p). A round-trip ride to Los Frailes (see below) should cost around $12 (£6.60), but be sure to coordinate your return pickup very well. If you can't flag down a taxi, call © **05/2300-127.**

ORIENTATION

Puerto López sits along the shores of a long, gently curving beach, with a seaside street, officially called Malecón Julio Izurieta, running the length of the town. The main coastal highway, E15, passes right through the center of town, where it is called Avenida Machalilla. This is where you'll find the town's Catholic church, its main market, and, just off of the market, its bus terminal. The ocean and the Malecón are 3 blocks east of here. Most of the town's hotels, restaurants, tour agencies, and Internet cafes are located on the Malecón, Avenida Machalilla, or one the few cross streets connecting them.

FAST FACTS   The **police station** is located on Avenida Machalilla, 1 block north of the market (© **05/2604-101**). There's a branch of **Banco Pichincha** on Avenida Machalilla and Calle Córdova (© **05/2300-140**). The **post office** is located on the Malecón between calles Sucre and Córdova (© **05/2604-236**).

You'll find a couple of Internet cafes along the Malecón as well as on the cross streets heading towards Avenida Machalilla.

WHAT TO SEE & DO IN & AROUND PUERTO LOPEZ

Puerto López makes a great base for a wide range of activities, but by far the greatest draw here is the annual humpback-whale migration, mating, and breeding event, as well as Machalilla National Park (see below). There are a host of tour agencies in town, and all the hotels here either have their own tour desk or work closely with some local tour operator. I highly recommend **Machalilla Tours** ★★ (© **05/2300-234** or 09/6109-185; machalillatours@yahoo.com), run by Fausto Choez Castro. In addition to whale-watching tours and visits to Isla de la Plata and Machalilla National Park, these folks have a number of tour offerings ranging from surf lessons and sea kayak trips, to sport fishing and horseback riding.

If you plan on enjoying the beach right here in Puerto López, I recommend you head, in either direction, away from the center of town, where all the fishing boats—and their detritus—congregate. However, by far the best beach in this area is found inside the national park at Los Frailes (see below).

Machalilla National Park ★★ includes the offshore island **Isla de la Plata (Island of Silver)** ★★★, as well as vast tracts of forest and a couple of ancient archaeological sites. Named Isla de la Plata because Sir Francis Drake is reported to have hidden a huge treasure here, the island is located 23km (14 miles) west of Puerto López. Isla de la Plata is often considered an alternative to the Galápagos Islands, especially for those short on time or money. The bird-watching and wildlife viewing on Isla de la Plata are top-notch: You will have the chance to see albatrosses; blue-footed, masked, and red-footed boobies; frigate birds; and sea lions, all in large numbers and all of which also live in the Galápagos. There are two major loop trails here that head around either end of the island. Each trail takes about 2 hours. Really hard-core tours will hike both of them. There are also some wonderful snorkeling spots here. All of the tour agencies and hotels in town offer trips out to Isla de la Plata for around $25 to $30 (£14–£17) including a guided hike, lunch, and snorkeling gear, but not including the park entrance fee.

On the mainland, Machalilla is made up of 55,000 hectares (135,910 acres) of mostly tropical dry forest. Within its boundaries lies **Los Frailes** ★★, a long, deep crescent of beautiful beach backed by high bluffs and thick forest. Los Frailes is widely reputed to be the most beautiful beach in Ecuador, and aerial photos of this spot are common on postcards and promotional materials across the country. Be sure to bring plenty of water and sunscreen. You can visit Los Frailes on your own, or as part of a guided tour, which will take you to a couple of nearby archaeological sites. From the park entrance gate at Los Frailes, there is a 3.2km (2-mile) trail down to the beach.

About 10km (6 miles) north of Puerto López is the village of **Agua Blanca,** which has a small archaeological museum and nearby ruins. The ruins and most of the artifacts in the museum are attributed to the Manteña people, who inhabited this region from 500 B.C. until around A.D. 1500.

Admission to Machalilla National Park, which includes access to Isla de la Plata, is $20 (£11). If you're just going to the island, the entrance fee is $15 (£8.25). A day pass to just visit Los Frailes costs $12 (£6.60). If you sign on for a tour, your tour operator will handle the park passes for you. If not, the national park has an **office** (✆ 05/ 2604-170) in Puerto López, on Calle Eloy Alfaro, a half-block east of the main market. The office is open Monday through Saturday from 8am to 5pm.

WHERE TO STAY IN PUERTO LOPEZ
MODERATE

Mantaraya Lodge (★   This sprawling hotel sits on a high hillside overlooking dry forest and the coastline. The buildings here feature faux-adobe walls, red tile roofs, and a quirky architectural style. There's a topiary whale and shark near the free-form pool which is fed by a waterfall flowing out of a large, unheated Jacuzzi. Most of the rooms have private balconies or terra-cotta tile patios. Room no. 15 is my favorite, with a great view from its second-story perch. Room no. 8 is another second-floor unit with a very large balcony-terrace. The rooms don't have air-conditioning, but they do have fans, and with tile floors, high ceilings, and good cross-ventilation, it's usually pretty comfortable, especially at night. The Mantaraya has an excellent tour operation, both here and in Quito (Advantage Travel), and a lot of the guests come as part of an organized package that includes room, board, and tours. A taxi here from town will cost just $2 (£1.10).

On the coastal highway, Puerto López. (℃ 02/2448-985 reservations office in Quito. www.mantarayalodge.com. 15 units. $80–$140 (£44–£77) double. Rates include full breakfast. Rates lower in the off season; higher during peak periods. AE, DC, MC, V. **Amenities:** Restaurant; bar; mid-size outdoor pool; tour desk; laundry service. *In room:* No phone.

INEXPENSIVE

Hostería Mandála (Finds   This unique lodging option is located on the Malecón, several blocks north of the center of town. The setting and extensive grounds and gardens here make the place feel more remote and isolated than it really is. The brick cabins—which come with a small front balcony or porch and a cloth hammock—feature artistic details and design elements made of wood, bamboo, and stone. There are rooms for couples, as well as two-story units that can hold up to six people. The hotel fronts a quiet section of beach, and they've built several thatch-roof shade huts on the sand for guests to commandeer while they're enjoying the sun, sand, and sea. Still, the best feature here is the Mandála's extensive and well-tended gardens, which show off a wide range of tropical flora.

Malecón Julio Izurieta, north end of town, Puerto López. (℃/fax 05/2300-181 or 09/9500-880. www.hosteria mandala.info. 20 units. $26–$30 (£14–£17) double. MC, V. **Amenities:** Restaurant; bar; tour desk; laundry service. *In room:* No phone.

Hotel Pacífico   With a privileged location right on the Malecón, near the center of town, this is a good option in Puerto López proper. Although only 10 rooms have air-conditioning—and they cost more—it's worth the splurge. The best rooms are the air-conditioned rooms facing the ocean, with big balconies equipped with hammocks and easy chairs. The older, more basic rooms with fans have less style, space, and definitely smaller bathrooms. There's a good-size kidney-shaped pool in a large garden area out back, as well as an unheated Jacuzzi and a basketball court. The hotel also has an oceanfront restaurant and a good tour agency that operates its own boat for trips out to Isla de la Plata.

Malecón Julio Izurieta, Puerto López. (℃ 05/2300-147 or 05/2300-133. www.hotelpacificoecuador.com. 30 units. $24 (£13) double with fan; $40 (£22) double with A/C. Rates lower in the off season; higher during peak periods. DC, MC, V. **Amenities:** Restaurant; bar; small outdoor pool; tour desk; laundry service. *In room:* No phone.

WHERE TO DINE IN PUERTO LOPEZ

All along the Malecón are simple restaurants serving excellent fresh seafood and Ecuadorian cooking at very reasonable rates. Of these, I like **Restaurante Carmita** (℃ 05/2604-146) and **Restaurante Spondylus** (℃ 05/2604-128).

Café Ballena/Whale Café ☆ SEAFOOD/ECUADORIAN   This beachfront place is located at the far southern end of the Malecón. Just head for the large whitewashed sculpture of a whale flipper emerging out of the sand. The best seats are found on their open-air balcony. Run by an American couple who have been here for nearly 20 years, the restaurant is famous for its filling breakfasts—in particular its fresh banana bread and banana pancakes. Lunch and dinner are just as satisfying. I always favor fresh grilled fish, but you can also get excellent pastas and pizzas. Save room for dessert, which might feature a fresh baked apple pie or flourless chocolate cake.

South end of Malecón Julio Izurieta. © 09/6284-047. Main courses $3.50–$14 (£1.95–£7.70). MC, V. Daily 8am–10pm. Often reduced hours in the off season.

PUERTO LOPEZ AFTER DARK

This is a quiet fishing town with very limited nightlife. The restaurant and bar at the **Hotel Pacífico** (see above) is one of the best spots to eat and drink in town. Aside from this, you can stroll the Malecón and see if any place calls out to you.

A NEARBY BEACH RETREAT

Hostería Alándaluz ☆ *(Finds)*   This place bills itself as a *pueblo ecológico* (ecological village), and makes every effort to be self-sustainable, low-impact, and environmentally friendly. The entire expansive complex here is constructed of bamboo, stone, palm thatch, wood, or some other renewable resource. Most of the toilets are self-composting. They've got organic gardens and a neighboring private reserve. The wide range in prices reflects the variance in style, luxury, and location of the *hostería*'s cabins. They even allow camping, in a comfortable little campground with shared bathrooms and showers. My favorite rooms are the Cabañas Torrecilla, which are classified as mini-suites. These are close to the beach, and feature private balconies and small fireplaces, which are really cosmetic since it's usually too hot to be of much comfort. The massive main lodge has a soaring thatch roof, polished wood floors, and homemade bamboo furniture. A full meal plan here will run $31 (£17) per person, per day. A host of tours and activities is offered.

In Puerto Rico, 12km (7½ miles) south of Puerto López on the coastal highway E15. © 04/2780-686 at the hotel, or 02/2440-790 for reservations office in Quito. www.alandaluzhosteria.com. 25 units. $29–$88 (£16–£48) double; $5 (£2.75) per person camping. DC, MC, V. **Amenities:** Restaurant; bar; tour desk; laundry service. *In room:* No phone.

5 Machala & South to the Peruvian Border

518km (322 miles) S of Quito; 191km (119 miles) S of Guayaquil; 73km (45 miles) N of Huaquillas

The capital of El Oro province, Machala is an agricultural city at the heart of Ecuador's banana belt. In fact, the city bills itself as "The Banana Capital of the World," and banana plantations extend for miles in every direction. Most of this massive banana production is shipped out of Puerto Bolívar, located about 6.5km (4 miles) west of Machala's downtown. Puerto Bolívar is a major port and shipping center. In addition to bananas, this region produces and ships large quantities of cacao, pineapples, and farm-raised shrimp. In many ways, Puerto Bolívar, its seafront Malecón packed with shops, restaurants, and bars, is more attractive to tourists than Machala.

Indeed, for most tourists Machala is simply a necessary transit stop from both Guayaquil and Cuenca on the way to Peru. While here, you can tour nearby mangroves, visit the beach at Jambelí, or take a tour of a unique petrified forest down near the Peruvian border.

Going Bananas

The banana has played a vital role in Ecuador's economic history. Following an epidemic blight that wiped out many of the banana plantations in Central America during the early 1940s, Ecuador was called upon to serve as an alternative supplier of the fruit to satisfy the growing demands of the U.S. market. After the end of World War II, Ecuador enjoyed a decade-long "banana boom" that brought with it an unprecedented period of peace and prosperity. From 1948 to 1952, annual exports increased from two million bananas to 20 million, and by 1955 they'd reached 26 million. Banana profits were used to improve the country's infrastructure, education, and health-care system, as well as to increase salaries.

Ecuador's political scene was also affected by the country's transformation into a **Banana Republic.** President Velasco served out three full consecutive terms in office, an unprecedented and unmatched feat in the country's history. Toward the close of the 1950s, however, world banana prices dropped, sparking an economic crisis marked by high unemployment and widespread social discord. The discovery of petroleum in the late 1960s helped alleviate the problem. (Bananas still rank as Ecuador's second-most-important export, after oil, and Ecuadorian bananas account for some 30% of worldwide consumption.)

The year-round tropical climate enjoyed by the country's southern coastal regions near Guayaquil is ideal for banana production. The majority of plantations are managed by private interests, the most well-known being those belonging to ex-presidential candidate and banana magnate Alvaro Noboa, owner of the world's largest export brand, Bonita. (Noboa, not coincidentally, is the wealthiest person in Ecuador.)

Despite being one of the world's most important exporters, Ecuadorian banana workers—who represent 12% of the nation's workforce—are some of the lowest paid in Latin America. Human-rights abuses on plantations continue to attract international media attention; there have been reports of violent attacks against workers and union organizers.

ESSENTIALS
GETTING THERE

BY PLANE   The closest airport with regular commuter service is located in Guayaquil. See "Guayaquil: Getting There: By Plane," on p. 234. There is a small airport in Machala, the **Aeropuerto General Manuel Serrano** (📞 **07/2935-677**; airport code: MCH), but it currently receives only occasional charter traffic.

BY BUS   There are a handful of direct buses from Quito to Machala each day on the **Cooperativa TAC** (📞 **02/2951-913** in Quito, or 07/2930-119 in Machala), **Occidental** (📞 **07/2930-820**), and **Panamericana** (📞 **07/2930-141**) bus lines. The ride takes around 12 hours, and the fare is about $10 to $12 (£5.50–£6.60).

Alternatively, you can make your way first to Guayaquil (see "Getting There," under "Guayaquil"), and make onward bus connections to Machala and the border.

Buses leave Guayaquil's main bus terminal at least every half-hour between 4:30am and 11:30pm, on three or four different bus lines, including **CIFA** (© 07/2933-735 in Machala, or 04/2140-379 in Guayaquil) and **Ecuatoriano Pullman** (© 07/2930-197 in Machala, or **04/2140-617** in Guayaquil). About half of these buses continue on to Huaquillas (see "Heading South to Peru," below). The ride takes 3½ hours to Machala, and 5 hours to Huaquillas. The fares run around $4.50 (£2.50) to Machala, and $6 to $7 (£3.30–£3.85) to Huaquillas.

Transportes Azuay (© 07/2930-539) has frequent service between Machala and Cuenca. The ride takes about 4 hours, and the fare is $4.50 (£2.25).

CIFA and **Ecuatoriano Pullman** make the run between Machala and the border at Huaquillas. The ride takes around 1½ hours, and the fare is $2 (£1.10).

There's no centralized bus station in Machala, but all the major bus lines arrive and depart from stops or terminals in the downtown area. For departures out of Machala, the terminal directions are as follows. To Guayaquil: **Rutas Orenses** leaves from Avenida 9 de Octubre and Calle Tarqui, while **Ecuatoriano Pullman** leaves from Avenida 9 de Octubre and Calle Colón, and **CIFA** leaves from Avenida Bolívar and Calle Guayas. To Quito: **Panamericana** and **Cooperativa TAC** buses both leave from Calle Colón and Avenida Bolívar, and **Occidental** buses leave from Avenida Buenavista between calles Sucre and Olmedo. To Cuenca: **Transportes Azuay** leaves from Calle Sucre and Calle Junín.

BY CAR   To reach Machala by car, follow the directions to Guayaquil (p. 236). From Guayaquil, take Highway E70 east out of town until the junction with E25. Just outside of the city center, E25 crosses E584, which will take you to Machala. E25 continues down to the town of Arenillas, where it connects with E50, which heads to Huaquillas and the Peruvian border.

GETTING AROUND

You should have no trouble flagging down a taxi in Machala. A ride anywhere in the city should cost less than $2 (£1.10), and a ride out to Puerto Bolívar should only cost $3 (£1.65). If for some reason you do have trouble finding a cab, you can always call **Cooperativa de Taxis Machala** (© 07/2920-271) or **Orotaxis** (© 07/2934-332).

Local buses run constantly along Avenida 9 de Octubre out to Puerto Bolívar. The fare is 30¢ (15p).

ORIENTATION

Machala's downtown features a central plaza with the city's Catholic church and a small park, bordered by avenidas Rocafuerte and 9 de Octubre and by calles Guayas and 9 de Mayo. Avenida 9 de Octubre is the main avenue running through the heart of town. As it heads out of Machala to the northwest, Avenida 9 de Octubre becomes Avenida Bolívar Madero Vargas, which takes you to Puerto Bolívar.

FAST FACTS   The main **police** station (© **101** or 07/2933-391) is located on Avenida 9 de Mayo and Calle Manuel Estomba, near the airport. For a medical emergency, call the **Cruz Roja (Red Cross;** © **07/2930-151).** The **Hospital Teófilo Dávila** (© 07/2935-570) is the best medical facility in the city, and is located close to downtown on Avenida Boyacá, between calles Colón and Buenavista.

The Ministry of Tourism operates a **tourist information office** (© 07/2932-106) at Avenida 9 de Mayo and Pichincha. The main **post office** is on Avenida Bolívar and Calle Montalvo. The **Peruvian Consulate** (© 07/2930-680) is on Avenida Bolívar and Calle Colón.

Most major Ecuadorian banks have a branch or two in downtown Machala. The main branches of both the **Banco de Guayaquil** (⦿ 07/2936-101) and **Banco Pichincha** (⦿ 07/2930-358) are located on Calle Guayas and Avenida Rocafuerte, and there's a branch of **Banco del Pacífico** (⦿ 07/2930-700) on Rocafuerte and Junín.

There are plenty of Internet cafes and phone cabins all over downtown Machala. Rates run around 80¢ to $1.50 (45p–85p) per hour. Your best bet is to find whichever Internet cafe seems most comfortable and well-equipped. I've had good luck at **Cyber Vagonet** (⦿ 09/3925-950) on Bolívar, between calles Guayas and Ayacucho; and at **Banana Net** (⦿ 07/2939-234) on Calle Sucre, between Santa Rosa and Ayacucho.

WHAT TO SEE & DO

There's little of interest to tourists right in Machala. If you end up spending any time here, you should probably contact the local branch of **Delgado Travel** (⦿ 07/2931-850) on Calle 9 de Mayo, between avenidas Rocafuerte and Bolívar. These folks can arrange day trips to a nearby banana plantation, to the colonial city of Zaruma, or to the Petrified Forest of Puyango (see below).

The most popular excursion from Machala is to the beach of **Jambelí,** which is located on the tip of a mangrove archipelago that lies just off the coast. On weekends and holidays, locals flock here. The beach is a long, narrow expanse of hard-packed gray sand; it's lined with palm trees and makeshift huts built to provide shade. Though very crowded on weekends and holidays, Jambelí is usually almost empty at other times. Be sure to bring plenty of sunscreen and mosquito repellent. There are some simple restaurants and *ceviche* shacks along the beach. Many visitors prefer to take a boat tour through the mangroves, where the bird-watching is excellent. Boat taxis leave throughout the day from the pier in Puerto Bolívar for Jambelí. Boats leave roughly every half-hour, or when they fill up, between 7am and 6:30pm. The ride takes around 20 minutes, and the fare is $1.40 (80p) each way. Alternatively, you can hire an entire boat for up to 10 people for around $12 to $18 (£6.60–£9.90) per hour.

Down south of Machala, right near the Peruvian border, sits the **Bosque Petrificado de Puyango (Petrified Forest of Puyango)** ⦿ (⦿ 07/2570-234), a unique dry-forest reserve with a vast collection of fossilized tree trunks, plants, leaves, flowers, fruits, and mollusks. Most of the fossils are approximately 100 million years old. The most common and impressive specimens here are the Araucarioxylon trunks, which are strewn across the landscape; the largest of these is some 15m (50 ft.) long, with a diameter of 2m (6½ ft.). Puyango is located 111km (69 miles) south of Machala. The reserve is open daily from 8am to 5pm. Admission is $1 (55p). The best way to visit here is on a guided tour out of Machala.

WHERE TO STAY IN MACHALA
EXPENSIVE

Hotel Oro Verde Machala ⦿   Part of a local chain, this is the plushest and best-equipped hotel this far south in Ecuador. The hotel has modern and extensive facilities and is very popular with business and conference travelers. The carpeted rooms feature contemporary furnishings and cheery fabric patterns. Those looking to stay active or fit can play tennis or squash, or work out in the small but well-equipped gym. Those looking for less strenuous pursuits can lounge by the large pool, or take a sauna or steam bath. The pool has a large children's area, and a nearby playground makes this a good choice for families traveling with the kids. There are several dining options in the hotel, including an informal deli with excellent fresh-baked breads and desserts. This Oro Verde is located on the eastern outskirts of downtown, in an upscale residential neighborhood.

Circunvalación Norte and Calle Vehicular, Machala. (℃) 07/2933-140. Fax 07/2933-150. www.oroverdehotels.com. 77 units. $90–$120 (£50–£66) double; $130–$150 (£72–£83) suite. Rates include breakfast buffet. AE, DC, MC, V. **Amenities:** 2 restaurants; 2 bars; outdoor pool; unlit outdoor tennis court; 2 indoor squash courts; small gym; sauna; Jacuzzi; steam room; tour desk; room service 7am-11pm; laundry service. *In room:* A/C, TV, minibar, safe, Wi-Fi.

MODERATE

Regal Hotel This is my favorite downtown hotel in Machala. I enjoy its bold architecture, with three columns of curving windows rising several stories over the busy Avenida Bolívar. The rooms vary greatly in size, and some can feel a bit cramped. All are done in a neutral, modern style familiar to anyone staying in a typical business-class hotel, with built-in wood-grained Formica furniture and matching headboard. Some come with comfortable leather sitting chairs. The hotel's restaurant is an American-style cafeteria that's popular with locals, especially for lunch.

Av. Bolívar, between Guayas and Ayacucho, Machala. (℃)/fax 07/2960-000. www.regalhotel.com.ec. 35 units. $55 (£30) double. Rates include full breakfast. AE, DC, MC, V. **Amenities:** Restaurants; bar; small gym; room service 7am–10pm; tour desk; laundry service. *In room:* A/C, TV.

INEXPENSIVE

Gran Hotel Americano *(Value)* This stately old dame shows her age in places, but remains a good choice and an excellent value. Most rooms come with a private balcony overlooking busy downtown Machala. The rooms themselves have received regular upgrading and upkeep and are quite up to snuff, especially at these prices. Heck, these folks even offer free valet parking. The higher up the room, the farther removed it is from street noise, which can be an issue at times. But altitude won't do anything to mute the noise generated by the older wall-mounted air-conditioning units. This is predominantly a business hotel, which fills up during the week, but empties out on weekends. Be sure to ask about their discounts for Friday and Saturday nights.

Av. 9 de Octubre and Calle Tarqui, Machala. (℃) 07/2966-400. Fax 07/2966-401. www.hotelesmachala.com. 60 units. $32–$36 (£18–£20) double; $50 (£28) junior suite. Rates include full breakfast. AE, DC, MC, V. **Amenities:** Restaurant; bar; tour desk; laundry service. *In room:* A/C, TV, safe.

WHERE TO DINE IN MACHALA

Downtown Machala has loads of restaurants serving inexpensive local fare and seafood. If you're looking for Chinese food, try **Chifa Central** (℃ 07/2932-961) on Calle Tarqui, between Avenida 9 de Octubre and Calle Sucre. The restaurant at the **Gran Hotel Americano** (see above) is also very good and popular with locals and visitors alike. The best thing to do, though, is to head to nearby Puerto Bolívar, which has a string of oceanfront options specializing in excellent *ceviches* and seafood. In addition to Pepe's, listed below, **Waikiki** (℃ 07/2929-810) is another top choice on Puerto Bolívar's Malecón.

INEXPENSIVE

Chesco Pizzería ITALIAN/PIZZA Don't come here for ambience. The fluorescent lights are dizzying, the decor relatively sterile. Still, the thin-crust pizzas here are the best in Machala. They also have a long list of pasta options and some steak and poultry main courses. Chesco offers delivery, and there's a new branch nearby on Avenida Pichincha, between calles Guayas and Ayacucho.

Calle Guayas, between Av. 9 de Octubre and Calle Sucre, Puerto Bolívar. (℃) 07/2936-418. Main courses $3.25–$8 (£1.80–£4.40). MC, V. Daily noon–10pm.

Pepe's ⚑ SEAFOOD/ECUADORIAN   The food here is very similar to what you'll find at any of the other *ceviche* and seafood joints along the Malecón in Puerto Bolívar, but this place, built on stilts over the water, definitely has the best setting. Grab one of the tables along the railing and order up a dish of the delicious shrimp *ceviche*. You can also get oysters on the half-shell, another excellent appetizer. For a main dish, find out what's the freshest catch, or splurge for some *langostinos* served in a rich garlic sauce. After dark, this place starts to resemble a bar scene, which is not necessarily a bad thing, and they even have karaoke on the weekends.

Malecón and Rocafuerte, Puerto Bolívar. No phone. Main courses $3–$12 (£1.65–£6.60). No credit cards. Daily 11:30am–midnight.

MACHALA AFTER DARK

Machala is a big city with a thriving nightlife. There are plenty of popular discos and dance clubs. My favorites include **Freedom Discotec** ⚑, on Avenida Madero Vargas and Circunvalación Sur (© 09/9404-538), and **Banana Disco,** on Avenida Bolívar and Calle Junín (© 07/2932-498). For a bar and karaoke scene that attracts a young crowd, head to **Tequila Bar** on Ayacucho, between avenidas 9 de Octubre and Rocafuerte (© 07/2937-435).

For a quieter time, I like **Golden Café Concert** (© 07/2933-555), a refined bar and club with frequent live music performances ranging from jazz to boleros to Latin folk. It's located on the corner of Avenida 9 de Octubre and Calle Junín. Another good option is **Tasca la Vara** (© 07/2923-551), a Spanish-style pub on Arizaga and Septima Oeste.

Gamblers can test their luck at the casino at the **Casinomar** (© 07/2960-258), on Circunvalación Norte and Vehicular 7, near the Hotel Oro Verde Machala.

HEADING SOUTH TO PERU

The road south to Peru passes right by Machala and heads down through Santa Rosa and Arenillas to the border town of Huaquillas, some 80km (50 miles) south of Machala. If you're going on to Peru, you should definitely use Machala, or even Guayaquil, as your final base in Ecuador because there are very limited services and no accommodations that I can recommend in Huaquillas. The Río Zarumilla forms the physical border between the two countries, and the Peruvian border town is Aguas Verdes. Both Ecuadorian and Peruvian immigration are always open. Keep in mind that the Ecuadorian immigration control point is located about 3.2km (2 miles) north of the actual border crossing, while its Peruvian counterpart is located about 2km (1½ miles) south of the river. Both are on the main road and readily identified by numerous signs.

If you are heading south by bus, you should get off at the Ecuadorian immigration office to have your passport stamped. You can keep your ticket and then catch the next bus farther into town after you complete your border formalities. I recommend, however, that you take a taxi, which will only cost around $1 (55p). As you walk across the bridge that serves as the border crossing, you will have to show your

---

⌐Tips Shameless Plug

If you're going on to Peru, you'll want to pick up a copy of **Frommer's Peru,** now in its third edition.

stamped passport to Ecuadorian and Peruvian authorities. From here you can grab another taxi to the Peruvian immigration office to get your entry stamp. Most travelers head immediately to the town of Tumbes, which has far more facilities, services, and accommodations than Aguas Verdes. At the border crossing, you can hire a taxi for around $7 (£3.85) to take you to Tumbes, which includes a stop at the immigration office for you to get your stamp.

Note: The border is a hectic mess on both sides, and is relatively dangerous for travelers. Peru and Ecuador have had border disputes in the past, which hasn't helped matters. Keep a careful eye on your belongings, and be wary of hucksters and scam artists. Try to avoid and discourage touts. Scores of individuals offer money exchange in the streets on either side of the border, but I recommend exchanging a minimal amount there, because these dealers often give unfavorable rates, use rigged calculators, and pawn off counterfeit bills. It's best to have a good grasp of the current official exchange rate ($1/55p was equivalent to 3.20 soles at press time), and to see if you can exchange dollars for Peruvian soles at a bank in Machala. If not, exchange what you need to get you through to Tumbes, where you'll find more reputable and less risky exchange houses.

10

Northern Pacific Coast & Lowlands

Ecuador's northern Pacific coast and its surrounding lowlands are often neglected or avoided by foreign visitors to the country. The region, however, is certainly not without its charms. The beaches of the northern Pacific coast are arguably the finest in the country. Long cherished by locals, they are also finding favor with international surfers, who can't get enough of the consistent beach break at **Canoa,** or the perfect point at **Mompiche.**

Manta is a major port and beach town that sits just about at the center of Ecuador's long stretch of Pacific coastline. The city has high-rise hotels, a seaside Malecón, and plenty of restaurants and nightlife, including a couple of ritzy casinos. Those looking for a more pastoral port city should head to the picturesque little peninsula that is **Bahía de Caráquez.** From Bahía, the coastline stretches north with mile after mile of pristine beaches backed at first by dry forest and cattle lands, which give way, as you enter **Esmeraldas** province, to lush rainforests and then dense mangrove forests. Esmeraldas is rightly known as "The Green Province." It is also the epicenter of the country's Afro-Ecuadorian population, a unique cultural community with distinct music, cuisine, and customs.

Inland, on the plains just below the Andes, lies **Santo Domingo de Colorado,** one of the country's major crossroads. From this hub, spokes head out in various directions to the coast, as well as straight south to Guayaquil. In the forests around Santo Domingo lie a couple of beautiful, isolated nature lodges.

1 Manta

419km (260 miles) W of Quito, 196km (122 miles) NW of Guayaquil

Manta is a city of many faces, but at its core it's an industrial port—the second largest port in Ecuador, after Guayaquil. Inhabited for centuries, Manta was a major trading port for the pre-Columbian Manteña people who gave the town its name. The conquering Incas also used Manta as a port. Today the city has a population of some 200,000 and is home to a large university, as well as a controversial U.S. airbase. It also makes a respectable stab at being a beach town, with a couple of good beaches located right near the center of the city. But Manta's appeal as a beach getaway is much more geared toward Ecuadorians looking for a quick, easy weekend or holiday spot than to foreign tourists in search of holiday bliss. The latter group generally uses the city's airport as a convenient gateway to beaches north and south of Manta.

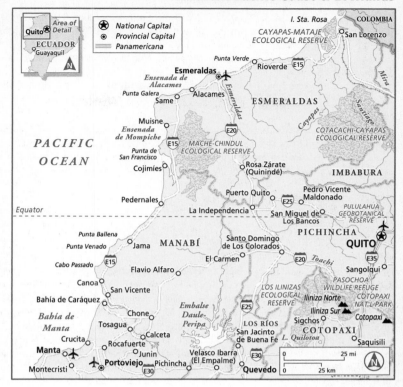

Northern Pacific Coast & Lowlands

ESSENTIALS
GETTING THERE & DEPARTING

BY PLANE Tame (ⓒ **02/2909-900** central reservation number in Quito, or
ⓒ 05/2613-210 in Manta; www.tame.com.ec), **Icaro** (ⓒ **1800/883-567** toll-free
nationwide, or 05/2627-327 in Manta; www.icaro.com.ec), and **Aerogal** (ⓒ **1800/
2376-425** toll-free nationwide, or 05/2628-899 in Manta; www.aerogal.com.ec) all
have daily flights into **Aeropuerto Eloy Afaro** (ⓒ **05/2622-812;** airport code: MEC)
in Manta. There are several daily flights in the morning and several in the afternoon.
However, there are somewhat fewer flights on weekends, particularly on Saturdays—
the schedule tends to fluctuate according to demand. The flight duration is 30 minutes, and fares run from $55 to $60 (£30–£33) each way.

The Oro Verde and Howard Johnson Manta hotels both have free shuttles await-
ing every flight. There are also taxis on hand when flights land. A taxi ride into town
should cost $4 to $5 (£2.20–£2.75).

BY BUS Buses leave from Quito's main terminal for Manta roughly every hour
between 6:30am and 11:30pm. The two main companies plying this route are **Cooperativo Carlos Aray** (ⓒ **02/2283-080** in Quito, or 05/2620-877 in Manta) and

Cooperativo Reina Camino (✆ 02/2572-673 in Quito, or 05/2695-818 in Manta). The ride takes around 9 hours and the fare runs from $8 to $10 (£4.40–£5.50). The return buses leave at roughly the same schedule.

There is also regular bus service between Manta and Ambato, Guayaquil, Puerto López, and Esmeraldas.

The main **bus terminal** in Manta is located just north of the Tarqui bridge, one block in from the Malecón, on Avenida 8 and Calle 7, behind the Banco Central building.

BY CAR   To reach Manta by car from Quito, you will need to start off heading south on the Pan-American Highway (E35) until the intersection at Aloag. From here, head west on E30 toward Santo Domingo de los Colorados. The quickest and best route is to continue on to Chone, Puerto Viejo, and finally Montecristi. In Montecristi, you will connect with E9 for the last few miles to Manta. The drive takes between 7 and 8 hours.

If you're driving from Guayaquil, take Highway E21 north out of town to the intersection with E9 north near the town of Nobol. From here it's a straight shot on E9 into Manta. The drive takes around 4 hours.

GETTING AROUND

You can rent a car in Manta at **Avis** (✆ 05/2626-680; www.avis.com), at the Centro Comercial Cocomanta on the Circunvalación; **Budget** (✆ 05/2629-919; www.budget-ec.com), on the Malecón between calles 15 and 16; and **Localiza** (✆ 05/2622-434; www.localiza.com.ec), on Calle Flavio Reyes and Avenida 21. Rates run around $45 to $90 (£25–£50) per day, including unlimited mileage and insurance.

Taxis are plentiful in Manta and constantly cruise Avenida Malecón. If you can't flag one down, call **Cooperativa de Taxis Jocay** (✆ 05/2922-860) or **Seguitaxi** (✆ 05/2628-215). A ride around downtown should cost just $1 (55p). A ride from downtown to the Howard Johnson should run around $3 to $4 (£1.65–£2.20).

FAST FACTS   If you need to contact the local **police,** dial ✆ 05/2920-900. In an emergency, call the **Red Cross** (✆ 05/2624-212), or head to the **Hospital de Manta** (✆ 05/2625-610), off the Vía Circunvalación a mile or so southwest of the Malecón.

There are loads of banks and ATMs all over Manta. You'll find branches of **Banco del Pichincha** on Avenida 2, between calles 11 and 12 (✆ 05/2626-844); **Banco Bolivariano** on Malecón Jaime Chávez Gutiérrez, next to the CAE building (✆ 05/2620-504; www.bolivariano.com); and **Uni Banco** on Avenida 102 and Calle 106 (✆ 05/2621-100). All these banks have 24-hour ATMs.

Most of the hotels in town, and a bunch of storefront Internet cafes, offer Internet access. My favorite of these is **Interactive,** on Avenida 3, between calles 12 and 13 (✆ 05/2625-400). Rates run around 50¢ to $1.50 (30p–85p) per hour. If your hotel can't do your laundry or you want to save a few bucks, try **Lavandería del Mar,** on Avenida 9 de Octubre (✆ 05/2636-638). For any photographic needs, there's **Konica Photo Express** in the Centro Comercial Paseo (✆ 05/2932-131).

ORIENTATION

The city of Manta is basically divided in two by the mellow Río Manta. The eastern half is usually described as Tarqui, as it is fronted by Playa de Tarqui (Tarqui Beach). This half of the city is predominantly residential and industrial. The western half is far more developed and of far more interest to tourists, with most of the city's hotels,

ATTRACTIONS ●
Malecón Esenico **9**
Museo del
  Banco Central **13**

DINING ◆
El Velero **11**
Las Velas **8**
Palmeiras **2**
Peces & Peces **10**
Rincón Criollo **4**
Topi Tu Pizza **12**

ACCOMMODATIONS ■
Hostel Manakin **3**
Hotel Balandra **5**
Hotel Oro Verde **7**
Howard Johnson Manta **1**
Vistalmar **6**

restaurants, shops, and businesses. Some folks call this half Murciélago, after the main beach here, Playa Murciélago.

The seafront Avenida Malecón is the defining avenue in Manta. It hugs the coastline and runs roughly east to west, from Playa de Tarqui, over a small bridge to Bahía de Manta (Manta Harbor) and Playa Murciélago. Just beyond the Hotel Oro Verde this avenue jogs inland slightly and becomes Avenida Flavio Reyes, which continues on toward Playa de Barbasquillo and the Howard Johnson hotel. Almost everything of interest to tourists is located either on the Malecón or Avenida Flavio Reyes. The airport is located about 15 minutes east of Playa de Tarqui.

INFORMATION

You'll find a **tourist information office** (☎ **05/2622-944**) in the town hall, or *edificio municipal,* on Avenida 4 and Calle 8. They usually have an English-speaker on hand and can offer good recommendations; they'll also give you a local map. There's another, smaller **tourist information office** (☎ **05/2624-099**) at the bottom of the steps that lead down to the Malecón Esenico. This one is run by the Universidad Laica Eloy Alfaro, and is much less organized and useful. Your best bet for local insight and tour information is the tour desk at your hotel, or the local branches of **Metropolitan Touring** (☎ **05/2620-728;** www.metropolitan-touring.com), which has its main

The Manta Airbase

Since its inception, Manta's Eloy Alfaro Air Base and the presence of U.S. military forces there have been the focus of dispute and controversy. In 1999, when Ecuadorian President Jamil Mahuad announced that he would allow the United States to operate at the base, some Ecuadorians argued that it would be an enormous affront to their country's sovereignty. Despite those protests, in 2000, a 10-year lease agreement was finalized between the United States and Ecuador.

Today, after $80 million (£44 million) in construction costs, the base in Manta is one of five primary Ecuadorian Air Force air bases. The base is also used by the U.S. Air Force for operations against illegal drug trafficking in northwestern South America. There are currently some 230 soldiers and 13 airmen stationed at the base. The effects of the base can be felt in the bars, restaurants, shops, and casinos of Manta. Some complain that the base has led to an increase in local crime, prostitution, and drug use; others herald the economic boom and well-paved roads it has brought.

Many Ecuadorians are convinced that the United States' real intention is to establish a permanent presence in Manta—essentially to take the place of the Howard Air Base, in Panama, which closed in 1999. However, following his 2006 election, incoming President Rafael Correa stated that Ecuador would not renew the agreement for use of the base by the U.S. military. Correa explained that the original agreement was an act "of unlimited betrayal," although he added that he would consider extending the lease— that is, if the United States let Ecuador set up a base in Miami.

offices at Avenida 4, between calles 12 and 13. These folks are the largest tour operator in Ecuador and offer a wide range of tours and activities around Manta and all along the Pacific coast. They also have another office in the small strip mall fronting the Howard Johnson hotel.

WHAT TO SEE & DO IN & AROUND MANTA

Aside from the beaches and beachfront promenades, and the activities they offer, there are very few attractions in Manta. The two main beaches in Manta are **Playa de Tarqui** and **Playa Murciélago.** Of these, Playa Murciélago is much better suited for those looking to do some sunbathing and swimming, or to join a pick-up game of beach volleyball or beach soccer. Most of Playa Murciélago is lined with a beachfront promenade called the **Malecón Esenico,** and features a concrete walkway lined with a steady string of open-air restaurants and souvenir stands. There's even a climbing wall at the western end of the Malecón Esenico. Playa Murciélago is the place to come if you want to rent a chaise lounge and shade umbrella on the sand. These are available for around $4 to $6 (£2.20–£3.30) per day.

Playa de Tarqui is in many ways a more atmospheric beach, where fishermen and boat builders still ply their trade. Of particular interest is the makeshift, open-air boatyard right on the beach just east of Río Manta; here you can watch as massive wooden commercial-fishing trawlers are built by skilled artisans. Be careful of any valuables in this area, and avoid the Tarqui Malecón at night, as it can be dangerous. If you walk a mile or more farther east along the beach, you can also find some beautiful and deserted patches of sand for sunbathing and swimming.

West from Playa Murciélago is **Playa Barbasquillo,** which is much less developed, although it's very rocky in places, with uninspiring brown sand in others.

If it's raining or you want a small dose of culture, you can head to the **Museo del Banco Central** (© 05/2612-878), on Avenida Malecón and Calle 7, in front of the bus station. The small museum here features a collection of pre-Columbian indigenous artifacts from the various tribes of the Manabí coast. The museum is open daily from 9am to 5pm. Admission is $1 (55p).

If you want to go sport fishing, inquire at your hotel desk, or head to the **Manta Yacht Club** (© 05/2623-505) and ask there. A full-day outing, with lunch and gear for up to four people fishing, should cost $400 to $900 (£220–£500), depending upon the size of the boat and the distance traveled to the fishing grounds. A wide range of game fish can be caught, including marlin, sailfish, wahoo, and tuna.

Perhaps the most popular side trip out of Manta is to visit the "Panama hat" weavers and shops in nearby **Montecristi** ★. The misnamed Panama hat is actually native to Ecuador. In a calculated move, much of the massive manufacture of these headpieces has shifted to Cuenca. Thirty years ago there were over 2,000 hat weavers in and around Montecristi; today that number has dwindled to less than 50. But hats woven in Montecristi are still widely considered the best and most authentic in the country. For more information on Panama hats, see p. 211. Montecristi is located just 16km (10 miles) south of Manta. You can rent a car (see above), or sign on for a guided tour at any of the hotels in town. In Montecristi you'll want to stop at **Manufactura de Sombreros de Paja Toquilla,** on Avenida 9 de Julio, the town's main street (© 09/7016-515). This place has a great selection, and will take you through the entire process of making one of these hats. Another good local hat shop is **Manufacturas de Sombreros Finos Bertha Pachay,** on Calle Rocafuerte and Avenida 10 de Agosto (© 09/3179-642). You'll find these hats for sale all over Manta, but if you want a wider selection, higher quality, and better price, it's worth a trip to Montecristi.

If you want to head farther afield, most hotel tour desks and tour operators in Manta also offer trips to **Machalilla National Park, Isla de la Plata,** and **Puerto López,** especially during whale-watching season. See chapter 9 for more information on these destinations.

No Hippies in These Hills

Even though the town of Jipijapa is pronounced "Hippy-Happa," don't come here expecting to find the ghosts of Abbie Hoffman or Janis Joplin. Despite its lyrical and suggestive name, this dusty roadside town south of Manta, on the highway to Guayaquil, offers little of interest to tourists. However, decades ago, Jipijapa rivaled Montecristi in the production of Panama hats. If you ask around you might still be able to find a local artisan crafting one of these Toquilla palm hats.

WHERE TO STAY IN MANTA

EXPENSIVE

Hotel Oro Verde ✦✦   This is the top resort-hotel in Manta, and it's often booked solid. The main building forms a sort of horseshoe around the pool and faces the beach. The rooms are everything you could want in this type of hotel, with plenty of space, cool tile floors, and plenty of amenities. The subdued cream- and eggshell-colored walls are nicely contrasted with patterned bedspreads. Every room includes a private balcony with an ocean view. I actually prefer the standard rooms and junior suites over the Grand Suites, which are in a separate wing. While these rooms have more square footage and a kitchenette, they have diminished views—in fact some of the Grand Suites have no ocean view at all. The Oro Verde has several restaurant options, including a lobby sushi bar, as well as the city's top casino. The pool is the center of activity here, and there's a separate children's pool, with a neighboring playground.

Malecón and Calle 23, Manta. ✆ **05/2629-200.** Fax 05/2629-210. www.oroverdehotels.com. 81 units. $110 (£61) double; $140 (£77) junior suite; $160 (£88) Grand Suite; $250 (£138) Master Suite. Rates include buffet breakfast. AE, DC, MC, V. **Amenities:** 3 restaurants; 2 bars; casino; midsize outdoor pool; small well-equipped gym; Jacuzzi; sauna; tour desk; room service 7am–midnight; shopping arcade; laundry service. *In room:* A/C, TV, minibar, safe.

Howard Johnson Manta ✦   This modern high-rise beach hotel isn't your parents' HoJo's. I actually find the rooms and facilities here slightly more appealing than those at the Oro Verde. However, the trade-off is a lack of direct beach access and an isolated setting north of the city. The hotel is set right on the ocean's edge, but the beach here is rocky and not very apt for bathing. Still, if you want some slight sense of isolation while still enjoying all the amenities and perks of a modern resort hotel, you might opt for this place. The rooms are simply furnished, and some might find them a bit too austere, but I like the bright white tile floors, white walls, and sleek beds and bureaus. Most rooms have good-sized balconies fronting the sea, and those on the higher floors have better views. Since the hotel is built into, and descending down, a steep hillside, the higher-floor rooms are actually closer to the lobby and restaurants. It's definitely worth the slight price increase ($10/£5.50) for an ocean-view room. The small gym here has modern machines and equipment set up fronting a wall of windows which look out over the sea.

Km 1.5, Vía Barbasquillo, Manta. ✆ **05/2629-999.** Fax 05/2629-989. www.ghlhoteles.com. 100 units. $85–$95 (£47–£52) double; $150 (£83) junior suite. Rates include buffet breakfast. AE, DC, MC, V. **Amenities:** 3 restaurants; 2 bars; casino; small outdoor pool; lit outdoor tennis court; small well-equipped gym; tour desk; shopping arcade; 24-hr. room service; massage; laundry service; free Wi-Fi. *In room:* A/C, TV, dataport; minibar, safe.

MODERATE

Hotel Balandra ✦ *Kids*   Although it's a couple of blocks inland from the beach, this is still one of the better vacation hotels in Manta. There's a cozy feel to the whole complex. The rooms are housed in a series of two- and three-story units. Each has a small balcony or porch, and the best include a hammock. Most of the rooms feature at least one wall of exposed brick and a small sitting area with a couch. A few have kitchenettes and several bedrooms, making them good options for families looking to do a little cooking on their own. A plus for those traveling with children is the hotel's small playground area, as well as its basketball court and game room with a Ping-Pong table and other distractions. The hotel also has a small gym with a sauna and a refreshing outdoor pool. The restaurant here, which serves good international fare, has three separate seating areas, including a beautiful outdoor terrace with views of the ocean.

Av. 7 and Calle 20, Barrio Córdova, Manta. (*C* 05/2621-671 or 09/9944-554. www.hotelbalandramanta.com. 31 units. $73 (£40) double; $127 (£70) cabaña for up to 5 people. Rates include full breakfast. MC, DC, V. **Amenities:** Restaurant; bar; small outdoor pool; small gym; sauna; laundry service. *In room:* A/C, TV, minibar, safe, free Wi-Fi.

Vistalmar ★★ *(Finds)* This unique boutique hotel is my top choice in Manta. As you come through the entrance gate you pass two large jade-covered horses and walk beside a pretty pond with a double Buddha fountain. The rooms and two-bedroom *cabañas* are all distinctly designed and decorated. I prefer the two rooms, which are located side-by-side and share a second-floor veranda overlooking the sea. These both feature an eclectic mix of African and Asian art and crafts. Each has one queen-size four-poster bamboo bed under mosquito netting and an exposed thatch roof. The three *cabañas* are done in a much more minimalist style, but with various accents and a sense of flair. These each have a sitting room and kitchenette, making them perfect for families. The small pool here is built along a steep cliff and features an infinity effect that makes it appear to blend in with the sea. Be sure to check out the artworks in the open-air, thatched-roof lounge, which include two giant marble Buddhas and a large painting of some sort of mythic bird riding a Galápagos tortoise while playing a harp. A path leads down to Playa Murciélago. There's no restaurant here, but breakfasts are served.

Calle M-1 and Av. 24, Manta. (*C* 05/2621-671 or 09/9944-554. www.vistalmarecuador.com. 5 units. $79 (£43) double; $106–$119 (£58–£65) 2-bedroom cabaña. Rates include full breakfast. DC, V. **Amenities:** Lounge; small outdoor pool; laundry service. *In room:* A/C, TV, coffeemaker.

INEXPENSIVE

Hostel Manakin *(Value)* There are plenty of real budget options in Manta, but most are run-down. Housed in a converted home in a residential neighborhood just a few blocks from the sea, this place is friendly, secure, and stylish. The rooms are simple yet sleek, with subdued colors on the walls offset by bright bedspreads with eye-popping geometric patterns. The common areas are very inviting, and include an indoor lounge area, an outdoor garden patio, and a simple restaurant.

Calle 20 and Av. 12, Manta. (*C* 05/2620-413. www.hostelmanakin.com. 9 units. $25–$50 (£14–£28) double. Rates include full breakfast. AE, DC, MC, V. **Amenities:** Restaurant; laundry service. *In room:* A/C, TV, no phone.

WHERE TO DINE IN MANTA

In addition to the more formal restaurants listed below, you really can't go wrong at any of the open-air seafood joints that line the Malecón Esenico on Playa Murciélago. All have a wide menu of *ceviches,* fish, shrimp, lobster, and mixed seafood plates for around $2.50 to $6 (£1.40–£6). Of these, **Las Velas** (no phone), toward the western end of the strip, is my favorite, with pretty patio tables under broad canvas umbrellas. Another good option, toward the eastern end of the walkway, is **Peces & Peces** (*C* 05/2623-574).

For Ecuadorian fare and local seafood, consider **Rincón Criollo** (*C* 05/2264-668), on Avenida Flavio Reyes and Calle 20.

MODERATE

El Velero ★ *(Finds)* INTERNATIONAL This place has arguably the best setting in Manta, on a canvas-covered wraparound deck overlooking the water at the Manta Yacht Club. The restaurant is ostensibly only open to yacht club members, but I've always been able to sweet-talk my way in as an eager tourist. The menu is simple, and very inexpensive. There's a wide range of *ceviches*—with everything from fish, octopus, and squid to lobster and langoustines—which locals have for breakfast, lunch, and afternoon snacks. The more substantial plates include a tuna steak in a pineapple sweet-and-sour sauce, and steak in a red-wine reduction. For a filling meal you can opt for a hearty plate of seafood linguine.

Av. Malecón and Calle 15, at the Manta Yacht Club. ℰ 05/2623-505. Reservations recommended. Ceviches $2.80–$17 (£1.55–£9.25); main courses $3.36–$5.75 (£1.85–£3.15). AE, DC, MC, V. Daily 9am–5pm.

Palmeiras ℱ INTERNATIONAL/STEAKHOUSE   Popular with locals and the nearby university crowd, this casual restaurant features a cool and funky open-air setting, with a stone patio floor, hanging wind chimes, and palms, ficus, and other lush tropical plants and flowers. The tables and chairs are plastic lawn furniture, although the tables do have faded tablecloths and glass-enclosed candles. The centerpiece of the menu, and of the restaurant itself, is the large, open, wood-fired grill. The menu features a wide range of grilled meats, poultry, fish, and seafood. You can get a whole grilled fish or a mixed seafood-and-meat platter. Portions are huge. I usually do just fine with a half-*cherna* (amberjack). The menu also features such varied options as quail breasts and a wide range of pizzas.

Vía Circunvalación and Av. Flavio Reyes, Manta. ℰ 05/2628-637. Main courses: $5–$22 (£2.75–£$12). AE, DC, MC, V. Daily 4:30pm–2am.

INEXPENSIVE
Topi Tu Pizza ITALIAN/PIZZA   Head for the second-floor of this lively open-air bar and restaurant. The tables overlook a busy round-about on the Avenida Malecón, but if you look beyond this, you'll have a view of the equally busy harbor. The pizzas here are excellent, and come with a wide range of toppings. You can also get some simple pastas, as well as more substantial seafood fare. I like the seafood spaghetti, which is loaded with fresh fish, crab, and shellfish in a tangy marinara sauce.

Av. Malecón and Calle 15. ℰ 05/2621-180. Main courses $3–$8 (£1.65–£4.40). MC, V. Daily 11:30am–1am.

MANTA AFTER DARK
Thanks to the city's steady and healthy local tourism industry, combined with the U.S. military base here, Manta actually has a relatively vibrant bar and club scene. The best and most popular bar and dance club in town is **Madera Fina** (ℰ **05/2610-507**), on Avenida Flavio Reyes and Avenida 23. **Tantra** (ℰ **05/2613-727**), on Avenida Flavio Reyes and Calle 20; and **Krug Pub** (ℰ **05/2624-700**), on Avenida Flavio Reyes and Calle 18, are two other popular clubs. For a more mellow night out, head to Malecón Esenico and grab a seat at one of the many outdoor restaurants and bars there.

If you want to try your luck at some gambling, head to the **Fantasy Casino** (ℰ **05/2629-200**) at the Hotel Oro Verde. This is a big, modern, glitzy casino with all the tables, games, and machines you could want. There's also a flashy new casino in the small strip mall attached to the Howard Johnson hotel.

AL NORTE: AN ISOLATED BEACH GETAWAY
The road north from Manta to Bahía de Caráquez passes a series of small, isolated beach towns, which get by on small-scale fishing much more than tourism. Still, if you really want to get away from it all and have a car or driver of your own, this might be right up your alley. The first major beach north is **San Jacinto,** which is precious little more than a few houses on either side of the highway. But the **Hotel San Jacinto** (ℰ **09/6218-407**) is an interesting option, in a worn old wooden building, with a

pool, restaurant, and weekend discothèque, not to mention a perfect location right on the beach.

North of San Jacinto lies San Clemente, which doesn't have much to offer tourists. However, when the tide is low, you can actually drive directly on the sand beach to Bahía de Caráquez, cutting many miles and quite some time off your trip. Most locals use this route, and even some of the bus companies take advantage of the savings in time and distance. You probably shouldn't try this on your own because the "exits" off the beach aren't marked, but ask around town, or flag someone down as they begin this route and ask to follow them.

2 Bahía de Caráquez ✦

340km (161 miles) W of Quito, 280km (418 miles) NW of Guayaquil, 120km (434 miles) N of Manta

BAHIA DE CARAQUEZ

Known simply as Bahía, or "the Bay," this quiet little port city is one of the safest, friendliest, and homiest spots in Ecuador. It's located at the mouth of the Río Chone, whose shifting bottoms and shallow channel have limited Bahía's usefulness as a port, while saving it from the woes that often accompany heavy industry and commercial shipping. In addition, a whole host of tours and adventures can be organized out of Bahía, ranging from bird-watching, to boating, to visiting an archaeological site.

In 1999, Bahía declared itself an "Eco-City," and efforts to promote recycling, conservation, and environmental awareness were instituted by a combination of local and outside actors.

ESSENTIALS
GETTING THERE & DEPARTING

BY PLANE   There is a small airport in San Vicente, just across the bay from Bahía. There are occasional charter flights into San Vicente, but for the nearest commercial airport, try Manta. See p. 269.

BY BUS   Cooperativo Reina Camino (© 02/2572-673 in Quito, or 05/2695-818 in Manabí province) has three buses daily to Bahía leaving at 10:30am, 1pm, and 11:30pm. The final bus is direct, with no stops, while the 1pm bus actually goes to San Vicente, a short ferry ride across the bay from Bahía. The ride takes about 8 hours. Return buses leave at 6:20am, 9am, and 10:15pm. Fares run $8 to $10 (£4.40–£5.50).

There's much more frequent bus service between Guayaquil and Bahía, with buses leaving roughly every hour around the clock. Both **Cooperativo Reina Camino** (© 04/2140-757 in Guayaquil) and **Coactar** (© 04/2140-078 in Guayaquil, or 05/2690-014 in Bahía) do this route. The ride takes about 6 hours, and fares cost $6 to $8 (£3.30–£4.40).

There is also regular bus service between Bahía and Puerto Viejo and Manta. The main bus terminal in Bahía is at the southern end of the Malecón, although most arriving buses drive into the center of town to drop off passengers before ending up at the terminal.

BY CAR   To reach Bahía by car from Quito, you will need to start off heading south on the Pan-American Highway (E35) until the intersection at Aloag. From here, you will head west on E30 towards Santo Domingo de los Colorados and then on to Chone. In Chone, there's a well-marked turnoff for the road to Bahía. The ride should take around 7 to 8 hours.

GETTING AROUND

BY TAXI   Taxis are abundant in Bahía, and largely unnecessary if you are sticking close to the downtown and Malecón area. There are actually two types of taxis to choose from: traditional car cabs, and what the locals call "eco-taxis," which are bicycle-powered rickshaw-type contraptions with the driver pedaling behind a small sitting area with two wheels on either side. There's a two-person maximum in the eco-taxis. A normal cab ride anywhere around town will run you $1 to $2 (55p–£1.10). The eco-taxis charge about half as much.

BY BOAT TAXI & FERRY   Bahía is connected to the small city of San Vicente, just across the bay, by a steady stream of boat taxis and ferries. The larger ferries, which carry vehicles, leave from a spot on the Malecón just across from a small triangular plaza, a block or so north of the passenger ferry or boat-taxi dock. Car ferries run roughly every half-hour between 6:30am and 9pm daily. The fare is $3 (£1.65) per car, and the crossing takes 20 to 25 minutes.

The boat taxis are small, faster boats that can carry around 10 passengers. Boat taxis run around the clock and basically leave whenever they are full. However, the frequency and number of ferries is greatly reduced in the wee hours. Rates are 35¢ (20p) per person on the boat taxis, with a slight surcharge after 10pm. If it's really late and there's no other traffic, you can hire a boat to take you across for $10 (£5.50). This crossing takes around 10 minutes.

FAST FACTS   The **post office** is located on Calle Aguilera, just off the Malecón. The Ministry of Tourism maintains an **information desk** (✆ 05/2691-124) at Avenida Bolívar 700 and Calle Mateus.

There are several banks and ATMs in the small downtown area. The biggest and best of the bunch is **Banco de Guayaquil** (✆ 05/2692-205), at the corner of Avenida Bolívar and Calle Río Frío.

There are a handful of Internet cafes all around the center of Bahía. Two of my favorites are **Genesis Net** (✆ 05/2692-400), on the Malecón across from the boat taxi dock, and **Multim@x** (✆ 09/9717-596), on Avenida Bolívar, between calles Mateus and Checa. Rates run around 50¢ to $1.50 (30p–85p) per hour.

ORIENTATION

Bahía is a long, narrow city that follows the inner coast of the bay out to the end of a jutting peninsula. All along the bay shore and out to the peninsula's point is a sidewalk promenade, the Malecón. The peninsula runs roughly north-south, with the point located at the northern end, where there's a small lighthouse. A few small parks, the ferry docks, and the Repsol service station, all located on the Malecón and the 2 blocks inland from here, define the heart of downtown. At its widest, Bahía is only 5 or 6 blocks wide. The central north-south avenue, located inland from the Malecón, is Avenida Bolívar, along which you'll find the town's greatest concentration of shops, banks, and other businesses.

WHAT TO SEE & DO IN BAHIA

My favorite thing to do in Bahía is walk around the quiet town and along the seafront Malecón. Be sure to stop in at the small Catholic church, inaugurated in 1906; it's made of zinc brought in from France. If you want something more engaging, several interesting tour and activity options are available.

The **Museo Arqueológico del Banco Central (Central Bank Archeological Museum)** ✿ (✆ 05/2690-817) is definitely worth a visit. Spread over three floors,

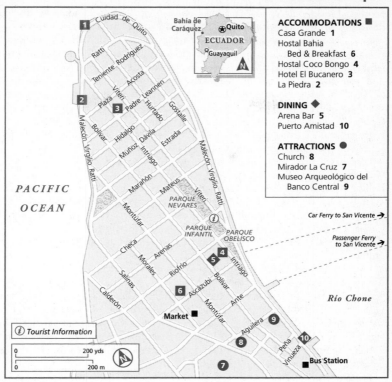

ACCOMMODATIONS ■
Casa Grande **1**
Hostal Bahia
  Bed & Breakfast **6**
Hostal Coco Bongo **4**
Hotel El Bucanero **3**
La Piedra **2**

DINING ◆
Arena Bar **5**
Puerto Amistad **10**

ATTRACTIONS ●
Church **8**
Mirador La Cruz **7**
Museo Arqueológico del
  Banco Central **9**

Car Ferry to San Vicente →
Passenger Ferry
to San Vicente →

PACIFIC
OCEAN

Río Chone

ⓘ Tourist Information

Market ■

Bus Station ■

the museum focuses on the history and archaeology of the coastal people of pre-Columbian Ecuador, although one large room is dedicated to modern art. Still, the heart and soul of the collection here are relics and artifacts of the Las Vegas, Machalilla, Valdivia, Tolita, Bahía, and Jama peoples who inhabited this coast for centuries before the arrival of the Spanish. At the entrance lobby, you'll find a massive balsa raft, with a mast and mannequins, believed to be a replica of those used in ancient times to navigate up and down the Pacific coast. The museum is open Tuesday through Saturday from 10am to 5pm, and on Sundays and holidays from 11am to 3pm. Admission is $1 (55p).

You should also take a trip to **Mirador La Cruz** ✦, a lookout located on a high hill directly behind the city. You can make the brisk hike up here in about 15 minutes, or you can grab a cab. The view is wonderful and really allows you to get a feel for the lay of the land and the bay. When I last visited, they were sprucing up the lookout area, building a small reception area to greet tourists, and adding a restaurant and small information center. The installations should be ready by mid-2007.

The beaches right in and around Bahía are passable but unspectacular. Both to the north and south, however, you will find excellent beaches. Heading south, you'll come to the beaches of **Chirije** ✦ (see below), **San Clemente,** and **San Jacinto,** which are really part of one very long stretch of almost deserted beach, broken up by the occasional rocky outcropping and small house or settlement. Heading north, you'll find a similar situation with the beaches of **San Vicente, Briceño,** and **Canoa** ★ (see below). Canoa can be easily reached by boat taxi and bus from Bahía. If you want to visit any other of these beaches, you'll have to hire a car or taxi. Be sure to bring some food and plenty of water and sunscreen, as there are very few restaurants or services.

If you want to get out on the water, check in with the folks at **Marina 69** (© 05/2691-057; www.marina69.com), who rent out small boats, sailboats, and jet skis ($40–$60/£22–£33 per hour). They will also take you waterskiing or parasailing ($30/£17), or, if you've got a group, they will tow you all behind a speedboat on a large, inflatable banana ($2/£1.10 per person, minimum six people). Marina 69 is located on the Malecón, next to the Repsol gas station.

Land-based tours center on bird- and wildlife-watching. The local tour agency, **Guacamayo Bahía Tours** (© 05/2691-412; www.riomuchacho.com), located on Av. Bolívar 902 and Calle Arenas, can arrange these types of tours and adventures. Their most popular tour is a 3-day/2-night participatory stay on their Río Muchacho organic farm, which is located up the coast from Bahía 10km (6 miles) north of Canoa. They also offer a 5-day program at the farm, which includes intensive language classes, and they have city tours as well as tours to visit an organic shrimp farm, located up the Río Chone estuary, or tours to nearby dry forests.

Bird-watchers will want to take a trip to **Isla del Corazón,** which is located in the Río Chone estuary upstream from Bahía. Isla del Corazón is a large mangrove island with a raised wooden walkway and trail through the mangroves. A wide range of water birds can be spotted here; there's a particularly healthy colony of frigate birds. The best way to visit these islands is on a guided tour. Check in with **Guacamayo Bahía Tours,** which offers a day tour for $26 (£14). Alternatively, boats can be hired near the docks in Bahía to tour these islands for around $12 (£6) per hour, although your captain and guide will most likely not speak English.

South of Bahía lies the archaeological site of **Chirije** ★. Although barely excavated, early indications are that Chirije was once a major indigenous settlement, and probably an important port and trading center. You can even stay at some simple beachfront cabins here (see below). To visit Chirije, you should sign up for a tour in town, or contact the hotel listed below directly.

Bahía is not a shopper's paradise. Along the Malecón you'll find a line of souvenir stands and kiosks that sell all sorts of trinkets, T-shirts, and arts and crafts. But the general selection and quality are rather lacking.

WHERE TO STAY
MODERATE
Casa Grande ★ *Finds*   Located in a converted home, this intimate bed-and-breakfast is a welcoming and homey option out on the northern end of the peninsula, right near the lighthouse. Rooms are large, with dark-stained wood floors, air-conditioning, and private bathrooms. A television can be requested but is not standard in all rooms. In a backyard garden, which has a view of the ocean, there's a pretty, free-form pool encircled by a broad brick deck, and the house is chock-full of excellent Ecuadorian art works. A large, common second-floor balcony offers a good sea view. These folks also have a unique beach hotel down in Chirije (see below).

Av. Circunvalación Virgilio Ratti, Bahía de Caráquez. © 09/9894-075. 5 units. $50 (£28) double. Rates include full breakfast. No credit cards. **Amenities:** Lounge; bar; tour desk; laundry service. *In room:* A/C, no phone.

La Piedra ⓚ *(Kids)*   The largest and fanciest hotel in town, La Piedra is located at the tip of the peninsula. The hotel is built in an open horseshoe around a midsize pool and deck area, and fronts a narrow patch of beach. All the rooms—sparsely furnished—are spacious with cool tile floors. I prefer those on the second story, which has high ceilings and slightly better views. Each rooms on the first floor has a table and chair set up on the shared veranda, which, inexplicably the rooms on the second floor lack—although they also have a shared veranda. The second-floor unit nos. 217 and 218, as well as room no. 302, are my favorite rooms, because each has a private seafront balcony. This is a good choice for families with kids since it's the only true beachfront hotel in Bahía, and they also have a game room, pool table, and beach volleyball court.

Av. Circunvalación Virgilio Ratti 802, Bahía de Caráquez. ℂ **05/2690-780.** Fax 05/2690-154. www.cialcotel.com. 42 units. $65 (£36) double; $70 (£39) suite; $80 (£44) presidential suite. AE, MC, V. **Amenities:** 2 restaurants; bar; tour desk; laundry service. *In room:* A/C, TV.

INEXPENSIVE
Hostal Bahía Bed & Breakfast   This longstanding budget option is located in a 140-year-old building in the heart of downtown. The building and most of the rooms, however, show their age. A few units have air-conditioning. What the hostel lacks in the way of refinement it makes up for in the knowledgeable and jovial attention provided by owner Jacobo Santos, who—if you can get him to do so—provides the best guiding services in the area.

Calle Ascazubi 322, Bahía de Caráquez. ℂ **05/2690-146.** hc4js@ecua.net.ec. 20 units, 14 with private bathroom. $12 (£6.60) double with shared bathroom; $16 (£8.80) double with private bathroom. Rates include full breakfast. No credit cards. **Amenities:** Lounge; laundry service. *In room:* A/C, no phone.

Hostal Coco Bongo *(Value)*   Located a block inland from the water, this is my top choice for a budget *hostal* in Bahía. All the rooms are located on the second story and feature wood floors and a variety of bed arrangements, although most have bunk beds. There's a large television in a common lounge area, as well as a shared balcony facing a small park and the bay. With its cheery *hostal* vibe, the Coco Bongo often has evening activities, which range from DVD movie nights to Latin dance and capoeira classes.

Malecón Alberto F. Santos 910 and Arenas, Bahía de Caráquez. ℂ **09/7390-897.** cocobongo@hotmail.com. 5 units. $20 (£11) double. Rates include full breakfast. No credit cards. **Amenities:** Lounge; laundry service. *In room:* No phone.

Hotel El Bucanero *(Value)*   Housed in a converted home toward the northern end of the peninsula, this place offers clean, cozy accommodations at a great price. All the rooms have tile floors, air-conditioning, and DirecTV, and those on the second floor feature high ceilings. Most rooms come with one twin and one queen-size bed. But if you can, get room no. 3, which is large with one king-size bed and a small private balcony—it's definitely worth a few extra dollars for a private bathroom. There's a big common living area on the ground floor.

Calle Laennen and Av. Intraigo, Bahía de Caráquez. ℂ **05/2690-016** or 09/8129-876. www.el-bucanero.com. 7 units; 5 with private bathroom. $25 (£14) double with shared bathroom; $30 (£17) double with private bathroom. Rates higher during peak periods (major holidays). Rates include full breakfast and taxes. AE, MC, V. **Amenities:** Restaurant; bar; tour desk; laundry service. *In room:* A/C, TV, no phone.

WHERE TO DINE
MODERATE
Puerto Amistad ⓚ *(Finds)* INTERNATIONAL   This is easily the best restaurant in Bahía. Set on a large, open-air dock extending out into the bay, the Puerto Amistad, with its bamboo-and-thatch roof, is a cool and pleasant place to be day or night.

Options range from sandwiches and quesadillas to a number of main courses. The restaurant claims to have the best hamburgers in Ecuador, and they are pretty good, as are their grilled steaks. Still, I prefer the excellent fish and seafood platters. And I usually start things off with some of their tasty vegetable fritters. For a main course, I recommend the shrimp curry over white rice, or the *filete a la Gloria,* a piece of fresh mahimahi in a caper sauce. There's a good wine list to go along with the extensive menu. The main operation here caters to cruising sailors who anchor just off the dock and use the shore facilities. For this reason, it's a great place to come and mingle with some water-worn old salts.

Malecón Alberto F. Santos, south of the passenger ferry dock. © 05/2693-112. Main courses: $5–$9.50 (£2.75–£5.25). DC, MC, V. Daily noon–midnight. Sometimes reduced hours in the low season.

INEXPENSIVE

Arena Bar ITALIAN/PIZZA   I like the funky, eclectic vibe of this simple pizza joint. The pizzas are pretty good, with a medium-thin crust and a wide range of topping choices. You can also get pasta dishes and homemade lasagna. Vegetarians will want to try the vegetarian parmesan, which is excellent. There are a few tables out on the sidewalk, and more inside two abutting dining rooms. Most of the tables are made of heavy cross-sections of tree trunks. The decor relies heavily on photo collages of various celebrities, ranging from Madonna, Marilyn Monroe, and Andy Warhol to Julio Cortázar, Compay Segundo, and Che Guevara. There's also some original art and a wall of masks over the small bar area.

Av. Bolívar. © 05/2692-024. Main courses: $3–$4.80 (£1.65–£2.65); large pizzas $8.50–$13 (£4.70–£7.40). No credit cards. Mon–Sat noon–2pm and 5pm–midnight; Sun 5pm–midnight.

AFTER DARK

Bahía is definitely a quiet town after dark. When locals want to really party, they usually head up the coast to Canoa (see below). The liveliest in-town bar and dance club is **Eclipse,** located on the Malecón, just north of the car-ferry dock. For a hip, late-night club scene, head to the tiny new **Mika Bar,** on Avenida Bolívar.

If you want a pleasant couple of drinks in a beautiful setting, head to **Expats,** on the Malecón just north of the passenger-ferry dock. If you do come here, be sure to head up the back stairs to the open-air rooftop bar and dining area.

A REMOTE BEACH HOTEL SOUTH OF BAHIA

Chirije *Finds*   This small collection of rooms and *cabañas* sits on a rise just off the beach a few miles south of Bahía, and is backed by a vast expanse of untouched tropical dry forest. Everything here is built with bamboo and thatch, and solar energy is used to heat the water and power some of the lights. The best rooms are the two A-frame units, which feature a sleeping loft and have a balcony and ocean view. There's a small museum here with some very interesting artifacts, as well as a display illustrating the process of archaeological digging in this area. The hotel's restaurant and bar overlook the sea. The restaurant features a huge tree trunk as its center support, and serves fresh seafood and local fare. Miles of deserted beach run in either direction from the hotel, and you will definitely feel far removed from everything if you stay here.

The best way to get here is to coordinate transportation with the hotel, which charges around $10 (£5.50) per person. You can drive here along the beach at low tide, and there is also a more circuitous inland route. No matter what, you need to reserve ahead.

On the beach in Chirije, Manabí. © 09/9754-773. chirije@telconet.net. 4 units. $40 (£22) double. Rates include full breakfast. No credit cards. **Amenities:** Restaurant; bar; tour desk; laundry service. *In room:* No phone.

3 Canoa ⟨★⟩

265km (164 miles) W of Quito, 299km (430 miles) NW of Guayaquil, 19km (12 miles) N of San Vicente

CANOA

Canoa is a long, straight stretch of salt-and-pepper-colored sand backed by a few dirt roads, which are packed with budget hotels, cheap restaurants, funky bars, and souvenir shops. Behind the town is a steep wall of low cliffs, with a high bluff atop. Parasailers and hang-gliders often use this bluff as a take-off point for their flights. Surfers come to Canoa for the miles of uncrowded beach breaks.

ESSENTIALS
GETTING THERE & DEPARTING

BY PLANE   There is a small airport in San Vicente, which is just 19km (12 miles) south of Canoa. There are occasional charter flights into San Vicente, but the nearest commercial airport is in Manta. See p. 269 for details.

BY BUS   There's no direct bus service to Canoa. You must first make your way to Bahía de Caráquez and then to San Vicente. See p. 277 for details. From San Vicente, local buses make the run to Canoa roughly every half-hour between 6am and 9pm. The fare is 50¢ (30p) for the 30-minute ride.

BY CAR   To reach Canoa by car from Quito, start off heading south on the Pan-American Highway (E35) until the intersection at Aloag. From here, you will head west on E30 toward Santo Domingo de los Colorados, and then on to Chone. After about 24km (15 miles), there's a well-marked turnoff for the road to San Vicente and Canoa. The ride should take around 8 hours.

GETTING AROUND

Everything in Canoa is within walking distance. There are always taxis around town, if you need a ride down to San Vicente, or to one of the hotels on the outskirts of town. If you can't flag one down, have your hotel call you a cab. The ride between San Vicente and Canoa costs around $5 (£2.75).

ORIENTATION

Canoa is a tiny beach town. The main highway between Bahía de Caráquez and the northern beaches of Esmeraldas runs parallel to the coastline and passes right through Canoa. Several dirt access roads run the 4 blocks through town, from the highway toward the sea.

FAST FACTS   Canoa has few services. There are no banks, so if you need to exchange or withdraw money, do so in San Vicente or Bahía (see above). You'll find a couple of Internet cafes in town, and some of the hotels provide Internet connections as well.

WHAT TO SEE & DO IN CANOA

Like Montañita to the south, this is a good beach for surfing, and in fact I prefer Canoa over Montañita—it's a much longer beach with far more peaks to choose from. When the waves are small, this is an excellent beach for beginning surfers. Several little stands and shops around town rent out surf and boogie boards, and if you ask around town you should even be able to find someone to give you lessons.

The bluff above and behind Canoa has become a popular take-off spot for hang-gliders and parasailers. The 150m (450-ft.) bluff, not to mention the frequent updrafts and miles of deserted beach for a landing site, makes this one of the top spots of aerial soaring in Ecuador. Occasionally you can find a local or visiting pilot with a tandem rig to take you for a ride. Ask around town or at your hotel, or head to Hotel Sol y Luna (see below).

Aside from surfing and the technical airborne sports mentioned above, there's not much to do in Canoa except for sunbathing, swimming, beachcombing, and crawling into a hammock. Locals sometimes rent out horses for horseback rides along the beach. Look for them on the beach, or ask at your hotel.

WHERE TO STAY
INEXPENSIVE

Hotel Bambú   This is the most popular budget hotel in town, and it's almost always packed to the gills with backpackers and surfers. Overflow traffic can pitch or rent a tent here, but I recommend trying to reserve a room in advance. Accommodations are rustic and show the effects of constant wear. The best feature here is the open-air restaurant and common area fronting the hotel and facing the sea. Tree-trunk tables are set in the sand under palm and sea-grape trees. There's also an area with hammocks and a beach volleyball court. A bonus: These folks offer up a free drink for every bag of beach trash you collect.

On the northern end of the beach, Canoa. ✆ **05/2616-370** or 09/9263-365. 17 units; 8 with private bathroom. $10 (£5.50) double with shared bathroom; $16–$20 (£8.80–£11) double with private bathroom. DC, MC, V. **Amenities:** Restaurant; bar; tour desk; laundry service. *In room:* No phone.

Hotel La Vista *⟨Value⟩*   I like the thatch and heavy timber construction of this beachfront hotel. Every room here has a balcony with a hammock. The choice room is the fourth-floor penthouse, which, thanks to the height, has the best view. Accommodations come with a variety of bed options from several twins or bunk beds to queen-size beds for couples. Be sure to ask for a fan, since there's no air-conditioning, and not every room is equipped with a fan. The hotel has a restaurant as well as a large sandy area in front with a thatch roof.

On the beach, near the center of town, Canoa. ✆ **08/6470-222.** 9 units. $16–$20 (£8.80–£11) double. DC, MC, V. **Amenities:** Restaurant; bar; tour desk; laundry service. *In room:* No phone.

Hotel Sol y Luna   Located about a half-mile south of Canoa, right on the beach, this is one of the older hotels in town, and one of the only ones with a swimming pool. Most of the rooms are quite large, although some show their age, with worn linoleum floors. The best rooms have tile floors and exposed wood-beam ceilings. I like nos. 7 and 8, which are large second-floor corner rooms with good views and a large shared balcony. Sol y Luna is frequented by surfers, parasailers, and hang-gliders. When I last visited they said they would be building a hotel up on the bluff behind town specifically to cater to airborne thrill-seekers.

On the beach, south of town, Canoa. ✆ **05/2616-363** or 09/8509-203. 19 units. $25 (£14) double. Rates include full breakfast. DC, MC, V. **Amenities:** Restaurant; bar; small outdoor pool; tour desk; laundry service. *In room:* No phone.

WHERE TO DINE
INEXPENSIVE

Café Flor *⟨Value⟩* INTERNATIONAL   Café Flor's owners used to run a popular restaurant in Macas, but they have been happily settled here on the coast for a few years. The menu covers a lot of ground, from vegetarian burritos to thin-crust pizzas, with main courses ranging from garlic shrimp over rice, to baked pork perníl served with two fried eggs on top. Breakfasts are excellent. You can get a shrimp, onion, and pepper omelet or homemade pancakes. Their fresh baked banana bread is delicious, and I like to buy a few extra slices to have as snacks on the beach. When the weather's cool and dry enough, grab one of the outdoor tables set in a sandy garden. When I last visited, the owners were fixing up a few budget rooms above the restaurant to rent out.

2 blocks inland, center of town. (C) 08/6959-928. Main courses $2.50–$4 (£1.40–£2.20). AE, DC, MC, V. Daily 8:30am–11:30pm.

Restaurante Costa Azul *(Value* SEAFOOD/ECUADORIAN There are lots of local restaurants serving seafood and Ecuadorian fare, but this is my favorite. The menu is quite long, with everything from steaks to pastas, but you should stick to the seafood. Start things off with mixed *ceviche* or fried calamari, and then inquire what's freshest. You can get lobster here—a great deal at $8 (£4.40). This open-air, beach-front joint is set on a raised wooden deck with plastic lawn chairs and long wooden tables covered with clear plastic sheets over lace tablecloths. Service is fast and professional, though a bit indifferent.

On the beach road, center of town. (C) 05/2616-376. Main courses $2.50–$8 (£1.40–£4.40). No credit cards. Daily 7am–9pm.

AFTER DARK

Although there are no major clubs or discos, the surfers, backpackers, and Quito vacationers like to party here in Canoa. Most of the action centers on the few open-air bars near the center of town, which include **Mambo Bar, Coco Bar,** and **Coco Loco.** One new place that is trying to regularly get folks dancing is the **Shamrock Dance Bar,** which takes up two floors of a three-story building right on the beachfront in the center of town. On any night, there might be live music or a DJ at any of the above. Ask around town to find out what's going on, or simply walk till you find something that suits you.

NORTH ALONG THE COAST: FROM CANOA TO ESMERALDAS

As you drive north along the coast from Bahía de Caráquez and Canoa toward Atacames and Esmeraldas, the lowland dry forest and scrub give way first to cattle ranches and farms, and then later to thick tropical rainforest and moist forests. The change is quite pronounced, and, in fact, happens almost immediately as you pass the sign announcing the start of Esmeraldas province.

At Km 342 is **Pedernales,** a rather undeveloped, and at times forlorn, little beach town—though one on the rise. Relatively new highways make this the closest Pacific beach to Quito, by car or bus. Pedernales is a long, straight beach of salt-and-pepper-colored sand, which almost disappears at high tide. Like Atacames (see below), the beach itself is strung with a line of simple, open-air thatch-roof restaurants and bars, and backed with a few low-end hostels and hotels. The town, located on a hill behind the beach, is a jumble of shops and businesses, with a busy central park that is fronted by an interesting modern church. If you decide to stay in Pedernales, I recommend **Hostal Teguendama** ((C) **05/3701-250** or 09/1989-819), a cute little beachfront hotel, with simple rooms, most of which share a common veranda facing the beach. Another option is **Hotel Mr. John** ((C) **05/2681-107**), which also fronts the beach and features many rooms with private balconies. For food, you'll definitely want to try the seafront **La Choza** ((C) **05/2680-388**).

Heading north, at Km 261, is the entrance to **Mompiche** ✹, which is a mile or so toward the sea from the highway. There's almost nothing going on in Mompiche right now, but that may change in the future—I hear that developers covet this mostly undiscovered gem. Currently, it's primarily surfers who know about Mompiche and its beautiful left point break. If you decide to stay here, try the new **Hostería Gabeal** (✆ **09/9696-543**).

4 Esmeraldas

319km (198 miles) W of Quito, 472km (293 miles) N of Guayaquil, 185km (115 miles) W of Santo Domingo

ESMERALDAS

When the Spanish first landed here in 1526, they were greeted by indigenous peoples wearing all manner of emerald jewelry and adornments, so they named the place Esmeraldas, meaning "emeralds." The local tribes never provided the Spaniards with much in the way of riches, and the conquistadors soon sought their fortunes elsewhere. Today Esmeraldas is the main port and transportation hub for this region and the capital of the province. It is also a major oil-processing and shipping point, with the recent completion of a Trans-Andean pipeline bringing in fresh crude from El Oriente.

And while there are scores of hotels and some decent beaches here, most visitors make a beeline to Atacames and its surrounding beaches (see later in this chapter). But if you're coming out to this neck of the woods, you'll almost certainly pass through Esmeraldas. Moreover, Esmeraldas serves as a good gateway for the very remote northernmost section of Ecuador's Pacific coast, which includes San Lorenzo and La Tolita.

ESSENTIALS
GETTING THERE & DEPARTING
BY PLANE **Tame** (✆ **02/2909-900** in Quito, or 06/2726-863 in Esmeraldas; www.tame.com.ec) and **Icaro** (✆ **1800/883-567** central reservation number, or 06/2727-951 in Esmeraldas; www.icaro.com.ec) both have daily flights between Quito and Esmeraldas's **Aeropuerto General Rivadeneira** (✆ **06/2729-119**; airport code: ESM). The schedules on these flights change frequently, and departure times vary from mid-week to weekends, so it's always best to check current schedules while booking. Flight time is 30 minutes, with fares running from $42 to $54 (£23–£30) each way.

Taxis meet all incoming flights. A taxi from the airport to Esmeraldas should run you around $10 to $15 (£5.50–£8.25).

BY BUS Several bus lines have regular daily service to Esmeraldas from Quito. Buses leave at least every half-hour all day and night. Bus lines running this route include **Transportes Esmeraldas** (✆ **02/2505-099** in Quito, or 06/2721-381 in Esmeraldas) and **Cooperativo Occidentales** (✆ **02/2502-735** in Quito, or 06/2723-772). All of Occidentales and about half of Transportes Esmeraldas buses leave from the main bus terminal in Quito (Terminal Terrestre). The rest of Transportes Esmeraldas buses leave from their own terminal on Calle Santa María 870 and Avenida 9 de Octubre. The ride takes around 6 hours and costs $5 to $6 (£2.75–£3.30). The buses in Esmeraldas all stop and leave from a variety of stops located within a 1-block radius of the town's main plaza.

There is also frequent bus service between Esmeraldas and Guayaquil, as well as periodic connections throughout the day between Esmeraldas and other major cities, including Manta, Ambato, and Santo Domingo.

Esmeraldas: Ecuador's African Coast?

Though only about 3% of Ecuador's population traces its roots to Africa, 70% of the people in Esmeraldas province are Afro-Ecuadorian. Most of its inhabitants are the descendents of maroons—escaped slaves who lived in free communities.

Legend has it that the first Africans arrived in Esmeraldas in 1553, when a slave ship ran aground off the coast and the captives escaped. What is certain is that by the late 16th century, the area had a thriving maroon population that attracted a steady trickle of runaways from the gold mines and sugar plantations of Colombia. The Africans mixed with local Indians, who shared their knowledge of the region's flora and fauna, and established communities known as *palenques* along the main rivers and the coast, some of which were fortified to fend off Spanish attacks.

Though the maroon leaders maintained sporadic relations with colonial authorities in Quito, for the better part of the 17th century, Esmeraldas virtually operated as an independent state ruled by a series of Afro-Amerindian kings. The Spaniards referred to the region as "La República de los Zambos," or "Zambo Republic," the term *zambo* being used to designate the offspring of an Indian and an African in the colonial caste system.

Though a few military campaigns made unsuccessful attempts to subdue the area, Esmeraldas's maroon communities lived in relative freedom and isolation for most of the colonial era, which allowed them to preserve a culture markedly different from that of the rest of Ecuador. It was one of dozens of areas in the Americas where escaped slaves managed to establish autonomous enclaves during the colonial era, but in terms of numbers and organization, Esmeraldas was one of the most important. It rivaled Palmares, a maroon kingdom near the Brazilian city of Bahía, which it took the Portuguese a century to subdue.

Just as the African traditions preserved in Palmares gave birth to the *samba* and *batucada*, Esmeraldas, too, has its traditional music, sometimes called *currulao*. This rhythmic style combines drums and marimbas—a xylophone-like instrument of African origin—and is usually accompanied by the gyrating hips of dancers, who are capable of shaking it for hours, despite the equatorial heat.

As it did in most of the world, the 20th century brought rapid change to Esmeraldas, eroding many of the region's traditions. Nevertheless, you can still get a taste of the province's African heritage by savoring an *encocado*—a coconut seafood stew—or by tracking down a bar with a band that plays *currulao*.

BY CAR   To reach Esmeraldas by car from Quito, you will need to start off heading south on the Pan-American Highway (E35) until the intersection at Aloag. From here, you will head west on E30 toward Santo Domingo de los Colorados, and from there follow the well-marked highway (E25) straight into Esmeraldas. The ride should take a little over 5 hours.

If you are coming from Manta or Bahía de Caráquez, I recommend taking the coastal road, which heads first to Jama and then to Pedernales, before continuing up the coast to Muisne, Atacames, and, eventually, Esmeraldas.

Esmeraldas is also connected by paved road to La Tola, Borbón, and San Lorenzo to the north. This paved road actually also hooks up with another paved road that loops around northern Ecuador, connecting San Lorenzo with Ibarra.

GETTING AROUND

Taxis are plentiful and inexpensive in and around Esmeraldas. Rides around town are just $1 (55p). A ride out to Las Palmas will cost around $2 (£1.10).

Frequent bus service connects Esmeraldas with Atacames and the beaches southwest down the coast. These buses leave from around the central plaza roughly every 20 minutes between 6am and 10pm. The direct buses to Atacames are the most frequent, although a dozen or more also continue on and stop in Sua, Same, Tonchigue, and Muisne. Some even continue on to Mompiche.

If you want to rent a car, **Localiza** (© **06/2711-761**) has an office on the Malecón and Calle Delgadillo.

FAST FACTS   There's a **tourism information office** on Av. Bolívar 221, between Calle Mejía and Calle Salinas (© **06/2714-528**). It is open Monday through Friday from 9am to 5pm. **Banco del Pichincha** (© **06/2728-741**) has a branch in downtown Esmeraldas, as well as one out in Las Palmas. Both have 24-hour cash machines.

The **Hospital Esmeraldas** (© **06/2710-012**) is located about midway between downtown and Las Palmas. The **post office** is located on Avenida Colón, between 10 de Agosto and 9 de Octubre. The main **police station** is on the corner of Avenida Bolívar and Calle Cañizares.

You'll find Internet cafes all over downtown and in Las Palmas. Rates run around 50¢ to $1.50 (30p–85p) per hour.

ORIENTATION

The center of Esmeraldas sits on the banks of the Río Esmeraldas, a few miles from the beach. A Catholic church faces the city's main central park, and 1 block east of this is the city's Malecón, which runs along the river. Most of the banks, shops, and services are located within a 2-block radius of this central park. The **Las Palmas** beach area, located 3.2km (2 miles) north of the town center, is reached by heading out Avenida Bolívar.

WHAT TO SEE & DO IN ESMERALDAS

The main attraction in town is the **Museo de Arqueología Regional (Museum of Regional Archeology;** © **06/2727-078;** admission $1/55p; Mon–Fri 9am–5pm, Sat–Sun 10am–4pm). Housed in the new Centro Cultural Esmeraldas (Esmeraldas Cultural Center), which also has a small library, bookshop, and gift store, this modern museum's collection features over 500 pieces of ceramic, bone, gold, and iron. There's a good selection of pieces from the La Tolita indigenous group.

The main beach area of Esmeraldas proper is **Las Palmas,** located 3.2km (2 miles) north of town. The beach at Las Palmas is a long broad stretch of brown sand, which usually has gentle waves and is good for swimming. The seaside Malecón here is packed with simple open-air restaurants and bars. During Esmeraldas's annual Carnaval, which celebrates the town's Afro-Ecuadorian heritage, Las Palmas is ground zero for some impressive revelry. Each year the celebrations coincide with the locally produced **Festival Internacional de Música y Danza Afro (International Festival of African Music and Dance),** and feature dancing in the streets, organized parades, and marimba band competitions. As with other Carnaval and Mardi Gras celebrations around the world, Esmeraldas's Carnaval occurs each year in the period prior to Lent.

If you want to do any organized tours, check in with your hotel desk or contact **Delgado Travel,** Calle Sucre 627 and Calle Cañizares (℃ **06/2723-723**), a large, national tour agency. Possible tours include sport fishing, whale- and dolphin-watching, and visits to La Tolita (see below) and the mangrove forests of the Cayapas Mataje Ecological Reserve.

WHERE TO STAY IN ESMERALDAS
INEXPENSIVE
Aparthotel Esmeraldas   This plush downtown hotel gives you plenty of space, comfort, and amenities for the price. The rooms are almost stylish, with shiny tile floors and modern furnishings. Located several blocks north of the central park, the Aparthotel Esmeraldas is popular with businesspeople. There's a good restaurant here, and they even have a small casino, for those in the mood to gamble.

Av. Libertad 407 and Ramón Tello, Esmeraldas. ℃ 06/2728-700. ℃/fax 06/2728-704. www.aparthotelesmeraldas.com. 44 units. $35–$38 (£19–£21) double; $48 (£26) suite. DC, MC, V. **Amenities:** Restaurant; bar; small casino; tour desk; laundry service. In room: A/C, TV, minibar.

El Cisne (Value)   This is a clean, dependable, and safe bet right in the heart of Esmeraldas. The rooms are decidedly simple and could use a bit more decoration and style, but they'll definitely do for a night or two. The restaurant serves good Ecuadorian cuisine and local specialties. El Cisne is located just a block and a half from the main plaza, close to a host of restaurants, shops, and bus stops.

Av. 10 de Agosto between Olmedo and Colón, Esmeraldas. ℃ 06/2721-588. ℃/fax 06/2723-411. 35 units. $20 (£11) double. DC, MC, V. **Amenities:** Restaurant; bar; tour desk; laundry service. In room: No phone.

Hotel Cayapas (✦)   Because I'd almost always rather stay at the beach than in town, this is my top choice in Esmeraldas. It's in Las Palmas, right on the beachfront, and the rooms here are cheerful and well-appointed. They even have a pretty little garden in back. The hotel's restaurant is very good, with excellent seafood and local specialties.

Av. Kennedy 100 and Valdéz, Las Palmas, Esmeraldas. ℃ 06/2721-318. Fax 06/2721-319. 17 units. $30–$40 (£17–£22) double. DC, MC, V. **Amenities:** Restaurant; bar; tour desk; laundry service. In room: A/C, TV.

WHERE TO DINE IN ESMERALDAS
The food in Esmeraldas province is distinct. Making ample use of the fresh seafood and other local ingredients, including coconuts, it is more like Caribbean cuisine than typical Ecuadorian fare. Local dishes include *encocado* (seafood in a slightly spiced coconut-milk broth), *empanadas de verde* (fried stuffed patties made with a plantain crust), and *tapao* (a fish and plantain stew).

Las Redes (Finds) SEAFOOD/ECUADORIAN   Facing the main plaza and church, this popular downtown joint can get packed, especially mid-week when local workers and businesspeople come for the daily *plato ejecutivo,* a three-course lunch for around $2 (£1.10). The seafood and local fare are top-notch here. Try the *encocado de camarones* (shrimp in a coconut-milk broth).

Av. Bolívar, fronting the main plaza. ℃ 05/2723-151. Main courses: $2.50–$8 (£1.40–£4.40). MC, V. Daily 7am–10pm.

Nuevo Amanecer SEAFOOD/ECUADORIAN This casual place fronts the beach in Las Palmas, and has an extensive menu of seafood dishes, including a wide range of *ceviches*. However, you can also get a thick steak or a chicken breast grilled over an open flame. But I recommend that you stick with the seafood. The *tapao* (fish and plantain stew) here is excellent.

Malecón, Las Palmas. (© 06/2725-339. Main courses: $3–$9 (£1.65–£4.95). DC, MC, V. Daily 8am–9pm.

ESMERALDAS AFTER DARK

The best nightlife to be had in Esmeraldas is on the coast in **Las Palmas.** Your best bet is to simply walk the Malecón here and stop into a few of the many open-air beachfront bars.

If you stay in the city itself, I recommend sticking very close to the bars, clubs, and restaurants around the central plaza. Esmeraldas has a reputation of being somewhat unsafe after dark. Single women should take particular caution. **Bar Asia,** on Avenida Bolívar near the main plaza, is a good option. If you're feeling lucky, you can always head to the casino at the **Aparthotel Esmeraldas** (see above).

NORTH FROM ESMERALDAS: SAN LORENZO & LA TOLITA

Heading north from Esmeraldas, the vegetation and terrain turn quickly from forest and pastureland to an immense area of mangroves, rivers, and canals. The main town up here is **San Lorenzo,** an Afro-Ecuadorian city that feels a world apart from the rest of the country. San Lorenzo was once connected by railroad to Ibarra, but the train no longer runs, and a road has been built to take its place.

There aren't many recommended places to stay in San Lorenzo. The surest bet in town is the **Gran Hotel San Carlos,** calles Imbabura and Juan José Flores (© 06/2780-284), which offers acceptable rooms—some that even have air-conditioning and televisions.

One of the most unique places to visit in Ecuador, however, is situated on a small island in the midst of mangrove forests outside of San Lorenzo. **La Tolita** 🎯 is an archaeological site, believed to be the remnants of one of the oldest pre-Columbian cultures in Ecuador. The people here smelted and worked with platinum, silver, and gold. It's not clear if La Tolita was a residential site or purely ceremonial one. "Tola" is the word for a small, elevated mound or grave. When the area was first discovered, there were over 50 tolas on the island, although many have been plundered and destroyed. One of the most fascinating parts of a visit to La Tolita is Santiguero Beach, where, instead of sand or stones, the shore is littered with millions of shards of pre-Columbian pottery.

Most of the mangrove forests around San Lorenzo are protected as part of the **Cayapas-Mataje Ecological Reserve.** There are no real services or trails in this reserve; in fact it is principally accessible by boat. A boat ride through the rivers, canals, and lagoons here is an excellent opportunity to spot hundreds of waterfowl, as well as caiman and other wildlife. The mangrove trees in this reserve are the tallest in the world, with some reaching nearly 60m (200 ft.).

You can hire a boat in San Lorenzo to take you to La Tolita or through the Cayapas-Mataje Reserve. **Coopseturi** (© 06/2780-161) will provide a boat and guide for around $12 (£6.60) per hour. But I think it's best to make day-trip arrangements through a hotel or tour agency in Esmeraldas or Atacames.

Warning: Although San Lorenzo is practically on the Colombian border, it is not recommended that you cross into Colombia here. Ongoing guerrilla activity and drug trafficking activities make the area on the Colombian side rather dangerous for tourists.

By far, the best place to stay in this region is **Kumanii Lodge** ⭐ (📞 **800/747-0567** in the U.S. and Canada; www.kumanii-lodge.com), located in the Chocó Rainforest. The lodge is run by members of the local Chachi indigenous and Afro-Ecuadorian tribes. Accommodations are a bit rustic, but the wildlife-viewing, cultural interaction, and sense of isolation make it definitely worthwhile. You can either fly directly into a small airstrip near the lodge, or take a 2½-hour boat ride upriver from the coastal mangrove town of Borbón.

5 Atacames & the Beaches West of Esmeraldas ⭐/⭐

349km (216 miles) W of Quito, 442km (274 miles) N of Guayaquil, 30km (19 miles) SW of Esmeraldas

ATACAMES & THE BEACHES WEST OF ESMERALDAS

This is probably my favorite stretch of beaches in Ecuador. Leaving Esmeraldas and heading west, or, more precisely, southwest along the coastline, you'll come to a string of beaches, most of which have broad swaths of white or cream-colored sand fronting a blue-green sea. These beaches run the gamut from bustling tourist resort towns, to isolated getaways with just a few cabins, to secluded secret spots where surfers pitch tents and ride wave after wave.

Just outside Esmeraldas is **Tonsupa** ⭐, a beautiful wide beach that is just starting to receive a fair amount of attention and development, which makes sense, since it is so close to the city. Heading a little farther southwest is **Atacames** ⭐, the most developed beach resort town on this coast. The seafront Malecón in Atacames is jam-packed with hotels, bars, restaurants, and shops.

Sua ⭐ is around 6.5km (4 miles) southwest of Atacames, **Same** ⭐⭐ around 8 miles (13km) southwest of Atacames. One of the most undeveloped beaches along this coast, Sua is located between two high bluffs, with a handful of fishing boats anchored offshore. Much larger is Same, with its broader beach backed with scores of vacation condos. Many of these condos are whitewashed and set on the surrounding hillside in such a way that Same has a Mediterranean feel.

Beyond Same lie ever more remote and out-of-the way beaches and small fishing villages, including Tonchigue and Galera. At Galera the coastline turns and heads south to the isolated little island of Muisne (see below).

ESSENTIALS
GETTING THERE & DEPARTING

BY PLANE   The nearest airport to these beaches is in Esmeraldas (p. 286). There are always taxis waiting for incoming flights. A taxi from the airport in Esmeraldas costs about $20 to $30 (£11–£17).

BY BUS   **Transportes Esmeraldas** (📞 **02/2505-099** in Quito, or 06/2721-381 in Esmeraldas) buses leave from Quito for Atacames roughly every hour between 7am and 11pm. The 6½-hour trip costs $5 to $8 (£2.75–£4.40). About half of Transportes Esmeraldas buses leave from the main bus terminal in Quito (Terminal Terrestre), with the rest leaving from Esmeraldas's own terminal, on Calle Santa María 870 and Avenida 9 de Octubre. While not a hard and fast rule, the departure site alternates pretty much one-for-one throughout the day. Your best bet is to call Transportes Esmeraldas to confirm the schedule before leaving. The bus stops in Atacames are all near the main park and Catholic church, east of the main bridge.

Local buses run between Atacames and Esmeraldas roughly every 20 minutes between 6am and 10pm. Those between Esmeraldas and destinations farther down the coast also leave consistently throughout the day. These buses stop in Atacames, Sua, Same, Tonchigue, and Muisne. Some continue on to Mompiche.

BY CAR   To reach Atacames and the surrounding beaches, follow the directions to Esmeraldas (p. 286). On the outskirts of the city of Esmeraldas, you will see a well-marked exit for the coastal road that passes by Atacames, Same, Sua, and Muisne.

GETTING AROUND

You'll have no trouble flagging down a taxi or one of the open-air motorcycle-powered cabs in Atacames. You can also call **Taxis Alfa Omega** (© 06/2760-710) or have your hotel call for you. Taxis to the neighboring beaches cost $5 to $10 (£2.75–£5.50) each way . If you do get a ride to one of the neighboring beaches, it's a wise idea to arrange a specific pickup for your return trip.

FAST FACTS   There's a branch of **Banco del Pichincha** (© 06/2731-029) on Calle Cervantes, between calles Montalvo and Espejo. While there's no bank in Same, there is a cash machine in the small convenience store just outside the Club Casablanca hotel (see below).

There are a handful of **Internet cafes** all over Atacames. Just head to the Malecón and pick one that has working air-conditioning and modern-looking equipment. Rates run around 50¢ to $1.50 (30p–85p) per hour. When I last visited, none of the other surrounding beach towns had an Internet cafe, although that could change at any time.

ORIENTATION

The town of Atacames is divided into sections by the curving Río Atacames, which enters the town as a narrow river but broadens considerably as it flows parallel to the ocean, toward the north end of town, before finally joining the sea. The main coastal highway runs through the center of Atacames and then southwest down the coast, with well-marked turnoffs for all of the other beach towns mentioned here.

WHAT TO SEE & DO IN & AROUND ATACAMES

Sunbathing, swimming, and relaxing are the main activities here. While there are sometimes good waves to be caught at the beach breaks all up and down this section of coast, serious surfers will want to head to the point break at **Mompiche** (see above). You can rent jet skis and Hobie Cats from a variety of stands set up on the beach. Rates run from $10 to $20 (£5.50–£11) per hour.

If you want to do any organized tours, check in with your hotel desk, or contact **Delgado Travel** (© 06/2723-723) a large, national tour agency with an office in Esmeraldas. Possible tours include sport fishing, whale- and dolphin-watching, and visits to La Tolita and the mangrove forests of the Cayapas-Mataje Ecological Reserve (see above).

GOLF   Club Casablanca (© 06/2733-159) has a 9-hole regulation course designed by Jack Nicklaus, but it doesn't get much use or upkeep. In fact, the course was in extremely bad shape the last time I visited. Still, if you're an avid golfer, or if you want to add an exotic course location to your list of places played, you can certainly head out for a round. The course is supposed to be reserved for members and guests at the Club Casablanca, and you may not be able to get a tee time or permission to play during very busy weekends or holidays. But I've found they'll usually let outside guests play during the week and slow periods. Greens fees are $50 (£30) for a round of 18 holes (twice around the course). Club rentals will run an extra $20 (£11), and a cart is $15 (£8.25).

WHERE TO STAY IN & AROUND ATACAMES

The beach hotels here tend to fill up on Friday afternoon and empty out on Sunday. If you're arriving on the weekend or during a holiday week, I recommend you have a reservation. Mid-week, almost every place is nearly empty.

MODERATE

Club Casablanca   This place has the reputation as being one of the top beach resorts on Ecuador's northern Pacific coast—a somewhat sad commentary on what's available along Ecuador's best beaches. The Casablanca sits on a beautiful stretch of beachfront, in the midst of a major condominium and apartment complex. The rooms are perfectly acceptable, though most were in dire need of some upkeep and remodeling when I last visited. The best rooms directly front the beach, with a small porch between you and the sand. There's a midsize rectangular pool in the center of the hotel, as well as a small children's play area and a beach volleyball net. The Casablanca has four tennis courts, two clay courts, which are lit, and two synthetic-surface courts, which are not. Guests have access to the neighboring golf course (see above). The restaurant, which is a delightful open-air space fronting the beach, serves good local cuisine and excellent thin-crust pizzas from a wood-fired brick oven. The hotel also rents out fully equipped apartments.

On the beach, Same. ℂ **06/2733-159** at the hotel, or 02/2252-488 reservations in Quito. Fax 02/2253-452. www.ccasablanca.com. 43 units. $65–$90 (£36–£50) double. Rates include full breakfast. AE, DC, MC, V. **Amenities:** Restaurant; bar; midsize outdoor pool; 4 tennis courts; tour desk; laundry service. *In room:* A/C, TV, no phone.

Hotel Juan Sebastián   One of the most popular beach hotels in Atacames, this massive place caters to Ecuadorian families as well as Quiteño revelers. Accommodations come in a variety of sizes, with several multiroom options, many featuring bunk beds for large families or student groups. In my opinion, the best rooms are the individual cabins; they give a slightly greater sense of privacy and isolation, which is welcome when this place is really cranking. The hotel claims to have the largest pool in Ecuador, a free-flowing affair built to resemble a series of connected lagoons. The bar, located right near the pool, even has a giant TV screen for karaoke.

On the Malecón, Atacames. ℂ/fax **06/2731-606** in Atacames, or 02/2240-364 in Quito. 65 units. $80–$120 (£44–£66) suite. Rates include breakfast buffet. Lower rates in the off season. DC, MC, V. **Amenities:** Restaurant; bar; large free-form outdoor pool; tour desk; laundry service. *In room:* A/C, TV, minifridge, safe.

INEXPENSIVE

In addition to the places listed below, if you want to stay in picturesque and isolated Sua, your best bet is the simple **Hostal Chagra Ramos** (ℂ **06/2731-006**), which is beautifully located on a piece of land that stretches right from the beach up a small hillside.

Hotel Cielo Azul 🜢 *(Kids*   This great option on the beach. The hotel is built in an L-shape around a small pool and Jacuzzi, and faces the sea. Rooms are plenty spacious and kept spotless, with cool tile floors and private balconies or patios. I prefer the second-floor rooms, with ocean view. However, most of the offerings here are actually two-bedroom suites, set up for families, with a master bedroom for the parents and a mix of twins and bunk beds in the second bedroom. The rooms don't have air-conditioning, but they all come with fans, and most of the beds come with mosquito netting. The pool area is very popular with guests, and features a small stone waterfall as well as a poolside restaurant serving excellent seafood and local cuisine.

Av. 21 de Noviembre, near the stadium, Atacames. ©/fax 06/2731-813 or © 09/4662-783. 11 units. $46 (£25) double; $88–$136 (£48–£75) suite. Rates include 12% IVA tax. Lower rates in the off season. Children under 12, 50% discount. DC, MC, V. **Amenities:** Restaurant; bar; small outdoor pool; tour desk; laundry service. *In room:* TV, minifridge, no phone.

Hotel Der Alte Fritz This German–Ecuadorian-owned-and-run hotel is located in a five-story building on the Malecón, painted bright white. The rooms are large and immaculate, with plenty of light. Most have a private balcony. You'll definitely want one of the rooms in the taller section of the building, toward the rear. Those fronting the Malecón can get a lot of the local partying noise at night. The hotel has a good tour operation with a wide range of available tour options, as well as a popular restaurant on the ground floor, facing the beach.

On the Malecón, Atacames. ©/fax 06/2731-610. www.deraltefritz-ecuador.com. 20 units. $20–$35 (£11–£19) double. Rates include full breakfast. DC, MC, V. **Amenities:** Restaurant; bar; tour desk; laundry service. *In room:* No phone.

Villas Arco Iris *(Finds* This is a cozy collection of two-story cabins on the slightly quieter, eastern end of Atacames. The units have thatched roofs, whitewashed walls, and a small front porch with a hammock. Rooms are simple, and slightly rustic inside, but they feature private bathrooms, air-conditioning, and small fridges. Some come with kitchenettes. The whole complex is set in a lushly planted garden area, with tall palms overhead and a central sandy lane. In the back is a pretty little pool with a large deck area around it. The owners have just finished building a major high-rise resort and condominium nearby, called the **Arco Iris Resort** (www.arcoirisresort.com), but, in many ways, I find that the older rooms here have more character.

On the Malecón, east end of Atacames. © 06/2731-069. Fax 06/2731-437. 27 units. $25–$45 (£14–£25) double. MC, V. **Amenities:** Restaurant; bar; small outdoor pool; tour desk; laundry service. *In room:* A/C, TV, minifridge, no phone.

WHERE TO DINE IN & AROUND ATACAMES

All the beach towns here have their share of simple seaside restaurants serving fresh fish, *ceviche,* and local cuisine. Pick any one that seems sanitary and inviting, and you can't go wrong. In addition to the place listed below, you can get good pizzas and pastas, not to mention an excellent view of the ocean, at **Pizza Terraza** (© 06/2733-320) in Same.

MODERATE

Sea Flower Restaurant *★★★ (Finds* INTERNATIONAL   If these folks hadn't built up such a stellar reputation, it'd be a real surprise to find this type of dining in a simple restaurant in Same. They focus on fresh seafood—as most beach restaurants do—but this place stands out for its creative dishes. Salads are served in a giant abalone shell, which itself is set in a massive slab of wood. A wide range of seafood is served in a variety of styles—in a spicy coconut milk broth, over spaghetti, simply grilled, or sautéed with garlic. The *pescado a la portuguesa,* a fresh filet of mahimahi baked in a terra-cotta bowl with a subtle passion-fruit and tomato sauce, is served piping-hot in the same clay bowl in which it was cooked. All meals come with a salad and hearty fresh-baked bread. But save room for dessert: delicious and decadent. The service is casual yet professional, and the ambience is a sort of rustic beach elegance, with thick cotton tablecloths, heavy Mexican glassware, and an eclectic mix of jazz, blues, and world music.

1 block inland from the beach, Same. © 06/2733-369 or 09/8147-536. Reservations recommended. Main courses: $7–$25 (£3.85–£14). DC. Daily 11am–10pm. Hours reduced in the low season.

ATACAMES AFTER DARK

Atacames has a well-deserved reputation as a party town. The beachfront Malecón is lined with an almost uninterrupted string of open-air thatch-roof bars that compete for your business nightly with loud reggae and Latin music, and cheap drink specials. This is the perfect strip for a leisurely pub crawl, stopping in at whichever spot seems the most happening or appealing. Many of these shacks have celebrity-sounding knock-off names like **Friend's Bar, Cheer's, Hard Rock Cafe,** and **Planet Atacames.** Two of the more established dance clubs include the **Scala Disco Club** (© 06/2730-131) and **Ludos** (© 09/9666-269), both on the Malecón.

There's much, much less nightlife to be had at the beaches west of Atacames; in fact, they are rather dead after dark. Though that can be a good thing to some travelers.

MUISNE: ALMOST YOUR OWN ISLAND

One of the most remote beach destinations in Ecuador, **Muisne** is a small island fishing community located some 42km (26 miles) southwest of Atacames. There's no road directly here, although the buses leaving Esmeraldas and Atacames will say MUISNE. The buses leave you at a small pier in the village of El Relleno, from which you take one of the nearly constant little boats across the Río Muisne to the island. The fare is 20¢ (10p). The boat-taxis run throughout the daylight hours and often into the early evening. Pedal-powered Ecotaxis await the boat-taxis and will take you to the tiny village, and anywhere else on the island, for $1 (55p). There are only a couple of places to stay on the island. The beachfront **Hostal Playa Paraíso** (© 06/2480-192) is your best bet, with rustic rooms and individual cabins going for $10 to $20 (£5.50–£11) for a double. The beach in Muisne is long, broad, and almost always nearly deserted. Ask at the hotel or around town, and you should be able to organize a boat tour through nearby mangroves. Aside from that and sunbathing, there's not much else to do here except enjoy the beach, sea, and tranquillity.

6 Santo Domingo de los Colorados

134km (83 miles) W of Quito, 287km (178 miles) N of Guayaquil, 185km (115 miles) E of Esmeraldas

Set in the lowlands just below the western slope of the Andes, Santo Domingo de los Colorados is a major transportation hub connecting coastal and southern Ecuador with Quito and the rest of the country. It is also set in the center some of the country's most productive agricultural lands, where bananas, palm nuts, pineapples, cacao, and more are grown.

The city gets its name from the local indigenous group, the Tsachilas, who paint their hair a bright red using an achiote paste. Seeing this, the early Spaniards dubbed them *los colorados* (the colored ones). When the area was colonized and converted by Dominican priests, the town was christened Santo Domingo de los Colorados.

ESSENTIALS

GETTING THERE & DEPARTING

BY BUS   Buses leave Quito for Santo Domingo roughly every 15 minutes between 4:30am and 10pm. Two bus lines work this route with equal frequency, **Cooperativo Aloag** (© 02/2570-020 in Quito, or 02/2758-750 in Santo Domingo) and **Cooperativo Zaracay** (© 02/2570-244 in Quito, or 02/2763-716 in Santo Domingo), with some smaller companies also running fewer buses. All buses leave from the main terminal (Terminal Terrestre). The ride takes about 3 hours. The fare is around $3 (£1.65).

Santo Domingo is also connected by frequent bus service to cities such as Guayaquil, Ambato, Ibarra, Esmeraldas, Manta, Pedernales, and Puerto Viejo. Less-frequent direct service runs between Santo Domingo and Bahía de Caráquez, Cuenca, Lago Agrio, Coca, Mindo, and Riobamba.

Santo Domingo's main bus terminal is located about 3.2km (2 miles) north of the center of town, just off Avenida Abraham Calazacón, near this avenue's intersection with Avenida Esmeraldas and Avenida de las Tsachilas. Taxis are always available at the bus station. A ride to downtown will cost $1 (55p).

BY CAR   If you're driving from Quito, start off heading south on the Pan-American Highway (E35), until the intersection at Aloag. From here, you will head west on E30 straight to Santo Domingo de los Colorados. The road from Aloag descends precipitously and provides a mix of hair-raising white-knuckle switchbacks and spectacular views. On a clear day, you can even see the Pacific Ocean in places. The ride should take about 2½ hours.

From Guayaquil, you can head to Quevedo on either Highway E23 or E25. From Quevedo, E25 continues on direct to Santo Domingo. From Guayaquil, the trip takes around 3½ hours.

GETTING AROUND

Taxis are plentiful in and around Santo Domingo. A ride to or from the bus station, or anywhere around downtown, should cost $1 to $2 (55p–£1.10). If you can't simply flag one down on the street, have your hotel call one for you, or try **Taxis Sudamericano** (© **02/2752-567**).

For a cheap city tour, you can hop on any bus marked CENTRO or TERMINAL, which will run a short circuit around town, and between the central plaza and the main bus terminal. The fare is 20¢ (10p).

If you want to rent a car while here, **Localiza** has an office on Avenida 29 de Mayo, between San Miguel and Las Provincias (© **02/2742-315**; www.localiza.com.ec). Rates run around $45 to $90 (£25–£50) per day, including unlimited mileage and insurance.

FAST FACTS   The **post office** is located on Avenida de los Tsachilas, near Calle Río Baba. There's a branch of **Banco de Guayaquil** at the corner of avenidas Quito and Abraham Calazacón (© **02/2769-033**), and a branch of **Banco del Pichincha** at Avenida La Paz and Calle Santa Rosa. Both have 24-hour ATMs (© **06/2722-300**).

Several Internet cafes are located around the downtown area, as well as near the bus station, and most hotels in town also offer access. Rates run around 50¢ to 1.50 (30p–85p) per hour.

ORIENTATION

The main road from Quito enters Santo Domingo and becomes Avenida Quito, which passes through the heart of the downtown area. The central plaza is bordered by Avenida Quito on the south, and has the city's Catholic church on its north side. The park here is large, with paths and benches set amid gardens and grass lawns. There's a large market area several blocks west of the main plaza.

WHAT TO SEE & DO

There is very little of interest to tourists right in Santo Domingo, although you can use this busy city as a base for a reasonable range of activities, including rainforest hikes, bird-watching excursions, visits to a Tsachila community, and white-water rafting trips. For any organized tours or activities around Santo Domingo, contact

Red-Haired Boys

Although they only number some 3,000, the Tsachila are one of the most distinctive indigenous groups in Ecuador, well-known for their healers and shamans. Today, the Tsachila live in eight community groups in the area surrounding Santo Domingo. Most dedicate themselves to farming and cattle ranching. As part of their traditional dress, the men use a thick paste made from the achiote seed to mat down and color their hair, and wear a knee-length wraparound skirt, with black and white horizontal stripes, tied at the waist with a red belt. For ceremonies and healings, both the men and women paint their bodies with horizontal black lines said to be indicative of the snake or serpent spirit. It is rare, but not unheard of, to see Tsachila in their traditional garb walking around Santo Domingo.

Delgado Travel, Avenida Quito and Calle Cocaniguas (© **02/2760-036**), or **Turismo Zaracay,** Avenida 29 de Mayo and Cocaniguas (© **02/2750-546**).

The best attraction close to Santo Domingo is the **Jardín Botánico La Carolina (La Carolina Botanical Gardens)** ℛ (© **02/3761-380**), located just a few miles outside the city center at the Km 2 marker on the road to Chone. The gardens have a broad series of well-marked, self-guided trails, and they will even provide a bilingual guide if you reserve in advance. Exhibits include ornamental and medicinal plants, orchids, and native and introduced hardwoods. The bird-watching here is often excellent. The Jardín is open daily from 9am to 4pm, and admission is $1.50 (85p), children half-price.

Even if you're not staying there, bird-watchers and nature enthusiasts can tour the trails and forests at **Tinalandia** ℛ (see below). Both of the tour agencies mentioned above offer day trips here for around $24 (£13) per person. Alternatively, you can head directly to Tinalandia, which offers lunch and free run of its trails and facilities for $12 (£6.60) per person.

WHERE TO STAY & DINE IN SANTO DOMINGO

There's no great dining scene in Santo Domingo. In many cases, your best bet will be your hotel restaurant. If you find yourself in the city and hungry, head to **D'Marco,** on Calle Río Mulaute near Calle Río Baba (© **02/2751-741**), or to **Restaurante Timoneiro,** on Avenida Quito near Tsachila (© **02/2751-642**).

MODERATE

Gran Hotel Santo Domingo ℛ   This is easily the plushest hotel in steamy Santo Domingo. It's hard to miss this four-story white-concrete behemoth with tinted windows, which seems a bit out of place in this hot and rugged agricultural city. Inside, though, you'll find a cool oasis. Rooms have an almost stately feel, with subdued tones and dark-wood furniture and trim. Most have private balconies or patios overlooking the central pool area. The restaurant here is the fanciest in town, and certainly one of the most dependable.

Rio Toachi and Galápagos, Santo Domingo de los Colorados. © **02/2767-948.** Fax 02/2750-131. www.grand hotelsd.com. 40 units. $45–$65 (£25–£36) double; $75–$85 (£41–£47) suite. AE, DC, MC, V. **Amenities:** Restaurant; bar; small outdoor pool; Jacuzzi; sauna; small gym; tour desk; 24-hr. room service; laundry service. *In room:* A/C, TV, dataport, minibar, safe.

INEXPENSIVE

Hotel Del Pacífico   This is your best option right in downtown Santo Domingo. This new hotel offers modern, comfortable accommodations just 2 blocks in either direction from the main plaza and main market. All the rooms are spacious and well-appointed, but the presidential suites are especially large, with separate sitting areas and upgrades like a king-size bed, air-conditioning, 74cm (29-in.) television, minibar, and hair dryer, which aren't included in the standard accommodations. Every room does come with either one, two, or three queen-size beds, a small wooden desk and chair, and a fan.

Av. 29 de Mayo 510, between Ibarra and Latacunga, Santo Domingo de los Colorados. ℭ 02/2752-806. srpacifico@ plus.net.ec. 40 units. $26–$28 (£14–£15) double; $65 (£36) suite. AE, DC, MC, V. **Amenities:** Restaurant; bar; tour desk; laundry service. *In room:* TV.

Hotel Zaracay   Located just on the outskirts of Santo Domingo, this is a sprawling complex with extensive grounds and pleasant gardens. The least expensive rooms here are rather dated, and only come with a fan. It's worth the splurge for one of the newer units, which are roomier and come with air-conditioning and a minifridge. In addition to the tennis court and pool, there are volleyball and basketball courts. This is a popular place for Ecuadorian business conferences and weekend retreats, and there's even a small casino. The hotel is named after Joaquin Zaracay, a famous contemporary Tsachila chief.

Km 1.5 on the road to Quito, Santo Domingo de los Colorados. ℭ 02/2750-316. Fax 02/2754-535. www.hotel zaracay.com. 61 units. $28–$36 (£15–£20) double; $50–$75 (£28—£41) deluxe. AE, DC, MC, V. **Amenities:** Restaurant; bar; casino; small outdoor pool; unlit outdoor tennis court; tour desk; laundry service. *In room:* TV.

SANTO DOMINGO AFTER DARK

There's plenty of nightlife in Santo Domingo, although much of it is rough and ragged. Prostitutes hang around the main plaza after dark, and tourists should be very careful about walking around then. I recommend that you take a taxi to and from any bar or nightclub. **Aruba Disco,** on Avenida de los Tsachilas and Avenida 29 de Mayo; and **Salsoteca,** out on Avenida Quito, are two of the better dance clubs in town.

NEARBY NATURE LODGES

Kashama ★★ *(Finds* This delightful jungle lodge and spa is set in lush forests on the shore of the Río Blanco. Located just 20 or so minutes away from Santo Domingo, it feels much, much more isolated. The rooms are all distinctively designed and decorated, with an emphasis on local materials. All units are spacious and bright, with white walls offset by colorful wood and paint accents. There's a large outdoor pool here with a tall sculpted waterfall filling one end. The Cascada Spa offers a wide range of traditional spa and massage treatments, many of them integrating local herbs, muds, or ritual into the deal. Nearby nature trails include a hike to a beautiful waterfall with a perfect wading pool below it. Rafting, horseback riding, and trips to the local indigenous communities are also offered.

Km 26 on the road to Esmeraldas, Valle Hermoso, Santo Domingo de los Colorados. ℭ 02/2773-193. ℭ/fax 02/ 2773-465. www.kashama.com. 20 units. $90–$120 (£50–£66) double. Rates include 3 meals daily. DC, MC, V. **Amenities:** Restaurant; bar; outdoor pool; Jacuzzi; sauna; tour desk; laundry service. *In room:* TV.

Tinalandia ★   Unlike Kashama, which lies in the lowlands west of Santo Domingo, Tinalandia is in the foothill slopes of the Andes east of the city in moist cloud forest. The bird-watching here is spectacular, with over 350 species recorded. The main lodge sits high on a steep bank over a small river. I find the rooms a tad dark and dated, but they are certainly plenty comfortable. A wide range of tours and activities are offered, but bird- and wildlife-watching are the strong suits. They actually have a little 9-hole "jungle" golf course, but it gets more use as a bird-watching zone. There's a pretty mid-size pool, with a great views of the surrounding forests. A full meal plan here, which is basically necessary, will run you $30 (£17) per person per day.

Km 16 on the road to Santo Domingo. ℭ/fax **02/2449-028,** or 09/9467-741. www.tinalandia.com. 16 units. $85 (£47) double. DC, MC, V. **Amenities:** Restaurant; bar; midsize outdoor pool; 9-hole golf course; tour desk; laundry service. *In room:* No phone.

El Oriente

The vast territory of Ecuador that stretches from the eastern slopes of the Andes to the border with Peru is known as El Oriente, which means "the east." This area contains over 25% of the nation's territory and is commonly called the Amazon region (Las Amazonas) because the rivers here—created by melting snow from the Andes—flow into the Amazon. The rainforests of El Oriente have been home to Native Americans for thousands of years. Because of the natural barrier formed by the Andes, the people here have lived in almost complete isolation. Some tribes have only had contact with the "outside world" since the 1970s, when oil was discovered. Since then, development has increased dramatically with the construction of new roads—such as the controversial Macas-to-Guamoote road, which runs through national parkland. Various tribes inhabit Ecuador's Amazon basin, including the Shuar, Cofán, Huaorani, and Quichua. Their languages and lifestyle are markedly different from that of Ecuadorians on the opposite side of the Andes. In order to adapt to somewhat harsh conditions, inhabitants of El Oriente have developed a special relationship with the natural resources of the area. When you take a trip to this region, you'll have the opportunity to meet some of the indigenous people, who will share their land with you and teach you some of their age-old secrets, such as how to farm, fish, hunt, or use medicinal herbs and plants.

In addition to learning about the local cultures, you can explore the incredible biodiversity that exists here. Fifty-seven percent of all mammals in Ecuador live in the Amazon basin, and there are more than 15,000 species of plants in Ecuador's rainforest. You'll have the chance to see more than 500 different species of tropical birds, as well as fresh-water dolphins, monkeys, sloths, anacondas, boas, turtles, and, if you're extremely lucky, the rare and elusive jaguars.

A healthy eco-tourism business has developed here over the past 15 years. Several excellent jungle lodges were built to blend in with the natural environment. Naturalist guides from these lodges take visitors on all sorts of excursions: walks through the forest to learn about the medicinal properties of the local plants; fishing trips to catch piranhas; early-morning bird-watching expeditions to see parrots, macaws, and other tropical species; visits to traditional villages; night-time canoe rides in search of caimans; and outings where you can paddle downriver in an old-fashioned canoe. Just be sure to bring plenty of mosquito repellent!

El Oriente comprises six provinces, but it is generally divided up into two areas: the **northern Oriente** and the **southern Oriente.** For the purposes of this guide, the lodges on and around the Río Napo, Río Coca, and Río Aguarico—which are reached by the gateway cities of Lago Agrio, Coca, and Tena—constitute the northern Oriente. This area has been most affected by the oil industry; charges of environmental destruction and uncompensated profit from indigenous lands and resources have been common,

and conflicts and protests have periodically occurred (see "Down & Dirty in the Jungle" on p. 303). This is also the area that has been most developed for tourism, and all the lodges listed here are quite safe and secure. The southern Oriente, which includes everything south and east of the gateway city of Puyo, is much less developed. However, this area is quite accessible by land from Ambato, Riobamba, and Baños, making it a good place to visit if you plan to be in one of those cities.

HOW TO VISIT EL ORIENTE: JUNGLE LODGES & INDEPENDENT TRAVEL

By far, the easiest way to visit El Oriente is with an organized trip to one of the well-established jungle lodges. These trips usually last 4 or 5 days. Depending on where you're staying, the journey generally involves a commercial flight to Coca or Lago Agrio. Some lodges, like **Kapawi** (p. 322), can only be reached by a charter flight. All the jungle lodges listed below either include transportation from Quito in their packages, or they can arrange transportation for you. *Note:* Because many of these lodges are extremely isolated and difficult to reach, I strongly encourage you to book your trip in advance, either before you come to Ecuador or while you're in Quito.

En Route: A Stop at Papallacta Hot Springs

If you're traveling to Lago Agrio or Coca by land, you might want to consider coordinating your trip so that you stop here for the night, or at least take a soak in the Papallacta Hot Springs. These **soothing sulfur springs** 𝒦𝒦 are perhaps the best hot springs in Ecuador. For more information on the springs and its namesake resort, see p. 137.

If you're looking to reduce costs—or if you want to conveniently combine some time in Baños or Riobamba with a visit to an Amazon-basin nature lodge—consider staying at one of the lodges in or around Tena or Puyo. Most of the lodges listed in these sections are easily accessed by bus, taxi, or rental car.

CLIMATE

Guarded by the high Andes mountains to the west, the lowland rainforests of El Oriente have a climate that's hot and wet most of the time. Well, it's *always* hot, and often wet. Annual rainfall throughout much of this region ranges from 3,000 to 4,500mm (120–175 in.), with some areas getting even more. The wettest months are March through June, the driest August through November. During the rainy season you'll find swollen rivers, muddy trails, and frequent downpours. In the drier months, things dry up some—but never completely. Some of the smaller rivers, canals, and lagoons either dry up, or become impassable. Rain is possible throughout the year, and it's a good idea to pack rain gear and fast-drying clothes. All of the lodges listed in this chapter provide thick rubber boots for hiking.

1 Lago Agrio & Cuyabeno Nature Reserve

Lago Agrio: 259km (161 miles) NE of Quito, 674km (418 miles) NE of Guayaquil, 700km (434 miles) NE of Cuenca

LAGO AGRIO

Sitting on the shores of the Aguarico River, **Lago Agrio** is the main port city and access point for Ecuador's northern Amazon Basin. It is the capital of Sucumbíos province. Officially known as Nuevo Loja (New Loja) because the early settlers were predominantly from Loja, the town is almost universally known now as Lago Agrio, or simply Lago. The name Lago Agrio was given to the town by Texaco oil-company workers, since the home base for this firm is in Sour Lake, Texas.

Today, Lago Agrio is a rough, dirty, and generally unappealing industrial town, and most of the forests and rivers immediately surrounding the town have been clear-cut or polluted by the oil industry. The town serves almost entirely as a necessary transportation hub for those seeking to visit the **Cuyabeno Wildlife Reserve** 𝒦𝒦 and the remote jungle regions further down the Aguarico and Zabalo rivers.

ESSENTIALS

GETTING THERE & DEPARTING

BY PLANE   Tame (🕾 **02/2909-900** central reservation number, or 06/2830-981 in Lago Agrio; www.tame.com.ec) has two daily flights from Quito to the small **Lago Agrio airport** (🕾 **06/2830-442;** airport code: LGQ). This flight originates in Guayaquil and stops in Quito to pick up passengers. There is also one flight from Cuenca to Lago Agrio Monday through Friday, which also stops en route in Quito to pick up passengers. The flight takes 30 minutes one-way from Quito, 90 minutes one-way from Guayaquil, and 2 hours one-way from Cuenca. The fare is $53 (£29) each way from Quito, $106 (£58) from either Guayaquil or Cuenca.

The airport is located about 3.2km (2 miles) southeast of town. Taxis are always waiting to meet incoming flights, and a cab ride between the airport and downtown should cost around $2 (£1.10).

Down & Dirty in the Jungle

For most travelers, Lago Agrio is simply the gateway to Cuyabeno Wildlife Refuge and some of Ecuador's remote jungle lodges. But this Ecuadorian oil town is also the battleground for a billion-dollar lawsuit filed by a coalition of environmental groups against U.S. oil giant Chevron.

The suit's 88 Ecuadorian plaintiffs claim to represent 30,000 people affected by water contaminated by oil operations in the area. It accuses Texaco, which merged with Chevron in 2001, of improperly dumping 18.5 billion gallons of wastewater into pits, swamps, and streams in the Lago Agrio area between 1971 and 1992.

Chevron claims that Texaco's Ecuadorian subsidiary, working together with the state-owned oil company PetroEcuador, operated within the local laws when it dumped oil-contaminated water. (The alternative would have been to use the more-expensive process of re-injecting wastewater, as is mandated in the United States.) The company, which extracted 1.5 billion barrels of oil from the area over the course of 3 decades, points out that it paid $40 million to "remediate" oil sites when its concession expired, and was subsequently given a release by the Ecuadorian government.

Environmentalists say the U.S. company cleaned up very little of the mess it made and claim the company dumped more oil in the Ecuadorian rainforest than was spilled during the Exxon *Valdez* disaster. They say Chevron-Texaco— the second-largest U.S. oil company—should spend billions to clean up the oil it left behind and provide medical care for communities affected by it.

The lawsuit was originally filed in New York in 1993, but after a decade of languishing in the U.S. legal system, an appellate court ruled that the case should be heard in Ecuador. A group of environmental lawyers consequently filed suit in Lago Agrio, *Aguinda vs. Chevron-Texaco,* in which they hope to apply a relatively new Ecuadorian law that mandates that companies cover the cost of cleaning up their pollution.

Environmentalists believe a victory against Chevron would set an important precedent for the developing world, where big corporations often get away with mistreatment of the natural environment. Tragically, despite all the noise made about Texaco, oil companies working in the Amazon basin continue to dump wastewater into streams and rivers, even though they could easily inject it back into the earth at a cost of just a few dollars per barrel. See the websites **www.chevrontoxico.org**, **www.texacorainforest.org**, **www.texacotoxico.org**, and **www.amazonwatch.org** for updates and information on the case.

⟨ Warning   Stay Away from the Border

The Colombian border is only 15km (9 miles) north of Lago Agrio. Instead of being an attraction, though, the border is mostly a source of trouble. The Colombian side of the border is a particularly lawless area, marked by guerrilla and drug-trafficking activity. Some of this spills over from time to time into Ecuador, and this region is a periodic scene of tension between the two countries. The most recent flare-up involves Ecuadorian protests over the Colombians' spraying herbicides on coca plants close to the border. Allegedly the spraying has affected the crops and health of innocent Ecuadorian farmers. What this all means for tourists is that the border area, and any crossing, should definitely be avoided. Moreover, Lago Agrio itself is best used only for transfers in and out of the hotels and jungle lodges listed below.

BY BUS   Buses leave from Quito's Terminal Terrestre for Lago Agrio roughly every half-hour between 6am and 11:30pm. Two main bus lines, **Transportes Baños** (✆ 02/2570-884) and **Putumayo** (✆ 02/2583-316 in Quito, or 06/2833-819 in Lago Agrio), make the run. About half of these buses continue on to Coca. The ride takes about 8 to 9 hours, and the fare is around $8 (£4.40). In Lago Agrio, the Putamayo station is located on the south end of town, on Avenida Río Amazonas and Avenida 12 de Febrero, while the Transportes Baños terminal is north of downtown on Avenida Progreso. Return buses follow roughly the same schedule.

BY CAR   To get here by car, take the highway (E20) east out of Quito to the remote town of Baeza. Here the road forks, with the well-marked northern fork (E45) heading to Lago Agrio. It's 88km (56 miles) from Quito to Baeza, and another 170km (105 miles) from Baeza to Lago Agrio. To get to the highway toward Baeza from downtown Quito, head north on Avenida Eloy Alfaro to Avenida de los Granados and then turn right. This road becomes Highway E20. Follow any signs to Papallacta, Tumbaco Baeza, or El Oriente. The ride should take about 7 hours.

GETTING AROUND

Taxis are readily available all around town. If you can't flag one down on the street, call Taxis Río Napo (✆ 06/288-169) or have your hotel call for you. Fares should be just $1 to $2 (55p–£1.10) anywhere in town.

FAST FACTS   To contact the local **police,** dial ✆ 06/2830-101. There are branch outlets of **Banco de Guayaquil** (✆ 06/2832-314; Av. Quito and 12 de Febrero) and **Banco de Pichincha** (✆ 06/2831-602; Av. Quito and 12 de Febrero). Both have 24-hour cash machines.

If you need any medical care, head to **Clínica González** (✆ 06/2830-728; Av. Quito and 12 de Febrero).

ORIENTATION

Lago Agrio is a compact little city. There is a small park or plaza at the corners of avenidas 12 de Febrero and 18 de Noviembre, which more or less defines the center of the city. However, most of the hotels, restaurants, and tour agencies are located a few blocks south of here, along avenidas Quito and Colombia.

WHAT TO SEE & DO

There's very little to do or see in Lago Agrio itself. For a vast majority of tourists, the town is essentially a transfer point on an itinerary into the deeper reaches of Ecuador's Amazon basin. Just outside of town is the namesake lake, where local authorities have undertaken a small tourism project dubbed **Parque Ecológico Recreativo Lago Agrio (Lake Agrio Ecological Recreation Park),** or **PERLA.** When completed, hopefully sometime in 2007, there will be a few nature trails, a swimming pool, lakeside picnic tables, and other recreational facilities, including canoe or rowboat rentals.

If you're not already traveling here as part of a package tour to one of the lodges listed below, the best way to explore this area is to sign up for a trip with one of the local tour agencies in Lago Agrio. In addition to the two agencies mentioned below, you might try **Cuyabeno Tours** (*C* **06/2831-737**).

Magic RiverTours *☆☆* (*C* **06/2831-003;** www.magicrivertours.com; Av. 21 de Mayo 301) offers a 5-day tour of the Cuyabeno Wildlife Reserve for $285 (£157) per person. Travel is by non-motorized canoes, and accommodations are in a mix of rustic lodges and tents. They will also customize longer or shorter custom tours to your liking.

For something even more unique, you might check out tours offered by the **Cofán Nation** *☆☆* (*C* **02/2470-946;** www.cofan.org). Led by a naturalized American chief, Randy Borman (see box below), the Cofán indigenous people offer multiday guided tours that allow visitors a firsthand experience of the lifestyle, culture, and ecology of this forest-dwelling tribe. Depending on group size and tour duration, trips cost between $65 to $100 (£36–£55) per person per day. *Tip:* The Cofán Nation website includes an extensive online dictionary of the Cofán language.

The **Cuyabeno Wildlife Reserve** *☆☆* is one of the largest and richest in Ecuador, with over 655,781 hectares (1.5 million acres) of protected land. The terrain is very

---

Cofán Chief Randy Borman

Born to American parents in the oil town of Shell, Ecuador, in 1955, Randall Bruce Borman is the current chief of the Cofán Nation. Randy's parents were missionaries who lived with the Cofán. They learned and spoke the language and adopted most trappings of the local lifestyle. Randy was raised almost entirely as a Cofán, although he did receive a modern Western education, including studies at Michigan State University and the Universidad Católica in Quito.

Seeing the destruction of the traditional Cofán lifestyle and ecosystem, Randy led a group of Cofán downriver and founded the village of Zabalo, on the banks of the Zabalo River. Since the establishment of this village, Randy and the Cofán Nation have fought hard to protect not only their heritage, customs, and language but also to preserve the natural habitat that gives them sustenance.

Founded in 1977, the Cofán Community Ecotourism project is often considered the first true community-based tourism project in the world. Today the Cofán Nation, with only some 1,000 people, continues its struggle to survive.

Fun Fact **Calling All Ironmen & Ironwomen**

Each year, El Oriente hosts El Desafío de la Selva (The Jungle Challenge). This 5-day event is based on similar endurance races, often called Eco-Treks. Here, 3-person teams of two men and one woman cover some 280km (174 miles). In addition to the "traditional" tests of mountain biking, kayaking, trekking, swimming, and rope climbing, challenges on this course include fishing for piranha, blowgun target competitions, and the performance of Quichua cleansing rituals. For more information (in Spanish), check out www.hcpo.gov.ec or call © **06/2880-896** or 06/2889-304.

wet, with numerous lagoons, rivers, and lakes. These waters are home to fresh-water river dolphins, as well as to piranha, manatee, anaconda, and five species of caiman. The rainforest canopy and dry land are home to a wide range of tropical flora and fauna. The Siona, Shuar, Cofán, and Secoya indigenous people live here. Almost all tours offered out of Lago Agrio, as well as those from the remote lodges listed below, either take part entirely or partially within the Cuyabeno Wildlife Reserve. There's a $20 (£11) entrance fee to the reserve, which is usually collected by your hotel, tour agency, or canoe captain.

WHERE TO STAY & DINE IN LAGO AGRIO

There are no notable dining options around Lago Agrio. Most travelers choose to simply eat in their hotel restaurant, call it a night, and wake early for a tour into the Cuyabeno Wildlife Reserve. Of the hotel restaurants in town, the Italian fare at **D'Mario** (see below) is a local favorite. When it's not too hot and muggy, their street-side tables are a great spot to sit and people-watch while enjoying a drink or meal.

INEXPENSIVE

In addition to the places listed below, **Hotel Araza** (© **06/2830-223**; Av. Quito 610 and Av. Narvaez) is another good option, in this price range, with clean, air-conditioned rooms.

Hotel D'Mario *Finds* This is my top choice in Lago Agrio. Accommodations are kept immaculate, though the least expensive rooms are rather small and don't have hot water. It's worth a bit of a splurge for more space, hot water, newer furnishings, and more modern decor, as well as—in most cases—a minibar and unlimited Internet access. The hotel has a small pool in a central courtyard area, plus a small but surprisingly well-equipped gym. The restaurant here is one of the better and more popular spots in town.

Av. Quito 263 and Pasaje Gonzanama, Lago Agrio. ©/fax **06/2830-172** or 06/2830-156. www.hoteldmario.com. 17 units. $17–$45 (£9.35–£25) double. Rates include continental breakfast. DC, MC. **Amenities:** Restaurant; bar; small outdoor pool; small exercise room; sauna; tour desk; laundry service. *In room:* A/C, TV.

Hotel El Cofán *Value* This well-located and neat little hotel is a good value. If you end up having to overnight in Lago Agrio and can't find space in D'Mario, you'll appreciate the tidy air-conditioned rooms, which come with cable television to boot. You might also enjoy the ample common areas, the small gym, or the billiards table in the bar. The restaurant here serves good Ecuadorian and international fare.

12 de Febrero 1915 and Av. Quito, Lago Agrio. ℂ **06/2830-526.** Fax 06/2830-456. 30 units. $24–$30 (£13–£17) double. Rates include full breakfast. DC, MC, V. **Amenities:** Restaurant; bar; tour desk; room service 7am–10pm; laundry service. *In room:* A/C, TV, minibar, safe.

NEARBY JUNGLE LODGES
INEXPENSIVE
Cuyabeno Lodge ⋐   While still decidedly rustic on many levels, this humble rainforest lodge provides the most comfortable accommodations inside or near the Cuyabeno Wildlife Reserve. Set on a small rainforest island in the middle of the reserve's Laguna Grande (Big Lagoon), the individual bungalows feature loads of darkstained wood and high thatch ceilings. All units have private bathrooms, mosquito netting over the beds, and large screened windows. Tasty, simple meals are served family style in the main lodge building. A host of tour and activity options are offered.

Laguna Grande, Reserva Faunística Cuyabeno. ℂ **02/2521-212** office in Quito, or 09/9803-395. Fax 02/2554-902. www.neotropicturis.com. 12 units. 5-day/4-night tour $355 (£195) per person, double occupancy. Rates include round-trip transportation from and to Lago Agrio, all meals, nonalcoholic beverages, daily tours, and taxes. Rates do not include the $20 (£11) park entrance fee. MC, V. **Amenities:** Restaurant; bar; laundry service. *In room:* No phone.

Jamu Lodge   This jungle lodge sits on the Cuyabeno River a few minutes downstream from the Laguna Grande. Accommodations are a series of raised duplex wooden bungalows with thatch roofs. The whole complex is connected by a series of raised wooden walkways. The cabins have private bathrooms, shared verandas, and no electricity. Light is provided by candles and oil lanterns. All the standard wildlife-viewing hikes and canoeing are offered. On their trip to the local Siona community, you can learn how to make cassava bread from the yuca root.

Laguna Grande, Reserva Faunística Cuyabeno. ℂ **02/2220-614** office in Quito, or 09/8139-472. www.cabanas jamu.com. 18 units. 5-day/4-night tour $250 (£138) per person. Rates include round-trip transportation from the Cuyabeno bridge, all meals, nonalcoholic beverages, daily tours, and taxes. Rates do not include the $20 (£11) park entrance fee. MC, V. **Amenities:** Restaurant; bar; laundry service. *In room:* No phone.

LAGO AGRIO AFTER DARK
There's really not a lot of action that's of interest to tourists here. If you're looking for a fun time, you could head to **Xavier's Karaoke** (ℂ **09/1880-434**), on Avenida Quito and Avenida 24 de Mayo.

EN ROUTE: SALTO DE SAN RAFAEL & VOLCAN REVENTADOR
Along the main route to Lago Agrio lies the spectacular Salto de San Rafael (San Rafael Falls). At 145m (475 ft.), San Rafael Falls is the tallest waterfall in Ecuador. But these falls are not only tall; they're raging and powerful. The trail head to the falls is marked CAMPAMENTO SAN RAFAEL Y LAS CASCADAS. It's a hike of a little over 1.6km (1 mile) to the lookout across from the base of the falls. The trail can be slippery and muddy at times. Sometimes a local guard will charge $1 admission (55p), though at other times you'll just waltz on through. The rich rainforest and cloud forest here are excellent for bird-watching.

Across the road from the entrance to San Rafael Falls, and just a little to the east, is a trail leading up the Volcán Reventador (Reventador Volcano). At 3,485m (11,430 ft.), Reventador is one of the most active volcanoes in Ecuador. If you want to hike the trail, and even attempt a summit, you should definitely go with a guide who knows the area and who is up-to-date on current volcanic activity. Any of the tour agencies out of Quito, Lago Agrio, or Coca should be able to set you up with a qualified guide.

San Rafael Falls and the Reventador Volcano are located just off Highway E45 on the way to Lago Agrio, about an hour and a half outside of Baeza.

2 Coca & the Lower Río Napo ⟨★⟨★

Coca: 300km (186 miles) E of Quito, 60km (37 miles) S of Lago Agrio

Although officially known as **Puerto Francisco de Orellana,** this riverside port city is known universally as **Coca.** The capital of Orellana province, Coca, like Lago Agrio, is a tiny boomtown carved out of the jungle to service the oil industry. Not surprisingly, it's seedy and rough around the edges. And, like its northern neighbor, Coca is also a gateway to several isolated jungle lodges.

Coca sits on the banks of the Río Napo, which, along with its tributaries, canals, and lagoons, is home to some of the best nature lodges in Ecuador's Amazon basin. Most of the lodges listed below are located a 2- to 3-hour boat ride downstream from Coca. The wildlife viewing here is top-notch.

ESSENTIALS
GETTING THERE & DEPARTING
BY PLANE   Coca is just a 30-minute flight from Quito, and there are numerous flights connecting the two cities. **Tame** (© **02/2909-900** in Quito, or 06/2881-078 in Coca; www.tame.com.ec) has two flights from Quito to Coca Monday through Friday, one in the morning, one in the afternoon, and just one morning flight on weekends. **Saereo** (© **02/3302-280** in Quito, or 06/2880-064 in Coca; www.saereo.com) has one daily flight at 9:15am, returning at 10:05am. **Icaro** (© **1800/883-567** central reservation number, or 06/2883-384 in Coca; www.icaro.com.ec) has five daily flights from Quito, with a reduced schedule on weekends. These schedules are extremely flexible and frequently altered according to demand. Fares run from $52 to $68 (£29–£37) each way.

The **Aeropuerto Francisco de Orellana** (© **06/2880-185;** airport code: OCC) is located on the northern outskirts of town. Taxis meet all incoming planes; a ride from the airport into town should cost $2 (£1.10).

BY BUS   **Transportes Baños** (© **02/2570-884**) runs four buses daily from the main terminal in Quito to Coca; departures are at 7, 8:20, 9:10, and 10pm. These buses go via Loreto, and the ride takes about 9½ hours. Buses to Coca via Lago Agrio leave every half-hour between 6am and 11:30pm. Both **Transportes Baños** and **Putamayo** (© **02/2583-316**) make this run, which is longer and takes about 11 hours. The fare via either route is around $15 (£8.25). Return buses follow roughly the same schedule.

BY CAR   To get here by car, take the highway (E20) east out of Quito to the remote town of Baeza. Here the road forks, with the well-marked northern fork (E45) heading to Lago Agrio, the southern fork to Tena. You can get to Coca via either route, although it's faster to head south toward Tena, and then take the turnoff for Coca. To get to the highway to Baeza from downtown Quito, head north on Avenida Eloy Alfaro to Avenida de los Granados and turn right. This road becomes Highway E20. Follow any signs to Papallacta, Tumbaco Baeza, or El Oriente. The ride should take about 8 hours.

ACCOMMODATIONS & DINING ■
La Selva Jungle Lodge 2
Napo Wildlife Center 4
Sacha Lodge 1
Sani Lodge 3
Yuturi Lodge 5

ATTRACTIONS ●
Cuyabeno Wildlife
  Reserve 6
Yasuní National Park 6

GETTING AROUND

Taxis are relatively plentiful around Coca; no ride, including out to the airport, should cost more than $2 (£1.10). If you can't find a cab on the street, have your hotel call one for you.

Most travelers come here as part of an organized tour, or sign on for an organized tour with one of the local agencies. In this case, transportation down the Río Napo is included. However, it is possible to either jump on one of the regular water taxis that ply this river, or rent one for yourself. Motorized launches can be hired at the main dock at the end of Calle Napo. A boat holding 8 to 10 passengers should cost around $50 (£28) for a ride to most destinations along the Napo.

FAST FACTS   **Banco de Pichincha** (*©* **06/2811-103**), near the corner of Avenida 9 de Octubre and Bolívar, has a 24-hour cash machine. The **post office** is located on Calle Napo, near the corner of Cuenca. You can actually get film developed in under an hour here, at **Foto Coca** (*©* **06/2880-179;** Av. Amazonas and Rocafuerte).

ORIENTATION

Unlike Lago Agrio, Coca has a riverside promenade, or Malecón, which actually received recent cosmetic improvements. These improvements include a mix of brick and wooden walkways, strewn with park benches and minor attempts at landscaping,

Orellana's Journey of Discovery

In a time when even the most remote regions of the Amazon basin seem to be easily accessible, it is hard to comprehend the challenges faced by the Spanish conquistadors. Few of that era's stories are as incredible as **Francisco de Orellana**'s—a man for whom an Ecuadorian province and its capital city are named, and who "discovered" and navigated the length of the Amazon.

That amazing journey began in Quito, but Orellana's tale started several decades earlier, in the south of Spain. Like most conquistadors, he came from the Spanish province of Extremadura, where conditions were grim enough to make joining expeditions to the Americas—from which few people returned—seem like a good idea. Orellana traveled to the West Indies at age of 17 and cut his teeth in Central America. In 1535, he joined an expedition led by his cousin Francisco Pizarro that conquered the Inca empire and captured unfathomable amounts of gold.

Orellana was rewarded for his military service with the governorship of Guayaquil, but the desire for glory, or perhaps simple greed, drove him to join an expedition to find El Dorado: a mythical empire awash with gold. That expedition, led by Francisco's brother Gonzalo Pizarro, departed Quito for the jungles east of the Andes in February of 1541, with 220 Spaniards, horses, indigenous porters, llamas, and livestock. By the time the group reached the confluence of the Coca and Napo rivers, half the men had deserted or died, and the food stores had run out. They built two boats and Pizarro sent Orellana downriver with 50 men to raid indigenous villages for food. But once he had the goods, Orellana was unable to return against the strong current, so he decided to go with the flow. What followed was an 8-month journey down increasingly wide and voluminous rivers, ending at the Atlantic Ocean. They floated past countless indigenous settlements, including one where the riverbank was lined with human heads skewered on posts. But the mythical golden city was not to be found. Some Indians were friendly, but for the much of the trip, the conquistadors' boats were attacked by poison arrows. According to Orellana, one such attack was led by fierce women, like the Amazons of Greek mythology, for whom the big river was subsequently named.

On August 26, 1542, Orellana and the remnants of his crew reached the Atlantic, where they sewed their blankets into sails and made their way to a Spanish outpost in the Caribbean. Orellana then returned to Spain, where he regaled the king and aristocracy with tales of his discovery and obtained a grant to establish two colonies on the river. In 1544, he set sail with four ships and 400 men, but Orellana's luck had run out. One ship sank en route, and disease, hunger, and enemy arrows claimed most of his crew once they reached the Amazon delta. Unable to establish a viable colony, Orellana fell ill and died in November 1546. The expedition's 44 survivors sailed to the Caribbean, where a Spanish ship rescued them.

running along the riverbank. The downtown area of Coca is about 6 square blocks, with the Río Napo defining its southern boundary, and the bus terminal defining its northern limits.

WHAT TO SEE & DO

There is very, very little for a tourist to do or see in Coca. If you've got some time to kill before heading down the Napo River on a tour or to a lodge, you should head to the riverfront **Malecón** for a pleasant stroll, and then stop at one of the simple bars or restaurants for refreshments or a bowl of *ceviche*.

Yasuni National Park ✦✦   While the Galápagos National Park actually covers more area, **Yasuni National Park** is Ecuador's largest land-based park, with some 962,000 hectares (2,376,140 acres). Yasuni encompasses several parks and reserves, including the Huaorani Reserve, and has been declared a UNESCO Biosphere reserve. The park—much of which has seen little or no human presence—comprises vast tracks of lowland tropical rainforest, swampland, rivers, and lagoons. Several indigenous groups have their lands and homes protected within the park, and still live very simple lives as subsistence farmers, hunters, and gatherers.

Yasuni's wildlife is astonishing, and hasn't yet truly been fully studied or counted. Among the more striking denizens are the jaguar, tapir, harpy eagle, and anaconda. Tours through Yasuni must be made with a guide, either through one of the remote lodges in this region, or as part of a tour out of Coca. There's a $20 (£11) entrance fee to visit, which is usually collected by your lodge or tour operator and is good for the length of your stay in the region. Yasuni National Park is located to the east and south of Coca, with the Río Napo forming its northern boundary.

WHERE TO STAY & DINE

The restaurants at the two hotels listed below are by far the best and most dependable in town. If you want good pizza and pastas, head to **Pizzería Restaurante Fellini,** calles Quito and García Moreno (✆ **06/2881-748**). You can get good burgers, burritos, and bar food at **Papa Dan's** (see below).

MODERATE

Hotel Auca ✦   This six-story brick-and-glass building towers over Coca. As you approach the fancifully carved front doors, you can almost feel the cool air-conditioning that awaits inside. This place has by far the most modern and comfortable accommodations in town, but it lacks the riverfront setting of the other option listed here. Still, if comfort is your top priority, I'd choose this place over La Misión (see below). There's a range of room styles here, with the less expensive units lacking air-conditioning and minibars—you'll get both of these if you splurge, which I'd recommend doing. Behind its imposing facade is a relatively large garden area, with hammocks for lounging, although the loud pet macaws might make it hard to take a siesta. The restaurant serves safe and dependable Ecuadorian and international fare. The Hotel Auca—as well as its restaurant—is a favorite of oil workers, and is set right in the middle of town, about 4 blocks from the waterfront Malecón.

Napo, between Rocafuerte and García Moreno, Coca. ✆ **06/2880-127** or ✆/fax 06/2880-600. 35 units. $30–$50 (£17–£28) double. AE, DC, MC, V. **Amenities:** Restaurant; bar; tour desk; laundry service. *In room:* TV.

INEXPENSIVE

Hotel La Misión *Kids*   This longstanding riverfront hotel is the major social and transportation hub in Coca. Units vary widely in terms of comfort and style; the best rooms are nos. 1 through 5, which are newer, second-floor rooms facing the river. These have much more modern furnishings than those in the rest of the hotel, which can feel rather worn and threadbare, although they are kept clean and presentable. All accommodations have televisions and air-conditioning, but only about half of the televisions have an international feed, for which you'll have to pay more. The hotel's best feature is its riverfront pool and boardwalk area, with three midsize pools, one with a spiral water slide, and separate children's pool. There are also several shady thatch-roof areas and an unheated Jacuzzi. The worst feature here? The sad little zoo of domesticated toucans, monkeys, and other local fauna.

On the waterfront Malecón and 12 de Septiembre, Coca (mailing address: 18 de Septiembre E4-76 y Amazonas, Quito). © 02/2553-674 reservations in Quito, or 06/2880-544 in Coca. Fax 06/2880-263. www.hotelamision.com. 85 units. $29–$33 (£16–£18) double; $50 (£28) suite. DC, MC, V. **Amenities:** Restaurant; bar; 3 outdoor pools; tour desk; laundry service. *In room:* A/C, TV, no phone.

COCA AFTER DARK

The most popular place in town for late-night fun is the downstairs bar and disco at the Hotel La Misión (see above), called appropriately **El Bunker.** If you're lucky, you'll be in town on an evening when this same hotel's floating bar, the **Big Bang,** heads out onto the Napo River for a night of partying. The floating barge features an airplane fuselage for the bar's structure. Check with the hotel (© **06/2880-260**) to get the barge-bar's current schedule, and to reserve a spot. My favorite bar in town is **Papa Dan's** (© **06/2880-907**), a simple, open-air joint on the Malecón facing the river; they have good bar food and rocking music.

JUNGLE LODGES ON THE LOWER RIO NAPO

In addition to the options listed below, the folks at the Hotel La Misión have a floating-barge hotel, similar to the *Manatee* listed below. The **Flotel La Misión** (© **02/ 2553-674** for reservations in Quito, or 06/2880-544 in Coca; www.hotelamision. com) is much more rustic, and I prefer the *Manatee* for this type of trip.

EXPENSIVE

La Selva Jungle Lodge   This place has been in business over 20 years, and is still going strong. The cabins are a bit more basic than those at the two other lodges listed in this price category, but accommodations here are still quite comfortable by jungle-lodge standards. The cabins are made of wood and thatch; each has a large, screened picture window for cross-ventilation, as well as a private bathroom. At night, light is provided by a pair of kerosene lanterns. For the adventurous, these folks offer camping expeditions into the rainforest. La Selva Jungle Lodge is located about 2 hours downriver from Coca; from the disembarkation point on the Napo River, it's a half-hour hike across a rickety raised pathway to the shores of Garzacocha (Heron) Lagoon, where you will be met by a dugout canoe to transport you across to the lodge.

Río Napo (office address: Calle Mariana de Jesús E7-211 y Pradera, Quito). © 02/2226-840 reservations in Quito, or 09/9724-723. www.laselvajunglelodge.com. 17 units. 4-day/3-night tour $697 (£383) per person; 5-day/4-night tour $832 (£458) per person. Additional nights $170 (£94) per person. Rates include round-trip transportation from and to Coca, all meals and nonalcoholic beverages, daily tours, and taxes. AE, MC, V. **Amenities:** Restaurant; bar; laundry service. *In room:* No phone.

Napo Wildlife Center *(Finds)*   This is perhaps the best-run, and most environmentally and socially conscious, of the area's lodges. A joint venture with the local Añangu Quichua community, the Napo Wildlife Center is actively involved in conservation efforts. The lodge consists of 10 lakefront bungalows, which are quite large and come with one king-size bed in the main living area and a twin-size bed in a small nook separated by a half-wall. The best feature here is the hammock hung on each bungalow's private balcony overlooking the lake. A favorite of bird-watchers, the Napo Wildlife Center's resident guides are excellent. The lodge is very close to two parrot licks—exposed clay riverbanks—where on sunny days you can find hundreds, if not thousands, of parrots of various species gathering to extract salt and other nutrients from the clay. The sight and sound of a parrot lick is not to be missed. The 36m (120-ft.) observation tower is one of the tallest in the area, and there's another, more convenient observation tower just off the bar area. In all, over 560 bird species have been spotted here so far. No motorized vehicles are allowed anywhere near the lodge, which is located inside the Yasuní National Park. This means from Coca it's a 2-hour motor-boat ride on the Río Napo, then either a 2-hour paddle or 2km (1.2-mile) hike in to the lodge.

On Añangu Lake, off the Lower Río Napo, Coca (Quito office: Calle de las Magnolias 51 y Los Cristantemos, Cumbaya, Quito). ©/fax 02/2897-316 reservation office in Quito, or 09/8349-087 cellphone. www.napowildlifecenter.com. 10 units. 4-day/3-night tour $650 (£358) per person; 5-day/4-night tour $795 (£437) per person. Rates include round-trip transportation from and to Coca, all meals and nonalcoholic beverages, daily tours, and taxes. Rates do not include $10 (£5.50) entrance fee to Yasuní National Park. AE, DC, MC, V. **Amenities:** Restaurant; bar; laundry service. *In room:* No phone.

Sacha Lodge ⍟ This is a another upscale lodge on the lower Napo River, though only so much luxury is possible in these parts. The large rooms feature high thatch ceilings, varnished wooden floors, relatively modern bathrooms, ceiling fans, and two double beds. But don't expect to find air-conditioning, televisions, or Wi-Fi. Located on Pilchicocha Lake, the cabins are connected to the main lodge via a network of raised and covered walkways; there's an observation tower here, and you'll have sweeping views of the rainforest and excellent bird-watching. Sacha Lodge is also very close to a clay parrot lick. Meals are served family style in a gorgeous open-air dining room and bar area, and the food served is plentiful, varied, and very tasty. This is one of the lodges closest to the town of Coca, the boat trip taking about 2½ hours.

On a small lagoon off the Lower Río Napo, Coca (mailing address: Julio Zaldumbide 397 y Valladolid, Quito). © 800/706-2215 in the U.S. and Canada, 02/2566-090 reservations in Quito, or 09/9733-182 cellphone. Fax 02/2236-521. www.sachalodge.com. 26 units. 4-day/3-night tour $645 (£355) per person; 5-day/4-night tour $790 (£435) per person. Rates are for double occupancy and include round-trip transportation from Coca, all meals and nonalcoholic beverages, daily tours, and taxes. Children under 12, 30% discount. AE, DC, MC, V. **Amenities:** Restaurant; bar; laundry service. *In room:* No phone.

MODERATE

Sani Lodge This newer option is entirely owned by the local Sani Island indigenous community, who, with some outside help, run the property and keep all the profits. While you are here, you will hear a lot about "the community," and you will almost certainly visit the home of one or more members. The lodge is set on a pretty, narrow black-water lagoon that is home to a healthy population of black caimans, as well as to the odd piranha, electric eel, anaconda, and fresh-water sting ray—so, of course, swimming is discouraged. The lodge also has miles of excellent trails and a 30m-tall (98-ft.) bird observation tower. Bird- and animal-watching are indeed excellent here. The rooms consist of 10 individual wooden bungalows arranged in a circle around a well-kept lawn. The bungalows are simple, with firm beds under mosquito netting, tiny porches, and cold-water showers. A solar-heated "shower bag" is hung inside the shower each afternoon. If it's a sunny day, you'll get a nice warm shower out of it; if it's cloudy, or if you wait too long, you're stuck with the cold water. Of course, it's so hot here that this isn't an issue for most visitors. Filling and tasty meals are served family-style in the main lodge, which features nice sunset views over the lagoon. Though overall the Sani is a good lodging option, the operation and coordination can be rough around the edges. The trip to the lodge takes about 3 to 4 hours by boat from Coca.

On a small lagoon off the Lower Río Napo, Coca (mailing address: Roca E4-49 y Av. Amazonas, Quito). © 02/2558-881 reservations in Quito, or 09/4341-728 cellphone. Fax 02/2765-472. www.sanilodge.com. 10 units. 4-day/3-night tour $450 (£248) per person; 5-day/4-night tour $600 (£330) per person. Additional nights $150 (£83) per person. Rates include round-trip transportation from and to Coca, all meals and nonalcoholic beverages, daily tours, and taxes. AE, MC, V. **Amenities:** Restaurant; bar; laundry service. *In room:* No phone.

INEXPENSIVE

In addition to the lodge listed below, the same folks in Quito also run trips to a similar place, **Yarina Lodge** (www.yarinalodge.com), which is closer to Coca, though I prefer the remote location and sense of greater isolation offered at Yuturi.

Yuturi Lodge   This rustic lodge caters to more budget-minded travelers. The bamboo-and-thatch cabins are arranged in neat rows facing each other across a small grassy central garden. Every cabin has a tiny front porch, anywhere from two to four twin beds—each with mosquito netting—and a private bathroom. All sorts of tour options are available, including visits to local Quichua communities and overnight camping excursions in the jungle. Food is well prepared and plentiful. This is one of the more remote lodges, located some 5 hours by boat from Coca, on the banks of the Río Yuturi.

Río Napo, Coca (mailing address: Av. Amazonas N24-240 y Colón, Quito). ©/fax 02/2504-037 reservations in Quito, or 09/9935-322 cellphone. www.yuturilodge.com. 16 units. 5-day/4-night tour $425 (£234) per person. Children under 12, 30% discount. Rates are for double occupancy and include round-trip transportation from Coca, all meals, daily tours, and taxes. DC, MC, V. **Amenities:** Restaurant; bar; laundry service. *In room:* No phone.

A UNIQUE RIVERBOAT LODGE ON RIO NAPO

Manatee Amazon Explorer ★ *(Finds*   For a different experience of Ecuador's Amazon basin, you might consider booking a berth on this converted river barge. The boat is based out of Coca, and cruises up and down the Napo and Aguarico rivers. Side trips to hike in the rainforest, to visit parrot licks, to paddle on isolated lagoons, and to visit local communities are all offered. The cabins are compact yet cheerful, and there are plenty of common areas and deck space, which you can enjoy during the cruise. By boat, you actually see more of the Amazon basin than by staying at a land-based lodge. The longer itineraries here include visits to both Yasuni National Park and Cuyabeno Wildlife Reserve, as well as to Limoncocha Biological Reserve and the flooded area of Lagartoc(ha. A cruise on the *Manatee* provides one of the better chances of seeing the unique fresh-water river dolphins of the Amazon.

Río Napo, Coca (mailing address: El Telégrafo E10–63 y Juan Alcántara, Quito). © 02/2448-985 reservations in Quito, or 02/2447-190. Fax 02/2437-645. www.manateeamazonexplorer.com. 13 units. 4-day/3-night tour $460 (£253) per person; 5-day/4-night tour $615 (£338) per person. Rates are for double occupancy and include round-trip transportation from Coca, all meals and nonalcoholic beverages, daily tours, and taxes. Rates do not include $20 (£11) entrance fee to Yasuni National Park. AE, DC, MC, V. **Amenities:** Restaurant; bar; laundry service. *In room:* A/C, no phone.

3 Tena & the Upper Napo River ✦

Tena: 186km (115 miles) SW of Quito; 79km (49 miles) N of Puyo

The capital of Napo province, Tena is an attractive and quiet city in the Ecuadorian lowlands. In addition to holding the provincial seat, Tena claims to be the "cinnamon capital" of Ecuador, and there are cinnamon farms in and around Tena. The town sits at the convergence point of the Tena and Puno rivers. Because of its location close to the Andean foothills, Tena has emerged as one of the top spots in Ecuador to go white-water rafting or kayaking.

Unlike the jungle lodges listed above, the rainforest lodges, tours, and adventures available from Tena are often accessible by car or 4WD vehicle, and do not necessarily involve long boat journeys. Also, since Tena is located in the Andean foothills, slightly above sea level, it's a bit cooler here than in the true lowland regions of El Oriente.

ESSENTIALS

GETTING THERE & DEPARTING

BY PLANE Club VIP (© 1800/847-847; www.vipec.com) flies from Quito's international airport to the **Aeropuerto Galo de Torre** (© 06/2886-895; airport code: TNA), in Tena, on Tuesday and Thursday at 11:10am. The flight takes 30 minutes and costs $60 (£33) each way. The return flight to Quito leaves Tena at 11:55am.

BY BUS Several bus lines leave from Quito's main bus terminal (Terminal Terrestre) for Tena. The main bus lines serving this route include **Transportes Baños** (© 02/2570-884), **Express Baños** (© 02/2953-479 in Quito, or 06/2886-256 in Tena), **Cooperativa Amazonas** (© 02/2571-747 in Quito, or 06/2887-213 in Tena), and **Flota Pelileo** (© 03/2849-544 main offices, or 06/2886-502 in Tena). Buses leave at least once per hour—often more frequently between 5am and 11pm—and the trip takes about 5 hours; return buses follow roughly the same schedule. Fares run from $5 to $8 (£2.75–£4.40). There is also frequent bus service between Tena and Ambato, Coca, and Puyo, as well as less frequent direct service between Tena and Baños, Misahualli, Lago Agrio, and Guayaquil.

BY CAR To get here by car, take the highway (E20) east out of Quito to the remote town of Baeza. Here the road forks, with the well-marked southern fork (E45) heading to Tena. It's 88km (56 miles) from Quito to Baeza, and another 98km (61 miles) from Baeza to Tena. Tena can also be reached from Baños, via Puyo. To take this route, follow the directions to Puyo below, and then head north 79km (49 miles) on E45 to Tena.

GETTING AROUND

Taxis are plentiful around Tena. No ride around town should cost more than $1 or $2 (55p–£1.10). Most of the taxis are white pick-up trucks, which are well-suited for rides on the rough dirt roads that abound off the main thoroughfares all around the area. If you can't easily flag one down or have your hotel call one for you, try **Vinicio Paredes** (© 09/8789-498) or **Daniel Aviles** (© 09/7527-387).

FAST FACTS The main **police station** (© 06/2886-101) is located on the main plaza. The **post office** is located at Calle Olmeda and García Moreno, northwest of the vehicular bridge. For emergencies, there's the **Hospital Tena** (© 06/2886-302), south of town on Avenida 15 de Noviembre.

Banco de Pichincha (© 03/2887-600) has a branch at the corner of Avenida Amazonas and Calle Juan León Mera, with a 24-hour cash machine. There are several Internet cafes located in the downtown area, especially around the central plaza.

ORIENTATION

Tena is spread out on both sides of the Río Tena, with one pedestrian and one vehicular bridge connecting the two halves of the city. The Río Tena makes a severe "S" right in the heart of downtown, so you're never very far from the river. Tena's main plaza is located just over the western end of the pedestrian bridge. The airport is 5 blocks north of this plaza. The bus station, on the other hand, is a little over 1km (½ mile) south of the pedestrian bridge on Avenida 15 de Noviembre, between Avenida Montero and Calle del Chofer.

WHAT TO SEE & DO

Tena is a quiet city, but an often pretty and safe town in which to stroll. The cathedral fronting the main plaza is an attractive blue-and-white building with two steeples. There are several stone-and-sand beaches on the Tena and Puno rivers, where locals like to wash their clothes or swim. The main attraction in town is the **Parque Amazónica** (© 09/9800-463), a small zoo and botanical garden located on a tiny island at the confluence of the Tena and Puno rivers. It is reached via a small bridge located on the riverfront a couple of blocks south of the main pedestrian footbridge. The park is open daily from 8am to 5pm. Admission is $2 (£1.10).

Many folks enjoy heading to the nearby town of **Archidona.** Located just 10km (6 miles) north of Tena on the road to Baeza, this quaint town maintains a sense of timeless tranquillity, with architecture evocative of its colonial past. The two-tone black-and-white-striped church is said to be an imitation of the main Catholic church in Siena, Italy, and while Archidona's is nowhere near as majestic, it's worth a quick visit.

Just a few miles north of Archidona are the **Cuevas de Jumandy (Jumandy Caves;** © 06/2889-185). This extensive cave system is a popular tourist destination. There's a basic little recreation complex near the entrance, with a couple of pools, slides, and playground areas. The main cave entrance is lit with floodlights, but the caves are best seen as part of guided tour, which not only allows you to explore much farther but includes a strong flashlight or headlamp and rubber boots—a help on the moist and muddy hike here. Bring a bathing suit: One of the more adventurous parts of the guided tours is the chance to swim in the cool interior pools and rivers. In fact, if you intend to explore the caves deeply at all, you'll have to wade or swim. Most guided tours combine the Jumandy Caves with a stop in Archidona. The caves are open daily from 8am to 6pm. Admission is $2 (£1.10).

While a host of guided tours of the local rainforests are possible, I recommend signing up for a visit to the **Jatun Sacha Biological Station** (© 02/2432-240; www.jatun sacha.org) a 2,500-hectare (6,180-acre) private reserve and field station. Developed to promote environmental education and conservation, Jatun Sacha has a well-maintained system of trails and a rotating stable of biologists, guides, and volunteers. Over 500 species of birds and nearly 800 species of butterflies have been spotted here. Jatun Sacha is located about 25km (15 miles) south of Tena, and can be reached by road or by river.

If you want to do any adventure or organized tours, check in with **Agencia Limon-cocha** ✿, at Avenida del Chofer and Sagrado Corazón de Jesús (© 06/2887-583; limoncocha@andinanet.net); **Hakmatecuad Travel Agency,** at 12 de Febrero and

Marañón 167 (© **06/2886-853;** hakmatecuad@gmail.com); or **Amarongachi Tours,** at Av. 15 de Noviembre 438 (© **06/2888-204;** www.amarongachi.com). All offer full- and multiday tour options.

GET WET

Tena provides access to some of the best **white-water rafting and kayaking** ✹✹✹ in the country. You have the choice of everything from Class III to Class V rapids. The most popular rivers are the Upper Napo, or Río Jatunyacu, a long and almost constantly moving Class III affair, and the Río Misahuallí, a rough and rugged Class IV+ that is wet and wild. The Misahuallí in particular is gorgeous, passing through virgin forest and a deep gorge, and includes a portage around the rushing Casanova Falls. The scenery along both rivers is quite beautiful. The Jatunyacu is no slouch, either; its name is Quichua for "Big Water." For beginners, children, or timid adventurers, there's the Río Anzu, a much more gentle, yet still moving, Class II and Class III ride.

The best local rafting operators are **Agencia Limoncocha** ✹ (© **06/2887-583;** limoncocha@andinanet.net), **Ríos Ecuador** ✹✹ (© **06/2886-727;** www.riosecuador. com), and **River People Rafting** ✹ (© **06/2888-349;** www.riverpeopleraftingecuador. com). Rafting trips run $35 to $70 (£19–£39) per person, depending upon which river you run and the size of your group. If you are an experienced kayaker, any of the above companies can arrange for you to kayak these rivers.

WHERE TO STAY IN TENA
INEXPENSIVE

Hostal Limoncocha   There's absolutely nothing fancy about this budget hostel in downtown Tena. But the rooms are clean and spiffy, with hand-painted murals, and they're definitely inexpensive. Given the very modest price increase, I definitely recommend one of the rooms with a private bathroom. These rooms also have small televisions with a handful of cable channels. In addition, you can use air-conditioning in these rooms for an extra $2.50 (£1.40) per day. The best reason for staying here is the fact that these folks run one of the better local tour and rafting agencies. There's no restaurant, but breakfast is served for $2 (£1.10) per day, and guests can use the communal kitchen. Limoncocha also has a rustic jungle lodge set beside a beautiful river, some 28km (17 miles) outside of Tena, in the Quichua area of Serena.

Av. del Chofer and Sagrado Corazón de Jesús, Tena. © 06/2887-583. limoncocha@andinanet.net. 12 units. $9 (£4.95) double shared bathroom; $12 (£6.60) private bathroom. No credit cards. **Amenities:** Bar; tour desk; laundry service. *In room:* No phone.

Hostal Los Yutzos ✹   This riverfront hotel should definitely be your first choice in Tena. Wonderfully located, beautifully maintained, and delightfully managed, the place stands head and shoulders above the competition in town. The rooms are simple but most are quite spacious, with firm beds, large windows, and a homey vibe. The more expensive units have air-conditioning and more room, and the best have riverview balconies. Other perks include free Wi-Fi access in the main lobby, and nightly turn-down service. Still, the best features at this hotel are the riverside location, open-air lounge with a great view of the river, and lush gardens. Los Yutzos also has a slightly less expensive and more basic annex, where the rooms have no air-conditioning or televisions, but you still get Wi-Fi access.

Augusto Rueda 190 and Av. 15 de Noviembre, Tena. © 06/2886-717 or 06/2887-897. Fax 06/2886-769. www.geocities. com/losyutzos. 30 units. $25–$80 (£14–£44) double. DC, MC, V. **Amenities:** Bar; tour desk; laundry service; nonsmoking rooms; free Wi-Fi in lobby. *In room:* TV, minibar.

WHERE TO DINE IN TENA

In addition to the places listed below, you can try the **Pizzería La Massilia** (© 06/2887-897), on the corner of Calle Olmedo and Calle García Moreno, for good pizza and pastas served up in a beautiful riverside setting.

MODERATE

The Marquis Restaurant *Finds* INTERNATIONAL/STEAKHOUSE   This is the fanciest place in town, although that's not exactly a monumental achievement since no one else is trying to fill this niche. In fact, the atmosphere in this open-air, family-run restaurant is quite relaxed and informal. That said, they do an excellent job, especially on grilled steaks and chicken. You can also usually get homemade pasta, or perhaps a Spanish-style tortilla. They have the only decent selection of wine in town. Portions are quite large, and you can opt for a fixed-price menu, including appetizer, main course, and dessert, for around $12 (£6).

Av. Amazonas 251 and Calle Olmedo. © **06/2886-513**. Reservations recommended. Main courses: $4–$12 (£2.20–£$6.60). DC, MC, V. Mon–Sat noon–3pm and 6–11pm.

INEXPENSIVE

Café Tortuga *Finds* INTERNATIONAL   Located beneath the Hostal Brisa del Río, this homey cafe specializes in iced coffees, fresh-baked desserts, and homemade crepes. For more filling fare you can get a hearty fresh salad, a sandwich served on a baguette, or an American-style hamburger. For a snack, I also like the *empanada de verde,* with a meat filling and "dough" made from ripe plantains. The large, open front door and windows face the Malecón and river below.

On the Calle Orellana (Malecón), just south of the footbridge. © **09/5295-419**. Main courses: $1.50–$3.50 (85p–£1.95). No credit cards. Mon–Sat 7:30am–9pm; Sun 7:30–11am and 4–9pm.

Chuquitos *ECUADORIAN*   This place fronts the main plaza on one side and the Río Tena on the other. You'll want to grab a river-view table in the open-air dining room, or on the open deck below it. The food here is simple but well-prepared and ample. The menu is quite extensive, and on top of the standard meat, poultry, and seafood dishes, they have such odd options as frog's legs and *cuy* (guinea pig). The fresh-water fried fish—see if they have piranha—is excellent. This is one of the most popular places in town, and justifiably so.

On Calle García Moreno, fronting the main plaza. © **06/2887-630**. Main courses: $3–$6.50 (£1.65–£3.60). DC, MC, V. Mon–Sat 7:30am–9:30pm.

Cositas Ricas ECUADORIAN/INTERNATIONAL   This is another popular spot, especially with tourists, because it's attached to the **Hostal Traveller's Lodging,** a budget hostel. The broad menu here caters to its built-in international youth crowd, with a good selection of vegetarian options in addition to the typical Ecuadorian and diner-style fare. Breakfasts here are filling and a good deal at around $2 (£1.10). Be sure to try the fresh juices or fruit smoothies. You can also get pizzas and pastas at their new neighboring addition, the **Pizzería Dolce Vita.**

Av. 15 de Noviembre, between 9 de Octubre and Calle Tarqui. © **06/2886-372**. Main courses: $2.50–$7 (£1.40–£3.85). DC, MC, V. Daily 7am–10pm.

JUNGLE LODGES OUTSIDE TENA

A couple of the lodges listed below are located on the upper Río Napo. All these lodges use both Tena and the tiny river outpost town of Misahualli as transportation points, although by far most tourists arrange for their transportation via Tena.

MODERATE

Hacienda Hakuna Matata   This family-run place sits on the banks of the gentle Inchillaqui River. There are two types of rooms here—it's worth the slight price increase to get one of the "Lodge" cabins, which are larger and have wraparound, covered verandas. Units have wood furnishings, large picture windows, and private bathrooms. Horseback riding, hiking, and river rafting are a few of the many popular activities. A lunch and dinner package will run you an extra $16 (£8.80) per person per day.

10km (6 miles) northwest of Tena (mailing address: Apartado Postal 165, Correo Central, Tena), Napo. ℂ/fax 6/ 2889-617. www.hakunamat.com. 9 units. $45–$53 (£25–£29) double. Rates include full breakfast. AE, MC, V. **Amenities:** Restaurant; bar; laundry service. *In room:* No phone.

INEXPENSIVE

Cabañas Aliñajui *Finds*   This pretty jungle lodge offers clean and comfortable rooms in a great setting fronting the Río Napo. The rooms are housed in a series of duplex cabins. Each cabin is built high up on raised stilts, with a hammock and lounge area on a concrete platform below the rooms. Each duplex has one common bathroom. The rooms are spacious, with wood floors and walls, thatch roofs, and large screened picture windows. Most rooms have either two or three twin beds. Meals are served buffet-style in a large, open-air dining room with a view of the river. Tours include rainforest hikes, trips to the adjacent Jatun Sacha Biological Station (see above), and canoe trips. One of my favorite activities here is floating an inner tube on the Napo River.

On the Río Napo, 25km (15 miles) south of Tena (mailing address: Inglaterra 1373 y Av. Amazonas, Edificio Centro Ejecutivo, Piso 7, Quito), Napo. ℂ/fax 02/2274-510. www.ecuadoramazonlodge.com. 11 units. 3-day/2-night tour $145 (£80) per person; 4-day/3-night tour $165 (£91) per person. Rates are based on double occupancy and include all meals and nonalcoholic beverages, daily tours, and taxes. 40% discount children under 10 years of age. Rates do not include round-trip canoe transportation from Tena ($40/£22). AE, MC, V. **Amenities:** Restaurant; bar; laundry service. *In room:* No phone.

Cotococha Amazon Lodge 🐾   I find the wood-and-thatch bungalows here some of the most inviting in this region. Request one of the few cabins that front the river. A couple feature a cozy second-floor bedroom nestled into the high peak of a thatch roof. None have electricity, although they all have hot-water showers and private balcony areas. A host of tour and activity options are available. As at the nearby Cabañas Aliñajui (see above), one of the most popular activities here is taking an inner tube out on the Napo. *Tip:* If you're booking direct, be sure to mention Frommer's and ask for a direct booking discount.

On the Río Napo, 10km (6 miles) south of Tena, on the Puerto Napo-to-Ahuano road (mailing address: Av. Amazonas N24-03 y Wilson, Segundo Piso 3, Quito), Napo. ℂ/fax 02/2234-419. www.cotococha.com. 17 units. 3-day/2-night tour $160 (£88) per person; 4-day/3-night tour $267 (£147) per person. Rates are double occupancy and include all meals, daily tours, and taxes. Rates do not include beverages, nor transportation to the lodge, which can be arranged as an add-on. AE, MC, V. **Amenities:** Restaurant; bar; laundry service. *In room:* No phone.

Huasquila Amazon Lodge *Value*   This newer lodge offers excellent opportunities to enjoy Ecuador's Amazon basin at a great price, with the added perk of easy road access. The wood-and-thatch cabins are a good size, and their decor features work by local artisans. Each unit comes with two twin beds and a private bathroom. Available tours and activities include rainforest hikes, horseback riding, visits to indigenous communities, and a tour to see nearby stone hieroglyphics. For an additional fee, white-water rafting can be arranged. The lodge provides round-trip land transportation from Quito for $30 (£15) per person, with a four-person minimum. From Quito, you can get to the lodge in 4 hours.

3km (2 miles) west of Cotundo, about halfway between Baeza and Tena (mailing address: Av. Amazonas 743 y Veintimilla, Edificio Espinoza, 801, Quito). © 02/2908-491. Fax 02/2237-224. www.huasquila.com. 6 units. 4-day/3-night tour $224 (£123) per person; 5-day/4-night tour $274 (£151) per person. Rates are double occupancy and include all meals and nonalcoholic beverages, daily tours, and taxes. Children under 12 years of age, 50% discount. AE, MC, V. **Amenities:** Restaurant; bar; babysitting; laundry service. *In room:* No phone.

4 Puyo & the Southern Amazon Basin ★

Puyo: 237km (147 miles) SE of Quito; 79km (49 miles) S of Tena; 61km (38 miles) SE of Baños

Puyo is the capital of Pastaza province and the principal gateway to the southern Amazon basin. It sits on the banks of the small Río Puyo, at the major road junction connecting Tena and the northern Oriente with Macas and other points in the southern Oriente. Despite not having any major oil industry—like Coca's or Lago Agrio's—Puyo is nevertheless the largest city in El Oriente, with nearly 25,000 inhabitants.

Located at the edge of the Andean foothills at an altitude of some 950m (3,100 ft.), Puyo has a slightly cooler and more pleasant climate than you'll find at the lower elevations of the Amazon basin. But it is very humid and moist here.

ESSENTIALS
GETTING THERE & DEPARTING
BY PLANE   Although the small airport here receives some charter traffic, no regular commuter service is offered to Puyo. The closest airport with regular service is Tena. See p. 315 for details.

BY BUS   Various bus lines leave from Quito's main bus terminal (Terminal Terrestre) for Puyo. The main bus lines servicing this route include **Cooperativo San Francisco** (© **02/2570-022** in Quito, or 03/2885-327 in Puyo), **Express Baños** (© **02/2953-479** in Quito, or 03/288-756 in Puyo), and **Cooperativa Amazonas** (© **02/2571-747** in Quito, or 03/2886-696 in Puyo). Buses leave at least once per hour, and often more frequently between 4am and 10:30pm. The trip takes about 5 hours, with fares costing $5 to $8 (£2.75–£4.40). Return buses follow roughly the same schedule. There is also frequent bus service between Puyo and Ambato, Macas, Riobamba, and Tena, as well as less frequent direct service between Puyo and Baños, Coca, Lago Agrio, and Guayaquil.

BY CAR   The most direct route to Puyo from Quito is via Baños, and, in fact, most visitors driving to Puyo come through Baños. Leaving Quito, take the Pan-American Highway (E35) south to Ambato. Just south of Ambato, take the well-marked turnoff for Pelileo, Patate, and Baños. This road continues on through Baños to Puyo. The drive should take around 4½ hours. Alternatively, you can reach Puyo from Tena. To take this route, follow the directions for reaching Tena (p. 315) and continue south on E45 to Puyo, which is a little over an hour's drive.

GETTING AROUND

Taxis are plentiful and inexpensive in Puyo. Any ride around town should be $1 to $2 (50p–£1). If you can't readily flag down a taxi, call **Taxi Puyo** (© **03/2885-231**) or **Taxi 12 de Mayo** (© **03/2885-185**).

FAST FACTS   The **Ministry of Tourism** (© **03/2883-681**) has an information booth at their offices on Avenida Francisco de Orellana, between Calle Vilamil and 27 de Febrero. They can give you information on local tours and accommodations.

To reach the local **police,** dial © **03/2885-101.** In the case of an emergency, head to the reasonably well-equipped **Hospital Puyo** (© **03/2885-335**), on Calle Ramiro Fernández, between Calle Espejo and Calle Juan de Velasco.

Banco de Pichincha (© **03/2886-795**) and **Banco del Austro** (© **03/2883-923**) both have branches in downtown Puyo, with 24-hour ATMs.

ORIENTATION

The main road from Baños enters Puyo from the south and becomes Avenida Alberto Zambrano. You'll find the main bus terminal along this avenue, a few blocks before hitting the heart of downtown. The central part of the downtown area is north off Zambrano, and its hub is the central park and main Catholic church found at the intersection of Avenida Bolívar and 9 de Octubre.

WHAT TO SEE & DO

The main attraction right in town is the **Parque Acuático Morete Puyu (Morete Puyu Aquatic Park)** 🌟 (© **03/2885-877**). This water playground is located just behind the main bus terminal and features a series of pools and water slides. There's even a wave pool here. Open daily from 8am to 6pm, the park has a $4 (£2.20) entrance fee. This place is very popular with local families and kids, especially on weekends and holidays.

Just off the main plaza in town is the small **Museo Etnoarqueológico (Ethno-Archaeological Museum)** Atahualpa, between 9 de Octubre and 10 de Agosto (© **03/2885-605**). The museum has a collection of artifacts, tools, and ceramics from the various indigenous communities of the region, as well as informative displays in Spanish. The museum is open Monday through Saturday from 9am to 5pm. Admission is $1 (55p).

Jardín Botánico las Orquídeas 🌟 (© **06/2884-855**) is a pretty little privately run botanical garden with well-groomed paths, ponds, and an extensive collection of tropical orchids. These botanical gardens are located about 3.2km (2 miles) south of Puyo, on the road to Macas. They are open daily from 8am to 5pm, but it's best to call ahead and confirm. Admission is $4 (£2.20).

If you're coming here independently and want to organize a trip into the rainforest, or if you want to sign up for adventure sports, you should definitely check in with **Madre Tierra** (© **09/7269-724;** www.madreselvaecuador.com). They offer a range of single-day adventures and tours, as well as multiday combination tours. Options include river rafting, mountain biking, canyoning, rainforest excursions, and tours of local indigenous communities. They can also arrange for Spanish classes and a home-stay with a local family, or set you up with a volunteer gig.

WHERE TO STAY & DINE IN PUYO

Puyo is a bustling town in the heart of the lowland jungle. It's not nearly as much of a tourism gateway as its northern neighbors, but it is starting to catch up. There are a number of unmemorable but acceptable budget lodgings in town, many of which are rock-bottom accommodations for backpackers; I recommend that you spend a few extra dollars for the comfort offered by the places listed below, which are still pretty inexpensive.

Aside from the restaurant at the **Hostal El Jardín** (see below), you might try the **Restaurante Carihuela** (② 03/2883-919), which is located near the bus station and specializes in grilled meats.

INEXPENSIVE

Hostal El Jardín   The outgrowth of a popular river-view restaurant, this newer *hostal* offers tidy, spacious rooms on large, well-tended grounds on a hillside over the Río Puyo. The rooms are pretty bare, with little more than their varnished wood floors and walls, a couple of beds with fluffy comforters, and large picture windows. I'd opt for one of the second-floor units, just to be above and away from the restaurant, but those on both the first and second floors have access to shared verandas with sitting areas and some hammocks. The hotel's restaurant is probably the best in town.

Paseo Turístico del Río Puyo, Barrio Obrero. ②/fax **03/2887-770**. www.eljardin.pastaza.net. 10 units. $30 (£17) double. Rates include full breakfast. MC, V. **Amenities:** Restaurant; bar; tour desk; laundry service. *In room:* No phone.

Hostería El Pigual *(Kids)*   This place is just outside downtown Puyo, yet it feels worlds away. It is reached via a small bridge over the Puyo River. The complex is a sort of country club and weekend retreat for Ecuadorians. All rooms are plenty large, with tile floors, white walls, dark stained-wood furniture and exposed beam ceilings, and minimal decor. You'll pay a little more for a deluxe room, but this will get you a minibar and, more importantly, a private balcony or porch. I recommend units on the second floor, with views of the river. There are two-floor units with a queen-size bed below and several twins upstairs, making this a good option for those traveling with children. On the grounds are a good-size outdoor pool, a children's playground, and a game room. One of the nicer features here is the large indoor sauna, steam, and Jacuzzi facility, with high ceilings and brick walls, built in imitation of ancient Roman baths. The extensive grounds, spacious rooms, and relatively modern facilities not only make this a good choice for families but for anyone looking for a respite from the congestion and bustle of the town.

At the end of Calle Tungurahua, Barrio Obrero. ②/fax **03/2886-137**. www.elpigualecuador.com. 21 units. $46 (£25) double; $64 (£35) deluxe. Rates include breakfast and dinner. Rates slightly lower midweek. AE, MC, V. **Amenities:** Restaurant; bar; midsize outdoor pool; Jacuzzi; sauna; steam bath; tour desk; babysitting; laundry service. *In room:* TV.

A VERY ISOLATED NATURE LODGE

Located in Ecuador's southern Amazon basin, Kapawi is only accessible via a charter flight from Quito.

Kapawi Ecolodge & Reserve ⭐⭐⭐   Kapawi is an excellent example of sustainable tourism in action. This lodge has been developed with the cooperation and participation of the local Achuar community, who will become the owners in 2011. In the meantime, the current owners—the company Canodros—pays monthly rent for use of the land and provides business and tourism training to the community.

All the structures here were built using traditional methods and environmentally friendly technology. The 20 cabins, which are set on stilts over a black-water lagoon, are rustic in a handsome way; they're extremely comfortable, with polished wood floors, thatched roofs, and bamboo walls. After a hard day of hiking or canoeing, you

Farther Down the Road: Macas

Macas is the southernmost major town in the Oriente. It's a quaint little jungle town on the banks of the Río Upano with very little in the way of tourism infrastructure. Indeed, it's really only for those looking to get as far away from it all as possible.

There are a handful of budget lodgings around the small downtown area. Of these, I recommend the **Hotel Heliconia** (© 07/2701-956), in the heart of downtown on Avenida Soasti and 10 de Agosto. You can't miss this six-story building, the tallest in Macas.

If you want to arrange any tours or adventure activities out of Macas, check in with **Planeta Tours** (© 07/2701-328), on Calle Domingo Comin and Avenida Soasti.

You can get to the town by bus from Quito, Cuenca, or Puyo, but the ride involves taking one bus as far as a narrow footbridge over the Río Puyo, and then transferring to a waiting bus on the other side.

For those looking to for a quick ride to Macas, **Saereo** (© 02/3302-280; www.saereo.com) has flights at 11:30am Sunday through Friday from Quito to the **Aeropuerto Coronel Edmundo Carvajal** (© 07/2700-258; airport code: XMS). The flight takes 40 minutes and costs $60 (£33) each way. The return flight leaves Macas at 2pm.

---

can relax in a hammock on your own balcony as you gaze down at the river. The bathrooms are small, but the showers have solar-heated hot water (a rarity in the jungle). The food here is so good that it's hard to believe you're in the middle of the jungle.

In addition to the excellent accommodations, the lodge offers well-organized, fun excursions. Two guides—a local from the Achuar community and an English-speaking naturalist—lead the trips, pointing out wildlife and discussing the area's trees and plants. When you visit the local village, don't worry—the Achuar people won't be offended if you don't drink the *chicha* (an alcoholic beverage made from corn by the women of the community). Spend a few days at Kapawi and you will leave with memories that last a lifetime. To get you here, the lodge will arrange a private charter flight on a light propeller plane.

On the Río Pastaza, Pastaza province (mailing address: Urbanización Santa Leonor, Manzana 5, Solar 10, Guayaquil). © 800/613-6026 in the U.S. and Canada, or 04/228-5711 in Ecuador. Fax 04/228-7651. www.kapawi.com. 20 units. 4 days/3 nights $650 (£358) per person; 5 days/4 nights $870 (£479) per person; 8 days/7 nights $1,340 (£737) per person. Round-trip airfare from Quito is an additional $224 (£123) per person. Rates are for double occupancy and include accommodations, all meals, all nonalcoholic beverages, guide services, and daily excursions. Rates do not include a $10 (£5.50) usage fee, given to the Achuar community, or government taxes. Half-price for children under 12. AE, DC, MC, V. **Amenities:** Restaurant; bar; library; laundry service. *In room:* No phone.

12

The Galápagos Islands

The Galápagos Islands offer some of the best wildlife viewing in the world, not only because the animals themselves are beautiful and interesting but because they are virtually fearless of humans. Through a quirk of evolution, large predators failed to evolve here, meaning, for example, that the famous blue-footed booby will perform its awkwardly elegant two-step mating dance right under your nose, oblivious to your camera. Mockingbirds will hop onto your shoes. Sea lions will do figure eights to show off their swimming prowess as you snorkel among them. The local penguins are, admittedly, a bit aloof, but even they aren't above using a snorkeler as a human shield as they attempt to sneak up on schools of fish. In the Galápagos, you don't have to get downwind and peer through the bushes to glimpse the wildlife; you do, however, have to be careful not to step on sea lions sleeping on the beach as you position yourself to take a photo.

The islands' geographic isolation, over 960km (600 miles) off the continental coast, has led to the evolution of numerous endemic species here. This, combined with the animals' fearlessness of humans, played a key role in Charles Darwin's development of the theory of natural selection.

Nearly every visitor to the Galápagos arrives by plane, and only two airlines make the flight from the mainland. Seats are often booked solid far in advance, and fares are certainly not cheap. The best way to see the islands is to book a package tour out of Quito or Guayaquil. Most packages will include airfare and a berth on a local cruise ship, or a planned land-based itinerary. The ships that tour the islands vary widely in size and quality. My advice: Spend as much money as you can afford. But no matter what you can pay, you won't be disappointed. The wildlife here, which so beguiled Charles Darwin and Herman Melville in the 19th century, is no less astonishing now than it was when they visited.

The Galápagos Islands were formed over 5 million years ago by volcanic eruptions. These (and the ongoing formation and development of the islands) occur primarily over a relatively localized hot spot. However, due to continental drift, the islands are slowly but steadily migrating eastward. Today, the most active islands are Fernandina and Isabela, the westernmost islands, although several others have ongoing volcanic activity.

The first European to discover the Galápagos Islands was the Spanish priest Father Tomás de Berlanga, who landed here in 1535. In the centuries that followed, the islands were frequented by various settlers, pirates, fishermen, and whalers. Today only five of the islands are populated—Santa Cruz, San Cristóbal, Floreana, Isabela, and Baltra.

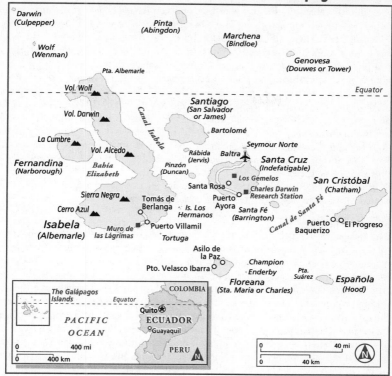

1 Essentials

GETTING THERE & DEPARTING

With rare exceptions, travelers come by plane to the Galápagos Islands. **Tame** (✆ 02/ 2909-900; www.tame.com.ec) and **Aerogal** (✆ 1-800/2376-425; www.aerogal.com.ec) now offer daily flights to both **Baltra Airport,** right off Santa Cruz island, and **Puerto Baquerizo Moreno,** on San Cristóbal island. Note, however, that there are sometimes last-minute changes to flight schedules owing to inclement weather. Always check and double-check with your airline and the cruise company to confirm the airport that will be used for your particular itinerary.

During the low season (mid-Sept through mid-Dec and mid-Jan through mid-June), flights from the mainland cost around $350 (£193) round-trip. In the high season, they cost just below $400 (£220).

Upon arrival you must pay a $100 (£55) fee to the **National Park** (www.galapagos park.org), which is good for the duration of your stay. This fee must be paid in cash, so be sure to plan ahead and have it ready. Children under 12 pay $50 (£28).

If you booked a boat tour before you arrived, the airfare and ticket booking should already be included. You can usually expect someone to pick you up at the airport and escort you through the logistics of arriving in the Galápagos and finding the way to your ship. If you're traveling on your own and you have a choice of flights (and airports), I don't recommend flying into San Cristóbal; there is very little tourist infrastructure here. There are a handful of hotels on the island, and you can book last-minute tours and day trips from its port city of Puerto Baquerizo Moreno. But if you plan to base your touring out of a hotel on land, or if you're looking for a last-minute berth on a boat, the place to be is Puerto Ayora, on Santa Cruz, which is accessed from the Baltra airport.

All flights from the mainland originate in Quito and stop in Guayaquil. If you plan on flying to the Galápagos the day after you arrive in Ecuador, I recommend spending the night in Guayaquil. Most flights to the Galápagos leave Quito early in the morning and then stop for more than an hour to pick up passengers in Guayaquil. You can count on a much more relaxed morning, and gain precious sleep time, if you board the plane there.

In addition to the two airports mentioned above, a small airstrip on Isabela island is used for provisioning and inter-island commuter traffic.

GETTING AROUND

The Galápagos archipelago consists of 13 big islands, six small islands, and more than 40 islets. **Santa Cruz** is the most populated island; its main town, Puerto Ayora, is the major city in the Galápagos. From here, you can arrange last-minute tours around the islands, day trips, and scuba-diving excursions. Santa Cruz is also home to the Darwin Research Station, where you can see giant land tortoises. **San Cristóbal** is the second-most populated island. Several tour boats begin their journeys from the its port, Puerto Baquerizo Moreno. While serving as the official capital of Galápagos province, the town of Puerto Baquerizo Moreno is small. Moreover, there's not much to see on this island. **Isabela** is the largest island, but only the third-most populated. In general, most visitors only stop here on a guided tour. For more information about individual islands in the Galápagos, see the appropriate sections below.

To enjoy the best of what the Galápagos have to offer, I recommend exploring the islands by boat. More than 100 tourist ships ply the seas. All boats need a permit and must register with the national park, so it's very difficult to use your private craft. If you're prone to seasickness, you can take day trips from Puerto Ayora to Santa Fe, Plaza Island, North Seymour, and Bartolomé.

Flights between the islands aren't frequent, but the local Galápagos airline **EME-TEBE** (✆ **05/2526-177**; emetebe@ecu.net.ec) offers service on tiny propeller planes between Santa Cruz, San Cristóbal, and Isabela islands. Fares are $100 to $120 (£55–£66) for each flight segment.

VISITOR INFORMATION

The main **tourist information office** (✆ **05/2526-613**; turismo@santacruz.gov.ec) in the Galápagos is located in Puerto Ayora, on Avenida Charles Darwin, close to the corner of Charles Binford. It is open Monday through Friday from 8am to noon and 2 to 5:30pm.

Note: the Galápagos Islands are 6 hours behind GMT, 1 hour earlier than mainland Ecuador.

EXPLORING THE GALAPAGOS
WHEN TO GO

There's never a bad time to visit the Galápagos. The peak season lasts from mid-June through early September and from mid-December through mid-January. It's almost

> ## (Tips) Bring Your Own Gear & Wear Some Rubber
>
> While most of the ships and boats and all of the dive shops in the Galápagos have snorkeling and diving gear for rent, you might consider bringing your own. If nothing else, bring your own mask. A good, properly fitting mask is the single most important factor in predicting the success of a dive or snorkeling outing. Faces come in all sizes and shapes, and I really recommend finding a mask that gives you a perfect fit. Fins are a lesser concern—most operators should have fins to fit your feet. But I definitely prefer to have my own snorkel. If you plan on going out snorkeling or diving more than a few times, the investment will more than pay for itself.
>
> Even during the dry season, the waters of the Galápagos are much cooler than you'd expect this close to the equator. Most scuba companies dive with full 6mm wet suits year-round. Even if you are snorkeling, a full or "shortie" wet suit will make the experience much more enjoyable, especially from June to November, when the Humboldt Current makes the water significantly colder. I highly recommend that you find out in advance if your ship or tour operator can provide or rent you a wet suit. If not, consider buying one.

impossible to find a last-minute deal at these times. The national park limits the number of visitors to each island and coordinates each ship's itinerary, so the Galápagos will never feel like Disney World. But if you visit in the summer, you are less likely to feel a sense of solitude and isolation. Below is a brief summary of the seasons to help you decide what time of year is best for you:

DECEMBER THROUGH MAY During these months, the water and the air are warmer, but this is the rainy season. It drizzles almost daily for a short period of time. Ironically, this is also the sunniest time of year. The end of December through the beginning of January is still the high season, so expect more crowds than during the rest of the year.

Because the water is warmer at this time, swimming and snorkeling are more enticing. On the flip side, there aren't as many fish to see as there are later in the year. This is the breeding season for land birds, so it's a good time to watch some unusual mating rituals. If you're into turtles, this is when you want to be here; you can watch sea turtles nesting on the beach, and March through May, you can often see land tortoises searching for mates around the lowland areas of the islands. Sea lions also mate in the rainy season—it's entertaining to watch as the males fight for the females. Around March and April, you'll see the adorable newborn pups crawling around the islands.

In February, March, and April, as the rains dissipate, flowers start to blossom and the islands are awash in bright colors. Another benefit of traveling to the Galápagos at this time of year: The ocean is much calmer, so you'll have less chance of getting seasick.

JUNE THROUGH NOVEMBER June through November, the Humboldt Current makes it way up to the Galápagos from the southern end of South America. The current brings cold water and cold weather, but it also brings water rich in nutrients and plankton, which attracts fish and birds. During this season there always seem to be clouds in the air, but it rarely rains. It's also quite windy, and the seas tend to be rougher.

Experienced divers claim that this is the best time of year to visit the Galápagos. Unfortunately, to see the wide variety of underwater marine life, you have to brave the cold water. Because there are more fish in the sea at this time of year, there are also more seabirds searching for these fish. Albatrosses arrive on Española in June and stay until December. Penguins also like the cold water and the abundance of fish, so you're more likely to see them here during this season. On Genovesa, the elusive owls mate in June and July, and you have the best chance of spotting one during this time. Blue-footed boobies also mate now, so it won't be difficult to witness their beautiful mating ritual known as the "sky point."

THE ISLANDS IN BRIEF

Every island in the Galápagos has its own allure. The more time you have, the richer your experience will be, but even if you have only a few days, with proper planning you'll come home with a lifetime of memories. When you're choosing a tour operator, you should always examine the itinerary. Note that 7-day trips often make frequent stops at Santa Cruz or San Cristóbal to collect and drop off passengers. The best trips head out to far-flung places, such as Genovesa, Española, and Fernandina, and spend only 1 day docked in Puerto Ayora, on Santa Cruz. To help you decide which trip might be best for you, here's a list of what each island has to offer.

Santa Cruz   You will most likely begin and end your trip to the Galápagos on Santa Cruz. If you plan to arrange your trip on your own, you should use Santa Cruz as your base. The main city here, **Puerto Ayora,** is a bustling and attractive little burg, with a variety of small hotels, restaurants, gift shops, and tour operators. If you're looking for a luxury getaway, this island offers the only such choices, with both the Royal Palm Hotel (p. 346) and Finch Bay Hotel (p. 345). This island is also home to the **Charles Darwin Research Station,** where you can observe tortoises firsthand. Tours of the island include stops at **Los Gemelos (The Twins),** two sinkholes that stand side by side. As you walk around Los Gemelos, you will have a good chance of spotting the beautiful vermilion flycatcher. Some companies will take you to a farm in the highlands, where you can see tortoises in the wild. It's exciting to see these enormous creatures crawling about, but I must warn you, it's either hot and sunny up here or cool and drizzly (depending on the seasons). After you see the tortoises, the tour continues on a long, boring hike to a small, unattractive lake. If you can, try to turn back after you see the tortoises. Finally, most trips make a stop at the lava tubes, where you can wander though underground tunnels created by the movement of hot lava. On the north side of the island is **Cerro Dragon,** which is a great place to see the unique Galápagos land iguana.

Bartolomé   Bartolomé (or Bartholomew) is famous for its dramatic vistas and barren volcanic landscape. The most common anchorage here is near the oddly shaped **Pinnacle Rock.** From here, you can climb 372 steps of a wooden walkway to reach the top of an extinct volcano. The vigorous but technically easy climb is a lesson in volcano geography, with cooled-off lava flows and parasitic spatter cones clearly visible along the route to the main cone. On the way up, you will certainly see lava cactuses and lava lizards. The panoramic view from the lookout up top is beautiful, with Pinnacle Rock below you. Be sure to ask your guide to pick out a few of the lava rocks to show how light they are. This island has one of the larger colonies of Galápagos penguins, and many snorkelers have spotted penguins off this island.

San Cristóbal Most boats only stop on San Cristóbal to pick up and drop off passengers. In 2006, work began to renovate the downtown Malecón, or boardwalk, of the island's main town, Puerto Baquerizo Moreno. By the time you read this, the new Malecón will feature a string of bayside restaurants, cafes, and gift shops. The main attraction on the island is the **Centro de Interpretación (Interpretive Center),** a small, interesting museum with exhibits on the natural, human, and geological history of the island. If you spend any time on San Cristóbal, you will probably stop at **El Lobería,** a beach with sea lions, red crabs, and colorful lava gulls. It's also worth visiting **La Galapaguera de Cerro Colorado,** a natural giant-tortoise reserve. If you sail into or out of Puerto Baquerizo Moreno, you will probably pass through **Kicker Rock**—a unique rock formation set about 1.5km (1 mile) offshore. Take note of San Cristóbal's fishing and commuter craft; many are ringed with strands of barbed wire to keep off sea lions. Boats without the barbed wire almost always have one or two of these large sea mammals lounging around on the aft deck or sunning on the prow.

Santiago 🌟 Also called **James Island,** Santiago was a major base where early buccaneers and pirates stocked up on fresh water and food. Santiago is also a case study in the potential destruction caused by introduced species. Supposedly a couple of pairs of feral goats, left here as a future source of food by buccaneers in the 18th century, reproduced to the point where they numbered over 100,000. Recent efforts have greatly reduced the size of the herds of wild goats, but they are still wreaking havoc on certain native species, including giant tortoises. Most of the sea lions in the Galápagos are California sea lions. But on Santiago island, you will have the chance to see the only endemic species of sea lion in the Galápagos, which is incorrectly called the Galápagos fur seal. After you see the fur seal, you will have an opportunity to take advantage of the excellent snorkeling here. If you're lucky, you'll see sea turtles. The island is also full of coastal birds such as great blue herons, lava herons, oystercatchers, and yellow-crowned night herons.

Española 🌟🌟 May through December, albatrosses settle down here to mate and take care of their young. In May and June, if you arrive early in the morning, you can witness the beak-cracking mating ritual of the albatross. Later in the season (Sept–Dec), you can see the little chicks. There must be some sort of aphrodisiac on this island because this is also a great place to see blue-footed boobies doing their mating dance, where the male extends his wings and lifts his beak at his prospective mate. If the female likes what she sees, she mimics her suitor.

Fernandina 🌟🌟 This is the westernmost island in the archipelago, and one of the best for wildlife encounters. The largest colony of marine iguanas live here. These cold-blooded animals hug and cuddle with each other to warm up after swimming. Flightless cormorants also inhabit the island; even though these birds can't fly (they are the only flightless cormorants in the world), they still dry their wings in the sun, just like their flying ancestors used to do millions of years ago. At something around 1 million years of age, Fernandina is the youngest of the Galápagos Islands, and one of the most volcanically active. Major eruptions here were recorded as recently as 1995.

Isabela Just to the east of Fernandina, this is the largest island in the Galápagos, formed by the volcanic activity and eventual joining of six different volcanoes—five of which are still active. Darwin's Lake provides an excellent backdrop for dramatic photos of the sea. The island is home to several different species of the giant Galápagos land tortoise, although you might not be able to see them in the wild. You should, however, be able to spot the land iguanas here, and you can take a long hike to a scenic point, from which you can see for miles. Isabela is particularly prized by bird-watchers; owing to its size, the island has a high species count. One of the common species here is the flamingo, found in its namesake **Pozo de los Flamingos (Flamingo Pond),** close to the main town of Puerto Villamil. Among the main attractions on Isabela is **El Muro de Lágrimas (The Wall of Tears),** a stone wall that was used as a torture

mechanism for prisoners kept in a penal colony here during the mid-20th century. In town, you can also see graffiti that dates all the way back to 1836. Tour companies in town and ships stopping here usually offer *panga* (dinghy) rides around Tagus Cove, where you will have the opportunity to see the Galápagos penguins.

Rábida Rábida, also known as **Jervis Island,** has a beautiful red-sand beach that is almost always heavily populated with sea lions. If you get too close to a female or child, the local bull male will probably make his presence known. Just behind the beach is a small salt-water lagoon that is a good place to see flamingos. A small loop trail leads to the top of a hill, with some good views of the island's coastline. In my opinion, the waters off Rábida offer the

Not Your Typical Passenger: Charles Darwin & the Galápagos Islands

Charles Darwin was only 22 years old when he set sail on an around-the-world cruise aboard the HMS *Beagle* in 1831. After several years surveying the coast of South America, the *Beagle* reached the Galápagos Islands in September of 1835 and spent 5 weeks charting the archipelago. While there, Darwin made careful note of the biology and geology of the islands and collected numerous specimens. Darwin only visited four of the islands—San Cristóbal, Santiago, Isabela, and Floreana. But his observation of species differentiation, particularly among the tortoises and finches, intrigued and inspired the young scientist. While Darwin is often credited with the discovery of the theory of evolution, what he really developed was the theory of natural selection, which explains how and why evolution occurs. Central to Darwin's theory was his recognition of the geological age and isolation of the volcanic islands; he was convinced that wildlife on the Galápagos came from mainland South America, changing and adapting over time to fill in specific niches defined by the particular ecosystem of the islands. Even though Darwin had formulated most of his most important ideas in just the few years following his visit to the Galápagos, he didn't publish his seminal work, *The Origin of Species,* until 1859. Prior to that, in 1839, he published *The Voyage of the* Beagle, which chronicled his trip.

(Tips Ship or Shore?

For many, the most important decision to make when planning a trip to the Galápagos is whether to take a cruise or visit the islands from a hotel base on land. The standard advice is that those very prone to seasickness are better off staying on land. This may be true, but if you plan to take day trips from Santa Cruz island to any of the other popular island sites, you will most likely be doing so on a very small boat. Conversely, if you book a cruise on one of the larger ships, you will be on a boat that is much more stable in rough seas, and most of the travel is done at night, while you are hopefully asleep, or, at the very least, supine.

If you're looking to avoid a regimented experience with a bit of the cattle-car feel, avoid the larger ships, and be sure to ask in advance the number of passengers per naturalist guide. I recommend you find a tour with no more than 10 tourists per naturalist guide.

Yogi Berra said: "When you come to a fork in the road, take it." I personally think the best way to go is to do both. My ideal Galápagos tour is a 4- or 5-night cruise, followed by 3 nights in Puerto Ayora.

---

best snorkeling in the islands. I recently found myself swimming simultaneously with sea lions and penguins here. Unfortunately, I arrived too late in the day, and the marine iguanas weren't interested in joining us; otherwise I would have scored a wonderful trifecta.

Genovesa (Tower) ℛ Home to **Darwin Bay** and the popular hiking trail known as **"Prince Philip's Steps,"** Genovesa is located on the far northeastern end of the archipelago. It's a long, often rough sail here, and only the longer tours include a visit to Genovesa. Almost every Galápagos tourist brochure has a picture of a frigate bird puffing up its red neck in an attempt to attract females; on Genovesa you'll have ample opportunities to see these birds in action. This island is also home to the largest colony of red-footed boobies on the archipelago. On another side of the island, you can see masked boobies and storm petrels. If you're lucky, you might spot the elusive short-eared owl—since these guys don't have predators, they are the only owls in the world that are diurnal. Genovesa is also home to both sea lions and the endemic Galápagos fur seal.

Floreana ℛ This small island, the first to be inhabited, is rich in lore and intrigue. Today, some 100 people live on this island, which is seldom visited by tourists. If you do come here, be sure to stop at **Post Office Bay,** where a barrel full of letters and postcards sits on the beach. It's a tradition begun by early whalers: If you see a letter or card addressed to someone in your town or country, you are supposed to carry it and post it from home. In exchange, feel free to leave a letter or postcard of your own for someone else to return the favor.

2 Cruises

CHOOSING A BOAT TOUR

Hundreds of companies offer trips through the Galápagos, and trying to sift through all the tourist brochures is a daunting task. First and foremost, let me warn you that

> ⌒**Tips** **Scuba-Diving Trips**
>
> The waters surrounding the Galápagos offer some of **the best diving in the world** ✦✦✦. If you want to dive here, you have two options: Book a tour on a dedicated dive boat—and dive every day—or take a nondiving cruise and then spend a couple of extra days in Puerto Ayora and arrange diving excursions from there. Two of the best diving outfitters in Puerto Ayora are **SCUBA Iguana** ✦ (✆ 05/2526-497; www.scubaiguana.com), located at the Hotel Galápagos on Avenida Charles Darwin, right below the Darwin Research Station; and **Sub-Aqua** (✆ 05/2526-633; www.galapagos-sub-aqua.com), on Avenida Charles Darwin and Avenida 12 de Febrero.

you tend to get what you pay for here. There are four classes of boats: economic, tourist class, first class, and luxury. The **economic boats** have shared dormitories and bathrooms, inexperienced (and non-English-speaking) guides, and mediocre food. On a **tourist-class boat** you may have your own private quarters, but expect them to be cramped. You probably won't have air-conditioning or hot water, and your guide might not have a good command of the English language. **First-class ships** have excellent guides, small but private cabins with hot water and air-conditioning, and passable food. The main difference between first-class and **luxury** service is the food; some luxury boats also have swimming pools or Jacuzzis, but the cabins are not necessarily much bigger.

Another word of caution: Don't expect your cruise in the Galápagos to be a typical pleasure cruise; the boats are used mainly for lodging and transportation purposes. During the day, small dinghies, known as *pangas,* will transport you to the actual islands. Once you're on land, the excursions often involve long, uphill hikes. The Galápagos are not a place for relaxing—expect to participate in strenuous activities. The larger ships, while very pleasant, accommodating, and efficient, definitely have a slight cattle-car feel. If you're looking for a more intimate experience, you'll want to book one of the smaller yachts.

Trips to the Galápagos venture out to the high seas, and the waters can be rough. Be sure to bring Dramamine or another anti-seasickness medication with you. Candied ginger also helps settle small stomach upsets, and is an alternative to medication. If you know that you are prone to sea sickness, you'll definitely want to book on one of the larger ships, which are much more stable and comfortable. Also note that although the lower cabins tend to be a bit darker, with portholes as opposed to larger windows, these cabins are also the most stable. (In other words, it's easier to get seasick when you're sleeping higher up.)

RECOMMENDED TOUR OPERATORS & SHIPS

Every travel agency and tour operator in Quito and Guayaquil offers package tours to the Galápagos, as do many international operators. In most cases they just book space, either by reserving in advance or on a first-come, first-served basis, on the set number of boats touring the archipelago. Profit margins are very low, and prices tend to be standardized—meaning it's very rare for any agency or operator to severely undercut another for the same berth on any one boat or ship. Below I list recommended Ecuadorian and international tour operators that specialize in Galápagos trips, as well as descriptions and direct contact information, when possible, for my favorite boats and ships.

ECUADORIAN & INTERNATIONAL TOUR OPERATORS

Butterfield & Robinson ⚜ (© **866/551-9090** in the U.S. and Canada; www.butterfield. com) specializes in the very high-end market. One of its most interesting options is a trip designed for families with children over 8 years old. The trip provides a wealth of activities and adventures for parents and children to enjoy both together and apart. These folks charter out the luxury cruise ship *Isabela II,* and pay particular attention to the small details. Of course, this level of service and luxury doesn't come cheap. A 9-day/8-night trip costs around $7,500 to $11,600 (£4,124–£6,380) per person.

Galacruises Expeditions (©/fax **02/2509-007** in Ecuador; www.galacruises.com) runs four ships of their own and can book passage on a wide range of other boats and ships. Their boats range from tourist-class monohulls to modern luxury catamaran yachts. They do full-service tours around Ecuador and the region.

Linblad Expeditions ⚜⚜ (© **800/397-3348** in the U.S. and Canada; www. expeditions.com) is another luxury-oriented tour agency with decades of experience in the Galápagos, and a particular commitment to protecting the environment and raising environmental awareness. The company operates two small, luxurious cruise ships here, the M/V *Islander* and the M/V *Polaris.* Their 10-day program costs $3,650 to $6,280 (£2,008–£3,454) per person. Various extensions are available, as is a Machu Picchu combination tour.

Metropolitan Touring ⚜⚜ (© **02/2988-200** in Ecuador; www.metropolitan-touring. com) runs two luxury ships (M/V *Santa Cruz* and M/V *Isabela II)* and one luxury hotel (Finch Bay Hotel), and is one of the largest and most professional tour agencies in Ecuador. Consider booking with them especially if you want to mix and match time on shore with time on a ship, or if you want to design a package that includes a Galápagos excursion as well as trips to other destinations in Ecuador.

Overseas Adventure Travel ⚜ (© **800/493-6824** in the U.S. and Canada; www. oattravel.com) offers good-value itineraries, often combining a Galápagos cruise with time in Ecuador's Amazon or a side trip to Machu Picchu. Tours are limited to 16 people and are guided by experienced naturalists. Their 11-day Galápagos-and-Amazon package is a very good deal at $2,795 (£1,537) per person, including round-trip airfare from Miami.

Surtrek ⚜ (© **02/2231-534;** www.surtrek.com) is one of the better Quito-based general tour-and-adventure tour operators. And their Galápagos connections and experience are top-notch. They can book a wide range of cruises and mixed itineraries, and are often good at finding last-minute bargain berths on ships.

Tauck ⚜⚜ (© **800/788-7885** in the U.S. and Canada; www.tauck.com) is a well-established soft-adventure tour company, catering to higher-end travelers. They do an excellent job across the board, and have various itineraries, ranging from a combination Galápagos-and-Peru trip to a family excursion through the Galápagos. Tauck always charters an entire ship, usually one of the better luxury cruise ships plying these waters.

LUXURY & FIRST CLASS

Ecoventura *Moments* FIRST CLASS   A successful trip to the Galápagos depends on your guide; great ones will share the secrets of the islands with you, spot the rare animals, and treat you like a friend. You can expect this and more from the guides on Ecoventura's boats. The company operates four ships: the 16-passenger dive boat M/Y

Sky Dancer (see below), and the three identical 20-passenger boats M/Y *Eric, Flamingo I,* and *Letty.* Each of the latter three has two guides for every 20 people, a large sun deck, a bar, two sea kayaks, and snorkeling equipment. In addition to providing personalized service, Ecoventura is environmentally friendly. Don't expect super-luxurious cabins or over-the-top food, but you can count on this operation having the most experienced guides in the islands.

5805 Blue Lagoon Dr., Miami, FL 33126. © 800/633-7972 in the U.S. and Canada, or 02/2907-396. Fax 305/262-9609. www.ecoventura.com. 4 boats. *Eric, Flamingo,* and *Letty:* 7 nights $2,450–$2,995 (£1,348–£1,647) per person based on double occupancy. *Sky Dancer:* 7 nights $2,895–$3,095 (£1,592–£1,702) per person; 10 nights $4,035–$4,235 (£2,219–£2,329) per person. Rates include accommodations, all meals, nonalcoholic beverages, guide services, snorkeling equipment, wet suits, sea kayaks, and transfers between the dock and airport. Rates do not include airfare, hotel-to-airport transfers in Quito or Guayaquil, gratuities, or the $100 (£50) national park fee.

KLEIN Tours *R* FIRST CLASS   KLEIN Tours is one of the oldest companies operating boats in the Galápagos, and their experience shows. The company maintains three ships: the 20-passenger M/Y *Coral,* the 26-passenger M/Y *Coral II,* and the 110-passenger M/V *Galápagos Legend.* The smaller boats offer comparable services to those offered by Ecoventura's fleet, but KLEIN Tours' food is better. The guides are excellent and knowledgeable. The M/Y *Coral* is the more deluxe option of the two smaller vessels, with a top-deck Jacuzzi and fine rooms. The *Legend* has large cabins, a swimming pool, massage service, a 24-hour coffee bar, and a jogging track. I prefer the intimate feel of the smaller boats, but on the *Legend,* you won't be lacking for any personal comforts.

Av. Eloy Alfaro N 34–151 and Catalina Aldaz, Quito. © 888/50-KLEIN in the U.S., or 02/2430-345 in Ecuador. Fax 02/2442-389 in Ecuador. www.kleintours.com. *Coral* and the *Coral II:* 3 nights $978–$1,477 (£538–£812) per person; 4 nights $1,304–$1,969 (£717–£1,083) per person; 7 nights $2,282–$3,446 (£1,255–£1,895) per person. *Legend:* 3 nights $978–$1,600 (£538–£880) per person; 4 nights $1,304–$2,133 (£717–£1,173) per person; 7 nights $2,282–$3,733 (£1,255–£2,053) per person. Rates include accommodations, all meals, nonalcoholic beverages, guide services, snorkeling equipment, and transfers between the dock and airport. Rates do not include airfare, hotel-to-airport transfers in Quito or Guayaquil, gratuities, or the $100 (£55) national park fee.

M/V *Galápagos Explorer II* *RR* LUXURY   The *Galápagos Explorer II* is arguably the most luxurious ship in the Galápagos. The 100-passenger cruise ship offers all the amenities you could ever want: swimming pool, Jacuzzi, bars, first-class food, research center, nightly naturalist lectures, library, game room, and even a medical center. Most importantly, all the accommodations are exterior-facing suites, with small sitting areas, a minibar, and a TV/VCR. But in my opinion, when you're on a ship like this, you sacrifice personal attention for comfort. I'm just not a big fan of the large-cruise-ship experience in the Galápagos. When you're exploring the islands with 100 other people, the islands lose some of their mystique. Plus, you always feel a bit rushed, because there is always a group behind you, waiting for you to continue on your way. It's all a matter of taste, of course—if you like big cruise ships, you'll love the *Galápagos Explorer II.* But if you want to linger on the islands and ask your guide questions, you'll be better off on a smaller ship.

Urbanización Santa Leonor, Manzana 5, Solar 10, Guayaquil. © 04/2514-750. Fax 04/2287-651. www.galapagos explorer.com. 3 nights $1,225–$1,900 (£674–£1,045) per person; 4 nights $1,635–$2,540 (£899–£1,397) per person; 7 nights $2,715–$4,205 (£1,493–£1,397) per person. Rates include accommodations, all meals, guide services, and transfers between the dock and airport. Snorkeling equipment is $5 (£2.75) extra. Rates do not include airfare, hotel-to-airport transfers in Quito or Guayaquil, gratuities, or the $100 (£55) national park fee.

S/S *Mary Anne* *RR* (Finds) FIRST CLASS   This is the most unique vessel touring the Galápagos. Launched in 1997, the *Mary Anne* is a true three-masted square-rigged barkentine. Over 60m (200 ft.) long, including her bowsprit, she carries over 93 sq. m (1,000 sq. ft.) of sail, and a maximum of 16 passengers. That's a lot of ship for very few passengers. When all her sails are set, she's an impressive sight. Heck, even at anchor she's pretty special. If you choose this vessel you'll truly feel transported back in time. The air-conditioned cabins aren't quite as large and luxurious as those on the more modern-luxury cruise ships listed above, but the *Mary Anne*'s food is good, and what you sacrifice in creature comforts you more than make up for in character and ambience. The ship carries kayaks for guest use, and one naturalist guide, which is a bit thin if they are booked to capacity. For a sailing vessel (with motor assist), the *Mary Anne* is surprisingly swift, and her itinerary is quite extensive and complete.

Mariana de Jesús E7–113 (326) y Pradera, Quito. © **02/3237-186** in Quito. Fax 02/3238-309. www.angermeyer cruises.com. 7 nights $2,592–$2,880 (£1,426–£1,584) per person. Rates include accommodations, all meals, nonalcoholic beverages, guide services, snorkeling equipment, and transfers between the dock and airport. Rates do not include airfare, hotel-to-airport transfers in Quito or Guayaquil, gratuities, or the $100 (£55) national park fee.

M/V *Santa Cruz* ୧୧୧ LUXURY   This is my favorite of the large, luxury cruise ships working the Galápagos. The entire ship was refitted and updated in 1998. Almost every cabin has an ocean view—many with large picture windows, and a couple with balconies. The common areas are inviting and the 90-passenger maximum is just small enough that it's easy to interact with other guests and not feel overwhelmed by the masses. Well-done buffet meals are served for breakfast and lunch, while dinners are more formal, with a limited selection of nightly a la carte items. The guides are all well-trained and very pleasant. The main deck area features a large, open-air bar and a popular, well-heated Jacuzzi. There's even free Internet access from a common computer in the small library, which has a good selection of natural history and general fiction to keep you busy reading during your trip.

Av. de la Palmeras N35–74 7 Av. de las Orquídeas, Quito. © **02/2988-200** reservations in Quito, or 874/37-350-5910 direct satellite number on ship. Fax 02/2464-702. www.mvsantacruz.com. 3 nights $1,264–$2,022 (£695–£1,112) per person; 4 nights $1,685–$2,696 (£927–£1,483) per person; 7 nights $2,949–$4,718 (£1,622–£2,595) per person. Rates include accommodations, all meals, guide services, and transfers between the dock and airport. Rates do not include airfare, hotel-to-airport transfers in Quito or Guayaquil, gratuities, or the $100 (£55) national park fee.

Quasar Náutica ୧ LUXURY/SUPERIOR TOURIST   These folks operate five luxury ships in the Galápagos, most of which are small and intimate. Their largest ship, the M/V *Evolution*, is a beautiful small cruise ship with 16 double staterooms. This vessel harkens back to the early 20th century, and features a wonderful aft-deck dining room. The M/S *Alta* is a regal three-masted motor ketch, while the M/V *Parranda* is an elegant 38m (125-ft.) classic motorized yacht. The M/V *Mistral* is their most humble and economical option, with just six bunk-bed staterooms.

7855 NW 12th St., Suite 221, Miami, FL. © **800/247-2925** in the U.S. and Canada or 02/2446-996 in Ecuador. www. quasarnautica.com. 7 nights $2,350–$4,400 (£1,293–£2,420) per person. Rates include accommodations, all meals, nonalcoholic beverages, guide services, snorkeling equipment, and transfers between the dock and airport. Rates do not include airfare, hotel-to-airport transfers in Quito or Guayaquil, gratuities, or the $100 (£55) national park fee.

TOURIST & ECONOMY CLASS

M/S *Angelique* SUPERIOR TOURIST   This is a beautiful 23m (74-ft.) wooden schooner that was entirely refurbished in 2001. Her foremast even carries a couple of square sails, making her seem like a classic sailing ship. The berths near mid-ship are larger than those closer toward the bow, but the mid-ship cabins are also closer to the engine, so it's a trade-off. I'd opt to be a bit further away from the engine. Scuba diving is possible from this vessel and costs $75 per dive, with all equipment included.

Ramírez Dávalos 117 y Av. Amazonas, Quito. 🕐 **02/2505-599**. Fax 05/2226-715. www.kempery.com. 3 nights $615–$675 (£338–£371) per person; 4 nights $770–$845 (£424–£465) per person; 7 nights $1,230–$1,350 (£677–£743) per person. Rates include accommodations, all meals, nonalcoholic beverages, guide services, and transfers between the dock and airport. Rates do not include airfare, hotel-to-airport transfers in Quito or Guayaquil, gratuities, or the $100 (£55) national park fee.

M/Y Sea Man SUPERIOR TOURIST   Of the small tourist-class motor yachts plying the Galápagos Islands, this is one of the best. This boat carries a maximum of 16 passengers in eight double staterooms. Totally refurbished in 2003, the wood-paneled cabins are a bit small, but they all have air-conditioning, which is not always the case with tourist-class yachts. And the intimate boat and excellent crew help compensate for the lack of space. Plus, when you're awake you don't spend that much time in the cabins, anyway. There's a large sun deck on the *Sea Man*'s uppermost level. This is a fully equipped dive boat, and scuba diving will run you an additional $75 (£41) per dive, with all equipment included.

Galacruises Expeditions, N22–118 9 de Octubre y Veintimilla, Edificio El Trébol, Quito. 🕐/fax **02/2509-007** in Quito. www.galacruises.com. 4 nights $985 (£542) per person; 7 nights $1,575 (£866) per person. Rates slightly lower in the off season. Rates include accommodations, all meals, nonalcoholic beverages, snorkel gear, guide services, and transfers between the dock and airport. Rates do not include airfare, hotel-to-airport transfers in Quito or Guayaquil, gratuities, nor the $100 (£55) national park fee.

M/S Sulidae ⭐ TOURIST   This is one of my top choices among the tourist- and economy-class options, but then again, I'm partial to sailboats—or at least to motor-sailers. This 19m (63-ft.) motor-sailer features teak decks, red sails, and the feel of a working sailboat. Down below, there's plenty of varnished wood, and the boat is well maintained. The bunks are compact, but all have private bathrooms and even air-conditioning. Traditional sailboat enthusiasts will find her massive aft quarters a bit unsightly, but they greatly increase the room and comfort inside. This boat also works as a dive boat, with a surcharge of $70 (£39) per dive, including all of your equipment.

Portugal 600 y Av. 6 de Diciembre, Quito. 🕐/fax **02/2250-553** in Quito, or 05/2526-526 in Puerto Ayora. www.hotelsilberstein.com. 3 nights $573 (£315) per person; 4 nights $726 (£399) per person; 7 nights $1,257 (£691) per person. Rates include accommodations, all meals, nonalcoholic beverages, guide services, snorkeling equipment, and transfers between the dock and airport. Rates do not include airfare, hotel-to-airport transfers in Quito or Guayaquil, gratuities, or the $100 (£55) national park fee.

DEDICATED DIVE BOATS

In addition to generally having better equipment and dive masters, the dedicated dive boats tend to design their itineraries in order to visit the archipelago's top dive sites, particularly those around Wolf and Darwin islands. Most feature an average of four dives per day, although some days you may go down five times. Night diving is not allowed in the Galápagos.

Caution: Diving in these waters is not for beginning divers. There are often strong currents, cold waters, and limited visibility. Much of the diving is relatively deep diving. The payoff comes in the size, number, and diversity of large marine life. Due to the nature of the diving here, I personally recommend taking a boat with Nitrox facilities. If you are not already Nitrox certified, you can take a course onboard and dive with Nitrox tanks the entire time.

M/V Galápagos Aggressor I & II ⭐⭐ *(Finds* LUXURY   Part of the worldwide *Aggressor* fleet, these identical live-aboard vessels provide state-of-the-art dive technology and guiding services along with top-notch accommodations, cuisine, and creature comforts. Living, dive, and common areas are all well-designed and roomy. These

Not a Yachtie—Travel by Sea Kayak

Perhaps the most unique way to experience the Galápagos is with **Row International** ⭐⭐ (📞 **800/451-6034** in the U.S. and Canada; www.rowinternational. com), which offers multiday excursions in which sea kayaks are the principal means of touring and transport. Sea kayaks get you right down close to the action, and your encounters with sea lions and penguins become even more special. Accommodations are a mix of modest hotels and beach camping. Travel between the different islands is on small commuter planes or speedboats. An 11-day/10-night trip with these folks runs around $3,400 (£1,870) per person, not including airfare to Ecuador, to the Galápagos, or between the islands, nor the $100 (£55) national park fee.

30m-long (100-ft.) ships carry a maximum of 14 divers, so the experience is always intimate and personal. While scuba diving is the focus, several land tours are included in the weeklong itinerary. This boat has Nitrox facilities, as well as full film-developing equipment. Underwater still and video cameras can be rented.

P.O. Box 1470, Morgan City, LA 70381, USA. 📞 **800/348-2628** in the U.S. and Canada or 04/2681-950 in Ecuador. www.aggressor.com. 7-day itinerary $3,300–$3,600 (£1,815–£1,980) per person double occupancy. Rates include accommodations, all meals and beverages, unlimited diving, and transfers between the boat and airport. Rates do not include airfare, hotel-to-airport transfers in Quito or Guayaquil, gratuities, or the $100 (£55) national park fee and $70 (£39) port fee.

M/S *Lammer Law* LUXURY   This large, stable trimaran makes an excellent base for diving. It is also a fast and comfortable means of transport while you tour the islands. The *Lammer Law* carries a maximum of 16 passengers in eight private staterooms. All the rooms have two twin beds—which can be joined together or used separately—a private bathroom, porthole windows, and a small skylight. The broad, spacious interior area makes the rooms feel more like standard, albeit small, hotel rooms than like staterooms on a ship. The large deck area, perfect for sunbathing, is also a topside dining area, where all of the meals are served.

7855 NW 12th St., Suite 221, Miami, FL 33126, USA. 📞 **800/247-2925** in the U.S. and Canada or 02/2446-996 in Ecuador. www.quasarnautica.com. 7-day itinerary $2,750–$3,050 (£1,513–£1,678) per person double occupancy. Rates include accommodations, all meals and beverages, unlimited diving, and transfers between the boat and airport. Rates do not include airfare, hotel-to-airport transfers in Quito or Guayaquil, gratuities, or the $100 (£55) national park fee.

M/V *Sky Dancer* ⭐ LUXURY   Like the *Aggressor* boats above, the *Sky Dancer* is part of an international chain of live-aboard dive boats—in this case the Peter Hughes Diving fleet. In Ecuador, the *Sky Dancer* is administered by the very capable Ecoventura company (see above). This modern 30m (100-ft.) vessel carries a maximum of 16 divers in eight staterooms. The air-conditioned staterooms are certainly comfortable, but I find the accommodations and amenities a notch better across the board on the two *Aggressors*. Still, this is a very well-run and reputable operation, and serious divers will not be disappointed here. Food and diving services are excellent, and they have top-notch facilities, including Nitrox tanks and training.

5723 NW 158th St., Miami Lakes, FL 33014, USA. 📞 **800/932-6237** in the U.S. and Canada, or 04/2207-177 in Ecuador. www.peterhughes.com. 7-day itinerary $3,195–$3,395 (£1,757–£1,867) per person double occupancy. Rates include accommodations, all meals and beverages, unlimited diving, and transfers between the boat and airport. Rates do not include airfare, hotel-to-airport transfers in Quito or Guayaquil, gratuities, or the $100 (£55) national park fee and $100 (£55) fuel surcharge.

(Tips) Organizing a Last-Minute Trip to the Galápagos

There's no way around it—trips to the Galápagos are expensive. But if you book a cruise at the last minute, you can save substantially off the regular rates. Unfortunately, it's not easy to find a last-minute price, and you run the risk of not finding space. During the high season (June–Sept and late Dec to early Jan), you shouldn't even waste your time looking for one. Even during the low season, you shouldn't expect to come to Ecuador and immediately find a boat that's leaving the next day. In some cases, you may have to wait a week to 10 days before you find an opening. The following list will help you plan a last-minute trip to the Galápagos.

Websites

- **TOPPSA** , also known as Travel Opportunities South America (www. toppsa.com), manages a website that specializes in offering last-minute trips throughout Ecuador (including to the Galápagos). If you plan to travel to Ecuador within the next 60 days, it's worth a look to see whether special offers are available.

Travel Agencies in Quito

Note: **Galasam,** on Avenida Amazonas and Cordero, specializes in wildly inexpensive last-minute trips to the Galápagos. But I have heard complaints about the level of service and the inefficiency on its ships. The prices are low, but so is the quality.

- **Ecoventura** operates five ships and yachts in the Galápagos. Through the website (www.ecoventura.com) they sometimes offers last-minute deals at reduced rates. If there are no special discounts on the website, stop in or call their local offices in Ecuador. In Quito they have an office at Almagro N31–80, Edificio Venecia (© 02/2907-396); and in Guayaquil they have an office on Av. Central 300A, Cdla. Miraflores (© 04/2207-177). At both offices, you can try to book a last-minute berth at last-minute prices.
- **Zenith Ecuador Travel** , Juan León Mera 452 y Roca (© 02/2529-993; www.zenithecuador.com), has access to information about 100 boats that ply the waters around the Galápagos Islands. Give the staff your dates and your requirements, and they'll talk to their contacts and try to find you a special last-minute deal. Ask to speak to the owner, Mr. Marcos Endara, and tell him you are a Frommer's reader.
- **Enchanted Expeditions,** Av. de las Alondras N45-102 y Avenida de los Liros, Floral Building, Office no. 104 (© 02/3340-525; www.enchantedexpeditions. com), operates several boats in the Galápagos. If there's space, you won't have trouble negotiating a discounted last-minute price.

Travel Agencies in Puerto Ayora

- Bargain hunters should make **Moonrise Travel Agency,** Av. Charles Darwin, near the corner of Charles Binford (© 05/2526-402), your first stop. They specialize in booking last-minute trips on a number of different vessels (all classes and all sizes).

3 Puerto Ayora & Santa Cruz Island 🖈🖈

Santa Cruz Island is the principal base for tourism operations around the Galápagos, and Puerto Ayora is the main city on Santa Cruz. In fact, Puerto Ayora is the largest settlement in all of the archipelago. If you're arriving on your own, this the best place to base yourself and organize your trip.

Puerto Ayora is a bustling little port, with almost 12,000 inhabitants. It is home to the Galápagos National Park headquarters, as well as to the Charles Darwin Research Station.

Just off the north coast of Santa Cruz lies the small but very crucial island of Baltra. It's home to both the busiest airport on the Galápagos and to the most important deepwater port, where cruise and cargo ships come to refuel, unload cargo, and pick up and discharge passengers. The only major paved road on the island, outside of the city streets, is the road that connects Puerto Ayora with the dock at the narrow Canal de Itabaca (Itabaca Canal), which separates Santa Cruz and Baltra islands.

ESSENTIALS

GETTING THERE & DEPARTING

All flights from Quito and Guayaquil to Santa Cruz land at the **Aeropuerto Seymour** (© 05/2521-187; airport code: GPS), on the small island of Baltra, just off Santa Cruz's northern coast. In addition to desks at the airport, **Tame** (© 02/2909-900 in Quito, or 05/2526-165 in Puerto Ayora; www.tame.com.ec) has its main local offices on Avenida Charles Darwin and 12 de Febrero, while **Aerogal** (© 800/2376-425 toll-free nationwide, or 05/2526-797 in Puerto Ayora; www.aerogal.com.ec) has its offices on Avenida Baltra, between 10 de Marzo and Indefatigable.

Once you land at the airport, a free shuttle bus will take you to a ferry crossing of the Itabaca Canal to Santa Cruz. If you are going to the town of Puerto Ayora, take the bus marked CANAL. The ferry costs 80¢ (45p), and a regular bus will be waiting for you on the other side. From here to Puerto Ayora, the ride takes about 40 minutes and costs $2 (£1.10). You can also go to Puerto Ayora by taxi—a host of them will meet you at the crossing. The fare should run you from $15 to $20 (£8.25–£11).

If you are going to directly board a boat or ship and are not being met by a representative of that ship, you may need to take the free bus from the airport terminal marked MUELLE. This bus takes you to the dock in Baltra, where many of the ships wait to pick up passengers. Be sure to check this out in advance with your ship.

VISITOR INFORMATION

The Ministry of Tourism runs a **tourist information office** (© 05/2526-613; turismo@santacruz.gov.ec) on Avenida Charles Darwin, close to the corner of Charles Binford. It is open Monday through Friday from 8am to noon and 2 to 5:30pm. There are some small local tour operators along Avenida Charles Darwin. All of these offer a range of tour options and can help you try to find a last-minute berth on a boat or cruise ship.

FAST FACTS   To contact the local **police,** dial © 05/2526-101. Their headquarters are located on Avenida Charles Darwin and 12 de Febrero. For the local **fire department,** dial © 05/2526-111.

You can get a cash advance, exchange traveler's checks, or use the ATM at **Banco del Pacífico,** Av. Charles Darwin, near the corner of Charles Binford (© 05/2526-073).

The hospitals in the Galápagos can provide for emergency care, but any serious condition or long-term treatment should be dealt with on the mainland, or back at home. If you need a pharmacy, try **Farmacia Edith** (© 05/2526-487) or **Farmacia Vanessa** (© 05/2526-392) on Avenida Baltra and Tomás Berlanga.

Internet access is slower and more expensive here than on the mainland, but it has improved in recent years. Reliable Internet cafes include **Galápagos Online** on Avenida Charles Darwin, between Baltra and Islas Plaza (© 05/2527-169), and **Choza.Net,** on Avenida Baltra (© 05/2527-010). Rates run $1 to $3 (55p–£1.65) per hour. The

Unwanted Guests

While visiting friends in the Galápagos, I wondered why their house was surrounded by a ring of powder. The answer: "To stop the bloody fire ants." Anyone who has been bitten by one of these buggers will understand my friends' preventive measures. But fire ants on the Galápagos Islands? What were these unwanted critters doing here?

Along with some 300 invertebrates, 24 vertebrates, and 480 or so plants, those fire ants were introduced—either on purpose or unintentionally— throughout the archipelago. Since the early 19th century, even as Darwin made his groundbreaking visit, the Galápagos Islands has seen populations of feral goats, pigs, cattle, and donkeys established to supplement food sources for passing ships or for the incipient resident communities. These species were accompanied by a whole host of accidental tourists—rats and insects stowed away on ships, escaped pet cats and dogs, and discarded fruit and vegetable seeds.

Prior to 1964, no objective scientific studies had been made to reveal the full impact of the invasive plants and fauna that compete against, dominate, or just plain decimate the delicate native and endemic species here. Increasingly expansive introductions, lack of control, and less-than-transparent government interests reached such a point that UNESCO, in 1995, threatened to list the Galápagos as an "endangered World Heritage site." This surely would have meant stringent outside regulations and reduced tourism income for the Ecuadorian government. The Special Law for the Conservation of the Galápagos Islands was passed in 1998 by the Ecuadorian Congress.

And the result? Depressingly, despite some attempts at control and eradication, the problems are ongoing. The complexity of the situation stems from increased human populations, ongoing fishing issues, the near impossibility of eradicating even a single species, such as goats, and funding difficulties.

With two primary objectives—the eradication of existing feral species and the prevention of further introductions—UNESCO has received multimillion-dollar funding for community education programs, quarantines, and rapid-response actions when new and unwelcome "settlers" are identified.

But this is not a situation that can be fixed quickly—it's likely, in fact, that *Frommer's Ecuador 2050* will include a sidebar similar to this one in its Galápagos chapter.

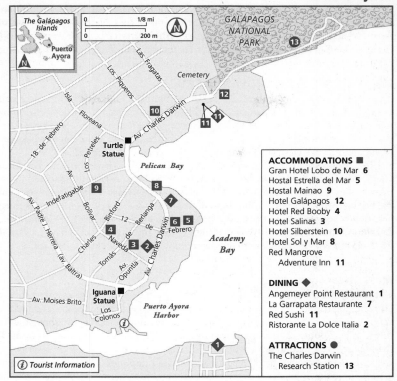

post office (© **05/2526-575**) is located at the far end of Avenida Charles Darwin, right across from the main dock.

ORIENTATION

Puerto Ayora is a port town set around a broad and deep harbor known as Bahía Academia (Academy Bay). The principal road in town, Avenida Charles Darwin, pretty much hugs the coastline, and runs from the main dock in town to the Charles Darwin Research Station. All along its length, Avenida Charles Darwin is peppered with restaurants, shops, tour agencies, bars, and hotels. Almost everything of interest to tourists in Puerto Ayora is within walking distance, although a few tourist attractions and destinations on the island do lie outside of town.

GETTING AROUND

Everything in Puerto Ayora is within easy walking distance, including the Charles Darwin Research Station. If you're really lazy, you can take a taxi around town for about $1 (55p). If you want to tour other sites around the island on your own, you can hire a taxi for about $10 (£5.50) per hour. If you can't flag one down on the street, have your hotel arrange one for you. Alternatively, you can rent a bike, which will only cost you around $10 (£5.50) per day.

If you're staying on one of the boats at anchor, or if you just want to visit someplace more easily reached by watercraft, head to the main dock at the southern end of Avenida Charles Darwin and grab one of the many water taxis. Rides run about $1 (55p) per person to any boat at anchor or any nearby pier. There's a slight surcharge for rides after dark.

WHAT TO SEE & DO ON SANTA CRUZ

There's plenty to see and do here. By far the most popular and convenient way to visit the various attractions and partake in the different active adventures listed below is by signing up for a tour. A host of tour agencies are located along Avenida Charles Darwin, and most local hotels can arrange any tour on Santa Cruz, on surrounding islands, and on the water, including every tour and activity listed below.

I like **Moonrise Travel Agency** ⚑⚑, Avenida Charles Darwin near the corner of Charles Binford (© **05/2526-402**), an excellent local tour outfit and source of information. The staff are friendly and they can help you arrange a last-minute cruise of the Galápagos, independent tours around the islands, and any of the local tours listed below. Another good agency, especially for adventure tours, is **We Are The Champions,** Avenida Charles Darwin, between 12 de Febrero and Tomás de Berlanga (© **05/ 2526-951;** www.wearethechampionstours.com).

ON THE ISLAND
Main Attractions
CHARLES DARWIN RESEARCH STATION ⚑   This is the primary tourist attraction on Santa Cruz, and a major player in the protection and propagation of the very endangered Galápagos tortoise. The main attraction here is an interpretive walk through the grounds of the active breeding center. The guided tour takes you through the life cycle and natural history of these massive land reptiles. You'll see juveniles as well as representatives of the 11 Galápagos tortoise subspecies. This is a great place to actually note the difference in shell shapes of the various subspecies. As you walk the trails you'll find various corrals holding the tortoises; with a guide's supervision, you can enter some of these for a close encounter with the denizens.

The Charles Darwin Research Station (© **05/2526-146;** www.darwinfoundation. org) is located at the end of Avenida Charles Darwin, about a 10- to 15-minute walk from the main dock in Puerto Ayora. It is open daily from 7am until 6pm. There is no entrance fee, and bilingual guides are provided. To offset the free admission, however, I recommend that you make a small donation to the Charles Darwin Foundation.

CERRO CHATO TORTOISE RESERVE   After you've learned about the giant tortoise and seen a few captive specimens at the Charles Darwin Research Station, you might want to head out to see these fascinating reptiles in their natural environment. This reserve, located southwest of the small inland town of Santa Rosa, is best visited as part of a guided tour. Most of these tours also stop at the bulk of the other attractions listed in this section. Some include horseback riding or mountain biking.

CERRO CROCKER, MEDIA LUNA & PUNTUDO   These three volcanic peaks are the highest spots on the island, and more or less clustered together near the center of the island. Although it's only 864m (2,864 ft.) high, it's still a vigorous hike to the top of Media Luna (Half Moon), the tallest of the three. The rewards, however, include excellent bird-watching on the way, as well as a wonderful panoramic view from the top.

Fun Fact **I'm So Lonely**

Discovered in 1971 by a National Parks expedition out hunting feral goats, Lonesome George was believed to be the sole survivor of the Isla Pinta tortoise subspecies. Previously, the last recorded sighting of an Isla Pinta tortoise had been in 1906. Lonesome George was brought to the Charles Darwin Research Station for a variety of reasons. Scientists, for example, are frantically trying to find a mate for him so that the species doesn't become extinct. They've even offered a $10,000 reward to anyone who finds another Isla Pinta tortoise. They have also tried to breed Lonesome George—estimated to be between 70 and 80 years old—with closely related female species, but so far these attempts have been unsuccessful. As this book went to press, however, biologists were speculating that, based on recent genetic evidence, a female Pinta tortoise was likely to be found on Isla Isabela.

CERRO DRAGON ☞   Cerro Dragon (Dragon Hill), on the north side of Santa Cruz, was established as a breeding and protection area for the endangered and unique Galápagos land iguana. There's a great loop trail here that offers excellent opportunities to see the land iguanas as well as many bird species, including the Darwin finch. If you're lucky, you may see flamingos in the large, brackish mangrove lagoon. Cerro Dragon is only accessible by sea, and you'll definitely need to sign up for a boat tour to visit here.

LOS GEMELOS (THE TWINS)   The Twins are two impressively large craters that straddle the main road almost halfway between Puerto Ayora and the Itabaca Canal. This popular destination sits at a high point on the island in an area of dense cloud forest. There are easily accessible lookouts for both craters just off the highway, and a couple of nearby trails through the forests offer excellent bird-watching. If you're lucky, you'll catch a glimpse of the brightly colored vermilion flycatcher.

PLAYA DE LOS ALEMANES & LAS GRIETAS ☞   Playa de los Alemanes (German Beach), a beautiful white sand beach, is good for sun bathing and swimming. A 15- to 20-minute hike from Playa de los Alemanes will bring you to Las Grietas (The Grottos), where a couple of steep, narrow canyons contain calm pools filled with a mix of fresh and salt water. Las Grietas is an excellent place for a refreshing dip. More adventurous types can jump off the surrounding rocks into the deep pools. To get here, take a water taxi at the main dock in Puerto Ayora and ask the driver to drop you at the trail head to Playa de los Alemanes. It's only about a 5-minute hike from there to the beach.

TORTUGA BAY ☞☞   Located just west of Puerto Ayora, Bahía Tortuga (Tortuga Bay) is one of the best and most beautiful beaches in the Galápagos. The first beach you come to is a long stretch of white sand. Be careful here: The waves and undertow are often very strong, and several drownings have occurred. If you really want to swim, head over to the far western end of the beach, where there is a calmer, protected area. Tortuga Bay is just 2.5km (1½ miles) outside of Puerto Ayora, and is reached via a well-marked and paved path. Ask anyone in town to point you to the trail head, from which a gentle hike should take you less than an hour each way.

ADVENTURE ACTIVITIES

CAMPING   October through July, the folks at the Red Mangrove Inn (see below) offer overnight camping excursions. **Galápagos Camping** (© 05/2526-564; www. galapagoscamping.com) has a relatively plush campsite inland on the island, in a spot where Galápagos tortoises can sometimes be found. Large, modern tents are set on platforms under a permanent roof. There's a large common dining area, as well as a small cave which is equipped with a built-in fireplace. The tour here leaves Puerto Ayora in the afternoon and returns the next morning. It costs $90 (£50) per person, including transportation, equipment, dinner and breakfast, and a cocktail.

MOUNTAIN BIKING & HORSEBACK RIDING   The largely uninhabited wild terrain of Santa Cruz Island is well suited for both mountain-bike and horseback exploration, and a variety of rides are possible. Several shops along Avenida Charles Darwin rent mountain bikes, although I think you're best off signing up for a tour. For those in less than competitive shape, I recommend one of the tours that take the gear and participants first by van to the highlands, so that most of the biking is downhill. Rates run from $10 to $20 (£5.50–£11) per day. Quality varies widely, so check out a few possibilities first. **Red Mangrove Adventure Inn** (see below) offers both full-day mountain biking and full-day horseback riding tours around Santa Cruz Island.

ON & UNDER THE WATER

BOAT TOURS TO OTHER ISLANDS   Water taxis are available for hire at the main dock, at the southern end of Avenida Charles Darwin. Rates run from around 80¢ (45p) for a short ride across Academy Bay, to around $10 or $15 (£5.50–£8.25) per hour for longer excursions. If you want to visit a specific island to do some wildlife-viewing or snorkeling, you're best off signing on for an organized tour with a reputable operator.

GLASS-BOTTOM BOAT   To see the underwater world of the Galápagos, check out **Aqua View Glass Bottom Boat** (© 05/2526-632), which has daily excursions at 9am and 2pm. The trips last 4 hours and include a stop or two to snorkel, as well as a snack. The ride passes around Punta Estrada and takes in Las Grietas (The Grottos). The cost is $35 (£19) per person.

PADDLING AROUND   The bays and mangroves around Santa Cruz are great spots for kayaking. Most of the tour agencies in town offer guided sea-kayak excursions. If you just want to rent one on your own, head to the **Red Mangrove Adventure Inn** (see below), which has a small fleet of them available for around $10 (£5.50) per hour, and also offers full-day guided kayak tours.

SURFING   The Galápagos Islands are not only one of the world's most exotic surf destinations; they are also blessed with numerous point, reef, and beach breaks. With the isolation of the archipelago, and the fact that most people come here to interact with wildlife or to scuba dive, these breaks are almost always uncrowded. While San Cristóbal is the islands' most popular surf destination, there are several good surf spots around Santa Cruz—and depending upon the swell direction, one or more is almost always working. Just beyond the Charles Darwin Research Station lie the spots of La Ratonera and Bazán. You'll almost always find locals surfing here, since they're so close to town. Farther afield, but still within walking distance, you can surf the break at Tortuga Bay. A short boat ride will bring you to prized surf spots like Ola Escondida (Hidden Wave) and Punta Barba Negra (Black Beard Point). You can easily hire a **water taxi** (see above) to take you to any of the more remote surf spots. There's no dedicated surf shop on the island yet, although if you ask around, you should be able to find a local tour agency with a beater board for rent. Still, you're best off bringing your own board and wet suit.

SNORKELING & SCUBA DIVING 🐟🐟🐟   The snorkeling and scuba diving around the Galápagos Islands is some of the best in the world. In addition to the vibrant fish life, you can often count on a close underwater encounter with a sea lion or sea turtle. Really lucky divers and snorkelers will catch glimpses of an underwater marine iguana or Galápagos penguin. For scuba divers the ante gets upped, and prized sightings include schools of scalloped hammerhead sharks, manta rays, and the occasional whale shark. Almost all the tour agencies and hotel tour desks in town can arrange for a snorkel or dive trip.

There's good snorkeling all around Santa Cruz. One of the most popular spots is called La Lobería (The Sea Lion Colony), which is a small island located about a 15-minute boat ride from Puerto Ayora. You are almost guaranteed a close in-water encounter with a playful sea lion here. Equipment rental runs around $7 to $10 (£3.85–£5.50) per day for fins, mask, and snorkel. A guided tour or boat excursion to snorkel will run you $20 to $45 (£11–£25), depending upon the length of the outing and the distance traveled to the snorkel spot.

For scuba diving, I recommend you use either **SCUBA Iguana** 🐟 (© 05/2526-497; www.scubaiguana.com), located near the old Hotel Galápagos, on Avenida Charles Darwin, right below the Darwin Research Station; or **Sub-Aqua** (© 05/2526-633; www.galapagos-sub-aqua.com), on Avenida Charles Darwin and Avenida 12 de Febrero. Both operations are very professional and have excellent gear and dive masters. A two-tank dive outing, including all gear, should run you $90 to $140 (£50–£77), including lunch. My favorite dive sites easily accessible from Puerto Ayora include Gordon Rocks, Mosquera Islet, and North Seymour Island.

SHOPPING

Most folks don't come to the Galápagos to shop, and most of what you will find here is pretty standard tourist fare. The entire length of Avenida Charles Darwin is strewn with simple souvenir shops and T-shirt outlets. But there are a few exceptions. If you're looking for jewelry, check out **Galápagos Jewelry** 🐟🐟, on Avenida Charles Darwin, between Isla Floreana and Indefatigable (© 05/2526-044; www.galapagosjewelry.com). They have excellent one-off pieces, many in the shapes and images of local flora and fauna. They also have storefronts in two high-end hotels in Quito, the J.W. Marriott and Swissôtel Quito. For good local art, head to **Galería Aymara** 🐟 on Avenida Charles Darwin and Los Piqueros (© 05/2526-835; www.galeria-aymara.com); or to **Angelique Art Gallery,** on Avenida Charles Darwin near the corner of Indefatigable (© 05/2526-656).

WHERE TO STAY

When I last visited, the long-standing **Hotel Galápagos** (©/fax 05/2526-330; www.hotelgalapagos.com) had been sold and was being torn down to make way for a new, luxurious boutique hotel. This place has a beautiful waterfront location, just below the Charles Darwin Research Station, and is expected to open sometime in 2008.

VERY EXPENSIVE

Finch Bay Hotel 🐟🐟 *Moments*   The only beachfront hotel in Santa Cruz opened in 2003 and is a 5-minute boat ride from Puerto Ayora. Secluded and serene among the mangroves with a magnificent pool and private beach, the Finch Bay also has over 30 species of resident birds, including red-footed boobies. Rooms are tastefully decorated with yellow walls and attractive wooden blinds; bathrooms are large and have spacious showers with good water pressure (rare in the islands). The hotel prides itself on being environmentally friendly, with solar power and a policy of conservation. There's a Zen garden where yoga is offered in the mornings; bikes, kayaks, and snorkeling equipment are available for guests, too. The friendly staff can organize day trips to the islands and scuba-diving excursions. The excellent restaurant serves three meals a day with an emphasis on healthy, organic ingredients; vegetarian offerings are also available. There's a computer with free Internet access for guests. None of the rooms have TVs, but a lounge offers satellite TV. To get here, take a water taxi from the dock; it'll cost you 80¢ (45p). When making your reservation, be sure to inquire about the all-inclusive packages that start at $839 (£461) per person for 3 nights, as well as about other promotional rates. Prices include transfers from the airport, all meals, and daily tours on the hotel's fast, private yacht, the *Sea Finch*.

Punta Estrada, Isla Santa Cruz. ⓒ 877/534-8584 in the U.S. and Canada, or 05/2526-297 at the hotel. Fax 02/3341-439. www.finchbayhotel.com. 21 units. $255 (£140) double. Rates include breakfast buffet. AE, DC, MC, V. **Amenities:** Restaurant; 2 bars; lounge; large outdoor pool; Jacuzzi; watersports equipment; bike rental; tour desk; limited room service; laundry service; smoke-free rooms. *In room:* A/C, dataport, safe.

Royal Palm Hotel 🐾🐾🐾 *(Finds)* The most exclusive resort in Ecuador sits on 200 lush hillside hectares (500 acres), a 20-minute drive from Puerto Ayora. The Royal Palm attracts a healthy dose of celebrities seeking the privacy and personalized service offered by this resort. There are 10 beautiful villas scattered on the hillside, four veranda studios, and three spectacular suites. The villas each have a separate living/dining area; a bedroom with a king-size bed and CD player; and a huge bathroom with large shower, dressing area, and separate room with a Jacuzzi tub. All villas come with gleaming hardwood floors and leather sofas. Windows face the serene countryside and the ocean at the bottom of the hill. The three suites are all different from one another—the two-bedroom, two-bathroom Imperial comes with its own Jacuzzi hidden in a private garden, while the Royal has a four-poster bed and an indoor sauna. The studios are the simplest (and least expensive) units but have charming patios with hammocks and spacious bathrooms with Jacuzzi tubs. Service is exquisite, friendly, and not at all stuffy. Anybody staying here will be made to feel like a VIP, from the special greeting at the airport to the private speedboat used for transfers from Baltra to Santa Cruz. The hotel is more than a half-hour from the port, so it is not the most convenient place to stay for visiting other islands.

Vía Baltra, Km 18, Isla Santa Cruz. ⓒ 05/2527-409. Fax 05/2527-408. www.royalpalmGalapagos.com. 17 units. $345 (£190) studio; $475–$575 (£261–£316) suite; $575 (£316) villa for 2; $825 (£454) Imperial Suite. Rates include American breakfast. AE, DC, MC, V. **Amenities:** Restaurant; bar; beautiful outdoor swimming pool; 2 outdoor tennis courts; exercise room; sauna; concierge; large business center; 24-hr. room service; massage; laundry service; same-day dry cleaning. *In room:* A/C, TV/DVD, dataport, minibar, hair dryer, safe.

EXPENSIVE

Hotel Silberstein 🐾 This longstanding institution, formerly the Hotel Anger-meyer, is a good choice downtown. The hotel is an attractive two-story structure set facing a delightful free-form swimming pool. Well-tended and relatively lush gardens give the grounds the feel of a small tropical oasis. The 22 rooms are large, with white-tile floors and built-in beds and nightstands. All share a common veranda. The hotel has a good restaurant serving Ecuadorian and international cuisine. In the Silberstein you'll find a dive center and tour agency, both of which are well run and respectable. Multiday tour and dive packages are available.

Av. Charles Darwin and Piqueros, Puerto Ayora, Isla Santa Cruz. ℂ 05/2526-277 at the hotel, or 02/2269-626 reservations in Quito. Fax 05/2250-553. www.hotelsilberstein.com. 22 units. $129 (£71) double. Rates include breakfast buffet. AE, DC, MC, V. Amenities: Restaurant; bar; small outdoor swimming pool; tour desk, laundry service. In room: A/C.

Red Mangrove Adventure Inn ⭐ (Finds) This unique little hotel oozes artistry and character. Owner Polo Navarro was a pioneering naturalist guide on Santa Cruz, and the hotel originally began as his personal home. The Red Mangrove is extremely close to both the Charles Darwin Research Station and downtown Puerto Ayora, yet it seems as if it's a world away. The hotel sits nestled in a grove of red mangroves on a calm and rocky bay. Rooms are a bit small and rather basic for this price range; the best units have views of the bay. All have funky colorful furnishings and decor, as well as adobe platform beds. There are delightful common sitting areas and a small tile pool and gazebo-covered hot tub. The open-air restaurant has fabulous views of the bay, and is the best sushi restaurant in the Galápagos (see below). Polo still organizes, and sometimes leads, guided tours of Santa Cruz and the surrounding islands. Tour options include mountain-bike, horseback, and kayak tours.

Av. Charles Darwin, Puerto Ayora, Isla Santa Cruz. ℂ 05/2527-011. Fax 05/2526-564. www.redmangrove.com. 10 units. $145–$205 (£80–£113) double; $275 (£151) suite. AE, DC, MC, V. Amenities: Restaurant; bar; small outdoor swimming pool; Jacuzzi; tour desk, mountain bike and kayak rentals; laundry service. In room: No phone.

MODERATE
Gran Hotel Lobo de Mar The rooms here are built around a small interior courtyard with a teardrop-shaped pool at its center. Everything here has been upgraded in recent years, and now all the rooms are modern and well kept. About half the units have private balconies that overlook either the pool and courtyard area, the street, or, in the case of the prize rooms, Academy Bay. The hotel actually has two swimming pools, both of which are small. You'll want to use the open-air courtyard pool—I find the indoor pool rather gloomy, claustrophobic, and uninviting.

Av. Charles Darwin and 12 de Febrero, Puerto Ayora, Isla Santa Cruz. ℂ 05/2526-188 in Puerto Ayora, or 02/2502-089 reservation office in Quito. ℂ/fax 05/2526-569. www.lobodemar.com.ec. 38 units. $70–$100 (£39–£55) double. Rates include breakfast buffet. DC, MC, V. Amenities: Restaurant; bar; one indoor and one outdoor pool; tour desk; laundry service. In room: A/C, TV, no phone.

Hostal Mainao This comfortable downtown option features bold Mediterranean-influenced architecture, with whitewashed stucco offset by red accents. The building itself features arched doorways and curved walls. Several of the rooms have private balconies. Decor is minimal, with white walls and thin white muslin curtains. My favorite rooms are Plazas and Genovesa—each comes with a large wraparound balcony. The Floreana is a huge suite, with a kitchenette, living room, and large balcony area as well.

Calle Matazarnos and Indefatigable, Puerto Ayora, Isla Santa Cruz. ℂ/fax 05/2527-029 in Puerto Ayora, or 04/2296-799 in Guayaquil. www.hostalmainao.com. 16 units. $55–$66 (£30–£36) double. Rates include continental breakfast. DC, MC, V. Amenities: Bar; tour desk; laundry service. In room: No phone.

Hotel Red Booby Although it's located a few blocks inland from Avenida Charles Darwin and the main strip, this newer hotel is an excellent choice. Rooms are spacious, with sparkling white-tile floors, simple wooden furnishings, and firm beds. You'll definitely want to ask for one of the "Isabela" rooms, which are located on the third floor around the pool. The best and most unique thing here is this open-air rooftop swimming pool, with a large terrace area all around and good views. The

slightly formal restaurant here serves respectable Ecuadorian and international fare, but I really like eating at the poolside grill, where you can get fresh fish, shrimp, or steaks prepared to order on their charcoal-fired grill.

Islas Plazas between Tomás de Berlanga and Charles Binford, Puerto Ayora, Isla Santa Cruz. © 05/2526-485 in Puerto Ayora, or 02/2221-505 reservation office in Quito. Fax 05/2526-486. www.hotelredbooby.com.ec. 26 units. $85 (£47) double. DC, MC, V. **Amenities:** Restaurant, bar; rooftop grill; small outdoor pool; tour desk; laundry service. *In room:* A/C, no phone.

INEXPENSIVE

Hostal Estrella del Mar   Located right off the water, fronting Academy Bay, this Norwegian-owned-and-managed hostel is a good budget option. You'll definitely want to reserve one of the four units that face the bay. About half the rooms have air-conditioning and televisions. Everything on-site is well-maintained and neat, and there's a relaxed vibe. A great feature here is the shared balcony overlooking the bay. There's no restaurant, but breakfast is served daily.

12 de Febrero, Puerto Ayora, Isla Santa Cruz. ©/fax **05/2526-080** or 05/2526-427. estrellademar@islasantacruz.com. 12 units. $30–$40 double (£17–£22). DC, MC, V. **Amenities:** Lounge; tour desk; laundry service. *In room:* No phone.

Hotel Salinas   This place offers some of the most popular backpacker accommodations in Puerto Ayora. The three-story hotel is built in a "U"-shape around a small garden courtyard. Rooms are fairly basic, with virtually no decor beyond some simple wooden beds and nightstands. The more expensive rooms are larger, and come with air-conditioning and private balconies.

Calle Isla Plaza between Av. Charles Darwin and Tomás de Berlanga, Puerto Ayora, Isla Santa Cruz. © **05/2526-107.** ©/fax 05/2526-072. 21 units. $22–$44 (£12–£24) double. Rates include continental breakfast. DC, MC, V. **Amenities:** Tour desk; laundry service. *In room:* No phone.

Hotel Sol y Mar *(Finds*   If you want an ocean view at budget prices, this place is even better than the Estrella del Mar (see above). Here, most of the rooms front Academy Bay, and the best of these have private balconies overlooking the water—you'll definitely want to pay a little extra and get a waterfront room with balcony. All units come with pleasant decorative touches, including Persian rugs and colorful bedspreads. Perhaps the hotel's best feature is its large bayfront patio and dining area. Pelicans, herons, and the occasional sea lion can often be found here.

Av. Charles Darwin between Tomás de Berlanga and Charles Binford, Puerto Ayora, Isla Santa Cruz. © **05/2526-139** or 05/2526-281. Fax 05/2527-015. 8 units. $20–$40 (£11–£22) double. DC, MC, V. **Amenities:** Restaurant; bar; tour desk; laundry service. *In room:* No phone.

WHERE TO DINE

The restaurants at the **Royal Palm Hotel** and **Finch Bay Hotel** (see above) are both excellent. If you're not staying at either of these, you might consider a splurge, and dine at one or both while in Puerto Ayora. In both cases, reservations are essential, and the food will be quite a bit more expensive than anything else you'll find around town.

EXPENSIVE

Ristorante La Dolce Italia *€* ITALIAN/PIZZA   If you're looking for a change of pace from the overabundance of *ceviche*, seafood, and sushi, try this simple trattoria-style Italian restaurant. You can start things off with some fried calamari or a plate of antipasti. If you want something lighter, the thin-crust wood-oven pizzas are excellent. The long list of pasta options includes several homemade fresh pastas. A variety of fresh seafood is served simply but expertly grilled. If you want something more elaborate, order the shrimp in a cream and cognac sauce. There's a slight maritime theme indoors, with some ship models and relics. I especially like the artfully placed panes of colored glass. La Dolce Italia offers delivery; in fact, they even deliver to ships docked in the bay.

Av. Charles Darwin and 12 de Febrero, Puerto Ayora. © 09/9848-666. Reservations recommended in high season. Main courses $6.50–$22 (£3.60–£12). AE, DC, MC, V. Daily 11:30am–10pm.

MODERATE

Angermeyer Point Restaurant *Moments* ECUADORIAN/INTERNATIONAL
This restaurant gets my vote for the best-located and most-atmospheric dining spot in Puerto Ayora. This old stone house, with a broad wraparound wooden deck, is set on a rocky promontory facing the bay. It was the former home of local legend and painter Karl Angermeyer, who arrived here in 1937. Weather permitting, you'll definitely want to grab one of the waterfront tables on the outdoor deck. You'll probably spend as much time enjoying the sight of sea lions, blue-footed boobies, and marine iguanas as you will enjoying your meal. In fact, this place is also known as La Casa de las Iguanas (The House of Iguanas), and there are always large groups of these remarkable reptiles here. The food, unfortunately, doesn't quite live up to the surroundings, but if you stick with grilled fish or a shrimp dish, you'll be just fine. To reach Angermeyer Point, you have to take a water taxi, which you can hire from the main dock in Puerto Ayora for around $1 (50p) each way. Or call the restaurant to make a reservation, and they should be able to arrange transport for you.

Angermeyer Point, Puerto Ayora. © 05/2526-452. Reservations recommended. Main courses $4–$17 (£2.20–£9.35). DC, MC, V. Daily noon–9:30pm.

La Garrapata Restaurante *(icons)* ECUADORIAN   This place is a local institution. It's where the expats eat—and all the foreign guides who work on the ships. There's a great selection of fresh juices and sandwiches. The open-air dining room features low wooden chairs and round tables with linen table-cloths. But there's nothing formal about either the vibe or service here. Main courses include a wide range of seafood and meat options, as well as some pastas. There's usually a *menú del día* (menu of the day) with soup, main course, and dessert for less than $5 (£2.75). They even have a pretty good wine list. On weekends, sometimes there's live music.

Av. Charles Darwin and Charles Binford, Puerto Ayora. © 05/2526-264. Main courses $4–$15 (£2.20–£8.25). AE, DC, MC, V. Mon–Sat 9am–4pm and 6:30–10pm.

Red Sushi *Finds* JAPANESE/SUSHI   The menu here is what you might expect to find at any typical sushi bar and Japanese restaurant. There's a wide range of sushi, sashimi, and maki options, as well as noodle dishes, tempura, and more substantial plates like chicken yakitori. The fish is extremely fresh, and overall they do a very good job. Presentations are artistic, with the dishes served on colorful plates or spread on large platters made from the cross-section of a log. The hip dining room and bar features floor-to-ceiling windows with a view of the bay, low tables and chairs, and a sprinkling of hammock-style swing chairs.

At the Red Mangrove Adventure Inn, Av. Charles Darwin, Puerto Ayora. © 05/2527-011. Reservations recommended. Main courses: $5–$15 (£2.75–£8.25). AE, DC, MC, V. Daily 12:30–3:30pm and 6–9:30pm.

PUERTO AYORA AFTER DARK

For such a seemingly sleepy little city, Puerto Ayora has a surprisingly lively, albeit limited, nightlife and bar scene. **Bongo Bar** *(icons)* (© 05/2526-264) is the most happening place in town at night. It's located on a rooftop above and behind La Panga (see below). Bongo Bar opens at 4pm, but usually doesn't get busy until after 8pm. Across the street, the **Limón Café** (© 05/2526-510) is popular early in the evening, and you can check e-mail from several computers. Limón Café often gets the crowds up and dancing, but if you're looking for the best dance club in town, head to **La Panga** (© 05/2526-264). If you want to find live music, try **La Taberna del Duende** (Finds (© 05/2527-320), which is popular with locals and is located inland from the main tourist strip on Calle Juan León Mera and San Cristóbal. It opens at 9pm and often doesn't get going till a bit later. Alternatively, you can see if there's any live music, theater, or poetry at **Casa del Lago** (© 09/9714-647), located on Calle Juan Montalvo and Calle Moises Brito.

4 Puerto Baquerizo Moreno & San Cristóbal Island

The second-most important island for tourism in the Galápagos, San Cristóbal is a large island at the eastern end of the archipelago. The main settlement here, Puerto Baquerizo Moreno, is the provincial capital of the islands. Still, it is a small city and much less developed and less active than Puerto Ayora, on Santa Cruz Island.

Aside from the capital city, there's only one other settlement of note on San Cristóbal, El Progreso. Located several miles inland from the port, El Progreso was actually the first spot settled on the island. In 1879, Ecuadorian businessman Manuel Cobo set up a notorious prison camp here, using the free prison laborers to farm sugar cane, harvest sea-turtle meat, and slaughter and skin the island's feral cattle. Conditions on Cobo's prison-farm were said to be cruel, and Cobo himself was a bit of a dictator; he even issued his own currency. An inmate uprising in January 1904, ended Cobo's life, although one of the town's main streets is still named after him.

ESSENTIALS

GETTING THERE & DEPARTING

All flights from Quito and Guayaquil to San Cristóbal land at the **Aeropuerto San Cristóbal** (© 05/2520-111; www.aeropuertosancristobal.com.ce; airport code: SCY), which is just a few blocks west of downtown Puerto Baquerizo Moreno.

Both of the major airlines, **Tame** (© 02/2909-900 in Quito, or 05/2521-351 in Puerto Baquerizo Moreno; www.tame.com.ec) and **Aerogal** (© 800/2376-425 toll-free nationwide, or 05/2521-118 in Puerto Baquerizo Moreno; www.aerogal.com.ec), have desks at the airport.

Taxis are always waiting to meet incoming flights. A taxi to any hotel in town should only cost $1 (55p).

VISITOR INFORMATION

The chamber of tourism runs a **tourist information office** (© 05/2521-124) on Avenida Charles Darwin and Teodoro Wolf. It is open Monday through Saturday from 8am to 5pm. They can provide orientation and some brochures, but you're probably better off going to one of the small tour operators that are concentrated around the tiny downtown area. All offer a range of tour options and can help you try to find a last-minute berth on a boat or cruise ship, or to book a hotel room.

FAST FACTS   To contact the local **police,** dial © 05/2520-101. Their headquarters are located on Avenida Charles Darwin and Calle Española. The **post office** (© 05/2520-373) is located on Avenida Charles Darwin and Calle Manuel Cobos.

> **Fun Fact Sinking Feeling**
>
> The popular bay and anchorage just off Puerto Baquerizo Moreno is called Bahía Naufragio, or Shipwreck Bay. Over the centuries, the bay has claimed several vessels, and today scuba divers—and marine life—get to enjoy the benefits.

The hospitals in the Galápagos can provide for emergency care, but any serious condition or long-term treatment should be dealt with on the mainland, or back at home. There is, however, a small **hospital** in Puerto Baquerizo Moreno (© **05/2520-118**), on Avenida Quito and Alsacio Northia. In an emergency, you can call the **Red Cross** at © **05/2520-125.** If you need a pharmacy, try **Farmacia Jane,** on Avenida Charles Darwin and Teodoro Wolf (© **05/2520-242**), or **Su Farmacia,** on Avenida 12 de Febrero and Alsacio Northia (© **05/2520-112**).

You can get a cash advance, exchange traveler's checks, or use the ATM at **Banco del Pacífico,** Aenida Charles Darwin, near the main dock (© **05/2520-365**).

There are several Internet cafes along the Malecón and scattered around the downtown area. Rates run from $1 to $3 (55p–£1.65) per hour.

ORIENTATION
Almost all the hotels, restaurants, shops, and tour operators of any importance on San Cristóbal are located in a compact area around Puerto Baquerizo Moreno's Malecón (the town's seafront promenade), which is about 10 blocks long. The main part of the downtown extends inland from the Malecón for just some 3 blocks, where it is bordered by Avenida Alsacio Northia, the town's primary east-west thoroughfare. At the far eastern end of the Malecón lies Playa de Oro (Gold Beach). A little bit beyond this is the island's small museum and interpretive center. The airport lies on the western outskirts of town.

GETTING AROUND
Almost everything in Puerto Baquerizo Moreno is within easy walking distance, including even the airport, although if you have any baggage you're best off taking a taxi. Taxis are readily available and a ride anywhere in town should cost $1 (55p). If you want to tour other sites around the island on your own, hire a taxi for around $10 (£5.50) per hour. If you can't flag one down on the street, have your hotel arrange one for you, or call **Coop La Galapaguera** (© **05/2520-900**).

If you're looking for a commuter flight to one of the other islands, contact **EMETEBE** (© **05/2521-427;** emetebe@ecu.net.ec), which has a desk at the airport.

WHAT TO SEE & DO ON SAN CRISTOBAL
As on Santa Cruz, there are plenty of land- and water-based tour options on San Cristóbal. If you're visiting the island on your own, and you're not part of a guided tour, you'll probably want to check in with one of the many tour agencies—there are a handful in Puerto Baquerizo Moreno, all located right around the downtown area. I recommend **Chalo Tours,** Española and Ignacio Hernández (© **05/2520-953;** www.chalotours.com); **Cristóbal Tours,** Avenida Charles Darwin and Española (© **05/2520-626;** www.cristobaltour.com.ec); or **Galakiwi,** Avenida Charles Darwin and Española (© **05/2521-562;** www.galakiwi.com). As the name implies, the latter agency

is a mix of locals (Gala, from Galápagos) and New Zealand transplants (Kiwi). These folks are particularly good at adventure activities and packages.

One of the most popular activities for travelers here is walking along the Malecón, which was spiffed up considerably in 2006 and features several shops and restaurants, as well as small plazas and sitting areas, all hugging the coastline along the bay.

MAIN ATTRACTIONS
On the island

CENTRO DE INTERPRETACION (INTERPRETIVE CENTER) ✦   This humble little museum features exhibits and displays on the human, natural, and geological history of San Cristóbal and the Galápagos Islands. It's actually worth a visit. There are several rooms, all well laid-out with a mix of dioramas, artifacts, illustrations, and written explanations (in English and Spanish). I particularly like the relief model of the entire Galápagos Archipelago, which shows both the underwater and above-sea-level topography. The **Interpretive Center,** Avenida Alsacio Northia, Sector Playa Mann (© **05/2520-358**), is open daily from 7am to noon and 1 to 5pm. Admission is free, and it's about a 15-minute walk from downtown. Alternatively, if you take a taxi here it should cost you just $1 (55p) each way.

EL PROGRESO   The only major road on the island connects the downtown port with El Progreso, the site of Manuel Cobo's infamous prison and work camp. If you visit, you can tour the ruins of the old farm house, and see Cobo's grave. **La Casa del Ceibo** (© **05/2520-248**) is a good place for a lunch break, and adventurous souls can inquire about the tree-house room for rent in the giant ceiba tree. Several buses a day leave downtown Puerto Baquerizo Moreno for El Progreso. The fare is just 20¢ (10p), and the ride takes about 10 minutes.

LA GALAPAGUERA DE CERRO COLORADO   On the far southeastern end of the island is this protected area of dry forest, which is also a wild-tortoise habitat. A hike along the trails here is an excellent way to do some bird-watching and wildlife-viewing; you'll also have the opportunity to see one of the endemic San Cristóbal giant tortoises in their natural habitat. At the entrance is a small information center, and a corral with one captive tortoise, Genesis. There are several well-maintained trails, with some bilingual self-guided information plaques. If you don't come here as part of a guided tour, a round-trip taxi should cost you $25 to $30 (£14–£17). *Tip:* This is a relatively new reserve, and should not be confused with La Galapaguera, another protected habitat of giant tortoises, which is located on the far northeastern end of the island.

LAGUNA EL JUNCO   Formed in the crater of a dormant volcano, this is one of the few fresh-water lakes in the Galápagos. It's only 240m (790 ft.) in diameter and barely 6m (20 ft.) deep. If you're lucky, you may observe the rare phenomenon of a giant frigate bird washing the salt off its wings in the fresh-water lagoon.

LA LOBERIA   La Lobería, or Sea Lion Colony, is a pretty crescent-shaped beach with a large colony of sea lions. You will probably also see some blue-footed boobies and an endemic mockingbird here, as well as marine iguanas. This is a popular surf spot and therefore a bit rough for casual bathing, so if you go swimming, try to choose a calm section of the beach—one that is also far from any territorial bull sea lion. La Lobería is located about a 40-minute walk northwest of downtown. You can hire a taxi here for around $3 (£1.65).

ADVENTURE ACTIVITIES

MOUNTAIN BIKING   The sparse car traffic, relatively subtle rise in altitude, and abundance of off-road trails and paths make San Cristóbal an excellent place to explore on a mountain bike. Most rides begin on the 6.5km (4-mile) paved road to El Progreso. But that's where the pavement ends, and a variety of destinations are possible from there. One of the more popular rides is to El Junco (see above). This 19km (12-mile) ride is mostly uphill on the way there, but welcomingly downhill on the way home. All the tour agencies and hotel desks in town can arrange a guided mountain-bike tour, or they can find you a bike to rent.

ON & UNDER THE WATER

KAYAKING   There's some great kayaking all around San Cristóbal. You can choose to either paddle around Bahía Naufragio, or to venture farther afield. If you want to rent a kayak, check at the **Hotel Orca** (see below), or with either of the tour agencies listed above. Rental rates run $5 to $8 (£2.75–£4.40) per hour, or $15 to $20 (£8.25–£11) per day. All the tour agencies in town offer guided half- and full-day kayak trips as well.

SURFING 𝍢𝍢   San Cristóbal has the most consistent and best-developed surf spots in the Galápagos, if not the entire country. They even have a local surf association, Asociación de Surf de San Cristóbal (ⓒ 05/2521-345). Some of the better-known breaks include **La Lobería, Punta Carola,** and **Tango Reef.** If you're a surfer, you should definitely contact the surf association. They can help get you orientated, and even provide you with permits and transportation to breaks that are located inside protected areas or offshore from San Cristóbal. *Caution:* The surf here is not for beginners, and there are no surf schools, board-rental outfits, or mellow beach breaks. If you come to the Galápagos to surf, you should probably know what you're doing, and bring your own gear. If you want to sign up for a surf tour with an operator that has lots of local experience, check out **Casa del Sol** (www.casasol.com).

SNORKELING & SCUBA DIVING 𝍢𝍢𝍢   As you'll find throughout the archipelago, the snorkeling and scuba diving out of San Cristóbal are excellent. Snorkelers often have close encounters with sea lions and sea turtles, while scuba divers frequently come across schools of hammerhead sharks, eagle rays, Galápagos sharks, and the rare whale shark. Some of the popular dive spots include **Roca Ballena (Whale Rock), Isla Lobos (Sea Lion Island), Punta Pitt (Pitt Point),** and the **Caragua Wreck.**

   Chalo Tours, Española and Ignacio Hernández (ⓒ 05/2520-953; www.chalotours. com), and **Wreck Bay Diving Center,** Avenida Charles Darwin and Teodoro Wolf (ⓒ 05/2521-663; wreckbay_divingcenter@yahoo.com), are the two most established dive operators on the island. Rates for a two-tank dive outing, including all gear and lunch, are $100 to $140 (£55–£77). A snorkel outing, including equipment, should cost $25 to $45 (£14–£25) per person. In both cases, the higher-priced trips involve greater travel time and distance to the dive or snorkel spot.

SHOPPING

The shopping options on San Cristóbal are quite disappointing, and nowhere near as interesting as those on Santa Cruz. All you'll find here are run-of-the mill souvenirs and T-shirts offered up at a host of small shops along the Malecón and scattered around downtown. If you venture inland from the Malecón, you can try your luck at the **Parque Ecológico Artesanal** (ⓒ 05/2520-240), a complex of shops arrayed around a small garden area located on Avenida Alsacio Northia, at the corner of Manuel Cobo. I find, however, that the offerings here are no better than those found near the waterfront.

WHERE TO STAY
MODERATE
Hotel Orca ⊕   This two-story yellow beachfront spot is the most upscale hotel in Puerto Baquerizo Moreno, although that definitely isn't saying a lot. It's located on Playa de Oro, at the eastern end of the bay, a short walk from the heart of downtown. The rooms are relatively plain and uninspiring, but large and well-kept. The best rooms are those on the second floor with large balconies and ocean views. You'll have to pay a little bit more for one of these, but it's well worth it. Reservations are often absolutely necessary here because tour groups frequently book up the entire place. The hotel has a good restaurant, as well as an excellent tour operation.

Av. Charles Darwin, on Playa de Oro, Puerto Baquerizo Moreno, Isla San Cristóbal. ℂ/fax **05/2520-233**. 20 units. $85–$95 (£47–£53) double. DC, MC, V. **Amenities:** Restaurant; bar; tour desk; laundry service. *In room:* A/C, minifridge, no phone.

INEXPENSIVE
Hotel Miconia *(Finds)*   This comfortable hotel is located right on the Malecón, facing the harbor, just steps away from the town's main dock. Rooms are simple—almost spartan, in fact—but they are certainly acceptable. The best units have colorful walls and some wall decorations. Facilities include a popular restaurant (see below), an Internet café, and a small gym with a shiny varnished wooden floor. In back of the hotel and restaurant is a small interior courtyard, which is concrete inlaid with creative tilework. Here you'll find a tiny pool and separate Jacuzzi, as well as a couple of hammocks.

Av. Charles Darwin, across from the main dock, Puerto Baquerizo Moreno, Isla San Cristóbal. ℂ/fax **05/2520-608** or 09/8330-493. www.miconia.com. 12 units. $40–$60 (£22–£33) double. Rates include breakfast. DC, MC, V. **Amenities:** Restaurant; bar; small pool; Jacuzzi; tour desk; laundry service. *In room:* A/C, TV, no phone

WHERE TO DINE
There are a host of simple local restaurants serving Ecuadorian cuisine and fresh seafood all around the downtown. Of these, **Deep Blue,** Avenida Charles Darwin and Española (℃ **05/2520-990**), is a good bet.

MODERATE
Miconia ⊕ *(Finds)* ITALIAN/SEAFOOD   This is my favorite restaurant in Puerto Baquerizo Moreno. Just the view from one of the second-floor bay-view tables would probably be enough to earn it this honor, but the food and service are also up to snuff. Most folks opt for the pizzas or pastas, but there's also a wide range of fresh seafood. This close to the water, I definitely recommend fresh fish or shrimp; they are best just sautéed in oil and garlic. There's actually seating in a ground-floor interior dining room, but you'll really want to walk up the stairs to the second floor, open-air dining area, which has both balcony seating as well as covered tables.

Av. Charles Darwin, across from the main dock, Puerto Baquerizo Moreno. ℃ **05/2520-608**. Main courses: $5–$12 (£2.75–£6.60). AE, DC, MC, V. Daily 7am–9:30pm.

PUERTO BAQUERIZO MORENO AFTER DARK
Puerto Baquerizo Moreno is a pretty quiet town when night falls. By far the best and most popular bar in town is **Iguana Rock** ⊕, located on Calle Juan José Flores and

An Island Whodunit?

Steel dentures, silk underwear, love triangles, food poisoning, and unaccounted-for corpses: The sordid details surrounding the early settlers on Floreana Island have all the trappings of a Carl Hiaasen murder mystery.

When German philosopher and dentist Dr. Friedrich Ritter set off with lover Dora Strauch in 1929, he foresaw the lack of dental facilities on his island Utopia, so he removed both his and Dora's teeth, replacing them with just a single set of steel dentures. Sharing is caring?

Their written dispatches tempted other dreamers to venture onto Floreana's arid shores. Most gave up quickly when faced with the daunting challenges of physical and spiritual survival there, but not Heinz and Margaret Wittmer. They established a home with Heinz's son Harry and soon enough gave birth to Rolf, the first Galápagos-born citizen.

This challenging idyll was shattered with the arrival of the self-described Baroness Eloise Wagner von Bosquet and her entourage of three "companions," Rudolph Lorenz, Robert Philippson, and Felipe Valdivieso. Valdivieso quit Floreana almost immediately. The newly self-enthroned "Empress of Floreana" exercised almost complete control over the tiny community's supplies and communications. Clad only in her favorite silk underwear, she controlled access to the supply ships, and bathed naked in the island's only reliable water source. She also played her various lovers against one other, and frequently denied visitors access to the island. Some say she brought Dr. Ritter into her complicated web of lovers.

Things came to a head in 1934. Primary lover Lorenz had been degraded to servant in favor of Philippson. After a violent dispute, Lorenz took refuge with the Wittmers. In March 1934, the Wittmers found Lorenz alone and hysterical, telling them that the Baroness and Philippson had left Floreana on an American yacht to seek new shores. Lorenz soon arranged to be taken to the mainland.

The Baroness and Philippson were never seen or heard from again. Lorenz and a Norwegian fisherman named Nuggerud disappeared. Dr. Ritter, a vegetarian, was poisoned from eating contaminated chicken.

Two desiccated corpses were eventually discovered 260km (160 miles) north on barren Marchena Island. Evidence suggests that they were Lorenz and Nuggerud, who apparently had starved to death.

Dora Strauch finally returned to Germany to publish her version in *Satan Came to Eden,* while Margaret Wittmer wrote *Floreana: A Woman's Pilgrimage to the Galapagos.* Both volumes contain firsthand accounts of the events mentioned above, but the early Floreana history remains, in many ways, a mystery.

Avenida Quito, about 4 blocks inland from the Malecón (© **05/2520-418**). This place occasionally has live music, and even when there's no band playing, the bar is lively and inviting—plus there's a pool table. Another good option is the **Voqui Bar,** located right near the water, on Avenida Charles Darwin (℗ 05/2520-154). For a relaxed vibe and the occasional jam session, check out what's happening at **El Barquero,** on Calle Ignacio Hernández and Calle Manuel Cobo (℗ 05/2520-516). Finally, for a quiet drink combined with stargazing, my favorite spot is the rooftop bar at **Arrecife de Coral,** on Avenida Alsacio Northia near Española (℗ 05/2520-429).

STAYING ON OTHER ISLANDS

While the vast majority of tourists stay either on boats or ships, or at one of the hotels on either Santa Cruz or San Cristóbal islands, it is possible to stay on the much-less developed islands of Isabela or Floreana. Staying at either of these will definitely give you the sense of being off the beaten path, while still allowing you access to all the same types of tour and activity options available to those who choose a more traditional route.

You can get to Isabela from either Santa Cruz or San Cristóbal on a commuter flight with **EMETEBE airlines** (℗ 05/2526-177; emetebe@ecu.net.ec), or via a boat ride from Puerto Ayora. Isla Floreana can only be reached by boat, and it's a slightly shorter ride to Floreana from Santa Cruz than from San Cristóbal. If you plan to stay on either one of these islands, you should probably reserve your room and arrange transportation in advance.

ON ISABELA ISLAND

La Casa de Marita ⚡ (Finds   Containing a delightful collection of rooms and suites, this little hotel fronts a beautiful crescent-shaped beach, a few blocks from the heart of downtown Puerto Villamil. Rooms vary in size and design, but all show the owner's attention to detail and style. The best room in the house is the large Mango Suite, with a private ocean-view terrace. But some prefer the Green House, a separate little two-story cottage right on the beach, with a full kitchen and living area downstairs, and a bedroom upstairs. Quite a few of the rooms have two twin beds, so be sure to specify if you want a queen or king. The third-floor dining room of the main house features modern glass-topped tables and a great view of the ocean.

Puerto Villamil, Isla Isabela. ℗ 05/2529-301. Fax 05/2529-201. www.galapagosisabela.com. 25 units. $80–$120 (£44–£66) double. Rates include full breakfast. AE, MC, V. **Amenities:** Restaurant; bar; Jacuzzi; tour desk; laundry service. *In room:* A/C, minibar.

ON FLOREANA ISLAND

Hostal Wittmer   This place is for the hard-core adventurer or real escape artist. The island has only around 100 inhabitants, and most are simple fishermen or farmers. The Wittmer, located near the beach and tiny town of Puerto Velasco Ibarra, is the hotel still owned and run by the descendents of Margaret Wittmer, who wrote the

---

Tips You Can Look, but You Better Not Touch

It seems like common sense, but in no case should you touch or in any way disturb the wild flora and fauna of the Galápagos. This includes plants, birds, reptiles, and mammals—every living thing, both on land and under the water. Be very aware of not encroaching upon any wild creature or habitat. Do not litter, and definitely do not attempt to feed any of the animals.

The Galápagos Tortoise

The giant Galápagos tortoise *(Geochelone elephantopus)* is the most distinctive animal on the entire archipelago. In fact, the name Galápagos comes from the Spanish word *"galápago,"* which is what the early Spanish explorers and conquistadores called these tortoises, because their shells resembled riding saddles. Fifteen subspecies of giant tortoise have been recorded. Of these, four are confirmed extinct, and another, the Isla Pinta subspecies, was thought to be on the verge of extinction, though recent genetic evidence indicates that there may be Pinta tortoises on Isla Isabela (see "I'm So Lonely," on p. 343).

Given the geological isolation and workings of evolution, almost every major island on the archipelago has one or more distinct subspecies. The various subspecies can be divided into two general classes, based on the shapes of their shells. Generally speaking, shells are dome-shaped or saddle-backed. The domed tortoises tend to live in higher, moister environments, and their plentiful food is found close to the ground. Their shells have very little curvature above their necks. Conversely, the saddle-backed tortoises live in more desertlike, arid environments, and often have to reach high for their favorite foods. Hence, their shells are characterized by the large open arch above their neck areas, allowing them to make these reaches. Domed-shell tortoises tend to be larger than their saddle-backed brethren, too—though most are large by nearly any standard.

For millions of years, the Galápagos tortoise had virtually no natural predators. Eggs and hatchlings were vulnerable to certain hawks and owls, but beyond that they lived a totally unthreatened life until the arrival of man. Early explorers, settlers, and pirates found the tortoise to be an invaluable and easy source of food, and thousands upon thousands of tortoises were slaughtered. These same early settlers introduced non-native species, like goats, pigs, dogs, and rats, that devastated the island's tortoise habitat, and, in some cases, the reptiles themselves. Today, several subspecies remain threatened or in danger of extinction, while many others have stable and growing populations, thanks to the efforts of conservationists, scientists, and the Charles Darwin Foundation.

book *Floreana,* a firsthand account of the life of early settlers here, which included the love-triangle and death mystery known as the Floreana Affair. The rooms here are simple and bare-bones. The best are individual cottages set off from the main building. Camping is also permitted here. A full meal package will run you around $28 per day.

Calle Ignacio Hernández, Puerto Velasco Ibarra, Isla Floreana. (C) **05/2529-506.** 18 units. $30–$40 (£17–£22) double. No credit cards. **Amenities:** Restaurant, bar; tour desk; laundry service. *In room:* No phone.

Appendix A:
Ecuador in Depth

Ecuador is much more than the Galápagos Islands. So, for a moment, forget about the giant tortoises, like the one on the cover of this book. Instead, think of a country that contains not only a part of the world's largest rainforest, the Amazon basin, but also a section of the world's longest mountain range, the majestic Andes. Imagine a place where you'll hear the sound of marimba music and taste an array of tropical fruits. And visualize yourself visiting craft and agricultural markets that have remained relatively unchanged over the past 1,000 years.

Now that you've gotten a tiny sense of mainland Ecuador, go ahead and picture those tortoises. Their home, the Galápagos Islands, is the site of some of the most startling biodiversity on earth. Some 1,000km (600 miles) off the country's Pacific coast, the islands are the nesting ground for giant tortoises that were around when Charles Darwin arrived here, in 1831. Among other species that call the Galápagos home are marine and land iguanas, sea lions, albatrosses, and the famous blue-footed boobies. It's not surprising that this magical archipelago inspired a scientific theory that would change how human beings understand the natural world.

Ecuador is a nation of extremes, a nexus of the Northern and Southern hemispheres, a link between the Old and New worlds. Centuries of Inca civilization and Spanish colonial rule, coupled with recent decades of tumultuous government, have given its economy, politics, crafts, architecture, languages, and religious customs one common trait: profound variety. With 13 million residents, Ecuador is one of the smallest countries in South America, but it's home to a diverse population that includes a sizable number of Amerindian, white, black, and *mestizo* people.

Ecuadorian politics is well-known for its own type of variety: The nation has had seven presidents in the last 10 years. Fortunately, large-scale violence has not accompanied the political turmoil, and, for travelers, Ecuador is one of the safest countries in Latin America.

During a visit here you won't fail to encounter your share of awe and adventure, whether you're floating down the Amazon in a dugout canoe; passing through colonial churches or plazas; hiking along snowcapped volcanic peaks or in dense jungles; dodging piranhas or anacondas; searching for howler monkeys in the rainforest or for giant condors soaring above the Andes; learning Quichua in a Quiteño language school (or listening to it spoken in a mountainous village near Riobamba); or viewing the woodcarvings, paintings, Panama hats, woven tapestries, and clothing of contemporary indigenous craftspeople or the stone temples, carvings, and fortresses of ancient Inca empires.

1 Ecuador Today

More than a quarter century after the end of military rule—despite the last decade's being somewhat tumultuous—Ecuador is on the road to recovery. But that road, like so many in the country, is bumpy, winding, and steep.

PEOPLE

Long-lasting Inca and Spanish empires, followed by centuries of unstable national governments, have produced an ethnically, linguistically, and economically divided Ecuador. Around 65% of the country's 13 million people are *mestizo*— of mixed Spanish-Amerindian heritage. Amerindians make up a full 25% of the population, with blacks accounting for 3%, and 7% falling into the "Caucasian/other" category.

There are 11 indigenous groups, each with its own language and customs. The largest is the Andean Quichua, over two million strong. They are joined in the equatorial Andes by the Otavaleños, Salasaca, and Saraguros. The shaman traditions of the Incas are carried on in the rainforest by the Huaorani, Zaparo, Cofán, lowland Quichua, Siona, Secoya, Shuar, and Achuar peoples. The nation's black population traces their ancestry to slaves who were brought to work on coastal sugar plantations in the 1500s. The Afro-Ecuadorian community is famous for its marimba music and lively dance festivals.

The population is about equally divided between the central highlands and the low-lying coastal region. Over the last few decades there has been a steady migration toward the cities, and today 60% of Ecuadorians reside in urban areas. Hundreds of thousands of people emigrated from Ecuador following the financial crisis at the beginning of the new millennium; the U.S. Department of State estimates that over 2 million Ecuadorians currently reside in the United States.

ECONOMY

The Ecuadorian economy depends heavily on the export of petroleum, which represents 40% of the country's earnings from exports and a third of the government's revenues. Agriculture is strong as well. Ecuador is the world's largest banana exporter, shipping out roughly 4 million metric tons of the fruit every year, which accounts for more than 30% of the world's bananas. Other crops include cocoa, coffee, cut flowers, rice, and sugar cane. Tourism and manufacturing are also increasingly important. In 2006, 2-year-old free-trade negotiations between Ecuador and the U.S. broke down after Ecuador passed a protectionist hydrocarbons law and seized the assets of Occidental Petroleum, the country's largest American investor. The U.S. Congress temporarily extended Ecuador's unilateral trade privileges at the end of 2006, but without a concrete agreement the climate for foreign investment is expected to remain volatile.

The nation's dependence on petroleum production has left it vulnerable to the frequent swings in the global market. It suffered a massive economic crisis in 1999, with GDP contracting by more than 6%. The adoption of the dollar as the national currency in 2000, replacing the rapidly devaluating sucre, was highly controversial and though it led to the end of hyperinflation, it also resulted in a perceived loss of national sovereignty.

The gap between rich and poor is wide. Estimates vary as to what percentage of the population lives below the poverty line, but most agree the rate is at least 40% and perhaps as high as 70%. Though social turmoil has been limited considering how vast the economic inequality is, economic weakness is not without its obvious social costs. The poverty rate helps explain, for instance, the number of young Ecuadorians in gangs: over 65,000, by some estimates.

POLITICS

Social and economic divisions have significantly affected Ecuador's political landscape. The 100-member National Congress is fractured along geographic, ethnic, and ideological lines. The main parties in the National Congress are the Ecuadorian Roldosist Party (Partido Roldosista Ecuatoriano, center-right populist), the Democratic Left (Izquierda Democrática, social democrat), and the Institutional Renewal Party of National Action (Partido Renovador Institucional de Acción Nacional, right-wing populist). In the 2006 election, the indigenous movement won only six seats in the National Congress, 11 less than during the previous term.

In recent years, the instability of Ecuador's executive branch has drawn international attention. Between 1996 and 2006, seven presidents attempted to govern the nation. They all failed to ameliorate the political volatility, either because of a hostile Congress, a military coup d'état, or what many Ecuadorians considered the presidents' sheer mental incompetence.

After a decade that saw power most often change hands through military intervention or presidential resignation, free, popular elections were held in the fall of 2006. Thirteen candidates ran for the nation's presidency. Because no candidate obtained a high enough percentage of the vote to win in the first round, a runoff election took place November 26, 2006. It pitted banana tycoon Alvaro Noboa, who had campaigned unsuccessfully in 1998 and 2002, against former finance minister Rafael Correa, an economic populist who resigned from President Alfredo Palacio's government after a disagreement with the World Bank.

Correa defeated Noboa, obtaining 56% of the vote; he subsequently announced plans to hold a referendum that would lead to the drafting of a new constitution. (In Latin America, as political movements routinely write new constitutions when they come to power.)

Correa's election has fueled the widely held belief that Latin American politics are shifting to the left, a perception reinforced by the election of Evo Morales in Bolivia in 2005, as well as the 2006 reelection of Hugo Chávez in Venezuela and of Daniel Ortega in Nicaragua.

Though Correa has denied being part of the Venezuela-led Bolivarian Movement, he does consider Hugo Chávez a personal friend. And his early remarks as president do not seem to foreshadow an administration that will be obsequious to the United States. For instance, Correa indicated that in 2009 he will not approve a renewal of the United States' lease on the Manta Airbase, a key outpost for operations against drug traffickers and the launching point for more than half of the U.S.-led drug seizures in South America.

The early months of Correa's term have been somewhat turbulent, although he enjoys a high approval rating among Ecuadorians. The legislative, executive, and judicial branches, at odds with one another, have been flexing their muscles. The most significant development so far has been the April 2007 national referendum in which more than 80% of voters approved a measure calling for a Constituent Assembly to rewrite the country's constitution.

2 History 101

EARLY HISTORY

Human presence in the Andes region dates perhaps as far back as 20,000 B.C.— making South America the last continent on earth, with the exception of Antarctica, to be inhabited. Evidence of the first hunter-gatherer societies in Ecuador dates back to 10,000 B.C., and methods of crop cultivation began to develop around 3600 B.C.

Though its partial influence began to spread from what is now Peru around

A.D. 1200, the Inca Empire only held uncontested dominion over the Andes region from 1438 to 1533. In Quichua it was known as *Tawantin Suyu,* or the "land of the four regions." At its height it encompassed an estimated 15 million people belonging to roughly 100 ethnic or linguistic communities; it covered an area of over 6,000 sq. km (2,300 sq. miles), within which were more than 25,000km (15,500 miles) of roads.

Inca warrior Pachacuti and his son Topa Yupanqui, descendants of the first Sapa Inca, Manco Capac, began to extend the empire into what is now Ecuador in 1463. The 11th Sapa Inca, Huayna Capac, completed the conquest of Ecuador, extended the empire into present-day Chile and Argentina, and took a special interest in the city of Quito, which his father, Tupac Yupanqui, had rebuilt. When Huayna Capac died of either smallpox or malaria during a military campaign in 1527, a war of succession began between his sons, Huáscar and Atahualpa.

Shortly after his father's death, Huáscar seized control of Cusco and captured Atahualpa. As legend has it, the crafty Atahualpa escaped with the help of a little girl, returned to Quito, and began recruiting his father's best generals to serve alongside him. Atahualpa's forces were eventually victorious, but the triumph was short-lived: While he was resting in hot springs near Cajamarca, a former swineherd from western Spain named Francisco Pizarro stopped by for a visit.

SPANISH CONQUEST

Francisco Pizarro set out from Panama at the end of 1531 with fewer than 200 men and arrived on the coast of Ecuador. He spent some months gathering precious stones and gold in order to finance reinforcements, and then he led his expedition inland.

On November 16, 1532, 168 Spaniards, led by Pizarro, attacked the imperial army of the Incas at Cajamarca, almost 80,000 soldiers strong. Despite reports of having felt quite scared the night before, the Spaniards slaughtered over 7,000 Incas and captured the emperor, Atahualpa. The supposed justification for the attack was Atahualpa's rejection of Christianity (a Spanish friar had presented him with a Bible, but the emperor said he could not hear what the book said and tossed it to the floor).

The Spaniards considered Atahualpa useful for subduing the rest of the population and kept him alive, though imprisoned. While under their watch he learned to speak some Spanish and play chess. But

Dateline

- **10,000–3600 B.C.** Preceramic Period. First hunter-gatherer societies in Ecuador.
- **3600–1800 B.C.** Early Formative Period. First signs of agriculture in Ecuador.
- **1800–1500 B.C.** Middle Formative Period. Further development of agricultural practices.
- **1500–500 B.C.** Late Formative Period. Economy becomes almost completely dependent on agriculture as advanced crop-raising techniques develop.
- **500 B.C.–A.D. 500** Regional Development Period. Growth and development of urban areas.
- **500–1500** Integration Period. Strengthening of regional, political, and economic structures.
- **1438–71** Pachacuti Inca Yupanqui expands kingdom of Cusco into a wide area of the Andes, including part of what is now Ecuador. Machu Picchu built in what is now Peru.
- **1471–85** Tupac Inca Yupanqui expands Inca control of Ecuador, conquers rival Chimor Kingdom, and rebuilds Quito with architects from Cusco.

(continued)

More like Dogs than Gods

Conventional wisdom holds that the Incas believed the Spaniards were gods, and capitulated to the invaders out of holy fear. This may have been true in some cases. Not so for Atahualpa. The Sapa Inca heard of these strange visitors who had wool on their faces, like an alpaca or a sheep, and considered them subhumans, akin to animals. They must have been fairly stupid, thought Atahualpa, if they walked around wearing metal pots on their heads—and they never even used the pots for cooking. It was the Inca's lack of fear, rather than his excess of it, that clouded his judgment, initially leading him to greet the Spaniards with dancers rather than soldiers.

after having received over 20 tons of gold and silver, Atahualpa's captors garroted him.

Quito fell to the Spanish in mid-1534, effectively ending resistance from the Inca armies. The conquistadores continued to loot, pillage, kill, and torture the indigenous population as they swept across the continent, though they were not able to implement a unified system of colonial rule until more than 20 years after capturing Atahualpa. Once established, Spanish dominion was largely peaceful, though in no way just.

COLONIAL RULE

When Spanish colonial rule began in 1544, Ecuador was part of the Viceroyalty of Peru. It joined the new Viceroyalty of Nueva Granada in 1720. Quito became an *audiencia real* in 1563, allowing for direct relations with the Spanish crown and circumventing the regional government in Lima. ("Quito" referred not just to the city but encompassed all of present-day Ecuador, reaching into northern Peru and southern Colombia.)

In Spanish colonial society, racial divisions were enshrined in law. *Peninsulares* (Spaniards living in the New World who were born in Spain) occupied the top of the economic and political pyramid, followed by *criollos* (descendants of Spaniards born in the New World), *mestizos* (those of mixed Spanish and Amerindian ancestry), *mulatos* (those of mixed Spanish and African ancestry), Amerindians, *zambos* (those of mixed Amerindian and African ancestry), and finally blacks. Individuals from the latter three groups were often enslaved outright. In Ecuador, the population soon became heavily *mestizo*, with less

- **1525** Huayna-Cápac dies, dividing the Inca kingdom between his sons Atahualpa and Huáscar.
- **1532** Expedition, led by Francisco Pizarro, "discovers" what is today Ecuador.
- **1534** Sebastián de Benalcázar begins the conquest of Quito.
- **1539** Spanish explorers set out from Quito and find the mouth of the Amazon River.

- **1563** By royal decree from Spanish King Felipe II, the Real Audiencia de San Francisco de Quito is created.
- **1809–10** Aristocrats in Quito declare independence, but their revolution is eventually suppressed by the Spanish crown. Many leading intellectuals are killed.
- **1820** Ecuador again declares independence from Spain; this time they are ultimately successful.

- **1822** Spanish rule ends. Quito becomes part of Gran Colombia, ruled by Simón Bolívar.
- **1830** Gran Colombia dissolves. The Republic of Ecuador is formed. General Juan José Flores becomes civilian and military ruler, convoking the first Ecuadorian Congress in the city of Riobamba in August 1830.
- **1832** Ecuador annexes the Galápagos Islands.

La Conquista: How Did it Happen?

How did 168 Spaniards, half a world away from their home, manage to defeat 80,000 veteran Inca warriors? As Jared Diamond explains in his Pulitzer Prize–winning bestseller *Guns, Germs and Steel* (W.W. Norton, 1997), the answer lies in a mix of historical and geographical factors. Fifteenth-century Spaniards were not inherently smarter or stronger than the Incas they conquered, but rather they were the beneficiaries of millennia of agricultural and technological development made possible by their geographic location.

First, the Spanish had horses and were expert riders, using a style called *jimeta*, known for its precision and utility for chasing down enemies. The Incas not only had never seen horses before; they had never seen people ride any animals. Second, the Spanish had the distinct advantage of steel (the indirect result, Diamond explains, of advances in agriculture and nutrition), which far overmatched the Incas' crude bronze and stone weapons. The Spaniards wielded well-tempered swords; the Incas had wooden clubs. The Spaniards had metal bolts fired by crossbows; the Incas had arrows with stone tips. The Spaniards even fired rounds from a primitive gun called the harquebus. It was far from an even fight.

indigenous predominance than in Peru or Bolivia but significantly more than in Argentina or Chile.

These racial divisions formed the basis for the economic system, the *encomienda*. In exchange for defending the territory, Spanish settlers were granted ownership not only of the land but also of the people living on it. The indigenous population, therefore, was forced into slavery on plantations. In 1542, Spanish friar Bartolomé de las Casas convinced the Spanish crown to institute the New Laws,

granting some protection to indigenous peoples. But despite these protections, forced labor largely continued.

And no law could protect against the most pernicious Spanish import: disease. The diseases the Europeans brought devastated the Incas and all other indigenous societies in the Western Hemisphere. Some scholars estimate that there were 20 million Native Americans in the New World prior to the arrival of the Spanish. Nearly 95% of them were wiped out after the conquistadors arrived, falling to diseases such as

- **1835** The HMS *Beagle*, with a young Charles Darwin aboard, reaches the Galápagos.
- **1860** Under conservative President Gabriel García Moreno, Catholicism becomes the official religion of Ecuador.
- **1895** Liberal revolution. García Moreno archrival Eloy Alfaro institutes liberal reforms such as freedom of

speech, civil marriage, and divorce.
- **1941** War between Ecuador and Peru. Peru occupies two-thirds of Ecuador, then withdraws after the signing of the Rio de Janeiro Protocol (1942), brokered by the U.S., Chile, Brazil, and Argentina. The border between the nations is only slightly better demarcated, leaving the door open for future conflict.

- **1948–52** Beginning of the banana boom. Exports of the fruit grow from $2 million to $20 million in 4 years.
- **1963** Military dictatorship begins.
- **1979** Pressured by instability in the global oil market, Ecuador returns to democracy. Jaime Roldós Aguilera elected president.

(continued)

plague, typhoid, and smallpox, to which they had no natural resistance. The Western Hemisphere was essentially emptied of its native population. While the Incas were vanquished militarily, after the imposition of colonial rule the effect of European diseases was severe and far-reaching.

INDEPENDENCE

Criollo discontent with the exclusive rule of *peninsulares* reached a boiling point in the early 19th century, and a mood of reform swept across New Spain. A sharp economic downturn contributed to that mood.

In October 1820, a *criollo* junta, led by José Joaquín Olmedo, declared Quito independent from Spain and appealed to the independence movements in Venezuela and Argentina for support.

At the time, rebellion was sweeping the Western Hemisphere. Simón Bolívar, El Libertador, defeated a Spanish army at Carabobo in Venezuela on June 24, 1821, clearing the way for the independence of modern-day Venezuela, Colombia, Panama, and Bolivia. On September 15, 1821, Gabino Gaínza, the Spanish captain general of Central America and a rebel sympathizer, signed the Act of Independence, which broke Mexico's and Central America's ties with Spain.

Bolívar sent troops and skilled officers to Olmedo, and an Ecuadorian army led by José de Sucre Alcalá won a decisive victory against the Spanish at Pichincha on May 24, 1822. Hours later, the Quito Audiencia formally surrendered to Sucre.

Ecuador immediately joined the Republic of Greater Colombia, led by Bolívar, but separated from that federation in 1830 following Bolívar's resignation as president. The Republic of Ecuador was born.

THE EARLY REPUBLIC

In 1832, Ecuador annexed an archipelago about 970km (600 miles) off its coast—the Galápagos. Originally used as a prison colony, the islands soon became populated by a group of farmers and artists. In 1835, the British survey ship HMS *Beagle* sailed by, carrying a young naturalist named Charles Darwin. He published *The Origin of Species,* a landmark in human thought, in 1859.

Following independence, Ecuador's political landscape was just as rocky as that of the Galápagos. It quickly came to be dominated by two parties, the Liberals and the Conservatives. Apart from the geographic differences between the two (the Liberals drew their strength from coastal populations, while the Conservatives represented the country's heartland), one issue defined their rivalry and Ecuadorian politics for more than a century after the creation of the republic: the role of the Roman Catholic Church in society.

- **1987** A devastating earthquake strikes. Oil exports are interrupted; the economy suffers.
- **1995** Cenepa War between Ecuador and Peru. The nations fight once again over the border established in 1942.
- **1998** Ecuador and Peru sign peace treaty (Montevideo Declaration), ending a half-century of conflict over the Amazon region.
- **2000** Under President Jamil Mahuad, Ecuador takes steps to adopt the U.S. dollar as its official currency during a severe economic crisis. Widespread popular unrest ensues. Military junta overthrows Mahuad, and Vice President Gustavo Noboa takes control.
- **1996–2006** Ecuador has seven presidents in 10 years.
- **2006** Leftist Rafael Correa wins presidential election in runoff against billionaire businessman Alvaro Noboa.
- **2007** In an April national referendum, the Ecuadorian people voted overwhelmingly for President Correa's measure calling for a Constituent Assembly to rewrite the country's constitution.

With backing from the Church, conservative politician Gabriel García Moreno rose to power in the 1860s. García Moreno strove to achieve universal literacy among the citizenry, and forged a close relationship with the clergy, granting asylum to exiled Jesuit priests.

Before being assassinated with a machete by a Colombian immigrant, García Moreno inspired deep resentment among the Liberals, who favored secular government, closer ties with the United States, and freer markets.

The political conflict soon became a military one: In 1895 Ecuador erupted in civil war between the Liberals and Conservatives. The Catholic Church urged their loyal members to take up arms against the Liberals, but later declared neutrality in the conflict. By the end of the year the Liberals were victorious, and formed a government under President Eloy Alfaro.

Intermittently serving until his bloody assassination in 1911, Alfaro was best known for instituting a firm separation of church and state. Whereas religious paintings had adorned the walls of public buildings during García Moreno's term, Alfaro replaced them with secular art. The president's other reforms included the establishment of civil rights such as freedom of speech, the legalization of civil marriage and divorce, the building of the first railroad from Guayaquil to Quito, and the construction of many public schools. Today he is remembered as a national hero in Ecuador.

A ROCKY CENTURY

All the while, Ecuador's economy was changing. By the early 20th century, cocoa had taken over as the dominant crop, responding to a worldwide boom in demand. But over-reliance on the crop led to trouble. In 1925, the cocoa market plummeted, and a bloodless political coup removed the Liberals from power. Contemporary observers might think today's political climate in Ecuador is volatile, but the 1930s were much worse: 14 chief executives served during the depressed decade.

The end of World War II and a global banana boom heralded a brighter future for Ecuador. Between 1948 and 1952, exports of the golden fruit grew from $2 million to $20 million. The political climate was relatively mild in the years following the war's end, with three freely elected presidents completing their terms between 1948 and 1960.

These stable conditions did not last, though. The banana boom ended in 1959, bringing a severe economic downturn in its wake. In 1963, a military junta deposed the sitting president, Carlos Julio Arosemena, who himself had pressured sitting president José María Velasco into resigning 2 years earlier. Velasco soon returned to the presidency, assuming dictatorial powers in 1970, only to be overthrown by another military junta in 1972.

Using revenues from Ecuador's newly successful oil export industry, the junta invested in land reform and industrialization. But in the midst of the global oil crisis of 1979, a successor junta allowed for a democratic transition to power. A charismatic young politician from Guayaquil named Jaime Roldós Aguilera won the presidency by a landslide, but his reform efforts were curtailed 2 years later when his plane crashed in heavy rain near the Ecuadorian border.

An economic and humanitarian crisis struck the country in 1987 in the form of a devastating earthquake in northeast Ecuador. The disaster interrupted oil exports, crippling the economy.

Though Ecuador's economy intermittently grew and contracted during the 20th century, the country itself followed a single trend: It shrank. Starting in 1904, Ecuador began to lose a substantial amount of its territory in small-scale conflicts with its neighbors. The most serious was the 1941 war with Peru, which resulted in Peru's temporarily occupying two-thirds of Ecuador. Though Peru eventually withdrew after the signing of the Rio de Janeiro Protocol in 1942, the ambiguous border between the two nations remained a point of contention. In 1995, the two countries began the so-called "Cenepa War," prompting shock and outrage from the international community. A ceasefire was quickly established, but a final treaty would not be signed for several more years.

A REVOLVING DOOR AT THE PRESIDENTIAL PALACE

Change seems to be a consistent factor in Ecuadorian politics—since the return to democracy in 1979, no party has captured the presidency through an election more than once—but the 1997–2006 period was as tumultuous as any during the last century. Seven presidents took office during that 10-year period, intermittently swept in and out of power by the ballot of the people, the vote of the National Congress, or the barrel of a gun.

In 1996, Ecuadorians elected Abdalá Bucaram, from the Guayaquil-based center-right Ecuadorian Roldosista Party (PRE), to what was supposed to be a 4-year term. He campaigned on promises to institute populist economic policies and check the influence of the nation's oligarchy, but once in office, his administration was widely criticized for corruption. Less than a year into his term, Bucaram was impeached by the National Congress on the grounds that he was mentally incompetent to serve. Fabián Alarcón, at the time the leader of the Congress, was named interim president, which was reinforced by the electorate in a May 1997 referendum.

A year later, the nation went to the polls once more to choose a replacement president to serve a full 4-year term. Quito Mayor Jamil Mahuad, of the Popular Democracy Party, narrowly defeated banana magnate Alvaro Noboa in a runoff election, taking office on August 10, 1998, the same day that a new constitution went into effect. Mahuad was lauded for negotiating a peace treaty with Peru to end the half-century-old border conflict, but his successes ended there. A sharp decline in the price of oil sent Ecuador's economy into a tailspin in 1999, leading Mahuad to propose adopting the U.S. dollar as the country's official currency in order to curtail inflation. Huge demonstrations swept Quito, and on January 21, 2000, protestors stormed the National Congress building, proclaiming a three-person junta to be Ecuador's new ruling body.

Military commanders intervened, and negotiated a deal whereby Mahuad would step down to make way for his vice president, Gustavo Noboa, to take office. Mahuad announced his resignation and endorsed his successor in a televised address, and Congress ratified the succession.

Noboa brought little in the way of policy change from his predecessor. He followed through on Mahuad's plan to dollarize the economy, and negotiated a deal for the construction of the country's second major oil pipeline using private financing.

Lucio Gutiérrez, formerly an army colonel and member of the ruling junta of January 21, won the presidential election of 2002 and took office in January of the following year. The conservative fiscal policies he implemented stood in stark contrast to his populist campaign promises, and when demonstrations began to shake the capital, Gutiérrez declared a state of emergency and replaced the Supreme Court. On April 20, 2005, Congress declared that he had "abandoned his post," and stripped him of it. Gutiérrez went into exile, leaving Vice President Alfredo Palacio to take over. He carried out no major reforms during his term.

In 2006, Ecuador went to the polls once more, and elected Rafael Correa. The eighth president in eleven years, Correa is a center-left former economist who considers himself a personal friend of Venezuela's Hugo Chávez. He is making waves early on in his presidency, with his plan to call a national assembly to rewrite the country's constitution. A referendum on Correa's plan is scheduled for April 15, 2007. The nation is holding its breath, and it's still too early to tell how things will shake out.

3 The Natural Environment

Ecuador sits near the top of the South American continent, straddling the equator. It covers an area of just under 256,000 sq. km (99,000 sq. miles), about the size of the state of Colorado. It is bordered on the north and east by Colombia, on the south and east by Peru, and on the west by the Pacific Ocean. The country includes the Galápagos Islands, 970km (600 miles) due west from mainland coast.

There are three primary geographic regions in Ecuador, plus the Galápagos. The first is La Costa (The Coast), the low-lying area that runs the length of the Pacific coastline. Fertile plains and rolling rivers lead into pleasant Pacific beaches.

The rugged center of the country is called La Sierra (The Mountains), with the **Andes Mountains** running all the way from north to south. The Andes, the longest mountain chain in the world, appeared around 5 million years ago. A German naturalist named Alexander von Humboldt visited Ecuador in the early 19th century and named this central region "Avenue of the Volcanoes." At an elevation of 5,897m (19,347 ft.), **Volcán Cotopaxi,** with its near-perfectly symmetrical cone—a beautiful one at that—is the world's fourth-highest active volcano. **Volcán Sangay** and **Volcán Guagua Pichincha** are numbers 9 and 10 in the world, respectively. (No. 1 is Ojos de Salado on the border between Argentina and Chile.)

Finally, El Oriente (The East), runs from the edge of the Andes to the borders with Colombia and Peru, and contains a chunk of the **Amazon rainforest.** This area covers over 25% of the country's landmass, but is home to less than 5% of its human population.

The Galápagos archipelago consists of 13 large islands, 17 islets, and several dozen ancient rock formations scattered over 7,500 sq. km (2,900 sq. miles) of ocean. Though famous for its beaches, active volcanoes also rise from several of the islands, reaching altitudes of up to 1,600m (5,250 ft.).

The biodiversity found within Ecuador's borders is stunning. While it only makes up .02% of the world's landmass, it contains an amazing 10% of the world's plant species. Cataloguing of the nation's biological treasures is far from complete, and already scientists have counted 3,800 species of vertebrates, 1,550 species of birds, 320 species of mammals, 350 species of reptiles, 375 species of amphibians, 800 species of freshwater fish, and 450 species of marine fish. Ecuador is a bird-watcher's paradise. A full 18% of the world's bird species can be found in Ecuador, more bird species per square meter than in any other Latin American country. In fact, although Brazil is 30 times Ecuador's size, Ecuador has just as many species of birds. And last but not least, there are over a million species of insects in Ecuador (they're not all ugly—4,500 species are butterflies).

See "Tips on Health, Etiquette & Safety in the Wilderness," in chapter 4, for additional tips on enjoying Ecuador's natural wonders. In appendix C you'll find an illustrated wildlife guide.

4 Ecuadorian Culture

Ecuador's culture is as varied as its population. Mainstream culture is a mix of Amerindian, Spanish, African, North American, and other Latin American influences. Its mixed heritage has ensured the existence of a wide array of crafts, literature, architectural styles, and musical rhythms.

ARCHITECTURE

Ecuador's buildings offer a charming mix of old and new. Quito is perhaps the South American colonial capital that has changed the least since Spanish rule. The city's very impressive colonial churches were built in the baroque style, including the Iglesia de Santo Domingo and the Iglesia de San Francisco. Several neoclassical and Beaux Arts buildings also survive from the beginnings of the republic.

Some of the most beautiful buildings in Ecuador are found in Cuenca. **La Inmaculada,** the city's main cathedral, was completed in 1885 and houses a famous painting of the Virgin Mary, along with modern stained glass. The city's other cathedral, **El Sagrario,** was completed in 1557 and built over Inca ruins, some of which are still visible. Several other colonial and colonial-esque buildings dot the historic city, including the district **Supreme Court.**

In Guayaquil, Ecuador's largest city, fire wiped out most of the old colonial buildings, and today modern high-rises co-exist with tin-roof slums, though poverty is not laid as bare as in other urban areas of Latin America.

Though not as elaborate as the structures in Peru, some Inca ruins are visible in Ecuador. The principal Inca site here is **Ingapirca,** near Cuenca. The stone structure is small but well-preserved. Other sites include **Rumicucho,** near Quito, **La Tolita,** near Esmeraldas, and **Tomebamba,** in Cuenca.

ART

Ecuadorian artists range from folk artisans working in a variety of forms, materials, and traditions to modern painters, sculptors, and ceramicists producing beautiful representational and abstract works.

Pre-Columbian artisans produced a wide range of pottery, paintings, sculpture, and gold and silver work. Intact pottery figurines dating to 3000 B.C. were discovered in the coastal village of Valdivia, and are still on display in several museums. After the arrival of the Spanish, art became increasingly influenced by Christianity. Paintings from colonial times can still be seen in many churches and museums. During the 17th and 18th centuries, painters of the Quito School began to combine Spanish and indigenous influences, but this movement fell out of favor following independence, when the focus shifted to formalist depictions of the great heroes of the revolution and the social elite.

Fun Fact **The Work of God, or of the Devil?**

As legend has it, a stonemason named Cantuña enlisted the Devil's help in constructing a chapel near the Iglesia de San Francisco in Quito in the late 18th century. When the Devil came to collect Cantuña's soul as payment for the work, thinking the project had been completed, the mason showed him that the church was in fact missing a single stone. The Devil returned to Hell angry and empty-handed.

Fun Fact A Man, a Plan, a Misnomer: The Panama Hat

Don't let the name fool you: Panama hats are made in Ecuador. The tradition of millinery in Ecuador is long and proud. By the 16th century, the Incas had used the *Carludovica palmata* plant to create headwear, and the hats continued to have a place in Ecuador's culture after the Spanish conquest. In a famous painting of St. James the Great from the 17th century, made by an anonymous artist of the Cusco School, the mighty apostle is portrayed wearing a typical Ecuadorian hat while bounding on his horse, slaying Moors. For more about these unique items, see p. 211.

Indigenous woven tapestries and clothing are still available for sale throughout the country, as are fine basketwork, leatherwork, woodcarving, ceramics, and jewelry. The most famous indigenous craft is the Panama hat, as much a must-buy in Ecuador as cigars are in Cuba.

Several galleries in Quito and Guayaquil carry a wide range of locally produced art; see chapters 5 and 9 for more information.

LITERATURE

Though Ecuador's literary tradition is not world famous, neither is it barren. Worth reading is Jorge Icaza's controversial 1934 novel *Huasipungo* (published in English as *The Villagers: Huasipungo*), an indictment of the oil industry, an exposé of the plight of indigenous peoples in the Sierra, and a pioneer in the "indigenous literature" movement. Another notable work is Jorge Enrique Adoum's *Entre Marx y una Mujer Desnuda* (Between Marx and a Naked Woman), a very clever novel about novels, and about Ecuadorian society as a whole. Although not yet translated, it was made into a 1995 film by Camilo Luzuriaga, and you can sometimes find a subtitled copy of the film at better video stores.

José Joaquín de Olmedo, famous for his role in the independence movement, was also a noted poet. Perhaps the most respected Ecuadorian author is Juan Montalvo, a political essayist. Others, such as Alfredo Pareja, Demetrio Aguilera, Enrique Gilbert, and Humberto Salvador, became known for their writings advocating social justice.

Quito is also saturated with a different kind of literature: graffiti. As a local saying goes, *No hay muros blancos*—there are no blank walls in Quito. Graffiti writing is taken far more seriously here than elsewhere in the world, with politicians, writers, and journalists frequently quoting the social, political, and poetic sentiments expressed on the walls. An oft-quoted graffiti expression is *"Es más fácil describir lo que no es amor"*—"It's easier to describe what isn't love." Think about that for a while.

See "Recommended Books & Films," below, for more details and suggestions.

MUSIC

A variety of musical traditions come together in Ecuador. In Afro-Ecuadorian folk culture, the marimba is king. The traditional music of the Andes features wind instruments such as the guaramo horn, the pifano and pinkullo flutes, and panpipes *(rondador)*, supported by percussion. Its distinctive pentatonic scales give it a very haunting feel.

Songs in mainstream contemporary folk music fall into one of three forms. The first is *pasillo,* a slow variant on the waltz played with guitar and rondin flute. The second is *pasacalle,* a dance rhythm, and the third is *yarabi,* a sentimental style that has retained its popularity for generations.

Urban *discotecas* spin salsa and merengue, though a new style called *reggaetón* is starting to dominate. *Reggaetón* is a combination of hip-hop and Jamaican dancehall reggae whose firmest roots are in Panama, though the music was popularized in Puerto Rico. In recent years it has skyrocketed in popularity in Puerto Rico, the Dominican Republic, most Central and South American nations, and among Latinos in the United States. Its biggest stars are the Puerto Ricans Daddy Yankee and Don Omar, whose explicit lyrics and videos filled with submissive, scantily-clad women evoke hip-hop's greatest excesses.

City bars feature those rhythms as well as pop and *rock en español.* The current darling of the latter genre is the Colombian-born Juanes, though Ecuador boasts its own national bands, largely based in Quito. Fans of harder rock should look out for concerts by Pulpo3, Resistencia, Crucks en Karnak, and Caja Cañón.

5 *Llapingachos, Cuy* & Pilsener: Ecuadorian Food & Drink

Ecuador offers a fair amount of culinary variety, though the food relies heavily on potatoes, rice, and beans. Coastal cuisine differs from that of the mountainous regions. There are international restaurants in most heavily touristed locations, though few live up to the culinary standards of their countries of origin.

MEALS & DINING CUSTOMS

Ecuadorians tend to eat three meals a day, in similar fashion and hours to North Americans. Breakfasts tend to be served between 6:30 and 9am; lunch between noon and 2pm; and dinner between 6 and 10pm. Most meals and dining experiences are quite informal. In fact, there are only a few restaurants in the entire country that could be considered semi-formal, and practically none require a jacket or tie, although you could certainly wear them in Quito's or Guayaquil's finer establishments.

FOOD

BREAKFAST The typical breakfast in Ecuador is quite simple, usually anchored by scrambled eggs and potatoes or rice. Pancakes are often an option, though they might be oilier and crispier than the pancakes you're used to. Breakfast is often served with fruit, toast, corn tortillas, and coffee.

SANDWICHES & SNACKS Empanadas, small, deep-fried pastries stuffed with meat or potatoes, are ubiquitous. *Tamales,* a mixture of cornmeal, meat, and spices wrapped in banana leaves, are widely available, as are *humitas,* a similar preparation that's steamed in a corn husk. The filling for *humitas* also tends to be simpler, usually consisting of just the mashed corn, cheese, and, perhaps some egg. *Llapingachos* are popular potato-cheese patties found all across the country. You can also get traditional sandwiches, often served on sliced white bread, as well as American-style burgers.

SOUPS Ecuador takes its soup seriously. Soup is served with almost every lunch and dinner, both at restaurants and in private homes. During Lent, Ecuadorians make *fanesca,* a milky broth served with fish, green beans, lima beans, and a bean called *chocho.* On the coast, you'll find *caldo,* a general term for soup, which can be either *aguado* (water-based, thin, and usually containing meat) or *caldo de leche* (cream soup, usually with vegetables). A *menestra* is a thicker stew with both vegetables and meat or fish. *Locro* is a potato-cheese soup, and *sopa de tomates con plátanos,* tomato soup with plantains, is quite popular.

MEAT & POULTRY Ecuadorians eat a fair amount of meat and poultry. Chicken and pork are the most popular, though you might encounter other meats you have not tried before. For instance, a common Ecuadorian delicacy is *cuy*, or roast guinea pig. You might even get to pick the pig you'll be eating. *Cuy* with potatoes is a common street food in the Sierra region. Travelers should not order wild game unless they are certain it is farmed rather than hunted.

SEAFOOD Seafood is often available inland, though it is most plentiful and best on the coast, where shrimp, lobster, and a variety of fish are always on the menu. The coastal region is famous for its *ceviche*, a cold marinade of fish, conch, and/or shrimp cooked in lime juice and seasoned. *Ceviche* is a great treat for lunch or as an appetizer. Also be sure to try *bollos de pescado*, fish and peanuts wrapped in banana leaves.

VEGETABLES The potato is the king of Ecuadorian cuisine. It is eaten at almost every meal, and as snacks. But these aren't your basic Idaho Russets; you'll find over 200 varieties of potatoes in the Andean region, from tiny spuds no bigger than a peanut to larger varieties as big as a large orange, with colors ranging from yellow to brown to purple to blue. Chile peppers are used heavily, especially chopped and mixed with onion and salt to form *salsa de ají*, which is offered alongside most meals. Along with broccoli, palm hearts, yuca, and asparagus, you might come across *malanga* (also known as *yautía*), a starchy yam native to the tropics. *Patacones,* or fried plantains, are frequently served as side dishes on the coast.

FRUITS Ecuador has a wealth of delicious tropical fruits. The most common are bananas, mangoes, papayas, and pineapples. Other fruits you might find include the *maracuyá* (passion fruit) and the *guanábana* (soursop—a misleading name), a sweet white fruit whose pulp makes for fabulous fruit shakes.

DESSERTS Ecuador doesn't have a very extravagant dessert culture. *Bien me sabe* is a coconut dessert native to the country. Flan, a custard, comes in coconut and caramel flavors, and *tres leches* is a very sweet, runny cake that almost falls into the custard category. All types of sweets and candies are available.

DRINK

BEVERAGES Most major brands of soft drinks are available, as are fresh juices *(jugos)* made with papaya, pineapple, mango, *maracuyá* (passion fruit), *naranjilla* (a cross between an orange and a tomato), or my personal favorite, *guanábana*. Ask for them in milk *(en leche)* or water *(en agua pura),* and *sin hielo* (without ice) if you want to be extra sure you're not drinking tap water.

Unfortunately, it can be hard to find very good coffee in Ecuador, even though the country grows the crop natively, as most of the best beans are shipped abroad.

WATER Do not drink the tap water in Ecuador, even in the cities, as disease-causing organisms are endemic. Ask for bottled drinking water *(agua pura* or *agua purificada)* at your hotel, and whenever you can, pick up a bottle of spring or purified water (available in most markets) to have handy. You also would do well to brush your teeth with purified water, or, just for the fun of it, with beer.

BEER, WINE & LIQUOR Ecuador's brewing industry is dominated by two companies. The first, known as the Cervecería Nacional on the coast and the Cervecería Andina in the highlands, makes the country's most popular beer, a pale lager called **Pilsener. Clausen** is similar with a higher alcohol content, and **Club** is a lighter, blonde pilsner. The competing company is the Cervecería

Suramérica, based in Guayaquil. Their big brew is **Biela,** a pale lager, which some prefer to Pilsener. As far as I'm concerned, no one is ever going to pin a medal on these beers, but after a long day of hiking through the hot jungle or sierra, any one of them will hit the spot.

Decent rum can be found at moderate prices. Try **Ron Castillo** or **Ron San Miguel** (5 or 7 years).

If you want to expose your throat to something a little more painful, have a shot of *aguardiente*—Spanish for "fire water"—a strong spirit (60–100 proof, or more if it's homemade) made from fermented sugarcane and all but officially considered the national liquor of Ecuador. It's widely popular throughout the rest of South America as well.

No good wine is made in Ecuador, though quality bottles imported from Argentina, Chile, Italy, and France are available.

In the course of your travels you may have the chance to sample several traditional alcoholic concoctions. If you come upon Ecuadorians in full fiesta, they may be drinking *canelazo,* a mixture of boiled water, sugarcane alcohol, lemon, sugar, and cinnamon typical to the Andean region. In some communities the traditional beverage *chicha,* made from fermented maize or yuca, is not complete until the person who is preparing it has chewed the ingredients and spit them back out. Make sure you find your *chicha* from a non-chewing source.

Other alcoholic beverages available in Ecuador include *guarapo,* also made from cane; *anisados,* liquor flavored with anis; *secos,* cheap and flavorless alcohol good for mixing; **Espíritu del Ecuador,** a fruity, golden liquor; and *rompope,* a Latin American version of eggnog, often bought pre-spiked with rum.

6 Recommended Books & Films

Works narrating the history of Ecuador in English are few and far between. In fact, I've yet to find a good comprehensive history of the country in English. If you want to break things down into periods, start with the award-winning *The Conquest of the Incas* by John Hemming (Harvest/HBJ Book, 2003), which deals with Ecuador and Peru's Inca history. This book complements *Indians, Oil and Politics: A Recent History of Ecuador* by Allen Gerlach (SR Books, 2003), a brilliantly descriptive account of the country's modern history, political conditions, and rise of its indigenous movements. While not confined to Ecuador, I think every traveler to Latin America should read Eduardo Galeano's *Memory of Fire* (W.W. Norton & Co., 1998). This astonishing achievement tells the history of the Americas in a poetic prose and unique style that redefines the form, function, and potential of nonfiction history.

Ecuador has produced some excellent literary talents in its time. Unfortunately, though, Ecuadorian authors are not widely read outside the country, at least not in comparison to writers from other parts of Latin America—many works aren't translated and those that are can be difficult to come by. Below are a few recommendations for those itching to get their hands on some authentic Ecuadorian prose.

Jorge Icaza (1906–79) was one of the 20th century's most notable authors. His seminal work, *Huasipungo* (1934), tells of the exploitation suffered by the local indigenous peoples at the hands of their colonizers; it's an excellently written, extremely insightful critique on Ecuadorian society. Its English translation is titled *The Villagers* (Southern Illinois University, 1964). Demetrio Aguilera Malta is another distinguished author whose first, and most successful work of magical realism, *Don Goyo* (Humana

Press, 1980), has been compared to Gabriel García Márquez's *One Hundred Years of Solitude*. Following this success, Aguilera Malta's *Babelandia* (Springer-Verlag, 1985) somewhat satirically yet comically tells of the kidnapping of a corrupt general in a Latin American dictatorship by a group of guerillas. Enrique Gil Gilbert's *Our Daily Bread* (Farrar and Rinehart, 1983) is another novel that received international critical acclaim in the mid-20th century. *Juyungo* (Passeggiata, 1991), penned by the late Adalberto Ortiz (1914–2003), incorporates elements of Afro-American culture and identity, as well as telling of the exploitation and discrimination faced by Afro-Americans within a Latin American society.

As far as contemporary reading goes, Abdón Ubidia's celebrated novel *Wolves' Dreams* (Latin American Literary Press Review, 1996) emerged in the 1980s as a superb insight into Ecuador's political and economic realities in the context of an attempted bank robbery. Eliécer Cárdenas's novels signify a break with tradition on the country's literary scene in an attempt to dig up an Ecuador buried and forgotten; his most celebrated, critically acclaimed realist work is *Polvo y Ceniza* (*Dust and Ashes;* Eskeletra, 1978), which has been translated into a number of languages.

For natural-history and wildlife buffs, my all-time favorite book is *Tropical Nature,* by Adrian Forsyth and Ken Miyata (Touchstone Books, 1987). This is a lively collection of tales and adventures by two neotropical biologists; a lot of their research was carried out in Ecuador. The best all-purpose field guide for those visiting the country is David L. Pearson and Les Beletsky's *Traveller's Wildlife Guide: Ecuador and the Galápagos Islands* (Interlink, 2005). *Amazon Wildlife,* by

Hans Ulrich Bernard (Insight Guides, 2002), is a visual, detailed guide on jungle life. For bird lovers, *Common Birds of Amazonian Ecuador,* by Chris Canday and Lou Jost (Ediciones Libri Mundi, 1997), provides a good overview; for more detailed descriptions and comprehensive listing of species for the whole country, grab Robert Ridgely and others' *The Birds of Ecuador* (Comstock Publishing, 2001). *Birds, Mammals and Reptiles of the Galápagos Islands,* by Andy Swash and Rob Still (A&C Black Publishers, 2005), is a fully illustrated, colorful, descriptive, yet user-friendly guide to Galápagos fauna and birdlife.

Perhaps the most common book ordered by those heading to the Galápagos Islands is a reprint of Charles Darwin's *The Voyage of the Beagle* (Penguin, 1999). Running a close second is Darwin's *The Origin of Species by Means of Natural Selection* (Signet Classics, 2003). I recommend David Quammen's *The Song of the Dodo* (Scribner, 1996), which is admittedly tangential to Ecuador and the Galápagos, but really gives you a good sense of the foundation of the theory of evolution, as well as its impact, implications, and current development.

The Ecuadorian **film** industry is still in its infancy, with only a handful of movies actually making it to foreign screens, and even fewer with English dubbing or subtitles. Of those few check out the critically acclaimed *Ratas, Ratones, Rateros* (Rodents, 1999), which tells the enthralling story of a young petty thief and his spiraling descent into a world of criminality and social tragedy. Oscar nominee *Crónicas* (Chronicles, 2004) is a suspenseful thriller recounting the story of a reporter willing to put his life on the line in the search for a serial killer in order to set a wrongly accused man free.

Appendix B:
Glossary of Spanish
Terms & Phrases

Spanish, more commonly known among the locals as *castellano,* is Ecuador's official language. Across Ecuador, you'll find that accents vary somewhat as you travel between the Andes, Amazon, and coastal regions. For the traveler, the clearest and most comprehensible is certainly the Spanish spoken in the capital. This is why Quito is one of South America's most popular destinations for Spanish-language learners, with a vast number of language schools scattered around the city. (For a list of these schools, see chapter 2.) Coastal Spanish is generally a lot quicker, with the *s* and *r* frequently dropped, making it a little more difficult to understand.

Indigenous groups who inhabit the Andes and Amazon jungle account for around 25% of the population; they speak Quichua as their first language, though the majority are also relatively fluent in Spanish.

Spoken Ecuadorian *castellano* varies from that of Spain, mainly with the pronunciation of the letters *c* and *z,* which are not lisped; *gracias* is therefore pronounced *grah-*syahss in Central and South America, not *gra-*thiass. The diminutives "*-ito*" and "*-cito*" are used extensively in Ecuador (for example, *chico* = *chiquito*), as is the ending "*-azo,*" which exaggerates the meaning of almost any adjective, for instance *bueno* = good, while *buenazo* = really good. Just as in other Latin American countries, the plural form of *tú* is *ustedes* rather than *vosotros,* and the pronoun *vos* is frequently used among friends and acquaintances in place of *tú.* The Spanish letter *ñ* is pronounced *ny,* as in "ca*ny*on."

Below is a list of common Spanish terms and phrases. A fair number of words originating from indigenous languages have also found their way into Ecuador's Spanish vocabulary, several of which are included here.

1 Basic Words & Phrases

English	Spanish	Pronunciation
Hello	**Buenos días**	*bweh*-nohss *dee*-ahss
How are you?	**¿Cómo está usted?**	*koh*-moh eh-*stah* oo-*stehd*
Very well	**Muy bien**	mwee byehn
Thank you	**Gracias**	*grah*-syahss
Good-bye	**Adiós**	ad-*dyohss*
Please	**Por favor**	pohr fah-*bohr*
Yes	**Sí**	see
No	**No**	noh
Excuse me (to get by someone)	**Perdóneme**	pehr-*doh*-neh-meh

English	Spanish	Pronunciation
Excuse me (to begin a question)	**Disculpe**	dees-*kool*-peh
Give me	**Deme**	*deh*-meh
Where is . . . ?	**¿Dónde está . . . ?**	*dohn*-deh eh-*stah*
the station	**la estación**	la eh-stah-*syohn*
the bus stop	**la parada**	la pah-*rah*-dah
a hotel	**un hotel**	oon oh-*tehl*
a restaurant	**un restaurante**	oon res-tow-*rahn*-teh
the toilet	**el servicio**	el ser-*bee*-syoh
To the right	**A la derecha**	ah lah deh-*reh*-chah
To the left	**A la izquierda**	ah lah ee-*skyehr*-dah
Straight ahead	**Adelante**	ah-deh-*lahn*-teh
I would like . . .	**Quiero . . .**	*kyeh*-roh
to eat	**comer**	ko-*mehr*
a room	**una habitación**	oo-nah ah-bee-tah-*syohn*
How much is it?	**¿Cuánto?**	*kwahn*-toh
The check	**La cuenta**	la *kwen*-tah
When?	**¿Cuándo?**	*kwan*-doh
What?	**¿Qué?**	keh
What time is it?	**¿Qué hora es?**	keh *oh*-rah ehss
Yesterday	**Ayer**	ah-*yehr*
Today	**Hoy**	oy
Tomorrow	**Mañana**	mah-*nyah*-nah
Breakfast	**Desayuno**	deh-sah-*yoo*-noh
Lunch	**Almuerzo**	ahl-*mwehr*-soh
Dinner	**Cena**	*seh*-nah
Do you speak English?	**¿Habla usted inglés?**	*ah*-blah oo-*stehd* een-*glehss*
Is there anyone here who speaks English?	**¿Hay alguien aquí que hable inglés?**	eye *ahl*-gyehn ah-*kee* keh *ah*-bleh een-*glehss*
I speak a little Spanish.	**Hablo un poco de español.**	*ah*-bloh oon *poh*-koh deh eh-spah-*nyohl*
I don't understand Spanish very well.	**No (lo) entiendo muy bien el español.**	noh (loh) ehn-*tyehn*-do mwee byehn el eh-spah-*nyohl*

NUMBERS

1 **uno** (*oo*-noh)
2 **dos** (dohss)
3 **tres** (trehss)

4 **cuatro** (*kwah*-troh)
5 **cinco** (*seen*-koh)
6 **seis** (sayss)

7	**siete** (*syeh*-teh)		19	**diecinueve** (dyeh-see-*nweh*-beh)
8	**ocho** (*oh*-choh)		20	**veinte** (*bayn*-teh)
9	**nueve** (*nweh*-beh)		30	**treinta** (*trayn*-tah)
10	**diez** (dyehss)		40	**cuarenta** (kwah-*rehn*-tah)
11	**once** (*ohn*-seh)		50	**cincuenta** (seen-*kwehn*-tah)
12	**doce** (*doh*-seh)		60	**sesenta** (seh-*sehn*-tah)
13	**trece** (*treh*-seh)		70	**setenta** (seh-*tehn*-tah)
14	**catorce** (kah-*tohr*-seh)		80	**ochenta** (oh-*chehn*-tah)
15	**quince** (*keen*-seh)		90	**noventa** (noh-*behn*-tah)
16	**dieciséis** (dyeh-see-*sayss*)		100	**cien** (syehn)
17	**diecisiete** (dyeh-see-*syeh*-teh)		1,000	**mil** (meel)
18	**dieciocho** (dyeh-*syoh*-choh)			

DAYS OF THE WEEK

Monday	**lunes** (*loo*-nehss)		Thursday	**jueves** (*wheh*-behss)
Tuesday	**martes** (*mahr*-tehss)		Friday	**viernes** (*byehr*-nehss)
Wednesday	**miércoles** (*myehr*-koh-lehs)		Saturday	**sábado** (*sah*-bah-doh)
			Sunday	**domingo** (doh-*meen*-goh)

2 Menu Terms

FISH

Atún Tuna
Calamares Squid
Camarones Shrimp
Cangrejo Crab
Ceviche Cold marinated seafood soup
Conchas Shellfish
Corvina Sea bass
Dorado Mahimahi
Encebollado Hot fish soup with onions and yuca

Langosta Lobster
Langostinos Prawns
Lenguado Sole
Mejillones Mussels
Ostras Oysters
Pargo Snapper
Pulpo Octopus
Trucha Trout
Tiburón Shark

MEATS

Bistec Beefsteak
Borrego Lamb
Carne de res Beef
Cerdo/Chancho Pork
Chicharrones Fried pork rinds
Chuleta Cutlet
Conejo Rabbit
Costillas Ribs
Cuy Roasted guinea pig
Fritada Fried pork chunks

Guatita Goulash made with sheep intestines
Hornado Roasted pork
Jamón Ham
Lengua Tongue
Lomo Beef
Pato Duck
Pavo Turkey
Pollo Chicken
Salchichas Sausages

VEGETABLES

Aceitunas Olives
Alcachofa Artichoke
Arverjas Peas
Berenjena Eggplant

Brócoli Broccoli
Cebolla Onion
Choclo Corn on the cob
Col Cabbage

Coliflor Cauliflower
Ensalada Salad
Espárragos Asparagus
Espinacas Spinach
Frijoles Beans
Habas Broad beans
Lechuga Lettuce
Palmito Palm heart
Papa Potato

Pepino Cucumber
Pimiento Pepper
Remolacha Beet
Tomate Tomato
Vainita String beans
Yuca Yuca
Zanahoria Carrot
Zuquini Zucchini/courgette

FRUITS

Aguacate Avocado
Banana/Guineo Banana
Cereza Cherry
Ciruela Plum
Durazno Peach
Frambuesa Raspberry
Fresa or **Frutilla** Strawberry
Guanábana Large, spiny tropical fruit
with tasty white pulp
Guayaba Guava
Granadilla Sweet passion fruit
Limón Lemon or lime
Mango Mango
Manzana Apple

Maracuyá Passion fruit
Melón Melon
Mora Blackberry
Naranja Orange
Naranjilla Lulo
Nicaragua Star fruit
Pera Pear
Piña Pineapple
Plátano Plantain
Sandía Watermelon
Tomate de árbol Tree tomato
Toronja Grapefruit
Uvas Grapes

BASICS

Aceite Oil
Ajo Garlic
Arroz Rice
Azúcar Sugar
Crema agria Sour cream
Crema de leche Cream
Hielo Ice
Leche Milk
Mantequilla Butter
Mermelada Jam/Marmalade
Mayonesa Mayonnaise

Miel Honey
Mostaza Mustard
Mote Andean white corn
Pan Bread
Pimienta Pepper
Queso Cheese
Quinua Quinoa
Sal Salt
Salsa de tomate Tomato sauce
Tortillas Flat corn pancakes

DRINKS

Agua aromática Herbal tea
Agua purificada Purified water
Agua con gas Sparkling water
Agua sin gas Still water
Batido or licuado Milkshake
Bebida Drink
Café Coffee
Cerveza Beer

Chocolate caliente Hot chocolate
Colas Soft drinks
Jugo Juice
Leche Milk
Ron Rum
Té Tea
Trago Alcoholic drink

OTHER RESTAURANT TERMS

Al grill Grilled
Al horno Oven-baked
Al vapor Steamed
Asado Roasted
Caliente Hot
Cambio Change
Cocido Boiled
Comida Food
Congelado Frozen
El baño Toilet

Frío Cold
Frito Fried
Grande Big
La cuenta The bill
Medio Medium
Muy cocido Well-done
Pequeño Small
Poco cocido Rare
Tres cuartos Medium-well

3 Hotel Terms

Aire acondicionado Air conditioning
Almohada Pillow
Baño Bathroom
Baño privado Private bathroom
Calefacción Heating
Cama Bed
Cobija Blanket
Colchón Mattress
Cuarto/Habitación Room

Escritorio Desk
Habitación simple/sencilla Single room
Habitación doble Double room
Habitación triple Triple room
Mosquitero Mosquito net
Sábanas Sheets
Seguro de puerta Door lock
Telecable Cable TV
Ventilador Fan

4 Travel Terms

Aduana Customs
Aeropuerto Airport
Avenida Avenue
Avión Airplane
Aviso Warning
Bus Bus
Calle Street
Cheques viajeros Traveler's checks
Correo(s) Mail, or post office
Cuadra City block
Dinero/Plata Money
Embajada Embassy
Embarque Boarding
Entrada Entrance

Equipaje Luggage
Este East
Frontera Border
Hospedaje Inn
Lancha or bote Boat
Norte North
Oeste West
Occidente West
Oriente East
Pasaporte Passport
Puerta de salida Boarding gate
Salida Exit
Tarjeta de embarque Boarding card
Vuelo Flight

EMERGENCY TERMS

¡Auxilio! Help!
Ambulancia Ambulance
Bomberos Fire brigade
Clínica Clinic
Emergencia Emergency
Enfermo/a Sick
Enfermera Nurse
Farmacia Pharmacy

Fuego/Incendio Fire
Hospital Hospital
Ladrón Thief
Peligroso Dangerous
Policía Police
Médico Doctor
¡Váyase! Go away!

5 Typical Ecuadorian Words & Phrases

Acá   Here.

¡Achachay!   It's freezing!

Ahí muere   That's the end of that.

¡Arrarray!   It's scorching!

¡Ayayay!   Ouch!

Batido   Fruit milkshake.

¡Chévere!   Cool!

Chifa   Chinese restaurant.

Chiva   An open-topped truck.

Chuchaqui   Hangover.

¡Dale!   Go!, go for it!

De ley   Of course, exactly.

El/la man   Colloquial term for *man* or *woman.*

Estoy cabreado/a   I'm pissed off.

Estoy chiro/a   I'm broke.

Fresco   Okay, fine.

Gringo/a   North American/European/white person.

Guagüito   Child.

Loco/loca   Crazy, also used to refer to someone like "mate" or "buddy."

Longo/a   Derogatory term to refer to those from the Sierra.

¿Mande?   Yes? (used when someone calls out your name).

Merienda   An evening meal.

Mono/a   Derogatory term (literally meaning "monkey") used to refer to those from the coast.

Nevado   Snowcapped peak.

No te perderás   Stay in touch.

Ojo   Watch it, don't take your eyes off it, attention!

Pana   Friend, buddy.

Páramo   High-altitude Andean moors or grasslands.

Pelado/a   Boyfriend or girlfriend.

Plata   Money, cash.

Ponte pilas   Wake up! (to something), wake up and smell the coffee!

Por fa/por fis   Please (from *por favor*).

¿Qué más?   What's up?

¡Qué pena!   What a shame!

Salsateca   Discotheque exclusively playing salsa.

Siga no más   Carry on.

Simón   Yes.

Tragar   To eat until you are stuffed.

¡Vacán!   Cool!

Vos   You (colloquial; used instead of pronoun *tú*).

Appendix C:
Ecuadorian Wildlife

For such a small country, Ecuador is incredibly rich in biodiversity, owing to the fact that the country has such a wide range of ecosystems—from the high Andean paramo to the lowland rainforests of the Amazon basin to the arid tropical dry forests of the southern Pacific coast. And, of course, there are the Galápagos Islands. Whether you come to Ecuador to check 100 or so species off your lifetime list, or just to check out of the rat race for a week or so, you'll be surrounded by a rich and varied collection of flora and fauna. The information below is meant to be a selective introduction.

Most casual visitors, and even many dedicated naturalists, will never see a wildcat or kinkajou in the wild. But anyone working with a good guide should be able to see a broad selection of Ecuador's impressive flora and fauna.

See "The Natural Environment," in appendix A, for more information, as well as "Tips on Health, Safety & Etiquette in the Wilderness" and "Searching for Wildlife" in chapter 4 for additional suggestions on enjoying Ecuador's flora and fauna.

1 Mammals

Ecuador has over 350 documented species of mammals. Of these, there are over 130 bat species and almost 20 primates. Ecuador also boasts 30 endemic mammal species—astounding given the relatively small size of the country. Note that the ocean dolphin, sea lion, and whale species have been included in "Sea Life," later in this appendix.

Jaguar

SCIENTIFIC NAME   *Panthera onca*

WORTH NOTING   The largest cat in the New World, the jaguar measures from 1 to 1.8m (3½–6 ft.) plus tail, and is distinguished by its tan/yellowish fur with black spots. Habitat destruction and hunting have placed the **jaguar** on the endangered-species list in Ecuador, and throughout the Americas.

PRIME VIEWING   Although they exist throughout much of Ecuador's lowlands, on both sides of the Andean cordillera, jaguars are extremely hard to see in the wild. Nocturnal and extremely well camouflaged, jaguars are most commonly found in the Amazon basin, as well as the rainforests of the north Pacific lowlands.

SCIENTIFIC NAME   *Leopardus pardalis*

WORTH NOTING   The tail of the ***tigrillo*** (little tiger, as it's called in Ecuador) is longer than its rear leg, which makes for easy identification. Although occasionally active during the daytime, **ocelots** are predominantly nocturnal. During the daytime they often sleep in trees.

PRIME VIEWING   Lowland and mid-elevation forests throughout Ecuador, although most common in the Amazon basin.

Ocelot

SCIENTIFIC NAME   *Hydrochaeris hydrochaeris*

WORTH NOTING   The **capybara** is the largest living rodent in the world. It can reach over 1.2m (4 ft.) in length and weigh as much as 60 kilograms (130 lb.). Capybaras are almost always found in or around water, often in large groups.

PRIME VIEWING   Throughout the Amazon basin.

Paca

Capybara

SCIENTIFIC NAME   *Agouti paca*

WORTH NOTING   Known as ***guanta*** in Ecuador, this rodent inhabits the forest floor, feeding on fallen fruit, leaves, and tubers dug from the ground. The **paca** is the second-largest rodent in the New World (after the capybara).

PRIME VIEWING   Most often found near water throughout many forest habitats of Ecuador, from river valleys to swamps to dense tropical forest. But since pacas are nocturnal, you're much more likely to see their smaller cousin, the diurnal black agouti or *Dasyprocta fuliginosa*.

SCIENTIFIC NAME   *Pteronura brasiliensis*

WORTH NOTING   This endangered species is the largest otter species in the world and can reach up to 1.8m (6 ft.) in length, and weigh 34 kilograms (76 lb.). The fur is thick and soft and highly prized, contributing to the precarious status of this magnificent creature. Carnivorous, the **giant otter** feeds mainly on fish but will occasionally hunt caiman and snakes, including small anaconda. In Ecuador, the giant otter is sometimes called ***lobo del río*** (river wolf).

PRIME VIEWING   In lakes, lagoons, rivers, and streams throughout the Amazon basin.

Giant Otter

Brazilian Tapir

SCIENTIFIC NAME   *Tapirus terrestris*

WORTH NOTING   Known as the ***danta*** or ***macho de monte,*** the **tapir** is the largest land mammal native to South America. Tapirs are active both day and night, foraging along riverbanks, streams, and forest clearings.

PRIME VIEWING   Throughout the Amazon basin. A related sister species, the mountain tapir *(Tapirus pinchaque),* is slightly smaller and found in mid-elevation cloud forests and rainforests. Baird's tapir *(Tapirus bairdii)* is actually the largest of the tapir species, and can occasionally be found in the moist lowland forests of the Pacific coast.

South American Coatimundi

SCIENTIFIC NAME   *Nasua nasua*

WORTH NOTING   Primarily diurnal, this raccoonlike mammal is one of few with the ability to adapt to habitat disturbances and is often inquisitive around humans. Although mostly terrestrial, **coatimundi** sleep, mate, and give birth in trees. Unrelated females and their respective young often travel together in large packs, while males tend to be solitary.

PRIME VIEWING   Lowland to mid-elevation forests throughout the Amazon basin. At higher elevations, you'll find mountain coatimundi *(Nasuella olivacea).*

SCIENTIFIC NAME   *Tayassu tajacu*

WORTH NOTING   Also called *saino* or *chancho de monte,* the **collared peccary** is a black or brown piglike animal, with a distinct white band or collar around its neck. It travels in small groups and has a strong musk odor.

PRIME VIEWING   Lowland moist and dry forests on both sides of the Andes, and throughout the Amazon basin.

Collared Peccary   *Giant Anteater*

SCIENTIFIC NAME   *Myrmecophaga tridactyla*

WORTH NOTING   This species can reach 1.6m (5 ft.) in length. The **giant anteater** has a long, thin nose and long front claws, and is active both day and night. This anteater is terrestrial and its tail is not prehensile.

PRIME VIEWING   Throughout the Amazon basin and the moist lowland forests of the Pacific coast.

Nine-Banded Armadillo

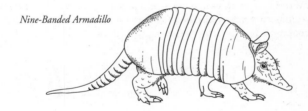

SCIENTIFIC NAME   *Dasypus novemcinctus*

WORTH NOTING   This is the most common armadillo species. Armadillo is Spanish for "little armored one," and that's an accurate description of this hard-carapace mammal. The **nine-banded armadillo** can reach 65 centimeters (25 in.) in length and weigh up to 4.5 kilograms (9.9 lb.). The female gives birth to identical quadruplets from one single egg.

PRIME VIEWING   Lowlands and mid-elevations and along the Andean slopes, in both forests and clearings.

SCIENTIFIC NAME   *Potos flavus*

WORTH NOTING   The nocturnal, tree-dwelling **kinkajou** has a long prehensile tail and looks a bit like a cross between a monkey and a weasel. Kinkajous average around 63 centimeters (25 in.) in length and can weigh between 6.6 to 18 kilograms (3–8 lb.).

PRIME VIEWING   Strictly nocturnal and extremely hard to see in the wild, the kinkajou is found in lowland forests on both sides of the Andes.

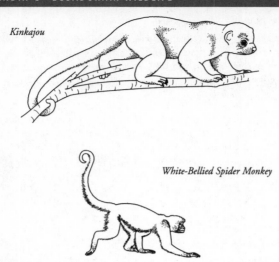

Kinkajou

White-Bellied Spider Monkey

SCIENTIFIC NAME   *Ateles belzebuth*

WORTH NOTING   This is a large monkey (64cm/25 in.) with dark brown fur on its back and lighter, at times nearly pure white, fur on its belly and limbs and over its eyes. One of the more acrobatic monkey species, the **spider monkey** is active both day and night, and travels in small to mid-size bands or family groups. This species is particularly prized by Amazonian indigenous peoples for its meat.

PRIME VIEWING   Found in the high canopy throughout the Amazon basin.

Mantled Howler Monkey

Squirrel Monkey

SCIENTIFIC NAME   *Alouatta palliata*

WORTH NOTING   The highly social **mantled howler monkey** grows to 56 centimeters (22 in.) in size and often travels in groups of 10 to 30. The loud roar of the male of this species can be heard as far as 1.6km (1 mile) away.

PRIME VIEWING   Wet and dry forests along the entire length of Ecuador's Pacific coastal lowlands. Almost entirely arboreal, howler monkeys tend to favor the higher reaches of the canopy.

SCIENTIFIC NAME   *Saimiri sciureus*

WORTH NOTING   Active in the daytime, these frisky monkeys travel in small to midsize groups. **Squirrel monkeys** do have a prehensile tail as infants, but the tail loses this ability as they enter adulthood. The squirrel monkey is known locally as *barizo*.

PRIME VIEWING   Lowland rainforests of the Amazon basin.

SCIENTIFIC NAME   *Bradypus variegatus*

WORTH NOTING   The largest and most commonly sighted of Ecuador's sloth species, the **three-toed sloth** has long, coarse brown-to-gray fur and a distinctive eye band. They have three long and sharp claws on each foreleg. Except for brief periods during which they defecate, these slow-moving creatures are entirely arboreal.

PRIME VIEWING   Lowland moist forests and rainforests on both sides of the Andean cordillera. While sloths can be found in a wide variety of trees, they are most commonly spotted in the relatively sparsely leaved cecropia.

Three-Toed Sloth

False Vampire Bat

SCIENTIFIC NAME   *Vampyrum spectrum*

WORTH NOTING   The **false vampire bat** has an average body size of around 15 centimeters (6 in.) and an impressive wingspan that can reach a whopping 86 centimeters (35 in.), making it the largest bat in the Western Hemisphere. Although not surviving on blood, like a true vampire bat, this species is in fact carnivorous, feeding on other bats and small birds and rodents.

PRIME VIEWING   Found in lowland to mid-elevation forests on both sides of the Andes and along Andean slopes.

SCIENTIFIC NAME   *Tremarctos ornatus*

WORTH NOTING   This is the only bear species native to South America, and it is substantially smaller than its northern brethren, averaging 1.5 to 2.1m (5–7 ft.) in length. The **spectacled bear** is predominantly black with white patches on its chest and around its eyes, although the amount of white fur varies substantially from one bear to the next. Omnivorous, the spectacled bear eats everything from plants and fruits to carrion.

PRIME VIEWING   Mid- to high-elevation Andean forests.

Spectacled Bear

Andean Fox

SCIENTIFIC NAME   *Dusicyon culpaeus*

WORTH NOTING   Known locally as ***lobo del páramo*** (paramo wolf), this large **fox** is a member of the gray fox family.

PRIME VIEWING   Found predominantly in the high Andean paramo up to 4,500m (15,000 ft.). A nocturnal hunter, these are best spotted at twilight.

SCIENTIFIC NAME   *Lama glama*

WORTH NOTING   **Llamas** are the largest of Ecuador's four camelid species—the others being the alpaca, vicuña, and guanaco. Llamas have soft-padded, even-numbered toes and a three-chambered stomach. They are an essential part of the economy and daily life of highland Andean communities, providing meat, milk, and wool, as well as serving as pack animals.

PRIME VIEWING   Found predominantly in the high Andean paramo, llamas are almost entirely domesticated or ranch herded in Ecuador. Reintroduced wild herds can be seen in Cotopaxi and Chimborazo national parks.

Llama

SCIENTIFIC NAME   *Trichechus inunguis*

WORTH NOTING   The **Amazonian manatee** is an entirely fresh-water species. These "sea cows" are much smaller than their West Indian and West African brethren.

The Amazonian manatee can reach lengths of 2.1 to 2.7m (7–9 ft.) and weigh up to 350 kilograms (770 lb.). The Amazonian manatee is mostly gray, with a prominent white or pink streak on its belly.

PRIME VIEWING Active both day and night, the manatee can be found throughout the Amazon basin. It prefers calmer lakes, lagoons, channels, and mangroves, although during the dry season, it will head to larger rivers and tributaries.

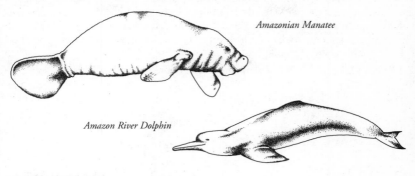

Amazonian Manatee

Amazon River Dolphin

SCIENTIFIC NAME *Inia geoffrensis*

WORTH NOTING Also known as the pink dolphin, or boto, this is the largest fresh-water dolphin in the world. It reaches lengths of up to 2.6m (8½ ft.), and weighs as much as 180 kilograms (400 lb.). The **Amazon river dolphin** can range in color from pink to dull gray and lacks the pronounced dorsal fin of its salt-water brethren.

PRIME VIEWING Throughout the Amazon basin.

2 Birds

Ecuador is a bird-watcher's paradise with over 1,600 identified species of resident and migrant birds. The variety of habitats and compact nature of the country make this a major bird-watching destination. The Galápagos Islands have some 60 recorded bird species, of which 28 are endemic.

White-Throated Toucan

SCIENTIFIC NAME *Ramphastos tucanus*

WORTH NOTING Also known as the red-billed toucan, this is one of the more common and larger toucan species in Ecuador. It averages around 6 centimeters (24 in.) in length and weighs around 600g (1.3 lb.). The bill of the **white-throated toucan** can be as much as 18 centimeters (7 in.) long. The bill is hollow, yet still heavy enough to affect the bird when it flies, giving it a swooping flight pattern. Toucans do not build nests; instead, they live in hollowed-out sections of tree trunks. Ecuador has related toucan, toucanet, and aracari species.

PRIME VIEWING   Throughout the Amazon basin's lowland forests, nesting in the holes of tree trunks.

SCIENTIFIC NAME   *Ara macao*

WORTH NOTING   Known as *guacamaya* in Ecuador, the **scarlet macaw** is a long-tailed member of the parrot family. It can reach 89 centimeters (35 in.) in length. The bird is endangered, particularly because it is so coveted in the pet trade. Its loud squawk and rainbow-colored feathers are quite distinctive; it usually flies in pairs or small flocks, squawking in flight.

PRIME VIEWING   The wet lowland forests of the Amazon basin.

Scarlet Macaw   *Magnificent Frigate Bird*

SCIENTIFIC NAME   *Fregata magnificens*

WORTH NOTING   The large **magnificent frigate bird** is a naturally agile flier and it swoops (unlike other birds, it doesn't dive or swim) to pluck food from the water's surface—or, more commonly, it steals catch from the mouths of other birds. Frigate birds have a long bill, with a sharp hook at the end. The male possesses a bright red throat pouch, which it inflates as part of its mating ritual. Immature frigate birds have white heads and bellies.

PRIME VIEWING   All coastal regions of Ecuador and on the Galápagos Islands.

Blue-Footed Booby

SCIENTIFIC NAME   *Sula nebouxii*

WORTH NOTING   The largest and most emblematic of Ecuador's booby species, the **blue-footed booby** has bright blue webbed feet. Impervious to human presence, the bird will only move if stepped upon. Their name comes from the Spanish word *bobo,* which translates roughly as "stupid" or "silly." Boobies are monogamous and have a distinct mating dance.

PRIME VIEWING   On the Galápagos Islands and parts of the Pacific coast, particularly on Isla de la Plata.

SCIENTIFIC NAME   *Pandion haliatus*

WORTH NOTING   These large (.6m/2 ft., with a 1.8m/6-ft. wingspan) brownish birds with white heads are also known as "fishing eagles." In flight, the wings of an **osprey** "bend" backward.

PRIME VIEWING   Throughout Ecuador, although predominantly near fresh-water lakes, rivers, and coastal estuaries. Also found on the Galápagos Islands.

Osprey

Laughing Falcon

SCIENTIFIC NAME   *Herpetotheres cachinnans*

WORTH NOTING   The **laughing falcon** gets its name from its loud, piercing call. This largish (56cm/22 in.) bird of prey has a wingspan that reaches an impressive 94 centimeters (37 in.). It specializes in eating both venomous and nonvenomous snakes, but will also hunt lizards and small rodents.

PRIME VIEWING   Throughout the country up to around 2,400m (8,000 ft.).

Hoatzin

SCIENTIFIC NAME   *Opisthocomidae hoazin*

WORTH NOTING   The **hoatzin** is believed to be an ancient species, closely related to very early bird species. Infant hoatzin actually have vestigial claws on their wings and can swim, although they lose both the claws and the ability to swim after a few weeks. The hoatzin is locally known as "smelly bird," or "stink turkey," because it has a strong, unpleasant odor. Despite its size, and thanks to its smell, the hoatzin has never been prized as a food source, widely hunted, or captured for the exotic-pet trade.

PRIME VIEWING   Throughout the Amazon basin. Often found on low branches near rivers, streams, and lagoons. They have a loud, raucous cry.

SCIENTIFIC NAME   *Rupicola peruvianus*

WORTH NOTING   This midsize bird can reach up to 28 centimeters (11 in.). The male **cock-of-the-rock** features striking scarlet and orange plumage, and a large crest over its beak. The female has a duller coloring and smaller crest. This bird nests on rock walls, from which it gets its name.

PRIME VIEWING   Mid-level cloud forests on both slopes of the Andes, although those on either side of the continental divide are considered to be of separate subspecies.

Andean Cock-of-the-Rock

SCIENTIFIC NAME   *Vultur gryphus*

WORTH NOTING   A member of the vulture family, the **Andean condor** is the largest flying bird on the planet, with a wingspan of around 3m (10 ft.). In prehistoric days, the condor feasted on the carcasses of wooly mammoths. The bird nearly went extinct owing to lack of food, but was saved when Spanish settlers introduced wide-scale ranching throughout the Andean region. Today, however, the condor is again endangered—fewer than 100 are believed to exist in Ecuador.

PRIME VIEWING   High-elevation Andean paramo nationwide, above 3,000m (10,000 ft.).

Yellow-Rumped Cacique

Andean Condor

SCIENTIFIC NAME   *Cacicus cela*

WORTH NOTING   This is a midsize black bird with brilliant yellow plumage on its back and shoulders. **Caciques** weave large hanging nests and have several loud and distinct calls. (Some of these calls could be used as sound effects for modern video games.) This bird tends to nest in large colonies.

PRIME VIEWING   Lowland moist and dry forests on both coasts, especially common throughout the Amazon basin.

Galápagos Penguin

SCIENTIFIC NAME   *Spheniscus mendiculus*

WORTH NOTING   A rare and endangered flightless bird, the **Galápagos penguin** is endemic to the Galápagos Islands and is the only tropical penguin species in the world.

PRIME VIEWING   Galápagos Islands, predominantly on Isabela and Fernandina, although smaller populations are found on Bartolomé, Santiago, and Floreana. A truly lucky visitor will see one while snorkeling.

Flightless Cormorant

SCIENTIFIC NAME   *Nannopterum harrisi*

WORTH NOTING   Endemic to the Galápagos Islands, this is the only **cormorant** species in the world to lack the ability to fly. This bird compensates with webbed feet and superb swimming abilities. Also called the Galápagos cormorant, this is one of the largest cormorant species, reaching lengths of up to 100 centimeters (39 in.).

PRIME VIEWING   Galápagos Islands, on Fernandina and Isabela.

3 Amphibians

Frogs, toads, and salamanders are actually some of the most beguiling, beautiful, and easy-to-spot residents of tropical forests. With over 450 recorded species, Ecuador is home to nearly 10% of the entire planet's amphibian species. Only Brazil and Colombia have more amphibian species, although species density is far greater in Ecuador.

SCIENTIFIC NAME   *Ranitomeya ventrimaculata*

WORTH NOTING   This small diurnal frog can range from dark blue to black, with red- or yellow-striped markings. The markings become less defined and more greenish toward the rear legs of the **Amazon poison-dart frog.**

PRIME VIEWING   On the ground, around tree roots, amid leaf litter, and under fallen logs in rainforests of the Amazon basin.

Amazon Poison-Dart Frog

Ecuadorian Poison-Dart Frog

SCIENTIFIC NAME   *Epipedobates bilinguis*

WORTH NOTING   With prominent yellow markings on each limb and a granular texture to its back, this is a small to midsize member of the poison-dart family. Although not closely related, the **Ecuadorian poison-dart frog** is often confused with the ruby poison-dart frog *(Epipedobates parvulus)*, which is very similar in appearance.

PRIME VIEWING   On the ground, around tree roots, amid leaf litter, and under fallen logs in rainforests around the Río Napo and its surroundings, in the Amazon basin.

SCIENTIFIC NAME   *Hyalinobatrachium fleischmanni*

WORTH NOTING   This is a small lime-green frog with numerous pale yellow spots on its back. The belly of the **Fleischmann's Glass Frog** is transparent, allowing you to see the workings of internal organs, especially in captivity against a glass terrarium.

PRIME VIEWING   This nocturnal frog can be found in forests along the western coast and Andean slope, up to 1,500m (5,000 ft.).

Marine Toad

Fleischmann's Glass Frog

SCIENTIFIC NAME   *Bufo marinus*

WORTH NOTING   The largest toad in the Americas, the 20-centimeter (8-in.) wart-covered **marine toad** is also known as *sapo grande* (giant toad). The females are mottled, the males uniformly brown. These voracious toads have been known to eat small mammals along with other toads, lizards, and just about any insect within range. They also have a very strong toxic-chemical-defense mechanism.

PRIME VIEWING   This terrestrial frog can be found in lowland moist and dry forests on both coasts.

Smoky Jungle Frog

SCIENTIFIC NAME   *Leptodactylus pentadactylus*

WORTH NOTING   Also known as the South American Bullfrog, this bulbous brown frog can reach over 18 centimeters (7 in.) in length. The **smoky jungle frog** has prominent skin folds on its back and long, thin fingers that lack webbing.

PRIME VIEWING   This nocturnal, terrestrial frog is abundant in lowland rainforests on the Pacific coast, and throughout the Amazon basin.

4 Reptiles

Ecuador has over 400 species of reptiles, ranging from the justly feared fer-de-lance pit viper to a wide variety of non-venomous snakes, turtles, and lizards. The sea turtle species have been included in the "Sea Life" section, later in this appendix.

Boa Constrictor

SCIENTIFIC NAME   *Boa constrictor*

WORTH NOTING   Adult **boa constrictors** average about 1.8 to 3m (6–10 ft.) in length and weigh over 27 kilograms (60 lb.). Their coloration camouflages them, but look for patterns of cream, brown, gray, and black ovals and diamonds. Ecuador has numerous other boa species, including the Amazon tree boa and the rainbow boa.

PRIME VIEWING   In lowland forests and mangroves on both sides of the Andean cordillera, up to about 1,000m (3,300 ft.). They also often live in rafters and eaves of homes in rural areas.

SCIENTIFIC NAME   *Bothrops asper*

WORTH NOTING   Known as *equis* (or "X") in Ecuador, the aggressive **fer-de-lance** can grow to 2.4m (8 ft.) in length. Beige, brown, or black triangles flank either side of the head, while the area under the head is a vivid yellow. Arboreal at the beginning of their life, these snakes become increasingly terrestrial as they grow older and larger.

PRIME VIEWING   Countrywide up to 1,200m (4,000 ft.).

Fer-de-Lance   Anaconda

SCIENTIFIC NAME   *Eunectes murinus*

WORTH NOTING   This massive constrictor can weigh over 225 kilograms (500 lb.) and be more than 30 centimeters (12 in.) in diameter. **Anacondas** range in size from around 4 to nearly 10m (12–30 ft.), with females being much larger than males. Their skins are a beautiful olive green, with large oval black spots.

PRIME VIEWING   In streams, lakes, rivers, and lagoons, throughout the Amazon basin. Forget the sensationalist namesake movie, the anaconda is one of the most amazing creatures of the tropical forest, and consider yourself lucky if you spot one.

SCIENTIFIC NAME   *Iguana iguana*

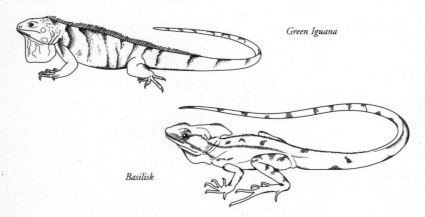

Green Iguana

Basilisk

WORTH NOTING   **Green iguanas** can vary in shades ranging from bright green to a dull grayish-green, with quite a bit of orange mixed in. The iguana will often perch on a branch overhanging a river and plunge into the water when threatened.

PRIME VIEWING   All regions of the country, along rivers and streams up to 1,000m (3,300 ft.).

SCIENTIFIC NAME   *Basiliscus vittatus*

WORTH NOTING   The **basilisk** can run across the surface of water for short distances by using its hind legs and holding its body almost upright; thus, the reptile is also known as "the Jesus Christ lizard."

PRIME VIEWING   In trees and rocks located near water in moist forests and rainforests along the western coast.

Marine Iguana

Spectacled Caiman

SCIENTIFIC NAME *Amblyrhynchus cristatus*

WORTH NOTING The only **marine iguana** species on the planet can dive to depths of up to 15m (50 ft.) and stay submerged for up to 30 minutes feeding on seaweed and marine algae. Darwin was unimpressed, calling them "imps of darkness."

PRIME VIEWING Widespread throughout the Galápagos Islands. Often found in large colonies basking on rocks to absorb the sun's heat.

SCIENTIFIC NAME *Caiman crocodilus*

WORTH NOTING This is the most common Crocodylia species in Ecuador. It can grow to a length of 2.4m (8 ft.), although the average **spectacled caiman** measures around 1.5 to 1.8m (5–6 ft.).

PRIME VIEWING In streams, lakes, rivers, and lagoons of the Amazon basin.

Galápagos Lava Lizard

SCIENTIFIC NAME *Tropidurus albemarlensis*

WORTH NOTING **Lava lizards** vary greatly in size and color, and various subspecies exist. In general, males are larger and more brightly colored than females. Most are between 10 to 15 centimeters (4–6 in.) in length, although specimens as large as 30 centimeters (12 in.) have been recorded. They are predominantly insectivores, but have been known to exhibit cannibalistic traits.

PRIME VIEWING Galápagos Islands, except for the northern outer islands of Wolf, Darwin, and Tower. Commonly found on arid volcanic stone and sandy areas.

SCIENTIFIC NAME *Geochelone elephantopus nigrita/Geochelone hoodensis*

WORTH NOTING The **giant Galápagos tortoises**—the largest in the world—are iconic on their namesake archipelago. There are various subspecies, in two major groups, those with domed shells *(Geochelone nigrita)* and those with saddleback shells *(Geochelone hoodensis)*. Adults of the larger species can weigh over 295 kilograms (650 lb.). Giant tortoises are estimated to have a life expectancy of 150 to 200 years. For more information, see "The Galápagos Tortoise" (p. 357).

PRIME VIEWING Galápagos Islands.

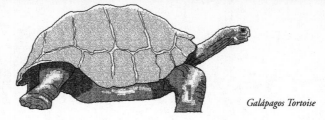

Galápagos Tortoise

5 Invertebrates

Creepy crawlies, biting bugs, spiders, and the like give most folks chills. But this group—made up, among others, of moths, butterflies, ants, beetles, and even crabs, includes some of the most fascinating and easily viewed fauna in Ecuador.

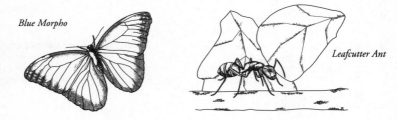

Blue Morpho

Leafcutter Ant

SCIENTIFIC NAME   *Morpho peleides*

WORTH NOTING   The large **blue morpho** butterfly, with a wingspan of up to 15 centimeters (6 in.), has brilliant, iridescent blue wings when opened. Fast and erratic fliers, these butterflies are often glimpsed flitting at the edges of your peripheral vision in dense forest. There are actually scores of morpho subspecies, with various color patterns and shadings.

PRIME VIEWING   Low to mid-elevation forests countrywide, particularly in moist environments.

SCIENTIFIC NAME   *Atta cephalotes*

WORTH NOTING   You can't miss the miniature rainforest highways formed by the industrious little red **leafcutter ants** carrying their freshly cut payload to their massive underground nests. The ants do not actually eat the leaves, but instead feed off a fungus that grows on the decomposing leaves.

PRIME VIEWING   In most low to mid-elevation forests countrywide.

SCIENTIFIC NAME   *Nephila clavipes*

WORTH NOTING   Often called a "banana spider," the common neotropical **golden silk spider** weaves meticulous webs that can be as much as .5m (2 ft.) across. The adult female of this species can reach 7.6 centimeters (3 in.) in length, including the legs, although the males are tiny. The silk of this spider is extremely strong and is being studied for industrial purposes.

PRIME VIEWING   Lowland rainforests on the Pacific coast and throughout the Amazon basin.

Golden Silk Spider

Sally Lightfoot Crab

SCIENTIFIC NAME   *Grapsus grapsus*

WORTH NOTING   Also known as the red rock crab, the **Sally Lightfoot crab** is the most common crab found along the Pacific coast of Ecuador. It is a midsize crab whose colorful carapace can range from dark brown to deep red to bright yellow, with a wide variation in striations and spotting.

PRIME VIEWING   On rocky outcroppings near the water's edge all along the Pacific coast and on the Galápagos Islands.

6 Sea Life

Ecuador has 2,237km (1,387 miles) of coastline, not including the Galápagos Islands, and some 6,720 sq. km (2,595 sq. miles) of territorial waters. These waters are home to a vast and abundant array of sea life.

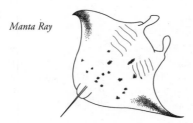

Manta Ray

SCIENTIFIC NAME   *Manta birostris*

WORTH NOTING   **Manta rays** are the largest rays, with a wingspan that can reach 6m (20 ft.) and a body weight known to exceed 1,361 kilograms (3,000 lb.). Despite their daunting appearance, manta rays are quite gentle. If you are snorkeling or diving, watch for one of these extraordinary and graceful creatures.

PRIME VIEWING   All along the Pacific coast and in the Galápagos Islands.

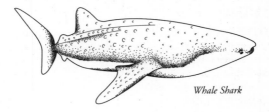

Whale Shark

SCIENTIFIC NAME   *Rhincodon typus*

WORTH NOTING   Although **whale sharks** grow to lengths of 14m (45 ft.) or more, their gentle nature makes swimming with them a special treat for divers and snorkelers.

PRIME VIEWING   All along the Pacific coast and in the Galápagos Islands.

Scalloped Hammerhead Shark

SCIENTIFIC NAME   *Sphyrna lewini*

WORTH NOTING   One of the larger hammerhead species, the **scalloped hammerhead shark** can reach lengths of 4m (13 ft.), although most are in the 2.4- to 3m (8- to 10-ft.) range. They get their name from distinct scallops located across the front of their signature hammer-shaped head.

PRIME VIEWING   All along the Pacific coast and in the Galápagos Islands. Large schools of these sharks are commonly sighted while diving in the Galápagos, especially off the outer northern islands.

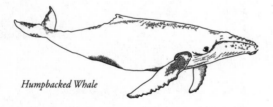

Humpbacked Whale

SCIENTIFIC NAME   *Megaptera novaeangliae*

WORTH NOTING   The migratory **humpbacked whale** (***ballena jorobada*** in Ecuador) frequents the waters off Ecuador's Pacific coast throughout the southern summer season. These whales mate and calve in the warm waters here. They have black backs and whitish throat and chest areas and can reach lengths of nearly 18m (60 ft.) and weigh as much as 48,000 kilograms (106,000 lb.).

PRIME VIEWING   Along the Pacific coast, particularly the central Pacific coast off of Puerto López and Machalilla National Park, from June through September.

Pacific Green Turtle

SCIENTIFIC NAME   *Chelonia mydas agassizii*

WORTH NOTING   Also known as the black sea turtle, the **Pacific green turtle** is the only sea turtle to mate and nest on the Galápagos Islands.

PRIME VIEWING   All along the Pacific coast, particularly in the Galápagos Islands.

SCIENTIFIC NAME   *Eretmochelys imbricata*

WORTH NOTING   The **hawksbill turtle** is a shy tropical species that feeds primarily on sponges. On the endangered species list, the turtle has a highly prized shell. Commercial exploitation and illegal hunting exacerbates the species' continued decline.

PRIME VIEWING   All along the Pacific coast and in the Galápagos Islands.

Hawksbill Turtle

Galápagos Sea Lion

SCIENTIFIC NAME   *Zalophus californianus wollebacki*

WORTH NOTING   Called ***lobo marino*** (sea wolf) in Spanish, this endemic species is plentiful throughout the Galápagos Islands and is seemingly fearless of humans. Large bull males are territorial, protecting a well-defined stretch of beach, which is usually populated by a large harem of females and their young. Males are much larger and have a pronounced bump on their forehead. It is not uncommon for snorkelers and scuba divers to have close encounters with **Galápagos sea lions.**

PRIME VIEWING   Widespread throughout the Galápagos Islands. Occasionally found along the north Pacific coast of the mainland.

Index

Abercrombie & Kent, 67
Accommodations, 46–47
  best, 9–13
Active vacations, 66–91
Adventure Planet Ecuador,
  69, 81, 168
Adventure trips
  best, 7–8
  organized, 66–68
  suggested itinerary, 61–63
Aeropuerto Internacional
  Mariscal Sucre (Quito),
  22, 92–93
African-American travelers,
  35–36
Afro-Ecuadorian people,
  287, 288, 290, 291
Agencia Limoncocha, 84
Aggressor Fleet Limited, 75
Agua Blanca, 259
Airport security, 24
Air travel, 22–26, 43–44
Altitude sickness, 31, 90
The Amazon, 190
Amazonas Spanish School
  (Quito), 42
Ambato, 180–185
American Express, 48
  Quito, 99
  traveler's checks, 28
American Express Travelers
  Cheque Card, 29
Andean Birding, 72
Andean condors, 155, 168–169
Andean Paths, 72, 77, 78
Andes Adrenaline
  Adventures, 72
Andes World Bike, 69
Años Viejos, 22
Antisana, 80
Arasha Resort, 81
Archaeological sites and finds
  Agua Blanca, 259
  Bahía de Caráquez, 278–279
  Baños, 185
  Chirije, 280

Cuenca, 208, 209
Esmeraldas, 288
Guayaquil, 241
Ingapirca, 220–221
Latacunga, 175
La Tolita, 290
Machalilla National Park,
  88, 258–259
Otavalo, 143–144
Puyo, 321
Quito, 121, 122, 127
Archbishop's Palace (Quito),
  120
Archidona, 316
Architecture, 368
Aries Bike Company, 69
Art, 368
Art galleries, Quito, 124–125
Art Marina, 76
Atacames, 291–295
ATMs (automated teller
  machines), 27–28, 48

Bahía de Caráquez, 277–282
Balneario Las Peñas
  (Baños), 189
Balneario Los Helenes (Santa
  Teresita), 198
Bananas, 262
Baños de Agua Santa,
  9, 15, 185–195
Bartolomé, 328
Basílica de la Dolorosa
  (Ibarra), 157
Basílica del Cisne, 224
Basílica del Voto Nacional
  (Quito), 118–119
Basílica de Nuestra Señora de
  Agua Santa (Baños), 188
Beaches, 5
  Bahía de Caráquez, 279–280
  Canoa, 283–284
  Chirije, 282
  Galápagos Islands, 343, 352
  near Guayaquil, 248
  Jambelí (near Machala), 264

Las Palmas, 288–289
Machalilla National Park, 259
Manta, 272–273
from Manta to Bahía de
  Caráquez, 276–277
Muisne, 295
Salinas, 250–251
west of Esmeraldas, 291–295
Beer, 371–372
Bellavista Cloud Forest
  Reserve, 135–136
Beraca Spanish School
  (Quito), 42
Beverages, 371
Bienal Internacional de Pintura
  (Cuenca), 209
Biking and mountain biking, 69
  Baños, 190
  Cotopaxi, 169
  Galápagos Islands, 344, 353
  Riobamba, 199
  Vilcabamba, 230
Biotours (Loja), 225, 227
Bipo & Toni's (Quito), 42
Bird Ecuador, 72
Bird-watching, 69–71
  Bahía de Caráquez, 280
  best places for, 8–9
  Cajas National Park, 220
  Cayapas-Mataje Ecological
    Reserve, 290
  Isla del Corazón, 280
  Podocarpus National Park,
    227
  Tinalandia, 298
  tour operators, 70–72
The Black Sheep Inn, 78
The Blue Marlin Lodge, 76
Boating (boat rentals). *See also*
  Kayaking; White-water rafting
  Bahía de Caráquez, 280
Boat trips and cruises, 73
  Cuicocha Lake, 146
  Galápagos Islands,
    331–338, 344
    last-minute trips, 338
    luxury and first class,
      333–335

recommended tour operators and ships, 332–333
tourist and economy class, 335–336
Lago Agrio, 305
San Lorenzo, 290
Books, recommended, 372–373
Bookstores, Quito, 99, 125
Borman, Randy, 305
Bosque Petrificado de Puyango, 264
Bosque Protector Cerro Blanco (near Guayaquil), 242
Bosque Protector Mindo-Nambillo, 136
Botanical Gardens (Guayaquil), 240
Bridge jumping, 189–190
Bucket shops, 24
Bugs and bug bites, 90
Bullfighting, 123
Bungee jumping, 72
Business hours, 48–49
Bus travel, 26, 44
Butterfield & Robinson, 333

Café Eucalyptus (Cuenca), 15, 217
Cajas National Park, 5, 85, 219–220
Calendar of events, 21–22
Cameras and film, 49
Camilo Egas Museum (Quito), 120
Camping, 72–73
Galápagos Islands, 344
Cañari people, 121, 203, 204, 208, 220
Canoa, 82, 280, 283–285
Canopy tours, 73
Canyoning, 189
Capilla del Hombre (Quito), 122
Carnaval (Carnival), 21
Esmeraldas, 288–289
Guaranda, 202
Vilcabamba, 231
Car rentals, 44, 45
Car travel, 26, 44–45
Casa de la Cultura (Latacunga), 175
Casa de la Cultura Ecuatoriana (Guayaquil), 248
Casa de la Cultura Ecuatoriana (Quito), 127
Casa de los Marqueses de Miraflores (Latacunga), 175

Casa de Montalvo (Ambato), 181
Casa Museo María Augusta Urrutia (Quito), 115
Casa Sol Surf Camp, 82
Casinos
Quito, 132
Tulcán, 163
Catedral, Loja, 223
Catedral Nueva (Cuenca), 6, 207
Catedral Vieja (Cuenca), 207
Cathedral, Latacunga, 174
Cathedral, Quito, 120
Cayambe, 80
Cayambe-Coca Ecological Reserve, 85
Cayapas-Mataje Ecological Reserve, 290
Cellphones, 38–40
Cementerio General (Guayaquil), 238
Cementerio Municipal (Tulcán), 162
Centers for Disease Control and Prevention, 30, 54
The Central Sierra, 17–18, 164–202
Centro de Interpretación (San Cristóbal Island), 352
Cerro Chato Tortoise Reserve, 342
Cerro Crocker, 342
Cerro Dragon, 328, 343
Cerro Santa Ana (Guayaquil), 239
Charles Darwin Research Station (Santa Cruz), 328, 342
Chevron oil company, suit against, 303
Chicha, 184
Children, families with, 35
best destinations for, 9
suggested itinerary, 60–61
Chimborazo mountain, 80, 195, 198–199
Chimborazo province, 195
Chirije, 279, 280, 282
Chiva, tours, 188
Chocó Rainforest, 85, 91, 291
Christmas Eve (Cuenca), 22
City Hall (Quito), 120
Ciudad La Mitad del Mundo, 134–135
Climate, 20–21
Climb Ecuador, 81
Climbing mountains and volcanoes, 79–81
Baños, 190
Chimborazo, 195, 198–199

Cotopaxi, 167–168
Reventador, 307
Tungurahua, 80, 190, 191
Cloud forests, 70
Intag, 148
Los Gemelos (The Twins), 343
Mindo and Bellavista, 135–136
Podocarpus National Park, 227
Tinalandia, 298–299
Coca, 308–312
Cofán Nation, 305
Colombia, 304
crossing into, 163
Compañía de Guías de Montaña, 81
Condor Bioreserve, 169
Condors, 155, 168–169
Consolidators, 24
Consulates, 50
Convento de la Concepción (Riobamba), 198
Correa, Rafael, 360
Cotacachi, 147
Cotacachi-Cayapas Ecological Reserve, 85
Cotopaxi.com, 68, 69, 77, 81, 84, 168
Cotopaxi National Park, 4–5, 86, 133, 164–173
Credit cards, 28
Cristóbal Colón Spanish School (Quito), 42–43
Cuenca, 15, 18, 203–221
accommodations, 212–215
getting around, 206
Internet access, 207
nightlife, 219
orientation, 206
restaurants, 216–219
shopping, 210
side trips from, 219–221
sights and attractions, 207–209
sports and outdoor activities, 210
traveling to and from, 204–206
visitor information, 206–207
Cuevas de Jumandy, 316
Cuicocha Lake, 4, 146–147
Cuisine, 370–371
Culture, 368–370
Currency, 27
Customs regulations, 49
Cuy, 1
Cuyabeno, 190
Cuyabeno Wildlife Reserve, 87, 302, 303, 305–306, 314

Darwin, Charles, 330
Darwin Island, 74
DECOIN, 148
Delgado Travel, 182, 289,
   292, 297
Día de los Muertos (Day
   of the Dead), 22
Disabilities, travelers
   with, 33–34
Diving, 74–75
   Galápagos Islands, 8, 74–75,
      332, 345, 353
      dedicated dive boats,
         336–337
Driving rules, 45
Drug laws, 50
Drugstores, 50

Earthwatch Institute, 90
Ecole Travel Ecuador, 69, 73, 77
Ecolodges, best, 11–12
Ecologically oriented volunteer
   and study programs, 90–91
Economy, 359
Ecotourism/sustainable
   tourism, 36–37. *See also*
   Adventure trips
Eco Trails, 77, 81
Ecuadorian Alpine Institute, 81
Ecuador Volunteer, 91
El Adoratorio/Castillo
   (Ingapirca), 220
El Altar, 80
El Angel Ecological Reserve,
   160–161
El Centro Cultural Metropoli-
   tano (Quito), 115
El Cisne, 224
El Desafío de la Selva, 306
Electricity, 50
El Oriente, 5, 18–19,
   70, 300–323
   climate, 21, 302
   jungle lodges and independ-
      ent travel, 301–302
Eloy Alfaro Air Base (Manta),
   272
El Pailón del Diablo
   (Baños), 188
El Panecillo (Quito), 115–116
El Progreso (San Cristóbal),
   350, 352
El Sagrario (Quito), 117
El Teleférigo (Quito), 9, 118
Embassies and consulates, 50
Emergencies, 50
Entry requirements, 19–20

Equitours, 78
Escorted tours, 41
Escuela de Español Atahualpa
   (Quito), 43
Esmeraldas, 286–290
Española, 329
Estadio Olímpico Atahualpa
   (Quito), 123
Etiquette, in the wilderness,
   89–90
Exclusive Hotels & Haciendas
   of Ecuador, 46
Exotic Birding, 70
Exploramar Diving, 75, 83

Families with children, 35
   best destinations for, 9
   suggested itinerary, 60–61
Fernandina, 329
Festivals and special events,
   21–22
Field Guides, 70
Fiesta de la Mama Negra
   (Latacunga), 175
Fiestas de Guayaquil, 21
Fiestas de Mama Negra
   (Latacunga), 22
Fiestas de Quito, 22, 128
Films, Ecuadorian, 373
Finca Punta Ayampé, 82
Fishing, 75–76
   Manta, 273
   Salinas, 251
Floreana, 331, 356–357
Food and drink, 370–372
Frommers.com, 37
Fundación Guayasamín
   (Quito), 6, 122–123

Galacruises Expeditions, 73,
   333
Galápagos
   climate, 20
   surfing, 82
Galápagos Divers, 75
Galápagos Islands, 5, 9, 19,
   324–357. *See also specific
   islands*
   cruises, 331–338, 344
      last-minute trips, 338
      luxury and first class,
         333–335
      recommended tour oper-
         ators and ships,
         332–333
      tourist and economy
         class, 335–336

   getting around, 326
   getting there and departing,
      325–326
   the islands in brief, 328–331
   scuba diving, 74–75
      Galápagos Islands, 8,
         74–75, 332, 336–337,
         345, 353
   seasons and climate, 326–328
   suggested itineraries, 59–61
   visitor information, 326
Galápagos Jewelry (Puerto
   Ayora), 15
Galápagos National Park, 88
Galápagos Spanish School
   (Quito), 43
Galápagos Sub-Aqua, 75
Gay and lesbian travelers, 34
   Quito, 132
Golf, 76
   Atacames, 292–293
Government Palace (Quito),
   119–120
Guacamayo Bahía Tours, 83
Guano, 198
Guaranda, 201–202
Guayaquil, 18, 233–248
   accommodations, 243–245
   beaches near, 248
   cinemas, 248
   getting around, 236
   nightlife, 247–248
   orientation, 236
   restaurants, 245–247
   rivalry between Quito
      and, 234
   shopping, 242
   sights and attractions,
      238–242
   traveling to, 234–236
   visitor information, 236
Guayatur, 83

Hacienda El Castillo
   (Guayas), 242
Hacienda La Alegría, 9, 79
Hacienda Leito (near Patate),
   183–185
Hacienda Manteles (near
   Patate), 185
Hacienda Pinsaqui, 79
Haciendas, best, 11–12
Hacienda Zuleta, 79, 154–155
Handicrafts. *See also specific
   towns and markets*
   Cuenca, 210–211
   Latacunga, 175
   Otavalo, 144, 145

Quito, 125–126
Riobamba, 198
Hang gliding and paragliding, 76–77
Health concerns, 30–32
in the wilderness, 89–90
Health insurance, 30, 32
Hidden Trails, 78–79
Hiking, 77–78
Baños, 190
Cuenca, 210
Otavalo, 148–149
Vilcabamba, 230
History of Ecuador, 360–367
Holbrook Travel, 67
Holidays, 21
Holy Week, 21
Horseback riding, 78–79
Baños, 190
Galápagos Islands, 344
Riobamba, 199
Vilcabamba, 230
Horseback-riding, Cotopaxi, 170
Hospitals, 50–51
Hotel Termas de Papallacta, 82
Hot springs
Balneario Los Helenes (Santa Teresita), 198
Baños, 188–189
Papallacta, 137, 302
Hualambari Tours (Cuenca), 206, 210, 219
Huaquillas, 266
Hummingbirds, 71

Ibarra, 155–161
The Idealist, 91
Iglesia de la Merced (Quito), 117
Iglesia del Carmen de la Asunción (Cuenca), 207
Iglesia de San Francisco (Quito), 6, 117–119
Iglesia de Santo Domingo (Loja), 224
Iglesia Santo Domingo (Ibarra), 157
Ilalo Expeditions, 79
Ilinizas National Park, 86
Independencia de Guayaquil, 22
Indigenous peoples, 359
Ingapirca, 6, 220–221
Instituto Otavaleño de Antropología, 143–144
Instituto Superior de Español (Quito), 43
Insurance, 29–30

Intag, 148
Intag Cloud Forest Reserve, 148
International Mountain Climbing School, 81
Internet access/e-mail, 40
Inti-Ñan Solar Museum (Ciudad La Mitad del Mundo), 134
Inti Raymi, 21
Isabela, 329–330, 356
Isla de la Plata, 5, 74, 258
Isla del Corazón, 280
Itineraries, suggested, 55–65

Jaguars, 227, 311
Jambelí (near Machala), 264
Jardín Botánico (Guayaquil), 240
Jardín Botánico La Carolina (Santo Domingo), 297
Jardín Botánico las Orquídeas (Puyo), 321
Jatun Sacha, 91
Jatun Sacha Biological Station, 316
Jervis Island (Rábida), 330–331
Jumandy Caves, 316

Kapawi Ecolodge & Reserve, 322–323
Kayaking, 7–8
Galápagos Islands, 3 37, 344, 353
Tena, 317

La Chocolatera, 251
La Compañía de Jesús (Quito), 6, 119
La Galapaguera de Cerro Colorado (San Cristóbal), 352
Lago Agrio, 302–307
Laguna de Colta, 198
Laguna de Yambo, 180
Laguna El Junco (San Cristóbal), 352
Laguna Quilotoa, 177
Lagunas de Atillo, 198, 199
Lagunas de Ozogoche, 198, 199
Laguna Yahuarcocha, 158
La Lobería (San Cristóbal), 352
La Mirage Garden Hotel & Spa, 81–82
La Mitad Del Mundo, 134–135
Lammer Law, M/S, 75
Language, 51

La Piscina de la Virgen (Baños), 188
La Proa Bar (Guayaquil), 247
La Quinta de Juan León Mera (Ambato), 182
La Ruta del Sol, 249
Las Grietas, 343
Las Palmas, 288–290
Latacunga, 173–180
La Tina (Peru), 228
Latin Trails, 68
La Tolita, 6, 290
Linblad Expeditions, 73, 333
Liquor laws, 51
Literature, 369
Loja, 221–228
Los Frailes, 259
Los Gemelos (The Twins), 328, 343
Los Molinos de Monserrat (Latacunga), 175
Lost and found, 51
Lost-luggage insurance, 30
Luna Runtun, 69, 78, 82

Macará, 228
Macas, 323
Machala, 261–267
Machalilla National Park, 5, 88, 256, 258–259
Machalilla Tours, 75, 76, 83, 258
Madre Tierra (Puyo), 321
Magellan Offshore Fishing Tours, 76
Malaria, 31
Malecón del Estero Salado (Guayaquil), 238
Malecón 2000 (Guayaquil), 238, 242
Malecón Esenico (Manta), 272
Manatee Amazon Explorer, 73–74
Manta, 268–277
Manta Airbase, 272
Maps, 19, 45
Maquipucuna, 91
Mariscal District (Quito), 15
Markets, best, 14–15
Media Luna (Santa Cruz), 342
Medical insurance, 30, 32
Mercado Artesanal (Guayaquil), 242
Mercado Artesanal La Mariscal (Quito), 124
Mercado de las Flores (Cuenca), 207–208

Metropolitan Touring, 73, 169, 170, 175, 182, 196, 199, 227, 242, 271, 333
Mindo, 135–136
Mindo Bird Tours, 72
Mindo-Nambillo Protected Forest, 136
Minga, 156
Mirador de la Virgen del Calvario (Latacunga), 175
Mirador de Turi (Cuenca), 208
Mirador La Cruz, 279
Moggely Climbing, 78, 81
Mojanda Lakes, 148
Mompiche, 82, 286, 292
Money matters, 26–29
Montañita, 15, 82, 254–256
Montecristi, 273
Monumento A La Primera Imprenta (Ambato), 182
Morete Puyu Aquatic Park, 321
Mountain and volcano climbing, 79–81
    Baños, 190
    Chimborazo, 195, 198–199
    Cotopaxi, 167–168
    Reventador, 307
    Tungurahua, 80, 190, 191
Mountain biking. See Biking and mountain biking
Muisne, 295
Museo Alberto Mena Caamaño (Quito), 115
Museo Antropológico y de Arte Contemporáneo (Guayaquil), 7, 240
Museo Arqueológico (Quito), 122–123
Museo Arqueológico del Banco Central (Bahía de Caráquez), 278–279
Museo Arqueológico del Banco del Pacífico (Guayaquil), 241
Museo Camilo Egas (Quito), 120
Museo de Arqueología Regional (Esmeraldas), 288
Museo de Arte Colonial (Quito), 123
Museo de Arte Moderno (Quito), 123
Museo de Arte Religioso (Riobamba), 198
Museo de Ballenas (Salinas), 251
Museo de Etnografía (Ciudad La Mitad del Mundo), 134
Museo de las Culturas Aborígenes (Cuenca), 209

Museo del Banco Central
    Cuenca, 6, 208
    Loja, 223–224
    Manta, 273
Museo del Banco Central de Ecuador (Ibarra), 157
Museo del Monasterio de la Conceptas (Cuenca), 209
Museo del Quito en Miniatura (Ciudad La Mitad del Mundo), 134
Museo de Tejidos El Obraje (Otavalo), 143
Museo Etnoarqueológico (Puyo), 321
Museo Fray Pedro Gocial (Quito), 120–121
Museo Histórico Militar/"Casa de Sucre" (Quito), 121
Museo Jacinto Jijón y Caamaño (Quito), 121
Museo Municipal de Arte Moderno (Cuenca), 209
Museo Municipal de Guayaquil, 241
Museo Nacional del Banco Central del Ecuador (Quito), 6, 121–122, 127
Museo Nahim Isaías (Guayaquil), 241
Museo Remigio Crespo Toral (Cuenca), 209
Museo Salinas Siglo 21, 251
Museo Solar Inti-Ñan (Ciudad La Mitad del Mundo), 134
Museum of Musical Instruments (Quito), 122
Music, 369–370

Napo River, 73–74, 83, 308, 309, 311
    lower, jungle lodges on, 312–314
    upper, jungle lodges on, 319–320
Napo Wildlife Center (Coca), 312–313
Nariz del Diablo train ride, 199
National parks and bioreserves, 84–88
Natural environment, 367
Newspapers and magazines, 52
Nightlife, best, 15
Northern Pacific coast and lowlands, 18, 268–299
The Northern Sierra, 17, 139–163

Olga Fisch Folklore (Quito), 14, 125
Orellana, Francisco de, 310
Otavalo, 139–155
    accommodations, 149–152
    getting around, 141–142
    nightlife, 154
    orientation, 142
    outdoor activities, 148–149
    restaurants, 153–154
    sights and attractions in and around, 143–148
    traveling to and from, 140–141
    visitor information, 142–143
Otavalo Institute of Anthropology, 143–144
Otavalo Market, 15, 133, 144–146
Overseas Adventure Travel, 68, 333

Pacific lowlands, 70
Package tours, 40–41
Panama hats, 126, 211–212, 242, 273, 369
Pan-American Highway, 142
Papallacta, 136–138
Parapente Crucita, 77
Parasailing, 280
Parque 21 de Abril (Riobamba), 198
Parque Acuático Morete Puyu, 321
Parque Amazónica (Tena), 316
Parque Calderón (Cuenca), 207
Parque Centenario (Guayaquil), 238
Parque Central (Loja), 223
Parque Condor, 148
Parque Ecológico Artesanal (San Cristóbal), 353–354
Parque Ecológico Recreativo Lago Agrio (PERLA), 305
Parque Guayaquil (Riobamba), 198
Parque Histórico Guayaquil, 241
Parque Infantil (Riobamba), 198
Parque Juan Montalvo (Ambato), 181
Parque La Libertad (Riobamba), 198
Parque Maldonado (Riobamba), 197–198
Parque Seminario (Guayaquil), 238

Parque Sucre (Riobamba), 198
Parque Vicente León
    (Latacunga), 174
Passports, 19, 52
Pedernales, 285
Peguche, 147
Peguche Waterfall, 147
People of Ecuador, 359
Peru
    consulate (Machala), 263
    crossing to, 228, 266–267
Pesca Tours, 76, 83
Petrified Forest of Puyango,
    264
Pinnacle Rock, 328
Piscina El Salado (Baños), 189
Piscinas Santa Clara (Baños),
    189
Piura (Peru), 228
Playa Barbasquillo, 273
Playa de los Alemanes, 343
Playa de Tarqui, 272
Playa Murciélago, 272
Playas General Villamil (near
    Guayaquil), 248
Plaza de la Independencia
    (Quito), 119–120
Plaza Foch (Quito), 130
Plaza San Francisco (Loja), 224
Plaza San Sebastián (Loja), 224
Plaza Santo Domingo
    (Loja), 224
Podocarpus National Park,
    86–87, 227–228
Politics, 358, 359–360
Post Office Bay (Floreana), 331
Post offices and mail, 53
Puerta de la Ciudad (Loja), 223
Puerto Ayora and Santa Cruz
    Island, 328, 339–350
    accommodations, 345–348
    adventure activities, 344–345
    getting around, 341–342
    getting there and departing,
        339
    invasive plants and fauna,
        340
    nightlife, 15, 349–350
    orientation, 341
    restaurants, 348–349
    shopping, 345
    sights and attractions,
        342–343
    visitor information, 339
Puerto Baquerizo Moreno,
    350–357
Puerto Francisco de Orellana
    (Coca), 308–312

Puerto Hondo (near
    Guayaquil), 242
Puerto López, 255–261
Puntudo (Santa Cruz), 342
Puyo, 190, 320–323

Quilotoa Loop, 177–180
Quinde Expeditions, 69
Quito, 1, 92–138
    accommodations, 102–108
    arriving in, 92–93
    casinos, 132
    cellphones, 99
    cinemas, 132
    climate, 20–21
    currency exchange, 99
    doctors and dentists, 100
    drugstores, 100
    emergencies, 100
    gay and lesbian scene, 132
    getting around, 97–99
    hospitals, 100
    Internet access, 100
    laundry and dry cleaning,
        100–101
    layout of, 93, 96
    neighborhoods, 96–97
    nightlife, 126–132
    outdoor activities and specta-
        tor sports, 123–124
    photographic needs, 101
    post offices, 101
    restaurants, 109–114
    restrooms, 101
    rivalry between Guayaquil
        and, 234
    shopping, 124–126
    side trips from, 133–138
    sights and attractions,
        114–123
    street-address system, 97
    suggested itineraries,
        56, 61, 63–65
    visitor information, 93
    weather, 102
Quitofest, 128
Quito School of art, 116
Quito Spanish Institute, 43
Quitsato Mitad del Mundo
    Monument, 1, 95

Rábida (Jervis Island),
    330–331
Rafting, 7–8, 83–84
    Baños, 189
    Tena, 317
Rainforests, 5, 367

Chocó Rainforest, 85, 91, 291
El Oriente, 300, 302, 306,
    307, 315, 316, 321
Podocarpus National Park,
    227
Regions of Ecuador, 17–19
Restaurants, 47–48
    best, 13–14
Restrooms, 53
Reventador Volcano, 307
Río Anzu, 84, 317
Riobamba, 195–202
Río Blanco, 83, 189
Río Chico, 82
Río Jatunyacu, 84, 317
Río Misahuallí, 83, 317
Río Mulaute, 83
Río Napo. See Napo River
Río Quijos, 84, 137
Ríos Ecuador, 84
Río Toachi, 83
Río Upano, 83–84
River People, 84
Road conditions, 44–45

Safari Ecuador, 68, 69,
    73, 78, 81, 169
Safety, 32–33, 53
    in the wilderness, 89–90
Salinas, 82, 249–254
Salto de San Rafael, 307
Same, 291
San Antonio de Ibarra,
    15, 157–158
San Clemente, 277
San Cristóbal, 329
San Cristóbal Island, 350–357
San Francisco Museum and
    Convent (Quito), 120–121
Sangay National Park, 87
San Jacinto, 276–277
San Jorge Eco-Lodge & Biologi-
    cal Reserve, 72, 79, 133–134
San Lorenzo, 290
San Mateo, 82
San Miguel de Salcedo, 179
San Pedro cactus, 230
San Rafael Falls, 307
Santa Cruz, 74, 328
Santa Cruz Island. See Puerto
    Ayora and Santa Cruz Island
Santa Elena Peninsula, 249
Santa Teresita, 198
Santiago (James Island), 329
Santo Domingo de los Col-
    orados, 295–299
Saquisilí, 177
Saraguro, 221

Scuba diving, 74–75
Galápagos Islands, 8, 74–75, 332, 345, 353
dedicated dive boats, 336–337
Scuba Iguana, 75
Seasons, 20
Senior travelers, 34–35
Shipping your luggage, 25
Shopping, best, 14–15
Simón Bolívar (Quito), 43
Sky Dancer, M/S, 75
Small World Adventures, 84
Smoking, 53
Snorkeling, 74–75
Galápagos Islands, 345, 353
South American Explorers (Quito), 93
Southern Amazon basin, 320–323
The southern coast, 18
The southern sierra, 18
Spanish-language programs, 42–43
Baños, 190–191
Cuenca, 209–210
Otavalo, 149
Spas, 81–82
Vilcabamba, 231
Student travel, 36
Study programs. See also Spanish-language programs
ecologically oriented, 90–91
Sua, 291
Sun exposure, 31, 90
Surfing, 7, 82
Canoa, 283–284
Galápagos, 82
Galápagos Islands, 344–345, 353
Montañita, 255
Salinas, 251
Surtrek, 68, 69, 72, 73, 78, 169, 333
Sustainable tourism/ ecotourism, 36–37
Swing jumping, 189–190

Tamarillo (tree tomato), 153
Tauck, 74, 333
Taxes, 53
Teatro Bolívar (Quito), 127
Teatro Nacional Sucre (Quito), 127
Telephones, 38
Tena, 315–320
Tennis, 123–124
Termas de Papallacta, 137
TerraDiversa (Cuenca), 206, 210, 219
Terranova Trek, 77
Textiles, Quito, 126
Tianguez (Quito), 14–15, 125–126
Time zone, 53
Tinalandia, 72, 297–299
Tipping, 54
Todos Los Santos, 208
Tomebamba Hall (Cuenca), 208
Tonsupa, 291
Tortoises, Galápagos Islands, 342–344, 352, 357
Tortuga Bay, 343
Transportation, 43–45
Traveler's checks, 28–29
Traveling to Ecuador, 22–26
Travel insurance, 29–30
Tree tomato (tamarillo), 4, 153
Tres Cruces, 220
Trip-cancellation insurance, 29
Tropic Journeys, 72
Tsachila people, 295–297
Tulcán, 161–163
Tungurahua, 80, 190, 191
Turisvision, 98
The Twins (Los Gemelos), 328, 343

VAT (value-added tax), 53
Victor Emanuel Nature Tours, 70
Vilcabamba, 1, 228–232
Virgin of El Cisne, 224
Visas, 19–20
Visitor information, 19

VoIP (Voice over Internet protocol), 40
Volcán Cotopaxi, 7, 80
Volcano climbing. See Mountain and volcano climbing
Vulqano Park (Quito), 9, 118

Water, drinking, 54, 371
Waterskiing, 280
Waterways Travel, 82
Wave Hunters Surf Travel, 82
Websites, best, 16
Whale Museum (Salinas), 251
Whale-watching, 7, 83, 257
Salinas, 251
White-water rafting, 7–8, 83–84
Baños, 189
Tena, 317
Wildlife, 380–399
amphibians, 391–393
birds, 387–391
invertebrates, 396–397
mammals, 380–387
reptiles, 393–395
sea life, 397–399
Wildlife viewing, 89. See also Bird-watching; Whale-watching
Bahía de Caráquez, 280
Yasuni National Park, 311
Wings, 71
Wolf Island, 74
Women travelers, 35

Yasuni National Park, 87–88, 311

Zoológico San Martín (Baños), 188

THE NEW TRAVELOCITY GUARANTEE

EVERYTHING YOU BOOK WILL BE RIGHT, OR WE'LL WORK WITH OUR TRAVEL PARTNERS TO MAKE IT RIGHT, RIGHT AWAY.

*To drive home the point,
we're going to use the word "right" in every single sentence.*

Let's get right to it. Right to the meat! Only Travelocity guarantees everything about your booking will be right, or we'll work with our travel partners to make it right, right away. Right on!

Here's a picture taken smack dab right in the middle of Antigua, where the guarantee also covers you.

The guarantee covers all but one of the items pictured to the right.

Now, you may be thinking, "Yeah, right, I'm so sure." That's OK; you have the right to remain skeptical. That is until we mention help is always right around the corner. Call us right off the bat, knowing that our customer service reps are there for you 24/7. Righting wrongs. Left and right.

For example, what if the ocean view you booked actually looks out at a downright ugly parking lot? You'd be right to call – we're there for you. And no one in their right mind would be pleased to learn the rental car place has closed and left them stranded. Call Travelocity and we'll help get you back on the right track.

Now if you're guessing there are some things we can't control, like the weather, well you're right. But we can help you with most things – to get all the details in righting,* visit **travelocity.com/guarantee**.

*Sorry, spelling things right is one of the few things not covered under the guarantee.

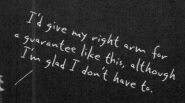

I'd give my right arm for a guarantee like this, although I'm glad I don't have to.

You'll never roam alone.

IF YOU BOOK IT, IT SHOULD BE THERE.

Only Travelocity guarantees it will be, or we'll work
with our travel partners to make it right, right away.
So if you're missing a balcony or anything else you
booked, just call us 24/7. **1**-888-TRAVELOCITY.

travelocity
You'll never roam alone